KT-168-849

Devon, Cornwall
& Southwest England

Oliver Berry
Belinda Dixon

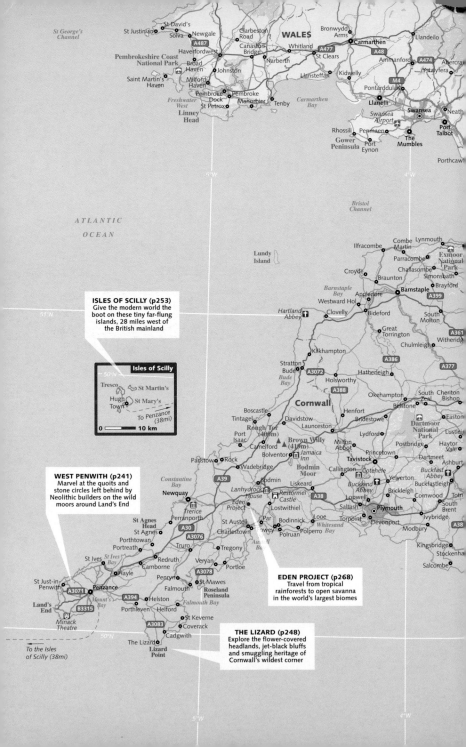

ATLANTIC
OCEAN

St George's
Channel

WALES

Pembrokeshire Coast
National Park

Freshwater
West
Linney
Head

Carmarthen
Bay

Gower
Peninsula

Swansea
Airport

Swansea

Neath

Port
Talbot

Porthcaw

Bristol
Channel

Lundy
Island

Exmoor
National
Park

Barnstaple
Bay

Barnstaple

Hartland
Abbey

Cornwall

Bodmin
Moor

Dartmoor
National
Park

Plymouth

ISLES OF SCILLY (p253)
Give the modern world the
boot on these tiny far-flung
islands, 28 miles west of
the British mainland

Isles of Scilly

Tresco   St Martin's

Hugh   St Mary's
Town
         To Penzance
         (38mi)

0 ——— 10 km

WEST PENWITH (p241)
Marvel at the quoits and
stone circles left behind by
Neolithic builders on the wild
moors around Land's End

EDEN PROJECT (p268)
Travel from tropical
rainforests to open savanna
in the world's largest biomes

THE LIZARD (p248)
Explore the flower-covered
headlands, jet-black bluffs
and smuggling heritage of
Cornwall's wildest corner

To the Isles
of Scilly (38mi)

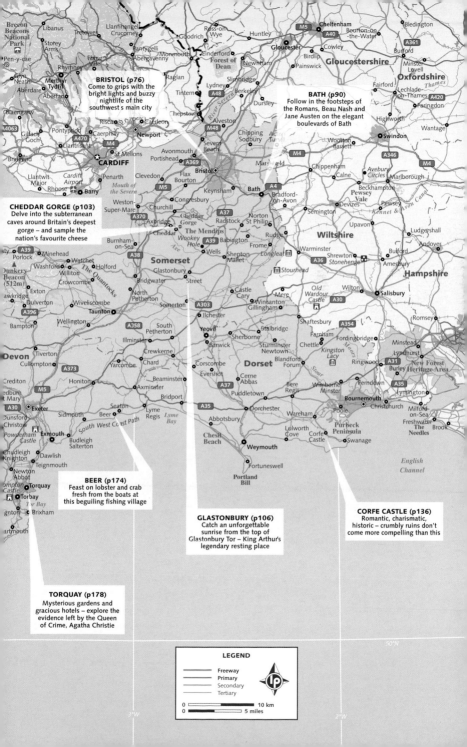

BRISTOL (p76)
Come to grips with the bright lights and buzzy nightlife of the southwest s main city

BATH (p90)
Follow in the footsteps of the Romans, Beau Nash and Jane Austen on the elegant boulevards of Bath

CHEDDAR GORGE (p103)
Delve into the subterranean caves around Britain's deepest gorge – and sample the nation's favourite cheese

BEER (p174)
Feast on lobster and crab fresh from the boats at this beguiling fishing village

GLASTONBURY (p106)
Catch an unforgettable sunrise from the top of Glastonbury Tor – King Arthur's legendary resting place

CORFE CASTLE (p136)
Romantic, charismatic, historic – crumbly ruins don't come more compelling than this

TORQUAY (p178)
Mysterious gardens and gracious hotels – explore the evidence left by the Queen of Crime, Agatha Christie

LEGEND

Freeway
Primary
Secondary
Tertiary

0   10 km
0   5 miles

On the Road

OLIVER BERRY Coordinating Author
Kynance Cove
Kernow's where I grew up and where I still live, so it's a place that's sort of in my blood. Here I'm on the cliffs above a beautiful little corner of the Lizard called **Kynance Cove** (p250), basking in the sunshine and drinking in the views. Cornwall's got a wild, grand edge that's different to the rest of Britain, and I miss it when I'm away.

BELINDA DIXON
Tidal Road
Sometimes in Devon you just have to wait for dinner. The stretch of water in front of the car is covering a tidal road on the way to a bistro near **Bigbury-on-Sea** (p195) in the south of the county. When the tide is high you can go the longer way around, but this route is much more fun. And if you haven't quite judged it right take a tip from the locals: take it easy, watch the boats bobbing on the river, wait for the water to fall and get them to hold that starter.

See full author bios page 302

THE SOUTHWEST

Welcome to England's wild, wild west. This far-flung corner of England has long been a source of inspiration for the nation and it's still our favourite place of escape: an Arcadian getaway, artistic haven, surfer's paradise and gastronomic trendsetter all rolled into one, where humpbacked crags and sea-smacked cliffs sit side-by-side with stately crescents, giant biomes and hip hotels. Catch a clifftop performance, paddle your toes in the briny blue, camp out under an un-cluttered sky, and feel your mind unwind – the southwest's a tonic for the heart.

Bristol, Bath & Somerset

From cutting-edge cities and mystical hills to underground caves and tumbledown abbeys, this is a region that indulges your every whim: a place where you can hit the clubs, hike the trails, wonder at the wildlife and feed yourself silly before laying your head down in a boutique hotel.

❶ Bristol

Feel the beats: Brizzle's buzzing. The south-west's biggest city (p76) has had a thorough polish in recent years (and frequently a paint job thanks to guerrilla graffitist Banksy). The harbour's alive, the centre's in flux, Clifton's kicking and Eastside's electric. Time to get in on the action.

❷ Bath

Break out the thesaurus: this stately, grand lady (p90) is a jewel in England's crown. A cultural icon, swish sophisticate and fashionable haunt for more than three centuries, Bath's a place to stroll the terraces, cherish the views and indulge your culinary cravings. Britain's most beautiful city, or maybe an overrated 'It' girl? You decide.

❸ Glastonbury Tor

King Arthur's tomb? A fairy kingdom? Ley-line terminus? Who cares – the sunset view from the top of this ancient hummock (p106) is enough to make you pack your bags, break out the tie-dye and book a one-way ticket to hippie central. Just don't forget to bring along the joss sticks.

❹ Somerset Levels

This little-explored corner of Somerset is one of Britain's last remaining wetlands (p111), and it's packed with heritage and wildlife: get to grips with traditional willowcraft, cycle along the traffic-free trailways and keep your eyes peeled for otters and great crested grebes.

❺ Cheddar Gorge

It's a tourist hot spot for good reason: Britain's deepest gorge (p103) also hides some of its most spine-tingling underground caves. Pull on an extra sweater and prepare to delve into Somerset's subterranean underbelly – and if you're feeling really brave, set out on a caving expedition.

Devon

Devon is the great escape: ditch a manic, modern world for tranquil, timeless Dartmoor; surf thrilling waves off the north shoreline; or swim in secluded coves on the south coast. From stone rows and cathedrals to crime writers, there's a densely plotted past to explore. Rediscover starlit skies, recharge in restful villages and your supper comes fresh from the fishing boats.

❶ Wild Wonderland

Dartmoor (p202): an elemental bolthole and the largest wilderness in southern England. Brooding and moody; expansive and exhilarating, it's packed with prehistoric sites, mossy woods, intimate villages and cracking inns. Hike, cycle, kayak or ride your socks off, then lord it up in a country-house hotel.

❷ Surf at Croyde

Surfer-chic doesn't come more chilled than Croyde (p213): the streets are lined with thatched cottages, fibreglass boards and funky bars. The north coast draws the waves: fast and steep, walls and barrels. Take lessons or just take time out – become a barefoot beach bum for the day.

❸ Detective Delights

Deduce the south Devon locations hidden in the books of Agatha Christie (p181), Queen of Crime – they lay a Jazz Age trail around tidal islands and grand hotels. Then hop on a ferry to the enchanting gardens of her home on the banks of the River Dart.

❹ Beer

A fishing village (p174), not a pint. Watch boats being pulled up onto the beach and the catch being landed – then picnic on succulent lobster on the pebbles alongside. Or don a hard hat and head deep into a network of chalky caves for tales of Romans, stonemasons and smugglers.

❺ Exeter Cathedral

Steep yourself in cloistered calm at this graceful Norman cathedral (p166). Marvel at its array of Gothic vaulting, evocative carvings and vividly coloured ceiling bosses. A fine centrepiece for a vibrant city.

Cornwall

Celtic culture, wind-blown bluffs and the great British seaside collide in Britain's most westerly corner. Cornwall's all things to all people: a foodie heaven, a natural wonderland, an adventurer's playground and a hub for artistic activities. Time to let a little Kernow into your soul.

❶ Island Hopping

The idyllic Isles of Scilly (p253): Cornwall's answer to the Caribbean, a scattering of 128 pocket-sized islands stranded 28 miles from the British mainland. Ditch the mobile, slap on the sunscreen and let island life dictate the pace – the outside world will feel a long, long way away.

❷ Eden Project

Environmental trendsetter, extraterrestrial ecopark and jungle wonderland all rolled into one, the Eden Project (p268) is one of Cornwall's must-see attractions. Marvel at gigantic plants, educate your senses, and gape at the biggest greenhouses on earth.

❸ Megalithic Monuments

Prehistoric settlers left their architectural mark on the Cornish landscape in the shape of countless stone circles, massive menhirs and tabletop quoits (p241), some of which predate their cousins at Stonehenge and Avebury by well over a millennium.

❹ Cornwall's Rooftop

Scan the scenery and feel the wind sting your cheeks from Kernow's highest point, Brown Willy, then set out deep into the wilds of Bodmin Moor (p273) – a primal landscape dotted with eerie tors, ancient churches and King Arthur connections.

❺ The Lizard

Everyone knows about the rugged cliffs and razzle-dazzle beaches of Cornwall's north coast, but for something wilder and grander head for the Lizard Peninsula (p248), where shipwrecks, cliff paths, gardens and creekside pubs are all crying out to be explored.

Dorset

Dorset's box-office draw is its 250-million-year-old Jurassic Coast. You'll love the scenery of rock arches, creamy-white cliffs and beaches strewn with fossils. Inland, Thomas Hardy's Wessex is a lush, lyrical landscape studded with a rich past: giant hillforts, crumbling castles and ancient, honey-coloured towns. And then comes Bournemouth – south-coast party central.

1 Fossil Hunting

A seriously addictive way to explore the Jurassic Coast: scour the shores around Lyme Regis (p160) and discover a latent passion for palaeontology.

2 Corfe Castle

This genuine jaw-dropper was the site of a Civil War stand-off between Parliament and the King – today its shattered ruins (p136) rear up out of a pastoral landscape like a magical movie set.

Contents

Regional Map Contents

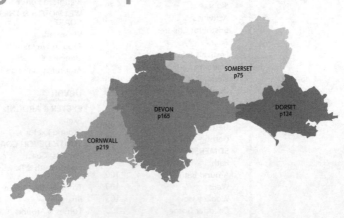

SOMERSET
p75

DEVON
p165

DORSET
p124

CORNWALL
p219

Destination Devon, Cornwall & Southwest England

The southwest's in flux. You can feel the crackle of change in the air. After decades of economic hardship and industrial decline, England's far-westerly peninsula has turned a corner and is chasing an upward curve. Regeneration is happening everywhere you look: futuristic greenhouses are springing up in abandoned clay pits, run-down docksides are being rejuvenated and designer bistros are setting up shop all along the coastline. For years it's been dismissed by snooty urbanites as a cultural backwater, but over the last decade or so there's been a profound shift in attitudes: the southwest has sloughed off its country-bumpkin image and reinvented itself as a hotbed of art, creativity and cutting-edge cuisine. There's a real interest in what's going on out west; people are yearning for a simpler, slower, more sustainable existence, and the region seems to offer a taste of the kind of life we all want to lead in the 21st century.

It's an ecohaven: home to the pioneering Eden Project and Britain's first plastic bag–free town, not to mention wind farms, wave hubs and farmers markets where you can be sure your fruit and veggies are 100% food-mile free. It's a creative trendsetter: Bristol's music scene is still basking in the post–trip-hop glow, while avant-folk artists are emerging from the region's murkiest corners, innovative chefs are taking the culinary world by storm, abstract painters are displaying their wares in converted telephone exchanges and world-class theatre companies are performing down disused mine shafts. And lastly, of course, it's an amazing outdoor playground, with natural charms to suit all-comers: heather-covered clifftops, surf-washed beaches, tree-clad lanes and wild moors. It's a place where people zip down the hillsides on mountainboards, strap themselves into inflatable zorbs and clamber across the cliffs in search of new coasteering spots.

And while much of the region is changing, it's also a place that remains reassuringly rooted in the past. History litters the landscape; tumbledown abbeys, ghostly mine stacks, crumbling keeps and spooky stone rings stand out against the horizon, and thatched villages and red-brick cottages nestle next to rushing brooks and village greens. You can still sip warm beer in a thatch-topped pub or down a pint of scrumpy made in the time-honoured fashion. Tractors trundle along the back lanes, birdsong fills the bridleways and sheep huddle together against knotted hedgerows. And, of course, the southwest remains by far the nation's favourite seaside getaway, where Britain's finest beaches rub shoulders with holiday towns and Victorian promenades. Thousands of holidaymakers flock to its shores to paddle in the surf and feel the sand between their toes, but they're certainly not all wearing Gucci shades – the southwest's beaches and clifftops have a broad appeal, and depending on which stretch of the coastline you choose to explore, you could find yourself building sand castles with the nippers, mixing it with the surfing fraternity or living it up in party-town hell.

FAST FACTS

Population: 3.2 million

Gross value added to the regional economy per person (2005): £16,685

Value of economy (2005): £84.6 billion

Unemployment: 3.8%

Total length of coastline: 711 miles

Proportion of energy from renewable sources: 3%

Average annual CO_2 output per person: 8.2 tonnes

Approximate number of second homes: 38,000

Percentage of journeys made by bus: 3%

Number of working fishermen (2005): 1020 (a 78% decline on the number of fishermen in 1938)

And it's that diversity that's one of the southwest's main draws. The four counties of the southwest covered in this book – Cornwall, Devon, Somerset and Dorset, plus the stand-alone city of Bristol – are a complex jumble of characters, where seaside resorts meet urban sprawl, country villages bump into buzzing cities and Georgian crescents commingle with concrete, plate glass and stainless steel. It's backward and forward in roughly equal doses; you can certainly buy a decent cappuccino on the St Ives harbourfront these days, but thankfully you can still buy a classic ice-cream cone and a paper-wrapped pasty too.

But life's not all rosy out west. There's no doubt that the region has seen a dramatic turnaround in its financial fortunes, buoyed up by the wider success of the British economy, the booming housing market, and major programmes of investment such as Objective One in Cornwall. Increased interest and booming investment in the region is obviously good news for an area that's historically been one of Britain's poorest, but it comes at a price. The southwest's always had a love–hate relationship with the summer influx of emmets and grockles (tourists); overflowing car parks, low-paid seasonal jobs and summer traffic jams have long been a fact of life out west. But new times have brought new tensions, and tourism isn't the silver bullet for all the region's ills as is sometimes claimed.

The spiralling property market and corresponding boom in second-home-ownership has priced many of the southwest's young people off the property ladder. Villages have had their hearts sucked out as the holiday lets and second-homers have moved in. The decline of traditional industries – fishing, farming, mining – has changed the character of much of the landscape, and certainly not always for the better. When a narrow sliver of land in south Dorset can command higher property prices than a penthouse apartment in downtown Manhattan, and villagers from a remote Cornish village are occupying Islington Green in an act of protest, you know strange things are afoot out in the west. And perhaps more worrying, many southwesterners still feel that decisions made in metropolitan-focused Westminster are made without any real understanding of the communities they'll affect – just look at the passionate feelings stirred up by fox hunting, the common agricultural policy or EU fishing quotas. The town and country divide is alive and well in the West Country, despite what the tourist brochures and development agencies will tell you.

Whatever you make of the arguments, there's no doubt that – at least for now – this is a region on the up. After years of economic neglect and downright metropolitan snobbery, the southwest feels like a place that's headed off down a new, exciting and unfamiliar road. Right now it is surfing the crest of a wave – how long it'll be before it breaks on the beach is anyone's guess, but for now most people seem happy just to enjoy the ride.

Getting Started

This is one region of Britain which really does suit every type of traveller, whether you're the kind of person for whom floating beds, fruit teas and flat-screen TVs are all essential items, or you're after just a rugged night under the stars with nothing but your backpack for company. Families, solo travellers and honeymooning couples will all find plenty to pique their interest, but even if you are a footloose nomad, it always pays to do a little bit of planning (and the odd bit of booking) before you set out on the road.

WHEN TO GO

With beaches and beauty spots galore, and countryside that's just crying out for galumphing, it's hardly surprising that the southwest is one of Britain's holiday hot spots. In fact, in the peak season during July and August, it can seem like half of the country is hightailing it to the southwest's shores, but despite the summer crowds and the region's reputation for having a peculiarly balmy climate, the weather is actually no more predictable than anywhere else in Britain. There's an old Cornish saying that sums it up pretty neatly: 'If you don't like the weather – wait a minute'. It's an adage that could happily be applied to the whole region; while it might be blazing sunshine over the coast, travel 10 minutes inland and you might well find yourself pulling on the Wellington boots and waterproofs.

For climate charts of the region, see p283.

Consequently, recommending the best time of year to visit is tough. Statistically speaking, July and August usually receive the most prolonged spells of sunshine – and by far the most visitors to boot – but both months can also be prone to sudden heavy downpours or more prolonged periods of rain. In general the most reliable periods are in late spring (April to May) or early autumn (September to October), when the crowds have eased and the weather is generally at its most settled. Other busy periods that might be worth avoiding – unless you're a fan of premium prices and mile-long traffic jams, of course – include the main bank holidays, especially Easter, May Day and New Year.

COSTS & MONEY

These days the southwest is popular with everyone from families on a bare-bones budget to city slickers in search of a luxury seaside getaway, and there are accommodation options to suit all-comers. As with any

---

DON'T LEAVE HOME WITHOUT...

- Swimming gear, snorkel, beach towel, windbreak and sunscreen – plus that all-essential bucket and spade
- Umbrella – equally handy for sunshine and showers
- Binoculars and camera
- Sturdy hiking shoes for tackling the tors, and comfy sandals or flip-flops for the beach
- Well-stocked picnic basket, some blankets and a Thermos flask
- A head for heights (cliffs)
- A nose for the country (cows)
- A taste for warm beer or strong cider – preferably both.

popular holiday destination, prices tend to take a hefty hike upwards in the high season, especially from June to August; consequently this is by far and away the most expensive time to visit, especially if you're travelling with the kids. To take advantage of the many out-of-season deals that tend to spring up in the shoulder months, it might be worth rescheduling your family trip.

No matter when you choose to visit, the region's big cities are always at the top of the price bracket, especially the must-see duo of Bristol and Bath. Here midrange travellers should budget between £80 and £100 per person per night, and between £30 and £50 for restaurant, transport and admission costs – so you're unlikely to see much change out of £150 per day.

Outside the cities, many upmarket country hotels can be just as pricey as their city cousins, but for most midrange travellers, chances are you'll be travelling by car and staying in small hotels and B&Bs. For a double room in a decent guesthouse, you're looking at between £40 and £60 per person per night (remember most B&Bs quote their tariffs per person, not per room, so what looks like a reasonable rate can actually be quite steep). Above £80 per person and you should be expecting something quite special; below £40 and you'll be exploring saggy-bed and shared-bathroom country. Single rates are often just a reduced rate on a double room (usually about 75%). Factor in meals, transport and admission charges, and you should be budgeting £100 to £120 per day for a pretty comfortable holiday.

If you're travelling with kids in tow, staying in B&Bs can be an expensive option, and some of the posher places won't accept younger children, so many people end up plumping for a self-catering holiday home instead – though this obviously means you'll be rooted in one spot. If you're aiming to travel more widely, ask for a family room or a large double, which often come with one or two extra single beds perfect for the kids.

Backpackers can get by for around £30 a day by staying in hostels, cooking your own grub and travelling by public transport (or better still by bike). If you need to cut costs, then bring your sleeping bag and a tent and head for one of the region's camp sites: prices average between £8 and £15 for a site for a tent and two people, depending on location and season.

ESSENTIAL LISTENING

Looking for an intro to southwest's rich and varies music scene? Here are a few titles from all ends of the spectrum with a solid southwest connection.

■ *Dummy* (Portishead)

■ *Protection* (Massive Attack)

■ *Flashlight Seasons* (Gravenhurst)

■ *Up All Night* (Razorlight)

■ *Contact* (Thirteen Senses)

■ *Freedom Fields* (Seth Lakeman)

■ *Kokopelli* (Kosheen)

■ *Tales of Grime and Grit* (Ruarri Joseph)

■ *Black Holes and Revelations* (Muse)

TOP READS

NOVELS, POEMS & STORIES

- *Jamaica Inn* and *Rebecca* (Daphne du Maurier)
- *Tarka The Otter* (Henry Williamson)
- *Northanger Abbey* (Jane Austen)
- *Kangaroo* (DH Lawrence)
- *The Mayor of Casterbridge* (Thomas Hardy)
- *Lorna Doone* (RD Blackmore)
- *The Hound of the Baskervilles* (Arthur Conan Doyle)
- *The Once And Future King* (TH White)
- *The Water Babies* (Charles Kingsley)
- *Collected Poems: 1951–75* (Charles Causley)

HISTORY & BIOGRAPHY

- *A Cornish Childhood* (AL Rowse)
- *Summoned by Bells* (John Betjeman)
- *The Imaginary Autocrat: Beau Nash and the Invention of Georgian Bath* (John Eglin)
- *Secret Underground Bristol* (Sally Watson)
- *Vanishing Cornwall* (Daphne du Maurier)
- *A Wild Life on Exmoor* (Johnny Kingdom)
- *Sir Francis Drake* (John Sugden)
- *Brunel: The Man Who Built The World* (Stephen Brindle)

GUIDEBOOKS

- *The South West Coast Path* (Official National Trail Guide)
- *Footprint Surfing Britain* (Chris Nelson and Demi Taylor)
- *South West Mountain Biking: Quantocks, Exmoor, Dartmoor Trail Guide* (Nick Cotton)
- *Pathfinder Walking Guides* (available for Cornwall, South Devon, Dartmoor and Somerset)
- *Complete British Birds: Collins Complete Photoguide* (Paul Sterry)
- *Fossils: A Collins Gem Guide* (Douglas Palmer)

There are several ways to cut costs if you're doing a lot of sightseeing. Membership of English Heritage (EH) and the National Trust (NT) can be a good investment, as these two organizations between them own many of the region's castles, country houses, gardens and monuments (with the added bonus that you'll also be able to park for free at all NT beaches). And it's worth remembering that many of the best attractions are completely free: sandy beaches, coastal walks and exquisite country scenes all come without an admission charge (although sadly the same can't always be said for the nearby car parks).

TRAVEL LITERATURE

There's plenty of reading material around if you want to get familiar with the southwest before you arrive. The region has inspired countless poets and writers down the years, and you'll come across a whole pantheon of colourful characters during your travels, from pioneering engineers and crackpot inventors to smugglers, explorers and sea captains. We've included some of our favourite titles in the boxed text, p19, but the list is by no means exhaustive – do a bit of digging and you're bound to turn up your own undiscovered gem.

INTERNET RESOURCES

You can't beat the net as a fount of preplanning information, but finding what you want can sometimes be a challenge. Your first port of call should be the main **Visit Southwest** (www.visitsouthwest.com) website, an excellent general resource put together by the southwest tourist board, with separate themed subsites on everything from heritage and nature to outdoor activities and romantic getaways.

The **Lonely Planet** (www.lonelyplanet.com) site is always a useful resource, and you can check out the Thorn Tree forum for tips from other travellers to the southwest.

Adventure Southwest (www.itsadventuresouthwest.co.uk) Comprehensive advice on adventure sports in the region.

Countryside Access (www.countrysideaccess.gov.uk) Find out which bits of the countryside you can (and can't) ramble over.

English Heritage (ET; www.english-heritage.org.uk) If you can't find the castle or monument you're after on the NT site, chances are it'll be here.

Good Beach Guide (www.goodbeachguide.co.uk) More sage and sandy advice on the region's best beaches.

National Trust (NT; www.nationaltrust.org.uk) Opening hours, prices and maps for all the NT's houses and gardens.

Surfcore (www.surfcore.co.uk) Surfers' site with links to lots of local blogs.

Youth Hostel Association (www.yha.org.uk) Plan your stay at one of the many fantastic YHAs dotted across the southwest.

Itineraries

CLASSIC ROUTES

THE GRAND TOUR
Four Weeks/Bristol to Bournemouth

This is the big one – end-to-end and top-to-bottom in one grand south-western adventure. Kick your trip off in the big city, **Bristol** (p76), then head to nearby **Bath** (p90) with its Georgian finery and 21st-century spa. Stock up on joss sticks in **Glastonbury** (p106); stroll around England's titchiest city, **Wells** (p100); delve into the caverns of **Cheddar Gorge** (p103); and explore **Exmoor** (p113), with its hilltop trails and red deer. Stop briefly in Devon at cliffside **Clovelly** (p216) before hitting the north coast of Cornwall – seafood central **Padstow** (p225), surf capital **Newquay** (p228) and art haven **St Ives** (p235).

Round the bend of **Land's End** (p243) and chase the curve of the **Lizard** (p248) to chichi **St Mawes** (p266) and the postcard-perfect harbour of **Fowey** (p269), allowing time for a side-trip via the **Eden Project** (p268). Then the home stretch: designer **Dartmouth** (p186), touristy **Torquay** (p178) and elegant **Exeter** (p166), rounded off with some fossil-hunting near **Lyme Regis** (p160), Hardy heritage in **Dorchester** (p138), and much-needed R&R in **Poole** (p129) and **Bournemouth** (p124).

The main event. A classic road trip around all the must-see sights the southwest has to offer: big cities, thatched villages, empty moors, boat-packed harbours and bone-white sands.

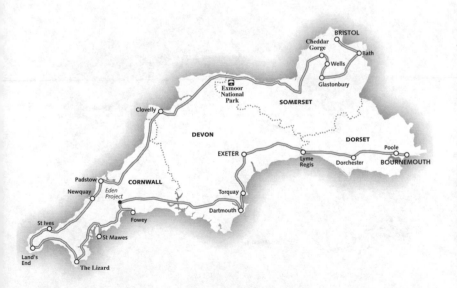

BIG CITY, LITTLE CITY   Two Weeks/Bristol to the Quantocks

This tour travels from big city to bucolic countryside in just under two weeks, taking in everything from Brunel's Bristol to tiny Wells and the wild Quantocks.

This one's more focused, concentrating on the main attractions in the region's major cities. Open up in **Bristol** (p76) at Brunel's **SS Great Britain** (p79), see what's afoot in the **Arnolfini Art Gallery** (p79), chunter around the boutiques and bars of **Clifton** (p87) and drink in the views from the **Suspension Bridge** (p81). Spend the next couple of days exploring the city's **museums** (p80) and the 320-hectare grounds of **Ashton Court Estate** (p82). Then swap the big city vibe for gentler Georgian **Bath** (p90), famous for its Roman **hot tubs** (p92) and regal **crescents** (p93), as well as a clutch of **museums** (p94) where you can view everything from classical art to period Americana and Jane Austen artefacts. Take a plunge at the luxurious **Thermae Bath Spa** (p93), catch a gig at **Moles** (p99), and spend a day strolling around the imagination of Capability Brown at **Prior Park** (p100), before heading on to the smallest city of all, **Wells** (p100), with its stunning scissor-arched cathedral and Bishop's Palace. And to round the trip off, leave the cities behind on the **Quantocks** (p110), where you can shake the smog out of your lungs, get down to some countryside hiking and tuck into plenty of hearty pub grub and real ale.

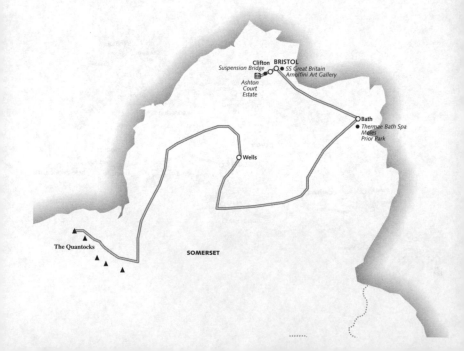

TAILORED TRIPS

LITERATURE LOVERS

England's far west has always attracted the nation's pen-pushers and poets. This route takes you on a whistlestop tour of the region's literary landmarks. Start in **Bath** (p90), the quintessential setting for Jane Austen's novels, before heading west across the Quantocks and Exmoor via **Nether Stowey** (p110), **Holford** (p110) and **Porlock** (p119), where Coleridge and Wordsworth wandered the hills in search of poetic inspiration. Further west is the hillside village of **Clovelly** (p216), where Charles Kingsley penned his classic children's tale *The Water Babies*, while the windswept cliffs of **north Cornwall** (p219) frequently informed the poems of John Betjeman. DH Lawrence briefly lived in **Zennor** (p240), while Virginia Woolf recalled her childhood holidays around **St Ives** (p235) in her groundbreaking novel *To The Lighthouse*. Follow in the footsteps of Daphne du Maurier in **Fowey** (p269), Agatha Christie in **Torquay** (p178), Arthur Conan Doyle on **Dartmoor** (p202) and John Fowles in **Lyme Regis** (p160), before finishing up in Thomas Hardy's Casterbridge – aka Dorset's county town, **Dorchester** (p138).

GREAT ESTATES

The southwest is stuffed with historical houses and (not so secret) gardens, and no matter which county you're in, a grand country seat is never far away. In Somerset, the finest examples are at **Montacute House** (p113) and **Barrington Court** (p113), joined by new-boy **Tyntesfield** (p90), currently undergoing a huge restoration programme. In Devon, there's Drake's former seat at **Buckland Abbey** (p206), the architectural mish-mash of **Knightshayes Court** (p173) and the last castle built in England, **Castle Drogo** (p210), as well as Agatha Christie's hush-hush hideaway **Greenway** (p187). Dorset has its fair share of stately homes, notably **Kingston Lacy** (p134), designed by the architect of the Houses of Parliament, and **Lulworth Castle** (p137), a crenellated chateau that's endured everything from tasteless owners to tragic fires. But it's Cornwall that has the greatest concentration of aristocratic estates. **Cotehele** (p277) and **Lanhydrock** (p275) are the finest, combining architecturally extravagant mansions with glorious landscaped grounds. Elsewhere in Cornwall the gardens take centre stage: the Fox family duo of **Trebah** (p252) and **Glendurgan** (p252) sit side-by-side along subtropical valleys, while the **Lost Gardens of Heligan** (p267) contain their own jungle ravine filled with exotic ferns and towering trees. Out to the west sits **St Michael's Mount** (p248), a craggy island abbey silhouetted against the skyline of Mount's Bay that's been variously used as a monastery, fortress and family seat.

WILD SOUTHWEST

If you want to get far from the madding crowd, then this backcountry tour's for you. First up is a spot of hiking around the high hills of the **Mendips** (p104) and the **Quantocks** (p110). There's wildlife, wetland and willow galore on the **Somerset Levels** (p111), while on **Exmoor** (p113), you can spend your days bombing down the bridleways on a mountain bike or hugging the hedgerows on a deer-spotting safari. South of Exmoor is the wild, windy, wet expanse of **Dartmoor** (p202), pocked by ancient bogs, granite tors and open heaths, and much loved by hikers, bikers and horse riders. Across the

border is **Bodmin Moor** (p273), home to Cornwall's highest peaks, Brown Willy and Rough Tor, as well as prehistoric remains and a fabled feline beast. If you haven't fulfilled your wild fix, then head for the rocky cliffs of the **Lizard Peninsula** (p248) or the quoits and stone circles of **West Penwith** (p241). For the ultimate escape head for the **Isles of Scilly** (p253), where you can while away the days exploring turquoise bays that would put most South Pacific islands to shame.

SEASIDE SPECIAL

For many people the southwest is all about the seaside, and there's somewhere to suit you whether you're after untouched beaches or stripy deckchairs on the sand. One of the most intriguing stretches is along the south Dorset coast; start off with a mosey around the **Purbeck Peninsula** (p134), before heading west via **Durdle Door** (p137) and **Lulworth Cove** (p136), where you'll find shiny white cliffs, circular coves and dramatic rock stacks. Take a wander around the promontory of **Portland Bill** (p158) and the huge bank of pebbles that makes up **Chesil Beach** (p159). Then make a beeline for rust-red **Lyme Bay** (p160), where the rapidly eroding cliffs are a paradise for amateur palaeontologists. For

a more classic vision of the English seaside, you can't beat **Weymouth** (p155), where King George III kicked off the fashion for seaside dipping in the 18th century and Punch & Judy booths still man the beaches. Further west you'll find more class around the swish harbour towns of **Salcombe** (p192), and **Dartmouth** (p186), and wild beauty at **Start Bay** (p190). If you're still keen for kitsch look no further than **Torquay** (p178) and **Paignton** (p178), where Victorian piers, jingling amusement arcades and candy-coloured bathing huts line the seafront. Grab a bag of chips, stroll the prom and find a handy bench as the fairy lights wink on for that quintessentially British finish.

ELEGANT ENGLAND

This tour steers a course through some of the southwest's quintessentially English towns. Top of the architectural heap is **Bath** (p90), with its concoction of Georgian crescents, landscaped gardens and palatial town houses; the gorgeous garden of **Prior Park** (p100) lies just outside the city, while the country house of **Tyntesfield** (p90), is to the northwest. The vintage cottages and quiet pubs of the Mendip villages are worth discovering, especially **West Harptree** (p105) and **Priddy** (p105), before heading south for the pocket-sized city of **Wells** (p100), still the official seat of the Bishop of Bath and Wells. Have a mosey around **Glastonbury** (p106) and take

a trip up the tor for views over the Somerset countryside, then veer south to the hilltop town of **Shaftesbury** (p152), where you'll find the classic English cobbled street on Gold Hill. Nearby **Sherborne** (p151) is blessed with a brace of imposing castles and a fabulous abbey dating from the early Middle Ages. Dorset's dotted with lots of smart market towns, including **Blandford Forum** (p153), **Wareham** (p134) and **Wimborne** (p133), and for more showiness there's also the elegant country house at **Kingston Lacy** (p134) and the rarefied ruins of **Corfe Castle** (p136). **Lyme Regis** (p160) still cuts a dashing figure, but it's outstripped in the style stakes by the red-brick streets of **Dorchester** (p138) and the cathedral city of **Exeter** (p166).

TASTEBUD TOUR

Time to think with your stomach. The southwest is becoming a destination of choice for people who appreciate fine wine and even finer food, so here's a quick rundown of the culinary cornerstones. Top on the specials board is the north Cornish coast, where you'll find Rick Stein's gastronomic empire in **Padstow** (p228), Jamie Oliver's spanking new restaurant on **Watergate Bay** (p232) and a bumper catch of seafood restaurants around **St Ives** (p238). Over at **Newlyn** (p244) you can buy lobsters and crabs straight from the pot, while there are loads of little farm shops dotted around the county worth seeking out. Across the Devon border you'll find another celebrity set-up run by TV chef John Burton Race in **Dartmouth** (p190), while **Torquay** (p182) is another good spot for a gourmet gander. Bristol's got some fantastic eateries, too – our favourites are **riverstation** (p86) and **Severnshed** (p86) for top-class waterside dining.

For tipplers, the **Camel Valley Vineyard** (p275) in Cornwall and the **Sharpham Vineyard** (p184) in Devon are brewing vintages that have even got the French sitting up and taking notice. The **Blue Anchor** (p249), in Helston, and the **Beer Engine** (p173), near Lyme Regis, both brew their own beer. Still not feeling too tipsy? Then take a gin tour in **Plymouth** (p198) or a spin around a traditional scrumpy farm in Somerset p114. Here's mud in your eye!

History

If you've got a penchant for the past, then you're in luck – the southwest of England packs an astonishing amount of history into a comparatively tiny space. Over the centuries the far west of Britain has played witness to many of the key events in British history, from Viking invasions and Spanish Armadas right through to the heyday of the Industrial Revolution. So no matter which period fascinates you, there's bound to be a historical sight that'll pique your interest – whether it's staring out from the battlements of a medieval castle, moseying around a stately country home or becoming all spiritual in a standing circle.

There's too much history to pack into one short chapter, so the timeline gives an overview of the major events, while in the main text, we delve into a few of the key periods, themes and people that have shaped the region's past.

ANCIENT STONES

It's thought that humans have inhabited the southwest of England for more than 100,000 years, but the first hard evidence of human settlement is a jawbone dating from around 35,000 BC, unearthed in Kent's Cavern (p180), near Torquay, during an excavation in 1927. (Academic opinion is divided as to whether the bone belongs to a Neanderthal or prehistoric ancestors of *Homo sapiens*.) The earliest southwest settlers were tribes of hunter-gatherers, living seasonally from the land and travelling in pursuit of game such as woolly mammoths, cave bears and rhinoceroses. Many of the region's caves were probably used by these primitive hunters as temporary shelters; the oldest human skeleton discovered in Britain was found in Cheddar Gorge (p103) and dates from around 7150 BC. Other notable Stone Age sites include an ancient settlement at Hengistbury Head in Dorset, but other archaeological evidence from this period is scarce, suggesting that the southwest was mainly used for itinerant hunting rather than permanent settlement.

As the great ice sheets melted at the end of the last Ice Age around 7000 BC, hunter-gatherers established themselves more firmly across the region, foraging across the grassy uplands and plains, and retreating to coastal sites during the colder months. The first signs of organised farming and animal domestication emerge around 4000 BC, and artefacts from this period, including stone axes, antler combs and flint arrowheads, have been discovered around the Mendips, Cheddar, Dartmoor, Bodmin Moor, Carn Brea, the Lizard and West Cornwall. Around this time prehistoric builders developed a taste for eye-catching architecture: stone rings, menhirs, stone

The Ancient Greeks referred to the British Isles as the Cassiterides, or Islands of Tin.

TIMELINE

To 4000 BC	3000–1800 BC	1000–500 BC
Region sporadically populated by nomadic hunter-gatherers and Neanderthals, followed by Mesolithic seasonal migrants. First evidence of organised farming and flint tools. Neolithic builders construct dolmens and quoits.	Many of the stone circles and menhirs dotted around Cornwall, Devon and Dartmoor are probably built around this time.	Arrival of the first Celts on British shores. Celtic warriors establish hillforts and fortified settlements and gradually begin to integrate with native Britons, bringing with them new iron tools and weapons.

rows, quoits and barrows, especially in Dorset, Devon, Dartmoor, Bodmin Moor, Penwith and the Isles of Scilly.

Quite what these ancient builders were up to with their curvy circles, wonky-topped henges and stone pillars is still a mystery, although that doesn't seem to have stopped people speculating – countless theories claim to explain their existence, ranging from celestial clocks to extraterrestrial landing pads. In reality, most were probably built to mark important sacred sites and burial mounds, and many seem to have been carefully aligned to coincide with the summer and winter solstices.

Thanks to its rich mineral deposits, the southwest began to attract settlers in increasing numbers with the advent of the Bronze Age, and there is evidence that by as early as 1800 BC there was a thriving trade with other parts of Europe in gold, tin, bronze and copper from Cornish mines. Many ancient artefacts, including beads, daggers, axes, bracelets and lunulae (crescent-shaped collars), bear a striking resemblance to similar items from Mycenae and ancient Greece, suggesting the southwest had already established trading links with the eastern Mediterranean; the most striking find was the 'Rillaton Cup', a golden chalice discovered in Linkinhorne on Bodmin Moor, now housed in the British Museum.

A new wave of settlers – the Celts – arrived around 1000 BC, mainly from northern France and the Netherlands, attracted by the region's mineral riches as well as its fertile agricultural land and temperate climate. Thanks to their sturdy iron weapons and warlike ways, they quickly conquered much of the area, establishing themselves in hilltop forts and coastal strongholds such as Chûn Castle (p241) near Zennor, Castle Dore (p270) near Fowey and Maiden Castle (p150) near Dorchester, as well as in small villages such as Chysauster (p241), just outside Penzance. Other settlers established communities near important water-courses, including the 'lake villages' of Glastonbury and Meare, probably founded in the 2nd century BC.

With their mix of martial prowess, artistic sensibility and religious dynamism, the Celts developed a culture, architecture and language entirely distinct from much of the rest of Britain, but their flourishing society lasted barely a thousand years. By the 1st century BC, a new wave of invaders had swept across the southwest landscape and brushed all but the hardiest Celtic defenders aside. *Veni, vidi, vici* – the Romans had arrived.

For a comprehensive overview of Cornwall's turbulent history, try *Cornwall: A History* by Philip Payton, or for something a little less weighty, pick up a copy of Daphne du Maurier's 1967 classic *Vanishing Cornwall*.

ROMAN RULE & THE COMING OF THE KINGS

The first Roman landings in Britain were led by Julius Caesar in 55 BC, but it was another century before the Roman conquest began in earnest. In AD 43 Aulus Plautius invaded Britain with around 20,000 troops, backed up by reinforcements from the stuttering Emperor Claudius. Over the next five years, under the orders of the genius military commander Vespasian,

55 BC	AD 55	410–600
Roman legions under Julius Caesar defeat native Belgic tribes ruled by their chieftain, Cassivellaunus. Over the next century the Belgae reassert control over southern England, pushing west towards Devon and Dorset.	Roman fortress built at Isca Dumnoniorum (Exeter). Other Roman towns are constructed at Bath, Dorchester, Ilchester and Gloucester. Construction of Roman roads including the Fosse Way from Exeter to Lincoln begins.	Arrival of Christianity in the southwest, probably brought from Ireland by some of the region's saints, including St Petroc, St Ia, St Keverne and St Piran, patron saint of Cornwall. Continuing conflicts between Saxons and Celts.

the legions rampaged through southern England, venturing as far as Exeter and capturing key strongholds such as Maiden Castle (p150) in Dorset.

At that time much of Dorset and Somerset was controlled by a Celtic tribe known as the Durotriges, while most of Devon and Cornwall was occupied by the Dumnonii (giving the region its Roman name of Dumnonia). A key fortress was built at Exeter (Isca Dumnoniorum to the Romans), which marked the western end of the vital Roman road to Lincoln known as the Fosse Way. Remnants of the original Roman fortifications can be still be seen around Exeter city centre.

While military matters where taken care of at Exeter, the legions could head for some R&R at Aquae Sulis (modern-day Bath), where the Romans established a complex series of bathhouses to take advantage of the natural hot springs (p92). Unsurprisingly, the town became a retirement hot spot for well-heeled Roman officials, and many grand villas sprang up around the city's outskirts, although sadly none have survived.

By the 4th century AD Rome's great empire was already in decline. Rebellions by recalcitrant Pictish warriors in the north, combined with Saxon invasions in the late 4th century, caused increasing pressure on Rome's dwindling resources. By AD 410 the last legions had been withdrawn from Britain, and the so-called 'Dark Ages' had begun.

Although detail about this period is patchy due to few written records, over the next 500 years southwest Britain was invaded by waves of Anglo-Saxon settlers, mainly tribes of Angles, Saxons, Jutes and Frisians from modern-day Germany, who first came as mercenaries in the Roman army. The native Celts were pushed back into their traditional strongholds in Wales, Dartmoor and Cornwall, creating pockets of Celtic culture, while the rest of the region was colonised by the Anglo-Saxons. About this time a fearsome war leader – supposedly by the name of Arthur or Arthurus – is said to have emerged to lead a counterattack against the invading Saxons, checking their progress over 12 great battles, and launching the enduring legend of King Arthur (p223). Whether Arthur ever existed is a matter of conjecture, but the next two centuries were marked by conflicts between indigenous Celts (occasionally helped by Danes and Vikings) and Anglo-Saxons. Finally, in the early 9th century, King Egbert and the armies of Wessex swept west and brought the whole of the southwest under Anglo-Saxon control. By the time of the death of King Alfred (of burnt cakes fame) in 899, the Vikings had been repelled, the Celts had been subdued, and the unified nation of England was on its way to being formed.

The town of Glastonbury is reputed to be the burial place of King Arthur and Queen Guinevere.

ALL AT SEA

With the largest stretch of continuous coastline in mainland Britain, it's hardly surprising that the southwest has one of the longest (and proudest) maritime histories in England. The region's past is peppered by all manner of salty sea-going characters, from ruthless pirates and cunning 'free traders'

814–38	878	939
Armies of Wessex under Egbert conquer most of southwest England, including Cornwall and Devon, although some isolated Cornish warriors fight on. Egbert defeats final alliance of Cornish and Viking warriors at Hingston Down.	Wessex is overrun by Vikings and King Alfred the Great goes into hiding in the marshes of Athelney (Somerset). He later musters an army and defeats the Viking king Guthrum.	Athelstan, king of Wessex and the first recognised king of all England, dies and is buried in Malmesbury Abbey.

to heroic sea captains and globetrotting explorers. The first in a long line of seaborne invasions began around 1000–500 BC, when Celtic migrants arrived from mainland Europe, followed in successive waves by the Romans, Irish and Vikings. The first Christian saints also arrived in the southwest by sea, probably from Ireland, although their vessels were a little unconventional – St Ia is supposed to have sailed up to the north Cornish coast on a giant leaf, while legend has it that St Piran, patron saint of Cornwall, arrived aboard a granite millstone.

Many of the region's key harbours had been founded in the days of the Roman occupation, and by the time of the publication of the Domesday book in 1086, there were already important ports at Plymouth, Fowey, Looe, Saltash and Bristol, although it wasn't until the reign of Henry VIII and the formation of the Navy Royal (later the Royal Navy) in 1509 that the region's maritime history really began in earnest.

His daughter, Elizabeth I, expanded the navy's power to counter the increasing strength of Spanish fleets, and also encouraged the practice of 'private enterprise' (otherwise known as piracy) on the open seas south of the British mainland. Many of her favourite sea captains were southwest lads, including the Cornish nobleman Sir Richard Grenville (born at Buckland Abbey in Devon); his cousin, Sir Walter Raleigh (born in Hayes Barton, East Devon); the aristocratic Sir John Hawkins (born in Plymouth); and his cousin, Sir Francis Drake, the first man to circumnavigate the globe in 1577 aboard his ship the *Pelican* (later renamed the *Golden Hind* – you can see a modern-day replica in Brixham Harbour, p183).

Elizabeth's military foresight proved prescient. In 1588 Philip II of Spain despatched an armada of 130 warships to invade Britain and bring the island under Catholic rule. The Armada was sighted off the Lizard on 19 July, and the message was carried to London via a series of specially-constructed beacons along the south coast. Whether Drake was really larking around bowling on Plymouth Hoe at the time of the invasion is unlikely, but that night he set sail from Plymouth with a fleet of 55 ships, accompanied by his cousin Hawkins and Lord Howard of Effingham. Over the next two weeks Drake fought a series of engagements against the Spanish fleet, culminating in the Battle of Gravelines on 29 July, in which 11 Spanish galleons were destroyed and the rest put to flight. Less gloriously, Drake and Hawkins were also instrumental in establishing the first slave-trafficking routes with Africa, a lucrative trade that underpinned the growth of several southwest ports (especially Bristol and Plymouth) over the two next centuries.

The southwest also played a key role in the move from Old to New Worlds. On 16 September 1620, a group of Puritan settlers set sail from Plymouth aboard the *Mayflower* for America, landing at Provincetown Harbour in present-day Massachusetts, where they founded the colony of New Plymouth.

Sir Francis Drake: The Queen's Pirate is an engaging examination of one of Britain's greatest sea captains, but it's not terribly complimentary. The upshot is that Drake was a ruthless pirate more interested in lining his own pockets with Spanish gold than protecting his country.

1050	1305	1337
Foundation of the first cathedral at Exeter, although the original building is substantially remodelled in the 12th and 13th centuries.	Edward I grants official charters to the Stannaries and establishes four stannary (tin-mining) towns in Cornwall (Truro, Lostwithiel, Launceston and Helston) and three more in Devon (Chagford, Ashburton, and Tavistock).	Edward III establishes the Duchy of Cornwall to provide an income for his son Edward, the Black Prince. The Heir Apparent subsequently inherits the titles of Prince of Wales and Duke of Cornwall.

BRISTOL & THE SLAVE TRADE

By the start of the 17th century Bristol had become the second busiest (and wealthiest) British port, behind only the port of London. Up until the late 17th century, the majority of its trade was based around local commodities, such as grain, wheat and especially cloth and wool, but the city's merchants had a notoriously keen eye for the latest market trends and, in 1698, they spotted a new money-making opportunity that was to dominate the city's fortunes for the coming century. That new trade involved shipping slaves across the Atlantic from countries on the west coast of Africa.

Prior to 1698 the slave trade was limited to a single Crown-owned monopoly known as the Royal African Company, but following vigorous lobbying the government opened up the trade nationwide, and Bristol's merchants seized the new opportunity with both hands. The first slaving ship set sail from Bristol's harbour in 1698, and over the next century the so-called 'Triangle Trade' grew into a fantastically lucrative enterprise for the city, along with other major slave-trading ports in London and Liverpool. Munitions, textiles and manufactured goods were carried to Africa, where they were sold for slaves; the slaves were transported to work in the booming colonies in the New World, principally in America and the Caribbean. In exchange for slaves British merchants carried back luxury goods produced on the plantations (especially sugar, tobacco, rum, indigo and cotton) to the markets in England and Europe. Needless to say, the conditions on the ships were horrific; it was routinely expected that more than 10% of the 'cargo' would be lost to disease or malnutrition on the 'Middle Passage' (Transatlantic crossing), but the actual figure was often far, far higher.

It was a brutal trade with potentially fantastic profits. In the hundred or so years until slavery was finally abolished in Britain in 1807, it's estimated that in excess of 2100 ships set sail from Bristol bound for the slave-trading ports, transporting approximately 500,000 Africans into slavery in the New World – around one-fifth of all the slaves transported by British vessels during the period.

The city is littered with reminders of the huge profits made by the city's slave-traffickers: many of the grand town houses in Clifton were built on the proceeds of the trade, and several of the city's most elegant edifices – such as the Theatre Royal on King St (also known as the Old Vic) – were partly financed by slave-trading investors. Many of Bristol's buildings and streets even bear names associated with the trade: Blackboy Hill is one of the most obvious examples, and it is claimed the hill was the site of slave auctions; while Colston Hall and Colston Ave are both named after the merchant Edward Colston, who had substantial interests in several slave ships operating from Bristol's docks, and was one of the original merchants behind the Royal Africa Company.

For more information about the city's murky slave-trafficking past, download the MP3 audio-tour from **Visit Bristol** (http://visitbristol.co.uk/site/sightseeing-and-tours/slave-trade-mp3-audio-tour) or pick up the printed booklet for the *Slave Trade Trail* (£2.95) from the tourist office, then explore for yourself.

You will find even more background in the galleries and interactive displays of the excellent British Empire and Commonwealth Museum (p81).

1348	**1497**	**1539**
The Black Death reaches the southwest, killing an estimated one-third of the population.	The 'An Gof' rebellion under Michael Joseph and Thomas Flamank against Henry VII marches on London, but is quashed and its leaders executed. A second Cornish rebellion under Perkin Warbeck fails later the same year.	Henry VIII initiates the Dissolution of the Monasteries; important monasteries and abbeys, including Glastonbury, Shaftesbury, Bath, Buckfast, Bodmin and Glasney College in Penryn, are stripped of their assets and later torn down.

The eastern seaboard of the USA is dotted with many other names reflecting the southwestern origins of the early settlers – Portland, Weymouth, Portsmouth, Dartmouth, Bideford and New Jersey, to name a few.

Following the turmoil of the Civil War in the mid-17th century, the southwest continued to expand its maritime traffic and cross-Atlantic trade. Between 1730 and 1745, Bristol had become Britain's second city and its leading slaving port (see the boxed text, opposite), while Plymouth consolidated its status as a key naval base and trading hub. Further west, the deepwater harbour of Falmouth had established itself as another important port thanks to the vital Falmouth Packet Service, which carried mail and goods to the far corners of the British Empire between 1689 and 1850.

In the late 18th century, rising customs duty on imported goods (especially luxury items such as brandy, gin and tea) led to a huge growth in smuggling all along the southwest coastline. Cornwall's remote coves were perfect hide-outs for the enterprising 'free traders', and the sight of government 'preventive' boats in pursuit of small smuggling vessels became fairly commonplace off the southern Cornish coastline. But the government operatives were often fighting a losing battle; widespread opposition to the punitive taxes, coupled with the lucrative returns that could be made from handling contraband goods, meant that collusion between the smugglers and onshore communities was widespread. Smuggling rapidly became a hugely profitable industry – according to some estimates, as much as four-fifths of the tea drunk in England in the late 19th century had escaped paying official duty – and some smugglers, such as Harry Carter and Jack Rattenbury, became local celebrities (Harry Carter even published his own autobiography).

The prospect of invasion loomed again during the Napoleonic wars in the early 19th century, but thanks to Messrs Nelson and Wellington, the vertically challenged Corsican general never managed to land any French boots on British shores. The latter years of the 19th century were a boom time for much of the southwest. The Industrial Revolution created a huge demand for the region's coal, tin and copper, much of which was shipped out from the region's ports or carried from Bristol to London on the new Great Western Railway, designed by the pioneering engineer Isambard Kingdom Brunel (p80). Brunel was responsible for designing the first great Transatlantic liners, including the *Great Western* in 1837 and the world's first iron-hulled steamer, the SS *Great Britain*, which was launched in Bristol in 1843 and can now be seen on the city's dockside (p79).

The growth in prosperity continued throughout the Edwardian and Victorian eras, largely thanks to the huge volume of goods flowing into the region's ports from Britain's colonies, but the boom time couldn't last forever. The hardships of WWI took a heavy toll, especially at the naval port of Plymouth, and as the British Empire began its long, slow decline, the region's once thriving harbours fell on hard times. Even worse, following the outbreak

Smuggling in the British Isles by Richard Platt is a rollicking journey through the history of free-trading around the southwest's shores and, as you might expect, there are frequent appearances from many local characters, including Jack Rattenbury and Harry Carter.

The lively website at www.smuggling.co.uk is packed with smuggling-related info, plus potted biographies and a useful guide to key locations.

1542	**1549**	**1588**
Bristol is granted its city charter, with the former Abbey of St Augustine becoming Bristol Cathedral.	Parliament passes the Act of Uniformity enforcing the use of an all-English Book of Common Prayer. Resistance culminates in a minor rebellion outside Exeter. It is put down in bloody fashion by Lord Grey; several clergymen and nobles are executed.	The Spanish Armada invasion fleet is first sighted off the Lizard Peninsula, but is defeated by the Royal Navy fleet under the command of Sir Francis Drake, who is stationed at Plymouth.

of WWII in 1939, British ports became key targets for German bombing raids, and many historic harbours were levelled by repeated Luftwaffe raids between 1940 and 1944. Some were never to recover, while others took the opportunity to rebuild and modernise; and though the great days of the ocean-going Empire had disappeared, the southwest's enduring links with the deep blue sea have lasted right through to the present day.

MINING & METHODISM

Humans have been digging around in search of precious metals since long before the first written records. Initially stone was more valuable than metal: minerals such as iron pyrites (used for fire-making) and flint (for making arrowheads, hunting knives and axe blades) were particularly prized, and natural ores such as copper, tin, bronze and gold were used to make decorative jewellery and ornaments. But it was in the Bronze Age, around 2000 BC, that mining really kicked into gear. Cornwall's rich deposits of tin and copper made it a valuable location for Bronze Age metalsmiths, and they settled here in large numbers; the ancient hilltop settlement of Carn Brea was certainly used by Bronze Age tribes, and there are other Bronze Age settlements around Dartmoor, Bodmin Moor and West Penwith.

Later Celtic and Iron Age settlers brought new types of tools and refined weapon designs from the Continent, and by 500 BC there were several thriving trading routes between Ireland, Wales, Cornwall and northern France. It's believed that during this period St Michael's Mount (p248) was used as a kind of 'clearing house' for locally mined ore and smelted metal. The Mount is also thought to have been the important trading island of 'Ictis', referred to by the Greek historian Diodorus in the 1st century AD. The Romans inevitably brought a degree of order to the proceedings, and no doubt made good use of the region's high-quality metals in keeping the legions supplied with those all-important weapons of warfare.

Early miners were forced to rely on a process of primitive open-cast mining, in which shallow pits or caves were dug to release metal ores just beneath the surface. Lighter metals such as tin were often extracted by streaming, where alluvial tin was collected from watercourses and river beds. By the early Middle Ages, tin had become a crucial part of the economy for much of Cornwall and Devon, and in 1201 King John granted the first charter to the Stannaries (key mining districts) in Cornwall, which by this time were already operating under their own Parliament and a semiseparate legal system. A century later in 1305 Edward I granted two further charters (one each for Devon and Cornwall) and founded a number of Stannary Towns, where tin was weighed, assayed and stamped, and coinage (a tax on smelted tin) was paid to the Crown.

Over the next few centuries the mining industry developed apace. The introduction of gunpowder in the late 17th century led to the introduc-

Brunel: the Man Who Built the World by Stephen Brindle is a lively and refreshingly unstuffy biography of the great inventor and engineer Isambard Kingdom Brunel, with some handy illustrations that reveal the true genius behind the man's pioneering designs.

1620	1642–46	1685
The Pilgrim Fathers set sail from Plymouth aboard the *Mayflower*, founding the colony of New Plymouth in Massachusetts in November the same year.	English Civil War divides loyalties; Cornwall declaring for the king, Charles I, other regions split. Early battles at Braddock Down, Stratton and Lansdown, near Bristol, and Plymouth. Royalist surrender at Tresillian, near Truro, in March 1646.	Protestant Monmouth Rebellion, led by the Duke of Monmouth, against the Roman Catholic James II defeated at Sedgemoor, the last battle fought on English soil. Its ringleaders are executed during the 'Bloody Assize' in Dorchester.

tion of 'blasting', allowing miners to access deep lodes of high-quality tin and copper, but it was during the 18th century that mining in Cornwall reached its apogee. Speculative investors, or 'adventurers', advanced huge amounts of capital to develop new mines in the hope they would strike it rich underground. Sometimes their investments paid out in astonishing fashion, as at Wheal Virgin ('wheal' is a Cornish word meaning 'mine') in Gwennap, near Redruth, which produced over £5700 worth of copper ore in its first fortnight in 1757 (equivalent to perhaps £100,000 today). Others were less successful – the ironically named Wheal Bounty, near Camborne, was developed at huge cost over several years, but eventually closed without ever having paid out a dividend.

While many mine-owners grew rich on their investments, conditions underground were altogether less pleasant. Most tinners worked for between eight and 12 hours a day, descending a hundred fathoms via metal ladders into dark, cramped tunnels where the temperature routinely reached 30°C, and explosions and rock falls were everyday hazards. For this, miners received an average weekly wage of around 4s, about £10 a year, barely enough to keep a family above starvation level. Consequently miners' wives and children were often roped into working at the mines as well, usually sorting or 'dressing' the extracted ore. At home things were scarcely any better: overcrowding, disease and malnutrition were widespread, and the average miner was lucky to make it into his late 30s. So it's hardly surprising that the tinners gained a reputation for drunkenness, lawless behaviour and hell-raising, especially at one of the many 'kiddleywinks' (pubs), which touted for their business. Fights and displays of public drunkenness were commonplace, and the fierce rivalry between neighbouring mining districts occasionally resulted in running street battles.

Cornwall was ripe for spiritual redemption when, in 1743, the Methodist preacher John Wesley arrived to deliver his first sermon at St Ives. Preaching the virtues of temperance, self-reliance and the promise of paradise in the next world in exchange for piety in this one, Wesley spent the next 20 years travelling the county, preaching to ever-larger crowds. In his journal in 1781, Wesley claims to have preached to around 20,000 people at Gwennap Pit, near St Day. Many Methodist chapels were built across the county, including several by the famous Cornish Methodist, Billy Bray (a former miner), and Methodism rapidly established itself as the county's predominant religion – by 1851, more than 60% of the county's residents considered themselves Methodist.

The beginning of the 19th century was another boom period for Cornish mining. In 1800 the county boasted 75 mines employing 16,000 people; by 1837, this had expanded to around 200 mines employing some 30,000 workers, in part thanks to the invention of the steam-powered engine by James Watt and, more importantly, the Cornish engineer Richard Trevithick, who

In the mid-18th century a pound of tea cost at least 8s – roughly the same as a bottle of champagne and the average weekly wage of a manual labourer.

The main online resource for the Unesco Cornish Mining World Heritage Site is www.cornish-mining.org.uk, with a list of Cornwall's famous mining sites and a history of the industry.

1720	1729	1743
Thomas Newcomen builds an 'atmospheric engine' at Wheal Fortune Mine, announcing the arrival of mechanised mining.	John Wood the Elder constructs Bath's first great Georgian terrace on Queen's Sq, followed by further Georgian masterpieces around the Circus and the Royal Crescent (both completed by his son, John Wood the Younger).	John Wesley delivers his first sermon in Cornwall and begins the long process of Methodist conversion in the county.

devised a steam locomotive. Another gifted Cornishman had also done much to improve the miners' lot; Humphry Davy, the brilliant Penzance-born chemist and engineer, invented the safety lamp in 1815, which prevented the lethal underground explosions caused by the ignition of flammable gases by miners' candles. But by the mid-19th century, the mineral lodes of many mines were already failing, turning previously rich mine shafts into 'knackt bals' (exhausted mines). Worse was to follow in 1866, when a financial crash across England bankrupted many mineowners and investors, and caused a catastrophic collapse in the Cornish mining industry. Just five years later, in 1871, every single one of the once-profitable copper mines around Redruth and Camborne had closed for good, and a subsequent slump in world tin prices resulted in the closure of countless others.

It was a disaster from which Cornish mining never recovered. Huge numbers of native Cornish migrated to the colonies, where their mining skills were still in demand, particularly in the gold and silver mines of California, Mexico and Australia, and the names of so-called 'Cousin Jacks' can be found on tombstones everywhere from Bolivia to Burra Burra. Today the pump houses and chimney stacks dotted across the Cornish landscape are the only remaining legacy of this once-mighty industry. Cornwall's last working mine – South Crofty, in Camborne – closed its gates in 1998, and despite several subsequent attempts to reopen the shafts, it seems Cornwall's mine shafts may well remain silent for good.

BRING OUT THE BATHING MACHINES

When you're sitting in a mile-long summer traffic jam on the A30, it might be hard to believe that much of the southwest was once a no-go area, but before the arrival of the railway in the mid-19th century, the Westcountry was about as popular with visitors as the American Wild West. Much of the region still required a journey of several days to reach, and roads were generally rough, muddy and poorly maintained, often navigable only on horseback rather than via the relative comfort of a horse-drawn carriage. It was also an astonishingly poor region; despite the plethora of grand town houses in prosperous cities such as Bristol, Exeter, Plymouth and Bath, the vast majority of people were still employed in hard manual-labour jobs, which were poorly paid, physically exhausting and often life threatening to boot. Even in the mid-19th century, many people were still living a largely subsistence lifestyle, eking a living from traditional industries such as fishing, farming, thatching and reed-cutting, while much of the countryside was given over to heavy industry, especially quarrying and mining.

The coming of the railway changed everything, opening up new markets in Britain's booming industrial cities. By the late 1850s the railway had reached coastal towns including Weymouth, Torquay and Dartmouth, and on 11 April 1859, the first train chugged out of Plymouth (crossing the

1768	1801	1831
James Cook sets out from Plymouth on his first voyage to the South Pacific. He is employed to record the transit of Venus across the Pacific Ocean, but inadvertently discovers Tahiti, New Zealand and Australia.	Richard Trevithick demonstrates his groundbreaking *Puffing Devil* steam locomotive on Fore St in Camborne. Jane Austen moves to Bath, using her time in the city to inform her novels *Northanger Abbey* and *Persuasion*.	Isambard Kingdom Brunel wins commission for the new Clifton Suspension Bridge; two years later he begins construction of the railway line from London to Bristol, and four years later launches the first transatlantic liner, the *Great Western*.

River Tamar via the Brunel-built Royal Albert Bridge) and travelled west to Truro. Within a few years the tracks had been extended west to Penzance. And where the railway went, the tourists inevitably followed – although to begin with it was more of a trickle than a tide.

The growth in seaside tourism is really down to the enterprising Victorians, who were the first to contemplate the idea of spending a spell by the sea for the good of one's health. The bracing sea air and warm coastal sunshine were believed to have beneficial effects for the body and mind, and during the late 18th and early 19th centuries strolling up and down the promenades of Britain's seaside resorts became a popular pastime. The practice of taking a public dip was initially frowned upon until King George III took to the Channel waters during his first visit to Weymouth in 1789 with the assistance of a new-fangled invention known as a 'bathing machine'. He must have enjoyed himself, as he returned to Weymouth 14 times over the next 16 years – and having received the royal seal of approval, soon bathing machines were being wheeled out at many other beaches along the south coast. Seaside holidays were very definitely *de rigueur*.

Over the next 50 years the southwest's coastal resorts continued to grow at an astonishing rate. Grand hotels, music halls and amusement arcades sprang up along the seafronts of many of the region's resort towns to cater for the influx of visitors, while donkey rides, ice sellers, minstrels, pierrots, street entertainers and 'oompah' bands kept the masses entertained. Unlike their more downmarket and solidly working-class cousins further north, such as Blackpool, Southend and Margate, the southwest's seaside towns deliberately set out to appeal to a more genteel clientele. Many towns, including Torquay, Paignton, Ilfracombe and Dawlish, prided themselves on their elegant architecture, carefully landscaped promenades and rarefied atmosphere (it was the Victorians who first gave the Torbay area the rather grand soubriquet of 'The English Riviera'). The Victorians even established their own purpose-built seaside settlement from scratch; in 1811 the first holiday home at Bournemouth had been built by the local landowner Louis Tregonwell. By the end of the 19th century the town had mushroomed into one of the largest Victorian resorts in Britain, famed across the country for its theatres and concert halls, as well as its lavishly landscaped Pleasure Gardens.

But tourism further west still had some way to go at the end of the 19th century – at least if the write-ups in Black's bestselling *Guide To The Duchy of Cornwall* are anything to go by. Take the review of St Ives in the 1876 edition, where the writer is struck by the 'accumulation of nastiness… The streets are narrow and crooked; the houses old and shattered; the shops mean and squalid; and everywhere pervades an intolerable fishy smell'. Despite the negative reviews, the Great Western Company (who

Britain joined the EEC (European Economic Community) in 1973. Three years later a major row over fishing rights in Europe had serious knock-on effects for fishing communities across the southwest.

1859	1940–41	1951
The Brunel-designed Royal Albert Bridge over the River Tamar opens, connecting Cornwall to Devon for the first time. Five years on, the Clifton Suspension Bridge opens, and Clifton becomes one of Bristol's most affluent and gentrified areas.	Bristol and Plymouth experience heavy bombing raids by the Luftwaffe, and both sustain heavy damage, especially around the docks and city centre.	Dartmoor becomes the southwest's first designated National Park, followed three years later by Exmoor.

had invested heavily in extending the main-line railway into Cornwall) quickly realised the attractions of the Cornish Peninsula, and by 1904 had produced its own guidebook, *The Cornish Riviera*, supplemented by an exotic poster campaign. Over the next 50 years, especially between the wars, tourism in Cornwall continued to grow, while other local industries steadily declined. Well-known visitors including DH Lawrence, Barbara Hepworth and John Betjeman also played their part in raising the profile of the county and encouraging trippers to visit its sparkling shores. Betjeman even penned his own guidebook to the county in 1964, published in the popular *Shell Guides* series, although he later claimed to have regretted opening up his beloved county to the ranks of the great unwashed.

Today the southwest remains one of the UK's most popular holiday destinations, and tourism still accounts for around 20% of the region's total annual income. The bathing machines and music halls may have disappeared, but some things never change – lounging around on a beach and larking about in the rockpools is as popular now as the days when linen parasols and whalebone corsets were in vogue.

The oil tanker *Torrey Canyon* ran aground off Land's End in 1967. With 120,000 tonnes of crude oil spilling onto the Cornish coastline, this was the worst oil disaster in Cornwall's history.

1998	2001	2007
Closure of South Crofty, the last working mine in Cornwall, marks an end to 4000 years of metal mining in Cornwall.	Foot and mouth epidemic strikes rural southwest. The Eden Project – the world's largest greenhouses – opens on the site of a disused clay pit in Cornwall. The Jurassic Coast becomes England's first natural World Heritage Site.	The MSC *Napoli* is beached off Beer Head on the east Devon coast, shedding hundreds of containers onto the beach and prompting a chaotic free-for-all to claim the salvage.

The Culture

If there's one thing that binds the four southwest counties together, it's their diversity. Britain is a nation of nations, and the strong regional distinctions between areas just a few miles apart remains one of the great pleasures of travelling around this pint-sized island kingdom. Nowhere is this truer than in Cornwall, Devon, Dorset and Somerset; to the casual outsider they may seem superficially similar, but scratch the surface and you'll be astonished at how different they are – and how proud they are to be so.

REGIONAL IDENTITY

Ask any British city-dweller what it's like out west and you'll instantly hit the stereotypes – once you get west of Bristol everyone suddenly turns into a corn-chewing yokel who drives around in a battered VW camper, speaks with a treacle-thick accent and is just a little *too* close to their pretty young cousin down the road. You don't need us to tell you that's a load of old cobblers. In truth the modern southwest is a complex mix of people of all ages, backgrounds and walks of life, from born-and-bred, died-in-the-wool Cornish nationalists to wealthy retirees seeing out their golden years on the Devon coast.

In general terms Cornwall has arguably the most coherent sense of itself in Britain. The county is deeply, abidingly proud of its Celtic roots, and while regional identity elsewhere in Britain seems to be growing more fractured, the reverse is true in Cornwall. You'll see St Piran's flags and bumper stickers everywhere you go, and there's a growing interest in revival of the Cornish language. There have even been calls for a de-volved Cornish assembly to match that of Scotland, Wales and Northern Ireland; Cornwall has its own political party devoted to promoting the nationalist cause, **Mebyon Kernow** (Sons of Cornwall; www.mebyonkernow.org). Devon has also laid claim to having some Celtic roots, although you'll find lit-tle sympathy for that view west of the Tamar; nevertheless it's still a proud and united county, with a strong sense of history to underpin its forward-looking attitude.

Elsewhere, people's loyalties are divided less along regional lines, and more around the town or area in which they're based – you're much more likely to hear about a Bathonian or a Bristolian than a Dorsetian or a Somersetian, for example. But most people still feel a strong sense of con-nection with their county. (For proof just pop along to a local rugby or cricket derby.) Outside of the cities, Somerset is still predominantly a rural community, with a strong agricultural heritage and a growing renaissance in traditional industries such as willow-craft and cidermaking, while Dorset is a real mix: sleepy rural villages, alongside big urban conurbations such as Bournemouth, Poole and Dorchester.

The Gorseth Kernow is an organisation that exists to promote Cornish culture, made up from specially invited Cornish bards who've made outstand-ing contributions to the cause. They even have their own natty outfits – check them out at www .gorsethkernow.org.uk.

LIFESTYLE

Despite the impression you'll get from some of the tourist brochures, the southwest isn't actually a place where everyone pops out for a quick surf in their lunchbreak before jumping on their mountain bike to attend a sea-shanty singalong down the local boozer. Having said that, there's no doubt that life down west is lived at a more leisurely pace than in many other parts of Britain. There's still a strong sense of community, especially in the more rural corners, which are often bound together by a shared tradition and history stretching back centuries. The idyllic scenery and quiet countryside outside the main towns naturally lends itself to a more laid-back pace, and it's hard not to find yourself getting caught up in it. Nevertheless, people still have to earn a crust, and for most people life still revolves around a standard nine-to-five day; in the southwest's urban areas life can be just as hectic, pressured and time-short as in any other big British city.

While it's difficult to generalise about such a diverse region, there does seem to be some concrete benefit to the lifestyle down west – the region is top of the table for female life expectancy in Britain, and joint-top for men. School results, educational provision and work-related skills are all rated better than the national average, while crime rates, environmental pollution and (perhaps surprisingly) unemployment are all rated below the national average. On the flipside, the rates for suicide, teenage pregnancy and chronic drug abuse are among the worst in Britain, and the region has the worst incidence of malignant melanomas and skin cancers anywhere in the UK, as well as a growing problem with childhood obesity.

Statistically southwesterners are also a cultural bunch – among the top three places in the UK in terms of attendance at cultural, artistic and sporting events.

The Dartmoor National Park Authority is helping compile a fascinating oral history of life on the moor – check out reminiscences with local Dartmoor folk at www .dartmoor-npa.gov .uk/laf-moormemories.

ECONOMY

There's no doubt that the southwest's economic golden boy is tourism. Depending on which statistic you use, tourism adds between £4.5 and £8 billion to the region's coffers every year, and in some areas more than half of the available jobs are related in some way to the wider tourist industry. But the division of wealth is incredibly varied; though Bristol is by far the biggest contributor to the regional economy, areas within Bristol itself are among the most economically deprived in the area. Bristol still has a strong manufacturing base, especially in the aeronautics industry – the major aeronautical firms of BAE Systems, Airbus and Rolls-Royce are all based in the Bristol suburb of Filton, where the pioneering Concorde aircraft was developed in the 1970s. Devonport Dockyard in Plymouth is also an important shipbuilding area – with 15 dry docks and more than 4 miles of waterfront, it's the largest naval base in Western Europe.

Historically traditional blue-collar industries such as farming, fishing and mining (of tin, copper and coal) were once massive industries, but these have almost completely disappeared over the last few decades. There are no working mines left in the southwest, and fishing and farming are both in severe decline, with only Brixham and Newlyn retaining sizeable fishing fleets. This has a knock-on effect for many rural communities, as the lack of well-paid work often forces families to migrate towards the cities or even move elsewhere. With the decline in traditional manual industries, local governments are making a slow transition towards a more 'knowledge-based economy'; the IT, internet, service and creative sectors are all identified as potential areas for growth.

In general terms the more regional areas are economically the poorest, with Cornwall the most deprived; in the 1990s the county was identified as one of the poorest areas in Europe and over the last decade has qualified for an emergency £350 million economic-aid package from the EU called Objective One, which ended in 2007. Average incomes in the southwest are around 10% lower than the rest of the Britain, but the massively overblown property market and the relatively high cost of goods and services

Cornwall's traditional drinking toast is to *kober, sten ha pesk* – or copper, tin and fish, historically the county's three most important industries.

means that, in real terms, the region's spending power is statistically one of the lowest in Britain.

POPULATION

The total population of the combined southwest area covered by this book is around 3.5 million people. The majority – around 80% – live either within a city or town or in its immediate environs, although that's partly due to the fact that the region covers a relatively small geographic area. According to the last census in 2001 (which we've used to gather all our population figures), Devon has by far the largest population (1,704,919), while Dorset has the smallest (390,980); Cornwall (501,267) and Bristol and Somerset combined (878,708) are somewhere in the middle.

There's been a general upward trend in population across the southwest, with a 10% (or sometimes higher) growth in population over the last 20 years. This is predicted to rise substantially by 2030, with the region identified as one of the UK's major growth areas, placing corresponding pressures on the need for housing, a problem that's been compounded in many areas by the increase in the growth of second homes and holiday lets. Perhaps the most worrying statistic is the southwest's rapidly ageing population: it has the oldest demographic of any region in Britain, with more than one third of residents aged 50 or more, and this is predicted to rise to 40% in the next decade.

SPORT

Like most of Britain, the southwest counties are passionate about their sport. In the winter months the twin giants of football and rugby reign supreme, and the counties' sports grounds are generally packed to capacity most weekends, despite the vagaries of the British weather.

Football

To tap into the fierce rivalry between the southwest's football sides, head for a local derby. Although none of the region's football teams plays in the top-flight Premier League, there are currently two playing in the Championship: Plymouth Argyle and recent success story, Bristol City. At the time of writing, Bournemouth, Yeovil and Bristol Rovers were playing in League One, while Exeter, Weymouth and Torquay were languishing in non-League football. League position aside, **Plymouth Argyle** (www.pafe.premiumtv.co.uk) tops the regional capacity rankings: its Home Park can accommodate 20,134 fans.

Tickets for Championship teams are pricey and generally scarce, but you can usually bag a seat to watch the lowlier sides – though derby games often sell out, especially for major events such as the clash between arch-rivals Bristol City and Bristol Rovers. There's usually a short-lived run for one of the region's teams in the FA and League cups, but it's been a while since anyone's got much further than the first few rounds.

Rugby

The sport that excites passion in the southwest, especially in Bath, Bristol and Cornwall, is rugby. Again local derbies are best to watch – only 13 miles separate rivals **Bath** (www.bathrugby.co.uk) and **Bristol** (www.bristolrugby.co.uk). A fiercely competitive trio of local sides play in National Division One – Exeter Chiefs, Plymouth Albion and the Cornish Pirates (formerly the Penzance Pirates), joined in the 2007/08 season by new boys Launceston.

Inter-region rivalry is particularly potent, with all four counties regularly meeting each other in the county championship. Cornwall has had particular success in this competition, and for a glimpse of Cornish pride at its fiercest

Cornwall is making a bid to become Europe's first region of culture – check out how the campaign's coming along at www .cornwallculture.co.uk.

you can't beat a home county match. The terraces are a sea of black and gold, the air resounds to the fruity songs of the supporting **Trelawny's Army** (www.trelawnysarmy.org.uk) and a giant Cornish pasty is paraded round the pitch and hoisted over the crossbar. In 1991, 54,000 Cornish fans made the trip to Twickenham to watch their side beat Yorkshire to the trophy (a feat they repeated in 1999 against regional rivals Gloucester).

Cricket

In the summer thoughts turn to inswingers, sticky wickets and maiden overs, especially for fans of key southwest sides **Somerset** (www.somersetcountycc.premiumtv .co.uk) and **Gloucestershire** (www.gloscricket.co.uk). Somerset is based at the County Ground in Taunton and have been hitting boundaries since 1875, notably lifting the Cheltenham and Gloucester Trophy in 2001. First-class games are sometimes played at the Bath Cricket Ground, which also hosts an annual cricket festival that's been running since 1897.

Gloucester has its headquarters at the County Ground in Bristol, and has notched up an unrivalled seven one-day trophies in just five years. But one of the delights of a Westcountry summer is a tranquil afternoon watching county or village matches, often in beautiful settings; local papers outline fixtures, or ask at the village pub.

'With more than a hint of quidditch, Cornish hurling has its origins in the mass fights'

Other Sports

Other sports and activities abound in the southwest, and range from mountain biking and kiteboarding to surfing around the north coasts of Cornwall and Devon (see the Southwest Outdoors chapter, for more information). More esoteric activities include Cornish wrestling (or 'wrasslin'), a curious cross between judo, ballet and old-fashioned brute force; jacket-wearing wrasslers grab hold of their opponents and try to trip or throw them to the ground. The **Cornish Wrestling Association** (www.cornishwrestling.co.uk) has lists of championship contests, or look out for demonstrations at events such as the Royal Cornwall Show, regattas and steam rallies.

With more than a hint of quidditch, Cornish hurling has its origins in the mass fights (thinly disguised as handball games) that used to occur between parishes and villages. The adult 21st-century version takes place at St Columb on Shrove Tuesday and sees two 'teams' (town and country) attempt to carry a silver ball to 'goals' 2 miles apart – there's no referee and no rules, and shops, wisely, are boarded up. A child-friendly version takes places in St Ives in February.

MEDIA
Magazines

There are plenty of glossy magazines produced in the region, mainly aimed at holidaymakers and corporate coffee tables; here's our low-down on the ones worth looking out for:

GIG RACING

Pilot gig racing has its origins in the six-oared wooden vessels used to ferry pilots to sailing ships. The vessels were also used as lifeboats and by smugglers to outrun the customs men. Today the boats are still made out of narrow-leaf elm to specifications laid down in 1838, and more than 50 clubs are registered with the **Cornish Pilot Gig Association** (CPGA; www.cpga.co.uk). The season runs between May and September and some of the most atmospheric races take place on Wednesday and Friday nights in the Isles of Scilly (p255), where boats from the different islands fight it out in heaving seas. The islands also host the World Pilot Gig Championships each May.

24-7 (www.twenty4-seven.co.uk) Free weekly listings mag covering Devon, Plymouth and Cornwall.
Cornwall Today (www.cornwalltoday.co.uk) The best of Cornwall's coffee-table magazines (£3.50) issued monthly.
Devon Life (www.devonlife.co.uk) Upmarket monthly (£3.25) with county-based features, listings and recipes.
Folio (www.foliomagazine.co.uk) Bristol-based free monthly mag with local listings and lots of ads.
Inside Cornwall (www.insidecornwall.co.uk) Cornish glossy (£3.50) with lots of listings; monthly.
Stranger (www.stranger-mag.com) Funky Falmouth-based monthly 'zine (£1.50) with features and an ecofriendly stance.
Venue (www.venue.co.uk) Bristol and Bath's top weekly magazine (£1.20) for listings and local features.
Wavelength (www.wavelengthmag.co.uk) Cornish surfer's mag (£3.50) with nice surfy pictures; nine per year.

Newspapers

The southwest has many regional and city-based newspapers, mainly covering local-interest news with some syndicated stories from the national press. One of the largest publishers is Devon & Cornwall Media, which produces *The Cornish Guardian*, *The Cornishman* and *The West Briton* (the most widely circulated newspaper in Britain), as well as the daily *Western Morning News*, covering Devon, Cornwall and the wider Westcountry.

The *Bath Chronicle* is Bath's main daily, while the *Bristol Evening News* and *Western Daily Press* cover Bristol and environs; look out also for the *Dorset Echo*; and the *Western Gazette* and *Weston Mercury* in Somerset.

Radio

The **BBC** (www.bbc.co.uk) has the strongest regional presence, with local radio stations for three of the counties as well as Bristol. Depending on where you are (and how many hills are in the way), you might have to fiddle around with the dial to get a decent signal. All the BBC stations are very local affairs, and are often listened to by a pretty mature audience – expect mild-mannered phone-ins rather than too much penetrating topical analysis.

There are also lots of independent commercial radio stations, usually hosting a mix of chart hits, oldies, news and chat-based shows. For a list of available radio stations, see p42.

TV & the Web

Britain has five main terrestrial TV channels: BBC1 and BBC2, both non-commercial channels paid for by an annual licence-fee, plus ITV, Channel 4 and Channel 5, which are financed by advertising. Many more channels are available via satellite or the digital 'Freeview' service. Currently terrestrial TV services in the southwest are analogue, but the government has decreed that Britain will switch over to all digital by 2012. Digital TV coverage can be patchy in the region, especially if you're relying on Freeview.

The Beeb broadcasts regional TV news magazines in prime-time slots at 1.30pm and 6.35pm on BBC1 (*Spotlight* for Devon and Cornwall, *Points West* for Bristol and Somerset and *South Today* for Dorset). On ITV, Britain's main commercial channel, Carlton is the main regional company, with some local-interest programming as well as regional news bulletins at 1.30pm and 6pm.

The BBC website (www.bbc.co.uk) has subsections with news, travel and weather specific to each county (add a forward slash to the BBC site address followed by the county's name). We've suggested useful local websites throughout the regional chapters; see also p20.

Bristol's most famous film company is Aardman Animations, best-known for cuddly plasticine heroes Wallace & Gromit. By far their most ambitious project to date is *The Curse of the Were-Rabbit*, a hilarious and hugely imaginative riff on everything from Hammer Horror to detective yarns.

OVER THE AIRWAVES

BBC Stations

- **Radio Bristol** – 95.5FM, 94.9FM and DAB Digital Radio
- **Radio Cornwall** – 103.9FM, 95.2FM, 96FM and DAB Digital Radio
- **Radio Devon** – 103.4FM, 94.8FM, 95.8FM, 96FM, 104.3FM and DAB Digital Radio
- **Somerset Sound** – 1566AM

Independent Stations

- **Atlantic FM** – 105.1–107FM (Cornwall)
- **Gemini FM Exeter** – 97FM
- **GWR Bath** – 103FM
- **GWR FM Bristol** – 96.3FM
- **Lantern FM** – 96.2–97.3FM (Devon)
- **Orchard FM** – 96.5, 97.1 and 102.6FM (Somerset)
- **Pirate FM** – 102.2–108.2FM (Cornwall)
- **Plymouth Sound** – 96.6–97FM

RELIGION

In keeping with its predominantly white population, the southwest is largely Church of England, although you'll find a few mosques, synagogues and Catholic churches dotted around the region's more diverse corners. During the 19th century John Wesley helped convert huge numbers of people across Devon and Cornwall to Methodism, although this sterling old faith has largely faded into history; for more background see p32. There are also plenty more esoteric faiths scattered around, especially around hippie hub Glastonbury, where you'll find everything from Goddess worshippers to Celtic druids and Wicca witches.

ARTS
Painting & Sculpture

For many, visual arts in the Westcountry are associated with the far west of Cornwall. The group of painters referred to as the Newlyn School (p244) were drawn to the port in the late 19th and early 20th centuries by the superb light, simpler life and cheap living. Themes were firmly those of social realism and included everyday life and work in local fishing communities. Among the key players were Lamorna Birch and Stanhope and Elizabeth Forbes, who founded the School of Painting at the turn of the century.

Willow bark was traditionally used as a medicinal remedy to treat rheumatism, chills and toothache, and the active ingredient, *salicin*, was eventually isolated and led to the development of aspirin.

Another Cornish artistic community is St Ives, which has attracted painters since JMW Turner's and Whistler's day. In the late 1920s it also inspired the extraordinary work of retired fisherman Alfred Wallis. Completely self taught, his paintings are beautiful examples of naïve art – they disregard perspective and apportion scale in relation to the subject's importance to the scene; Wallis' poverty meant his work was often painted on cardboard.

The abstract painter Ben Nicholson had been hugely impressed by Wallis' work on a visit to St Ives in 1928. Nicholson moved to the port in 1939 with his wife, the pioneering sculptor Barbara Hepworth. Others followed in their footsteps: Bernard Leach, the abstract artist Wilhelmina Barns-Graham, landscape painter Peter Lanyon and painter-designer Patrick Heron all helped establish the port as an avant-garde enclave; the Tate St Ives (p235) displays many of their works.

Expect a blend of the old masters, French and modern art at Bristol's City Museum and Art Gallery (p80), while the collection at the Victoria Art Gallery (p94) in Bath ranges from the 15th-century right up until the present day.

More recent artwork has been provided by Bristol-based Banksy (p83), a semi-anonymous, guerrilla graffiti artist, while north Devon has a splash of art by Damien Hirst, whose work preserving sharks and cows in formaldehyde propelled him to fame. His restaurant, 11, The Quay (p212; www.11thequay.com) in Ilfracombe, features chunks of his *Pharmacy* exhibit as well as rows of preserved fish, funky menus and great décor.

Literature

The southwest landscape is a literary one; everywhere there are places famous authors have used as inspirations for their work.

Devon was the birthplace of crime-writing legend Agatha Christie, who grew up in Torquay, lived near Dartmouth and wove countless local places into her novels. Many are clearly identifiable and can still be tracked down today; you can also visit the beautiful gardens of her holiday homes; see p181).

Another Westcountry writer inextricably linked with the landscape she loved is Daphne du Maurier (p269). Best known for romantic, dramatic novels such as *Rebecca*, she also wrote the short story that became the Alfred Hitchcock film *The Birds*. Du Maurier moved to Fowey in her early 20s and Cornwall's bleak moors and tree-fringed creeks feature strongly in her writings.

For many, Dorset is all about the Wessex wordsmith Thomas Hardy (p140), who used a thinly disguised version of the county throughout his writings. Dorchester is recognisably the title town of *The Mayor of Casterbridge*, while the modern use of the word 'Wessex' is entirely due to him.

The exquisite streets of Bath positively summon the elegant wit of Jane Austen (p94). Her discreet send-ups of middle-class life in Regency England include *Sense and Sensibility, Pride and Prejudice, Mansfield Park* and *Emma*, and she actually set *Northanger Abbey* and *Persuasion* in Bath.

Other southwest literary connections include John Fowles, who based *The French Lieutenant's Woman* in Lyme Regis (p160); the popular poet and broadcaster Sir John Betjeman, who is buried near his home in Trebetherick, north Cornwall (p225); and the poet Charles Causley, who lived in and was inspired by west Cornwall. The swashbuckling 17th-century epic *Lorna Doone* by Richard Blackmore is subtitled *A Romance of Exmoor*, and its atmosphere infuses the book. Henry Williamson featured the landscape of his north Devon home in *Tarka the Otter* and it's still called Tarka Country today. The historical novel *Westward Ho!*, written by Charles Kingsley in 1855, was such a hit that a village of the same name (p215) was actually built in the north Devon spot the book describes.

Music

Long tainted by images of Morris Dancers dancing round maypoles, turtle-necked folkies strumming out earnest tunes and tractor-tunesmiths The Wurzels just embarrassing everybody, the southwest's music scene has (thankfully) managed to carve out a more respectable niche for itself in recent years.

The region's best-known musical export, trip-hop, was born in the mid-90s by Bristol-based acts including Portishead, Tricky and Massive

In between decorating the nation's underpasses and flyovers, Banksy found time to collate *Wall and Piece,* a funky photographic journey through all his favourite work. Sadly there's no guidebook – mainly because many of the pieces had already been scrubbed off by the time the book was published.

Although there have been several attempts to analyse the mind of the 20th century's greatest thriller-writer, Agatha Christie's own *Autobiography* is by far the most revealing – and she even reveals some of the secrets behind her most famous plots.

Attack; its mix of dub-heavy beats, scratch-laden samples and digitally processed sounds was a massive commercial success, and continues to exert an influence, most clearly in the trippy beats of another big Bristol act, Kosheen. One of Bristol's other big musical names also shares a Massive Attack connection – Roni Size, the influential drum and bass artist, cut his musical teeth working with members of the band. Bristol's club scene is still at the cutting edge, with a number of high-profile DJs pushing the beat boundaries – legendary Brizzle club night Blowpop is still held monthly at the Thekla Social (p88).

On the flipside, there's been a recent revival in interest in that most maligned of musical genres, folk. A number of southwest singer-songwriters have found success reinventing the form with a 21st-century twist, most notably Seth Lakeman, whose songs are shot through with tales and locations drawn from his Dartmoor youth. Other names include James Hollingsworth and Gravenhurst (aka Nick Talbot), while down in Cornwall local singer-songwriters Luke Toms and Ruarri Joseph have recently been making waves. On the more traditional side of things, bands such as Dalla and sowena have used the sounds and instruments of Celtic music to craft their distinctive sound, often used as a soundtrack to traditional dance forms such as *noze looan* (Cornish for 'happy night').

Theatre

Despite being 200 miles from London's West End, the Theatre Royal Plymouth (p201) has the third highest financial turnover in the country – pipped only by the National Theatre and the Royal Shakespeare Company (RSC). It also has the futuristic TR2 rehearsal complex, which has helped attract a number of world premiers (such as Matthew Bourne's *Edward Scissorhands*) and produced key shows (*Jerry Springer – The Opera* and Yukio Ninagawa's *Hamlet*). The theatre's Drum performance space also produces innovative shows such as *pool (no water)* and *NHS – The Musical!*

The Theatre Royal Bath (p99) has three spaces: the Main Stage, the Ustinov Studio (which programmes fringe shows) and the Egg – a theatre especially for young children. The Tobacco Factory (p88) in Bristol is an intimate 250-seat space; highlights of its programming include and annual spring Shakespeare season. The Bristol Old Vic was the oldest continuously working theatre in the country until it closed for an 18-month refurbishment in mid-2007.

The southwest has long been used as a readymade set for film directors – www.visit southwest.co.uk/main /film_tv/filmtvhome .cfm has a guide to some of the most famous locations.

Further west, Cornwall's cliffside Minack (p243) has a season running from June to September. Nothing quite beats seeing *The Tempest* with a real raging sea as a backdrop.

Cornish-based theatre company **Kneehigh** (www.kneehigh.co.uk) has firmly established itself as one of most innovative and exciting in the UK. It uses words such as 'joyful anarchy', 'risk' and 'exhilaration' to define its work, and with good reason. Acclaimed productions include *Tristan & Yseult*, *Nights at the Circus*, *A Matter of Life and Death* and *Cymbeline*. Despite packing theatres nationwide it also keeps true to its Cornish roots; rehearsal space is a barn near Mevagissey, its offices are in Truro and it still tours Cornish village halls.

Architecture

Despite being a rural region, the sheer variety of the southwest's built environment can be a highlight of any trip. Many tourist offices provide town trail guides that outline places of interest; some stage guided walks. Or do it yourself and hunt out the blue plaques on the sides of architecturally and historically interesting buildings.

Dartmoor (p205), Bodmin Moor (p273) and the Penwith (p241) area of Cornwall have an unusually high number of prehistoric sites: Stone Age stone circles and Bronze Age settlements pop up everywhere. In Maiden Castle (p150), Dorset has an awe-inspiring Iron Age hillfort which, at 48 hectacres, is the finest in Britain. Bath has the pick of the region's Roman architecture (as well as a whopping 5000 listed buildings); the Roman Baths Museum (p93) affords glimpses of Roman pavements and the ruins of the 2000-year-old temple to Sulis-Minerva.

The murky events of the Dark Ages are evocatively conjured up by tumbling castle ruins across the southwest – most atmospherically in Cornwall at Tintagel (p223), where fragments of 6th-century walls grip the headland – prompting claims of links with King Arthur. The stunning remains of Corfe Castle (p136) in Dorset provide an insight not only into Norman building style, but also the destruction of the English Civil War – the castle was literally dynamited to pieces by the Parliamentarians.

The southwest has some of the finest smaller cathedrals in the country. The mostly Norman towers of Exeter Cathedral (p166) contain the largest collection of 14th-century sculpture in England. Wells Cathedral (p101), built between 1180 and 1508, boasts similarly stunning sculptures in its west front as well as several Gothic styles and striking scissor arches.

For 600-year-old townscapes head to Sherborne (p151) in Dorset or Totnes (p184) in Devon. Clustered around a fine abbey, Sherborne's central streets are full of exquisite, 15th-century, honey-coloured buildings, while Totnes' Fore St is lined with 60 Tudor merchants' houses faced with ancient tiles and propped up by pillars. Thatched cottages, often built from cob (a mixture of clay, sand and straw) are dotted across the region; Devon alone has 4000.

Elegant terraces, Palladian porticoes and sash windows also abound. In the Royal Crescent and the Circus (p93), Bath has some of the most jaw-dropping examples of Georgian buildings in the country. Blandford Forum (p153) in Dorset is an architectural oddity – rebuilt completely after a fire in 1731, the whole town centre dates from the same era.

Far grittier are the region's industrial heritage sites. Cornwall and West Devon's mining heritage has been recognised by Unesco and an underground tour of the mine at Geevor (p240) is memorable. Iconic and hugely atmospheric, the remnants of engine houses pepper the cliffs of Cornwall, and you can still see traces of the industry in the shape of mine-owner mansions and Methodist chapels.

There's more extraordinary engineering in the shape of the Clifton Suspension Bridge (p81), designed by Isambard Kingdom Brunel (see boxed text, p80), which spans the Avon Gorge at Bristol, and in several Victorian piers including those at Bournemouth (p126) and Teignmouth (p177).

Bath is the only UK city to be awarded a blanket Unesco World Heritage Site status.

Depending on your view, Prince Charles' very own architecture project, Poundbury (p149) in Dorset is either a mock-Georgian model town or a pioneering attempt at building better communities. Cornwall's Eden Project (p268) transformed a former clay pit into the biggest greenhouse in the world, while new city centre developments in Exeter's Princesshay (p166) and Plymouth's Drake Circus (p197) have drawn both praise and criticism.

Gardens

Blessed with an unusually temperate climate thanks to the Gulf Stream, the southwest is home to some of the nation's finest landscaped gardens. Cornwall is the horticultural hot spot; its unique coastal geography allows many exotic species to flourish here that simply wouldn't survive elsewhere in Britain. The most familiar names are the Eden Project (p268) and Heligan (p267), but you'll also discover a wealth of gardens left over by Edwardian and Victorian designers, including the valley gardens of Trebah and Glendurgan (p252), the rolling grounds of Trelissick (p262), the huge country estates of Cotehele (p277) and Lanhydrock (p275), and the National Magnolia Collection at Caerhays (p267).

'almost every self-respecting countryseat has its own glorious grounds attached,'

Across the border into Devon you can visit Agatha Christie's amazing garden retreat at Greenway (p187), while many country houses have beautiful grounds attached: Knightshayes Court (p173) and Buckland Abbey (p206) are particularly impressive. It's a similar story in Dorset – almost every self-respecting countryseat has its own glorious grounds attached, most notably at Kingston Lacy (p134) and the former hunting lodge and deer park around Lulworth Castle (p137).

Lastly, in Somerset, there's the Gertrude Jekyll–influenced garden at Barrington Court (p113) and the wonderful Elizabethan topiary and arboretum at Montacute House (p113). Top of the compost heap has to be the Palladian arcadia of Prior Park (p100), just outside Bath, which was laid out by the renowned landscaper Capability Brown, with input from poet Alexander Pope.

Food & Drink

If you can't find something to like here, you don't like food. Clambering with crustaceans, teeming with fine fish, packed with rich meats, oozing delicious cheese, studded with superb fruit and vegetables and awash with fine wines and robust ciders – the southwest is foodie heaven.

It's partly the geography. Few places are more than 30 miles from the sea, and undulating fields of rich farmland stretch between these productive shores. But it's also a matter of approach. There's determination here to keep food traditions alive, but also to diversify – particularly into speciality and chemical-free markets. One telling statistic: Devon has more organic producers and processors than any other county in the UK. Add steadily growing cities with evolving, diverse eating scenes, whisk in a miniboom of celebrity restaurants (Jamie Oliver and Rick Stein), and you have a recipe for a satisfied stomach.

There's also quirkiness by the trolley full. A miner's lunch turned cultural icon, a fish pie with eye contact, yellow – yes, yellow – bread, and a cheese that was originally made by dragging a mouldy horse harness through the milk. Of course quality varies, with restaurants in the southwest just as good as the rest of the UK at ruining a perfectly good meal, but inspired treatment of fabulous local ingredients and good value for money also abounds and we've selected the best of the southwest for this guide.

STAPLES & SPECIALITIES

If it's possible to capture the essence of a county in a type of food, the Cornish have done it with the pasty. More than just pastry-wrapped meat and veg, it's also a symbol of tradition and pride – and you'll see them everywhere. Early references to this crinkly edged, half-moon of carbohydrate and protein date from the 13th century. Its origins lie in tin-mining communities. Originally vegetables (but no meat) were wrapped in pastry with a pocket of fruit or jam at one end, making a portable, durable two-course lunch. Those working underground in grim, arsenic-laced conditions didn't eat the crimped seam – instead it allowed them to hold their food without contaminating it. When waves of impoverished Cornish miners emigrated, they took their food traditions with them, particularly to Australia and the USA, and you can now pop out for a pasty in Adelaide and Arizona, as well as across the UK. It means the economic pasty factor is huge; worth a staggering £150 million to the county each year. Yet the quality and the brand have suffered amid mass production and some stomach-churningly weird

Food from Cornwall (www.foodfromcornwall .co.uk) is a web guide to local producers and farmers markets in Kernow.

PASTY PERFECTION

With mass production and chain stores everywhere, how do you ensure a good 'un? Here's some advice from pasty purists:

- Head for the bakers, butchers or village shop
- Steer clear of those wrapped in cellophane, opt for paper bags instead
- Ask if it's home- or locally made and fresh that day
- Never, ever have it reheated in the microwave – it should be warm from baking
- Keep it simple – go for beef (or vegetables or cheese and onion); chicken tikka simply wasn't meant to be wrapped in pastry this way...

ingredients. It's prompted the Cornish Pasty Association to bid for official status – meaning only those pasties made in the county can have the title (think: Champagne versus sparkling wine). For some, the foodstuff is as much about identity as it is about lunch – a giant pasty is still hoisted over the cross bar at key Cornwall County rugby matches. Even the question of its invention stirs the blood, with rival claims from neighbouring Devon being fiercely rejected.

More than 80 million pasties made in Cornwall are munched annually, with the industry employing just under 2000 people.

Providing a tasty and tangible link between food and place, the fruits of the southwest's seas are likely to linger in your memory. Eating fish that's been landed a few yards away is special – still in buckets, it's sometimes even carried past diners by waterproofs-clad fisherman. To rejoice in these negligible food miles try the ports of Newlyn, Falmouth, Padstow and Mevagissey in Cornwall; Brixham, Salcombe and Dartmouth in Devon; and Lulworth Cove, Poole, Portland and Weymouth in Dorset. Despite a dramatic decline in the fleet, restaurant tables remain weighted with the 40 different species hauled in locally. Highlights include superb oysters, mussels, crab and lobster, line-caught sea bass and mackerel, and the freshest monkfish, John Dory and Dover sole. Around Bath and Bristol look out too for River Severn salmon.

It is worth scouring menus for samphire, a wild coastal plant with more than hint of asparagus; and laverbread, fried patties of boiled seaweed, oats and bacon. Also, don't neglect that great British staple: fish and chips. Wrapped in paper, dripping with vinegar and scattered with salt, this fast food can be surprisingly good – at its best in fishing ports where the day's catch ends up in batter.

Creamy, tangy, soft and hard, the southwest offers cheese lovers countless slices of gourmet heaven. The quantity is no surprise – the region is studded with dairy farms, but it's the quality and variety of cheese that astounds. Fittingly for a region that is home to Cheddar (the place), there are some mouth-puckeringly strong traditional varieties – try the Cheddar Gorge Cheese Company (p104), Green's of nearby Glastonbury or Quickes, near Exeter. There's also the gentle, nettle-wrapped, semihard Cornish Yarg; melting, local brie-type cheeses (try Sharpham Vineyard, p184); and full bodied, vein-laced offerings. Traditionally a mouldy horse harness was dragged through left-over milk to induce the 'blue' of the Dorset Blue Vinny; that or storing it next to mouldy boots or damp bags. Be reassured, these days a highly hygienic system involves a blue-mould solution. Other pungent delights to pick out for a picnic are the Exmoor (cow), Devon (cow), Harbourne (goat) and Beenleigh (sheep) Blues.

The Bath Oliver biscuit neatly spans the region. A Cornish physician (Dr William Oliver) who worked in Plymouth, moved to Bath for the therapeutic waters. Here, wanting to tempt his patients from more fattening options he

---

THE EYES HAVE IT

While the pasty is ubiquitous, another Cornish delicacy is much harder to find. It also requires a robust constitution. Stargazy (or starry) Pie is essentially fish and pastry – the twist is the heads and tails are kept on and stick out, disturbingly from the crust. Why? Tradition has it that one Christmas, people in the fishing village of Mousehole (p244) were starving – fierce storms having stopped them heading out to sea. One local man defied horrendous conditions and returned home a hero with a boat full of seven types of fish. Their heads were kept on in the resulting communal pie to show what was what. Even now the events are re-enacted in Mousehole the day before Christmas Eve, with a huge pie baked and served up at the Ship Inn. Stirring tales aside, you're unlikely to come across this dish on many menus – if you do prepare to look your dinner in the eye.

invented the savoury biscuit that took his name. Delicious with cheese, it can be found in good delis and supermarkets nationwide.

The organic sector is emerging, healthily, from the soil, as a speciality in itself. A whopping 41% of the UK's registered organic producers and growers are based in the southwest, with Devon heading the regional league table. Dairy, meat, fruit and vegetables – they're all produced locally. Look out especially for local venison and the kind of organic, handmade sausages that put the mass-produced variety deeply to shame. Somerset is home to one of the country's key organic dairy producers Yeo Valley Organics, while Riverford, behind one of the UK's biggest organic-box schemes where boxes of organic produce are delivered to customers, is based near Totnes in Devon. It has also set up a pioneering Field Kitchen where you eat food harvested from the furrows in front of you – picked to order (p186).

Bristol-based arbiters of all things organic; the Soil Association's online directory (www .whyorganic.org) lists hundreds of southwest producers, eateries and places to stay.

If the Cornish can claim pasties as their own, people in Devon can do the same for cream teas, although cross-county rivalry ensures that is disputed. Some historians date the sweet snack back to the 10th century, when monks fed bread, cream and jam to workers repairing a Devon abbey after a Viking raid. Hundreds of years later it's sold by most traditional teashops in the region. At its best a cream tea is a delightful combination of light scones, tasty, homemade jam, a steaming brew and utterly gooey, stand-your-spoon-up-in-it clotted cream. At its worst it's more reminiscent of an inflight meal – before ordering check what's coming out of the kitchen. Expect to pay about £4. The whole consumption process is also inexplicably the subject of furious debate about which to spread first: the jam or the cream. For a really interesting afternoon, pose the question to the tearoom, and watch it divide on aesthetic, taste and even county lines (in Cornwall traditionally it's jam on first, in Devon it's the cream). A Cornish variation that's seeing a resurgence is Thunder and Lightning, with treacle, syrup or honey replacing the jam.

Bakers' windows in Cornwall are dotted with a yellow fruit loaf in the form of saffron cakes and buns. Again food is also history. Early tin traders are said to have secured this exotic golden spice from the Phoenicians, but these days the dough could well be yellowed by more prosaic food colouring. Watch out too for the fruity Cornish Heavy Cake and more types of fudge than even the sweetest-toothed could manage in a lifetime.

More than just taste sensations, local farmers markets, farm shops and agricultural shows mean you actually meet the people who've made what you eat.

In keeping with its holiday image, the southwest has jumped on the luxury ice-cream bandwagon. Kiosks and frozen cabinets everywhere stock high-quality, local produce. Look out for Treleavens and Roskilly's Farm in Cornwall, Salcombe Dairy in Devon, Purbeck in Dorset and Lovington's in Somerset.

DRINKS

The most famous falling-down-water hereabouts is cider. The second-largest producer in the world, Gaymer, is based in Somerset, crushing 30,000 tonnes of fruit each season for brands including Blackthorn and Olde English. Farm orchards still exist, but centuries ago it was a very different story. No farm would have been without its orchard; apples were pressed then fermented to form the 'scrumpy', which was drunk like water. Actually, drunk more than water as the H_2O then was more toxic than alcohol. Dazed but delighted labourers were often partly paid in this golden currency – an average 4-pint (2.25L) allowance increasing to 8 pints during hay-making. Be aware: the mass-produced, bright-orange substance that jets from some bar pumps is not the same as the lovingly made, deeply flavoured elixir so evocatively dubbed 'wine of wild orchards' by the writer Laurie Lee. Thankfully it's still possible to connect with the past via this rich liquid. The apple names alone are enough to give you a warm, fuzzy glow: Slack ma Girdle, Sops in Wine and Quench. Excellent, small-scale producers include south Devon–based Luscombe and the Lyme Bay Winery. Somerset's Burrow Hill Cider comes in sparkling or scrumpy forms, and the same people make the 'cousin of Calvados' Somerset Cider Brandy range – which can retail at more than £35 a bottle.

A minirenaissance of real ale ensures the region can rejoice under a local influence, even if it does surprise some overseas visitors by being deliberately warm and flat. In Cornwall, St Austell has been brewing since 1851 and you're likely to find yourself in one of its 150 pubs drinking its distinctive Tribute and Tinners ales. Also worth sampling are Sharp's spicy and sweet Doom Bar Bitter, named after a treacherous sandbank, and the vividly titled range of Skinner's Ales (a pint of Cornish Knocker or Keel Over anyone?). The Bristol Beer Factory is based in an old city-centre fermenting block and produces Sunrise (smooth and pale) and the full-bodied, but lower-alcohol-content, Red (3.8%). The Atlantic Brewery joined the party in 2005 with organic ales, which are bottle-conditioned, and can be quaffed without conscience by vegetarians and vegans. The tiny Beer Engine (p173) is a pub that brews its own ale on the outskirts of Exeter. Bath Ales is an independent microbrewery between Bristol and Bath that produces high-quality ales.

The mild, southwest weather ensures good conditions for vineyards – many are so successful that demand far outstrips supply. Sipping a chilled glass of white on a sun-drenched terrace, overlooking neatly staked rows of vines feels more like Chablis than Cornwall and is an unforgettable experience. Set in 200 stunning hectares, Devon's Sharpham Vineyard (p184) produces highly acclaimed wines – prices range from £8 for a very decent off-dry white to £25 for its Beenleigh Red, a Cabernet Sauvignon–Merlot blend. Camel Valley Vineyard (p275), in north Cornwall, is another seriously good award winner. Look out for its aromatic and appropriately named Bacchus (£11). Visit both or search them out on local wine lists and in off-licences.

The Devon city of Plymouth has awarded itself the tag line 'Spirit of Discovery' – apt, considering it's home to Plymouth Gin (p198). For 200 years no British Royal Navy vessel left port without its own supply. Today the brand is available in pubs and bars around the world and a distillery tour allows you to sniff botanicals (the things that add flavour) and carry out your own taste tests. Be aware: the alcohol volume of the Navy Strength brand weighs in at a hefty 57%.

WHERE TO EAT & DRINK

Just a few decades ago a meal out in the southwest would have run the risk of the curse of the English – chronically unappetising food. But these days all those quality local ingredients demand quality eateries – and the region has delivered. Designer destination restaurants coexist happily with the trendy and the traditional. Of course you can still come across a bad meal, but you'll find crisp, quality and smart as much as you encounter dusty, dodgy and doily-ed. Parents with young children can expect menu choices similar to the rest of the UK: great if your little darlings can defy science and flourish on pizza and chips, more challenging if you seek child-friendly and nutritious. Again, it is possible and we've highlighted such options where they exist.

Cafés & Teashops

Multinational chains, frilly tearooms, greasy spoons and funky little oases of individuality – the southwest region has the full range. One of the key tourist staples, the cream tea, is resolutely unsuited to ubertrendy

---

Sidebar notes:

Exquisite, densely written prose-poetry; Laurie Lee's *Cider With Rosie* transports you via this drink of 'golden fire' to a Westcountry of russet summers, hazy days and the beginning of the end of childhood innocence.

Want to buy local and make the farmers and fishermen smile? Click on the great-for-gourmands www.tasteofthewest .co.uk, for events, awards and local producers.

THE ESPRESSO EFFECT

The world divides into two types of destinations: those that have espresso machines (and sometimes always have) and those that haven't – yet. Once they arrive the whole place changes inexorably and it cannot return to what it was. It's not just the coffee – it's the pastries, decor, language, attitude and expectations that are different too. The onward march of the barista has left you spoilt for choice in matters mocha in cities, towns and resorts across the southwest. Falmouth, Polzeath, Totnes and Salcombe bear witness to this expanding espresso culture, thankfully often in nonchain style. Elsewhere whole communities are without a gleaming, steaming machine. Even amid the brave new, roasted-bean world, individual outposts of instant and filter stubbornly remain – a visit is a good chance to play social anthropologist and see just what difference it makes.

---

caffeine havens, thankfully ensuring the preservation of the traditional teashop. Of course the quality varies, but at its best – with a dignified waitress serving properly brewed tea in a calm, knick-knack–packed interior, the cream tea is a wonderful way to satisfy your stomach and step back in time.

Another type of café, this one pronounced 'caff', is the no-nonsense home of all-day breakfasts, egg 'n' chips and baked potatoes. In the southwest hunt out the flavourfull ones around docks, ports and cattle markets. If you've never actually experienced a full breakfast of eggs, bacon, sausages, cooked tomato and fried bread at five in the afternoon, this might be the time to try.

Restaurants

Feeling the full force of a wave of celebrity restaurants, the food world of the southwest is changing. So much so that Padstow has been renamed 'Padstein' by locals – TV Chef Rick Stein has six eateries there (see p228). Nearby, celebrity chef Jamie Oliver has made a big impact with Fifteen Cornwall (p232) at Watergate Bay near Newquay, while another small-screen chef, John Burton Race (of *French Leave* fame), runs the New Angel (p190) in Dartmouth. This cult of celebrity tends to be a good thing for diners of good cuisine; even if a famous chef doesn't sauté your starter, overall the bar has been raised. But there's also a tide of identikit venues. More Westminster than Westcountry, their excessively 'fusioned' menus are surrounded by blonde wood and blue-and-white canvas. Standards in these tend to be good, although sometimes they're just standard and you can end up paying more for eating in the same town as a famous chef.

As ever the bigger towns and cities have the widest variety and fly diverse culinary flags. Be aware though: in less cosmopolitan areas it's not at all uncommon for service to stop at 9pm or earlier. Some do buck the trend – at Rick Stein's Seafood Restaurant, the summertime late sitting starts at 10pm, with some tables being reserved a year in advance. This is the exception rather than the rule, but it's still a good idea to book ahead on a busy summer evening.

A battle on the bookshelves: southwest TV chefs are vying for your eye. Rick Stein's *Food Heroes* champions small-scale producers while the mantra of Hugh Fearnley-Whittingstall in the *River Cottage Year* is seasonal and local.

Pubs & Bars

Despite a reputation as a sleepy backwater, the southwest also knows how to party. Hard. Too hard some locals would grumble. While you expect and get vibrant nightlife in the bars of Bristol, Bath, Bournemouth, Plymouth, Torquay and Exeter, you also encounter large numbers of boozed-up youths in sometimes surprising locations; many smaller towns and ports

---

GETTING SERVED

Times vary but in general you're likely to be fed and watered between the following hours. Where it varies we'll tell you in the text.

- Eating in pubs and restaurants: noon to 2pm and 6pm to 10pm
- Drinking in pubs and bars: 11am to 11pm, later at weekends

Counting the Cost

On a posh plate, or parcelled in paper, how much is that fish (or other) dish? (How long is a piece of string?) Here are some handy guides:

- Ice-cream cone £2 to £3
- Cream tea: £3 to £6
- Cornish Pasty £1 to £3.50
- Main meal £7 to £15
- Main meal at a celebrity chef's restaurant £20 to £45
- Proper pint (beer or cider) in a traditional pub £2.50
- Designer bottle of beer (half as much) in a city bar £2.50 to £3
- Fish and chips in newspaper £4 to £5
- Sunset sea views while enjoying the same: priceless

---

have taken steps to crack down on on-street and on-beach drinking. While some violence inevitably occurs, regionwide the scene is similar to the various degrees of beery, leery rowdiness you find all over the UK at chucking-out (and chucking-up) time.

Pubs range from old-fashioned city boozers to time-warp village locals where the welcome is genuine, the fire is real and that horse brass has hung on that hook for centuries. There are also bigger villages where the pub is still the epicentre of community life, and smaller hamlets and islands (St Agnes and Lundy Island) where the pub is the only sign of life. In discovering these gems you do more than have a pint; you tap into the region's soul, drink in its history and engage in a centuries-old continuum – memorable times indeed.

Regional pub-grub encompasses the ubiquitous scampi and chips, deeply satisfying cheese-rich ploughman's lunches and fancier gastropub fare. A fair percentage serve food all day – but equally many don't. Not all have a children's menu, but many have a family room or are happy to allow children in the bar until about 7.30pm. Expect to pay £6 to £8 for standard bar food, £11-plus for fancier fare.

> The southwest region has more Michelin stars than any other outside London. The coveted asterisk accompanies eateries in Chagford, Bath, Dartmouth, Padstow, Penzance, Taunton and Torquay.

VEGETARIANS & VEGANS

Menus list livelihoods as well as meals; sometimes asking for vegetarian food at a pub beside a cattle market or a fish restaurant on the quay can result in hunger and hard looks. That scenario is rare, although in some eateries the nonmeat option is fish or vice-versa. Generally if you prefer pulses to food that's eaten some, you should find enough possibilities to make your stay enjoyable, while judicious restaurant selections will often give vegetarians real menu options rather than that infamous 'choice' of one dish. Predictably, vegans fare worse except in larger towns and cities, but thankfully mini-alternative centres such as Glastonbury, Totnes and Falmouth boost prospects considerably.

COOKING COURSES

Although not quite rivalling the temptations of Tuscany, the region is home to some great places to hone your cooking skills.

Ashburton Cookery School (☎ 01364-652784; www.ashburtoncookeryschool.co.uk) In Devon these classes include a vegetarian one of between one day (£115) and a diploma-level month (£1999).

Bordeaux Quay (☎ 0117-904 6679; www.bordeaux-quay.co.uk) A Bristol not-for-profit group with a focus on local growers and suppliers. Workshops range from lunchtime demonstrations (£25) to planning a full dinner party (£200). Children's courses also available.

New Angel (☎ 01803-839425; www.thenewangel.co.uk) In Dartmouth New Angle runs one- and two-day courses costing from £195 for one day, to £550 for two days, residential.

Padstow Seafood School (☎ 01841-532700; www.rickstein.com) Rick Stein offers courses of one to six days covering a variety of national styles. Courses are residential and range between £175 and £2250.

Percy's (☎ 01409-211236; www.percys.co.uk) Percy's in north Devon offers bespoke lessons to hotel residents – courses are £100 per day, with double rooms from £170.

River Cottage HQ (☎ 01297-630302; www.rivercottage.net) In Dorset Hugh Fearnley-Whittingstall's centre is typically earthy and teaches everything from catching and cooking your own fish to butchering a whole pig. Prices range from £50 to £225 for one and two days.

Fighting for proper pints and proper pubs, the Campaign for Real Ale (www.camra.org.uk) lists brilliant boozers, festivals and tasting notes; it even evangelises about cider.

Environment

For most people the southwest is all about the great outdoors. From sea-smacked cliffs and bottle-green meadows to open moors, dense woodland and sandy dunes, the region's landscape is astonishingly varied and boasts one of the most diverse natural environments in Britain. Thanks to the Gulf Stream, which pushes up warmer air from the sun-baked countries on the opposite side of the Atlantic, the region has an unusually temperate climate that supports many plant and tree species that simply can't survive in the rest of Britain. It's particularly noticeable in the deep valley gardens of southern Cornwall and Devon, where exotic trees and towering rhododendrons grow in wild profusion, but you can see its effects practically everywhere you go – in the flower-filled hedgerows and gorse-covered clifftops, the lush river chines around the English riviera, or the tropical palms and monkey puzzle trees of Cornwall's great gardens. The legacy of industries, such as farming, mining and fishing, is also clear to see as you travel around the region; and while the heavy industries have largely faded into history, many of the old quarries, dams and reservoirs have since been transformed into nature reserves and havens for local wildlife.

THE LAND

First-time visitors are often bowled over by the sheer, searing *greenness* of much of the southwest, and there's no denying that the region contains some of Britain's most eye-popping countryside. But despite its pastoral façade, this is far from a pristine natural environment – the landscape has been continually shaped, worked and managed by generations of people over the centuries, and the countryside bears little resemblance to how it would have looked before the first people who arrived here pitched up. Prior to the arrival of the earliest settlers, much of the region was still carpeted by thick forests of elm, oak and yew – even the most barren areas (including Dartmoor and Bodmin Moor) were once covered with dense native woodland. But as industry and agriculture developed, trees were cleared for timber, crop cultivation and grazing, and the long process of taming Britain's wild places began in earnest. Hedgerows were planted to delineate fields and property boundaries; granite, slate and stone was removed to build houses and harbours; deep-shaft mines were sunk in search of gold, copper and tin. All of these activities have left an enduring mark on the terrain, whether it's in the chequerboard of arable fields or the ghostly remains of disused mine stacks, and the close relationship between people and the surrounding landscape continues to have a profound effect on the character of the whole southwest region.

Cornwall's granite rocks are rich in natural radioactive isotopes, including thorium, potassium and uranium, leading to speculation that they could possibly be used as a source of geothermal energy.

In geological terms, humans are just a tiny blip on the timeline. Some 400 million years before the first people arrived, Britain was still part of a large continental landmass (known as Pangaea) that included Europe and North America, and much of the southwest was covered by a deep tropical sea. Around 350 to 290 million years ago, violent volcanic activity sent sheets of ash and lava across the sea floor and caused the intrusion of a huge mass of granite that now runs down the middle of the region, and can today be seen at exposed high points such as Dartmoor, Bodmin Moor and the Isles of Scilly. Many of the region's rich mineral deposits were formed around the same time. Over the next 150 million years the entire area was thrust up by further volcanic eruptions, and contir uing periods of geological activity and marine submergence created many of the region's distinct geological features and laid down large areas of chalk, flint, sandstone, slate and clay. Most of the present-day landscape has been formed within the last two million years. Although the glaciers and ice sheets of the last great Ice Age never reached as far south as Devon and Cornwall, fluctuations in sea levels and rapid climate change were responsible for carving out many of the region's cliffs, beaches and bays. Intriguingly, it's thought that until relatively recently the Isles of Scilly were still joined to the main landmass by a narrow isthmus of land that was submerged when sea levels rose at the end of the last Ice Age – perhaps giving rise to the old legend of the lost Lands of Lyonesse (p243), and also explaining the submerged forests that are occasionally exposed at low tides around the peninsula's coastline.

All these geological comings-and-goings have done much to create the distinct differences between the four southwestern counties. Cornwall is famous for its pockmarked coastline, sweeping sands and plunging cliffs, while inland the county's large areas of heath and granite moorland have encouraged traditional industries such as agriculture and cattle farming. The two coastlines of Cornwall are markedly different; while the north coast is mainly wild, rugged and windswept, the south coast is altogether gentler, characterised by countless rolling green fields sloping gently into broad, shallow bays.

Across the Cornish border, Devon is rightly regarded as one of the greenest and most pastoral of Britain's counties, a bucolic landscape of meadows, moors and winding bridleways, framed by yet more glorious stretches of coastline. The huge expanse of Dartmoor occupies a vast area of southern Devon and contains some of the wildest land anywhere in the southwest, as well as a series of characteristic rock hummocks locally known as tors.

Further east is the rural county of Dorset – Thomas Hardy country – a famously sleepy place, which for centuries has been one of the country's great farming heartlands. Dorset is also famous for its unique southern coastline, the Unesco-protected Jurassic Coast, which is distinguished by its unmistakeable russet-coloured soil, frequent landslips and fossil-rich shoreline, as well as some lovely coves and unusual cliff formations, such as those at Lulworth Cove and Durdle Door.

On the other side of the peninsula, north Devon is linked to the county of Somerset by the fields and coombes of Exmoor. While Somerset's coastline might not be able to match its neighbours in terms of grandeur or good looks, the county still has plenty of other charms, including the hog-backed hills of the Quantocks and the Mendips, the gentle countryside around Glastonbury and Street and the ancient limestone caverns around Cheddar Gorge and Wookey Hole.

WILDLIFE
Plants
Nurtured by the balmy Gulf Stream, and bathed in equal measures of sustaining sunshine and drenching rain, it's hardly surprising that the southwest has such a wild profusion of plants, shrubs, trees and wildflowers. The region is at its most spectacular (and scented) in the summer months, when the hedgerows and meadows are awash with blossom – sorrels and speedwells, foxgloves and hawksweeds, crocosmia, campion, pennywort, cow parsley and ox-eye daisies – although spring and autumn have their fair share of colourful blooms too. Cornwall and Devon are especially well known for their country hedgerows, many of which stretch back to the days of the Domesday Book. Sturdy shrubs such as hawthorn, holly, hazel and elder were commonly used as hedgerow building materials, and you

The Jurassic Coast in Dorset and east Devon is one of the fastest-eroding stretches of coastline in Britain. It was also Britain's first natural Unesco World Heritage Site and the location of England's first complete ichthyosaur skeleton.

For a general overview of Britain's flora and fauna, www.wildaboutbritain .co.uk is a good place to start. There are sections on everything from British birds to wild fungi, and online diaries where you can record your sightings.

Tim Smit's *Eden* documents the many trials and tribulations of building the world's largest greenhouses in a Cornish clay pit, while you can find out about the beginnings of his Cornish cultural crusade in *The Lost Gardens of Heligan*.

can often see them twisted into weird shapes by the elements, especially around the exposed coasts and moorland of Cornwall. Gorse and heather are another ever-present sight around the region's heaths and clifftops.

The southwest is also famous for its landscaped gardens. Many of the deep river valleys of west Devon and Cornwall boast a semitropical climate – a unique phenomenon which allowed pioneering Edwardian and Victorian gardeners to populate their estates with exotic species brought back from the furthest corners of the Empire, including some of the finest collections of magnolia, azalea and rhododendron anywhere in Britain. The most impressive gardens are dotted along the south coast of Cornwall, including Trebah (p252), Glendurgan (p252) and Heligan (p267), while further west are the famous Abbey Garden (p256) on Tresco in the Isles of Scilly.

Animals
LAND ANIMALS
Wind the clock back a few centuries and you'd be astonished at some of the creatures that once roamed across the southwest landscape – everything from wolves and brown bears to wild boars – but these days the wildlife is altogether tamer. The region's most famous resident is probably the miniature Dartmoor pony, a stubby-legged, shaggy-maned little steed which rarely grows much above 12 hands (roughly 1.2m) high, and its slightly larger cousin, the Exmoor pony. Despite their pocket-sized proportions, both varieties are astonishingly strong, and have been used as pack animals, riding ponies and beasts of burden for many centuries. Red deer are also fairly widespread on Exmoor and Dartmoor, although they're notoriously skittish creatures, so your best chance to see one is probably on a local wildlife safari (p116).

The southwest's strong farming traditions mean that sheep and cattle can be seen scattered practically everywhere across the countryside – although falling farming revenues and the increasing pressure of supermarket economics could mean that they become a rather rarer sight in years to come.

The average southwest cow produces around 500L of methane every day, accounting for between 15% and 20% of the region's emissions of the gas. It's such a problem that the EU is even considering imposing an emissions limit on these flatulent Friesians.

The region's wilder inhabitants include badgers, hares, several types of bat and, of course, several million rabbits. Foxes are also widespread, and since February 2005 have been protected (along with stags) by a ban on the traditional country pursuit of hunting with horses and hounds (much to the delight of animal activists and much to the chagrin of many country folk; see p70 for more on the ban).

Along the region's riverbanks you might glimpse the odd stoat, vole or, if you're very lucky, a playful otter – a charming river animal that is now enjoying a slow growth in numbers after decades of decline. Sadly, the once-common native red squirrel hasn't been so fortunate – it's almost disappeared over the last 50 years thanks to the introduction of the more aggressive grey squirrel from the USA.

The hedgerows, coastlines and meadows of the southwest are also wonderful places for spotting butterflies and dragonflies – some of the more common varieties you might see include the tortoiseshell, hedge brown, red admiral and painted lady, as well as more elusive species such as the orange tip and silver-washed fritillary. Rarest of all is the Large Blue, which became extinct from the British Isles in 1979 but has since been re-introduced to five areas around the southwest.

Look out, too, for grass snakes, slow worms and adders (Britain's only poisonous snake), especially on areas of exposed moor- and heathland during warm weather.

SEA LIFE

The most spectacular visitor to southwest waters is undoubtedly the stately basking shark (the second-largest fish in the ocean after the whale shark), which can often be seen off the coast of Cornwall in the summer months. Despite its fearsome bulk – the average shark measures between 6m and 8m long – like many large ocean creatures it's entirely harmless to humans, somehow managing to sustain itself entirely on plankton and other forms of microscopic marine life. Some other species of shark including the mako, porbeagle and blue are rather less friendly, although you'll be unlikely to encounter them unless you happen to have hauled them up from the deep on a sea-fishing trip.

Grey seals are another common sight along the southwest coastline. You might occasionally catch sight of a grey head or two bobbing in the waters off the Devon and Cornish coasts, but most of the region's seal colonies tend to cluster on small offshore islands, especially around the coasts of Cornwall and Scilly.

Sightings of dolphins and porpoises are much rarer, but if you're really lucky you might occasionally find a pod of curious dolphins keeping you company on an offshore boat trip. The best places for land-based sightings are generally the far westerly coastlines around Land's End, Cape Cornwall and West Penwith. Dolphin numbers have declined drastically in recent years, probably due to falling fish stocks and commercial fishing techniques, although it's hoped that the blanket European ban on drift nets (colloquially known as 'walls of death') will provide a much-needed boost to dolphin populations.

Jellyfish occasionally venture into southwest waters in the warmer months, and, although poisonous or stinging species are very unusual, it's probably best to steer clear if you see one.

BIRD LIFE

The southwest is home to a fantastic array of bird species, so it's an absolute dream come true for twitchers. For a quick fix the coast is undoubtedly the best place to start: you're bound to catch sight of the most common birds, including the razorbill, guillemot, gannet, cormorant and, of course, one of several types of seagull. Most common of all is the herring gull, distinguished by its grey plumage, light-coloured feet and black wingtips; if you're being harassed by a gull for a bite of your pasty or you've just been blessed from above, chances are it's thanks to a herring gull. Less common are the slightly darker black-backed gull and the smaller common gull (which, despite its name, actually isn't all that common). Gulls of all descriptions have become something of a nuisance in recent years thanks to the attentions of unsuspecting tourists and the growth in rubbish tips and street litter – whatever you do, don't feed them, as it only makes them bolder and certainly won't win you any friends among the locals.

There are also puffin colonies on the Isles of Scilly, Durlston Head near Swanage, Long Island near Boscastle and, in much smaller numbers, on Lundy.

Inland, you might catch sight of the odd bird of prey hovering above farmland and stretches of open countryside. Species to look out for include the sparrowhawk, kestrel and, most common of all, the buzzard. By night keep an ear cocked for the hoot of the barn owl or tawny owl in remote countryside.

River estuaries are also good for a spot of bird-watching, especially for wading birds, and various species of duck, grebe and goose. The estuaries around the Rivers Tamar and Exe in Devon, Dawlish Warren near Exmouth,

One of Britain's classic children's tales, *Tarka the Otter*, written by Henry Williamson in 1927, is set on the River Torridge, near Bideford in Devon. It's a charming (if occasionally sentimental) evocation of life in the prewar Devon countryside, but be warned – it's a bit of a tearjerker, too, so a box of Kleenex might come in handy.

Baby herring gulls tap the red spot on their parents' beaks as a signal for them to regurgitate food.

THE CORNISH CHOUGH

While you certainly won't have any trouble spotting a seagull around the coastline of Cornwall, you'll be extremely lucky to catch sight of the elusive Cornish chough (pronounced chuff). A member of the crow family distinguished by its jet-black plumage and bright orange beak, this elegant bird is an enduring symbol of Cornish culture – legend has it that the chough embodies the spirit of King Arthur, and the bird even features on Cornwall's coat of arms. The chough was once a common sight around the county's shores, but suffered a huge decline in the 20th century, probably due to intensive farming and a general decline in habitat. Happily, the first pair of choughs to nest in Cornwall for more than 50 years arrived in 2002, and the success of recent breeding programmes has led to hopes that the chough will again establish itself along the county's clifftops.

---

the Avon Gorge near Bristol and Hayle in Cornwall usually promise especially rich pickings for twitchers. There's also a unique swannery at Abbotsbury (p160) that's well worth a visit.

The southwest branch of the **Royal Society for the Protection of Birds** (RSPB; ☎ 01392-432691; www.rspb.org.uk; Keble House, Southernhay Gardens, Exeter) operates a number of bird reserves around the region, and can provide plenty of useful info on the best places to see various bird species.

The devoted twitcher David Norman has published a number of guides to bird-watching in the southwest, including Where to Watch Birds in Devon and Cornwall, with handy advice on habitat, seasons and key sites. If you can't tell your gannet from your herring gull, this could come in handy.

NATIONAL PARKS & AREAS OF OUTSTANDING NATURAL BEAUTY

The region has two designated national parks: Dartmoor (p202), founded in 1951, and Exmoor (p113), declared in 1954. Britain's national parks operate in a slightly different way to those in many other countries: rather than operating as strict nature reserves, they are run more as areas of environmental protection and natural conservation, where human activity is allowed to coexist with areas of natural beauty in a managed way. Agriculture, forestry, residential housing and even some heavy industry (such as quarrying) are all theoretically allowed within the parks' boundaries, but strict rules on planning, land use and development ensure that the landscape remains largely unspoilt, offering some of the wildest and most pristine countryside anywhere in Britain. The parks are run by government-funded National Park Authorities (NPAs) who manage the landscape, ensure the welfare of the wildlife and natural environment, and oversee visitor activities within the parks' boundaries. Unsurprisingly, both Dartmoor and Exmoor are magnets for nature lovers and bird-watchers, as well as outdoor enthusiasts of all descriptions, including hikers, bikers, horse riders, rock climbers and canoeists.

The southwest also has 11 Areas of Outstanding Natural Beauty (AONBs): south, east and north Devon, the Quantocks, the Mendips, the Isles of Scilly, the Tamar Valley, the Cotswolds and the Blackdown Hills, as well as the whole of Dorset and Cornwall. AONBs are protected in a similar way to the national parks, although the rules and regulations governing development, land use and environmental protection are much less rigorous. For general information contact the **National Association for AONBs** (☎ 01451-862007; www.aonb.org.uk; The Old Police Station, Cotswold Heritage Centre, Northleach, Gloucestershire), which can put you in touch with local AONB offices, or check the contact details on the website.

There's a useful rundown of some of the southwest's most interesting birds, mammals, insects and sea creatures at www.naturesouthwest .co.uk/main/en/Wildlife .cfm.

Large sections of the southwest coastline are owned by the National Trust (NT), an independent charity that manages many important sites on behalf of the general public. There are also a number of smaller nature reserves and Sites of Special Scientific Interest (SSSIs), usually established to protect specific natural habitats such as meadows, riverbanks, reed beds, moors and mudflats.

ENVIRONMENTAL ISSUES

Not surprisingly, water pollution is top of the environmental agenda. A few decades ago some of the region's beaches were in a sorry state, and it wasn't uncommon to find raw sewage and industrial effluents being pumped straight into the sea just a few miles from the most popular swimming spots. Happily, thanks to pressure put on local government by environmental NGOs and local campaign groups such as **Surfers Against Sewage** (www.sas.org .uk), and helped along by the implementation of directives on water quality set by the EU, the southwest has cleaned up its act and now boasts some of the cleanest coastline anywhere in Britain. Thirty-two southwest beaches achieved the coveted Blue Flag award in 2006, more than ever before – for a full list visit www.blueflag.org.uk. Dogs are also banned on many beaches between April and October.

Other forms of pollution have proved more difficult to tackle than doggy-doo-doos. The region's agricultural industry has caused ongoing problems with pesticides and farming chemicals (especially nitrates and phosphates), which can seep into the water table, pollute river courses, poison fish and other river animals and cause unwelcome side effects, such as algal bloom. The growth in organic farming will hopefully go some way to addressing this issue in future years, but it remains a thorny problem. Waste disposal is another important issue, especially given the relatively small land area of the four southwestern counties; recycling is on the up everywhere, but the vast majority of waste still finds its way into landfill.

Coastal erosion is a problem in many areas, especially along the southern coastline of Devon and Dorset, where large landslips and rockfalls are a fact of life. Rising sea levels and changing weather patterns caused by global warming are predicted to exacerbate coastal erosion in future years, potentially threatening many buildings and natural beauty spots. Severe winter storms and coastal flooding are also predicted to become more commonplace as sea temperatures rise, and the migration patterns of marine life might also be affected. In the most dire forecasts, some scientists also believe the vital Gulf Stream, which is responsible for maintaining the southwest's temperate climate, might shut off altogether, with devastating effects for the natural environment.

Traffic and air pollution are also growing dilemmas, especially during peak holiday periods. The vast majority of visitors – around 80% – travel to the region by car, with all the attendant problems of parking, pollution and traffic jams. It's not always the easiest option, but you might well find you have a much less stressful time if you leave the car at home and investigate some other ways of exploring the region. Hopping on a bike, hitting the trail or catching a train might not be as quick or convenient as having your own wheels, but it will allow you to explore the countryside at a more laid-back

To find out about what the southwest is doing to clean up its environmental tracks, check out Future Footprints (www .futurefootprints.org.uk) and the Cornwall Sustainable Tourism Project (www.cstn.org.uk).

GOING GREEN

If you're looking for a more environmentally friendly getaway, you're in luck – the southwest has no end of ways to travel green. Budding ecotrippers could find themselves kipping in a Mongolian yurt (p225), learning traditional countryside skills such as coppicing or willowcraft, or building your own biodiesel reactor (p269). If you're after a few more mod-cons but still want to do your bit for the planet, look out for the Green Tourism Business Scheme (GTBS) award, designated by a small green leaf. In order to qualify, businesses have to make an effort to increase their energy efficiency, cut down on their carbon emissions, support local suppliers and ethical products, and generally act in more environmentally sustainable ways – you can search for qualifying establishments at www.visitsouthwest.co.uk/feelgood.

BRITISH SEA POWER

With concerns about global warming looming large on everyone's collective horizon, the search is on to find cleaner, greener, renewable sources of energy to help wean us off our insatiable addiction to fossil fuels. While wind farms and hydrogen-powered cars grab all the environmental headlines, a cutting-edge new project in Cornwall might just hold the key to cracking the carbon-emissions conundrum.

The **Wave Hub** (www.wavehub.co.uk) is a groundbreaking scheme, which aims to build an electrical connection point on the seabed 12 miles off the coast of St Ives, where several different wave-power technologies will be collected together in order to research their relative merits. Once the research phase is completed, the hope is that at least one wave-power technology will demonstrate the potential to provide for energy generation on an industrial scale – some scientists believe offshore wave power could satisfy up to one-sixth of the UK's energy demands by 2020. And since the Wave Hub is situated entirely below the sea's surface, there are no worries about ruining any natural beauty spots, and the Hub might even have unexpected knock-on benefits by providing a nursery ground and 'no-take zone' for local fish stocks, as well as diverting heavy shipping away from the Cornish coastline.

It's an exciting prospect, and one that certainly seems to have caught the imagination of the UK government, which has recently invested £21.5 million of the total £28 million budget required to get the project up and running. If things go according to plan, construction on the Wave Hub could be completed as early as summer 2008. But despite all the recent attention, in fact the Wave Hub isn't Britain's first wave farm. That honour belongs to the pioneering **Seaflow tidal turbine**, which was constructed a mile offshore from Lynmouth in Devon in 2003, and was the first commercial tidal turbine to be built anywhere in the world.

Surfers Against Sewage (www.sas.org.uk) is one of Cornwall's most active campaign pressure groups, and has scored a number of successes in cleaning up the region's beaches and waterways.

pace, and at the very least you won't have to spend the start of your holiday trapped in a 3-mile tailback on a sweltering summer day. See the Transport chapter for information on public transport and other suggestions on ways to travel green.

Lastly, the region suffers as much as anywhere else from the curse of food miles, especially thanks to the large supermarkets. But while the major chains are trying to clean up their act, you can do your bit by checking out the hundreds of farmers markets, village shops and small producers dotted around the region, all of which offer a wonderful opportunity to get to grips with local delicacies, ranging from freshly caught fish and award-winning ice cream to organic honey and home-grown veggies. By buying local you'll be helping the environment, supporting the local economy and enjoying the tastiest produce all in one go.

Southwest Outdoors

The southwest is one huge adventure playground. If you're an adrenaline junkie looking for a fix, or chilled-out kayaker itching for a wilderness escape you'll find it here. There's a lot to do with two national parks, hundreds of miles of coast and oodles of stunningly beautiful bits in between. Hike through the iconic, historic landscape of the South West Coast Path – England's longest national trail – or wander the tranquillity of the region's intimate hills and desolate moors. Surfing and its sister sports exert a magnetic pull on people of all ages, drawn to the southwest by the biggest and best waves in England. For cyclists there's a tempting variety of routes: from leg-testing gradients to hundreds of miles of level path. Trot sedately on a horse, escape on a yacht, paddle around tranquil coves, clamber up a rock face, dive some of the UK's most exciting sites or test your mettle in a frenzy of adventure – your break could be the start of a new passion or the rediscovery of an old one.

Information

Throughout this guide we've highlighted some of the very best opportunities to enjoy the great outdoors. This chapter can help focus a trip around a particular theme, or inspire a more detailed exploration of what's on offer. Across the southwest any tourist office can provide more details, while newsagents, outdoor-clothing shops and the local section of bookshops are also fertile hunting grounds.

In 1956 Somerset's Quantock Hills became the first place in England to be designated an Area of Outstanding Natural Beauty.

The regional **tourist board** (☎ 0870 442 0880) has several excellent websites; click on www.itsadventuresouthwest.co.uk or www.naturesouthwest.co.uk. Other key information points are the **Dartmoor National Park Authority** (DNPA; ☎ 01822-890414; www.dartmoor-npa.gov.uk) and the **Exmoor National Park Authority**, (ENPA; ☎ 01398 -323841; www.exmoor-nationalpark.gov.uk).

While the southwest brims with activity providers at peak times, demand can overwhelm supply; if you want to be sure of adventure, it's best to book.

WALKING

Whether you chose day trips or whole weeks of adventure, memorable hiking awaits. The South West Coast Path is a staggering (walk it and you will) 630 miles long and is arguably the pinnacle of the region's hiking world, but the rest isn't bad either. Another national trail – the Cotswold Way winds its captivating way out of Bath. Throw in three distinct moorland landscapes, a couple of World Heritage Sites and no fewer than 11 Areas of Outstanding Natural Beauty (AONB) and you've plenty to chose from.

At 630 miles the South West Coast Path is 360 miles longer than Britain's next biggest national trail, the Pennine Way – a trifling 270 miles.

Dartmoor National Park

At 368 sq miles, Dartmoor (p204) occupies a fair chunk of central Devon. Its rounded hills, or tors, pepper a rolling, primitive landscape – the emptiest, highest and wildest in southern England. Prehistory is also remarkably well preserved with an array of stones circles and rows, burial mounds and massive Bronze Age settlements. Be aware, the military stages training on parts of Dartmoor using live ammunition (see p203).

The DNPA can advise on day hikes and runs a programme of guided walks themed around history, legends and geology. They cost between £3 and £6 (free if you show your bus ticket); details are online and in the free *Dartmoor National Park Visitor Guide*. Longer, self-guided hikes include the 18-mile

OUTDOORS

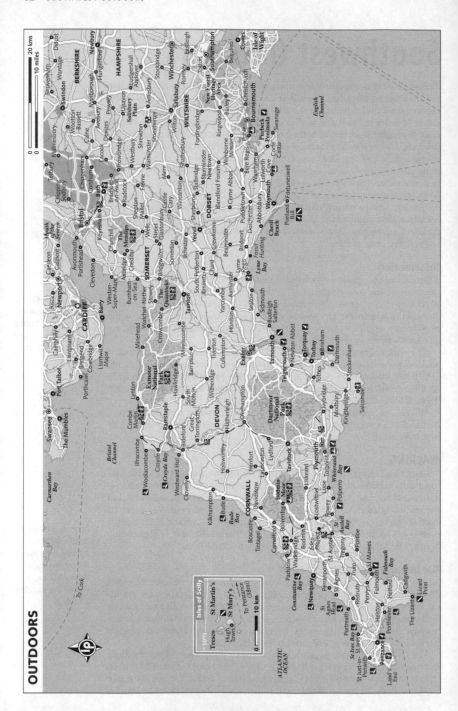

THE SOUTH WEST COAST PATH

Billed as the 630-mile adventure, this is one walk that lives up to all expectations. It is also Britain's longest national trail, snaking from Poole in Dorset around Land's End to Minehead in Somerset. Here there are cliffs crowned by tin mines, dazzling bays, pretty fishing villages and swathes of rural idyll. It's so gorgeous you'll forgive it the sometimes painful climbs that add up in total to the equivalent to climbing three Everests. Measuring it in metric makes it sound even more impressive: 1014km. Few people tackle it all in one go; leave around eight weeks (56 consecutive walking days) if you do. Stretches can provide exhilarating, if seriously testing, days or weeks.

You'll have plenty to stop and look at along the way. The bird life along the coast is particularly impressive – peregrine falcons, gannets, fulmars, kittiwakes and guillemots. Seals, dolphins and huge basking sharks are often seen close inshore, especially in the far west. The region's wildflower extravaganza is outstanding in spring and summer; a palette of pink thrift, creamy bladder campion, purple heather and yellow gorse. A healthy dose of the real world balances all this wilderness splendour in the shape of kiss-me-quick resorts, working ports and gritty cityscapes.

Where to walk? Where not to. A glance at some statistics reveals a lovely dilemma: 65% is within Areas of Outstanding Natural Beauty (AONBs), more than half is heritage coast and 5% is national park. Here are just some of the best bits:

- **Exmoor** (p113) – The realm of the red deer – a unique world of vertiginous cliffs where the moors meet the sea. This represents hefty hiking. Day walk: Lynmouth to Combe Martin (13 miles).
- **Hope Cove** (p194) – Take a happy wander towards this enchanting south Devon fishing village, all thatched cottages and lovely ice cream. Day walk: Salcombe to Hope Cove (8 miles).
- **Jurassic Coast** (p155) – Get to the highest point on England's south coast and experience crumbling cliffs that deposit fossils on the beach. Day walk: Lyme Regis (p160) to West Bay (10 miles).
- **Land's End** (p243) – More than a traveller's totem, a section of stunning surfing beaches and a theatre built into the spectacular cliffs. Day walk: Sennen Cove to Porthcurno (6 miles).
- **Levant Mine** (p240) – The remains of Cornwall's rich industrial heritage dot the path, including a still-steaming, restored mine and some engine houses. Day walk: Pendeen Watch to Sennen Cove (9 miles).

The trail's official website (www.southwestcoastpath.com) has an excellent overview, a very handy distance calculator and recommended day walks. There's also information about easier access options; some stages are suitable for wheelchair users. In part these are seafront promenades, but serious efforts have also been made to provide access to some more remote stretches too. The charity **South West Coast Path Association** (☎ 01392-383560; www.swcp.org .uk) produces the annual *South West Coast Path Guide,* which details the route, transport and on-trail accommodation.

The path can be walked all year but it's at its best from April to September – although in July and August beds and serenity can be at a premium. In winter, conditions are often very wet and muddy with severe gales. There are other potential dangers. Be sure to keep on the official path, especially around cliff edges, and to check locally before you wade across rivers; it can be fatal. You'll also need to carry water, a hat and weatherproof clothing. Follow detour signs warning of live military firing!

Waymarking along the path is in the form of acorn symbols; sometimes they're missing and crossing cities, towns and large villages can also be complicated – checking an Ordnance Survey (OS) map is advised. Accommodation is plentiful and ranges from glitzy five-star, through seaside chic and old-fashioned B&Bs, to youth hostels and camping. See p278 for a general guide on costs. The walking itself – in all its inspirational, exhausting glory – is absolutely free.

(two- to three-day) Templar Way which winds from Haytor on Dartmoor to seaside Teignmouth. Good bases for hikers are Princetown, with its key tourist office, Okehampton and Widecombe-in-the-Moor.

Exmoor National Park

While Dartmoor is bigger, 267-sq-mile Exmoor National Park (p113) has a different asset – the sea. A cracking 34 miles of jaw-dropping, leg-testing coastline. Add ancient woods, time-warp villages, red deer and Exmoor ponies and you have a winner.

The ENPA runs a wonderfully varied programme of guided walks (£3 to £5) and can suggest day hikes. Excellent bases include the gorgeside villages of Lynton and Lynmouth (p120); sleepy Dulverton (p116), a starting point for an superb 12-mile circular walk via Tarr Steps (p116); and picturesque Exford. The 117-mile (seven- to eight-day) Two Moors Way is an epic coast-to-coast traverse that cuts right across Devon from Wembury, just outside Plymouth, to Lynmouth on Devon's northern shores.

Bodmin Moor

Not to be outdone Cornwall has its own moor: Bodmin. Old tin mines dot an atmospheric, mystical landscape of bogs, Stone Age sites and high tors (hills), making for a moody hiking environment. Highlights include walks from the ancient mining village of Minions (p277), with its own stone circle, and the high tors of Brown Willy and Rough Tor (p275). A logical base is Bodmin, which has the distinct feel of a moorland settlement.

Other Routes

Amid a gentler landscape the Cotswold Way meanders for 102 delightful miles along a steep escarpment north from Bath. Here enchanting English villages are crafted out of warm, honey-coloured stone. The whole route has its challenges; allow at least seven to eight days, then revel in exhilarating views, country pubs and waves of rolling countryside. Although you can join the trail at various points along the route, Bath – with its spas, good restaurants and beautiful architecture – is the best option.

Other regional highlights include Somerset's Mendip (p104) and Quantock (p110) Hills. Offering patches of tranquillity and laced with history, both are AONBs. New Age Glastonbury and the village of Nether Stowey make good bases.

Safety & the Environment

Some of these walking environments, especially the moors, have their dangers. Live firing takes place on Dartmoor, and on some of the southwest's trails there's little signposting – carrying a map and compass, and knowing how to use them, is recommended. Regionwide the elements can catch people

More cattle and sheep live on Dartmoor than humans. People: 33,400; cows: 52,899; sheep: 239,930; goats: 46.

Inspired to wander further? Lonely Planet's *Walking in Britain* will guide you. It includes two weeks hiking the Cornish coast-path, Dartmoor day trips and the seven-day jaunt from Bath that is the Cotswold Way.

SAFER, HARMLESS HIKING

- Be safe – plan ahead and observe any instructional signs
- Leave gates and property as you find them
- Take care not to damage plants and animals
- Stick to existing tracks and avoid short cuts
- Take your litter home
- Keep dogs under close control, especially during lambing

WHERE DID YOU SAY WE WERE?

You've walked and cycled the region's wide open spaces to get away from it all – but sometimes you have to get back as well. Whether driven by needing a bed for the night, a pub lunch or a toilet, you're going to need a map. **Ordnance Survey** (OS; www.ordnancesurvey.co.uk) produces excellent charts of the region which can be bought in bookshops and often local stores. While its *Landranger* (1:50,000) series will suit many, the 1:25,000-scale *Explorer* range has more detail (£7 to £8). Alternatively, **Harvey Maps** (www.harveymaps.co.uk) makes an in-between 1:40,000-scale range for walkers (£10), which includes a map of the Cotswold Way and several on the South West Coast Path. By zooming in on walking routes a lot of ground is covered in one map, which can work out cheaper.

Across England, road and footpath signs are measured in miles. One quirk worth noting: while both OS and Harvey maps have a scale in both miles and kilometres, their grid lines are measured in the latter – calculations based on the wrong scale can have a big impact when dealing with long distances.

---

out: warm, waterproof clothing, water, hats and sunscreen are essential. See p300 for more on preventing and treating hypothermia.

You have a legal right to walk on footpaths, bridleways and byways. In national parks you can often walk on other areas deemed to be open country; check with NPAs and local authorities if you're in any doubt. Along with the usual guidelines, hikers are asked to leave historic sites undisturbed, to not feed ponies or other animals and to consider leaving the car behind.

Walking Festivals

These concentrations of guided walks are a great way to get under the skin of an area. North Devon and Exmoor's festival starts in early May (www .walkingnorthdevon.co.uk); Ivybridge and Dartmoor's in late April (www .ivybridge-devon.co.uk); and the fun on the compact Isles of Scilly, with a Monty Python–sounding website, www.walkscilly.co.uk, is in late March. Some firms specialise in walking tours – see p289 for a flavour.

CYCLING

For cyclists the southwest is one of the most appealing regions in the country – routes often have little or no traffic and the environments, and the challenges, are incredibly diverse. Here you can freewheel alongside meandering canals, potter through country lanes or push yourself to the limit down a precipitous moorland slope.

The best single source of information on cycle routes in England is **Sustrans** (☎ 0845-113 0065; www.sustrans.org.uk). With a name derived from 'sustainable transport', this pioneering, campaigning charity has been battling for a greener, healthier way to move around since 1977. It can provide details on the routes that follow and many others.

Cycling Routes

The biggest of the region's bike challenges is the West Country Way – stretching just over 250 bum-numbing miles from Bath or Bristol to Padstow. It takes in the Mendips, the Somerset Levels, Glastonbury, Exmoor and Bodmin Moor before propelling you onto the north Cornwall coast. Of the total, 75 miles are traffic free. Another epic is the 102-mile Devon Coast to Coast, with a cracking 71 miles without the curse of the car, which skirts Dartmoor to link Ilfracombe with Plymouth.

The region's shorter routes are particularly good for families. The Granite Way (p204) is a spectacular 11-mile, largely traffic-free, jaunt along a former

Walkers, cyclists and horse riders can all use the new 36-mile, Quantocks-Exmoor Coleridge Way. The website www.coleridgeway.co .uk helps you plan and explains that romantic poet connection.

Saddle up with *Cycling in the UK* (£12) – an official guide to the National Cycle Network with 150 of the country's best routes; 43 are family friendly, and there are colour maps and photos too.

ADVENTURE

Across the region there's a distinct whiff of adrenaline in the air. While not quite up there with the adventure capitals of the world, the southwest is still ready to thrill your socks off. Plunge from cliffs into the sea, skin a rabbit, drive a tank, squeeze into a cave. You can do it all here.

Coasteering

Among the maddest option is coasteering. The crash helmet, life jacket and wet suit give it away: an insane scramble around the world where the cliffs meet the sea combining abseiling, leaping off rocks, swimming, sea-cave exploring and climbing.

White-water Rafting

The region's Class II white-water rapids provide thrills, and spills, for rafters. Beginner-friendly and focused around the River Dart in Devon and the Rivers Barle and Exe on Exmoor, it's only allowed in the winter (October to February) to protect the environment. You can experience a white-knuckle half-day for about £30.

Survival

Whether your inspiration is *Robinson Crusoe, Survivor* or UK TV's survival expert Ray Mears, you can live out your bushcraft dreams here – be they flint-knapping (making stone tools), wild-food foraging, building a coracle (small skin or hide boat) or chopping up a chicken. Great for getting away from it all and helping kids and adults reconnect with nature, they're also the kind of experiences you really remember. **Bushcraft Expeditions** (☎ 01432-356700; www.bushcraftexpeditions .com) runs day courses in Dorset from £75; options at the Devon-based **Survival School** (☎ 0871-222 7304; www.survivalschool.co.uk) include a weekend for £175.

Dartmoor railway line between Okehampton and Lydford. There are no cars at all on the 7-mile Plym Valley route which winds from Plymouth to the moor. The DNPA also runs a free, seasonal bike-bus service: the Dartmoor Freewheeler ferries you and your cycle up to the moor for a largely downhill glide back. Routes range from around 6 to 41 miles but it does get booked up quickly and can't transport trikes and tagalongs for children. The DNPA sells a comprehensive map of moorland cycle routes (£10). Exmoor also has an exhilarating network of mountain-bike trails, recently graded ski-run style by the ENPA in a new map, *Exmoor for Off-Road Cyclists* (£9.95). Dunster makes a good base.

Linking Bristol and Bath, the Railway Path (p82) is 16 miles of carefree, car-free cycling; a route that passes plenty of lunch stops and is scattered with sculptures and a working steam engine. Also from Bristol it's an 11-mile pedal to Portishead along a mix of quiet road and traffic-free routes, including a sweep along the Avon Gorge under the Clifton Suspension Bridge. Off limits for drivers, the Camel Trail is 17 miles of gorgeous cycling between the western fringes of Bodmin Moor and the north Cornwall coast. Linking up with the tail end of the West Country Way, the 5-mile section between Wadebridge and Padstow is a particularly family-friendly, but sometimes crowded, stretch.

Starting at Braunton, the Tarka Trail (p213) is a delightful, traffic-free, 30-mile route through north Devon's lowlands. Running in parts alongside the River Taw, it's also great for bird-watching. You can cycle beside another great Devon river – the Exe, around Exeter, p169. In Cornwall the 3- to 5-mile Clay Trails (see www.claytrails.co.uk) connect with the heart of St Austell's mining heritage – one even goes to the Eden Project, allowing a suitably ecofriendly arrival. In Dorset, among miles of possible tracks, the Maiden

You can be towed at speed around some southwest waters. British Water Ski (☎ 01932-570885; www.british waterski.org.uk) or the tourist board can advise; prices start from about £20 for 15 minutes.

For a completely free wilderness experience head to Dartmoor, grab a pack and go wild-camping (so called by exponents to distinguish between what they term the 'mild-camping' of official sites). In parts of the moor pitching a tent for up to two nights in the same spot is allowed – provided you stick to some strict but simple rules. They're outlined in a free leaflet produced by the Dartmoor National Park Authority; pick one up, chose a legit camp site, then sleep under the stars with only the sheep for company.

And the Rest...

Abseiling, mountainboarding, kitebuggying, playing Tarzan on rope bridges (it's called 'high ropes', apparently) and zorbing (rolling down hills encased in an inflatable PVC ball) – there'll be things you won't have thought of, or even heard of. See the following for some details of providers; the regional **tourist board** (☎ 0870 442 0880; www.itsadventuresouthwest.com) can provide you with more companies.

Some Multi-activity Centres

Adventure Cornwall (☎ 01726-870844; www.adventurecornwall.co.uk) Near Fowey, Cornwall.
Adventurous Activity Company (☎ 0117-925 3196; www.adventurousactivitycompany.co.uk) Located in Bristol.
CRS Adventures (☎ 07891-635964; www.crsadventures.co.uk) Ashburton, Devon.
Essential Adventure (☎ 01395-271156; www.essential-adventure.co.uk) Exmouth, Devon.
Extreme Academy (☎ 01637-860840; www.extremeacademy.co.uk) Newquay, Cornwall.
Mountain Water Experience (☎ 01548-550675; www.mountainwaterexperience.com) Near Kingsbridge, Devon.
Outdoor Adventure (☎ 01288-362900; www.outdooradventure.co.uk) Near Bude, Cornwall.

Newton–Dorchester route is a fairly flat 8-mile countryside wander along quiet roads, bridleways and footways.

As well as the routes described here, hundreds of other personal explorations are possible. One of the delights of the region is hunting out those lanes signed 'unsuitable for motor vehicles', where the grass grows in the middle, the trees meet overhead and the banks rise improbably high either side. Self-discovered routes like this, on the way to the pub in the golden, slanting light of a warm summer's evening, are possibly the most delightful of all.

Rules & Practicalities

There are some basic rules governing where you can cycle in the UK. Bicycles are not allowed on motorways, but are allowed on other public roads. In reality, unless you like dicing with death, you won't enjoy pedalling along A roads, and many of the region's B roads are similarly unappealing; instead opt for cycle paths or C and unclassified roads. Cyclists can ride on public bridleways, but must give way to other users – be aware, too, that bicycles can alarm horses. You are not allowed to cycle on footpaths or across most open countryside. In moorland areas and on coastal paths this is a particular bone of contention – it's your responsibility to check where you can ride.

Although bicycles can normally be carried on the region's trains (see p294), restrictions or reservations sometimes apply – check when you buy the ticket. The most enjoyable cycling weather falls between spring and autumn, with July and August predictably busier. While not everywhere, cycle-hire shops are scattered around the region, often handily near trailheads – we list many in this guide. Expect to pay around £10 for a half-day's rental.

THRILL-SEEKER?

So you want to experience that ultimate adrenaline rush. Are you in safe hands? Will you get good tuition? Will your fun harm the environment?

Here are some top tips:

■ If the activity involves under-18s, check the operators are registered with the **Adventure Activities Licensing Authority** (AALA; ☎ 029 2075 5715; www.aala.org).

■ Ask if centres are approved by the individual activity's governing body. If not it doesn't mean it's a bad centre; if it is you know specific criteria have been met.

■ Check the instructors are qualified.

■ See if you're happy with the staff-student ratio – the lower it is the more time instructors have for you.

■ Check the company's environmental policy; some activities involve going to remote, sensitive environments.

■ See if you get a good vibe from the staff. If it feels like it's not pitched at your sort of person, it's probably not right for you.

SURFING

You've got the T-shirt, now take to the swells – with surf fashion exerting an illogical hold over the UK's urban, inland zones, this is your chance to actually ride the waves. The southwest's expansive beaches get the full force of the line-ups rolling in from the Atlantic. The result: the most-consistent quality surf conditions in England.

The self-styled capital of English surfing is Newquay (p230); it's also party central, with waves of clubbers washing up in its cafés and bars. More relaxed surf hubs include Polzeath p226), Bude (p220) and Sennen Cove (p242) in Cornwall, and Woolacombe (p212), Croyde (p214) and Bantham (p195) in Devon. In Dorset Bournemouth is bidding to increase the size of its waves – by sinking an ingenious artificial reef offshore (p126). It's worth noting that hordes of out-of-towners descending on the best breaks doesn't always go down well with the locals, who complain some holidaymakers don't respect their space.

Surf's Up. Or not. Review the best beaches and work out where the waves will be going off at www.a1surf.com. Or call ☎ 09063-620 004, 60p per minute.

Beginners are likely to spend a lot of time simply trying to stand up and lessons are highly recommended for safety's and sheer frustration's sake. The **British Surfing Association** (☎ 01637-876474; www.britsurf.co.uk) runs excellent courses from its **National Surfing Centre** (☎ 01637-850737; www.nationalsurfingcentre.com) in Newquay. Costs range from £30 for 2½ hours to £135 for seven sessions. It also approves scores of schools regionwide. If falling off a moving fibreglass lozenge doesn't appeal, try lying down – bodyboarding is a hit with children and adults alike. Expect to pay around £10 for a half- to full-day's hire for a wet suit; the same for surf- or bodyboards.

Thicker wet suits mean you can experience the waves at any time of year. Perversely the biggest tend to occur amid winter low pressures; good surf in the summer sunshine is not uncommon but can't be guaranteed. The north shores of Devon and Cornwall tend to enjoy better conditions, but wind and swell directions mean different beaches on either coast can be better on the day.

Kitesurfing & Windsurfing

A tricky but thrilling way of riding the waves propelled by a massive canopy, kitesurfing is the new kid on the block. The **British Kite Surfing Association** (☎ 01305-813555; www.britishkitesurfingassociation.co.uk) is its governing body. Prices start from around £75 for a half-day. Windsurfing is governed by the **Royal Yachting Association** (RYA; ☎ 0845 345 0400; www.rya.org.uk); expect to pay from £40 for a taster session. Exmouth in east Devon is a superb base for both (p177), as are Poole (p130), Christchurch (p133) and Weymouth (p159) in Dorset. See also the multi-activity centres we feature in the boxed text, p66.

CANOEING & KAYAKING

The southwest offers something for adrenaline junkies and laid-back paddlers alike – tranquil, slow-moving rivers, peaceful reservoirs, fierce white water and intimate coves.

White Water

The River Dart on Dartmoor is a big draw; heavy winter rains funnel into deep gorges en route to the sea – the result is foaming, fast-flowing water. Environmental concerns mean the rapids are only open broadly between October and March. Kayaking also takes place on the Exe and Barle on Exmoor – again only during the winter months. The DNPA and ENPA have more information.

Unless you're a real expert it's best to sign up with one of the many centres (see the boxed text, p66) for a day or two; the **British Canoe Union** (BCU; ☎ 0845 370 9500; www.bcu.org.uk) also approves training centres. If you are going it alone you'll need a permit as numbers are monitored; contact www.dartaccess .co.uk or the BCU.

White-water kayaking isn't suitable for beginners, so notching up some basics first is essential. Many courses specify being BCU two-star standard, although some introductory sessions do cover the 'slower-moving water' category. Expect to pay from £30 to £50 for a half-day. **CRS Adventures** (☎ 07891-635964; www.crsadventures.co.uk), based near Ashburton in Devon, runs a variety of courses. Postbridge or Widecombe-in-the-Moor make good places to stay.

Other Kayaking & Canoeing

White water aside, the region's slower-moving rivers and coasts are supremely tempting on a summer day. Generally no previous experience is necessary, and with kayaking courses often run from coastal sailing centres or inland reservoirs, the fun is available all over the region. Prices are around £25 to £40 for a half-day. In Devon, Plymouth (p199) is a possibility as are the Kingsbridge area (p192) of south Devon and Poole (p130) in Dorset.

Look out too for the Canadian canoe trips some firms specialise in. These often have a slightly New Age feel; Totnes is one possibility, p185.

For a surf movie Cornish style, try *Land of Saints*. This soulful epic was shot entirely in the Duchy and captures its chilled-out wave-riding spirit. It features awesome scenery and top UK surfers too.

Need to rest after that manic, adrenaline-charged activity? Or just want to chill-out? Breathe deeply and search www.relaxsouth west.co.uk for recharging, restorative inspiration.

SEA SAFETY

Advice from the life-saving charity the **RNLI** (www.rnli.org.uk):

■ Use beaches with lifeguards. Swim and bodyboard only between red-and-yellow flags.

■ Surfers with boards should stick to water marked by black-and-white chequered flags.

■ Follow the lifeguard's advice, don't go in the water alone and be aware of the tides.

■ Don't take inflatables into the sea. If you do, an adult should attach a line and hold onto it.

■ Make sure children are within easy reach at all times.

■ If you see someone in trouble tell a lifeguard or call ☎ 999 and ask for the coastguard.

THE HUNTING BAN

As you roam the rural southwest, signs proclaiming 'Fight Prejudice, Fight the Ban' dot the hedgerows. They are the legacy of years of fierce debate in the run up to legislation to outlaw fox hunting. After decades of discussion and sometimes violent confrontations, a bill banning hunting with dogs in England and Wales came into force in 2005 – not before a small group of prohunt demonstrators broke into the House of Commons Chamber.

What the Act does and doesn't allow remains highly controversial but it was always about much more than a piece of legislation. For many communities, urban and rural alike, it has become a defining characteristic; your views on hunting express something fundamental about who you are. While for many in the cities the concerns were over claims of cruelty and suffering, for many in rural areas it was seen as an assault on livelihoods and freedom. In the southwest, with a strong tradition of both fox and stag hunting, the issues had particular resonance. Years on, the fact that the signs are still up signifies feelings continue to run high. Although much more complex than an urban–rural divide, it's easy for some city dwellers to underestimate just how raw feelings are on the subject. If you want to bring it up in a country pub, expect heated arguments.

The southwest's rugged coast makes sea kayaking hard to resist. There's a reasonable chance of seeing seals, dolphins and basking sharks – especially off Cornwall. Some providers will require you to have moving-water experience; costs are similar to those for white-water kayaking. North Devon–based **Sea Kayaking South West** (☎ 01271-813129; www.seakayakingsouthwest .co.uk) does a two-day session for beginners for £150, and two-day expeditions for £180. At Lulworth Cove in Dorset you can paddle along the heritage-site Jurassic Coast (p137).

SAILING

Fittingly for a region that's waved off countless explorers, the southwest is a haven for sailors, fringed with wind-battered coasts, calm reservoirs and peaceful anchorages, as well as marinas, historic ports and quayside pubs.

You can sail all year but more courses are focused on the summer months – beating into the wind in heaving mid-November seas isn't always that much fun. All levels of experience are catered for; from a beginner's day course in a topper, to a week on board learning the basics, to chartering your own boat – with or without a skipper. The **Royal Yachting Association** (RYA; ☎ 0845 345 0400; www.rya.org.uk) can advise on approved training centres.

Predictably the key maritime centres and ports are excellent places to get on the water: Weymouth and Portland (p159) and Poole (p130) in Dorset; Dartmouth (p189) and Plymouth in Devon (p199); and Falmouth (p258) and Fowey (p269) in Cornwall. Reservoirs are another option, the **South West Lakes Trust** (☎ 01566-771930; www.swlakestrust.org.uk) has five water-sports centres in West Somerset, Devon and Cornwall.

Despite its reputation as a sport for toffs, sailing doesn't have to cost the earth. Half-day sessions in the smaller craft (eg a topper) cost about £25. A day's sailing in a yacht can cost from £50 per person or £360 a day for a seven-berth boat with skipper. A weekend, intensive live-aboard course for a RYA qualification can cost from £180 per person, while a seven-day sail to France will set you back around £750 per person.

ROCK CLIMBING

Granite, limestone and chalk: you can clamber over them all in the southwest and experienced climbers have plenty to choose from. Strings of fabulous crags are stretched across Dorset, Somerset, Devon and Cornwall – areas around Portland, Swanage, Torbay, Bodmin and Cheddar make par-

Sail off Weymouth and Portland and you'll get in before fleets of world-class yachtsmen. The Dorset ports are the sailing venues for the 2012 Olympics.

ticularly good focus points. Dartmoor alone has scores of accessible climbs with multi- and single-pitch routes, the DNPA can provide a free leaflet and further advice. Sometimes restrictions apply and you're required to book with the landowner for some crags; as ever it's the responsibility of the climber to check they should be there.

The **British Mountaineering Council** (☎ 0161-445 6111; www.thebmc.co.uk) has a database of climbing locations and also lists indoor walls. *South Devon and Dartmoor, a Climber's Guide*, by Nick White (£13), is an excellent information source. For tuition try the **Rock Centre** (☎ 01626-852717; www .rockcentre.co.uk; Rock House; per half-/full day £15/25) in Chudleigh, Devon. Many of the region's activity centres (see the boxed text, p66) also run climbing courses. To test muscles you never knew you had, expect to pay around £15 to £30 for a half-day.

HORSE RIDING

Many riders dream of cantering across open countryside and, in places, that can be realised in the southwest. In fact the range of horse-riding environments for all levels is huge: dappled bridleways, spectacular moorland or the ride-through-the-surf beloved of films. A pace thing, clip-clopping along sets you very much in tune with the rhythm of your surroundings.

Among the biggest draws are the region's expansive moorland landscapes and many stables are within easy reach of Exmoor (p115) and Dartmoor (p204). Other prime sites are the Mendips and the Dorset Downs. The region's extensive network of public bridleways is another boon, Exmoor alone has 400 miles of them. Centres cater to novices and more experienced riders alike – expect to pay from about £14 an hour. Throughout the chapters we've highlighted centres, while other good sources of information are tourist offices and NPA centres; the **British Horse Society** (☎ 08701-202244; www.bhs.org.uk) lists stables. Many riding centres offer accommodation, ranging from luxurious farmhouses to basic camping; some will put your horse up too.

> Searchable by region, www.equinetourism .co.uk lists events, stables, trekking centres and horse holidays. It even has details of a Devon equine spa.

DIVING

The number of wrecks off the southwest coast makes sailors nervous. But couple them with reefs and crystal-clear waters and you have a great area to dive. Wrasse, conger eels and dogfish will float past your face mask in a watery world that can take you to shallow reefs or deeper waters.

The region's most unusual underwater attraction is the **Scylla** (www.national -aquarium.co.uk/Scylla). This gutted, ex-warship was sunk in Whitsand Bay near Plymouth by the National Marine Aquarium in 2004 as part of a project to study how reefs form. Elsewhere thousands of ancient ships lie beneath the waves; the coasts of Devon and Cornwall are peppered with more than 4600 wrecks. Many make for excellent dives; the Isles of Scilly alone have a remarkable 150 recognised dive sites.

The **British Sub Aqua Club** (☎ 0151-350 6200; www.bsac.com) has a network of recognised training centres. Weymouth and Portland (p159) in Dorset, Exmouth (p177) in Devon and the Isles of Scilly (p255) are particularly good bases. Beginners will probably learn in the summer months. A half-day taster costs around £30 while a four- to five-day training course that takes you from pool to sea costs from around £325. You will need a medical statement saying you're fit to dive and be required to complete some safety homework before you start. The next level is around £250 for two days, while those with experience can opt for a two-dive weekend from £40, or an evening dive from about £20.

Responsible Diving

Consider the following tips when diving to help preserve the environment for the enjoyment of all.

- Ask about the environmental characteristics that can affect your diving and how local trained divers deal with these considerations.
- Avoid touching or standing on living marine organisms and reefs.
- Be conscious of your fins. Even without contact, the surge from fin strokes can damage delicate organisms. Take care not to kick up clouds of sand, which can smother organisms.
- Practise and maintain proper buoyancy control. Major damage can be done by divers descending too fast.
- Take great care in underwater caves. Spend as little time within them as possible as your air bubbles may be caught within the roof and thereby leave organisms high and dry. Take turns to inspect the interior of a small cave.
- Resist the temptation to collect or buy shells or to loot marine archaeological sites (mainly shipwrecks).
- Ensure that you take home all your rubbish and any litter you may find as well. Plastics in particular are a serious threat to marine life.
- Do not feed fish.
- Minimise your disturbance of marine animals.

UNWINDING

Sand-castle building, shell collecting, stone row wandering, tree hugging, deep breathing, deeper thinking – an unforgettable delight of all the southwest's wide open space is actually doing very little. Beachcombing (or 'reading the seaweed') is a local favourite. Bare feet on hot sand, the surge of a soothing sea and a transporting, tiny world of shells and driftwood – it's better than a spa. It's also completely free.

Beachcombers on east Devon and Dorset's Jurassic Coast (p155) can hunt for ancient treasures: fossilised chunks of 200-million-year-old plants and animals. Responsible fossil collecting here has an official thumbs-up. Freed from the cliffs by constant erosion, experts say these rock-hard nuggets of prehistory would otherwise be destroyed by the sea if not found by fossickers. Even children get a buzz from it. Lyme Regis has particularly fertile fossil hunting, but also keep an eye out at Charmouth and Portland in Dorset and also Minehead in Somerset. Official advice is to stay on public paths, check tide times, only pick up from the beach (never dig out from cliffs because it can cause rock falls), always leave some behind for others and be sure to tell the experts if you find a stunner.

For the cost of a shrimping net or a crabbing line, you can go rockpooling or sit dangling bait over a harbour wall. Here you head right back to childhood; captivating for the kids, utterly liberating for the rest of us.

Look out locally for leaflets detailing the superb programmes of outdoor events run by many local authorities and charities. Far from regimented outings ('are we having fun yet?') these gems are really worth hunting out – fireside storytelling, bat detecting, moonlight paddles, woodland thinning, deer watching, dry stone walling, night walks, farm visits and history hikes. The following run informative, fun programmes of events – normally for just a few pounds:

Dartmoor National Park Authority (www.dartmoor-npa.gov.uk)
Dorset AONB (http://dorsetaonb.org.uk)
Exmoor National Park Authority (www.exmoor-nationalpark.gov.uk)
National Trust (NT; www.nationaltrust.org.uk)
South Hams AONB (www.southdevonaonb.org.uk)
Torbay Countryside Trust (www.countryside-trust.org.uk)

Safe Diving

Before going scuba diving or snorkelling, consider the following points to ensure a safe and enjoyable experience.

- Possess a current diving certification card from a recognised scuba-diving instructional agency.
- Be sure you are healthy and feel comfortable diving.
- Get reliable information about physical and environmental conditions at the dive site (eg from a reputable local dive operation).
- Be aware of local laws, regulations and etiquette about marine life and the environment.
- Dive only at sites within your realm of experience; if available, engage the services of a competent, professionally trained dive instructor or dive master.
- Be aware that underwater conditions vary significantly from one region, or even site, to another. Seasonal changes can significantly alter any site and dive conditions. These differences influence the way divers dress for a dive and what diving techniques they use.

The Wrecking Season is a beautiful, lyrical film where beachcomber-playwright Nick Darke explores the origins of things washed up on Cornwall's shores. Amazonian seedpods and Canadian lobster tags connect the region to the world's coastal communities.

Bristol, Bath & Somerset

There's a kaleidoscopic feel to the southwest's uppermost corner. Part rural escape, part coastal retreat, part historical textbook, it presents multiple faces to the visitor: one minute you're travelling through a pastoral hotchpotch of cornfields, copses and willow-shaded bridleways, and the next you're steaming over a humpbacked hill, plumbing the depths of a limestone cavern, or tracing the curve of a windblown coastline. The accents may be laced with a burr that's thicker than butter, but don't be fooled into thinking this is a backward corner of Britain; the stately cities of Bristol and Bath have been setting trends, breaking rules and educating the rest of England for centuries.

It's a county of collision, where wild hill meets tourist town, Georgian crescent meets cobbled street and thatched cottage meets city skyline. Bristol – a gateway to the region – and Bath are essential stops, but Somerset's also the traditional home of cider, Cheddar cheese and Britain's tiniest city. In the east are the Mendips and Quantocks, choice walking country and a source of poetic inspiration for Messrs Coleridge and Wordsworth, while the centre of the county conceals the frying-pan flats of the Somerset Levels, a watery wetland and twitcher's paradise. Smack bang in the middle looms the emerald hump of Glastonbury – King Arthur's legendary resting place, the realm of a faerie king and the home of everyone's favourite musical mudfest. Out to the west, straddling the border with Devon, is Exmoor, Britain's oldest national park, where red deer stalk the hilltops, wooded coombes tumble seawards and trailheads crisscross the cliffs. Savour the sights, sip some scrumpy or get all spiritual – Somerset's a treat for the senses.

HIGHLIGHTS

- Head for the bright lights of the southwest's big city, **Bristol** (p76)
- Sink some scrumpy at a traditional **cider brewery** (p114)
- Scan the scenery from the top of **Glastonbury Tor** (p106)
- Do as the Romans did and have a bath in **Bath** (p93)
- Explore the quiet lanes and nature reserves on the **Somerset Levels** (p111)
- Head out on a wildlife-spotting safari around **Exmoor** (p113)

- POPULATION: 878,710
- EARLIEST SCRUMPY PRODUCTION: 1230
- RATIO OF SHEEP TO PEOPLE ON EXMOOR: 50:1

SOMERSET

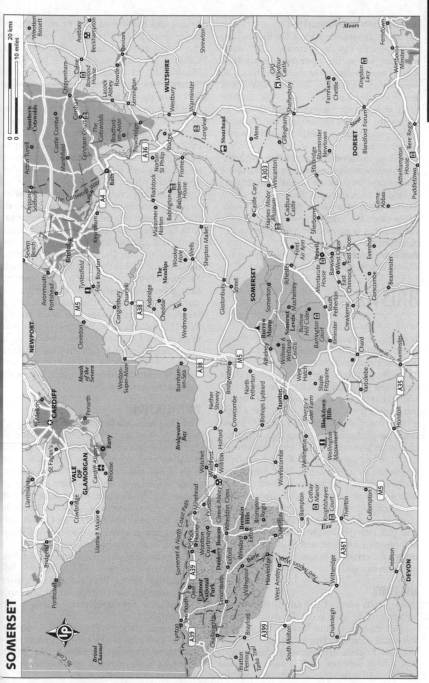

Orientation & Information

Somerset is bounded west by the Bristol Channel and east by Exmoor. The Mendips cut across the countryside between Bristol and Wells, while the Quantocks lie west towards Exmoor; Taunton, Yeovil and the Somerset Levels occupy the middle ground between Somerset and Dorset to the south. Wells, Glastonbury and Taunton make good bases for exploring the wider Somerset area.

The main **Somerset Tourist Office** (☎ 01934-750833; somersetvisitorcentre@somerset.gov.uk) is at the Sedgemoor Services on the M5 South near Axbridge. For regional info:

Heart of Somerset (www.heartofsomerset.com) Covers the Blackdowns, Quantocks and Somerset Levels.

Visit Somerset (www.visitsomerset.co.uk) The county's main tourist info site.

Visit South Somerset (www.visitsouthsomerset.com) Information on the Yeovil and south Somerset area.

BRISTOL

☎ 0117 / pop 380,615

For a big-city buzz, nowhere in the southwest can measure up to Bristol. This grand old girl has gone through a wardrobe of outfits down the centuries – river village, mercantile city, slave port, shipbuilding centre, industrial powerhouse and aeronautical hub – but despite her venerable history, she's been a little down-at-heel in recent years. However, her fortunes are changing; while the old industries have sailed into the sunset, over the last decade Bristol's rediscovered her sense of self-esteem. The run-down docks have been rejuvenated, the harbour's alive with media centres, museums and metropolitan *pieds-à-terre,* and the city's cultural scene is crackling with theatres, bars, clubs and galleries. She might not have the lolly of London or the beauty of Bath, but one thing's for certain – this old lady's got plenty of life in her yet.

HISTORY

Strategically sited at the confluence of the Rivers Frome and Avon, Bristol began as a small river port, and by the 11th century the small Saxon village of Brigstow (from the Old English for 'place by the bridge') was a busy harbour, with a lucrative trade in cloth and wine. By the mid-14th century

Bristol had blossomed into Britain's third-largest port. In 1497 'local hero' John Cabot (actually a Genoese sailor called Giovanni Caboto) set sail from the city for Newfoundland, and Bristol later became one of Britain's major transatlantic ports, growing fat on the proceeds of the 'Triangle Trade', in which commodities including textiles, munitions, copper and guns were shipped to African states, where they were sold in exchange for slaves who were then transported to the New World colonies. For more on Bristol's link to the slave trade, see the boxed text, p30.

By the 18th century the city was experiencing increasing maritime competition from Liverpool, Portishead and Avonmouth, so the city repositioned itself as an industrial centre and shipbuilding hub, as well as the terminus for the Great Western Railway, masterminded by the engineer Isambard Kingdom Brunel. In the early 20th century, Bristol became a centre for the aviation industry; unfortunately, this made the city a target for German bombing raids during WWII, and much of the city centre had been levelled by 1945. The postwar rush for reconstruction left Bristol with plenty of concrete carbuncles, but the city has undergone extensive redevelopment, especially around the harbour area.

ORIENTATION

The city centre, north of the river, is compact but hilly. The central area revolves around St Nicholas Market, the Corn Exchange and Broadmead shopping centre. Park St is lined with shops and cafés up to the university, while Whiteladies Rd is the hub of bar and restaurant life. The hilltop suburb of Clifton, with its Georgian terraces, cafés and boutique shops, is west of the centre. The Clifton Suspension Bridge spans the Avon from Clifton to Leigh Woods in north Somerset.

As in any big city, it's worth taking care at night, especially around Cheltenham Rd, Gloucester Rd, St Paul's and Montpelier (northwest of the centre), which all have a reputation for street crime. Grab a cab after dark.

The main station is Bristol Temple Meads, a mile southeast of the centre. Some trains use Bristol Parkway, 5 miles to the north. The bus station is on Marlborough St, northeast of the city centre.

BRISTOL

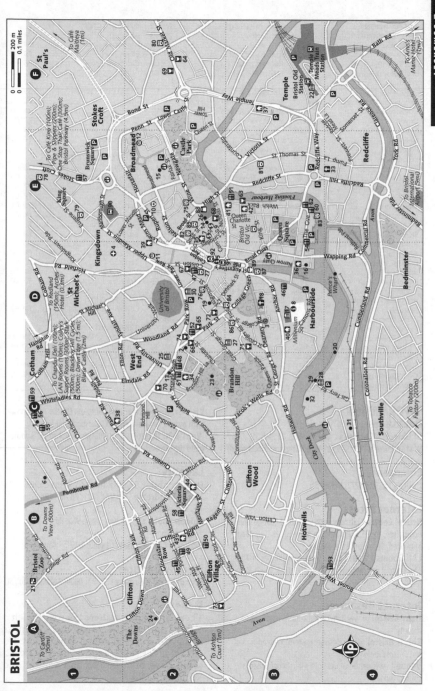

INFORMATION
Bookshops
Blackwell's/George's (☎ 927 6602; 89 Park St)
Waterstone's (☎ 925 2274; The Galleries, Broadmead)

Emergency
Police (☎ 927 7777; Nelson St)

Internet Access
Bristol Central Library (☎ 903 7200; College Green; access free; 9.30am-7.30pm Mon, Tue & Thu, 10am-5pm Wed, 9am-5pm Fri & Sat)
LAN Rooms (☎ 973 3886; 6 Cotham Hill; per hr £2.50; 10am-11pm Mon-Thu, 10am-10pm Fri, 10am-9pm Sat & Sun)

Internet Resources
Itchy Bristol (www.itchybristol.com) Web guide to the city.
This is Bristol (www.thisisbristol.com) Web edition of the *Bristol Evening Post*.
Venue (www.venue.co.uk) Online version of Bristol's listings guide.

Visit Bristol (www.visitbristol.co.uk) Official tourism site with events, accommodation, transport and sights.
What's On Bristol (www.whatsonbristol.co.uk) Another good listings webzine.

Laundry
It costs about £3.50 a load to keep clean.
Alma Laundrette (☎ 973 4121; 78 Alma Rd; 7am-9pm)
Golden Spot (☎ 973 2042; Alma Vale Rd; 8am-8pm)
Redland (☎ 970 6537; Chandos Rd; 8am-8pm)

Medical Services
Bristol Royal Infirmary (☎ 923 0000; 2 Marlborough St)

Money
There are banks scattered across the city. You'll find all the usual main culprits along Corn St, including Barclays at No 40, Lloyds at No 55 and NatWest at No 32; some have branches around Clifton and Whiteladies Rd.

Post
Post office (The Galleries, Broadmead)
Post office (Upper Maudlin St)

Tourist Information
Broadmead (The Mall Galleries; 9am-5.30pm Mon-Sat, 11am-5pm Sun)
City Centre (Colston Ave; 10.30am-5.30pm Mon-Fri, 10am-1pm Sat & Sun)
Clifton (in City Museum, Queens Rd; 10am-5pm)
Main tourist office (enquiries premium rate 0906 711 2191, for accommodation 0845 408 0474; www.visit bristol.co.uk; The Annexe, Wildscreen Walk, Harbourside; 10am-6pm Mar-Oct, 10am-5pm Mon-Sat, 11am-4pm Sun Nov-Feb) The main telephone number is used for all branches.
Temple Meads (in Empire & Commonwealth Museum, Clock Tower Yard, Temple Meads; 10am-5pm)

Travel Agencies
STA Travel (929 4399; 43 Queens Rd; 9am-6pm, noon-5pm Sun)
Trailfinders (929 9000; 48 Corn St; 9am-6pm)

SIGHTS
Harbourside
AT-BRISTOL
On Bristol's revived harbourside, At-Bristol (0845 345 1235; www.at-bristol.org.uk; Harbourside; adult/child £9/6.50; 10am-5pm Mon-Fri, 10am-6pm Sat & Sun) houses one of the country's leading science centres, Explore-At-Bristol. It's crammed with hundreds of hands-on exhibits demonstrating the everyday applications of science, with zones spanning ingenious inventions, optical illusions, outer-space technology and the human brain. Strum on a virtual harp, freeze your shadow, become a virtual sperm or journey across the solar system in the amazing domed Planetarium.

On your way out, look out for Pero's Bridge, which spans the river across to the Arnolfini Arts Centre, and was named after the African-born slave who served the Bristolian merchant John Pinney (see Georgian House, p80). On nearby Millennium Sq is a statue to Cary Grant, aka Brizzle boy Archibald Leach.

SS GREAT BRITAIN
Moored on the city's historic dry dock is one of the great monuments to Bristol's industrial past. In 1843 Brunel designed the SS Great Britain (929 1843; www.ssgreatbritain.org; adult/child £10.50/5.50; 10am-5.30pm Apr-Oct, 10am-4.30pm Nov-Mar;), the second of his trio of great transatlantic steamers, preceded by the Great Western in 1837 and followed by the monumental Great Eastern in 1852. In many ways the Great Britain was the most groundbreaking; the first luxury Atlantic liner constructed entirely from wrought iron and powered by the revolutionary system of screw propulsion. But as with many of Brunel's designs, she was ahead of her time. Huge running costs meant the ship ran at a massive loss, and when she was accidentally grounded off Dundrum Bay in Ireland in 1846, there was serious talk about whether she was worth the expense of saving. She was eventually sold off as a transport vessel, before being used as a troop ship and a lowly coal hulk; by 1937 she was no longer watertight and was abandoned near Port Stanley in the Falklands.

There the Great Britain remained, rusting and forgotten, until 1970 when she was finally towed back to Bristol aboard a floating pontoon. Since then a 30-year, £11.3 million restoration project has allowed the ship to rediscover her former splendour. The ship's rooms have been painstakingly refurbished, including the galley, surgeon's quarters, mess hall and the great engine room, but the highlight is the 'glass sea' on which the ship sits, enclosing an airtight dry dock that preserves the ship's delicate hull. Quite rightly, the museum's scooped a host of awards, and there are plans to include the whole dry dock in a forthcoming bid for Unesco World Heritage status.

Moored nearby is a replica of John Cabot's ship Matthew, built in 1997 to coincide with the quincentenary celebrations of the explorer's original voyage. The Maritime Heritage Centre (927 9856; Great Western Dockyard, Gas Ferry Rd; admission £6.25; 10am-5.30pm Apr-Oct, 10am-4.30pm Nov-Mar) houses various exhibits relating to the ship and her illustrious history. East along the river is Prince's Wharf, formerly the site of Bristol's main dock and the city's Industrial Museum (currently being redeveloped into a new Museum of Bristol).

ARNOLFINI ARTS CENTRE & SPIKE ISLAND
In a huge red-brick warehouse near Pero's Bridge is the Arnolfini Arts Centre (929 9191; www.arnolfini.org.uk; admission free; 16 Narrow Quay), Bristol's lively contemporary arts centre. Entry to exhibitions is free, but you'll have to pay for music events, screenings or dance performances.

Culture vultures can also visit **Spike Island** (☎ 929 2266; www.spikeisland.org.uk; 133 Cumberland Rd; ⊙ noon-6pm Tue-Sun), a centre for contemporary visual arts that's recently reopened after a £2.25 million revamp, with artists' studios, a light-drenched gallery and a great café.

City Centre

CITY MUSEUM & ART GALLERY

The city's municipal **museum** (☎ 922 3571; Queen's Rd; admission free; ⊙ 10am-5pm) is housed in a stunning Edwardian building near the university. There's a collection of British and French art on the 1st floor, along with galleries dedicated to ceramics and decorative arts – look out for the 'Bristol Boxkite' above reception, a pioneering canvas aeroplane built in Bristol and made famous in the 1965 film *Those Magnificent Men in their Flying Machines*. On the ground floor you'll find the archaeological, geological and natural history wings, as well as the refurbished Egyptian Gallery.

GEORGIAN HOUSE

For a taste of the aristocratic high life once enjoyed by Bristol's merchants, head for the 18th-century **Georgian House** (☎ 921 1362; 7 Great George St; admission free; ⊙ 10am-5pm Sat-Wed). This stunning six-storeyed mansion was the home of former sugar merchant John Pinney, along with his family and his slave Pero (after whom Pero's Bridge is named). The house is magnificently preserved, with a booklined study, sitting parlours, several Georgian-themed bedrooms and the original library containing the Pinney family Bible. But the true heart of the house is the basement kitchen, complete with jelly moulds, spice boxes and a roasting spit big enough to roast an ox.

RED LODGE

Arguably the southwest's finest slice of Elizabethan architecture, the **Red Lodge** (☎ 921 1360; Park Row; admission free; ⊙ 10am-5pm Sat-Wed) was built in 1590 but remodelled in 1730, and bears the hallmarks of Elizabethan, Stuart and Georgian architects. Originally built to accompany a great house that stood on the site of the Colston Hall, the lodge is an architectural feast, packed with wood carvings, original cornicing and delicate plasterwork, as well as a Tudor 'knot-garden' and the fabulous Oak Room, hardly changed since its Elizabethan builders first pinned up the panelling.

BRISTOL & BRUNEL

The year 2006 saw the 200th anniversary of the birth of one of Bristol's towering figures, Isambard Kingdom Brunel (1806–59) – industrial genius, pioneering engineer, and general all-round Renaissance man.

The precocious young Isambard was picked out for greatness from an early age. Educated at the Lycée Henri-Quatre in Paris and the University of Caen in Normandy, Brunel was barely 20 years old when he was appointed chief engineer of the Thames Tunnel, designed by his father Marc and located between Rotherhithe and Wapping in London. The project was fraught with technical difficulties; foul-smelling river water and explosive gases were a constant threat, and the tunnel was flooded twice in 1827 and 1828. Brunel was almost drowned during the second flood while trying to rescue trapped workers. While recovering, he entered a competition to design a bridge over the Avon at Clifton. His first submission was rejected, but the competition was run again in 1831 and this time Brunel's design was awarded first prize. The foundation stone was laid in June the same year, but Brunel died before his first major commission was completed.

Thankfully he had time to see plenty of other schemes to fruition. During his 30-year career Brunel was responsible for many landmark projects, including the construction of the Tamar Rail Bridge, the foundation of the Great Western Railway Line and the design of three of the world's greatest ships (see p79). He also built 1000 miles of railway lines, modernised the docks at Bristol, Plymouth and Cardiff, designed a prefabricated field hospital for use during the Crimean War and worked on railway projects everywhere from India to Italy.

Despite surviving on a daily diet of four hours' sleep and 40 cigars, and suffering from numerous bouts of ill health, Brunel's closest shave came when he nearly choked to death having accidentally swallowed a coin performing a conjuring trick for his children. His eventual end was more prosaic; he suffered a stroke in 1859, just before the *Great Eastern* made its first voyage to New York, and died 10 days later at the age of 53.

BRISTOL CATHEDRAL

Originally founded as the church of an Augustinian monastery in 1140, **Bristol Cathedral** (☎ 926 4879; www.bristol-cathedral.co.uk; College Green; ☺ 8am-6pm) has a fine Norman chapter house and gate, while the attractive chapels have eccentric carvings and impressive heraldic glass. Although much of the nave and the west towers date from the 19th century, the 14th-century choir has fascinating misericords depicting apes in hell, quarrelling couples and dancing bears. The south transept shelters a rare Saxon carving of the 'Harrowing of Hell', discovered under the chapter-house floor after a 19th-century fire.

ST MARY REDCLIFFE

Described as 'the fairest, goodliest and most famous parish church in England' by Queen Elizabeth I, **St Mary Redcliffe** (☎ 929 1487; www .stmaryredcliffe.co.uk; Redcliffe Way; ☺ 8.30am-5pm Mon-Sat summer, 9am-4pm Mon-Sat winter, 8am-7.30pm Sun year-round) boasts a soaring, 89m-high spire, a grand hexagonal porch and a vaulted ceiling decorated with fine gilt bosses.

CABOT TOWER

Built in 1897 to commemorate 400 years since Cabot's voyage to Newfoundland, the 150m-high **Cabot Tower** (admission free; ☺ 8am-7pm summer, 8am-4pm winter) stands in the small park on Brandon Hill and can be seen from across the city. Built in red sandstone and pale-cream Bath stone, the tower offers wonderful views from the top of its spiral staircase, but be warned – it's a long, puff-powered climb to the top.

Temple Meads

Bristol's slave-trading past is thoughtfully explored at the **British Empire & Commonwealth Museum** (☎ 925 9480; www.empiremuseum.co.uk; Clock Tower Yard; adult/child £7.95/3.95; ☺ 10am-5pm). Dealing with the history and consequences of British colonial conquest, the 16 galleries range over 500 years of British trade, exploration and exploitation, and while there's a conscious attempt at perspective, it's hard not to be moved by the stories of subjugation that underpinned Britain's imperial rise. Highlights include sepia-toned films from the Empire's heyday and a collection of outfits worn by colonial administrators, Indian viceroys and tribal chiefs. *Breaking the Chains*, marking the bicentenary of the Abolition of Slavery Act in 1807, interweaves film, music and audio testimony in an examination of the gruesome realities of the slave trade. For more on Bristol and the slave trade, see the boxed text, p30.

Clifton

Bristol grew rich on transatlantic trafficking, and during the 18th and 19th centuries the spa resort of Clifton was transformed into an elegant suburb where the city's well-heeled businessmen could live far from the squalid city docks. Clifton sits on a hilltop overlooking the Avon Gorge, stretching from Whiteladies Rd to the river; the further west you go, the posher the houses become, especially around **Cornwallis Cresent** and **Royal York Cresent**. These days Clifton is still the poshest postcode in Bristol, with a villagey mix of streetside cafés, upmarket boutiques and designer shops. See p89 for buses to Clifton and the zoo.

CLIFTON SUSPENSION BRIDGE

Clifton's most famous (and photographed) landmark is another Brunel masterpiece, the 76m-high **Clifton Suspension Bridge** (www.clifton -suspension-bridge.org.uk), which spans the Avon Gorge over to Leigh Woods in northern Somerset. It's a graceful sight, and one of Britain's most elegant bridges. Though construction work began in 1836, Brunel died before the bridge's completion in 1864. It was designed to carry light horse-drawn traffic and foot passengers, but these days around 12,000 motor vehicles cross it daily – testament to the quality of Brunel's original design. It's also a magnet for stunt artists and suicides; in 1885 Sarah Ann Hedley jumped from the bridge after a lovers' tiff, but her voluminous petticoats parachuted her to earth and she lived to be 85.

There's a **visitor information point** (☎ 974 4665; visitinfo@clifton-suspension-bridge.org; ☺ 10am-5pm) near the tower on the Leigh Woods side; guided tours (£2.50) are available by arrangement.

BRISTOL ZOO

In a lovely spot on Clifton Hill, **Bristol Zoo** (☎ 973 8951; www.bristolzoo.org.uk; Clifton; adult/child excl donation to projects £10.50/7; ☺ 9am-5.30pm summer, 9am-5pm winter) is one of the country's finest. Highlights include an underwater gallery for viewing seals and penguins, a huge open-air aviary, a gorilla island, a reptile house and the

Twilight World, populated by bizarre beasties such as two-toed sloths and naked mole rats. There's also a newly opened Monkey Jungle, with a forested enclosure of red-ruffed lemurs, lion-tailed macaques and howler monkeys.

THE DOWNS
The grassy parks of **Clifton Down** and **Durdham Down** (locally known as The Downs) make a fine picnic spot. Nearby, a scruffy observatory houses England's only **camera obscura** (☎ 974 1242; admission £1; ⊙ from 12.30pm Mon-Fri, from 10.30am Sat & Sun), which offers incredible views of the suspension bridge.

Outskirts
BLAISE CASTLE
Surrounded by tree-filled parkland in the northern suburb of Henbury, **Blaise Castle House Museum** (☎ 950 6789; Henbury Rd) offers a fascinating insight into Bristol's changing social history. The elegant manorhouse, built for merchant and banker John Harford between 1796 and 1798, contains a quirky collection of vintage toys (from spinning tops to model trains), as well as a 'Cabinet of Curiosities', whose contents include the scrimshawed armbone of a Bristol rioter and a 'scold's bridle' used to punish recalcitrant wives.

Bus 40/40A (45 minutes, every 15 minutes) passes the castle from Colston Ave; bus 1 (20 minutes, every 10 minutes) travels from Temple Meads via the city centre.

ASHTON COURT ESTATE
This huge **estate** (☎ 963 9176; cheri_seddon@bristol -city.gov.uk) is Bristol's 'green lung', with 345 hectares of woods, trails and public parkland. It's also the venue for many summer events, including the annual International Balloon Fiesta (opposite).

ACTIVITIES
Getting active in Bristol is easy. Skaters can swing by **Bristol Ice Rink** (☎ 929 2148; Frogmore St; ⊙ hours vary), while cyclists can take to the trails around Ashton Court or the **Bristol and Bath Railway Path** (www.bristolbathrailwaypath .org.uk), a 13-mile trail jaunt along a disused train track. For outdoorsy types, the **Bristol Orienteering Klub** (www.bristolorienteering.org.uk) arranges orienteering, while the **Avon Outdoors Activity Club** (☎ 949 7350; www.aoac.co.uk) and the **Adventurous Activity Company** (☎ 925 3196; www .adventurousactivitycompany.co.uk) runs climbing, biking, riding and windsurfing trips in the Bristol area.

BRISTOL FOR CHILDREN
Bristol has some fantastic activities to keep the whippersnappers happy. First off is a quick spin around the city by **boat** (below). Then it's off to **Explore-At-Bristol** (p79), where budding Einsteins can conduct experiments and push interactive buttons to their hearts' content. The **SS Great Britain** (p79) has audioguides specially designed for kids, centring around Tom (the ship's boy), Florence (an Australian emigrant) and Sinbad (the ship's cat), while the denizens of **Bristol Zoo** (p81) are always a huge hit. Other ideas include a **piratical tour** (below) of the harbourside – Long John Silver and Edward Teach (aka Blackbeard) both have Bristol connections – or a trip across to the **Ashton Court Estate** (left) for deer-spotting, mountain biking or horse riding.

The city has a dedicated festival for kids. The **Bristol Children's Festival** kicks off at the start of August on The Downs, with four days of puppetry, circus skills, magic and children's theatre, and there are also annual festivals for **hot-air balloons** and **kite-flying** (opposite).

And if after all that you just feel like handing them over to someone else for a day, contact **Bristol Babysitting Agency** (☎ 01454-851 960; www.bristolbabysitting.co.uk) who can recommend accredited local childminders, or try **Park Lane Nannies** (☎ 373 0003) or **Tinies** (☎ 300 5630; bristol@tinieschildcare.co.uk).

TOURS
Bristol Highlights Walk (☎ 968 4638; ⊙ 11am Sat Apr-Sep) A weekly tour (£3.50) of the old town, city centre and harbourside, run every Saturday by Bristol's Blue Badge guides from the tourist office. Tailor-made tours exploring Clifton, the slave trade and Bristol's wine merchants are available on request.

Bristol Packet Boat Trips (☎ 926 8157; www.bristol packet.co.uk; adult/child £4.25/2.75; ⊙ every 45min 11am-4.15pm Sat & Sun year-round & daily during school holidays) A fleet of wooden-hulled boats cruise around the harbour area. There are also day trips to Avon Gorge (£11.50/8.50) July to October, and to Bath (£20/15) one Sunday per month May to September.

Bristol Pirate Walks (☎ 07950 566483; adult/child £3.50/2.50; ⊙ 6.15pm Tue, Thu & Sat Apr-Sep, 2pm Sat & Sun Oct-Mar) Learn about Bristol's piratical past in the company of Pete the Pirate (dressed in suitably swashbuckling fashion) on this two-hour harbour walk. Book via the tourist office.

City Sightseeing (☎ 926 0767; www.bristolvisitor
.co.uk; adult/child 90p/50p, day ticket adult/child £9/5,
3-day ticket adult/1st child £14/free; ☾ 10am-4pm
Easter-Sep) An open-top hop-on, hop-off bus chugs past
all the major attractions, including the SS *Great Britain*,
Bristol Zoo, Clifton and Temple Meads. Buses leave Broad
Quay every 45 minutes June to September, and every 90
minutes October to May. If you can survive the stigma, it's
actually a useful way of buzzing round the city.

Visit Bristol MP3 Tours (www.visitbristol.co.uk) Free
downloadable audio tours are available on the tourist
office website, including guides to Brunel's Bristol, Clifton
and the Quayside Area.

Visit Eastside (www.visiteastside.co.uk) Two free
downloadable tours of the multicultural districts of St
Paul's and Easton, focusing on specialist shops, cafés and
art galleries.

FESTIVALS & EVENTS

Summer is the busiest time for live events
in Bristol.

Shakespeare Festival (www.bristolshakespeare
.homestead.com) This event runs from May to September
and is held at various venues, including the Ashton Court
Estate, Queen Sq and the zoo.

St Paul's Carnival (☎ 944 4176) A giant street party
held in St Paul's on the first Saturday of July.

Bristol Harbour Festival (☎ 922 3148) Brings bands,
theatre and DJs to the dockside in late July.

International Balloon Fiesta (☎ 953 5884; www
.bristolfiesta.co.uk) The Ashton Court Estate hosts this
balloon fest in August. The Ashton Court Festival recently
packed up after 33 years.

Bristol Flower Show Held in August.

Bristol Pride (www.bristolpride.org) The city's gay
festival, held in August.

International Kite Festival (☎ 977 2002; www.kite
-festival.org) Flies in September at Ashton Court Estate.

Bristol Poetry Festival This word fest is hosted at the
Arnolfini in September.

Encounters Festival (☎ 929 9188; www.encounters
-festival.org.uk) Bristol's biggest film festival is held at the
Watershed every November.

Christmas Market Late November and December.

SLEEPING

There's a wealth of places to stay in Bristol, but the city's still struggling to shake
off its corporate edge; with a little digging
you'll discover some fantastic upmarket
hotels and an ace YHA hostel. The tourist
office's free *Bristol Guide* has listings and a
fold-out map.

Budget

Bristol Backpackers (☎ 925 7900; www.bristolback
packers.co.uk; 17 St Stephen's St; dm/tw/tr £14/36/45; ☐)
This old-school hostel is not so fancy, but
it's still handy for the city centre. The dorms
and doubles are tiny, with cramped beds and
cheap nylon carpets. It gets rowdy thanks
to the on-site bar and the lack of a curfew,
but it's nothing the seasoned backpacker
shouldn't be able to handle.

   Bristol YHA (☎ 0870 770 5726; bristol@yha.org.uk;
Hayman House, 14 Narrow Quay; dm £19.95, s incl breakfast
£20-35, d incl breakfast £45-50; ☐ ☐) Housed in a

QUIRKY BRISTOL

One of Bristol's most mysterious exports is **Banksy**, a guerrilla graffitist, political prankster and
street stenciller whose provocative works have been gracing the city's walls for more than a
decade. Like any self-respecting antihero, Banksy's true identity is a closely guarded secret, but
rumour has it that he was born in 1974 in Yate, 12 miles from Bristol, and cut his teeth in a Bristol
graffiti outfit. Taking a wry, witty and protest-laced look at modern British life, Banksy's works have
sprung up everywhere from Brick Lane to the Palestinian West Bank – his more famous stunts
include spraying 'fat lane' on a Venice Beach sidewalk, painting Guantanamo Bay prisoners inside
Disneyland and building a Stonehenge made of portaloos at the Glastonbury festival.

   You can still see his most famous Bristol piece, a ghostly take on Charion, the River Styx
boatman, that graces the side of the Thekla (p88). His notorious 'love triangle' stencil (featuring an angry husband, a two-timing wife, and a naked man dangling from a window) is on the
wall of a sexual-health clinic on Frogmore St. There's also a large mural called 'Mild Mild West'
featuring a Molotov cocktail–wielding teddy bear on Cheltenham Rd opposite the junction with
Jamaica St.

   Somewhat ironically for such an anti-establishment figure, Banksy is almost mainstream these
days – his work has inspired think-pieces in the *Guardian* and the *New Yorker,* and some of his
work has sold at Sotheby's. For more info check out www.banksy.co.uk.

red-brick harbourside warehouse, this brilliant multistoreyed hostel is a YHA flagship. The accommodation is nothing extraordinary – expect easy-clean walls and identikit furniture – but the facilities are fantastic (games room, cycle store, net access) and the location is unbeatable.

Arches Hotel (☎ 924 7398; www.arches-hotel.co.uk; 132 Cotham Brow; s £28.50-45, d £50.50-58.50; ☒) Nine rooms in an ecoconscious guesthouse with huge veggie-only breakfasts.

Midrange

Premier Travel Inn, City Centre (☎ 910 0619; www.premiertravelinn.com; The Haymarket; s £61.50-69.50, d £57-77; P ☒) All right, all right – we know it's a Travel Inn, but bear with us, because this one's a find. First, it's in a brilliant spot by the harbour, steps from the Old Vic. Second, the rooms are (almost) stylish, with decent beds, workdesk and wi-fi. And third…well, it's dead, cheap. Insist on a harbour-facing room.

Downs View (☎ 973 7046; www.downsviewguesthouse .co.uk; 38 Upper Belgrave Rd; s £45-55, d £60-70) A handy, if outdated, Clifton guesthouse with venerable rooms, tatty furniture and a faintly Victorian air.

Downlands House (☎ 962 1639; www.downlandshouse .com; 33 Henleaze Gardens; s £48-52, d £68-75; ☐ ☒) A trad-brick B&B in northern Bristol, offering simple, inexpensive rooms in cosy cream and country prints (with bits of china and cornicing to spice things up). The location near Durdham Downs is quiet and residential and there's free broadband.

Ibis (☎ 989 7200; h5547@accor.com; Explore La; r from £70; ☒ ☐) Bristol's chain-hotel love affair continues at the Ibis, worth considering for its knock-down prices more than its flair for interior design. As always with the multinationals, you know what to expect – bland furniture, bland décor and bland bathrooms – but the more upmarket rooms could be from somewhere far posher.

Downs Edge (☎ 968 3264; www.downsedge.com; Saville Rd; s £48-57, d £71-78; ☒) A slice of rural Somerset with unusually tranquil views for a big-city B&B. Oil paintings and polished wood conjure an old-time feel, offset by frippery bedspreads, thick carpets and floral curtains. Breakfast includes porridge, compotes and yogurts, plus four cooked options (try the smoked haddock 'Dawntreader').

Victoria Square Hotel (☎ 973 9058; www.vicsquare .com; Victoria Sq; s £59-95, d £75-115; P ☒ ☐) Split

across two Victorian town houses overlooking a tree-shrouded Clifton square, this hotel is owned by Best Western, so function takes precedence over flair, but most rooms have traces of Victorian character as well as soft beds, Freeview TVs and wi-fi. Just ignore the odd clanking pipe or scruffy bathroom tile.

Clifton Hotel (☎ 973 6882; clifton@cliftonhotels.com; St Paul's Rd; s £64-74, d £79-84; ☒) This shabby old hotel is in the B&B-heavy area of St Paul's Rd, but the rooms are a real hit-and-miss affair – generally the top ones are quieter and larger, and the bathrooms are in better condition. The ground-floor Racks bistro is popular with Clifton's social set, and gets very busy on warm weekends.

Rodney Hotel (☎ 973 5422; rodney@cliftonhotels .com; 4 Rodney Pl; s £64-87, d £79-92; P) Standing in a terrace of Clifton town houses, this is another Bristol hotel that doesn't live up to its exterior promise. If the owners spent some cash on restoring the Georgian character, this could be one of the city's best; as it stands the rooms are disappointingly reminiscent of a Travelodge. Still, it's functional and the Clifton location is top.

Arno's Manor (☎ 971 1461; www.arnosmanorhotel .co.uk; 470 Bath Rd; s/d from £105/125; P ☐) Built for the Bristol magnate William Reeve in 1760, this smart hotel has an original crenellated chateau plus an extension tacked on the side. The poshest rooms are in the old building, and boast half-tester beds, spa baths and bags of space; the annexe rooms are more corporate, but still have wi-fi and rubber duckies in the bath.

Top End

City Inn (☎ 925 1001; bristol.reservations@cityinn.com; Temple Way; r £65-169; P ☐ ☒) It might look like a concrete car park, but once inside you're in for a surprise. The furniture here is sleek and contemporary, there are wall-to-ceiling windows in every room, and luxury extras such as mist-proof mirrors, hi-fis and White Company toiletries. It's a bit soulless and businesslike, but you could definitely do worse in Brizzle.

Berkeley Square Hotel (☎ 925 4000; berkeley @cliftonhotels.com; 15 Berkeley Sq; s £79-129, d £115-139; P ☐) This imaginative place sits on the edge of a fine Georgian square, and crosses period elegance with beetlejuice-baroque. Painted gazelle heads, day-glo settees and rococo mirrors are dotted around the lobby, while the bedrooms mix classy mod-cons (DVD players, widescreen TVs, gratis sherry) with classic finishes.

Mercure Brigstow Hotel (☎ 929 1030; H6548@accor .com; Welsh Back; s £99-175, d & tw £99-175, ste £250; 🖳) The charmless concrete skin of this riverfront hotel conceals a high-faluting heart. Curving gloss-wood walls, trendy floating beds, mood lights and big glass windows populate the rooms, and there are tiny plasma TVs lodged in the bathroom tiles. Insist on a river view for maximum impact.

our pick Hotel du Vin (☎ 925 5577; www.hotelduvin .com; Narrow Lewins Mead; d £130-195, ste £215; P) Located in six 18th-century sugar warehouses (check out the old chimney stack), this fantastically indulgent boutique hotel would be more at home in downtown Manhattan than dear old Bristol. Huge floating futon beds, claw-foot baths, frying-pan showerheads and a mix of chic furniture, industrial beams and iron pillars define the luxurious rooms, all christened after vintage wines. If you can afford them, the split-level loft suites are mind-blowingly cool. A three-course dinner is £40 plus wine.

EATING

Bristol's eating-out scene has taken a radical turn in recent years, and these days you'll find top-class British bistros and riverboat restaurants alongside the old greasy spoons, pie shops and curry houses. Clifton and Whiteladies Rd are the hot spots.

Budget

CAFÉS & QUICK EATS

Bar Chocolat (☎ 974 7000; 19 The Mall; 🕑 9am-6pm Mon-Sat, 11am-5pm Sun) Chocoholics beware – this shrine to the cocoa bean might be your undoing. Chocolate in every concoction is served in the cosy café, from chilled chocolate and chocolate brownies to fairtrade choc-chip cookies and petits fours.

Pieminister (☎ 942 9500; 24 Stokes Croft; pies £2.95; 🕑 10am-7pm Sat, 11am-4pm Sun) Ditch that stodgy steak and kidney – the British pie goes gourmet at this Brizzle stalwart. Chomp on ingenious creations such as Poussin Boots (red wine, chicken and pancetta) or veggie Bush pie (cheddar cheese, cabbage, mushroom and onion), all drowned in lashings of mash and gravy. There's another branch inside St Nick's market.

Café Kino (☎ 924 9200; 3 Ninetree Hill; lunch £3.25-6.50; 🕑 lunch Tue-Thu, lunch & dinner Fri-Sun) Run by all-vegan owners, this cooperative café is impressive – the food's organic and local, the coffee's ethical, and there's even an alternative to corporate coke. Veggie lasagnes, leek and bacon pie and portabella mushrooms characterise the menu.

Rocotillo's (☎ 929 7207; 1 Queens Row; mains from £4; 🕑 breakfast & lunch) This is Bristol's version of an all-American diner, with leather booths, open grill, chrome stools and jukebox tunes. It has a menu stocked with steak sandwiches, slap-up brekkies and the best milkshakes in the west.

Lockside (☎ 925 5800; 1 Brunel Lock Rd; breakfast £4.50-5.50, lunch £4.50-10.95; 🕑 breakfast & lunch) Bristolians swear this place serves the city's lushest breakfast. Bubble and squeak, dry-cure bacon and local sausages are washed down by as much toast, tea or filter coffee as you can handle.

RESTAURANTS

One Stop Thali Café (☎ 942 6687; 12A York Rd; set meal £6.95; 🕑 lunch) The bustle and buzz of an Indian street market comes to this cute Montpelier diner, which serves traditional thalis (multi-course Indian dishes) that change depending on what the chef's picked up. It's fresh, spicy and authentic, and the six-course £6.95 menu is ridiculously cheap.

Gourmet Burger Kitchen (☎ 316 9162; 74 Park St; burgers around £7-8; 🕑 noon-11pm Mon-Fri, 11am-11pm Sat, 11am-10pm Sun) A new boutique-chain burger joint with imaginative versions including chicken, camembert and curry or aubergine and goat's cheese, accompanied of course by doorstop fries and cold beers.

Midrange

Budokan (☎ 914 1488; 31 Colston St; mains from £8; 🕑 lunch & dinner) Pan-Asian food is cooked up at this exciting fusion restaurant, where diners sit at communal tables and indulge in handmade sushi, ho-fun noodles and Malaysian curries. It's particularly good pre-7pm for the 'Rapid Refuel' menu (sushi, side dish and main), all for a paltry £7.95.

Mud Dock (☎ 934 9734; 40 The Grove; mains from £8.50; 🕑 11am-11pm Mon-Sat, 10am-10pm Sun) This much-loved place has a split personality. On the ground floor is the city's top bike shop, while the 1st floor is an industrial-style café offering crispy pork, black-bean chilli or sausage and mash, perfect fare for keeping those wheels spinning.

Clifton Sausage (☎ 973 1192; 7-9 Portland St; mains £8.50-16.50; ☾ lunch & dinner) Fourteen types of banger are served at this much-vaunted Clifton gastropub, from pork, red onion and ginger to lamb, mint and apricot – but you'll also find St Mawes fish, Cotswolds beef and sticky toffee pudding on the Brit-centred menu.

Fishers Seafood Restaurant (☎ 974 7044; 35 Princess Victoria St; mains £9.50-16.95; ☾ lunch & dinner) Stripey tablecloths and storm lanterns conjure a ship-shape atmosphere at this Clifton seafooderie, which takes daily deliveries from Billingsgate Fish Market. The food is simple and superb, ranging from bream fillets to full-blown *bouillabaisse* – here the ingredients are the star, not the chef.

Picture House (☎ 973 9302; 44 Whiteladies Rd; mains £11-18; ☾ lunch & dinner) This converted cinema is another sign of how far British cooking has come. The dining room is light and sexy, with picture windows, chocolate-coloured seats and blonde-wood floors, and the menu mixes Albion classics (slow-cooked mutton, pig-in-a-blanket, Eton Mess) with esoteric fare (smoked eel, wild boar, squirrel).

Quartier Vert (☎ 973 4482; 84 Whiteladies Rd; mains £11.50-18.50; ☾ lunch & dinner) The QV has been a Whiteladies staple for two decades, and after several revamps has settled on Spanish and southern Med flavours, supplemented by designer cheeses, sausages, tapas and home-baked bread. Wine-tasting and Slow Food courses will knock that philistinic palate into shape.

Severnshed (☎ 925 1212; The Grove; mains from £12; ☾ lunch & dinner) Part bistro, part bar, part architectural experiment, this amazing eatery shelters inside a Brunel-designed boatshed. A hovering bar zips around the restaurant while foodie-types dig in to the cultured food, from corn-fed chicken to fish and chips with Yorkshire caviar. The 977 menu (served before 7pm) includes two courses for £9.77.

Primrose Café (☎ 946 6577; 1 Boyces Ave; mains £12-17.50; ☾ 10am-5pm & from 7pm Mon-Sat, 10.30am-3pm Sun) Hidden away down a Clifton cul-de-sac, this sweet neighbourhood bistro is a passionate proselytiser for the Slow Food campaign. The blackboard menu is strong on Cornish fish and British game, and the streetside tables are ideal for sampling the Primrose's trademark cakes.

riverstation (☎ 914 4434; The Grove; mains £12.50-18.50; ☾ lunch & dinner) A decade on and Bristol's original riverside restaurant is still setting the pace. Split over two levels (downstairs, a groovy bar-kitchen; upstairs, a barrel-roofed brasserie), the riverstation has a huge following among Bristol's fooderati, blending the best of British with exotic accents – think ravioli of wood pigeon or roast pollock with guacamole.

Top End

Cafe Maitreya (☎ 951 0100; 89 St Marks Rd; 3 courses £20.95; ☾ dinner Tue-Sat) Voted the UK's top vegetarian restaurant two years running, the Maitreya is one of the city's most inventive eateries. Forget veggie hotpots and bean casseroles, the seasonal menu is renowned for its culinary creativity, and dabbles in everything from red onion tartelet to cashew-nut roulade.

Glassboat (☎ 929 0704; Welsh Back; lunch mains £7-8, dinner mains £14-21; ☾ closed Sun) The most romantic table in the city, a thoroughly Gallic affair housed in a wooden-hulled riverboat lit by globe lanterns and tabletop candles. French cooking and British ingredients fuse into an enticing eating experience, and the watery views are divine.

Bordeaux Quay (☎ 943 1200; V-Shed, Canons Way; dinner 2/3 courses £21/23.50; ☾ lunch & dinner) Housed in a stonking great wharfside warehouse once used to store imported wine, this sexy, exciting and admirably ecofriendly restaurant is a treat. The vintage building has been converted with wit, imagination and plenty of environmentally friendly materials reclaimed from the original building; all the produce is deliberately chosen to cut down on food miles; and the menu gives an innovative spin to classic Provençal and Italian dishes. There's even a cookery school where you can learn how the magic happens. Thoroughly 21st century, and drop-dead cool.

Colley's Supper Rooms (☎ 973 0646; 153 Whiteladies Rd; 4-course menu from £25; ☾ dinner daily, lunch Sun) Who said dinner parties were dead? Supper at this swag-heavy restaurant feels like dining in his lordship's drawing room, with rich drapes and wine-dark colours and a stiff-backed waiter describing the dishes in painstaking detail – duck *à l'orange*, bread and butter pudding, roast fowl.

Self-Catering

Papadeli (☎ 973 6569; 84 Alma Rd) Everything from goat's-cheese tart and Serrano ham to damson jam and poppy-seed cake is stocked at this gorgeous deli, where the shelves are filled with more cheeses and charcuterie than a Provençal street market.

Chandos Deli (☎ 970 6565; Whiteladies branch; 121 Whiteladies Rd; Queens branch; 39 Queens Rd) Another excellent little deli, great for takeaway lattes and lunchtime baguettes, as well as stickier teatime treats. Judging by the queues, the Chandos certainly has the local seal of approval.

DRINKING

Bristol has loads of places to wet your whistle, with new bars opening up practically every week (and often closing as quickly). The fortnightly magazine *Venue* (www.venue .co.uk) details the latest tips (£1.20). The freebie mag *Folio* is published monthly.

Goldbrick House (☎ 945 1950; 69 Park St; ☺ 9am-11pm Mon-Sat, 10am-6pm Sun) Uberposh drinking emporium that combines the ambience of a private gentleman's club (squeaky leather sofas, armchairs, chandeliers) with the champagne and cocktails of a Soho celeb bar. A new fave among Bristol's moneyed-up 30-somethings and media crowd.

Elbow Room (☎ 930 0242; 64 Park St) Part dimly lit bar, part hustlers' pool hall, this is a favourite hangout for Bristol's style-conscious frat. Rack up the balls and knock back the bourbons to a soundtrack of jazz, funk and hip-hop. For budding Fast Eddies, there's a pool competition every Monday.

Ivory (☎ 927 2292; 20 St Nicholas St) Slate tables, deep seats and walnut furniture lit by designer lamps feature at this stylish new arrival. Superior beers – Staropramen, Hoegaarden, Becks – and fruit-flavoured vodkas attract a high-class crowd.

Woods (☎ 925 0890; 1 Park St Ave; ☺ 4pm-2am Sun-Thu, 4pm-4am Fri, 4pm-6am Sat) Cultured and cool, this is another haunt for Bristol's beautiful, crammed with glitter balls, refectory benches and Victoriana sofas, plus 50 whiskies behind the bar.

Stark (☎ 973 9522; 168 Whiteladies Rd) Burgundy walls, rich red settees and pop-art prints in a metropolitan-style bar, with backgammon, pool and table footie when the small talk runs dry.

Park (☎ 37 Triangle St West; ☺ 4.30pm-1am Sun-Wed, 4.30pm-2am Thu, 4.30pm-4am Fri & Sat) Longstanding choice with Bristol's night owls, with a scuffed-up aesthetic, banquette sofas and weekend DJs, plus globespanning drinks

(Wyborowa vodka from Poland and Makers Markbourbon from Kentucky).

Apple (☎ 925 3500; Welsh Back) Stocking more ciders than you could possibly hope to imbibe, this riverside retreat is a temple to traditional scrumpy. Chutney sandwiches and ploughman's lunches complete the apple-flavoured experience.

Pipe & Slippers (☎ 942 7711; 118 Cheltenham Rd) The Pipe is a solid bet for a solid pint and an equally solid meal – Bath Ales behind the bar and Pieminister pies make this ever popular with Bristol's boozer-cruisers.

White Lion (☎ 973 8955; Sion Hill) The fabulous panoramic platform at the Avon Gorge Hotel wins the views contest hands down. On hot days punters pack the terrace tables to watch the sun sink over the suspension bridge.

ENTERTAINMENT
Cinemas

Odeon (☎ 0871 224 4007; 29 Union St, Broadmead) The city's biggest mainstream cinema.

Watershed (☎ 927 5100; www.watershed.co.uk; 1 Canon's Rd) The leading arthouse cinema in Bristol, and venue for the annual Encounters film festival.

Cube (☎ 907 4190; 4 Princess Row) It's a wickedly offbeat little arts complex, with an eclectic programme that takes in 35mm classics, acoustic sets, burlesque shows and highbrow discussions.

Live Music

Big names play the Carling Academy (see p88), while a host of smaller venues feature emerging acts.

Fleece & Firkin (☎ 945 0996; www.fleecegigs.co.uk; 12 St Thomas St) A small, intimate venue, much favoured by indie artists and breaking names on the local scene.

Colston Hall (☎ 922 3686; www.colstonhall.org; Colston St) The biggest concert hall in Brizzle, hosting everything from big-name comedy to touring bands.

Croft (☎ 987 4144; www.the-croft.com; 117-119 Stokes Croft) Chilled venue with a policy of supporting new names and Bristol-based artists. There's usually no cover charge if you arrive by 10pm Sunday to Thursday.

Bierkeller (☎ 926 8514; www.bristolbierkeller.co.uk; All Saints St) A legendary place that has played host to plenty of rock stars down the years, and still gets packed out on weekends.

Nightclubs

The Bristol club scene moves fast, so check the latest listings to see where the big nights are happening.

Native (☎ 930 4217; www.nativebristol.com; 15 Small St; admission £5-8; ☺ 10pm-4am) Bristol's top ticket, this tiny 200-cover club is right on the cutting edge, with drum and bass, latin, jungle, dubstep, hip-hop and jazz all making the playlist, along with a revolving line-up of guest DJs.

Thekla Social (☎ 929 3301; www.theklasocial.com; The Grove; admission £5-7; ☺ gigs 7.30pm-11pm, club nights 10.30pm-3am) After a hefty refitting, Bristol's venerable club-boat is back with nights to cater for all tastes: electro-punk, indie, disco and new wave, plus live gigs and legendary leftfield night Blowpop once a month.

Timbuk2 (22 Small St; ☺ 9am-2pm; admission £5-10) This scruffy-chic club-venue is crammed underneath the arches off Corn St, and hosts a mixed bag of breaks, House, drum and bass and jungle.

Nocturne (☎ 929 2555; 1 Unity St) A hyperexclusive members club, part owned by Massive Attack, with a decadent designer vibe and notoriously fussy bouncers, so smarten up your act and start queuing early.

Carling Academy (☎ 0870 711 2000; Frogmore St; admission £6-10) Bristol's original superclub can hold a 2000-strong crowd, but it's practically never that busy. There's indie and R&B during the week and big House nights on weekends.

Theatre

Following ongoing financial problems, the landmark Bristol Old Vic is currently closed with no date set for its reopening. Check up on the latest news on the fundraising campaign (or sponsor a seat!) at www .savebristololdvic.co.uk.

Tobacco Factory (☎ 902 0344; www.tobaccofactory .com; Raleigh Rd) This small-scale theatre venue stages cutting-edge drama and dance. Catch bus 24 or 25 from Broadmead to the Raleigh Rd stop, south of the river.

SHOPPING

Shopophiles will find plenty to feed their habit in Bristol, whether it's a designer hand-me-down in a retro clothes shop or a choice cheese in a local food market. Top stop is the **St Nicholas Market** (Corn St; ☺ 9.30am-5pm Mon-Sat), a chaotic melee of wobbly stalls and indie shops selling everything from recycled clothes to handmade jewellery and artisan bread.

Outside, Corn St is the venue for regular markets, including a **farmers market** every Wednesday, where all the produce is sourced within a 40-mile radius, and the UK's only **slow food market** on the first Sunday of every month. There's also the **nails market** every Friday and Saturday, stocked with handmade cards, craftwork and quirky clothing.

GETTING THERE & AWAY

Air

Bristol International Airport (☎ 0870 121 2747; www.bristolairport.co.uk) is 8 miles southwest of town, with scheduled flights across the UK

GAY & LESBIAN BRISTOL

Bristol's gay scene centres around Frogmore St and the Old Market (locally known as Bristol's 'gay village'). The grand old dame is the **Queenshilling** (☎ 926 4342; www.queenshilling.com; 9 Frogmore St; ☺ 10pm-2am Wed & Sun, 9pm-3am Thu & Fri, 9pm-4am Sat), a lively club-bar specialising in burlesque nights and big cheesy tunes, while the **Old Market Tavern** (☎ 922 6123; Old Market St) attracts gay and straight punters in roughly equal numbers.

Other venues include the **Pineapple** (☎ 907 1162; www.pineapplebristol.com; 37 St Georges Rd; ☺ 3pm-midnight Mon-Fri, 3pm-1am Sat & Sun) with cabaret, quiz nights, karaoke and an annual street party, and the **Griffin** (☎ 930 0444; 41 Colston St), a popular preclub place decked out in day-glo shades and saucy artwork. New bars are springing up all over the Old Market – try **Bar Orchid** (☎ 373 8109; www.barorchid.co.uk; 49-51 West St; ☺ noon-11pm Mon-Thu, noon-1am Fri & Sat, noon-midnight Sun) and **Bar Prague** (50 Old Market St; ☺ noon-11pm Mon-Thu, noon-1am Fri & Sat, noon-midnight Sun).

On the club side the big nights are at **Flamingos** (☎ 07980 842438; www.flamingosbristol.com; 23-25 West St), with twin dance floors and five bars, and old favourite **Vibes** (☎ 934 9076; www.vibesbristol .co.uk; 3 Frog Lane; admission £2-5; ☺ 10pm-2am Mon & Tue, 10pm-3am Wed & Sun, 10pm-4am Sat). Check www.pridewest.co.uk/bristol for listings or ask around the Old Market for hot tips.

and Europe, plus daily flights to New York. Airlines operating from Bristol:

Air Southwest (☎ 0870 241 6830; www.airsouthwest .com) UK destinations including Leeds, Manchester, Newquay, Plymouth and Jersey.

EasyJet (☎ 0870 600 0000; www.easyjet.com) Budget flights to Edinburgh, Glasgow, Newcastle, Inverness, Belfast and European cities.

Ryanair (☎ 0871 246 0000; www.ryanair.com) Irish airports including Derry, Dublin and Shannon, plus European cities.

Skybus (☎ 0845 710 5555; www.ios-travel.co.uk) Flights to the Isles of Scilly.

Bus

National Express coaches go to Birmingham (£17, two hours, nine daily), London (£17, 2½ hours, at least hourly), Cardiff (£6.70, 1¼ hours, eight daily) and Exeter (£12, two hours, five daily).

The express bus X39/339 (55 minutes, four per hour Monday to Saturday, two per hour Sunday) and the 332/632 (one hour, hourly Monday to Saturday, seven on Sunday) are the quickest services to Bath. The 375/376 goes to Wells (one hour) and Glastonbury (1¼ hours) every half-hour, while the X1 goes to Weston-Super-Mare (50 minutes, two per hour Monday to Saturday, 10 on Sunday).

Train

Bristol is an important rail hub, with regular connections to London (£62.50, 1¾ hours) and the southwest, including Exeter (£19, 1¼ hours), Plymouth (£44, 2½ hours) and Penzance (£59.50, four hours). There are frequent trains to Bath (one way £5.60, 11 minutes, four per hour).

Cross Country Trains link the southwest with the north, including Edinburgh (£101, five to six hours, every two hours) and Glasgow (£101, five to six hours, five to seven direct daily) via Birmingham (£31, 1½ hours, two per hour).

GETTING AROUND
To/From the Airport

Bristol International Flyer runs shuttle buses (one way/return £5/7, 30 minutes, half-hourly 5am to 11pm, every 15 minutes at peak times, plus early buses at 3am and 4am) to the airport from the bus station and Temple Meads. An airport taxi costs around £25 to £30 depending on traffic.

Bicycle

Bikes can be rented from Mud Dock (p85) and **Blackboy Hill Cycles** (☎ 973 1420; 180 Whiteladies Rd; ⏰ 9am-5.30pm Mon-Sat) for £10 to £15 per day. Mud Dock also offers secure bike parking and a repair shop.

Boat

The **Bristol Ferry Boat Co** (☎ 927 3416; www.bristol ferryboat.co.uk) runs two ferry routes: city centre to Temple Meads (one hour, six to 10 daily April to October, weekends only November to March), via At-Bristol, Welsh Back and Castle Park (for Broadmead); and city centre to Hotwells (40 minutes, 12 to 16 daily year-round), via Mardyke and the SS *Great Britain*. A one-way fare is £1.80/1.50 per adult/child; a day pass is £7/5.

Bus

Buses run from the northern Parkway Station to the centre every 15 minutes (30 minutes). Buses 8 and 9 run every 15 minutes to Clifton (10 minutes), Whiteladies Rd and Bristol Zoo from St Augustine's Pde; add another 10 minutes from Temple Meads. Other useful services include the 48/49 via Eastville and the 76/77 via Gloucester Rd. The tourist office supplies bus maps and timetables.

FirstDay passes (adult/child £4.40/2.70) are valid for one day's travel across the Greater Bristol area. The FirstFamily ticket (£7) buys one day's travel for two adults and three children, but is only valid after 9am Monday to Friday. FirstDay Southwest tickets (£7/5) are valid throughout the southwest region.

Night buses are operated by Nightflyer every hour on Friday and Saturday night. There are eight routes, all leaving from St Augustine's Pde; useful numbers include N8 via Clifton and Henbury, N7 via Whiteladies Rd, and N2 via Easton.

Car & Motorcycle

Bristol's traffic can be a real headache – you're better off using the **park-and-ride** (☎ 922 2910; return before 10am Mon-Fri £3, after 10am Mon-Fri £2.50, Sat £2; ⏰ every 10mins Mon-Sat), which operates from Portway, Bath Rd and Long Ashton. They are well signed on routes into the city. If you do drive, expect to pay upwards of £10 per day in the city-centre car parks.

Taxi

There are several taxi ranks in the centre, including ones outside the Hippodrome, on St Augustine's Pde, on Baldwin St and Colston St. Official taxis have lights on top and operate to council-set rates; if you grab a minicab make sure you agree the fare beforehand. Reputable companies:

Bristol Brunel Taxis (☎ 947 7153)
Bristol Hackney Cabs (☎ 953 8638)
Bristol Streamline Taxis (☎ 9264 0001)

SOMERSET

Somerset's a county that neatly splits between town and country. While the flush, fashionable and beautiful flock to the streets of Bristol and Bath, the rest of rural Somerset ambles along in its own sleepy way, apparently unflustered by the onward march of the modern world. This is still largely an agricultural corner of England, a rustic landscape of copper-coloured fields, country churches and village greens, where cider's brewed in the time-honoured fashion and thatch still graces many a rooftop. But it's more than just a place to mooch the back lanes – you could plunge into the caves around Cheddar Gorge, hit the hills of the Quantocks and Mendips, interrogate your tarots in hippie-capital Glastonbury or even try your hand at traditional willowcraft.

BATH

☎ 01225 / pop 90,144

If Bristol's a grand old dame, then Bath is her slinkier, sexier, snootier little sister. Glittering with porticoed mansions, elegant crescents and Palladian terraces, this is unquestionably one of Britain's most stunning cities, and for more than 300 years she's been showing the rest of England what the high life is all about. Founded by the Romans, who came to indulge their passion for taking a public plunge in the city's hot springs, Bath came into its own in the 18th century, when trendsetters including Beau Nash, Jane Austen and the two John Woods (father and son) put the city on the cultural map. The dandies and debutantes may be gone, but there's still a rarefied air lingering around Bath's stately streets. Whether it's wandering along the Royal Crescent, admiring the vistas from Prior Park, or sink-

---

VICTORIAN SPECTACULAR

Tyntesfield (NT; ☎ 01275-461900; Wraxall; adult/child £9/4.50; ☒ 11am-5pm Mon-Wed, Sat & Sun Mar-Oct) Formerly the aristocratic home of the Gibbs family, this ornate Victorian pile has recently been acquired by the National Trust (NT). Prickling with spiky turrets and towers, the house was built in grand Gothic Revival style by the architect John Norton, and is crammed with Victorian decorative arts, a working kitchen garden and a magnificent private chapel. The house is currently undergoing extensive renovation, so it's still a work in progress – call ahead for the latest updates. Bus 354 between Bristol and Nailsea drops off at Tyntesfield.

---

ing into a hot tub in the city's spanking new avant-garde spa, it's impossible not to be bewitched by this radiant minx of a city.

History

Prehistoric people certainly knew about the natural hot springs around Bath, but the first organised settlers were the Celts, who founded a sacred site dedicated to the water goddess Sulis. The Romans followed, founding the spa town of Aquae Sulis in AD 44. Following the Roman withdrawal in the 5th century, the city was abandoned until the foundation of a Saxon monastery in the late 8th century, where King Edward the Peacemaker, the first king of unified England, was crowned in 973.

During the early Middle Ages Bath was devastated by plague, and it wasn't until the completion of Bath Abbey in 1616 that the city's fortunes were revived. By the late 17th-century the fashion for spa-bathing had once again taken Britain by storm, and Bath again became a boom-town; but it was during the Georgian era that Bath really hit its stride under the auspices of philanthropist Ralph Allen, architect John Wood (the Elder), and bon viveur extraordinaire Beau Nash. Together they made Bath the toast of British high society, constructing Prior Park (p100), laying out the city's Georgian terraces and laying on a social whirl for England's upper classes.

Despite a brief blip when the sudden fashion for sea bathing stole some of its thunder, Bath continued to grow during the 19th and early 20th centuries, and the entire city was named a World Heritage Site by Unesco in 1987.

Orientation

The city sits in a bowl-shaped valley ringed by seven hills (beautiful, but knackering). Right in the city centre are the Abbey, Pump Rooms, Roman Baths and the tourist office; the Royal Crescent overlooks the city's north side above Royal Victoria Park, while the Bath Spa train station sits at the southern end of Manvers St. The bus station is in a temporary location on Avon St while the Southgate area is redeveloped.

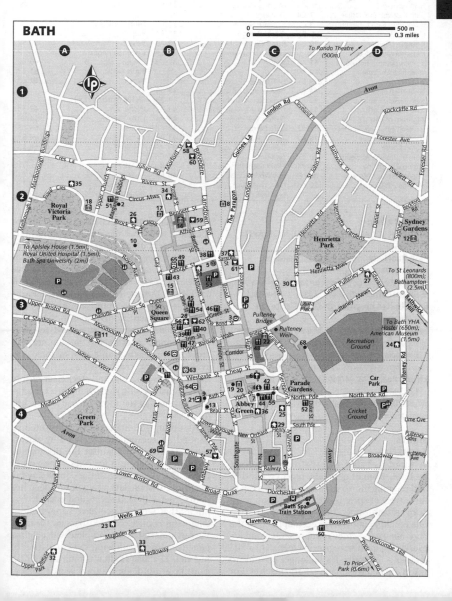

Information

@internet (☎ 443181; 12 Manvers St; per 20min £1; ☽ 10am-10pm)

Bath Quarterly Guide to sights, accommodation, restaurants and events.

Laundrette (4 Margarets Bldgs; per load £2; ☽ 6am-9pm)

Main post office (☎ 0845 722 3344; 25 New Bond St)

Royal United Hospital (☎ 428331; Combe Park; ☽ 24hr)

Tourist office (☎ 0906 711 2000 www.visitbath.co.uk; Abbey Churchyard; ☽ 9.30am-6pm Mon-Sat Jun-Sep, 9.30am-4pm Mon-Sat Oct-May, 10am-4pm Sun year-round) There is net access for 50p per minute.

Virtual Realm (☎ 447466; George St; per 10min 50p; ☽ 12.30-7.30pm)

What's On (www.whatsonbath.co.uk) Lists the city's events and nightlife.

Sights
BATHS

Without its baths, well, Bath just wouldn't be Bath. Roman generals, regency dandies and reigning monarchs have all taken a dip in the city's hot springs, which bubble up from deep underground at a constant 46°C. Various fanciful claims have been applied to the cure-all waters – they're supposedly good for everything from an ingrowing toenail to a foul temper – but sadly, it's no longer possible to take a dip in the Roman Baths themselves. For

modern-day dunks you'll have to head for the sparkling new Thermae Bath Spa (opposite).

The **Roman Baths** (☎ 477785; www.romanbaths .co.uk; Abbey Churchyard; adult/child £10.25/6.50, Jul & Aug £11.25/6.50, combined ticket with Museum of Costume £13.50/8; ☽ 9am-8pm Jul & Aug, 9am-6pm Mar, Jun, Sep & Oct, 9.30am-5.30pm Jan, Feb, Nov & Dec, last admission one hour before closing) now comprise one of the best-preserved ancient Roman spas in the world. Unfortunately, they're also a must-see item on everyone's itinerary and the summertime crowds can reach titanic proportions – to avoid the worst crush, visit as early or late in the day as possible, and steer clear of July and August – going sightseeing in a camera-wielding human stampede isn't all it's cracked up to be.

Assuming you manage to get in, you'll be handed an audioguide (narrated by actress Juliet Stevenson and author Bill Bryson), or you can hang around for one of the hourly tours. The centrepiece of the complex is the magnificent **Great Bath** a huge 1.6m-deep hot pool, lined with lead sheets and encircled by pillars that would once have supported an enclosing roof. Excavated passages lead to the **East** and **West Baths**, complete with original *pilae* (tile towers allowing the circulation of hot air). The **King's Bath** was built in the 12th century around the original sacred spring;

1.5 million litres of hot water still pour into the pool every day. Elsewhere you can see the Roman version of a sauna in the **Laconicum**, as well as the cold-water **Circular Bath**. There's also a small **museum** displaying archaeological finds, including a huge collection of votive coins thrown into the spring, as well as stone fragments from the lost Roman temple.

BATH ABBEY

The last great Gothic church to be built in England, **Bath Abbey** (☎ 422462; www.bathabbey .org; requested donation £2.50; 9am-6pm Mon-Sat Easter-Oct, 9am-4.30pm Nov-Easter, afternoons only Sun year-round) was built between 1499 and 1616 on the site of two former churches: an 8th-century abbey and a great Norman cathedral built around 1090. Like all Gothic cathedrals, it's a show stopper, resplendent with ornate stained glass, flying buttresses and a gorgeous fan-vaulted ceiling. But the most impressive feature is the elaborate west façade, where angels climb up and down stone ladders, commemorating the dream which inspired Bishop Oliver King to construct the cathedral. Inside are memorials to Isaac Pitman, (the inventor of Pitman shorthand), James Montague (Bishop of Bath and Wells in 1608–16) and Beau Nash, who's buried beneath the nave. On the abbey's southern side, the **Vaults Heritage Museum** (10am-4pm Mon-Sat) contains fine stone bosses, statuary and other archaeological artefacts.

THE ROYAL CRESCENT & THE CIRCUS

The crowning glory of Georgian Bath is The Royal Crescent, a semicircular terrace of 30 majestic houses overlooking the green sweep of Royal Victoria Park. Designed by John Wood the Younger (1728–82) and built between 1767 and 1775, the Grade I–listed terrace is the most important Georgian street in Britain. Despite the symmetry of Ionic columns and Palladian porticos, inside no two houses are the same; the original purchasers were allowed to re-jig the interior as long they preserved the Crescent's uniform exterior. Many were let out to socially suitable families visiting Bath for the summer season; these days most of the houses are split into flats, which command a quite staggering price tag.

For a flavour of the razzle-dazzle of Georgian life, head for **No 1 The Royal Crescent** (☎ 428126; www.bath-preservation-trust.org.uk; adult/child £5/2.50; 10.30am-5pm Tue-Sun Feb-Oct, 10.30am-4pm Nov). Only materials available during the 18th century were used during its refurbishment, so it's about as realistically Georgian as you can get. Sadly, the same can't be said for the endearingly hammy staff dressed in period costume.

Inspired by the Roman Colosseum, the **Circus** is a Georgian masterpiece of Wood the Elder's design. Arranged over three equal terraces, the 30 mansions here overlook a garden populated by plane trees; a German bomb fell into the square in 1942 and demolished several houses, although they've since been rebuilt in seamless style. Look out for plaques to Thomas Gainsborough, Clive of India and David Livingstone, all former Circus residents. To the south is the restored **Georgian Garden**, with formal terraces, period plants and gravel walkways, tidied everyday using an original 19th-century roller.

BATH'S NEW BATH

Larking about in the Roman Baths might be off the agenda, but thankfully you can still sample the city's curative waters at the **Thermae Bath Spa** (☎ 331234; www.thermaebathspa.com; Hot Bath St; spa sessions Cross Bath adult/child £12/9, New Royal Bath per 2hr/4hr/day £20/30/50, spa packages from £65; New Royal Bath 9am-10pm, Cross Bath 10am-8pm). Incorporating the old **Cross Bath** into a shell of Georgian stone, stainless steel and plate glass, the ferociously modern building has ruffled the feathers of many Bathonian purists, but whatever you make of the architecture, the hot springs themselves are a treat. Packages range from a dip in one of the heated pools (choose from the Cross Bath or the New Royal Bath, which includes a choice of pools, steam rooms and waterfall shower) to exotic treatments including peat baths, body cocoons, Vichy showers and the ominous-sounding 'Kraxen stove' (an Alpine hay chamber, apparently). Best of all is the amazing open-air rooftop pool, where you can admire the cityscape dressed in nowt but a bathrobe and fluffy slippers.

Across the street are treatment rooms above the old **Hot Bath**, while the Hetling Pump Room houses a **visitor centre** (10am-5pm Mon-Sat, 10am-4pm Sun) exploring the history of Bath bathing.

ASSEMBLY ROOMS & MUSEUM OF COSTUME

The city's glorious **Assembly Rooms** (☎ 477785; www.museumofcostume.co.uk; Bennett St; ☿ 11am-6pm Mar-Oct, 11am-5pm Nov-Feb) were built in 1771 under the supervision of Beau Nash. Chamber concerts, card games and public balls were held in the gloriously furnished rooms, and welcomed many famous visitors including Jane Austen, Charles Dickens, Haydn and Strauss. You can stroll around the card room, tearoom and ballroom, all lit by their spectacular 18th-century chandeliers (one of which nearly crushed the artist Thomas Gainsborough in 1771).

In the basement is the **Museum of Costume** (adult/child £6.75/4.75, incl Roman Baths Museum £13.50/8), which houses a huge wardrobe of vintage outfits including some lavish 18th-century embroidered waistcoats, a collection of 500 handbags and several whalebone corsets which are, frankly, alarming.

JANE AUSTEN CENTRE

Though Bath only features in two Jane Austen novels (*Persuasion* and *Northanger Abbey*), for many people the city is the quintessential Austenesque setting, the perfect place for dashing young beaus to sweep retiring young dilettantes off their feet. Austen lived in the city from 1801 to 1806, residing at various houses including No 4 Sydney Pl (marked by a blue plaque opposite the Holburne Museum). The **Jane Austen Centre** (☎ 443000; www.janeausten .co.uk; 40 Gay St; adult/child £6.50/3.50; ☿ 9.45am-5.30pm Apr-Sep, 11am-4.30pm Oct-Mar) explores the author's connections with the city through costumed guides, pictorial prints and Austen-themed exhibits – there's even a Regency tearoom and a gift shop stocked with lace parasols. But sorry ladies – no sign of Mr Darcy...

OTHER MUSEUMS

Sir William Holburne, the 18th-century aristocrat, aesthete and art fanatic, amassed a huge collection, which now forms the **Holburne Museum** (☎ 466669; Great Pulteney St; adult/child £4.50/free; ☿ 10am-5pm Tue-Sat, 11am-5pm Sun), beautifully situated in the tree-shaded Sydney Gardens. Works by Turner, Gaudi, Stubbs and Thomas Gainsborough litter the palatial rooms, supplemented by a hoard of majolica, porcelain and portrait miniatures (look out for one of Beau Nash).

More glorious artwork lines the walls of the **Victoria Art Gallery** (☎ 477233; www.victoriagal

---

A DEDICATED FOLLOWER OF FASHION

While Ralph Allen and the two John Woods were responsible for moulding Bath's architectural legacy, Richard 'Beau' Nash was busily transforming the city from an inconsequential spa town to the toast of British high society.

Born in Swansea in 1674, Nash had an inauspicious start. An Oxford University drop-out, failed soldier, rubbish lawyer, inveterate gambler and insatiable womaniser, his only saving grace was his knack for organising a good knees-up. Attracted by the booming social scene, Nash became Bath's Master of Ceremonies in 1705 when his master, Captain Webster, was killed in a duel over a card game.

For five decades Nash set about reinventing fashionable Bath society, organising balls and tea dances, arranging chamber concerts and imposing strict regulations on behaviour, dress and social conduct. His rakish fashion sense – black wig, beaver-trimmed hat, ruffled shirt and florid waistcoat – earned him his dandyish nickname of 'Beau', while his 'Rules' set down the conduct of polite society. Among his dictates were a ban on swearing and the wearing of sabres (which tended to cause duels), and an eccentric fixation with male footwear (he thought calf-length boots vulgar, preferring daintier shoes). Though the rules seemed strict, snooty and frequently daft, they actually helped encourage mixing across the classes – since everyone knew how to behave, no one had any fear stepping out of line. A lifelong gambler, he was even known to bail out people's debts just to keep the social waters smooth.

But inevitably Nash fell short of his own strict standards. He financed his extravagant social life on prodigious gambling profits and, following tightened gaming rules in the mid-18th century, he fell on hard times, and eventually died in abject straits in 1761. But Bath hadn't forgotten its debt to Nash; most of the fashionable city turned out for his lavish funeral at Bath Abbey, where he's now buried beneath the nave and commemorated by a surprisingly understated plaque.

.org.uk; Pulteney Bridge; admission free; 10am-5pm Tue-Sat, 1.30-5pm Sun), the city's main art museum. There are fine canvases by Gainsborough, Turner and Sickert, as well as biting Georgian caricatures from the pens of James Gillray and Thomas Rowlandson.

The **Museum of East Asian Art** (☎ 464640; www.meaa.org.uk; 12 Bennett St; adult/child £4/1.50; 10am-5pm Tue-Sat, noon-5pm Sun) has a collection of more than 2000 artefacts gathered from Cambodia, Japan, China and other parts of Southeast Asia, including Japanese sculptures, ornate hand fans and bamboo carvings.

For the back-story on Bath, head for the **Building of Bath Museum** (☎ 333895; www.bath-preservation-trust.org.uk; The Vineyards, The Paragon; adult/child £4/2; 10.30am-5pm Tue-Sun mid-Feb–Nov), which traces the city's evolution from a sleepy spa town into one of the centres of Georgian society. Its eclectic displays detail everything from how to build a Georgian sash window to a guide to the most fashionable wallpapers of 18th-century society.

The classical composer turned telescope maker William Herschel lived in a town house on King St, now the **Herschel Museum of Astronomy** (☎ 311342; 19 New King St; adult/child £3.50/2; 1-5pm Mon, Tue, Thu & Fri, 11am-5pm Sat & Sun Feb-Nov). Herschel's achievements included the discovery of Uranus in 1781 and the construction of several pioneering telescopes, including a gargantuan 40ft (12m) refractor built in 1785. Unfortunately the reality never quite lived up to the design: the mirror quickly fogged up and the elaborate mechanics, which required several operators who communicated via a speaking tube, ultimately proved unworkable. His 7ft (2m) models were more successful – a replica of one can be seen in the museum's lobby.

Tours

BALLOON TRIPS

Bath Balloons (☎ 466888; 8 Lambridge, London Rd) See the city from a more elevated angle. Balloon tours take off from a launch-base in Royal Victoria Park. Prices range from £99 to £139, and flights are obviously dependent on the British weather playing ball.

BOAT TRIPS

Various boat trips cruise the River Avon. Both the following operate from Pulteney Weir. For cruises to Bristol, see p82.

Avon Cruising (☎ 0779 191 0650; pulteneyprincess@tiscali.co.uk)

Bath City Boat Trips (☎ 07974 560197; www.bathcityboattrips.com)

BUS TOURS

Bath Bus Company (☎ 330444; www.bathbuscompany.com) A hop-on, hop-off city tour (adult/child £10/6 running between 9.30am and 5pm, later in summer) on an open-top bus that stops all over the city. There's also a second route, the Skyline tour, out to Prior Park (p100); the same tickets are valid on both routes.

Heritage Hopper Tour (☎ 838621; incl 4 children £19.95; spring-autumn) Includes bus travel and admission to the Holburne Museum, American Museum and Prior Park.

GUIDED TOURS

Bath Carriage Company (☎ 07916 177149; 10.30am-4pm Mon, 10.30am-11pm Tue-Sat) Stylish half-hour tours in an open-top, horse-drawn carriage (per adult £10, children free).

Bizarre Bath Comedy Walks (☎ 335124; www.bizarrebath.co.uk; adult/child £7/5; tours 8pm Mar-Sep) For something less reverential; a chaotic blend of street theatre, live performance and guided tour. The 1½-hour tours leave from outside the Huntsman Inn on North Pde Passage.

Jane Austen's Bath (☎ 443000; adult/child £4.50/3.50) Bibliophiles can join up with this tour conducted by bonneted guides dressed in suitably frilly fashion. The tour takes in various Austen-linked sites, including her former houses and the Assembly Rooms. Tours leave from the Abbey Churchyard at 11am on Saturday, Sunday and bank holidays. You can download a free MP3 tour to Jane Austen's Bath at www.visitbath.co.uk/janeausten/audio-tour.

Mayor's Guides (☎ 477411; www.thecityofbath.co.uk) Free historical tours leave from outside the Pump Room at 10.30am and 2pm Sunday to Friday, and 10.30am on Saturday. From May to September there are tours at 7pm on Tuesday, Friday and Saturday.

Tourist Tracks (www.tourist-tracks.com/tours/bath.html) Has two MP3 tours (£5) to the city's architectural highlights. If you haven't brought your iPod, you can hire one from the tourist office (half-/full day £6/10).

Quirky Bath

Commemorating everything from the Puritan pioneers to the Wild West frontier, the **American Museum** (☎ 460503; www.americanmuseum.org; Claverton Manor; noon-5pm Tue-Sun mid-Mar–Oct) houses a huge collection of Stateside artefacts in the grand environs of Claverton Manor, 2 miles outside the city. Established in 1961, the museum's displays range from First Nation handiwork to vintage revolvers, pioneers' maps and a collection of American quilts. You can also stroll around 15 period-themed rooms, including a New Orleans plantation villa, a Shaker room and a flashy 18th-century parlour room from a Maryland farmhouse. Bus 18 and most university buses stop nearby.

Festivals & Events

Bath's annual calendar is still packed with enough events to satisfy the most discerning socialite. All bookings are handled by the **Bath Festivals box office** (☎ 463362; www.bathfestivals.org .uk; 2 Church St; ⏱ 9.30am-5.30pm Mon-Sat).

Bath Literature Festival (☎ 463362; www.bathlit fest.org.uk) Book readings, signings and big-name authors. Recent attendees have included John Mortimer, Margaret Atwood and Terry Pratchett. Held in early March.

Bath International Music Festival (www.bath musicfest.org.uk) From mid-May to early June, with a main programme of classical music and opera, as well as jazz, world and folk gigs in the city's smaller venues.

Bath Fringe Festival (www.bathfringe.co.uk) Hits town mid-May to early June as well; it's the biggest fringe festival in Britain after Edinburgh, with all kinds of theatre shows and street acts around town.

Guitar Festival (www.igf.org.uk) Concerts, workshops and much more from the end of July to early August.

Jane Austen Festival (www.janeausten.co.uk) The highlight of this festival in September is a grand Georgian costumed parade through the city's streets all the way to Royal Cres.

Bath Film Festival (www.bathfilmfestival.org.uk) Takes place in the last two weeks in September.

Mozartfest (www.bathmozartfest.org.uk) An annual celebration of the musician in mid-October.

Christmas Market Beside the Abbey. There are also Yuletide happenings at the American Museum and the Jane Austen Museum.

Sleeping

Unsurprisingly, beds command a premium in Bath. If you're stuck, the tourist office can usually winkle out somewhere for a £3 fee, but it might not be the Regency palace you were banking on.

BUDGET

Bath Backpackers' Hostel (☎ 446787; bath@hostels .co.uk; 13 Pierrepont St; dm £12-13; 🖳) Bath's indie hostel has seen better days. Chewed-up carpets, peeling paint and sticky-floored kitchen aside, it's still a central base, and the party 'dungeon' can be fun with the right crowd – but the no-curfew rule means late-night noise,

and the saggy bunk-beds could do with a dose of Botox.

Bath YHA Hostel (☎ 465674; bath@yha.org.uk; dm £13, d from £35; P 🖳) This wonderful high-ceilinged hostel is housed in an Italianate pile uphill from the city, encircled by grassy gardens and overgrown trees. Choose from period rooms in the main house, or modern dorms in a separate lodge; there's bike hire, coin-op internet and a convivial bar.

YMCA (☎ 325900; www.bathymca.co.uk; International House, Broad St Pl; dm £13-15, s £25-29, d & tw £38-46; 🖳) Swap swishness for centrality at the city's YMCA. The furniture's prefab and the décor's hardly designer, but it's dirt cheap and near the sights. There's a cut-price café serving jacket potatoes and casseroles, and a health gym where you can atone for the calorie intake.

Abbey Rise (☎ 316177; www.abbeyrise.co.uk; 97 Wells Rd; s £38-48, d £50-70; P ✗) The owner of this smart little B&B cut her teeth as a Buckingham Palace housekeeper, and it shows; cute rooms in corn yellows, bluebell and cream, spotty cushions and snow-white sheets on the beds, and a fine brekkie of kong-sized proportions.

MIDRANGE

The midrange bracket contains most of Bath's hotels; some are central, but most dot the city's residential outskirts.

Henry (☎ 424052; 6 Henry St; www.thehenry.com; s £40-45, d £65-75; ✗) Bath doesn't have to break the bank at the cheery, central Henry, a tip-top budget hotel linked with Three Abbey Green. Theatre posters, quilted bedspreads and simple colourways define the rooms, though you'll have to share bathrooms and the street noise is taxing. Still, this close to the centre it's a steal.

Oldfields (☎ 317984; www.oldfields.co.uk; 102 Wells Rd; s £49-99, d £65-115; P 🖳) A heritage honey with boutique touches. Spacious rooms and deep, soft beds for comfort; brass bedsteads, patterned wallpaper and antique chairs for character; and Laura Ashley fabrics and Molton Brown bathstuffs for luxury, all wrapped up in a lemon-stone house with views over Bath's rooftops.

Paradise House (☎ 317723; www.paradise-house .co.uk; 86-88 Holloway; d £65-170; P) If the tourist hordes are too much, beat a retreat to this chimney-crowned villa and its charming walled garden. It's an old-world treat, with half-tester beds, glided mirrors and oil paintings in the drawing room, and a lighter palette in the bedrooms (plus Jacuzzis and four-posters for the high-rollers).

Ayrlington (☎ 425495; www.ayrlington.com; 24/25 Pulteney Rd; d & tw £75-175) This magnificent villa-style hotel has something for everyone: Chinese chests and Buddha prints for the style-conscious, gloss-wood and clean lines for the urbanites, heavy curtains and half-testers for the purists. And there's a walled garden that would have Capability Brown weeping into his grass cuttings.

Kennard Hotel (☎ 310472; www.kennard.co.uk; 11 Henrietta St; d £79-118) Keep this one quiet – it's a covert gem. On a terraced street this tidy you'd expect a heftier price tag, but the understated rooms and straightforward service keep the tariffs realistic. Extra cash buys more character – a canopied bed, plaster cornice or vintage desk.

Three Abbey Green (☎ 428558; www.threeabbey green.com; 3 Abbey Green; d £85-125; ✗) You'll have to forgo the flashy antiques, but this wonderfully central town house is unbeatable for the sights, on a tree-shaded terrace steps from Bath Abbey. Despite the ornate Georgian exterior, simplicity and smartness are the watchwords; plain whites offset by tartan checks or colour-tints.

Apsley House (☎ 336966; www.apsley-house.co.uk; 141 Newbridge Hill; d £85-160; P 🖳) This imposing Georgian mansion was built by the Duke of Wellington for his mistress, and it's got illicit style in abundance; lofty ceilings, rich drapes, sexy swags and chaise longues, with modern spoils such as flat-screen TVs, wi-fi and top-end bath goodies. Perfect for that romantic *liaison dangereuse*.

Haringtons Hotel (☎ 461278; www.haringtonshotel .co.uk; Queen St; d £98-140) Bath's classical trappings aren't to everyone's taste, so things are kept modern and minimal at this city-centre crash pad: clean lines, crisp colour schemes and LCD TVs, with a choice of sizes depending on the depth of your wallet.

Brocks (☎ 338374; www.brocksguesthouse.co.uk; 32 Brock St; r £79-99) Get the regal postcode without having to remortgage; spic-and-span rooms steps from The Royal Crescent.

Milsoms Hotel (☎ 750128; www.milsomshotel .co.uk/bath; 24 Milsom St; d from £85) Cocoa-bean colours and superchic furnishings at a dead-central metropolitan-style hotel.

TOP END

our pick Queensberry Hotel (☎ 447928; www.the queensberry.co.uk; Russell St; d £115-215, ste from £395; P) Where to begin? This boutique barnstormer is sexy, swanky and super. The city's coolest rooms are hidden in four side-by-side town houses where modern fabrics, muted colours and funky throws meet burnished wardrobes, feature fireplaces and Zen-tinged furniture. Gleaming bathrooms hide his-'n'-hers sinks and posh smellies, designer-print cushions sprinkle sofas and oversized beds. There are several lounges, and the walled garden is a chilled asylum from the city fizz. Prepare to be pampered.

Dukes (☎ 787960; www.dukesbath.co.uk; Great Pulteney St; d £155-175; ste £198-215; P) Slightly more affordable than the Royal Crescent, but no less exclusive, this is a Palladian pile that pulls out all the stops; original cornicing and Regency furniture, frilly four-posters and Toile du Jouy fabrics. Rooms range from over-the-top Oriental to extravagant Louis XVI. Not for the shy and retiring.

Royal Crescent Hotel (☎ 823333; www.royalcrescent .co.uk; 16 Royal Cres; d £305-405, ste £545-865; P) Say goodbye to the pension fund – you'll be dining on dry crackers if you stay here, but for true baronial splendour there's only one choice. Paintings by Gainsborough and Joshua Reynolds, a sweeping secret garden and opulent suites crammed with more chaise longues, chandeliers and sash windows than your average royal palace.

Eating

CAFÉS & QUICK EATS

Blackstones Kitchen (☎ 338803; 10 Queen St; mains £2-7; ⏰ 7.30am-4pm Mon-Sat) Takeaway with a twist in a concept kitchen. Daily changing mains are cooked up before your eyes and packed up for the ultimate gourmet picnic. The menu's wide-ranging – one day it's Boston beans with cornbread, the next it's chorizo sausage casserole – and the quality matches any sit-down supper-house.

Kindling (☎ 442125; 9a Claverton Bldgs; sandwiches £3-5; ⏰ 7.30am-4.30pm Mon-Fri, 10am-4.30pm Sat & Sun; 🖳) Another locals' favourite renowned for its carefully crafted café food and Manhattan coffee-shop vibe; plus free wi-fi for you and toys for the nippers (or maybe the other way round).

Adventure Café (☎ 462038; 5 Princes Bldgs; mains £3-6) Californian bohemia mixes with urban chic at this groovy café-cum-hangout, all picture windows, distressed wood and deep sofas. Cappuccinos by morning, ciabattas at noon and cocktails after dark.

Boston Tea Party (☎ 313901; 19 Kingsmead Sq; lunch £3-6; ☺ Mon-Sat) The city's original lunch stop is still jamming in the punters with its zingy citrus drinks, fruit smoothies and gourmet wraps, soups and sandwiches.

Sally Lunn's (☎ 461634; 4 North Pde Passage; lunch £5-6, mains from £8) Sally Lunn's Famous Bun is synonymous with the city – it's been served at this superfrilly tearoom for three centuries. Actually more a bread than a cake, the bun can be eaten with either sweet or savoury toppings – and don't confuse it with the Bath Bun, which is smaller, sweeter and studded with currants.

Café Retro (☎ 339347; 18 York St; mains £5-11; ☺ breakfast & lunch) A café from the old school, harking back to prelatte days. Settle in among arty types, earth mothers and truanting students for a slap-up burger or a veggie lasagne. Sarnies and takeaway coffees are available from Retro2Go next door.

RESTAURANTS
Parisien (☎ 447147; Shires Yard; mains £6.50-12; ☺ 8am-6pm Mon-Sat, 9am-5pm Sun) *Oh la la* – a little *soupçon* of Paris in the heart of Bath. It's all authentically Gallic – tables on the terrace, *moules frites* (mussels and chips) on the menu and the crispiest *frites* this side of the English Channel.

Walrus & the Carpenter (☎ 314864; 28 Barton St; mains £7-15; ☺ lunch & dinner) Another Bath classic, eschewing snootiness in favour of a homelier mix of mismatched furniture, chummy service and down-home food. The menu's divided into 'befores' and 'afters' – the kebabs, chillis, moussakas and huge burgers are old faves.

Yum Yum Thai (☎ 445253; 17 Kingsmead Sq; mains £7.95-11.95; ☺ lunch & diner Mon-Sat, dinner Sun) Bangkok canteen food served up fast and fresh in a light, very-white interior. Pad Thai noodles, stir-fried sea bream and curried mussels with nary a dash of MSG in sight.

Gascoyne Place (☎ 445854; www.gascoyneplace .co.uk; 1 Sawclose; mains £10.95-16.95; ☺ lunch & dinner) A stylish new restaurant on Sawclose, housed inside a renovated gentleman's club, and split into sections: two starchy-white dining rooms, plus a mezzanine, cosy snug and a candlelit bar with original medieval wall. The menu's classic British, the ambience authentic Bath.

Firehouse Rotisserie (☎ 482070; 2 John St; mains £11-15; ☺ lunch & dinner Mon-Sat) Not as starry as some of Bath's restaurants, perhaps, but Fireworks is still a winner, especially if you like your flavours hot 'n' spicy. Cajun cooking, Louisiana chicken and brick-fired pizza are the trademarks.

Demuth's (☎ 446059; 2 North Pde Passage; mains £11.50-12.50; ☺ lunch) Veggie food's all very well, but it's about as tasty as cold tea, right? Wrong. This wonderful place dispels all the myths about vegetarian cooking – it's one of Bath's most innovative eateries, churning out exciting dishes such as vegetarian dharamsala thali or Marrakech chickpea tagine.

Blackstones Restaurant (☎ 444403; 2-3 Queen St; mains £11.50-16.75; ☺ lunch & dinner Tue-Sat, lunch only Sun) The Blackstones team has expanded operations into this groovy restaurant across the street. The food flits from Cumberland sausage to Catalonian stews, and most of the produce is certified southwest.

ourpick **Le Petit Cochon** (☎ 421251; 11 Margarets Bldgs; mains £11.95-£16.95; ☺ lunch & dinner Tue-Sat) This place offers French farmhouse cooking on one of Bath's smartest streets, with ingredients imported from across the Channel. Escargots, cassoulet and lobster bisque are served in a Gallic-chic atmosphere, full of hand-chalked menus and pine furniture. There's a less formal café-deli across the city on Widcombe Pde.

FishWorks (☎ 448707; 6 Green St; mains from £13; ☺ lunch & dinner) This restaurant (half fishmonger, half seafood bistro) has proved so popular it's spawned 12 other outposts, but this is the original and best. Piscatorial treats sit on ice-packed trays; choose something to cook at home or let the chefs do the work while you soak up the street-market vibe.

Onefishtwofish (☎ 330236; 10a North Pde; mains £13-18; ☺ dinner Tue-Sun) Lights twinkle overhead and the tables are crammed in under a barrel-brick roof at this extraordinary cellar restaurant, which ships in its seafood from Devon ports, and cooks up everything from wonton salmon to Marseillaise *bouillabaisse*.

Hole In The Wall (☎ 425242; 16 George St; mains £14.95-19.95; ☺ lunch & dinner Mon-Sat) This place is another refined refectory that adventures through Anglo-French flavours – braised pork with Puy lentils, or Chew Magna lamb with potato fondant – in a cellar dining room that's half country restaurant, half urbane elegance.

Olive Tree Restaurant (☎ 447928; Queensbury Hotel, Russell St; 2-/3-course lunch £15/17.50, dinner mains £15-26; ☺ lunch Tue-Sun, dinner Mon-Sun) Break out the glad-rags – the Queensberry Hotel's restaurant is a posh, pricey extravaganza, studiously minimalist and sparkling with boutique British cuisine. It's the kind of place where you'll need a gastronomic glossary – expect galantine of wood pigeon and dark chocolate panacotta with Grottine cherries.

SELF-CATERING

Self-caterers are spoilt for choice at the Guildhall Market, where you'll find small specialist shops offering all kinds of sweet and savoury treats.

Paxton & Whitfield (☎ 466403; 1 John St; ☺ Mon-Sat) You can smell this place long before you see it – a gourmet cheese shop selling everything from Cheddar cheddar to Cornish brie and French camembert.

Chandos Deli (☎ 314418; George St; ☺ Mon-Sat) Fresh pasta, chunktastic sandwiches and Italian cakes are the mainstays at this excellent deli that's perfect for stocking up on picnic supplies.

Deli Shush (☎ 443563; 8a Guildhall Market) Serrano ham, antipasti, samosas and 20 types of olives fill the shelves of this designer deli.

Drinking

Belvedere Wine Vaults (☎ 330264; www.belvedere winevaults.co.uk; 25 Belvedere, Lansdown Rd) Built by a celebrated 18th-century oenophile, this 30-somethings' hangout is carrying on the gourmet grape tradition with a 50-strong wine list, plus frozen vodka, Becks beer and a welcome absence of those fruit machines.

Common Room (☎ 425550; 2 Saville Row) Swish and sexy bar for swish and sexy people, near the Assembly Rooms and next door to a retro antiques shop. Stripped wood, potted plants, leather sofas and cool cocktails – you know the score.

Grappa (☎ 448890; 3 Belvedere, Lansdown Rd) Hemingway's favourite spirit takes top billing at this Continental-style bar, but at anywhere between 40% and 70% proof, it's not for lightweights.

Raven (☎ 425045; Queen St) Recently given the nod by the Camra crowd, this fine city drinking den commands a devoted following for its real ales and authentic British-boozer décor.

Pig & Fiddle (☎ 460868; 2 Saracen St) Fave with the Bath Spa students, especially for big-screen sports and table footie.

Bath Tap (☎ 404344; 19-20 St James Pde; ☺ to 2am Thu-Sat) The classic pub hangout for Bath's gay community, with a late weekend licence and a fun range of theme nights ranging from drag to cabaret.

Entertainment

Venue (www.venue.co.uk) is the main source of info for clubs, gigs and cinemas in Bristol and Bath – it's sold all over town for £1.20.

LIVE MUSIC & CLUBS

Moles (☎ 404445; www.moles.co.uk; 14 George St; admission £5-7) Bath's main music venue commands a nationwide reputation – loads of big-name bands have played here, from The Smiths to Massive Attack, and it still has a reputation for breaking new acts.

Porter Cellar Bar (☎ 424104; George St) Just across the street and also run by the Moles folk, this is a rustic, spit-and-sawdust affair that hosts the bands who aren't yet big enough to play Moles; the cellar venue gets very crowded on gig nights.

Delfter Krug (☎ 443352; Sawclose) A massive, rambling pub opposite the theatre equipped for all eventualities – upstairs club for Housey tunes and DJs, downstairs bar for dedicated drinkers, and a street terrace for when the weather's fine.

THEATRE & CINEMAS

Theatre Royal (☎ 448844; www.theatreroyal.org.uk; Sawclose) This posh provincial theatre features comedy, drama, opera, ballet and world music in the main auditorium, and more experimental productions at its smaller Ustinov Studio.

Rondo Theatre (☎ 463362; www.rondotheatre.co.uk; St Saviours Rd, Larkhall) This small rep theatre mixes up a varied programme of comedy, music, dance and drama.

Little Theatre (☎ 466822; St Michael's Pl) Bath's arthouse cinema, screening mostly fringe and foreign-language films.

Getting There & Away

BUS

Most National Express coaches require a connection via Bristol (£3.60, 45 minutes, at least eight daily) or Swindon (£5.90, one hour, eight daily), although there are direct coaches to London Victoria (£17, 3½ hours, 10 to 12 daily).

The fastest bus to Bristol is X39/339 (55 minutes, four per hour Monday to Saturday, two per hour Sunday) or 332/632 (one hour, hourly Monday to Saturday, seven on Sunday). The 173 (one hour 20 minutes, hourly Monday to Saturday, six on Sunday) travels to Wells.

The bus station on Manvers St is closed during the redevelopment of the Southgate area; it's temporarily located at Avon St car park.

TRAIN

There are direct services from Bath Spa to London Paddington and London Waterloo (£60.50, 1½ hours, at least hourly) and several per hour to Bristol (£5.60, 11 minutes), where you can connect to northern and southwestern England.

There are also local trains to Frome (£7.30, 40 minutes), Dorchester West (£12.30, 1¾ hours) and Weymouth (£12.60, two hours) every two hours Monday to Friday, with some services at weekends.

Getting Around
BICYCLE

Hire bikes from **Avon Valley Cyclery** (☎ 461880; www .bikeshop.uk.com; Arch 37; half-/full day £10/15; ☒ 9.30am-5pm Mon-Sat, till 8pm Thu) near the train station.

See p82 for details on the Bristol and Bath Railway Path.

BUS

Bus 18 runs from the bus station, High St and Great Pulteney St up Bathwick Hill past the YHA to the university every 10 minutes. Bus 4 runs every 20 minutes to Bathampton from the same places. A FirstDay Pass for unlimited bus travel in the city costs adult/child £4/2.60.

CAR

Bath has a serious traffic problem (especially at rush hour) and an infuriating one-way system. **Park-and-ride services** (☎ 464446; return £1.70; ☒ 10min to centre, every 10-15min, 6.15am-7.30pm) operate at Lansdown to the north, Newbridge to the west and Odd Down to the south.

AROUND BATH
Prior Park

The celebrated landscape gardener Capability Brown and the satirical poet Alexander Pope both had a hand in the creation of **Prior Park** (NT; ☎ 01225-833422; adult/child £4.80/2.70; Ralph Allen Dr; ☒ 11am-5.30pm Wed-Mon Feb-Nov, 11am-dusk Fri-Sun Dec & Jan), an 18th-century ornamental garden dreamt up by the local entrepreneur Ralph Allen. Cascading lakes, a Gothic temple and a Palladian bridge can be found around the garden's winding walks, and the sweeping views over the Bath skyline are something to behold.

Prior Park is 1 mile south of the centre; it can be reached on foot or by bus (2 or 4, every 10 minutes), as well as the City Skyline tour (p95).

WELLS

☎ 01749 / pop 10,406

Even by England's proportionally challenged standards, Wells is a miniscule city – it only qualifies for the 'city' title thanks to its medieval cathedral, the main seat of ecclesiastical power in this part of Britain since the 12th century, and still the official residence of the Bishop of Bath and Wells. The cathedral forms the centrepiece of one of the best-preserved medieval closes in Britain, an alluring collection of cobbled streets, cloistered walkways and a moat-fringed Bishop's Palace where the swans order their supper by tinkling a bell. Don't be surprised if it

---

THE LAST WORD IN LUXURY

our pick **Babington House** (☎ 01373-812266; www.babingtonhouse.co.uk; near Frome; r £210-325; P ⌨ ♿) Golly gosh – you won't forget this one in a hurry. Dripping with Georgian architecture and zinging with urban invention, this designer's playground is like a cross between *Homes & Gardens* and *Wallpaper*. Angle-poise lamps meet reclaimed beams; floating beds sit beside plasma TVs and vintage towel-racks; carved marble fireplaces face zebra-print seats; and the bathrooms are like something out of *Blade Runner*. Choose from rooms in the manorhouse, a stable block, twin-storeyed lodge or the mezzanine-floored coach house. Dine in the amazing Log Room restaurant, or have a brainstorming session in the Kubrickesque 'Play Room'. It even has its own 45-seat cinema, for heaven's sake.

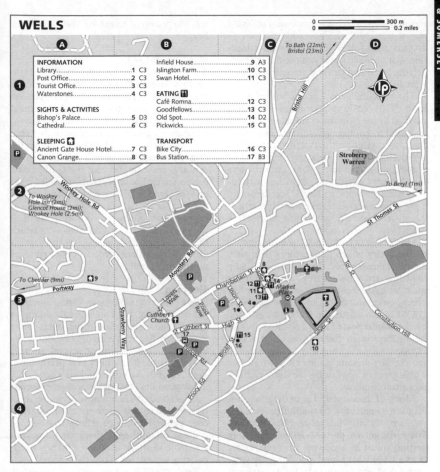

WELLS

0 —————— 300 m
0 —————— 0.2 miles

INFORMATION	
Library	1 C3
Post Office	2 C3
Tourist Office	3 C3
Waterstones	4 C3

SIGHTS & ACTIVITIES	
Bishop's Palace	5 D3
Cathedral	6 C3

SLEEPING	
Ancient Gate House Hotel	7 C3
Canon Grange	8 C3

Infield House	9 A3
Islington Farm	10 C3
Swan Hotel	11 C3

EATING	
Café Romna	12 C3
Goodfellows	13 C3
Old Spot	14 D2
Pickwicks	15 C3

TRANSPORT	
Bike City	16 C3
Bus Station	17 B3

To Bath (22mi);
Bristol (23mi)

Stroberry
Warren

To Beryl (1mi)

To Wookey
Hole Inn (2mi);
Glencot House (2mi);
Wookey Hole (2.5mi)

To Cheddar (9mi)

Portway

St
Cuthbert's
Church

Market
Place

To Bath (22mi);
Bristol (23mi)

looks weirdly familiar – the cathedral close has featured in countless films and costume dramas, most recently in the cult Brit comedy *Hot Fuzz*. Despite the starry connections, it's a quiet, sleepy city, and a good base for further forays around the Mendips and northern Somerset.

Information

Library (Union St; closed Sun)

Post office (Market Pl)

Tourist office (☎ 672552; www.wells.gov.uk; Market Pl; 9.30am-5.30pm Apr-Oct, 10am-4pm Nov-Mar) Stocks the *Wells City Trail* leaflet (30p) and sells discount tickets to Wookey Hole and Cheddar Gorge.

Waterstone's (Market Sq; 9am-5.30pm Mon-Sat, 10am-4pm Sun) The town's main bookseller.

Wells Laundrette (39 St Cuthbert St; 8am-8pm) Opposite St Cuthbert's Church.

Sights

WELLS CATHEDRAL

The southwest has some stunning ecclesiastical architecture, but few places can match the **Cathedral Church of St Andrew** (☎ 674483; www .wellscathedral.org.uk; Chain Gate, Cathedral Green; requested donation adult/child £5/2; 7am-7pm Apr-Sep, 7am-6pm Oct-Mar), otherwise known as Wells Cathedral. Built in several stages between 1180 and 1508, Wells bears all the hallmarks of classic Gothic church-building, but is most famous for the ornate **west front**, an intricately carved sculpture gallery depicting various lords, notables and saintly characters. The façade was designed to conjure up a vision of divine majesty for approaching worshippers, but it's actually a shadow of its former self; restoration work revealed many of the figures were originally painted in vivid colours and laced with gold leaf.

The cathedral's central spire burned down in the 15th century; its original position is marked by the twin **scissor arches**, which were installed to counter subsidence caused by the tower. High in the north transept is a wonderful **mechanical clock** dating from 1390, the second-oldest in England after the one in Salisbury Cathedral. The clock is particularly notable for its medieval face, depicting a pre-Copernican universe with the earth at its centre; jousting knights and a quarter jack mark every quarter-hour.

Other highlights include the 15th-century **chained library**, which houses more than 6000 medieval manuscripts (the chains were to stop light-fingered scholars from carting off the most valuable tomes); it's only open a few afternoons in summer. The elegant **lady chapel** (1326) is also worth a look, but it's eclipsed by the **Chapter House** (1306), reached via spiralling steps worn down by centuries of feet. Flooded with light, ringed by carved seats and crowned by delicate ceiling ribs, it feels like a little piece of *The Lord of the Rings* plonked into rural Somerset.

Much of the cathedral is undergoing restoration as part of a £6 million project, but you can still visit the cloisters and the **Chain Bridge**, designed to prevent clerical robes from getting soiled in a downpour. Free hourly **tours** are available Monday to Saturday year-round, and you can drop by for evensong or a Sunday service to hear the **cathedral choir** in action. Photo permits (£2) are sold in the cathedral shop.

CATHEDRAL CLOSE

Surrounding the cathedral is a cluster of ecclesiastical buildings that form the medieval Cathedral Close. The **Vicars' Close** is a cobbled alley of 14th-century houses, thought to be the oldest medieval street in Europe; nearby is the 15th-century **Old Deanery** and the **Wells Museum** (☎ 673477; 8 Cathedral Green; www.wellsmuseum.org.uk; adult/child £3/1; ☯ 10am-5.30pm Mon-Sat, 11am-4pm Sun Easter-Oct, 11am-4pm Nov-Easter), with exhibits on local life, cathedral architecture and the archaeological finds of Wookey Hole. **Penniless Porch**, a corner gate leading onto Market Sq,

was the preferred haunt for Wells' medieval beggars.

BISHOP'S PALACE

A short stroll from the cathedral is the 13th-century **Bishop's Palace** (☎ 678691; www.bishops palacewells.co.uk; adult/child £5/1; ☯ 10.30am-6pm Mon-Fri, noon-6pm Sun Apr-Oct), ringed by a moat and fortified with a medieval drawbridge as a result of various heated disputes between the city's bishops and burghers. Though the original Great Hall fell into ruin in the 16th century, you can still visit the Gothic state rooms which house portraits of Wells' bishops; the ceremonial Coronation Cape; and the 'Glastonbury Chair', the prototype for a folding oak chair much-copied during the Middle Ages. The four natural wells after which the city is named bubble up in the palace's grounds; the palace gardener conducts tours on summer evenings.

Sleeping

Infield House (☎ 670989; www.infieldhouse.co.uk; 36 Portway; s/d £45/58; **P**) You'll feel the bump as you slide down the price ladder, but if you're keeping the financial reins tight try this pleasant, spacious B&B, one of several on busy Portway road. It's flouncy and pretty unremarkable, but the buffet brekkie's good.

Islington Farm (☎ 673445; www.islingtonfarmatwells .co.uk; s/d £45/60; **P**) Farmhouse-style digs in an ivy-covered cottage surrounded by Somerset countryside. It has original fireplaces, beamed ceilings and authentic character galore, but a notable shortage of space – there's a self-catering annexe for extra elbow room.

Beryl (☎ 678738; www.beryl-wells.co.uk; Hawkers Lane; s £65-80, d £75-120; **P** ⚲) Another spoil – an enormous country manor dotted with ticking grandfather clocks, dolls' houses and walnut dressers, run by an endearingly eccentric English family. The 10 old-fashioned country rooms cover several floors (each with kitchen, washing machine and fridge) and most overlook the wooded grounds. It's a mile outside Wells – ask for directions or you'll get lost.

Swan Hotel (☎ 836300; www.swanhotelwells.co.uk; Sadler St; d from £130) Yes, it's owned by Best Western, but this 15th-century coaching inn is far from an anonymous corpo-hotel. Expect heritage wallpaper, polished wood and padded armchairs in the rooms, plus hunting memorabilia and a charming gentlemen's lounge downstairs.

our pick Glencot House (☎ 677160; www.glen
cothouse.co.uk; r £165-260; P Ⓛ) This one's a jaw-
dropper – a slice of Jacobean magnificence,
dripping with ornamental vases, inglenook
fireplaces and wood-panelled walls. The
stately bedrooms are period-packed, with
half-testers, vintage rugs and leaded windows,
but come with mod-cons including wi-fi and
LCD TVs. Outside there's a 1.3 hectare park,
a croquet lawn and, of course, a helipad. What
do you mean you're arriving by car? How
common.

Canon Grange (☎ 671800; www.canongrange.co.uk;
s £31-40; d £52-68) Ancient B&B harking back decades
décor-wise, but central and cheap; the Walnut Suite has
some antique class.

Ancient Gate House Hotel (☎ 672029; www.ancient
gatehouse.co.uk; Browne's Gate; s £72.50, d £91-97.50;
⊠) Expect musty rooms and wood-panelled character at
this old inn built into the cathedral's West Gate.

Eating

our pick Wookey Hole Inn (☎ 676677; www.wookey
holeinn.com; mains £8-16) Glorious, much-vaunted
gastropub between Wells and Wookey Hole,
where half-timbered heritage meets Belgian
beers and top-notch modern British grub –
think pestorib of beef, coconut sea bass and
Merguez sausages. If you can't tear yourself
away book a groovy room (£80 to £100), with
freestanding bath, Oriental bed and DVDs on
demand. Lovely.

Pickwicks (☎ 676697; 25-27 Broad St; ☾ breakfast &
lunch Mon-Sat) Soup of the day, paninis and sarnies are the mainstays at this little pine-finished
café; it's also a good bet for afternoon tea and
sweet-tooth spoils.

Café Romna (☎ 670240; 13 Sadler St; mains £10-15;
☾ lunch & dinner Mon-Sat) Serves fusion Bangladeshi cuisine in contemporary surroundings
(banquette seats, razor-edge tables, abstract
art), where old Indian staples are joined by
zingy mains such as *maas oori* (*boowal* fish
in runner-bean sauce) and king josh (lamb
with tomato and bullet chillies).

Goodfellows (☎ 673866; 5 Sadler St; mains £14.50-
24, 6-course menu £49; ☾ lunch & dinner Tue-Sat) Half
upmarket patisserie and artisan baker, half
superswanky seafood bistro, where the food
is Anglo-French laced with Somerset ingredients. If it's a bit rich for supper, there's an ace
£10 lunch menu.

Old Spot (☎ 689099; 12 Sadler St; menus £21.50-26.50;
☾ lunch Wed-Sun, dinner Tue-Sat) This new bistro's
quietly stunning food has been getting stellar

write-ups, and quite rightly. It's a straight-
forward British delight, run by a chef with
London credentials and a sharp sense for
country flavours – *brandade* (garlic purée)
of cod, braised rabbit or smoked eel.

Getting There & Around
From the bus station on Princes Rd, bus
375/376 goes to Bristol (one hour) at least
hourly from Monday to Saturday, while the
29 travels to Glastonbury (20 minutes, five to
seven daily) and Taunton (one hour). Bus 126
runs to Cheddar (25 minutes) hourly Monday
to Saturday and every two hours on Sunday.

Bike City (☎ 671711; 31 Broad St; ☾ 9am-5.30pm
Mon-Sat) charges £15 per day if you need to
hire a bicycle.

WOOKEY HOLE
The limestone rock around northern Somerset is riddled with a series of deep fissures and
subterranean caves, many used as temporary
shelters by prehistoric people. Just north of
Wells, the River Axe has carved out **Wookey
Hole** (☎ 01749-672243; www.wookey.co.uk; adult/child
£12.50/9.50; ☾ 10am-5pm Apr-Oct, 10.30am-4pm Nov-Mar),
where a guided tour descends through a network of underground chambers. Highlights
include an underground lake and some fantastic stalagmites and stalactites (one of which
is the legendary Witch of Wookey Hole, who
was turned to stone by a local priest). Prehistoric hunter-gatherers were using the site at
least 50,000 years ago, and because many of
the caves are now under water, no-one's quite
sure how far they extend – the deepest subterranean dive ever recorded in Britain was made
here in September 2004, when divers reached
a depth of 45.5m.

In addition to the natural wonders on offer,
there's also a tacky mirror maze, an Edwardian penny arcade and a paper mill. Most of
the site's prehistoric finds are on display at
the Wells Museum (opposite).

Bus 670 runs from Wells (10 minutes, nine
daily, four on Sunday).

CHEDDAR GORGE
Carved out by glacial forces during the last
Ice Age, the deep ravine of Cheddar Gorge is
the largest in England, in places towering over
138m above the twisting road. It's strikingly
reminiscent of the gorge and cave systems
of southwestern France, and like its French
cousins the area was extensively used by

prehistoric hunters. The oldest complete skeleton in Britain was discovered here in 1903; it dates from 7150 BC. Genetic tests have revealed that the 'Cheddar Man' still has descendants living in the area.

At the heart of the valley are the **Cheddar Caves** (☎ 01934-742343; www.cheddarcaves.co.uk; Explorer Ticket adult/child £14/9; ☉ 10am-5.30pm Jul & Aug, 10.30am-5pm Sep-Jun), a series of limestone caverns carved out over the millennia by geological forces. **Gough's Cave** is the largest, stretching more than 1.3 miles underground through a network of stalactite-draped 'rooms', including the Diamond Chamber, Aladdin's Cave and Solomon's Temple (where the cave lights are usually extinguished to freak out the claustrophobes).

Further down the valley is **Cox's Cave**, discovered in 1837 when a local mill worker fell through a hole in the roof. There are seven main chambers, including the 'Home of the Rainbow', where mineral deposits have created a multicoloured sheen on the surface of the rock.

The Explorer ticket also includes admission to the **Cheddar Man & Cannibals Museum**, which explores the alleged cannibalistic habits of our ancestors, and the 274-step slog up **Jacob's Ladder** to the **Lookout Tower**, from where you can see Exmoor on a clear day. Nearby a signposted 3-mile-round walk follows the edge of the Gorge, and is a good place to escape the crowds; you might even glimpse a peregrine falcon if you're lucky. More adventurous souls should contact **Rocksport** (☎ 01934-742343; caves@cheddarcaves.co.uk), which arranges abseiling and climbing trips (£16 for 1½ hours), and caving expeditions (from around £20) into subterranean areas that are otherwise off-limits to visitors.

The **tourist office** (☎ 01934-744071; cheddar.tic @sedgemoor.gov.uk; ☉ 10am-5pm Easter-Sep, 10.30am-4.30pm Oct, 11am-4pm Sun Nov-Easter) is at the southern end of the gorge.

None of the nearby hotels is up to much – you're better off basing yourself in Wells or Glastonbury – although the **Cheddar YHA** (☎ 0870 770 5760; cheddar@yha.org.uk; Hillfield; dm £14) offers pleasant hostel digs in an old stone house in Cheddar Village.

Bus 126 runs to Wells (25 minutes) hourly Monday to Saturday and every two hours on Sunday.

THE MENDIPS

Stretching for around 200 sq km between Weston-Super-Mare, a typically tacky seaside resort on the northern Somerset coast, and the market town of Frome, the Mendip Hills are a range of limestone humps offering fantastic views all the way to the Somerset coast. Usually just called the Mendips, it's an area that's dripping with history – prehistoric people sheltered in the area's many caves, and the remains of Bronze Age barrows and Iron Age forts are scattered across the hilltops. The Mendips later became an important mining district, especially around Midsomer Norton and Radstock; the quarrying of Mendip stone continues to the present day.

Since becoming an Area of Outstanding Natural Beauty (AONB) in 1972, the Mendips has developed into a hiking, mountain-biking and rambling heartland. Many trails wind their way across the grassy hilltops, including excellent walks around **Burrington Coombe**, the old mines and woodlands around **Blackmoor Reserve**, the steeply wooded ravine at **Ebbor Gorge**, and the Mendips' highest point at **Blackdown** (326m).

A CHEESY STORY

As well as its spectacular cave system, cheddar is the spiritual home of the nation's favourite cheese. Cheddar's strong, crumbly, tangy cheese is the essential ingredient in any ploughman's sandwich, and has been produced in the area since at least the 12th century. Henry II proclaimed it 'the best cheese in Britain', and the king's accounts from 1170 record that he purchased 10,240lbs (around 3650kg) of the stuff. In the days before refrigeration, the Cheddar caves made the ideal cool store for the cheese, with a constant temperature of around 7°C, but the powerful smell attracted rats and the practice was eventually abandoned.

These days most cheddar is made far from the village, but if you're interested in seeing how the genuine article is made, head for the **Cheddar Gorge Cheese Company** (☎ 01934-742810; www.cheddargorgecheeseco.co.uk; Cheddar; admission £1.85; ☉ 10am-5.30pm). You can take a guided tour of the factory from April to October, and pick up cheesy souvenirs at the on-site shop.

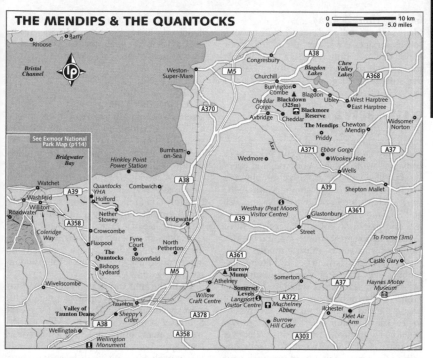

THE MENDIPS & THE QUANTOCKS

Trail cards detailing popular routes are available from local tourist offices or the **Mendips AONB Office** (☎ 01761-462338; www.mendip hillsaonb.org.uk) near Blagdon. If you fancy something more hands-on, there are regular courses in traditional skills such as hedge-laying and dry stone walling – contact the office for details.

Until the Middle Ages, large tracts of the Mendips lay beneath swampy meadows, and the remaining wetlands provide an important wildlife habitat. **Chew Valley Lake** is one of the best places for bird-spotting, and there's also a small tourist office and teashop selling cakes, sandwiches and bickies.

There are some gorgeous thatched villages to explore around the Mendips, including **Chewton Mendip** with its delightful church from the 15th-century, and the chocolate-box village of **Priddy**, famous for its annual **Folk Festival** (www.priddyfolk.org) and **Sheep Fair** (www.priddysheep fair.co.uk), held on the village green since 1348. Just north is **East Harptree**, where you can visit the ruins of the Norman-era Richemont Castle, and **West Harptree**, with a village pub and an elegant 12th-century church.

Sleeping & Eating

The accommodation within the AONB itself is limited; Wells or Glastonbury make better bases.

Harptree Court (☎ 01761-221729; www.harptree court.co.uk; East Harptree; s £65, d £80-90; P) This ab-fab manor is a Mendip gem, ensconced down a private drive and surrounded by lush parkland. There are only three rooms, so it never feels crowded, and while the colour-coded rooms aren't particularly lavish, the country house setting is straight from *Brideshead Revisited*.

Ring O' Bells (☎ 01761-221284; Compton Martin) Butcombe Bitter and Chew Valley trout are served beneath hefty beams and hanging plates, with a huge grassy beer garden out back. A thoroughly lovely place for a plough-man's or a plate of ham and eggs before heading out on the trail.

New Inn (☎ 01749-676465; Priddy) This is a popular local's pub much-favoured by cavers and hill-baggers, stocked with ales from Bath Ales. It has classic English pub games (shove ha'penny and skittles) to keep the kids out of mischief.

Getting There & Away

Many of the Mendip villages are quite remote, so bus services are scarce; the 672/3 'Chew Valley Explorer' (four daily) is about the only transport. It runs between Bristol and Cheddar, stopping at Blagdon, Ubley and East and West Harptree.

GLASTONBURY & AROUND

☎ 01458 / pop 8429

Break out the tie-dye and the tarot cards – you've just landed in hippie central. Ley-lines converge, white witches convene, and every shop is filled with the aroma of smouldering joss sticks in good old Glastonbury, where the spirit of the Summer of Love is alive and well and England's ragtag band of mystics, travellers and part-time bongo players are rolled together in one great countercultural bundle. Famous for its annual musical mudfest, held on Michael Eavis' farm in nearby Pilton, Glastonbury was a centre for New Age culture long before the traveller buses rolled in. The green hump of Glastonbury Tor was an important pagan site and is rumoured to be the mythological Isle of Avalon, where King Arthur was legendarily borne after his death. Whatever you make of Glastonbury's many legends, one thing's for sure – if you need to knock your chakras into shape, this is the right place.

Information

Oracle (www.glastonburyoracle.co.uk) Free guide to Glastonbury events.
Post office (☎ 831536; 35 High St)

Tourist office (☎ 832954; www.glastonburytic.co.uk; The Tribunal, 9 High St; ☾ 10am-5pm Apr-Sep, 10am-4pm Oct-Mar) Walking guides, maps, travel timetables and accommodation lists. The Lake Village Museum is on the 1st floor.

Sights

GLASTONBURY TOR

There's a bewildering maze of myths associated with Glastonbury Tor. To some it's the stronghold of Gwyn ap Nudd (ruler of Annwyn, the Faerie Kingdom), while to others it's the Celtic site of *Ynys Witrin,* the Isle of Glass. Wearyall Hill, just below the tor, is supposedly where Joseph of Arimathea buried the Holy Grail following Christ's crucifixion. But the most famous legend identifies the tor as the Isle of Avalon, where King Arthur was taken after being mortally wounded by his nephew Mordred, and where Britain's 'once and future king' sleeps until his country calls again.

Until the land was drained for agriculture in the 13th and 14th centuries, much of the countryside around Glastonbury (as on the Somerset Levels) was surrounded by marshy wetland; many of the area's high hills would have appeared to local people to be islands, which probably explains its legendary status as an 'isle'.

The tor has long been a site of pilgrimage for Christians heading for the ruins of the church of St Michael, and possibly for prehistoric pilgrims, too: two twisted oak trees, **Gog** and **Magog**, are believed to mark an ancient pro-

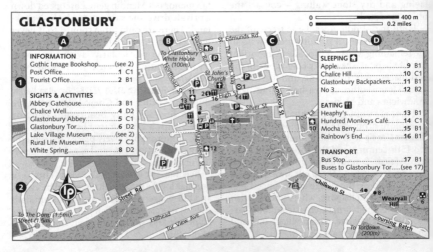

GLASTONBURY

0 — 400 m
0 — 0.2 miles

cessional avenue. Various other unexplained remains have been found around the tor, including an ancient sacred maze, constructed around the same time as Stonehenge.

It's a 45-minute round trip on foot from town, or you can catch the Tor Bus (£1) that runs from Dunstan's car park half-hourly between 10am and 7.30pm May to September and until 3.30pm the rest of the year. It also stops at Chalice Well and the Rural Life Museum.

GLASTONBURY ABBEY

Somerset is littered with medieval abbeys, but the largest and most powerful was **Glastonbury Abbey** (☎ 832267; www.glastonburyabbey.com; Magdalene St; adult/child £4.50/3; ☼ 9.30am-6pm Apr-Sep, 9.30am-5pm Mar & Oct, 9.30am-4.30pm Nov, 10am-4.30pm Dec). By the time of the Domesday Book, Glastonbury was the richest monastery in England, but it was destroyed by fire in 1184 and later rebuilt before being ransacked during the Dissolution. It's still possible to make out the nave walls, the ruins of St Mary's chapel, and the remains of the crossing arches, which may have been scissor-shaped like those in Wells Cathedral. In the 13th century, monks uncovered a tomb inscribed with the legend *Hic iacet sepultus inclitus rex arturius in insula avalonia,* or 'Here lies buried the renowned King Arthur in the Isle of Avalon', along with a pair of side-by-side skeletons (supposedly Arthur and Guinevere). The bones were buried beneath the altar in 1278, but were lost following the plundering of the abbey; the site of the tomb is marked in the grass.

The **Holy Thorn** in the Abbey grounds is supposedly an offshoot of the thorn tree that sprang from Joseph of Arimathea's staff on Wearyall Hill. The tree mysteriously blooms twice a year, at Christmas and Easter. Elsewhere you'll find a cider orchard, duck pond and herb garden, as well as a small museum with a scale model of the abbey in its prime.

CHALICE WELL & GARDENS

People have been dunking, drinking and paddling at the **Chalice Well & Gardens** (☎ 831154; Chikwell St; www.chalicewell.org.uk; adult/child £3/1; ☼ 10am-5.30pm Apr-Oct, 10am-4pm Nov-Mar), a natural spring just below Glastonbury Tor, for at least 2000 years. The rust-red waters from this ancient well are rumoured to have healing properties, good for everything from eczema to smelly feet. Their distinctive crimson col-

our supposedly stems from the burial of the Holy Grail nearby, although it's actually a result of iron deposits in the soil. The well is surrounded by lovely gardens dotted with babbling pools and gnarled yew trees, and you can fill up your flasks with the sacred water from a lion's-head spout.

The Chalice Well is also known as the 'Red Spring' or 'Blood Spring'; its sister, **White Spring**, surfaces across Wellhouse Lane, and there's often a queue of people waiting to fill containers.

RURAL LIFE MUSEUM

Somerset's agricultural heritage is explored at the **Rural Life Museum** (☎ 831197; Abbey Farm, Chilkwell St; admission free; ☼ 10am-5pm Tue-Fri, 2-6pm Sat & Sun Apr-Oct, 10am-5pm Tue-Sat Nov-Mar), which contains tools and memorabilia relating to willow growing, peat-digging, cidermaking and cheesemaking.

LAKE VILLAGE MUSEUM

Inside the 15th Tribunal building, on the 1st floor above the tourist office, the **Lake Village Museum** (EH; admission £2) collects together various artefacts from the prehistoric swamp village discovered in nearby Godney in 1892. The village comprised five to seven groups of circular houses, built from reeds, hazel and willow, and was probably occupied by summer traders who lived the rest of the year around Glastonbury Tor.

SHOE MUSEUM

A couple of miles south of Glastonbury is Street, once the site of Britain's largest shoe factory, **Clark's**. The footwear factory has long since hiked overseas, but the town's shoe connections continue at the huge Clark's factory-outlet shop and a rather odd **Shoe Museum** (☎ 43131; High St; ☼ 10am-4.45pm Mon-Fri), which explores the history of shoemaking from Roman sandals to high-heeled stilettos.

Tours

Goddess Tours (☎ 275084; kathy.jones@ukonline .co.uk) Visiting white witches will want to join one of the tours offered by the Priestesses of Avalon, devotees of the matriarchal 'Goddess' religious order.

Mystical Tours of Glastonbury (☎ 831453; www .gothicimagetours.co.uk; 7 High St; per person £60) Guided tours to Wearyall Hill, Gog and Magog and Glastonbury Tor, offered by suitably alternative types based at the Gothic Image bookshop (next to the tourist office).

GLASTONBURY'S FESTIVAL(S)

For many people the name of Glastonbury is synonymous not with the town but with the extravaganza of music, mud and general mayhem otherwise known as the **Glastonbury Festival of Performing Arts** (www.glastonburyfestivals.co.uk), held (most) years on Michael Eavis' dairy farm. What started as a few ragtag bands playing on a ramshackle stage in the 1970s has now mushroomed into the world's largest, longest-running and best-loved music festival, and despite the appalling weather that's recently blighted the festival, it still packs in more than 120,000 music-lovers, and tickets sell faster than a whippet on water skis.

But Glastonbury's not the only festival in these 'ere parts. The **Big Green Gathering** (☎ 01458-834629; www.big-green-gathering.com) is an August festival that focuses on alternative technology, ecoliving and general greenness (with a few bands thrown in for good measure). Meanwhile the yearly **Goddess Conference** (www.goddessconference.com) is a celebration of the Crone Goddess, the earth mother-cum-matriarch who's been worshipped around Glastonbury since the days of Stonehenge; expect prancing, chanting, talks, readings and a culminatory pilgrimage up to Chalice Well and Glastonbury Tor. There's also a **dance festival** in July, a **children's festival** in August, a **street carnival** in November, and an annual **cultural 'extravaganza'** in the Abbey grounds, topped off with fireworks. Far-out, man.

Sleeping

Glastonbury Backpackers (☎ 833353; www.glaston burybackpackers.com; 4 Market Pl; dm/tw/d £14/35/40; Ⓟ ⌨) The original Glastonbury crash pad has recently had a lick of paint and some fresh furnishings; choose from simple-but-comfy dorms or proper doubles, all reached via a spiral staircase. It's really friendly and there's coffee and net access at the café.

Apple (☎ 834547; 5 Norbins Rd; applebnb@ukonline .co.uk; d £50-60) This traditional red-brick Victorian town house has had a contemporary refit at the hands of its bubbly owners: mix-and-match furniture and abstract artwork in the rooms (two share a bathroom), and an apple-tree garden where you can have your Fairtrade brekkie.

Glastonbury White House (☎ 830886; www.glaston burywhitehouse.com; 21 Manor House Rd; d £50-66; Ⓟ) Glastonbury character meets London style at this refined B&B, with two perfectly formed rooms boasting painted wood-floors, cast-iron bedsteads and vintage pull-chain loos. Breakfast is served either in-room or at one of the High St cafés.

Tordown (☎ 832287; www.tordown.com; 5 Ashwell Lane; s £28, d £54-62; Ⓟ) New Agers will love this cross between a classic English guesthouse and higher-self hideaway, which offers everything from Reiki massage to Egyptian ear-candling, plus a chill-out hydrotherapy spa. Bizarrely, the rooms are anything but calming, with a surfeit of granny patterns and florid eiderdowns.

Dorm (☎ 841943; www.the-dorm.co.uk; Glaston St; d £60-75; Ⓟ) Down the road in Street this converted dormitory is basic but fun, and run by funky owners. Three, small chintz-free rooms have white sheets, DVD players and breakfast-in-a-basket; the Honeymoon Suite has its own robotic massage chair. Weird.

Chalice Hill (☎ 838828; www.chalicehill.co.uk; Dod Lane; s/d £70/90; Ⓟ) Captivating Georgian B&B near Chalice Hill, run by an artistic owner. Gilded mirrors, book-filled shelves and the odd Indian fabric downstairs; upstairs three peaceful rooms in corn yellow and watery blues, all looking over oak-filled grounds. A real retreat.

No 3 (☎ 832129; www.numberthree.co.uk; 3 Magdalene St; s £85-95, d £110-120; Ⓟ) The next best thing is this luxurious town house just off the main Glastonbury drag. Frills and drapes aplenty in the rooms (most named after trees); the Walnut Room is lacy pink and looks over the willow-filled garden, while the Blue Room has Abbey views.

Eating

Rainbow's End (☎ 833896; 17A High St; mains £4-7 ❤ 10am-4pm) The hippie café to end them all, decked out in rainbow shades, scuffed-up furniture and a profusion of beads and potted plants. Expect bean chillies, quiches lentil soups and umpteen varieties of jacket spud, chased down with carrot cake and choc-chip muffins.

Heaphy's (☎ 837935; 16 Market Pl; mains £4.95-9.95 ❤ breakfast & lunch) Squeeze into one of the benches at this chaotic Glasto fave and settle in; the food might take a while. When it does arrive you'll find hearty pizzas, doorstop sarnies and hot chillies on your plate, washed down with English tea or fresh-squeezed fruit juice (organic and ethical, of course).

Mocha Berry (☎ 832149; 14 Market Pl; mains £5-8; ☺ Sun-Wed) Just because you're in Glastonbury doesn't mean you can't get a decent cappuccino, but the milkshakes and multipurpose breakfasts (pancakes, fry-ups, muffins) aren't bad either.

Hundred Monkeys Café (☎ 833386; 52 High St; mains £5-11; ☺ lunch & dinner Mon-Sat) No Indian throws or bean bags, here it's all wood tables, chalkboard menus and pared-back interiors. Gourmet sandwiches are supplemented by cakes, salads and upmarket mains.

Getting There & Away
Bus 29 travels to Glastonbury from Taunton (50 minutes, five to seven daily), and to Wells in the opposite direction. The hourly 375/6 goes to Bristol (one hour 20 minutes) via Wells, and to Yeovil (one hour) in the opposite direction.

TAUNTON & AROUND
☎ 01823 / pop 58,241
Taunton is in the heart of Somerset in more ways than one; it's bang in the middle of the county geographically, and is also the area's county town and commercial centre. Originally founded by Saxon king Ine, the town became infamous in the 17th century during the Monmouth Rebellion, an uprising against ruling monarch James II. The rebellion was crushed at the Battle of Sedgemoor and its leaders were tried and condemned during the Bloody Assizes under Judge Jeffreys. These days it's a solid red-brick shopping town, and a useful gateway to the Quantocks.

The **tourist office** (☎ 336344; tauntontic@tauntondeane .gov.uk; Paul St; ☺ 9.30am-5.30pm Mon-Sat) is next door to the library.

Sights
The 12th-century **Taunton Castle** where the Assizes were held houses the **Somerset County & Military Museum** (☎ 320201; Castle Green; admission free; ☺ 10am-5pm Tue-Sat), with displays of uniforms, weapons and cannon belonging to Somerset's military regiments, as well as local archaeological artefacts, including an ichthyosaur skeleton and the Shapwick coin hoard, a col-

lection of 9238 Roman denarii – the largest ever found in Britain. Taunton's other famous landmark is the **Church of St Mary Magdalene** (☺ 10am-4pm Mon-Fri, 10am-1pm Sat), which has the tallest church tower in Somerset.

BLACKDOWN HILLS
To the west of Taunton are the **Blackdown Hills** (www.blackdown-hills.net), a range of limestone humps topped by a 53m monument to the Duke of Wellington, with fine views across the Vale of Taunton Deane and lots of hiking, biking and horse-riding opportunities. The tourist office stocks trail leaflets and cycling guides, and can put you in touch with the **Blackdown Hills Hedge Association** (www.blackdown hills-hedge.org.uk), which offers courses in rural skills such as hedge-laying and coppicing.

To the north of the Blackdowns is the 15th-century **Cothay Manor** (☎ 672283; www.cothay manor.co.uk; adult/child £4.50/2.50; ☺ gardens 2-6pm), worth visiting for its shady yew walk and medieval cottage garden.

WEST SOMERSET RAILWAY
Chimneys chuff and steel wheels clatter aboard the **West Somerset Railway** (☎ 24hr talking timetable 01643-707650, other information 01643-704996; www.west-somerset-railway.co.uk), a classic old steam-powered railway that's been chugging through the Somerset countryside since 1859. It's a real slice of old England, with vintage carriages and time-warp stations along the line from Bishops Lydeard (near Taunton) to Minehead, 20 miles away (£12.40 return, 1¼ hours), with stops at Crowcombe Heathfield (for the Quantocks), Watchet and Dunster – depending on the time of year. There are several daily trains from April to October, with a weekend-only service in winter.

Bus 28 runs to Bishops Lydeard from Taunton (15 minutes, 11 daily Monday to Saturday), or you can catch the 50 'Steamlink' service to Taunton's town centre.

Sleeping & Eating
Blorenge House (☎ 283005; www.blorengehouse.co.uk; 57 Staplegrove Rd; d £58-75; P 🐾) A stonking great detached villa (complete with gardens and a backyard pool) near the town centre. The house is Victorian and the décor's mid-'70s, so it won't scoop any awards for originality, but it's dead-good value.

Salisbury House Hotel (☎ 272083; 14 Billetfield; s/d from £58/65; P) There's a country-club air around this solid guesthouse, with big, comfy rooms heavy on heritage patterns, and a pleasant location near Vivary Park. It's the best option if you want to base yourself in the town proper.

Greyhound Inn (☎ 480277; info@thegreyhoundinn .fsbusiness.co.uk; d from £80; P) Six miles south from Taunton in Staple Fitzpaine, this is a gem of a country pub – fishing tackle and hunting prints carpet the walls, log fires roar in flagstoned hearths and creepers cover the 16th-century inn. The food is fab – venison, guinea fowl and Somerset lamb – and there are sweet rooms with views of the Blackdown Hills.

our pick **Farmer's Inn** (☎ 480480; www.farmersinn westhatch.co.uk; West Hatch; d £90-110; P) The rustic overcoat of this Somerset inn conceals boutique undergarments. The stunning rooms, all named after Somerset hills, are a wonder – our faves are the Blackdown, with its freestanding bath, mahogany furniture and exposed stone, and the Quantock, with wetroom shower, chaise longue and Bergère bed. Lovely country food (mains £10.75 to £14.95), too (pork-and-cider bangers, homemade fishcakes). It's 4 miles east from Taunton in Higher West Hatch.

Castle (☎ 272671; www.the-castle-hotel.com; Castle Green; d £185-265; P ▢) Once a Norman fortress, now a plush (but overpriced) hotel, the Castle is Taunton's poshest place to stay. Pocket-sprung beds, *Homes and Gardens* colours and bags of space in the rooms, but it's the glitzy Anglo-French restaurant that most people come for, stuffed with country classics from Barrow boar to Brixham scallops.

Getting There & Away

Taunton is a main transport hub for Somerset. Bus 29 travels to Glastonbury (50 minutes, five to seven daily), and Wells (one hour 10 minutes), while the 28 (hourly Monday to Saturday, nine on Sunday) crosses the Quantocks to Minehead (1¼ hours). The hourly 54 goes to Yeovil (one hour 10 minutes).

Trains from Taunton run to London (£41, two hours, every two hours), to Exeter (£9, 30 minutes, half-hourly) and to Plymouth (£23, 1½ hours, half-hourly).

THE QUANTOCKS

Running along a sharp 12-mile ridge between the Vale of Taunton Deane and the north Somerset coast, the rusty-red hills of the Quantocks (from the Celtic word *can-*

tuc, meaning 'circle') are 3 miles wide and just 384m at their highest point, Wills Neck. Bronze Age settlements and burial mounds litter the hilltops, and the high heathland is an important habitat for rare birds of prey; the area is also well known for its Coleridge connections, as the poet lived for six years in Nether Stowey. You can follow in his footsteps along the **Coleridge Way**, a 36-mile trail from Nether Stowey to Porlock – see Exmoor, p115, for details.

The **AONB Service** (☎ 01278-732845; www.quan tockhills.com; Castle St, Nether Stowey; ☒ 10am-12.30pm & 2-5.30pm Mon, Wed & Fri, 10am-1pm & 2-4pm Sat) is in the library at Nether Stowey. There's another tourist office at **Fyne Court** (NT; ☎ 652400; fynecourt@nationaltrust.org.uk; ☒ 9am-6pm or dusk), a National Trust nature reserve in Broomfield, at the Quantocks' southern end.

Nether Stowey & Holford

Most of the Quantock villages feel like forgotten corners of England. Nowhere is this truer than Nether Stowey, Coleridge's former home village, where the most eventful happening is usually the daily postal delivery. Other than a couple of country pubs and a village shop, there's nothing to disturb the peace other than the twitter of birdsong and the occasional rumble of a passing tractor.

Coleridge moved here in 1796 with his wife Sara and son Hartley, setting up home in **Coleridge Cottage** (NT; ☎ 01278-732662; admission £3.20; ☒ 2-5pm Thu-Sun Apr-Sep). William Wordsworth and his sister Dorothy followed a year later, moving into Alfoxden House in Holford. During that year the two poets began work on *Lyrical Ballads* (1798), the short pamphlet that kickstarted the British romantic movement. The artefacts are sparse, but you can wander around several original rooms, and it's a curious feeling to stand in the place where Coleridge probably composed *The Rime of the Ancient Mariner* and *Kubla Khan*.

For accommodation you could try **Stowey Brooke House** (☎ 01278-733356; www.stoweybrooke house.co.uk; 18 Castle St, Nether Stowey; s/d from £35/55; P), with a couple of cottagey rooms set back from a bubbling brook on the main street, but the nicest rooms are at the **Old Cider House** (☎ 01278-732228; www.theoldciderhouse.co.uk; 25 Castle St, Nether Stowey; s £42-55, d £60-80; P), an Edwardian red-brick affair that specialises in breaks for ale enthusiasts; owner Ian runs his own microbrewery.

For more luxury, head half a mile to the **Castle of Comfort** (☎ 01278-741264; www.castle-of -comfort.co.uk; s £40-88, d £99-135; **P** **ℛ**), a Grade II–listed manor set in rolling fields on the northern slopes of the Quantocks.

The small **Quantocks YHA Hostel** (☎ 01278-741224; reservations@yha.org.uk; Sevenacres; dm £11.95; **P**) is 1.5 miles west of Holford. There are only three dorms and a couple of private rooms, so book ahead.

Tucked away in a wooded valley is **Combe House** (☎ 01278-741382; www.combehouse.co.uk; Holford Combe; s £65, d £90-130; **P** **ᗃ** **ℛ**), one of the best-known Quantock retreats. It certainly isn't shy about pampering its guests; the best rooms boast huge four-poster beds and views over wooded gardens, and there's a heated indoor swimming pool, sauna and a country restaurant in gleaming Cornish oak.

Crowcombe

One of the prettiest Quantock villages, Crowcombe still has cottages made of stone and cob (a mixture of mud and straw), many with thatched roofs. The ancient **Church of the Holy Ghost** has wonderful carved 16th-century bench ends with surprisingly pagan themes (the Green Man is common). Part of its spire still stands in the churchyard where it fell when lightning struck in 1725.

Crowcombe is a little short on places to stay and eat – the best option is the **Carew Arms** (☎ 01984-618631; www.thecarewarms.co.uk; s/d £40/65; **P**), which has six newly refurbished upstairs rooms and serves up pub grub (mains £10 to £17.50) including Brixham scallops and four varieties of steak.

There's also a good camp site, the **Quantock Orchard Caravan Park** (☎ 01984-618618; www.quantockorchard.co.uk; Flaxpool; site per tent or caravan £11-18).

Getting There & Away

Bus services around the Quantocks are very limited. Bus 14 travels from Bridgwater to Nether Stowey (40 minutes, four daily Monday to Saturday) en route to Watchet and Williton. Half-hourly bus 28 runs from Taunton to Minehead but only stops at Crowcombe (30 minutes) once daily.

SOMERSET LEVELS

Covering around 250 sq miles to the east and northeast of Taunton, the Somerset Levels is one of the largest wetlands in Britain. Pan-flat, largely treeless and only just above sea level,

it's an important haven for all kinds of rare wildlife, but it's actually not a natural landscape; the environment has been created by centuries of cultivation, and without human intervention the land would quickly return to the natural status quo – peat bog, marsh and reed bed. The fields and pastures are divided by drainage channels known as *rhynes* (pronounced 'reens') and traditional industries such as peat-cutting, reed-harvesting and willow-growing are still practised much as they were during the Middle Ages.

It's a little-explored and beautiful corner of old England, especially in winter when the floods are up and the mists roll in across the wetlands. Until the drainage of the Levels in the early 14th century, the whole area was covered by shallow marsh; hills such as **Burrow Mump**, a 24m-high mound near Burrowbridge, would once have been islands. King Alfred supposedly had his headquarters on the island of **Athelney**, where he legendarily crisped his cakes before defeating the Danes and taking the English throne.

Athelney was once home to an important abbey, which was torn down during the Dissolution along with **Muchelney** (EH; adult/ child £3.20/1.60; ⓧ 10am-6pm Jul-Aug, 10am-5pm Apr-Jun & Sep, 10am-4pm Oct), once the largest abbey in Somerset after Glastonbury. Though largely in ruins, Muchelney has a couple of intriguing features, including the old Abbot's House and a two-storeyed monk's lavatory – one of the only known monastic loos in England.

Important populations of otters, water voles, butterflies, dragonflies and beetles live on the Levels, as well as a huge bird population ranging from sedge warblers to wagtails. Being mostly flat, it's also great for hiking or cycling – various bike trails crisscross the wetlands, including the **Withy Way** (28 miles), the **Peat Moors Cycle Route** (24 miles) and the **Avalon Marshes Cycle Route** (28 miles); the long-distance **River Parrett Trail** between Cheddington and Combwich also crosses the Levels.

You can hire bikes from the **Langport & River Parrett Tourist Office** (☎ 01458-250350; cycling@bowbridgecycles.enta.net; ⓧ 10am-6pm Tue-Sun Apr-Sep, 10am-4pm Oct-Mar), handily plonked along the Withy Way, with several small exhibitions exploring local industries and wetland wildlife, as well as a café that's locally renowned for its home-baked cakes.

THE WONDERFUL SOMERSET WILLOW

The most important local industry around the Somerset Levels is **willow** (locally known as *withy*), a naturally sustainable crop that's been used for centuries to make everything from baskets to beehives, fish traps and pigeon panniers. It's an industry that goes back at least as far as the Iron Age, when settlers used willow crops to build pathways across the boggy marshland – one example, the **Sweet Track**, is thought to date back 6000 years (you can see a replica at the Lakes Village Museum (p107) in Glastonbury – the real McCoy is in the British Museum).

Willow was used by the Romans (who used it for chariots and furniture) and the Celts (who used it for shield-making and coracle-building), and until the arrival of disposable plastics in the mid-1950s it was still used widely across Britain. It's a quintessentially English material – without it the bearskin caps of the Grenadier Guards wouldn't stand up, thatched roofs would be blown off in a breeze, and Marcus Trescothick would find himself playing without a cricket bat. Willow is even a potential solution for tackling climate change – many Swedish villages use it as a biomass fuel, and it's being considered by several British councils as a possible energy resource.

To get to grips with this wonder crop, head for the **Willows & Wetlands Visitor Centre** (☎ 01823-490249; adult/child £2.50/1.25; ☻ 9am-5pm Mon-Sat) in Stoke St Gregory, run by a local family who have been harvesting willow for 175 years. There's a fascinating exhibition with lots of willowy artefacts – look out for the school cane, once known to British schoolkids as the 'Sally Rod', a derivation of its Latin name, *Salix*. If you're lucky, local basket-makers might even be conducting a demonstration.

And if you're driving north along the M5 near Bridgwater, look out for the southwest's answer to the Angel of the North – the **Willow Man**, built by Serena de la Hay in 2000. Unfortunately, the Willow Man has proved less durable than his northern cousin – he was burnt down in 2001, rebuilt, and then rebuilt again in 2006 when it was discovered local birds were plundering him for nest-building materials.

The **Peat Moors Centre** (☎ 01458-860697; Westhay; adult/child £2.50/1.75; ☻ 10am-4.30pm Apr-Oct) explores the history of peat cultivation on the Levels and has replicas of Iron Age houses based on those uncovered at the Glastonbury Lake Village (p107).

Getting There & Away

There's almost no public transport across the Levels, and hardly any proper roads – so you'll either be walking or cycling.

YEOVIL & AROUND

☎ 01935 / pop 41,871

Named after the River Yeo, Yeovil grew up along the old Roman road, the Fosse Way, and during the Middle Ages became a hub for glove-making (hence Yeovil Town Football Club's nickname, the Glovers). During the 20th century it was an important manufacturing centre for the defence industry, which made it a prime target for WWII bombing raids; the scars of postwar reconstruction can still be seen all over town. While there's not much to see in Yeovil itself, it's a useful launch pad for exploring the surrounding area, and has plenty of busy shops to browse on a wet Somerset day.

The **tourist office** (☎ 462991; yeoviltic@southsomerset .gov.uk; Petter's Way) stocks the usual selection of guides, walking booklets and leaflets that list attractions.

Sights

There are several pretty villages around Yeovil, including **East Coker**, famous as the birthplace of William Dampier, the buccaneering sea-captain who was the first Englishman to set foot on New Holland (Australia). The village also contains the ashes of TS Eliot, whose ancestors emigrated from here in the 17th century (one of the *Four Quartets* is named after the town). Just to the west is **West Coker**, once a centre for flax and rope-making, while 5 miles northwest is the Iron Age fort of **Cadbury Castle**, locally rumoured to have been King Arthur's fabled stronghold of Camelot.

Motorheads everywhere will already be acquainted with the name of Haynes, the publisher of ubiquitous car-repair manuals and spiritual guru to many an amateur car restorer. The **Haynes Motor Museum** (☎ 01963-440804; www.haynesmotormuseum.com; Sparkford; adult/child £7.50/4; ⏰ 9.30am-5.30pm Apr-Oct, 10am-4.30pm Nov-Mar) houses a collection of more than 300 vintage motors, from classic Morris Minors through to a huge 'Red Room' filled with scarlet-tinted Lamborghinis and Ferraris. There's also a room devoted to British and American classics – seeing a Mini Cooper and a full-size Cadillac side-by-side is quite an odd experience. The museum is in Sparkford off the A359, around 6 miles northeast from Yeovil.

If you still haven't had your petrol fix, the **Fleet Air Arm Museum** (☎ 840565; www.fleetairarm .com; adult/child £10.50/7.50; ⏰ 10am-5.30pm daily Apr-Oct, 10am-4.30pm Wed-Sun Nov-Mar) houses a huge collection of naval aircraft, spanning the history of sea-going aviation from Sopwiths to Phantom fighters. You can walk onto the flight-deck of the first British-built Concorde and take a simulated flight onto the aircraft carrier HMS *Ark Royal*. The museum is four miles north of Somerset, near Yeovilton.

This extraordinary Elizabethan **Montacute House** (NT; ☎ 823289; montacute@nationaltrust.org.uk; adult/child house £8.80/4.40, garden only £5/2.20; ⏰ house 11am-5pm Wed-Mon mid-Mar-Oct, garden 11am-6pm Wed-Mon mid-Mar-Oct, 11am-4pm Wed-Sun Nov-Mar) was built in the 1590s for Sir Edward Phelips, a Speaker of the House of Commons, and contains some of the finest 16th- and 17th-century interiors in the country. The house is renowned for its plasterwork, chimney-pieces and magnificent tapestries, but the highlight is the Long Gallery, decorated with Elizabethan-era portraits borrowed from the National Portrait Gallery. Bus 681 from Yeovil (20 minutes, hourly Monday to Saturday) to South Petherton passes close by.

The first property acquired by the National Trust, **Barrington Court** (NT; ☎ 01460-241938; Ilminster; adult/child £7/3; ⏰ 11am-5pm Thu-Tue Apr-Sep, 11am-4.30pm Thu-Tue Mar & Oct) packs an impressive Tudor punch. Built in the 16th century for a wealthy London merchant, the house has suffered severe ups and downs (including fires and interior demolitions), but it's been painstakingly restored with original Stuart furnishings and working kitchen gardens. The highlight is the magnificent grounds, laid out by the famous English landscaper Gertrude Jekyll in a series of outside 'rooms' (including a rose and lily garden and a colourful arboretum).

Sleeping & Eating

Greystones Court (☎ 426124; www.greystonescourt .com; 152 Hendford Hill; d £56.50-62) Decent townhouse accommodation in Yeovil itself, with small, traditional B&B rooms that are showing their age (old carpets and dated pine aplenty). Still it's handy for town and won't break the bank.

Barrows Farmhouse (☎ 864576; www.barrowsfarm house.com; East Chinnock; d £64-74; Ⓟ) A sweet double-gabled farmstay 4 miles from Yeovil, run with chaotic attitude by its friendly owner, who's dead proud of the spic-and-span rooms in icy blues and rose pinks. Boutique it isn't, but sometimes a down-home experience is all you're after.

Lord Poulett Arms (☎ 01460-73149; www.lordpoulett arms.com; Hinton St George; s/d £55/89; Ⓟ) This is a glorious stone-fronted Crewkerne pub that's been reinvented with 21st-century flair. It's a hotchpotch of characters; rustic trusses and elm bench seats meet retro sofas and polished chess sets, while the rooms boast Roberts radios, roll-top baths and quirky wallpapers.

Getting There & Away

Bus 54 travels to Taunton (one hour 10 minutes, hourly). Other options are the hourly 60/1 to Ilminster (one hour) via West Coker (10 minutes) and Crewkerne (30 minutes), and the hourly 376 to Bristol (2½ hours) via Glastonbury and Wells. Buses also go to Sherborne and Shaftesbury in Dorset.

EXMOOR NATIONAL PARK

Straddling the borders of Somerset and Devon, one of Britain's original national park – founded in 1954 – is a far gentler (and greener) place than Dartmoor to the south. Crisscrossed by dry stone walls, bottle-green fields and meandering bridleways, it's one of the country's agricultural heartlands, with some farms dating back to the Norman Invasion. Sturdy horned sheep, Exmoor ponies and red deer mill on the hilltops, while stout pubs and country hotels nestle in the steeply wooded coombes. Unsurprisingly, it's a fantastic place for hiking, biking and bird-spotting, and is less well known than some of Britain's other national parks, so it's a great place for walkers who

SCRUMPY STORY

The classic Somerset tipple is **cider**, a traditional drink made from fermented apples that's been getting the English tiddly for at least eight centuries. It comes in many varieties, ranging from dark and sweet to light and tart, but nearly all traditional cider has one thing in common – it's deceptively strong, often twice (or thrice!) the strength of traditional beer. Quaffers beware...

Cider making was most likely introduced to England after the Norman invasion. The name **scrumpy** derives from the practice of using 'scrumped' apples; initially, the term referred to windfall apples, but later came to mean illicitly acquired fruit. Once practically every Westcountry farm – and many a garden shed – had its own cider brewery on the go, but these days most cider is brewed in commercial plants. Though apples are usually the main ingredient, many fruits can be used – one local alternative is **perry**, made from pears.

Though every cider maker has his own practices, the fundamental principles are the same. Once picked (or scrumped!), apples are scratted (ground down) into a pomace (pulp) and then pressed into a firm cake, rather confusingly called the **cheese**. Several cheeses are piled into the cider press and squeezed; the pressed juice is then left to ferment (traditionally in oak casks) for several weeks, et *voilà*, – you've got your scrumpy.

If you fancy trying some true Somerset cider, **Sheppy's Cider** (☎ 01823-461233; www.sheppys cider.com; Bradford-on-Tone; 8.30am-6pm Mon-Sat, 11am-1pm Sun) near Taunton and **Burrow Hill Cider** (☎ 01460-240782; www.ciderbrandy.co.uk; Kingsbury Episcopi; 9.30am-5.30pm Mon-Sat) both have breweries you can visit and, of course, sample the produce. Consult www.somersetcider .co.uk for more ideas.

prefer their trails tranquil. Ditch the mobile and dig the solitude – Exmoor's an escape. We're covering the whole of Exmoor National Park in this section, including Lynton, Lynmouth and the western part of the moor (despite the fact they're actually in Devon).

Orientation

Compared with Britain's other national parks, Exmoor is tiny – 21 miles wide from west to east and just 12 miles from north to south. Waymarked trails crisscross the park and the South West Coast Path runs along the northern side between Minehead and Lynton; the coastline is where you'll also find most of the main towns.

Information

There are five **National Park Authority (NPA) tourist offices** (10am-5pm Easter-Oct, limited hours Nov-Easter):

Blackmoor Gate (☎ 01598-763466; NPCBlackmoorGate@exmoor-nationalpark.gov.uk) This tourist office is planning to move to a new site in Lynmouth soon.

Combe Martin (☎ 01271-883319; NPCCombeMartin@exmoor-nationalpark.gov.uk; Cross St)

County Gate (☎ 01598-741321; NPCCountyGate@exmoor-nationalpark.gov.uk; A39 Countisbury)

Dulverton (☎ 01398-323841; NPCDulverton@exmoor -nationalpark.gov.uk; 7-9 Fore St)

Dunster (☎ 01643-821835; NPCDunster@exmoor -nationalpark.gov.uk; Dunster Steep)

The **Exmoor NPA administrative offices** (☎ 01398-323665; www.exmoor-nationalpark.gov.uk; Exmoor House, Dulverton) publishes the free *Exmoor Visitor* newspaper, which details accommodation, organised activities and contains a handy map. Walking leaflets, trail maps, Ordinance survey (OS) maps and nature guides are sold at the national park centres. The *Golden Walks* series (75p) detail several useful day hikes.

INTERNET RESOURCES

There are several good websites covering Exmoor, in addition the that of the NPA office:

Active Exmoor (www.activeexmoor.com) Info on outdoor sports and listings for upcoming events.

Exmoor Tourist Association (www.exmoor.com) This site has details on accommodation and activities.

Visit Exmoor (www.visit-exmoor.co.uk) Excellent information site with advice on activities, events, accommodation and eating out.

What's On Exmoor (www.whatsonexmoor.com) Local listings and information.

Activities

ADVENTURE & WATER SPORTS

You can sail, windsurf and kayak at **Wimbleball Lake Watersports Centre** (☎ 01398-371460; www.swlakes

trust.org.uk), while **Exmoor Adventure** (☎ 01271-830628) can arrange rock climbing, canoeing and abseiling.

CYCLING

The network of bridleways and quiet lanes makes Exmoor great cycling country, but you're not going to get away without tackling some hills. NPA centres have leaflets on specific routes; popular trails travel through the Brendon Hills, the Crown Estate woodland and along the old Barnstaple railway line.

A new map, *Exmoor for Offroad Cyclists*, rates the main off-road trails using a ski-run-type system ranging from green (easy) to black (terrifying). Pick it up at NPA centres.

Several sections of the National Cycle Network (NCN) cross the park, including the **West Country Way** (NCN Rte 3) from Bristol to Padstow, and the **Devon Coast to Coast Cycle Route** (NCN Rte 27) between Exmoor and Dartmoor. See p116 for details of bike hire.

FISHING

Exmoor's clear rivers are excellent for anglers, stocked with everything from brown trout to wild salmon. You'll need a rod licence and a fishing permit (available from post offices, tourist offices and NPCs). Alternatively, arrange a guided fishing trip for around £80 to £100 per day including equipment:

John Dawson (☎ 01398-331498; Bampton)
Nick Hart (☎ 01398-331660; www.hartflyfishing.co.uk) Near Tiverton.

PONY TREKKING & HORSE RIDING

There are lots of places to hop up on horseback – see the *Exmoor Visitor* for full details. Expect to pay £25 for an hour's lesson, and around £40 for a two-hour hack.

Brendan Manor Stables (☎ 01598-741246) Near Lynton.
Burrowhayes Farm (☎ 01643-862463; www.burrowhayes.co.uk; Porlock)
Dean Riding Stables (☎ 01598-763565; www.deanridingstables.co.uk) Near Blackmoor Gate.
Knowle Riding Centre (☎ 01643-841342; www.knowleridingcentre.co.uk; Dunster)
Outovercott Stables (☎ 01598-753341; www.outovercott.co.uk; Lynton)

WALKING

For most people the best way to explore the park is on foot, and there are any number of routes to test your trail legs. The best-known routes are the **Somerset & North Devon Coast Path** (part of the South West Coast Path) and the Exmoor section of the **Two Moors Way**, which starts in Lynmouth and travels south to Dartmoor.

Part of the 180-mile **Tarka Trail** traverses the park. Join it in Combe Martin and walk to Lynton/Lynmouth, then inland to Brayford and Barnstaple.

The **Coleridge Way** winds for 36 miles through Exmoor, the Brendon Hills and the Quantocks, taking in Coleridge's home at Nether Stowey as well as the village of Porlock.

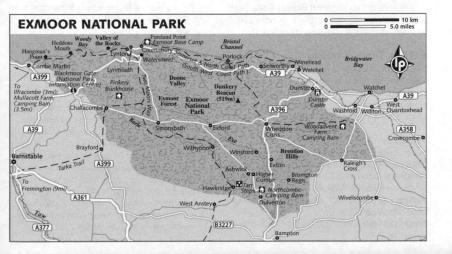

Organised walks run by the NPA are held throughout the year. Contact one of the NPA centres, visit www.exmoor-nationalpark.gov .uk, or see the listings in the *Exmoor Visitor*. The walks take in everything from gentle nature trails to full-blown hikes; costs are £3 for a short walk, £5 for longer walks of four hours or more.

Moorland Tours

Several companies offer 4WD 'safari' trips across the moor. If you're a nature lover or a keen photographer, bespoke bird-watching and deer-watching safaris can be arranged. Half-day trips start at around £25.

Barle Valley Safaris (☎ 01643-851386; www.exmoor wildlifesafaris.co.uk; Dulverton & Minehead)

Discovery Safaris (☎ 01643-863080; www.discovery safaris.com; Porlock)

Exmoor Safari (☎ 01643-831229; www.exmoorsafari .co.uk; Exford)

Sleeping & Eating

Hotels, B&Bs, restaurants and inns are dotted all over the park. If you're backpacking, there are YHA hostels in Minehead and Exford, camp sites along the coast and **YHA camping barns** (☎ bookings 0870 770 8868; per person £6.50) at Woodadvent Farm near Roadwater, Mullacott Farm near Ilfracombe, and Northcombe near Dulverton. The NPA runs **Pinkery Bunkhouse** (☎ 01643-831437; pinkery@exmoor -nationalpark.gov.uk) near Simonsbath, while the NT has **Exmoor Base Camp** (☎ 01598-741101; karen .elkin@nationaltrust.org.uk) near Lynton.

For longer stays, **Exmoor Holiday Group** (www .exmoor-holidays.co.uk) rents cottages, or have a look at www.exmoor-acco mmodation.co.uk.

Getting There & Around

Green travellers will have a tough time on Exmoor, as the bus services leave a lot to be desired. The main routes chunter up and down the coast, and there are practically none to the park's west side.

BICYCLE

Several places around the park hire mountain bikes, including hardtails and full-sus rigs.

Fremington Quay (☎ 01271-372586; www.biketrail.co.uk; Fremington; per day £6.50-24) Delivers bikes to your door.

Pompys (☎ 01643-704077; www.pompyscycles.co.uk; Minehead; per day £12.50-25)

Tarka Trail Cycle Hire (☎ 01271-232 4202; Barnstaple; per day £7-15)

BUS

The *Taunton & West Somerset Public Transport Guide*, free from tourist offices, contains timetables for all the main bus routes.

DULVERTON & AROUND
☎ 01398

Solid country types in Barbour jackets and gumboots stalk the streets of Dulverton, which sits at the southern edge of the park at the meeting of two main rivers, the Exe and Barle. If you're after country equipment, you're in luck – there are tackleshops and gun sellers all over town. The main **NPA tourist office** (☎ 01398-323841; dulvertonvc@exmoor-na tionalpark.gov.uk; 7-9 Fore St; ☻ 10am-5pm Easter-Oct) is opposite the town hall.

Five miles north of Dulverton is one of Exmoor's sweetest time-trap villages, **Winsford**, with a collection of thatch-crowned cottages and wisteria-clad pubs collected around nine packhorse bridges. It's a slice of little England, and makes a gorgeous spot for a pub lunch. The six-belled church is the village's most obvious landmark, but Winsford's main claim to fame is as the birthplace of Ernest Bevin, wartime Minister of Labour and later British Foreign Secretary.

The **Exmoor Pony Centre** (☎ 323093; www.exmoor ponycentre.org.uk; rides £35), in nearby Ashwick, offers rides on Exmoor's diminutive ponies, but they can only carry 76kg, so larger lads will have to settle for feeding them carrots.

To the east of Dulverton is **Wimbleball Lake** (☎ 371460; www.swlakestrust.org.uk), a popular spot for windsurfing, canoeing and other water sports, as well as trout fishing for more leisurely souls.

DULVERTON TO TARR STEPS

There's a stunning 12-mile circular walk that goes along the river from Dulverton to Tarr Steps – an ancient stone clapper bridge haphazardly placed across the River Barle and shaded by gnarled old trees. The bridge was supposedly built by the devil for sunbathing. It's a four- to five-hour trek for the average walker. You can add another three or four hours to the walk by continuing from Tarr Steps up Winsford Hill for distant views over Devon.

Sleeping

Town Mills (☎ 323124; www.townmillsdulverton.co.uk; High St; s incl breakfast £32-46, d incl breakfast £54-60) A smart converted millhouse which trades on its vintage architecture; roof beams and sloping walls make for snug and cosy rooms, and the décor's fittingly rustic. Local jams and fresh-baked loaves on the brekkie table.

Three Acres (☎ 323730; www.threeacrescountryhouse .co.uk; Brushford; s £55-70, d £80-110; ℗) Another peaceful retreat surrounded by woods and lanes a short drive from Dulverton, sprinkled with country essentials: log fires to lounge by, armchairs to sink into, and big linen-wrapped beds to rest those weary bones. It's a tad old-fashioned in places, but full of charm.

Tarr Farm (☎ 01643-851507; www.tarrfarm.co.uk; s/d £65/130; ℗) One of the loveliest getaways on Exmoor, hidden in a birdsong-filled valley near Tarr Steps, 5 miles from Dulverton. Despite the farmhouse appearance, this is a top-class treat: nine rooms in rich creams and yellows, with throw-draped beds, organic bath goodies and old-fashioned bath taps, plus spoils such as home-baked cookies, in-room fridges and DVD players.

Ashwick House (☎ 323868; www.ashwickhouse .com; d £100-150; ℗ 🖳) Still boasting its original William Morris wallpaper and galleried hallway, this handsome Edwardian pile was built for a Bristol merchant and has real historical pizazz. Edwardian fixtures mix with Oriental pieces and gilt Buddhas, while the bedrooms blend silky fabrics with rich colour schemes, cast-iron fireplaces and sparkling bathrooms.

Eating

Lewis' Tea Rooms (☎ 323850; 13 High St; ☼ breakfast & lunch Mon-Sat, dinner Thu-Sat) Cream teas, gooey cakes and piping-hot Welsh rarebits are the top choices at this Exmoor tea-room, where the tables are pine, the china's white and the waitresses are friendlier than Mary Poppins.

Royal Oak (☎ 851455; Winsford; mains £6.50-10) Winsford's thatch-roofed packhorse inn has been doling out pints and pies since the Middle Ages, and it's still a lovely place for Sunday lunch; nestled next to the bubbling Win Brook, with a couple of bars, a tranquil beer garden and solid baguettes.

Tongdam (☎ 323397; 26 High St; mains £8.50-12.50; ☼ lunch & dinner) Probably not what you'd expect to find in rural Dulverton, but this little res-

---

WHEDDON CROSS TO DUNKERY BEACON

The highest point on Exmoor (and in Somerset) is **Dunkery Beacon** (519m), about 4 miles northeast of Exford. The best route up to the summit is from Wheddon Cross; start out at the village car park and follow the back lanes to Dunkery Gate, where you can hike straight up the hill or take a more circuitous route to avoid the worst of the gradient. From the top of the Beacon there are 360-degree views along the Exmoor Coast, inland to the Quantocks and Dartmoor, and even to Wales on the right day. The round-trip walk from Wheddon Cross is 8 miles, and is quite steep in places; wear good shoes and take a picnic for the top.

---

taurant does the best Thai food on Exmoor – classic pad Thai noodles plus adventurous mains, such as deep-fried red snapper and black tiger prawns.

Woods (☎ 324007; 4 Bank Sq; mains £11-17; ☼ lunch & dinner) Rough wood and old oak characterise this much-loved little eatery, which has carved out a devoted local following thanks to its solid country dishes – pork belly, lamb shank, samphire and lentil soup. It's rich, rustic food made for a hiker's tummy.

Getting There & Away

Bus 398 stops at Dulverton six times daily on its way from Minehead (50 minutes) and Dunster (40 minutes) to Tiverton.

EXFORD

☎ 01643

Even by Exmoor standards Exford is a sleepy place, little more than a knot of cottages, a couple of shops and two country inns arranged around a quiet English green. To people on the moor it's best-known for its hunting connections; the Devon and Somerset Staghounds have had their kennels here since 1875, and meets still take place despite the hunting ban. A couple of miles east is **Wheddon Cross**, the best starting point for the slog up to the top of Dunkery Beacon (see the boxed text above).

Sleeping & Eating

Exford YHA Hostel (☎ 0870 770 5828; exford@yha.org .uk; Exe Mead; dm £13; ℗) A brilliant spot near Exford's shops mean this hostel is usually packed with cyclists and walkers; it's a sweet little place, with latticed windows, a convivial lounge and kitchen and Victorian character to boot.

Exmoor House (☎ 841432; www.exmoorhouse.com; Wheddon Cross; s/d £35/70; **P**) Over in Wheddon Cross, this swish little place punches way above its weight; for this kind of cash you wouldn't normally expect so much individuality. Light, contemporary colours and modern furniture in the rooms, chrome taps and checked tiles in the private bathrooms.

Edgcott House (☎ 831495; www.edgcotthouse.co.uk; s £40-42.50, d £70-78; **P**) Bona-fide English eccentricity in a beautiful Exmoor house. Bikes, wonky pictures, abandoned Wellies and antique gramophones are scattered throughout the muddled house, and the owners mix fluster and friendliness in equal doses. It's all ramshackle charm – big tile bathrooms, vintage beds and an amazing 1.5m 'Long Room' await – and then there's the Edgcott marathon for breakfast…

Crown Hotel (☎ 831554; www.crownhotelexmoor .co.uk; Chapel St; s £67.50, d £105-135; **P**) Exford's old 'sporting hotel' has been plying huntsmen and horse riders with sustenance for centuries, but these days you're more likely to see weekend hikers in Gore-Tex. Huge rooms rich with drapes, thick carpets and country prints make this Exford's choicest rural hideaway, and the bar serves up hearty haddock kedgeree, grilled chicken and champ mash.

Exmoor White Horse (☎ 831229; Exford; r £130; **P**) The town's second inn lacks the historical punch of its neighbour, but with its ivy-covered frontage, deer heads and preserved birds, it's still light years away from a Wetherspoon's. Stout food – ham hock, liver terrine, baked fowl – and a great Sunday carvery (mains from £12) keep the bar busy.

Getting There & Away

The 398 bus from Tiverton to Minehead stops at Exford once daily Monday to Saturday. The open-top vintage 400 from Minehead stops at Dunster, Exford and Porlock twice daily on Tuesday, Thursday and summer weekends.

DUNSTER

☎ 01643

After the tourist fizz and family fun of Minehead, Dunster comes as something of a culture shock. Centred around a scarlet-walled castle

and an original medieval yarn market, it's one of Exmoor's oldest villages, sprinkled with bubbling brooks, packhorse bridges and a 16th-century dovecote.

The most obvious landmark is **Dunster Castle** (NT; ☎ 821314; admission castle £6.80, garden & park only £3.70; 🕙 11am-5pm Sat-Wed Mar-Oct, 11am-4pm Nov), originally owned by the aristocratic Luttrell family whose manor encompassed much of northern Exmoor. It's been the subject of repeated remodelling; the gateway is 13th century, but most of the castle (including the turrets and exterior walls) were added during a romantic makeover in the mid-19th century. The interior contains glorious Tudor furnishings, 17th-century plasterwork and a ridiculously grand central staircase, while the terraced gardens have fine views across Exmoor and the coastline. And look out for spooks – the castle's supposedly one of England's most haunted.

Dunster's other attractions include the **St George's Church**, home to the longest rood screen in England, as well a blossom-filled walled garden and a red-brick dovecote, once used for breeding edible squabs (young pigeons) for the castle dinner table. Nearby is a working **watermill** (☎ 821759; Mill Lane; admission £2.60; 🕙 11am-4.45pm daily Jul-Sep, 11am-5pm Sat-Thu Apr-Jun, Oct & Nov). The marshy expanse of **Dunster Beach** is about a mile from the village.

The **NPA tourist office** (☎ 821835; Dunster Steep; 🕙 10am-5pm Easter-Oct) is in the main car park.

Sleeping & Eating

Yarn Market Hotel (☎ 821425; www.yarnmarkethotel .co.uk; s £40, d £60-80; **P**) Mod-cons replace medieval trappings at this modest little hotel. Despite the old-fashioned exterior, the rooms are all motel-modern, finished in plain yellows and off-whites, with generously proportioned bathrooms, deep tubs and well-stocked treat trays.

Millstream Cottage (☎ 821966; www.millstreamcot tagedunster.co.uk; 2 Mill Lane; d £65) Perched above a rushing stream, this Dunster cottage is a delight; it's been newly redone in gingham checks and country creams, with cast-iron bedsteads and dinky furniture jammed in under low-beamed ceilings. There's a private lounge and a grassy garden where owner Sue plies you with homemade cakes and piping-hot tea.

Luttrell Arms (☎ 821555; www.luttrellarms.co.uk; d from £100; **P**) Blimey – this one's a medieval marvel. Huge flagstones, wood trusses and an exposed fireplace in the master suite, while the other four-poster rooms drown in swags, chaises longues and chequered armchairs; the cheaper rooms have less wow-factor. The rustic bar's great for grub and ale, too.

Cobblestones Café (☎ 821595; lunch £5-10; ☺ breakfast & lunch Mon-Fri, dinner Sat) This dinky little café is best for light lunches and tea-time cakes. Baguettes, pâtés and homemade pies dominate the lunchtime menu, and it's also open on Saturday for a set three-course supper.

Reeve's (☎ 821414; mains £14.25-18.95; ☺ dinner) Table tealights, hefty oak girders and worn-wood tables create a bewitchingly cosy atmosphere in this pocket-sized bistro, which conjures up some rustic specials including guinea fowl, fillet of brill and baked onion tartlet.

Getting There & Away

Bus 28 runs from Minehead to Taunton via Dunster hourly Monday to Saturday, and nine times on Sunday. Bus 398 travels from Dunster to Exford (30 minutes, once daily except Sunday) and Dulverton (40 minutes, six daily except Sunday), and to Minehead (50 minutes, six daily except Sunday).

The West Somerset Railway (p109) stops at Dunster during the summer.

MINEHEAD
☎ 01643 / pop 10,300

The classic British seaside is alive and well in Minehead, a vintage seaside resort originally developed for Victorian holidaymakers, and still a favourite summertime getaway for swathes of knobbly-kneed British tourists. Historically a fishing and trading port, Minehead's maritime trade was soaked up by Portishead and Bristol in the 18th century, and the town reinvented itself as a seaside resort following a devastating fire in 1791. With its sweeping promenade, pebbly beach and faded 19th-century air, it's something of an Exmoor oddity – cornets, beach-breaks and paddling on the sands are higher on the agenda than natural splendour, but it's still fun for a sunbathe.

Minehead's best-known landmark is **Butlins** (www.butlins.co.uk), the southwestern outpost of Britain's superkitsch holiday camp. Most of the resort is (believe it or not) booked out throughout the summer, but you can still visit the tourist-friendly facilities, which include a fun fair, go-karts and 10-pin bowling alley.

Nearer town are the flower-filled terraces of **Blenheim Gardens** and peaceful **North Hill**, a small nature reserve where you can wander the walkways or stroll around the 15th-century Church of St Michael. But it's the **beach** that's the main Minehead draw: a mile of pebbly shingle packed with spade-wielding nippers and sunburned trippers in summer, and eerily devoid of life during the winter season. Around the old harbour, kayaks, dinghies and windsurfers are all available for hire.

The West Somerset Railway (p109) terminates in Minehead.

The **tourist office** (☎ 702624; info@mineheadtic .co.uk; 17 Friday St; ☺ 10am-12.30pm & 1.30-5pm) has local brochures and can help out with accommodation.

Sleeping

Beverage trays and battered kettles define most of Minehead's old-school B&Bs; there are lots of places collected around Tregonwell Rd.

Marston Lodge (☎ 702510; www.marstonlodgehotel .com; St Michaels Rd; d £60; ℗) Revel in the kitsch surroundings of this flock-walled, pattern-carpeted guesthouse, overlooking the town near North Hill. The house itself is huge, with double bay windows and a canopied entrance porch; but inside the rooms are pretty standard affairs.

Glendower House (☎ 707144; www.glendower-house .co.uk; 30-32 Tregonwell Rd; d £75-80) The pick of a mixed bag along Tregonwell Rd with clean, chintz-free rooms livened up by wicker chairs, flowers and views of the Exmoor Hills from the rear rooms; ask for the four-poster for the most space.

Getting There & Away

There are lots of buses to and from Minehead, including the 39/300 to Porlock (30 minutes, 11 daily Monday to Saturday) and Lynmouth (one hour, four daily), and the 28/ X28 to Taunton (one hour 20 minutes, at least hourly) via Dunster and Crowcombe.

PORLOCK
☎ 01643

Thatched pubs, cob cottages and quiet shops line the main street of Porlock, the most attractive village in the north of Exmoor.

Historically Porlock was a hub for Exmoor's country communities; farmers tended flocks on the hillsides while fisherman plied their trade from Porlock Weir. It was a favourite stop-off for the romantics, who adored its authentic rural charm; Coleridge was famously interrupted by a mysterious 'person from Porlock' during the composition of *Kubla Khan,* and he subsequently never finished the poem. These days the country atmosphere is still the main attraction, and the village is ever-busy with sightseers and coastal strollers.

The village of **Selworthy**, 2.5 miles east of Porlock, forms part of the 19-sq-mile Holnicote Estate, the largest NT-owned area of land on Exmoor. Though its cob-and-thatch cottages look ancient, in fact the village was entirely rebuilt in the 19th century by the local philanthropist and landowner Thomas Acland to provide accommodation for elderly workers on his estate.

Porlock's **tourist office** (☎ 863150; www.porlock.co.uk; West End, High St; ☷ 10am-5pm Mon-Sat, 10am-1pm Sun Apr-Oct, 10.30am-1pm Tue-Fri, 10am-2pm Sat Nov-Mar) is a mine of local knowledge, and is also the point of contact for info on the Coleridge Way.

The tiny **Dovery Manor Museum** (High St; admission free; ☷ 10am-1pm & 2-5pm Mon-Fri, 10am-noon & 2.30-4.30pm Sat May-Oct) is housed in a pretty, 15th-century building, and exhibits artefacts and interesting photos of the village.

Sleeping & Eating

Reines House (☎ 862913; www.reineshouse.co.uk; d £47) Cute and ridiculously cheap rooms in a brick B&B opposite Porlock's church; the colours and fixtures are all standard-issue (pine, pastel, plain), but it's brilliant value this near to the village.

Ship Inn (☎ 862507; www.shipinnporlock.co.uk; High St; s/d £30/70; Ⓟ) Coleridge and pal Robert Southey both downed pints in this venerable thatched Porlock pub, so you'll be in illustrious company if you drop by – you can even sit in 'Southey's Corner'. Substantial pub food – mainly steaks, roasts and stews – are served in the wood-filled bar, and there are 10 surprisingly light rooms in pine and cream.

Andrews on the Weir (☎ 863300; www.andrewsontheweir.co.uk; Porlock Weir; 2-/3-course menu £31.50/38.50) Exmoor's most famous restaurant is nestled behind the Porlock breakwater, and it's a sophisticated spoil. The much-lauded

chef Andrew Dixon sources all his produce from local farms and fishing boats; expect ham hock, Cornish brill and Devon duck in superstarchy surroundings. The rooms (£100 to £180) are less starry, but most have weir views.

Getting There & Away

Bus 39/300 runs from Lynmouth to Porlock (50 minutes, four daily Monday to Saturday) and on to Minehead.

LYNTON & LYNMOUTH
☎ 01598

Sheltering under tree-clad cliffs on Exmoor's northwestern corner, the bustling little seaside town of Lynmouth – known to Victorian holidaymakers as 'Little Switzerland' – boasts one of the prettiest locations on the north Devon coastline. It's a picture of peace and tranquillity today, but in 1952 the village was devastated by a sudden flash flood that swept most of the town into the sea and killed 34 people. Even now the flood is a surprisingly common topic of conversation. But these are happier times for Lynmouth; it's a must-see stop for Exmoor coach tours and day-trippers, filled with ice-cream sellers, fudge shops and doily-clad tearooms. Slightly more sophisticated is the twin town of Lynton, which sits on the bluffs above Lynmouth. Catch the water-operated cliff railway or test your legs on the twisting cliff path.

The **tourist office** (☎ 0845 660 3232; info@lyntourism.co.uk; Lynton Town Hall, Lee Rd; ☷ 10am-4pm Mon-Sat, 10am-2pm Sun) is in Lynton and publishes the *Lynton & Lynmouth Scene* (www.lyntonandlynmouthscene.co.uk), a free newspaper with accommodation, eating and activities listings.

There's a small **NPA tourist office** (☎ 752509; The Esplanade; ☷ 10am-5pm Apr-Jun, Sep & Oct, 10am-9pm Jul & Aug) near Lynmouth harbour.

Sights

For background on the flood, head for the **Lyn & Exmoor Museum** (☎ 752317; St Vincent's Cottage, Market St, Lynton; adult/child £1/20p; ☷ 10am-12.30pm & 2-5pm Mon-Fri, 2-5pm Sun), where you can view a scale model of the village and browse through an archive of photos and newspaper clippings.

Just inland from the harbour is the **Glen Lyn Gorge** (☎ 753207; adult/child £4/3; ☷ Easter-Oct), the steepest of the two valleys into Lynmouth. Several lovely river walks follow the course of the shady valley; look out for the miniature hydroelectric power station, which feeds electricity back to the national electricity grid.

The **Cliff Railway** (☎ 753486; www.cliffrailway lynton.co.uk; one way/return £1.75/2.75; ☒ 8.45am-7pm Easter-Nov) is an amazing piece of Victorian engineering designed by George Marks, a pupil of Brunel. Two cars linked by a steel cable descend or ascend the slope according to the amount of water in their tanks. It's been running like clockwork since 1890, and it's still the best way to commute between the two villages. The views aren't bad, either.

If you wish to continue into Devon along the north coast, turn to p211.

Sleeping

The twin towns have plenty of places to stay; most of the B&Bs are on Lee Rd in Lynmouth, while there are touristy hotels are near the Lynton waterfront.

Sea View Villa (☎ 753460; www.seaviewvilla.co.uk; 6 Summer House Path; s £40, d £50-90; ☒) This place isn't shy about showing off – it's a luxury pamper-pad, housed in a fine Georgian villa near the Lynmouth waterfront, with rooms in sophisticated stripes and regal shades of 'champagne', 'berry' and 'ginger', plus deluge showers, inch-thick carpets and bathstuffs sealed with champagne corks.

Victoria Lodge (☎ 753203; www.victorialodge.co.uk; Lee Rd; r £60-90) Another B&B with regal ambitions – all the rooms are named after royal princesses and strut with patterned pelmets, frills and padded cushions, while the choice of breakfasts is fit for a king – eggs Benedict, maple pancakes and an Exmoor 'Works' that'll keep you stuffed till suppertime.

St Vincent Lodge (☎ 752244; www.st-vincent-hotel .co.uk; Castle Hill; d £65; ℗) No sea view, but this classy lodge hotel is still our favourite Lynton base. The house has plenty of history – it was built by a sea captain who sailed alongside Nelson – and the décor's suitably classic, with plenty of glossy antiques, vintage chairs and oil paintings dotted around. Downstairs there's a sophisticated bistro run by the hotel's Belgian owner, where Somerset ingredients are served with a Gallic twist.

Hunters Inn (☎ 763230; www.thehuntersinn.net; Heddon Valley; r £80-130; ℗) Beside the main road up the Heddon Valley, this is one of Exmoor's best-known coaching inns, and if you're looking for country character you won't be disappointed; choose a rear room for views over tumbling hills, and sample venison steak in the oak-crammed bar.

Tors Hotel (☎ 753236; www.torslynmouth.co.uk; Tors Park; r per person £102-144; ℗ ☒) It's a little faded, but this grand old Victorian getaway still has the most stunning position in Lynmouth, perched in woods on the hillside, with three levels of rooms ranging from dated 'Countisbury' to a fab baronial suite.

LYNTON WALKS

Lynton has excellent short walks and easy access to some longer routes; the South West Coast Path, the Coleridge Way and the Tarka Trail all pass through, and Lynmouth is the official starting point of the Two Moors Way.

The most popular walk is the mile-long hike to the dramatic **Valley of the Rocks**, described by the poet laureate Robert Southey as 'rock reeling upon rock, stone piled upon stone, a huge terrifying reeling mass'. Many of the tortuous rock formations have been named over the years – look out for the Devil's Cheesewring and Ragged Jack – and the valley is also home to a population of feral goats. Continuing west you'll reach the beautiful rocky cove of **Woody Bay**, and real trail junkies can strike out for **Hangman's Point**, the highest point on the South West Coast Path – it's 8 miles west of Lynton near Combe Martin.

There are other trails to the lighthouse at **Foreland Point**, and to **Watersmeet**, 2 miles upriver from Lynmouth, where there's a handily placed National Trust (NT) teashop housed in a Victorian fishing lodge.

Inland from Lynton towards Parracombe is the **Heddon Valley**, a beautiful NT valley, with a trail leading down to the isolated cove of Heddonsmouth. The **NT centre** (☎ 763402; heddonvalley@ nationaltrust.org.uk; ☒ 11am-5pm Mar-Oct) is next to the Hunter's Inn, and organises regular walks, as well as courses in rural skills such as hedge-laying and coppicing.

You're paying a lot for the view – but it *is* quite a view.

Eating

Vanilla Pod (☎ 752460; Queen St; coffee & cakes £5) This lively café is more about lattes and patisseries than cream teas and scones; the décor's bright and modern and the tables are reassuringly frill-free.

Greenhouse Restaurant (☎ 753358; 6 Lee Rd; mains £5-12) Brit classics are the mainstays at this Lynton lunch room, filled with armchairs, old barometers and original leaded windows. Hand-cut sandwiches (prawn with brandy mayo, stilton and bacon, cheese and onion marmalade) are available, plus steak pie and pork bangers, all washed down with a pot of Darjeeling.

Eat Moor (☎ 752424; 3 Watersmeet Rd, Lynmouth; mains from £8) Lynmouth's top heavy on teashops, so this bold new entry makes a welcome change. Fiery colours and the odd Eastern knick-knacks complement the spicy flavours – tuck into a Cajun steak, Moroccan tagine or pan-seared monkfish.

Getting There & Away

Bus 39/300 runs from Lynmouth to Minehead (one hour 10 minutes) via Porlock (50 minutes) four times daily Monday to Saturday. Bus 300 also goes west to Ilfracombe.

The most scenic route to Porlock is the steep, twisting road that hugs the coast all the way from Lynmouth. The stunning scenery along the way is worth the £2 toll, and you get to avoid the notoriously steep descent via Porlock Hill.

Dorset

Bypassed by many heading west, Dorset is actually the essence of England – a lush, rippling chessboard of fields sprinkled with ancient villages and fringed by a silver sea. It evokes Shakespeare, Hardy – and the British TV classic the *Vicar of Dibley*. Bards and kindly curates aside, Thomas Hardy was born here and a thinly disguised Dorset weaves through his writings like a literary seam, while his notebooks, possessions and former homes can be seen in Dorchester.

The county's shoreline also inspires: a glittering World Heritage Site Jurassic Coast, extraordinary for its beaches, beauty and an exposed geological timeline which covers 185 million years in just 95 miles. This coastal classroom presents a dizzying variety of landscapes: beaches with fossils ripe for the picking, an awe-inspiring 17-mile pebble ridge, atmospheric limestone quarries and exquisite sea-carved coves and stacks around Durdle Door. It's a coast to get stuck into; hike precipitous paths, kayak under creamy white cliffs and skim around Olympic-class sailing venues.

Tear yourself away from the sea to find a monumental Iron Age hillfort, bewitching ruined castles, stately churches and an audacious chalk figure who leaves nothing to the imagination. Then amid all this history, seek out the epitome of modern England: Bournemouth. This former preserve of the blue-rinse brigade is now a hedonistic paradise or stag-and-hen party hell. Whatever your view, it certainly makes a statement.

HIGHLIGHTS

- Unearth your own ammonite in **Lyme Regis** (p160), fossil epicentre of the **Jurassic Coast** (see the boxed text, p155)
- Swim under the spectacular rock arch at **Durdle Door** (p137)
- Explore **Maiden Castle** (p150), an awe-inspiring Iron Age hillfort
- Soak up the serenity of the mellow, yellow abbey town of **Sherborne** (p151)
- Fall in love with **Corfe Castle** (p136), an utterly romantic ruin
- Giggle at the supermacho **Cerne Giant** (p150) chalk figure
- Trace through Thomas Hardy's lyrical landscape around **Dorchester** (boxed text, p140)

■ POPULATION: 701,800	■ ICE CREAMS SOLD ON SUNNY DAY, BOURNEMOUTH: 90,000	■ AVE SUMMER HOURS OF SUNSHINE: 619

DORSET

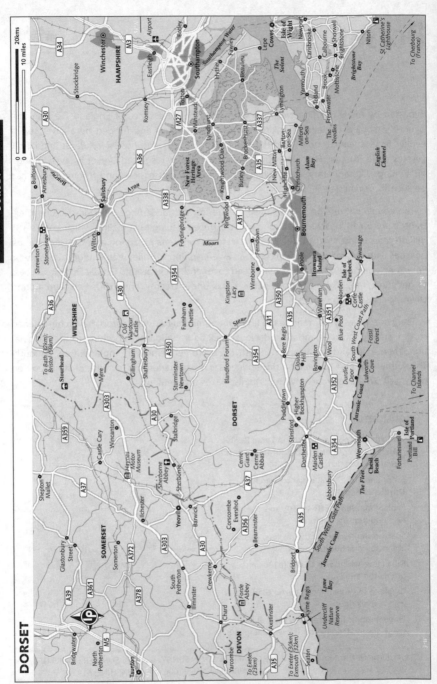

Orientation & Information

Dorset spans the coast from Lyme Regis on the western (Devon) border, to Christchurch; meeting Hampshire on the east. Dorchester, the county town, sits in between and is the most central base for exploring, but Lyme Regis, Bournemouth or Weymouth will suit those who prefer the coast. For Dorset-wide transport, see p296 and p298.

There are several useful Dorset websites to help with planning your explorations:

Dorset County Council (www.dorset-cc.gov.uk) Find information about services available across Dorset.

Rural Dorset (www.ruraldorset.com) A guide to Dorset's lesser-known spots.

West Dorset (www.westdorset.com) District council's guide to all things in the west of the county.

BOURNEMOUTH & AROUND

Dorset's big conurbation and its hinterland form a heady holiday cocktail – a rich mix of contrasting ingredients that conjure wildly different atmospheres. With its candy floss and carousels, beaches, bingo and arcades, Bournemouth is classic British seaside with one heck of a twist. At times it parties so hard it's a nation's drinking problem personified. Poole, a few miles west, is less manic and also more moneyed – its Sandbanks district has some of the most expensive properties in the world. Christchurch, on Bournemouth's eastern fringe, is different again; leafy, calm and graced by a fine priory church. A few miles west of Poole, layered drinks are replaced by a layering of geological time – boat trips along the Jurassic Coast shuttle past 140-million-year-old rocks sculpted, especially around Durdle Door, into extraordinary shapes by the sea. Inland, prosperous Wimborne boasts a fine Norman minster, Corfe a bewitching ruined castle, while red-brick Wareham offers the chance to get on the trail of one of the 20th century's most enigmatic figures, Lawrence of Arabia.

BOURNEMOUTH

☎ 01202 / pop 163,600

In Bournemouth four worlds collide: old folks, families and corporate delegates meet club-loads of boozers out on a bender.

Sometimes the edges rub – painfully. On weekend evenings parts of town transform into a massive stag-and-hen party frenzy; full of angels with L plates and blokes in frocks, blonde wigs and sling backs. Although the party-goers clearly revel in it, the extent of the binging is causing a headache for some guesthouse owners who are fed up with having to nurse the damage hangover. But there's also a much sunnier side to the town. In 2007 a nationwide survey revealed Bournemouth had the happiest residents in the UK – thanks partly to its glorious 7-mile sandy beach. The visiting bucket 'n' spade brigade loves that coastal strip too; delighting in promenading, sand-castle-building and swimming. And Bournemouth has just added another attraction – Europe's first artificial surf reef is set to bring even bigger barrels and amped-up board riders to the town.

History

Bournemouth was effectively born around 1810 when local landowner Lewis Tregonwell built a summer residence here. Initially the select settlement grew slowly – shops weren't allowed and tradesmen had to visit from neighbouring Christchurch and Poole. By the mid-1800s Bournemouth had grown into one of the largest Victorian resorts in Britain, noted for its chines (sharp-sided valleys), which were lined with holiday villas. The ornamental Pleasure Gardens in the heart of Bournemouth, and at Boscombe and Alum Chine, are the most obvious reminder of its genteel golden age, although most of its Victorian architecture has been smothered by 20th-century development.

Orientation & Information

Bournemouth stretches out, like so many sunbathers, along the coast towards Poole in the west and Christchurch to the east. The pier marks the central seafront area, the town centre and train station are to the northeast.

Bournemouth Library (☎ 454848; 22 The Triangle; ⊙ 10am-7pm Mon, 9.30am-7pm Tue, Thu & Fri, 9.30am-5pm Wed) Free internet access.

Cyber Place (☎ 290099; 25 St Peter's Rd; per hr £2; ⊙ 9.30am-midnight)

Tourist office (☎ 0845 051 1700; www.bournemouth .co.uk; Westover Rd; ⊙ 10am-5.30pm Mon-Fri, till 6pm Jul & Aug, 10.30am-5pm Sun year-round)

DORSET

Sights & Activities

Backed by 3000 deck chairs, Bournemouth's big draw is its 7-mile sandy **beach**. Regularly clocking up seaside awards, it stretches from Southborne in the far east to Alum Chine in the west – an immense promenade backed by ornamental gardens, cafés and toilets. It also prides itself on two piers (Bournemouth and Boscombe). Around Bournemouth Pier you can be part of centuries of tradition and hire beach **chalets** (☎ 451781; per day £22.50; ⏰ 9am-6pm Apr-Oct), deck chairs (per day £2), windbreaks (£2) and parasols (£4), as well as sit-on-board **kayaks** (☎ 07970 971867; per 30min £5). **Bournemouth Surf School** (☎ 0800 043 7873; www.bournemouthsurf school.co.uk; ⏰ Feb-Nov) operates from the beach just east of Bournemouth Pier and runs surf

lessons (per three hours £35) and half-day bodyboarding sessions (£25).

Bournemouth has been busy building itself an **artificial surf reef** – the first one in Europe. It involves 60m-long sausage-shaped bags being lowered into the sea just east of Boscombe Pier, then being pumped full of 1000 tonnes of sand. The aim is to produce heavy-breaking, barrelling 3m waves – a challenging ride. The accompanying £8 million redevelopment at Boscombe Spa Village is set to add a new wave of surf shops and restaurants to the mix.

The **Oceanarium** (☎ 311933; www.oceanarium.co .uk; adult/child £8/5.50; ⏰ 10am-6pm) brings you eye-to-eye with mean-looking sharks, massive moray eels and giant turtles. Underwater tunnels, touch-screen games and feeding

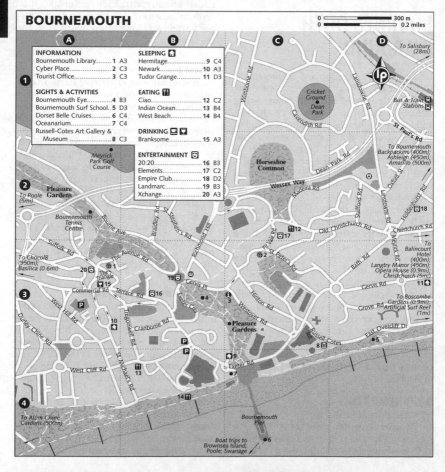

BOURNEMOUTH

0 — 300 m
0 — 0.2 miles

INFORMATION	
Bournemouth Library	1 A3
Cyber Place	2 A3
Tourist Office	3 C3

SIGHTS & ACTIVITIES	
Bournemouth Eye	4 B3
Bournemouth Surf School	5 D3
Dorset Belle Cruises	6 C4
Oceanarium	7 C4
Russell-Cotes Art Gallery & Museum	8 C3

SLEEPING 🏠	
Hermitage	9 C4
Newark	10 A3
Tudor Grange	11 D3

EATING 🍴	
Ciao	12 C2
Indian Ocean	13 B4
West Beach	14 B4

DRINKING 🍺 🍷	
Branksome	15 A3

ENTERTAINMENT 🎭	
20:20	16 B3
Elements	17 C2
Empire Club	18 D2
Landmarc	19 B3
Xchange	20 A3

To Salisbury (28mi)

Bus & Train Stations

To Bournemouth Backpackers (400m); Ashleigh (450m); Amarillo (500m)

To Balincourt Hotel (400m); Langtry Manor (450m); Opera House (0.9mi); Christchurch (5mi)

To Boscombe Gardens (0.9mi); Artificial Surf Reef (1mi)

To Poole (5mi)

To Chocol8 (950m); Basilica (0.6mi)

To Alum Chine Gardens (500m)

Boat trips to Brownsea Island; Poole; Swanage

Bournemouth Pier

Pleasure Gardens

Meyrick Park Golf Course

Cricket Ground • Dean Park

Horseshoe Common

Bournemouth Tennis Centre

sessions mean you meet fish from habitats ranging from the Amazon to Key West, via the inky depths of the deep-sea abyss. Huge fun and educational too.

Between April and September **Dorset Belle Cruises** (☎ 558550; www.dorsetcruises.co.uk) operates a range of trips from Bournemouth Pier. The pick is a 2½-hour cruise (adult/child £12/6, two to three daily) to the sheer white chalk cliffs at Old Harry – the start of the Jurassic Coast (boxed text, p155). It also runs ferries to Swanage (return adult/child £12/6, one to three daily), Poole (£7/2, one to two daily) and Brownsea Island (p130; £7/2, two to four daily).

The **Russell-Cotes Art Gallery & Museum** (☎ 451858; www.russell-cotes.bournemouth.gov.uk; Russell-Cotes Rd; admission free; ☺ 10am-5pm Tue-Sun) is an ostentatious mix of Italianate villa, Scottish baronial pile and Japanese gardens. It was built at the end of the 1800s for Merton and Annie Russell-Cotes as somewhere to showcase the remarkable range of souvenirs gathered on their world travels – look out for the plaster version of the Parthenon frieze by the stairs, Maori woodcarving and Persian tiles. The house is also dripping with Victorian art and paintings by Rossetti, Edwin Landseer and William Frith.

Bournemouth's **Pleasure Gardens** are one bit of the Victorian town that has survived – they're even Grade II–listed. This colourful belt of greenery, shrubs and herbaceous perennials stretches 1.5 miles northwest from the seafront. Tucked into the gardens is the **Bournemouth Eye** (☎ 314539; www.bournemouthballoon.com; Lower Gardens; adult/child £10/6; ☺ 7.20am-11pm Apr-Sep). Some say a trip in this hot-air balloon can cure vertigo. As ascents to 150m last only about 15 minutes, at least you'll find out really fast if they're right or not. The views from the top encompass 25 miles and are amazing.

Sleeping

Bournemouth overflows with hotels and B&Bs. While many aren't going to win design awards, there are a few winners as well. There's a range of budget B&Bs on Frances and St Michael's Rds.

Bournemouth Backpackers (☎ 299491; www.bournemouthbackpackers.co.uk; 3 Frances Rd; dm £13; ☐) The dorm rooms in this hostel inside a small suburban house may be plain (expect aluminium bunk beds), but it's cheap and friendly. Reception is only open from 5pm to 6pm between Sunday and Friday.

Newark (☎ 294989; www.thenewarkhotel.co.uk; 65 St Michael's Rd; s from £28, d £35-50) A courtyard packed with flowers leads into lashings of Victoriana: gold-flock wallpaper, deep-red carpets, glinting chandeliers and gilt picture frames. It's toned down a touch in the bedrooms, but the modern fabrics and wicker chairs are still comfy. Some rooms share bathrooms.

Amarillo (☎ 553884; www.amarillohotel.co.uk; 52 Frances Rd; s £25-45, d £50-90, f £80; P ☐) A rarity: a budget Bournemouth B&B with style. Neutral tones are complemented by tweaks of minimalist chic: abstract painting, beige throws and arrangements of willow. Rooms include two singles, a triple and one sleeping four – some have shared bathrooms.

Ashleigh (☎ 558048; www.ashleighhotels.com; 6 Southcote Rd; s £40, d £50-73; P ☐) Largely anonymous décor (think lots of pine) is jazzed up by bright curtains and bedspreads; the bathrooms are modern and gleaming. There are touches of B&B nostalgia as well, with trouser presses in some rooms and wall-mounted, boxlike hairdryers.

Tudor Grange (☎ 291472; www.tudorgrangehotel.co.uk; 31 Gervis Rd; s £45-52, d £60-80, f £100; P) A superb, pint-sized baronial pile where hundreds of years of history waft from the panelled walls and grand staircase. Rooms are either antique and flowery or historic with a twist – old oak meets buff throws. Bizarrely, the whole house was moved, brick by brick, from Berkshire in 1927.

Balincourt Hotel (☎ 552962; www.balincourt.co.uk; 58 Christchurch Rd; s/d from £50/80; P ✗) Impeccable attention to detail sets this late Victorian B&B apart from the rest – even the china on the tea tray is hand painted to match each room's colour scheme. The décor is bright and tasteful, respecting both the house's heritage and modern antifrill sensibilities.

our pick **Langtry Manor** (☎ 553887; www.langtrymanor.com; Derby Rd; s £79-148, d £98-236; P ☐) A hotel with a delicious whiff of royal indiscretion. Built by Edward VII for his mistress Lillie Langtry, it immerses you in a world of opulent grandeur – from the red carpet rolled out in the entrance to the immense chandeliers and intricately carved woods inside. The rooms are named after Lillie's friends and contemporaries (Oscar Wilde, Ellen Terry, Sarah Bernhardt) and ooze Edwardian elegance, with modern touches – recessed lights and Jacuzzi

DORSET

DORSET

baths. The King's Suite is a real jaw-dropper: a monumental, climb-up-to-get-in four-poster bed and a wood-and-tile fireplace big enough to fit two seats inside.

Hermitage (☎ 557363; www.hermitage-hotel.co.uk; Exeter Rd; s £58-69, d £116-150; P 🖳) Around 100m from the sea, the public rooms of this cream and blue hotel are all cosy elegance – think soft leather armchairs, gold brocade and wood panels. The airy bedrooms are more modern and feature light fabrics and gold tassels – about half have pier views.

Eating

Bournemouth really can't be described as awash with fine eateries, but you can still tuck into a good meal in town.

Chocol8 (☎ 766000; Westbourne Arcade, 61 Poole Rd; ☻ 10am-5.50pm Mon-Sat) Heaven: a café that doubles as a chocolatier. Sip your cappuccino surrounded by shocking-pink walls, tiny tables and hundreds of multicoloured, gift-wrapped sweet temptations.

Indian Ocean (☎ 311222; 4 West Cliff Rd; mains £8-13; ☻ lunch & dinner) Don't be fooled by this place's unimpressive glass frontage – the interior is modern and funkily lit and the menu includes unusual Karai and Bangladeshi specials, as well as tried and tested Indian favourites.

Ciao (☎ 555657; 144 Old Christchurch Rd; mains £8-14; ☻ lunch & dinner) A cool hangout with slabs of red paint on the walls, a huge glass-backed bar piled high with bottles and tables that spill out onto the street. The food is firmly focused on pizza, pasta and gourmet panini.

Basilica (☎ 757722; 73 Seamoor Rd; 3-course menu £13.95; ☻ Mon-Sat) The menu at this groovy bistro visits more Mediterranean countries than your average InterRailer – expect meze, Parma ham parcels, grilled haloumi and pasta with chorizo. The brick-lined interior

is dotted with jars of olives bigger than your head and tables hacked out of single chunks of wood.

ourpick West Beach (☎ 587785; West Promenade; mains £21) A firm favourite with the foodie crowd, this buzzy restaurant delivers both the best views and the best meals in town. The seafood is exemplary: rock oysters with shallot vinegar; monkfish medallions with Parma ham; and a seafood platter crammed with crab claws, lobster, razor clams and crevettes (£30 per person). The décor is deliciously crisp – whites, blues and blond wood – and it's so close to the beach, the sand drifts up to the doorway.

Drinking & Entertainment

Trying to find a traditional pub in the centre of Bournemouth is like trying to find a sober soul on a Saturday night – instead it's all chain bars and cheesy clubs. Most of the main venues are clustered around Fir Vale Rd, St Peter's Rd and Old Christchurch Rd.

Landmarc (☎ 589868; www.thelandmarc.com; Exeter Rd; ☻ 7pm-1am daily plus noon-5pm Sat & Sun) The preacher wouldn't recognise it. This vibrant bistro-cum-music venue is set in a massive former church – now the stained glass merges with red neon. Acts are a mix of acoustic and tribute bands, with comedy on Wednesday. The menu's full of tasty café staples (mains £9): Swiss burger and fries, grilled tuna steak and Thai chicken curry.

Opera House (☎ 399922; www.operahouse.co.uk; Boscombe Arcade, 570 Christchurch Rd) This gorgeously renovated 19th-century theatre mixes Victorian design with an ultracool lighting system. The line-up features a cross-section of music (jazz meets rude-boy punk) and comedy.

Other clubs:

Elements (☎ 311178; Fir Vale Rd; ⊙ till 3am or 4am) Massive queues and club anthems are the mainstays at Bournemouth's biggest club.

Empire Club (☎ 554566; 24-26 Holdenhurst Rd) This is the home of techno, trance House as well as Drum and Bass.

20:20 (☎ 317818; 4 Terrace Rd) Former casino with varied programme – DJ sets and rock, breakbeat, house and hip-hop.

Getting There & Away

National Express runs from most major towns and cities, including Bristol (£15, four hours, one daily), Exeter (£16.60, 3½ hours, three daily), London (£18, 2¼ hours, hourly), and Oxford (from £31, three hours, two daily).

Bus X3 runs half-hourly from Salisbury (1¼ hours) and on to Poole (20 minutes) every hour. The X34/35 comes from Southampton (two hours, five daily Monday to Saturday, plus two on Sunday). Many buses go between Bournemouth and Poole (15 minutes). Bus 150 goes to Sandbanks (30 minutes, hourly Monday to Saturday, six on Sundays) and on to Swanage (one hour).

Trains run every half-hour from London Waterloo (£35, two hours); half of these continue on to Poole (10 minutes), Dorchester South (£8.60, 45 minutes) and Weymouth (£10.90, one hour).

POOLE

☎ 01202 / pop 138,288

Just a few miles to the west of Bournemouth at Poole, the smell of chip vinegar is replaced by the heady aroma of money – the town's Sandbanks district constitutes one of the most expensive chunks of real estate in the world. The centre of Poole also has a smarter air than at breezy Bournemouth – impossibly pricey motor cruisers tie up alongside yachts and pleasure boats; a bobbing backdrop to an agreeable old quay packed with pubs and restaurants. The town is also the gateway to miles of sandy beach, some exhilarating water sports and a fantastic island, all ready for your exploration.

Orientation & Information

Poole gathers round an immense natural harbour, with Sandbanks 3 miles southeast beside the sea.

Central Library (☎ 262421; Dolphin Centre; 30min free; ⊙ 9am-5.45pm Mon-Fri, till 4.45pm Sat) Has internet access.

Tourist office (☎ 253253; www.pooletourism.com; Poole Quay; ⊙ 9.15am-6pm Mon-Fri Jul & Aug, 10am-5pm Mar-Jun, Sep-Nov, till 4pm Sat year-round) On the central quay.

Sights & Activities

BROWNSEA ISLAND

This 200-hectare **island** (NT; ☎ 707744; www .nationaltrust.org.uk/brownsea; adult/child £4.70/2.30; ⊙ 10am-6pm late Jul & Aug, 10am-5pm late Mar-late Jul & Sep, 10am-4pm Oct) played a key role in a worldwide movement famous for three-fingered salutes, shorts and toggles. Lord Baden-Powell staged the first ever scout camp here in 1907. Slap-bang in the middle of Poole Harbour, the island's heath and woodlands are home to peacocks, red squirrels and red deer. There are trails to explore as well as guided walks (at 2pm in July and August) on subjects ranging from the island during the war to smugglers and pirates.

Several operators ply the ferry route to the island – try **Brownsea Island Ferries** (☎ 01929-462383; www.brownseaislandferries.com; Poole Quay), whose boats run from Poole Quay (adult/child return £7.50/5) and Sandbanks (£4.50/3.50). Both services operate when the island is open – the last boat is about 4.30pm.

BOAT TRIPS

Brownsea Island Ferries runs boats to Sandbanks from Poole Quay (adult/child return £7.50/4.50, half-hourly, late-March to October) and cruises along the coast (£12.50/5); look out for the Old Harry Rocks trip. These limestone stacks have been separated from each other by sea erosion and signal the start of the Jurassic Coast.

POOLE OLD TOWN & HARBOUR

A pleasant place to dawdle, Poole's old town and harbour are lined with pubs, restaurants and shops, often in grand old 18th-century buildings. The **Waterfront Museum** (☎ 262600; 4 High St; admission free; ⊙ 10am-5pm Mon-Sat, noon-5pm Sun Apr-Oct) charts the town's history, with exhibits on smuggling, pirates and the distinctive Poole Pottery. It also displays an intriguing hand-chiselled, Iron Age log boat, dredged up from the harbour.

DORSET

DORSET

WATER SPORTS

Courses in windsurfing and power-kiting (£45/79 per three hours/day) are offered at **H₂O Sports** (☎ 733744; www.h2o-sports.co.uk; 91 Salterns Rd). **FC Watersports Academy** (☎ 708283; www .fcwatersports.co.uk; Sandbanks) hires out kayaks (£10 per hour) and sailing dinghies (£20 per hour). It also offers tuition in windsurfing (from £25 per hour), has kitesurfing classes (£100 per day) as well as a two-day starter sailing course (£165).

Sailing courses held at **Moonfleet** (☎ 0800 091369; www.moonfleet.net; Cobbs Quay Marina, Hamworthy) include those for beginners (£180/395 per two/five days). You can also cling to a jet ski with **Absolute Aqua** (☎ 666118; www.abso luteaqua.co.uk; Parkstone Marina, Hamworthy) from £135 a day, or try a bit of wakeboarding with **Surface2Air** (☎ 738448; www.s2as.com; 14 Station Rd; per 30 min £40).

Sleeping

Beacon Hill (☎ 631631; www.beaconhilltouringpark .co.uk; Blandford Rd North; sites £20; ☻ Apr-Sep; ▯ ☻) Campers should head to this site 3 miles northwest of town.

Burleigh (☎ 673889; www.theburleigh.co.uk; 76 Wimborne Rd; s £27-35, d £45-50; ▯ ▯) It's a good, budget B&B. Bright bedrooms feature floral fabrics, dark pine and peach; some are enlivened by rocking chairs and dashes of orange. It has parking and free wi-fi and is popular with visiting members of the Bournemouth Symphony Orchestra.

Quayside (☎ 683733, 07710 249609; 9 High St; s/d/f £40/70/80) Just the length of a yard arm from the harbour, this ancient, cosy B&B is a warren of zigzag passageways. Few rooms are square; the steeply slanting ceilings on the top floor are a real duck-your-head zone. It's a pleasing effect, topped off by a delicate pink-and-green colour scheme.

our pick Saltings (☎ 707349; www.the-saltings .com; 5 Salterns Way; d £70-85; ▯ ▯ ▯) You can almost hear the languid drawl of Noël Coward in this utterly delightful 1930s B&B. Art Deco charm is everywhere, from the curved windows and arched doorways to the decorative uplights. Immaculate rooms feature dazzling white, spearmint and pastel blue. There's a hint of decadence too – minifridges, digital radios and free Lush toiletries in the

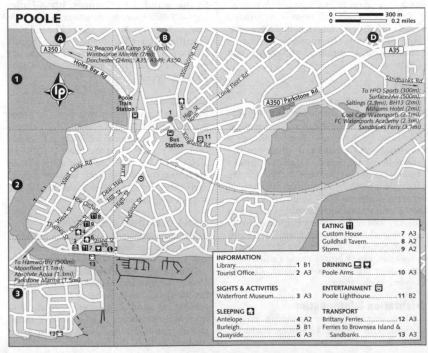

POOLE

0 ———————— 300 m
0 ———————— 0.2 miles

To Beacon Hill Camp Site (3mi);
Wimbourne Minster (7mi);
Dorchester (24mi); A35; A349; A350

Holes Bay Rd

Wimborne Rd

Long Fleet Rd

A350   Parkstone Rd

Sandbanks Rd

To H²O Sports (300m);
Surface2Air (500m);
Saltings (1.1mi); BH13 (2mi);
Milsoms Hotel (2mi);
Cool Cats Watersports (2.1mi);
FC Watersports Academy (2.3mi);
Sandbanks Ferry (3.1mi)

Poole
Train
Station

High St North

Bus
Station

Kingland Rd

West Quay Rd

Dear Hay Lane

Hill St

High St

Ladland Rd

New Orchard

Church St

Strand St

Thames St

West St

To Hamworthy (500m);
Moonfleet (1.1mi);
Absolute Aqua (1.3mi);
Parkstone Marina (1.5mi)

LOCATION, LOCATION, LOCATION

A surprising thought: a property in the **Sandbanks** area of Poole costs more than one in New York's Fifth Ave. In fact the Dorset suburb is the fourth-most expensive place to lay your head in the world. Sandbanks real estate costs £689 per square foot – only pipped by Shoto in Tokyo's Shibuya district (£895), Barker Rd in Hong Kong (£859) and Eaton Sq in London's Belgravia (£775). Those expensive inches add up – in 2005 a Sandbanks 1950s bungalow, in need of some TLC, went for a shade under £3 million.

So what's so hot about Britain's millionaire's row in miniature? Curling round Poole Harbour, Sandbanks is a 2-mile, wafer-thin peninsula with a bobble of land at the end whose houses may make you wonder what all the fuss is about: it's a suburb, admittedly a superposh one, by the sea. You're more likely to be impressed by the tempting water sports on offer (see below), its glorious beach and the stunning views over Poole Bay towards the Jurassic Coast. What's more, you don't have to carry a gold card to enjoy its golden sands; wandering one of the most expensive shorelines in the world is free.

A fleet of buses and ferries shuttle to this home of the superrich, see p132.

ultramodern bathrooms, not to mention big fluffy towels and complimentary chocolate snacks. One room is more like a little suite, with its own seating area and pocket-sized balcony. Saltings is part way between Poole and Sandbanks.

Milsoms Hotel (☎ 609000; www.milsomshotel.co.uk; 47 Haven Rd; d £75-95; P ⑤) Eight subtle and supremely stylish rooms fill this minihotel. Off-white fabrics and painted wood are paired with light purple throws and a terribly restrained scattering of cushion; bathrooms are glam in chrome and cream. It's owned by the Loch Fyne seafood-restaurant people – its white wood and pine restaurant, open for breakfast, lunch and dinner, is just downstairs, dishing up excellent fish (mains £10 to £15): intensely flavoured kiln roast salmon, smoked haddock and homemade stews.

Antelope (☎ 672029; www.antelopeinn.com; 8 High St; s/d/f £70/90/110; P) A 15th-century inn full of cosy rooms – colour schemes range from terracotta and cream to deep reds and browns, while CD players and sparkly new bathrooms ratchet up comfort levels. The family rooms have plenty of space – some of the others are a tad on the small side.

Sandbanks (☎ 707377; www.fjbhotels.co.uk; Sandbanks; s £45-110, d £90-220, f £105-270; P ☒) A place to play spot the millionaire, and be one – set in some of the most expensive land in the world, it ain't cheap. Patios back directly onto the beach and the best rooms have spectacular views of the sea or the harbour. The smoothly comfy bedrooms (plasma-screen TVs, bright throws and double sinks) are a touch uniform. There's a kids activity pro-

gramme and an indoor pool, sauna, gym and in-house spa.

Eating & Drinking

Custom House (☎ 676767; Poole Quay; mains £8; ☺ lunch & dinner) This chilled venue has a fabulous harbourside terrace and a downstairs bistro with flagstones on the floors, trendy art on the walls and a menu full of quirky favourites: chilli and coriander mussels or gnocchi with brie. Upstairs the décor is more elegant, as is the food (two courses £28) – try fresh crab salad or monkfish with smoked salmon in white-wine sauce.

BH13 (☎ 701101; 37 Haven Rd; mains £12; ☺ lunch & dinner Tue-Sat, lunch Sun) A sleek and chic bar-restaurant with brown suede settees, chrome lights and the odd dash of purple, backlit glass. The menu travels the Med – chicken and chorizo meets slow-cooked lamb in cumin, and paella.

Guildhall Tavern (☎ 671717; 15 Market St; mains £15-20; ☺ lunch & dinner Tue-Sun) More Provence than Poole, the grub at this French-run brasserie is Gallic gourmet charm at its best: unpretentious and top notch. Expect char-grilled sea bass flambéed with pernod, or beef with Roquefort sauce. Exquisite aromas fill the dining room, along with the quiet murmur of people enjoying very good food.

Storm (☎ 674970; 16 High St; mains £17; ☺ dinner) The tables here are rustic: huge and rough-hewn – the menu is similarly robust and changes according to what the owner (a keen fisherman) catches. Flavour combos include baked halibut with Welsh rarebit topping and Goan fish curry.

Poole's harbour is lined with waterside watering holes. The green, tiled **Poole Arms** (☎ 673450; The Quay; ☒ lunch & dinner) is the oldest pub on the quay and is thankfully unmessed-about-with – framed knot-samples and deeply worn wooden tables still rule. It also serves tasty bar food (mains £6) of the homemade fish soup and pie variety.

Entertainment

The town's arts hub, **Poole Lighthouse** (☎ 08700 668701; www.lighthousepoole.co.uk; 21 Kingland Rd) hosts a lively events calendar including live music, theatre, film and exhibitions.

Getting There & Around

Countless buses cover the 20-minute trip to Bournemouth. National Express runs hourly to London (£18, three hours). Train connections are as for Bournemouth (see p129), just 13 minutes closer to London Waterloo.

Bus 152 goes from Poole to Sandbanks (15 minutes, hourly July and August plus Saturday and Sunday May to September, three daily Monday to Saturday, October to June). Ferries also make the same journey, see Boat Trips (p130).

Sandbanks Ferry (☎ 01929-450203; www.sandbanks ferry.co.uk; per pedestrian/car 90p/£3) shuttles across to Studland every 20 minutes. This is a short-cut from Poole to Swanage, Wareham and the west Dorset coast, but the summer queues can be horrendous. **Brittany Ferries** (☎ 0870 366 5333; www.brittany-ferries.com) sails between Poole and Cherbourg in France (2¼ to 6½ hours, one to three daily); expect to pay around £86 per foot passenger, £330 for a car and two passengers.

Cool Cats Watersports (☎ 701100; www.coolcats watersports.com; Sandbanks; per day adult/child £10/9), next to the Sandbanks hotel, rents bikes.

For a taxi try **Dial-a-Cab** (☎ 666822).

CHRISTCHURCH

☎ 01202 / pop 44,865

With its elegant 11th-century priory, Norman castle ruins and grassy parks, Christchurch is dramatically different from brash Bournemouth and bustling Poole. The most eastern of the seaside conurbations, it's also the calmest and its shaded, ancient buildings lend it a collegiate, established air. But, tucked in at the head of an intricate harbour, Christchurch also offers an enticing range of maritime activities – choose from adrenaline-fuelled water sports off fine sandy beaches or boat trips to a picturesque sandbank and quay.

Orientation & Information

The town's high street, home to the **tourist office** (☎ 471780; www.visitchristchurch.info; 49 High St; ☒ 9.30am-5.30pm Mon-Fri, 9.30am-5pm Sat Jul & Aug, 9.30am-5pm Mon-Fri, 9.30-4.30pm Sat Sep-Jun) leads north from the priory in the town centre. Castle St, with its range of restaurants, branches off to the east. Christchurch Quay is a few minutes' walk south, while Mudeford Quay and Sandbank lie 1 to 2 miles away towards the mouth of the harbour.

Sights & Activities

The magnificent lines of **Christchurch Priory** (☎ 485804; www.christchurchpriory.org; Quay Rd; suggested donation £2; ☒ 9.30am-4pm or 5pm Mon-Sa, 2.15pm-5.30pm Sun, subject to services) rise from a cluster of compact parks in the middle of town. Started in 1094 by Ranulf Flambard, one of King William II's right-hand men, it only escaped destruction during the Reformation after a plea from the townspeople. The 1360 altar screen in the Great Quire wasn't quite so lucky – a few of its figures were hacked out but it's still a beautiful piece of carving and depicts a peopled version of Christ's family tree. Look out for the exquisite Norman arches in the nave and check to see if the West Tower is open – 176 steps lead to first-class views over the town and sea.

Slightly north of the priory, the evocative ruins of **Christchurch Castle** cling to a tiny rise. The stone keep of these Norman defences dates from the 12th century – before coming to a crumbling end after the Civil War. Hunt out the quintessentially English bowling green next door, and the stocks.

The **Red House Museum** (☎ 482860; Quay Rd; admission free; ☒ 10am-5pm Tue-Sat, 2-5pm Sun) whisks you through thousands of years of Christchurch's past, from Iron Age spears and knives to Saxon grave goods and early-20th-century domestic devices. Imaginatively displayed, some of the exhibits are tucked away in drawers ensuring you get to make some discoveries of your own. Check out the massive wood and iron mangle – remarkably still in use in a local convent until 1963.

Christchurch Quay is a blend of bandstands, tearooms and yachts with pinging rigging. It's also home to the beautifully preserved Saxon **Place Mill** (☎ 487626; admission free; ☒ 11am-

5.30pm Tue-Sun Apr-Sep), which displays local art as well as cutlasses, guns and the pebbles used in Iron Age sling shots. You can hire **motorboats** (☎ 429119) from the quay (£20 per hour) between April and October.

Bournemouth Boating Services (☎ 429119) runs ferries from Christchurch Quay to **Mudeford Sandbank** (return £5.30; 5 sailings daily Apr-Oct), a slender spit of grass-backed beach that curls across the mouth of the harbour. Incredibly, garden-shed-sized huts here have sold for £165,000. The same boat crosses the mouth of the harbour to **Mudeford Quay**, an unreconstructed jumble of boats, lobster pots and a fresh fish stall – look for the pub, which is renowned for its crab salad. The **Mudeford Ferry** (☎ 07968-334441; Mudeford Quay; adult/child return £2/1; ☼ Apr-Oct) is a continuous shuttle between the quay and the sandbank.

Ocean Sports (☎ 07801-813228; www.oceansports .info) runs windsurfing (from £90 per eight hours) and power-kiting classes (from £25 per two hours).

Sleeping

Ashborne (☎ 475574; fax 482905; 47 Stour Rd; s £35-45, d £45-60; P) A simple, classic British B&B: there are printed flowers on the bedspreads, fringes on the lampshades and family photos on the walls. Some rooms share bathrooms. It's a 10-minute walk to town and there's a string of similar options near by.

Druid House (☎ 485615; www.druid-house.co.uk; 26 Sopers Lane; s £45-60, d £70-90; P ✗) The décor in this small hotel is certainly distinctive – white leather sofas, peach walls, brown throws and plenty of cappuccino-coloured drapes. The restful patio makes a top coffee-sipping spot. Town is a few minutes' walk away.

Lord Bute (☎ 01425-278884; www.lordbute.co.uk; 179 Lymington Rd; s £78-88, d £98-108, ste £180-225; P) Classy name, classy place. Rooms range from contemporary (all oatmeal fabrics, slim leather sofas and ultramodern sinks) to traditional, plastered with plush drapes and peppered with antiques. Some of the suites even have their own garden areas. The Lord Bute is 3 miles east of Christchurch.

Eating

Soho (☎ 496140; 7 Church St; mains £8; ☼ lunch & dinner) A funky bistro with immense squishy sofas, swirling art and a compact sun terrace to lounge on. Big clay ovens bake tasty pizza and the open-plan kitchen serves up pastas (try the blue cheese tagliatelle) and rustic salads.

Fish Works (☎ 487000; 10 Church St; mains £12; ☼ lunch & dinner Tue-Sat) Great idea – a fishmonger that also cooks the food. Take away ready-to-eat crab and lobster or settle down to feast on skate in black butter or roasted sea bass with rosemary. There are steak and veggie options too.

Splinters (☎ 483454; 12 Church St; mains £12, 2 courses £19; ☼ lunch & dinner Tue-Sat) A wholesome place, with rustic furnishings of wicker and lots of wood. The food is simple and tasty; try the leak and potato seafood chowder or the chicken breast wrapped in Parma ham.

Getting There & Away

Buses 1A/1B/1C/3A go to Bournemouth (30 minutes, every 10 minutes). Christchurch is linked by train at least hourly to Bournemouth (seven minutes), London Waterloo (£35, two hours) and Weymouth (£11.10, 1¼ hours).

Buses 121/123 go to Mudeford (15 minutes, half-hourly), which can also be reached by ferry (see left).

WIMBORNE

☎ 01202 / pop 14,844

Just 10 miles from Bournemouth, but half a world away, Wimborne sits in the middle of a peaceful, pastoral landscape. Its imposing minster, complete with an intriguing chained library, oversees a central array of Georgian houses, sedate tearooms and creaky old pubs. With the impressive ancestral pile of Kingston Lacy nearby, it makes for a soothing antidote to a sometimes cocksure coast.

The helpful **tourist office** (☎ 886116; wimborne tic@eastdorset.gov.uk; 29 High St; ☼ 9.30am-5.30pm Mon-Sat Apr-Sep, 9.30am-4.30pm Mon-Sat Oct-Mar) is based near the minster and sells a good town trail leaflet (£1). Wimborne's annual **folk festival** is held in June.

Sights
WIMBORNE MINSTER

A patchwork of honey-grey and worn red stone, **Wimborne Minster** (☎ 884753; donation suggested; ☼ 9.30am-5.30pm Mon-Sat, 2.30-5.30pm Sun) was started by the Normans in 1120. It contains a rare **chained library** (☼ 10.30am-12.30pm & 2-4pm Mon-Fri, 10.30am-12.30pm Sat Easter-Oct) in a tiny room at the top of a winding staircase. Established in 1686, it's filled with some of the

DORSET

country's oldest medieval books, as well as 12th-century manuscripts written on lambskin, and ancient recipes for making ink from oak apples.

The minster's 15th-century west tower is home to the **Quarter Jack** – a red-jacketed soldier who strikes the hours and quarters. Inside the minster lies the tomb of the infamous smuggler Isaac Gulliver, who conducted a lucrative racket smuggling gin, silk, lace and tea along the south Dorset coastline. A reformed character, he ended up a respectable wine seller in the town and a church warden.

KINGSTON LACY

Looking every inch the setting for a period drama, **Kingston Lacy** (NT; ☎ 883402; adult/child house £10/5, grounds only £5/2.50; ☉ house 11am-4pm Wed-Sun late Mar-Oct), became home to the aristocratic Bankes family when it was evicted from Corfe Castle (p136) by the Roundheads. This grand, 17th-century country mansion was later clad in stone by Charles Barry, architect of the Houses of Parliament, but it's best known for its resplendent Spanish Room, which is hung with gilded leather. The property's wonderfully preserved interior is dotted with paintings by Titian, Brueghel and Van Dyck. Outside, the extensive landscaped gardens encompass the Iron Age hillfort of Badbury Rings. Kingston Lacy is 2.5 miles west of Wimborne off the B3082.

Sleeping & Eating

Old George (☎ 888510; chrissie_oldgeorge@yahoo .co.uk; 2 Corn Market; d £60-70) A charming 18th-century house on a tiny square right beside the minster. Chic rooms are done out in light greens and russets with a scattering of dinky cushions and elegant armchairs. The bathrooms are splendid in black and gold.

Old Merchant's House (☎ 841955; 44 West Borough; s/d £50/70) Creeper-clad and stuffed full of antiques, this Grade II–listed house is set around a delightful walled garden, offering exactly what you'd expect from a rural British B&B – clean, well-appointed rooms, a hearty cooked breakfast and just the occasional burst of chintz.

ourpick Percy House (☎ 881040; www.percyhouse .jazzland.co.uk; 4 East Borough; s/d/f £60/80/100) A hot tub in the garden and a river to fish in set this B&B way above the rest. Gorgeously Georgian, an impressive staircase sweeps up

to rooms where the style is rustic meets elegant: raspberry-red walls, antique furniture and stripped woods. There's also seriously slanting accommodation above a compact former stable. In the centre of town.

Blue Fig (☎ 884321; 9 Leigh Rd; mains £12-17; ☉ lunch Thu-Sun, dinner Wed-Sun) The walls are lemon yellow, the chairs are chocolate brown and the food is seriously good. The flavours are local with eclectic inspiration: pork glazed with muscovado sugar and Dorset Blue Vinny cheese (p48), and goat's cheese soufflé with fig chutney.

Getting There & Away

Bus 3 goes to Poole (30 minutes, two to four per hour). Bus 13 connects with Bournemouth (50 minutes, hourly Monday to Saturday, six on Sunday).

ISLE OF PURBECK

The Isle of Purbeck boasts arguably the most beautiful stretch of shoreline in all of Dorset. Curling underneath Poole, this is the start of the Jurassic Coast (see the boxed text, p155) and the rocks here have been carved by the sea into glittering bays and towering cliff formations – making swimming irresistible and hiking memorable. Lulworth Cove, Durdle Door and the Fossil Forest are just a few highlights. The 'Isle' is really a peninsula; inland the immense, fairy-tale ruins of Corfe Castle sit amid verdant hills, while the area around Wareham sheds light on the mysterious figure of Lawrence of Arabia.

Wareham & Around
☎ 01929 / pop 5665

The red-brick market town of Wareham has a bustling, established air – its houses are still laid out along an original Saxon grid system and the centre is encircled by the low, grassy remains of its 10th-century ramparts. It makes an attractive base for two fabulously diverse attractions, encompassing monkeys and the military, and is the start of the TE Lawrence trail.

Purbeck tourist office (☎ 552740; www.purbeck .gov.uk; Holy Trinity Church, South St; ☉ 9.30am-5pm Mon-Sat, 10am-1pm & 1.45-4pm Sun Apr-Sep, 10am-3pm Mon-Sat Oct-Mar) stocks free leaflets of the Lawrence Walking Route – a 7-mile stroll from his army base at Bovington, via his home at Clouds Hill to St Nicolas Church in Moreton, where his funeral took place.

LAWRENCE IN DORSET

British scholar, military strategist and writer, Thomas Edward Lawrence (1888–1935) is legendary for his role in helping unite Arab tribes against Turkish forces in WWI. His hit-and-run guerrilla raids, particularly on railway lines, proved a crucially telling drain on the enemy. Having risen to the rank of colonel, by the end of the war he'd become fiercely disillusioned by what he saw as a British betrayal of Arab independence. As a result he rejected his rank and enlisted in the services under a batch of assumed names. But he failed to achieve the anonymity he craved and was exposed in a series of press articles. His actions ensured he was a source of fascination for many during his lifetime. David Lean's 1962 epic *Lawrence of Arabia* assured his mythical status for decades to come.

While stationed at Bovington, 6 miles from Wareham, Lawrence worked on his epic account of the desert campaign *Seven Pillars of Wisdom* and eventually retired to Clouds Hill nearby. In 1935 he had a motorcycling accident on the Dorset roads. He died six days later at the age of 46 – conspiracy theories have abounded about his death ever since. The **TE Lawrence Society** (www.telsociety.org.uk) was founded in 1985.

DORSET

SIGHTS

An isolated cottage 7 miles northwest of Wareham, **Clouds Hill** (NT; ☎ 405616; adult/child £4/2; ☽ noon-5pm Thu-Sun mid-Mar–Oct) was Lawrence's rural retreat. Its evocative, spartan rooms hint at his cryptic personality – and include some relics underlining his interest in Middle Eastern culture and fascination with the Arab world. Packed with photos, there's also an exhibition detailing his life.

Lawrence was stationed at nearby Bovington Camp, now a **Tank Museum** (☎ 405096; www .tankmuseum.org; Bovington; adult/child £10/7; ☽ 10am-5pm), and died at its military hospital. The museum's collection of tanks means fierce armour and caterpillar tracks are everywhere – from lumbering WWI giants to those that saw action in the Middle East's 20th-century conflict of Desert Storm.

Wareham's delightful Saxon **St Martin's Church** in North St dates from about 1020. Inside there's a 12th-century fresco on the northern wall and a marble effigy of Lawrence of Arabia.

The two-room **Wareham Museum** (☎ 553448; East St; admission free; ☽ 10am-4pm Easter-Oct) provides a good potted history of Lawrence's life, along with press cuttings on the speculation surrounding his death.

Overflowing with the 'aah' factor, **Monkey World** (☎ 462537; www.monkeyworld.co.uk; Longthorns; adult/child £10/7; ☽ 10am-5pm, till 6pm Jul & Aug) is a noisy, irresistible sanctuary for rescued chimpanzees, orang-utans, gibbons, marmosets and some ridiculously cute ringtailed lemurs.

SLEEPING & EATING

our pick **Trinity** (☎ 556689; www.trinitybnb.co.uk; 32 South St; d £50-60 f £80; ✗) This 15th-century B&B oozes so much character, you wouldn't be surprised to meet a bloke in doublet and hose here. Bedrooms are framed by fantastic brickwork and inglenook fireplaces; the staircase is a swirl of ancient timber; floors creak under stately rugs and rooms are alive with nooks and crannies. The old-meets-new bathrooms are reassuringly modern, all yellow and green tiles and smart shiny fittings.

Old Granary (☎ 552010; The Quay; mains £6-10; ☽ lunch & dinner) Right beside the riverbank (which has been known to flood in), it's great for a pint and dose of rustic charm and old woods; the menu is full of pub-food standards.

Anglebury (☎ 552988; www.angleburyhouse.co.uk; 15 North St; mains £9-13; ☽ lunch daily, dinner Tue-Sat) Lawrence of Arabia and Thomas Hardy have, apparently, both had cuppas in the coffee shop attached to this 16th-century inn. Simple but quaint rooms (singles/doubles £35/60) are done out in creams, floral fabrics and pine. Squishy sofas line the stone-walled bar and the restaurant does substantial food – trout wrapped in bacon and lamb in pernod, as well as simpler snacks.

GETTING THERE & AWAY

Wareham is on the main line from London Waterloo to Weymouth (£38.50, 2½ hours); trains run hourly.

Buses 142/143 run between Poole and Swanage via Wareham hourly (35 minutes, every two hours on Sunday).

DORSET

Corfe Castle
☎ 01929

The massive, shattered ruins of Corfe Castle loom so dramatically from the landscape it's like blundering into a film set. The defensive fragments tower over an equally photogenic village, which bears the castle's name and is built out of the same gold-grey stone. The combined effect is a cinematographer's dream and with the ruins acting as an ever present backdrop to some good hotels, it's a romantic spot for a meal or an overnight stay.

Corfe Castle (NT; ☎ 481294; adult/child £5.30/2.70; ⏰ 10am-6pm Apr-Sep, 10am-5pm Mar & Oct, 10am-4pm Nov-Feb) was begun in 1068 by the compulsive castle-builder William the Conqueror, then extended by Kings John, Henry III and Edward I. By the time of the English Civil War it was home to Sir John Bankes, Charles I's right-hand man. It was besieged by Cromwell's forces for six weeks, during which time its robust defence was directed by the formidable Lady Bankes and the castle only fell after being betrayed from within. The Roundheads then blew it up with gunpowder – up close it's clear they did a good job; remnants of turrets and soaring walls sheer off at precarious angles. Conservation and safety requirements inevitably mar some views but it's still ideal for peeping through slit windows and prowling the fractured battlements. Among the child-friendly gory bits, try hunting out the 'murder holes' or prescribing medieval medicine in the main NT tourist office. Some of the best views of the castle are from the west; from the junction of a cluster of trails leading off the circular Castle Walk.

SLEEPING & EATING

Bankes Hotel (☎ 481288; www.dorset-hotel.co.uk; East St; s £40-60, d £55-85; [P]) This cosy, village-centre inn is steeped in its 450-year past – bedrooms are a mass of mullioned windows, creaking floors and slightly worn bathrooms. Feast on local fish pie or venison stew (mains £8 to £14) in the bar alongside huge fireplaces and the odd heraldic crest.

Mortons House (☎ 480988; www.mortonshouse.co.uk; East St; s from £130, d £154-255; [P] [&]) A place to break open the Bollinger: a romantic, luxurious 16th-century, mini–baronial pile. The rooms are festooned with red brocade and gold tassels with the occasional chaise longue thrown in, while a grand staircase leads to an elegantly English dining room (mains £20,

open lunch and dinner) where the food is all French flair.

GETTING THERE & AWAY

Buses 142/143 run hourly and link Corfe Castle with Swanage (20 minutes), Wareham (15 minutes) and Poole (45 minutes).

The **Swanage Steam Railway** (☎ 425800; www.swanagerailway.co.uk; adult/child day rover £9.50/5.50; ⏰ hourly Apr-Oct plus many weekends in Nov, Dec, Feb & Mar) runs between Swanage and Norden (20 minutes) and stops at Corfe Castle.

Blue Pool

Sometimes green, sometimes turquoise the **Blue Pool** (☎ 01929-551408; www.bluepooluk.com; Furzebrook; adult/child £4.80/2.40; ⏰ 9.30am-dusk Mar-Nov) has an extraordinary knack of changing colour in different conditions – it's all down to tiny particles diffracting light through the water in this former clay pit. The surrounding woods are home to green sand lizards and shy Dartford warblers. The pool is signposted from the A351; buses 142/143 from Wareham (10 minutes) stop nearby.

Lulworth Cove & the Coast
☎ 01929 / pop 938

South of Corfe Castle the coast steals the show. For millions of years the elements have been creating an intricate shoreline of curved bays, caves, stacks and weirdly wonderful rock formations – most notably the massive natural arch at Durdle Door. This chunk of shoreline is towards the eastern tip of the Jurassic Coast (see the boxed text, p155) and is an ideal spot to begin investigating its awe-inspiring past.

The best base is Lulworth Cove – a perfect circle of white cliffs broken only by a distant segment of sea. This miniresort is sprinkled with thatched cottages and has a happy-go-lucky feel. A pleasing jumble of fishing boats and gear winds to the beach, and every now and then shops and cafés spring up in what look like sheds. In the height of summer visitor numbers risk making Lulworth a victim of its own success, but otherwise it's a charismatic springboard for some superb hikes and activities.

The **Lulworth Cove Tourist Office** (☎ 40087 admission free; ⏰ 10am-6pm Apr–mid-Sep, 10am-4pm or 5pm late Sep-Mar) is a useful information source and has excellent displays on the geological story of the shore. A mile inland, the village of West Lulworth has a range of accommodation options, while Durdle Door is 3 miles west by road.

SIGHTS & ACTIVITIES

A half-mile hike east along the coast path from Lulworth Cove leads to the **Fossil Forest**. Here huge, raised donuts of rock sprout from the cliff – all that's left of the tree trunks of a 144-million-year-old Jurassic jungle. The forest is just inside an army firing range – the path tends to be open most weekends and school summer holidays, but it does vary. Check with the tourist office, or by calling ☎ 404819.

Jurassic Coast Kayaking (☎ 01305-835301; Lulworth Cove Tourist Office) offers an unforgettable view of the cliffs on a three-hour paddle (£40) from Lulworth Cove to Durdle Door on sit-aboard kayaks. Weather dependent, it's available most weekends in summer.

A creamy, dreamy, white, **Lulworth Castle** (EH; ☎ 400352; www.lulworth.com; East Lulworth; admission £7; ◷ 10.30am-6pm Apr-Oct, 10.30am-4pm Nov-Mar) looks more like a French chateau than a traditional English castle. Built in 1608 as a hunting lodge, it has survived extravagant owners, extensive remodelling and a disastrous fire in 1929. It's now been sumptuously restored – check out the massive four-poster bed, and the suits of armour in the basement.

SLEEPING & EATING

Durdle Door Holiday Park (☎ 400200; durdle.door@ lulworth.com; tent sites £10-20; ◷ Mar-Oct) A well-equipped camping area (bar, restaurant and BBQs) set just back from the famous rock arch. Some of the tent sites are in woodland – others border a busy track.

Lulworth YHA Hostel (☎ 0870 770 5940; School Lane; dm £12; ℗) This single-storey wooden hostel has a basic, prefab feel, but it's in a good spot: on the edge of West Lulworth and a mile from the coast path.

Bishops Cottage & Café (☎ 400880; www.bishop scottage.co.uk; Main St, Lulworth Cove; s £35-45, d £60-90, f £160; 🖳) As cool as the coolest kid in the year, this three-room B&B throws together antique furniture and sleek modern fabrics – and makes it work. Chill out on your own window seat or in the funky café downstairs where big wooden tables sit on scuffed floorboards and chefs rustle up spicy seafood or ploughman's with cider (mains £3 to £8; open 9am to 5pm May to September). Wi-fi connection is available.

Cove House (☎ 400137; www.covehouse.net; Main St, West Lulworth; d £65-75; ℗ ✗) Full of space and calm, this mid-Victorian gabled house is tucked back from the coast in West Lulworth. Its two bedrooms have high ceilings, minichandeliers and marble fireplaces – the best room looks out over the hill leading to Durdle Door.

Rose Cottage (☎ 400150; www.rosecottage.fsworld .co.uk; Main St, Lulworth Cove; s £35-50, d £70-80) The archetypal thatched B&B – flowers adorn the door, it has thick walls and incredibly low lintels frame the interior. The décor is homely charm, one bedroom has a sea view, two share a lovely dark-wood bathroom.

Beach Hotel (☎ 400404; www.lulworthbeachhotel .com; Main St; d £90-105, f £105) An oh-so-stylish hotel 200m from the beach. Rooms feature blonde woods, coconut matting and flashes of leather and lime – the best has its own private sea-view deck. The restaurant serves locally caught fish (try the baked citrus sea bass), as well as steak and veggie options (mains £15). Dinner is normally served nightly in the summer – check for times.

SCULPTED BY NATURE

Extraordinary even by this coast's standards, the massive Portland Stone arch of the **Durdle Door** plunges into the sea near Lulworth Cove. The name 'durdle' may come from the Anglo-Saxon 'thirl' – a pierced hole or opening, and that's actually how it began. Massive earth movements tilted the rocks up, softer layers were exposed and a cave was formed. Over millions of years, pounding seas expanded the hole to form the sweeping arch. The next stage was an eventual collapse of the top, to leave just a standing pillar. Either side of the arch, hundreds of steps lead down to a perfect bay – bring a swimsuit, then take a dip beside this 150-million-year-old limestone arch carved out by the sea.

There's a car park at the top of the cliffs – to get to it you drive through a camp site. Better still, hike along the cliffs from Lulworth Cove (1 mile), passing the delightfully named Lulworth Crumple en route – here layers of rock have been forced into dramatically zigzagging folds.

In the summer look out to see if the **Lulworth Beach Café** (☎ 400404; The Beach; ⊗ dinner Fri, Sat & sometimes Sun) is open. Right by the shore, it sells whatever fish is freshest. There's £2 corkage on bring-your-own wine and it only takes cash and cheques.

GETTING THERE & AWAY
Lulworth is not well served by public transport. Bus 103 (three daily, Monday to Saturday) connects Lulworth to Wool (on the X53 Weymouth–Wareham–Bournemouth bus route), but buses only leave Wool in the morning, and Lulworth in the afternoon. Services only go on to Durdle Door by request; phone ☎ 0845 602 4547.

DORCHESTER & INLAND DORSET

The country around Dorchester is Thomas Hardy country. It seeped into his books and now the landscape is steeped in his writings. Here you can see the lush, gentle hills that inspired him and the towns and buildings that hide in his novels. Interestingly, Hardy himself is now an attraction: the area boasts a museum with a world-class collection of his manuscripts and artefacts, as well as two of his former homes. Literature aside, the landscape around Dorchester also contains the most impressive Iron Age hillfort in England, the sauciest chalk figure in the country and a string of bewitching, ancient towns – Sherborne is a particular delight.

DORCHESTER
☎ 01305 / pop 16,160
With Dorchester you get a real-life, bustling county town and Thomas Hardy's fictional Casterbridge side by side. The writer was born just outside Dorchester and clearly used it to add authenticity to his works – literary locations can be found amid the town's white Georgian terraces and red-brick buildings. The Hardy connection becomes even more tangible when you visit his houses and, in the exhibits in the town museum, study some of his original manuscripts, complete with corrections. Then there's another intriguing town on the fringes of Dorchester: Poundbury, a mock-Georgian development dreamt up by Prince

Charles as a model housing scheme. Incredibly varied museums, from teddy bears to terracotta warriors via Tutankhamen, and some attractive places to sleep and eat combine to make an appealing base for a night or two.

Information
Dorchester's **tourist office** (☎ 267992; www.west dorset.com; Antelope Walk; ⊗ 9am-5pm Mon-Sat Apr-Oct, 10am-4pm Mon-Sat Nov-Mar) is a great source of Hardy information. It stocks a *Dorchester Town Walks* (£1.30) brochure, which features a stroll themed around the novelist.

Sights
THOMAS HARDY SIGHTS
Dorset County Museum (☎ 262735; www.dorsetcounty museum.org; High West St; admission £6; ⊗ 10am-5pm daily Jul-Sep, 10am-5pm Mon-Sat Oct-Jun) The Hardy collection here is the biggest in the world and offers an extraordinary insight into his creative process – reading his cramped handwriting it's possible to spot where he's crossed out one word and substituted another. There's also a letter from Siegfried Sassoon, asking Hardy if Sassoon can dedicate his first book of poems to him, and a wonderful reconstruction of his study at Max Gate.

A trained architect, Hardy was responsible for the design of **Max Gate** (NT; ☎ 262538; Alington Ave; adult/child £3/1.50; ⊗ 2-5pm Mon, Wed & Sun Apr-Sep), where he lived from 1885 until his death in 1928. *Tess of the D'Urbervilles* and *Jude the Obscure* were both written here, and the house contains several pieces of original furniture, but otherwise it's a little slim on items of interest. The house is a mile east of Dorchester on the A352.

The small cob-and-thatch **Hardy's Cottage** (NT; ☎ 01297-561900; admission £3.50; ⊗ 11am-5pm Sun-Thu Apr-Oct), where the author was born, is again short on attractions, but it makes an evocative stop for Hardy completists. It's in Higher Bockhampton, 3 miles northeast of Dorchester.

Look out for **Hardy's statue** at the top of High West St in Dorchester. You can also try and track down what's thought to be the red and grey brick inspiration for the Mayor of Casterbridge's house, now a Barclays Bank branch, in South St, and visit the Maumbury Rings (p140); the location of Henchard's secret meetings in the same book.

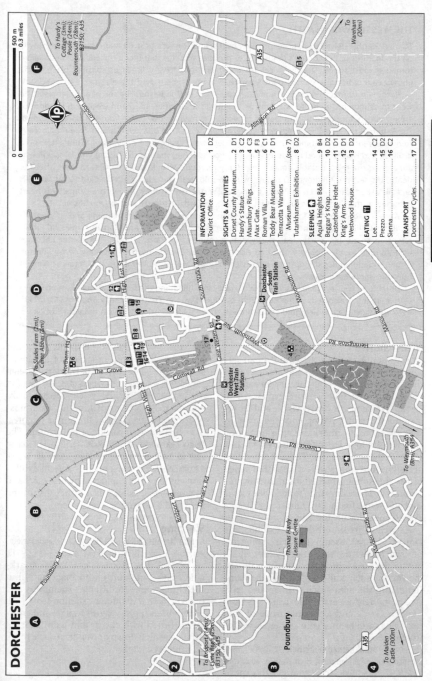

DORCHESTER

DORSET

0 500 m
0 0.3 miles

INFORMATION	
Tourist Office............................	1 D2

SIGHTS & ACTIVITIES	
Dorset County Museum............	2 D1
Hardy's Statue...........................	3 C2
Maumbury Rings.......................	4 C3
Max Gate...................................	5 F3
Roman Villa..............................	6 C1
Teddy Bear Museum.................	7 D1
Terracotta Warriors
Museum.............................	(see 7)
Tutankhamen Exhibition.........	8 D2

SLEEPING	
Aquila Heights B&B.................	9 B4
Beggar's Knap..........................	10 D2
Casterbridge Hotel...................	11 D1
King's Arms..............................	12 D1
Westwood House.......................	13 D2

EATING	
Lee...	14 C2
Prezzo.......................................	15 C2
Sienna.......................................	16 C2

TRANSPORT	
Dorchester Cycles....................	17 D2

DORSET

THE WESSEX WORDSMITH

Thomas Hardy (1840–1928): poet, prolific novelist and Dorset's best PR man. Hardy drew heavily on the features of the county's landscape to produce writings that blend bucolic idyll and reality, romance and tragedy. Deeply lyrical, his books not only have a firmly established place in the literary canon, but also elicit groans from generations who studied them as set texts at school.

Hardy was born at Higher Bockhampton, just north of Dorchester. The son of a stonemason, he went to school in Dorchester, became an architect's apprentice at 16 and worked in London for a few years before returning to Dorset to write. The novels flowed: *Far from the Madding Crowd, The Return of the Native, The Mayor of Casterbridge, Tess of the D'Urbervilles* and *Jude the Obscure*. *Jude* received some scathing reviews, largely because it challenged conventional morality, and a disillusioned Hardy turned to poetry instead – *Poems of the Past and the Present* and *Wessex Poems* are among the most notable collections. Hardy married twice; first Emma Gifford then, after her death, his secretary Florence Dugdale, who was 40 years his junior. Hardy died in his late 80s and his ashes were placed in Poet's Corner at Westminster Abbey. Rather gruesomely his heart is buried in the same grave as his first wife in Stinsford, just northeast of Dorchester.

Wessex hadn't existed for around 1000 years when Hardy revived the name and used it as a location for his stories – he also borrowed specific features (forts and Roman ruins) and whole towns to create his 'partly real, partly dream-country'. In Hardy's books Dorchester becomes Casterbridge, Cerne Abbas is dubbed Abbot's Cernel, Sherborne gets the new name Sherton Abbas and Higher Bockhampton is rechristened Upper Mellstock. The result is a literary scavenger hunt for Hardy enthusiasts.

Dorchester tourist office has a wealth of Hardy info including the free *Exploring Thomas Hardy's Dorset* leaflet. It also sells pamphlets (30p) produced by the **Thomas Hardy Society** (☎ 251501; www.hardysociety.org), which guide you through the real-life locations of each individual book.

OTHER SIGHTS

Dorchester was once a thriving Roman settlement and excavations have uncovered the foundations of a 1st-century **Roman villa** behind the town hall on Northern Hay. The layout of the house is clearly visible and the remains of the main building, enclosed in a glass structure, boast remarkable mosaic floors. Also worth a look are the **Maumbury Rings**, just south of the town centre. These steep-sided, grass-covered ridges were a Neolithic henge before the Romans turned them into an amphitheatre. These days they're an idyllic picnic spot and venue for open-air music and drama events; check locally for listings.

As well as its superb Hardy exhibits, the Dorset County Museum (p138) has some impressive **fossils** from the Jurassic Coast – look out for the huge ichthyosaur on the wall, and the 1m dinosaur skull hanging over the stairs. Reflecting the area's rich Bronze and Iron Age past, there are archaeological finds from Maiden Castle and a treasure trove of gold neck rings and bronze coin cashes, as well as Roman mosaics.

At the **Tutankhamen Exhibition** (☎ 269571; www .tutankhamun-exhibition.co.uk; High West St; adult/child £6.75/4.95; ⊗ 9.30am-5.30pm) you get to experi-ence the sights, sounds and smells of ancient Egypt in a fake-gold mock-up of the Pharaoh's tomb. The **Terracotta Warriors Museum** (☎ 266040; www.terracottawarriors.co.uk; East Gate, East High St; adult/child £5.50/3.75; ⊗ 10am-5.30pm) whisks you off to 8th-century China for an atmospheric reconstruction of the famous figures, as well as assorted costumes and armour. The **Teddy Bear Museum** (☎ 266040; East Gate, East High St; adult £5, 1st 2 children free; ⊗ 10am-5.30pm Apr-Oct, till 4.30pm Nov-Mar) rounds off this surreal exhibition combo – it's populated by historical and famous bears, as well as a rather disturbing family of life-sized teddies.

Sleeping

Aquila Heights B&B (☎ 267145; www.aquilaheights .co.uk; 44 Maiden Castle Rd; s £34, d £66-74, f £80-110; P ⊠ ⛨) The décor's not that remarkable (dark pine and photo placemats) but the choices are: 16 different shampoos and breakfasts that include cinnamon toast with caramelised apple, veggie sausages and croissants stuffed with cheese and ham. Work it off on a walk to town or Maiden Castle (both 15 minutes away).

(Continued on page 149)

BEST OF THE SOUTHWEST

The southwest of England is an all-year, all-ages destination with a range of holiday options that gives an insight into the various characters of the region, from family-based water fun to adrenaline-pumping extreme sports; from fine dining to traditional country food; from prehistoric stone circles to modern architecture; and from Roman history to literature for the romantic.

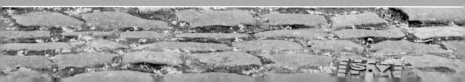

The Great Outdoors

Whether it's wind-, pedal-, foot- or hoof-power you're after on your trip, getting out and enjoying the countryside is easy around these parts. And for some much-needed R & R after your exertions, there are plenty of eating and drinking options in which to recover.

1 South West Coast Path
Pick a favourite section or hike all 630 miles of it – whatever you choose, this long distance trail, hugging the coastline of the whole region, offers some vigorous walking and plenty of spectacular views (p63).

2 Riding
Let the rein take the strain and saddle up for a gentle trot around some of the best scenery the southwest has to offer (p71).

3 Surfing in Cornwall
Newquay (p228) might be the most famous surfer hang-out, but there are plenty of other excellent spots around the county for beginners and experts alike.

4 Cycling
Avoid the summer traffic jams and get out and about on two wheels. There are plenty of (often car-free) routes to enjoy at your own pace including the Tarka Trail (p213).

5 Sailing
Practise tying a cleat hitch and learn how to hoist up the mainsail (and pronounce it 'mains'l') on a sailing course on the beautiful waters off the southwest coast (p70).

Food & Drink

Pasties and scrumpy might be the first things that come to mind when you think of West Country food (and pretty fine they can be too), but whether it's some award-winning wines or internationally famous restaurants, the contemporary culinary scene is an equally good reason to visit.

❶ Devon Cream Teas

You can pretend you're replenishing those calories lost through outdoor activities or say it's only because you're on holiday, but to be honest you don't really need an excuse to have a nice cup of tea (or two) and a scone (or three); see p49.

❷ Pasties

Forget pale imitations, it's the home of the pasty (Cornwall that is, whatever Devon might try to claim) where you can best sample the real thing (p47).

❸ Scrumpy

Cider, Jim, but not as we know it. If you're used to the carbonated stuff you find in pubs then get ready for the superior, tastier and considerably stronger local brew (p114).

❹ Southwest Wine

So popular locally that it's difficult to find a bottle outside the region, the Southwest's wine output is getting a justifiably good name for itself. Try Devon's Sharpham (p184) or Cornwall's Camel Valley (p275) vineyards.

❺ Rick Stein in Padstow

Jamie Oliver might be getting the attention at the moment with his *Fifteen Cornwall* down the road, but Rick Stein started the foodie revolution round these parts and Padstow (aka Padstein) has plenty of options for trying one of his dishes (p225).

Rainy Days

Contrary to what local tourist boards may tell you, the southwest isn't exempt from the usual chilly and wet British weather. A heavy downpour can ruin the best-laid plans, so having a backup for a rainy day is always a good idea and visitors are spoilt for choice.

1

❶ Eden Project

It doesn't matter what the weather's doing when you've got two huge indoor gardens to explore (p268). Check out the steamy tropics and then chill in the temperate zone.

❷ Thermae Bath Spa

For a contemporary spin on the city's oldest attraction, spend a day at Bath's luxury new spa (p93), which uses the local therapeutic waters in its pools.

❸ National Maritime Museum, Falmouth

Boats suspended from ceilings, interactive displays and a wonderful view across the town make the National Maritime Museum (p259) a great first resort if the weather's not playing ball.

❹ Dorchester

With more than its fair share of interesting museums – from local history to Tutankhamun – Dorchester (p138) should have something to keep everyone singing in the rain.

❺ At-Bristol

Massive, hands-on science museum (p79) that will appeal to kids of all ages (including the over 18s) thanks to its range of involving exhibits including a trip to the stars in the planetarium.

(Continued from page 140)

Slades Farm (☎ 264032; www.bandbdorset.org.uk; Charminster; s/d £45/60; P ⊠) Barn conversions don't come much more tasteful and airy than this – done out in oatmeal and cream, tiny skylights dot ceilings which meet walls in gentle curves. The riverside paddock is perfect to laze in, while breakfasts are full of local delicacies. Two miles north of Dorchester on the Cerne Abbas road and bus route.

our pick Beggar's Knap (☎ 268191; beggarsknap @hotmail.co.uk; 2 Weymouth Ave; s £45, d £60-65) Far from impoverished, this utterly fabulous, vaguely decadent guesthouse spins the clock back to the Victorian era. Opulent, raspberry-red rooms drip with chandeliers and red-and-gold brocades while the beds are covered in fine cottons and range from French sleigh to four-poster. It's all supremely stylish and has a spacious, uncluttered feel – from the high-ceilings and bay windows to the occasional, well-placed classical figurine. The breakfast room, with its towering plants and a huge harp, is gorgeous.

Westwood House (☎ 268018; www.westwoodhouse .co.uk; 29 High West St; s £45-50, d £60-85, f £120) An elegant Georgian B&B whose seven rooms are dotted with wicker furniture painted to match the colour schemes – choose from gentle lemon, light blue or red. The two basement bedrooms are still perfectly acceptable, but have a slightly subterranean feel.

Kings Arms (☎ 265353; www.kingsarmsdorchester.com; 30 High East St; s £69, d £79-109; P ⊠ 🖥) Downstairs this hotel is all 18th-century charm. A huge heraldic crest hangs over reception and the ceiling is lined with elaborate plasterwork. Bedrooms are more modern, featuring sleek armchairs and ultratrendy sinks. The bar is definitely different: riding boots, stuffed fish and a ship's figurehead hang from the walls.

Casterbridge Hotel (☎ 264043; www.casterbridgeho tel.co.uk; 49 High East St; s £55-75, d £99-125; P 🖥 &) In the 1780s this hotel was the town jail. Now marble fireplaces, ruched furnishings and Thomas Hardy books in the rooms make it worth spending a night in an old prison. Breakfasts are brim-full of local ingredients and are served in a lovely conservatory. Six bedrooms are in a 1980s annexe.

Eating

Lee (☎ 756088; 34 High West St; mains £8; ☺ lunch & dinner) Ornate, carved tables and chandeliers dominate this popular eatery which specialises in Peking, Szechwan and Thai food. Try the sliced squid Cantonese style, or the sizzling tofu in black bean sauce.

Prezzo (☎ 259678; 6 High West St; mains £8-11; ☺ lunch & dinner) A typically reliable outpost of this Italian chain; the baroque interior is filled with black leather sofas and twisted willow – top-notch pizzas and pastas are on the menu.

Sienna (☎ 250022; 36 High West St; 2-course set lunch /dinner £16.50/27.50; ☺ Tue-Sat) Indulge in some fine, pan-European cooking which combines complex flavours: rare roast Scottish sirloin with mushrooms sits on the same menu as fresh tagliatelle with roasted artichokes, and a goat's cheese and pepper tart with sherry

---

IDEAL HOMES?

Poundbury (www.poundburytown.com) has a lot to live up to. The brainchild of arch-architecture critic Prince Charles, it aims to be the perfect 21st-century housing development: a thriving community of homes, shops and light industry, which combines traditional architecture and modern town planning.

Building started in 1993, on land which actually forms part of the Prince's Duchy of Cornwall estate. The style is modern mock-Georgian – red-brick, cream stone and flint houses line up in a series of cul-de-sacs, dinky squares and sweeping crescents. The streets are deliberately narrow and serpentine to slow cars down. Dotted among them are minifactories producing chocolate or cereal and chichi shops selling bridal gowns, wine or cakes. At times it's a model village in more than one sense and is reminiscent of a pristine collection of dolls houses – it's even been lambasted by one critic as 160 hectares of pastiche. Poundbury's ever-expanding boundaries have also caused concern among some locals, who question whether the original design ideals are still being adhered to. Others suggest it's infinitely better than many built-from-scratch towns and, while it may not be perfect, at least it's trying to solve the knotty problem of creating new communities in a people-friendly way.

Dorchester's tourist office sells a Poundbury map (£1), to guide you through this unusual cityscape, the development is 15 minutes walk west of Dorchester town centre.

vinegar. The décor is simpler – light woods and red padded seats.

Getting There & Around

There's a direct daily National Express coach to London (£19.20, four hours).

Bus 31 travels hourly from Dorchester to Weymouth (30 minutes) and to Lyme Regis (1¾ hours). Bus 10 also goes to Weymouth (35 minutes, three per hour Monday to Saturday, two hourly on Sunday). Bus 387 goes to Poole (one hour, three daily Monday to Friday).

There are two train stations, Dorchester South and Dorchester West. Trains run at least hourly from Weymouth (11 minutes) to London Waterloo (£39.40, 2½ hours) via Dorchester South, Bournemouth (£8.60, 45 minutes) and Southampton (£17.70, 1¼ hours).

Dorchester West has connections with Bath (from £13.50, 1¾ hours) and Bristol (£13.40, two hours), running every two hours.

Dorchester Cycles (☎ 268787; 31 Great Western Rd; per day £15) hires bikes.

AROUND DORCHESTER
Maiden Castle

Occupying a massive slab of horizon on the fringes of Dorchester, Maiden Castle is the largest and most complex Iron Age hillfort in Britain. The huge, steep-sided chalk ramparts flow along the contour lines of a hill and surround 48 hectares – the equivalent of 50 football pitches. The first hillfort was built on the site around 500 BC and in its hey-day was densely populated with clusters of roundhouses and a network of roads. Despite being strengthened in 250 BC, the Romans besieged then captured it in AD 43. It was a fierce battle: an ancient Briton skeleton with a Roman crossbow bolt in the spine was found at the site. After their capture, the inhabitants were moved to the then Roman new town of Durnovaria – modern Dorchester. The sheer scale of the ramparts is awe inspiring, especially from the ditches immediately below, and the winding complexity of the west entrance reveals just how hard it would be to storm. Finds from the site are displayed at Dorset County Museum (p138). Maiden Castle is 1.5 miles southwest of Dorchester.

Cerne Abbas & the Cerne Giant
☎ 01300 / pop 732

Cerne Abbas is the epitome of a sleepy Dorset hamlet. Houses run the gamut of architectural styles and centuries, climbing roses adorn countless doorways and half-timbered houses frame a honey-coloured, 12th-century church.

But it also packs one heck of a surprise – a real nudge-nudge, wink-wink tourist attraction in the form of the **Cerne Giant**. Nude, full frontal and notoriously well endowed, this chalk figure is revealed in all his glory on a hill on the edge of town. And he's in the kind of stage of excitement that wouldn't be allowed in most magazines. Around 60m high and 51m wide, the figure's age remains a mystery, some argue he's a depiction of the Roman god Hercules, but the first actual reference to him is in 1694, when three shillings were set aside for his repair. The Victorians found it all deeply embarrassing and allowed grass to grow over his most outstanding feature. Today the hill is grazed by sheep and cattle – only the sheep though are allowed to do their nibbling over the giant – the cows would do too much damage to his lines.

Away from the giggling crowds, its worth searching out the remains of Cerne's Benedictine abbey, near the village church. Founded in 987, it was destroyed by that architectural vandal Henry VIII, but it's still possible to see the remnants of the **Abbot's Porch** (adult/child £1/20p); an exquisite red-gold structure complete with lattices, shields and oriel windows.

SLEEPING & EATING

Badger Hill (☎ 341698; 11 Springfield; s £27-32, d £54-70; **P**) A huge cedar-wood bungalow with sedate bursts of B&B chintz – little posies of fresh flowers and some draped doilies. It's on the edge of the village – a minute's walk takes you to the giant, four delivers you to the pubs.

New Inn (☎ 341274; www.newinncerneabbas.co.uk; 14 Long St; s/d £40/80; **P** ✗) The New Inn was 'new' when the Plantagenets were on the throne. Its 13th-century rooms are rustically comfy: exposed stone, bits of old furniture and sparkling new bathrooms. A proper, local pub (look out for the village cricket team), the grub is good (mains £8) – try the flavoursome steak and ale pie.

Royal Oak (☎ 341797; 23 Long St; mains £11-13; ✆ lunch & dinner) This thatched pub dishes up superb food – whole crab or lobster salad, Dartmouth smokehouse eels and Lyme Bay scallops in lemon butter. It's gorgeously atmospheric with flagstone floors, wonky beams and a great collection of old stone beer bottles.

GETTING THERE & AWAY

Bus D12 runs to Cerne Abbas from Sherborne (30 minutes) and Dorchester (20 minutes) two to three times a day, Monday to Friday only.

SHERBORNE

☎ 01935 / pop 9350

Sherborne gleams with a mellow, orangey-yellow stone – it's been used to build a central cluster of 15th-century buildings, and the impressive abbey church at their core. This serene town exudes wealth. The five local fee-paying schools include the famous Sherborne School and its pupils are a frequent sight as they head off to lessons from boarding houses dotted around the town. The boutique shops and the number of convertibles in the car parks reinforces the well-heeled feel. Evidence of big expenditure, 16th- and 18th-century style, lies on the edge of town – two castles, one a crumbling ruin, the other a marvellous manorhouse complete with a Capability Brown lake.

Sherborne's **tourist office** (☎ 815341; sherborne .tic@westdorset-dc.gov.uk; Digby Rd; ☷ 9am-5pm Mon-Sat Apr-Oct) stocks the free *All About Sherborne* leaflet with a map and town trail. **Walking tours** (£3) depart from the tourist office at 11am on Friday from May to September, and last 1½ hours . The Green Hill area of town, a cluster of eateries and B&B options, is at the top of Cheap St, while the town's two castles are a 15-minute walk east from the centre.

Sights

SHERBORNE ABBEY

At the height of its influence the magnificent **Abbey Church of St Mary the Virgin** (☎ 812452; suggested donation £2; ☷ 8.30am-6pm late Mar-late Oct, 8.30am-4pm Nov–mid-Mar) was the central cathedral of the 26 Saxon bishops of Wessex. Established early in the 8th century, it became a Benedictine abbey in 998 and functioned as a cathedral until 1075. The church has the oldest fan vaulting in the country, solid Saxon-Norman piers support the central tower and the main entrance has a Norman porch built in 1180. There are also several intriguing tombs – look out for the elaborate marble effigy on the one belonging to John Lord Digby, Earl of Bristol, while both of Alfred the Great's elder brothers, Ethelred and Ethelbert, are buried in the corner.

On the edge of the abbey lie the beautiful, 15th-century **St Johns' Almshouses** (admission £1.50; ☷ 2-4pm Tue & Thu-Sat May-Sep). Notice the six-sided **conduit** now at the foot of Cheap St. This arched structure used to be the monks' lavatorium, or washhouse, but was moved to provide the townsfolk with water when the abbey was disbanded.

OLD CASTLE

These days the epitome of a picturesque ruin, Sherborne's **Old Castle** (EH; ☎ 812730; adult/child £2.40/1.80; ☷ 10am-6pm Jul & Aug, 10am-5pm Apr-Jun & Sep, 10am-4pm Oct), was built by Roger, Bishop of Salisbury, in around 1120. Queen Elizabeth gave it to her one-time favourite Sir Walter Raleigh in the late 16th century – he spent large sums of money modernising it before opting for a new building instead, moving across the River Yeo to start work on the next Sherborne Castle. The old one became a Royalist stronghold during the English Civil War, but Cromwell reduced the 'malicious and mischievous castle' to rubble after a 16-day siege in 1645.

SHERBORNE CASTLE

Having had enough of the then 400-year-old Old Castle, Sir Walter Raleigh began building **New Castle** (☎ 813182; www.sherbornecastle.com; house adult/child £8/free, gardens only £4/free; ☷ 11am-4.30pm Tue-Thu & weekends Apr-Oct) in 1594. Really a splendid manorhouse, he got as far as the central block before falling out of favour with the royals and ending up back in prison – this time at the hands of James I. In 1617 James sold the castle to Sir John Digby, the Earl of Bristol, who added the wings we see today. In 1753, the grounds received a mega-makeover at the hands of landscape gardener extraordinaire, Capability Brown. Visit today and marvel at the massive lake he added, along with a remarkable 12 hectares of waterside gardens.

SHERBORNE MUSEUM

A digital version of the *Sherborne Missal*, the most exquisite illuminated manuscript to survive from the Middle Ages, can be viewed at the **Sherborne Museum** (☎ 812252; www.sherbornemu seum.co.uk; Church Lane; adult/child £2/free; ☷ 10.30am-4.30pm Tue-Sat Apr-Oct). With this high-tech copy you can turn the virtual pages and zoom in on sections of text.

DORSET

Sleeping

Cumberland House (☎ 817554; sandie@bandbdorset
.co.uk; Green Hill; s £45, d £59-69) A 17th-century B&B
with few straight lines – instead walls un-
dulate towards each other. Charming rooms
are done out in white, beige and tiny bursts
of vivid pink. Breakfast is either Continental
(complete with chocolate croissants) or full
English – either way there's freshly squeezed
orange juice.

Antelope (☎ 812077; www.theantelopehotel.co.uk;
Green Hill; s £54-60, d £60-85) A creaking 18th-
century coaching inn, which shows its age
slightly; some corners are a little scuffed,
some paint peels, but it's actually all part of
the charm. The beamed rooms are simple
with sash windows and there are old prints
on the walls.

Stoneleigh Barn (☎ 815964; www.stoneleighbarn
.com; North Wootton; s £45-56, d £70-80, f £80-100;
P X ⚡ &) Outside, this 18th-century barn
delights the senses – it's smothered in bright,
fragrant flowers. Inside, exposed trusses frame
rooms tastefully decorated in cream and gold
and crammed with books and jigsaws. One
room is suitable for those with disabilities.
Two miles southeast of town.

Eastbury Hotel (☎ 813131; www.theeastburyhotel
.co.uk; Long St; s £68, d £120-140) The best rooms
here have real wow factor – black and gold
lacquer screens sit discreetly in front of minimalist free-standing baths; shimmering fabrics swathe French sleigh beds. The standard
rooms are much more standard, but are still
elegant with stripy furnishings and paired-
down wicker chairs.

Eating & Drinking

Pear Tree Deli (☎ 812828; Half Moon St; mains £4-8;
9am-5pm Mon-Sat, 10am-4pm Sun) Full of mouth-
watering aromas, this delectable deli is an
ideal place to stock up on gourmet picnic supplies. Spinach and feta pie, homemade soups
and a wealth of local cheeses are coupled with
irresistible cakes and puds.

Paprika (☎ 816429; Half Moon St; mains £7-12;
lunch & dinner) Expect excellent, well-spiced
food in this Indian restaurant. The menu is
a mix of the usual fare and some surprises:
honey and cashew-nut chicken, garlic marsala
and Thai prawn risotto.

Green (☎ 813821; 3 The Green; 2/3 courses £25/30;
lunch & dinner Tue-Sat) Local food features
strongly at this intimate, cream and green
restaurant at the top of Cheap St. Tempting
flavour combinations include Dorset venison
and butternut squash, or local crab with tar-
ragon and avocado.

Half Moon Inn (☎ 812017; Half Moon St) The
town's liveliest pub – best appreciated on
the streetside terrace as the sun sets over the
abbey nearby.

Getting There & Away

Bus 57 runs from Yeovil (30 minutes, half-
hourly Monday to Saturday), as does bus 58
(15 minutes, every two hours Monday to Saturday, six on Sunday), which sometimes continues to Shaftesbury (£5.10, 1½ hours). Buses
D12 and D13 run to Dorchester (one hour,
three to six daily Monday to Saturday).

Hourly trains go to Exeter (£13.80, 1¼
hours), London (£36.60, 2½ hours) and Salisbury (£9.60, 45 minutes).

SHAFTESBURY & AROUND
☎ 01747 / pop 6665

Crowning a hilltop and gathered around its
historic abbey ruins, Shaftesbury is somehow both typically English and reminiscent
of a walled European settlement. Its compact
centre and bird's-eye views lend it the self-
contained air of an ancient French hill town,
but the jumbling of British architectural styles
is much more Dorset than the Dordogne.
Oddly, there's a fair chance you'll know one
of Shaftesbury's streets even if you've never
been there – it features in one of Britain's
most famous TV ads.

The **tourist office** (☎ 853514; www.shaftesburydor
set.com; 8 Bell St; 10am-5pm daily Apr-Sep, 10am-3pm
Mon-Sat Oct-Mar) is by the Bleke St car park.

Sights

Irresistibly pretty **Gold Street** is Shaftesbury's
best-known landmark – its steep cobbled
slope is lined with chocolate-box cottages
topped by thatch and tile roofs. It's the setting for Hovis' *Boy on the Bike* commercial,
where a young lad struggles up the street to
the strains of a brass band, before bobbling
down again having got his loaf. Interestingly
Hovis also contributed £10,000 to the restoration of the cobbles.

Shaftesbury Abbey (☎ 852910; www.shaftesburyab
bey.co.uk; Park Walk; adult/child £2.50/£1; 10am-5pm
Apr-Oct) was founded by Alfred the Great in
888 and was the first religious house in Britain built solely for women; Alfred's daughter,
Aethelgifu, was its first abbess. King Knut

died at the abbey in 1035, and it's thought his heart is buried here. Before Henry VIII's dissolution of the monasteries in 1539, the abbey was home to the largest community of nuns in England – most buildings now are in ruins, but you can still wander around its foundations with a well-devised audioguide.

The small **Gold Hill Museum** (☎ 852157; Gold Hill; adult/child £2.50/1; ☾ 10.30am-4.30pm Thu-Tue) is worth visiting for its local exhibits, including an 18th-century fire engine, a collection of Dorset decorative buttons, and an ornamental Byzant coin, used during the town's ancient water ceremony.

There's a touch of the Continental about the hexagonal **Old Wardour Castle** (EH; ☎ 870487; adult/child £3.40/1.70; ☾ 10am-6pm Jul & Aug, 10am-5pm Apr-Jun & Sep, 10am-4pm Oct, plus Sat & Sun Nov-Mar). It was built in lavish French style in the 14th century – primarily for entertainment rather than defence. Severely damaged during the English Civil War, its towering part-ruins are a romantic spot today – it even featured in the film *Robin Hood, Prince of Thieves*. Bus 26 runs the 4 miles from Shaftesbury (three daily, Monday to Saturday).

Sleeping

Cobwebbs (☎ 853505; www.cobwebbs.me.uk; 14 Gold Hill; d £70; ☐ ✗) Half-way up Gold Hill and postcard perfect; roses climb up the white-washed front, a thatched roof sits on top. You get access to a sitting room as well as double bedroom. The patio doors lead onto the lovely rear terrace.

Retreat (☎ 850372; www.the-retreat.org.uk; 47 Bell St; s/d/f £40/80/115; P) The rooms in this Georgian town house are large and stately, if a little staid – all moulded ceilings, antique chairs and pieces of 19th-century china. Two minutes' walk from town.

Fleur de Lys (☎ 853717; www.lafleurdelys.co.uk; Bleke St; s £75, d £100-120, f £155; P ✗ ☐) For a lovely dollop of luxury immerse yourself in the world of Fleur de Lys. Fluffy bathrobes, minifridges and laptop computers ensure you click into pamper mode. Pop downstairs for an aperitif on the terrace, before dining in the elegant restaurant (two/three courses £24/29) for lunch Wednesday to Sunday or dinner Monday to Saturday. The menu includes quail with raspberry and apple, and smoked salmon and samphire. Two hundred metres from the centre of town.

Eating & Drinking

Green Rock (☎ 858550; Swans Yard; mains £4; ☾ 9am-5pm Mon-Sat) Tasty meat-free food in a modern building tucked off the high street. Try its bean and veggie casserole.

Mitre Inn (☎ 852549; 23 High St; mains £6-10; ☾ lunch & dinner Mon-Sat, lunch Sun) An atmospheric town-centre pub, which combines wooden floors and stunning hill views with good beer and bar food – smoked haddock fish cakes and butternut-squash risotto.

Bell Street Café (☎ 850022; 17 Bell St; mains £10-15; ☾ lunch Tue-Sat, dinner Wed-Sat) A funky bistro where the flavours are from Lombardy, Gascony and Burgundy but the ingredients are often local, seasonal and organic. Ancient wooden stairs and whitewashed walls give it a cool feel – helped by regular live bands (flamenco and swing).

Getting There & Away

Buses 309/310 run to Blandford (1¼ hours, two to four Monday to Saturday). Bus 58 goes to Sherborne (1¾ hours) and onto Yeovil (two hours, five daily, Monday to Saturday), while buses 26/27 and 29 go to Salisbury (1¼ hours, five to seven Monday to Saturday).

One National Express bus a day runs direct from Shaftesbury to London Victoria, via Heathrow (£17.20, three hours 50 minutes).

BLANDFORD FORUM

01258 / pop 8755

Today a charming architectural curiosity, Blandford Forum's history was actually forged by fire. The town was consumed by a massive conflagration in 1731 and the monumental rebuilding programme that followed has resulted in a rarity – a town centre that dates from just one period. Local builders the Bastard brothers (coyly pronounced 'B'stard' locally) were commissioned to do the work and did a fine job; these days Blandford is a satisfying collection of porticoes, sash windows, walled gardens and graceful streets. Architecture aside, the town also offers two unusual attractions: an army signals museum, and the chance to wander around a brewery.

The **tourist office** (☎ 454770; blandfordtic@bt connect.com; 1 Greyhound Yard; ☾ 10am-5pm Mon-Sat Apr-Sep, till 3pm Oct-Mar) is located by the West St car park and sells an excellent town trail leaflet (£1).

Sights

Blandford's fire began in a tallow chandlers on the site of the Kings Arms at the foot of White Cliff Mill St – 13 people lost their lives and 480 families were made homeless. Over the next 30 years a remarkable concentration of Georgian architecture developed; everywhere you look oriel windows and mathematical tiles perch over white colonnades and weathered red bricks. There's also the delightful, Georgian **Parish Church of St Peter and St Paul**. Among the first buildings to go up, it was finished in 1739 and has an arched white cupola on the tower instead of a spire. The colonnaded former **town pump** is just outside. Turned into a monument to the work of the Bastard brothers, it notes 'Divine Mercy has raised this town like a phoenix from the ashes'.

At the **Hall and Woodhouse Badger Brewery** (☎ 486004; www.hall-woodhouse.co.uk; Blandford St Mary; adult/child £6/4; ☉ visitor centre 10.30am-5.30pm Mon-Sat, plus 11am-2pm Sun Apr-Oct, tours at 11am & 2.30pm Mon & Wed-Sat, plus 11am Sun Apr-Oct) you get to watch ale being made. Set up by a Dorset farmer in 1777, the firm secured the contract to supply beer to the army camped at Weymouth during the Napoleonic Wars and moved to Blandford in 1899. Guided tours wind past huge vats and you get to taste the malt, smell the hops and sup such delights as Tanglefoot and First Gold. The brewery is on the southwest fringes of Blandford – book if you want to be sure of a tour.

The **Royal Signals Museum** (☎ 482084; www.royal signalsmuseum.com; Blandford Camp; adult/child £6.50/4; ☉ 10am-5pm Mon-Fri, plus 10am-4pm Sat & Sun Feb-Oct) is located inside the corp's base and is very hands-on-war – the tone is set at the start when you report to the guardroom for directions. Exhibits chart the history of army communications from the Crimean War to the Gulf, feature the work of women spies during WWII and include one of the famous Nazi Enigma code machines. The museum is 2 miles east of Blandford; some buses on the 184 route stop there (20 minutes, two to four daily).

Sleeping & Eating

St Martin's House (☎ 451245; www.stmartinshouse .co.uk; White Cliff Mill St; s/d £40/60; ℗ ☒) A cosy, Victorian B&B where brass bedsteads and cast-iron baths sit snugly alongside heavy embroidered fabrics and old wood furniture. Handily placed, it's a five-minute walk from the town centre – its owners speak French and Spanish.

our pick Portman Lodge (☎ 453727; www.portman lodge.co.uk; White Cliff Mill St; s/d £45/65; ℗) The perfect place to swap travellers' tales, this 19th-century house is stuffed to its high ceilings with an astounding collection of souvenirs amassed during the owner's 40 years working abroad. Thai figurines, Egyptian bridal jewellery and huge Angolan masks (check out the one with the grass beard) all jostle for space. Bedrooms are only slightly more subdued. Flowery furnishings are topped off with lace and fabric canopies or brown leather and white linen. Get the owner to talk you through the collection and head off on a virtual tour of the world.

Crown Hotel (☎ 456626; West St; thecrownhotel @blandforddorset.co.uk; s £80, d £110-125, f £130; ℗) Built immediately after the fire, the décor is sensitive to its grand age. Thick drapes hang the elegant length of its tall ceilings, gold picture frames and brown leather armchairs surround brass beds. The Georgian bar is encircled by tapestries, dark wood and leather-bound books – its varied dinner menu (mains £9 to £18) ranges from stuffed aubergine or ham, eggs and chips, to classic peppered steak.

Getting There & Away

Bus 83 goes to Shaftesbury (40 minutes, three daily, Monday to Friday) and Wimborne (30 minutes). The X8 bus runs to Poole (40 minutes, hourly Monday to Friday, four on Sunday), while bus 184 travels to Salisbury (1¼ hours, five daily Monday to Saturday, two on Sunday), Weymouth (one hour) and Dorchester (45 minutes).

WEYMOUTH & THE WEST COAST

The stretch of shoreline between Weymouth and Devon is like a living, breathing TV documentary on an epic scale. Here the Jurassic Coast really comes into its own. The pebble ridge of Chesil Beach spreads along a breathtaking 17 miles of shore. Inland lies a massive lagoon at Abbotsbury, which is home to an absolutely unique attraction – a swannery of 600 nesting birds. Lyme Regis summons up an irresistible whiff of fossil fever, while the Isle of Portland juts proudly out from its picture-postcard neighbours, providing an engrossing insight into a historic quarrying community. Geology aside, the Georgian resort of Weymouth is busy reinventing itself as an Olympic-class water-sports centre.

WEYMOUTH

☎ 01305 / pop 50,917

At just over 200 years old, Weymouth is a grand dame of a resort with a few tricks up her faded sleeve. Candy-striped kiosks and deck chairs line a beach where Punch still screams at Judy – chuck in cockles and chippies and prepare to promenade down seaside memory lane. But just as Weymouth lurches towards pastiche, the old girl pulls a couple of surprises: the resort has revitalised its historic harbour and secured the 2012 Olympic sailing events. Then there are natural assets that always endure: masses of golden sand, a deep blue arch of bay, green headlands and distant white cliffs.

King George III put Weymouth on the seaside map when he took an impromptu dip here in 1789 to cure his 'nervous disorder' and so launched the resort's Georgian heyday. Its legacy is a line of tall, white, seafront buildings with a huge, peeling statue of the king, from a decidedly grateful town, in the middle.

Orientation & Information

Weymouth is strung along the seafront. To the west is the rejuvenated harbour, a vibrant jumble of brightly painted Georgian town houses, restaurants and pubs.

The **tourist office** (☎ 785747; www.visitweymouth .co.uk; The Esplanade; ⏰ 9.30am-5pm Apr-Oct, 10am-4pm Nov-Mar) sells discounted tickets to many local attractions.

Sights & Activities

Weymouth's **beach** is a chance to surrender to your inner kitsch and rent a deck chair, sun lounger or a pedalo (£5 per hour). Alternatively, go all Californian and join a volleyball game.

The recently revamped, 19th-century **Nothe Fort** (☎ 766626; www.fortressweymouth.co.uk; Barrack Rd; adult/child £5/1; ⏰ 10.30am-5.30pm May-Sep, 2.30-4.30pm Sun Oct-Apr) is all martial magnificence – 12-in coastal guns, cannons, rifles and searchlights. It also details the Roman invasion of Dorset, a Victorian soldier's drill and Weymouth in

DORSET

A BOX-OFFICE COAST

The kind of massive, hands-on geology lesson you wish you had at school, the Jurassic Coast is England's first natural World Heritage Site – putting it on a par with the Great Barrier Reef and the Grand Canyon. This exquisite section of shoreline, stretching from Exmouth in East Devon to just beyond Swanage in Dorset, encompasses 185 million years of the earth's history in just 95 miles. This means you can walk, sometimes in just a few hours, many millions of years in geological time.

It all began with earth movements tilting the rocks from west to east. Newer layers formed on top then erosion exposed the different strata, leaving the oldest formations in the west and the youngest in the east. And the differences are very tangible. The rusty-red Triassic rocks in the Devon section are some 200 to 250 million years old; their colour is down to the presence of iron. The dark-clay Jurassic cliffs around Lyme Regis (p160) ensure superb fossil hunting, while the bulk of the coast from Lyme to the Isle of Purbeck (p134) is around 200 to 140 million years old. Pockets of much younger, creamy-coloured Cretaceous rocks (a mere 140 to 65 million years old) also pop up, notably around Lulworth Cove (p137), where erosion has sculpted a stunning display of cliffs, coves, rock arches and stacks – particularly visible at the Durdle Door (see the boxed text, p137).

Good sources of information are www.jurassiccoast.com and the local tourist offices. They also sell the *Official Guide to the Jurassic Coast* (£4.95) and the child-friendly *Explorers Guide to the Jurassic Coast* (£2.95); both are excellent for helping to interpret the landscape. Responsible fossil hunting is positively encouraged by the authorities as these nuggets of prehistory would otherwise be destroyed by the sea. But the coast is highly unstable in places and the official advice is to keep away from the cliffs, stay on public paths, check tide times, only pick up from the beach (never dig out from cliffs), always leave some behind for others and tell the experts if you find a stunner.

WWII. The coast views are fabulous, and commanding an armoured car and clambering around the magazine prove popular with regiments of children.

The red-brick Brewer's Quay has a shopping centre as well as **Timewalk** (☎ 777622; Hope Sq; adult/child £4.25/3; ⏰ 10am-5.30pm Feb-Nov), a sensory journey through the sights, sounds and smells of Weymouth's history from the Black Death and the Spanish Armada to a Georgian ballroom. Next door, the **Weymouth Museum** (☎ 777622; admission free; ⏰ 10am-5pm) is strong on the Great Western Railway, as well as smuggling, paddle steamers and shipwrecks.

Deep Sea Adventure (☎ 0871 222 5760; www.deep sea-adventure.co.uk; 9 Custom House Quay; adult/child £4/3;

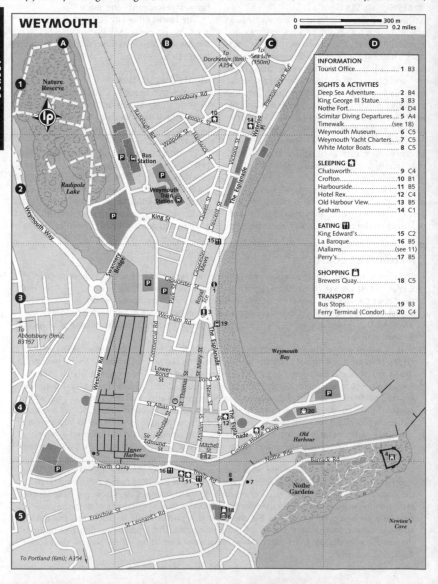

WEYMOUTH

0 _____ 300 m
0 _____ 0.2 miles

☑ 9.30am-5pm Sep-Jun, till later in high season) uses models and computer games to detail the history of diving. To stop it getting too serious there's a kids' play area and laser shootout zone.

Seals, otters and sea horses meet you at **Sea Life** (☎ 761070; www.sealife.co.uk; Lodmoor Country Park; adult/child £11.50/8; ☑ 10am-5pm). Look out too for the deadly striped sea snakes.

White Motor Boats (☎ 785000; www.whitemotor boat.freeuk.com; adult/child return £7/5) run a cracking 35-minute jaunt across to Portland Castle (p158) from Cove Row on the harbour. There are three to four a day between April and October.

The range of water sports available locally is superb; see the boxed text, p159.

Sleeping

Crofton (☎ 785903; fax 750105; 36 Lennox St; s/d with shared bathroom £23/40; ℗) A classic British B&B – carpets clash with the furnishings and each other and only sometimes match the wallpaper. In a street full of its counterparts, it's also cheap, cheerful, clean and disarmingly friendly.

Seaham (☎ 782010; www.theseaham.co.uk; 3 Waterloo Pl; s £30-38 d £60-76; ✗) Bright and fresh, the pink rooms get a style boost from floating drapes and sleek TVs; the breakfast room is crisp and finished in blue and white. The front bedrooms have window seats, sea glimpses and a low rumble of traffic noise.

Chatsworth (☎ 785012; www.thechatsworth.co.uk; 14 The Esplanade; s £35-45, d £72-108) With big bay windows and squishy settees, this B&B's great location means you choose to see the harbour or the seafront. The furnishings are super-trendy with purple satin, leather armchairs, vanilla candles and worn wood. There's also a lovely waterside terrace – watch yachts cast off just metres away as you breakfast.

Old Harbour View (☎ 774633; fax 750828; 12 Trinity Rd; d £75-80) Boats right outside the front door and boating themes in the bedrooms – the headboards are in the tall, paired-down shape of a prow. Set in a Georgian terrace, rooms are fresh with lots of white-painted wood – one overlooks the harbour, the other faces the back.

our pick Harbourside (☎ 777150; www.harbour side2let.co.uk; 5 Trinity Rd; 2/4 people £80/125) So close to the water you can almost hear it lapping. Regency meets modern in this stylish apartment – elegant antique chairs and brass bedsteads combine with maplewood

and Egyptian cotton. The twin and double bedrooms and the lounge look out directly onto the bustling harbour. It's often rented as a weekly let (£300 to £700) but the nightly rates are a bargain.

Hotel Rex (☎ 760400; www.kingshotels.co.uk; 29 The Esplanade; s £59-68 d £86-120; ☐) Reminiscent of bonnets and Empire silhouettes, this Regency hotel sits sedately on the seafront. The best five rooms have fantastically high ceilings, balconies and superb views over Weymouth Bay while the others are pleasant but more uniform – bright fabrics, light woods and only glimpses of period charm.

Eating & Drinking

It's got to be done: sit on Weymouth seafront and scoff fish 'n' chips. For a waterside drink you're best heading off to the pubs and bars lining the harbour.

King Edward's (☎ 786924; 100 The Esplanade; mains £6; ☑ lunch & dinner) A classic chippy – all burgundy tiles and wrought iron, eat inside or out. Then chase it down with an ice cream from the kiosks dotting the prom.

La Baroque (☎ 750666; 19 Trinity Rd; tapas £4, mains £13; ☑ lunch & dinner) Baroque by name, baroque by nature. Munch tapas surrounded by raspberry walls and heavy gilt pictures in the wine bar. Or pop upstairs to sturdy tables, sleek chairs, Toulouse Lautrec prints and classy dining – beef with truffled lentils, mushrooms and spinach.

our pick Perry's (☎ 785799; 4 Trinity Rd; mains £12-17; ☑ lunch Tue-Fri & Sun, dinner Tue-Sat, plus Mon & Sun in summer) Effortlessly elegant, but also relaxed, this Georgian town house is a study of snowy-white tablecloths and flashes of pink. For a fabulous harbour view ask for the window table on the 1st floor. The fish comes from local merchants, the shellfish is direct from Portland. Just try and resist the Lyme Bay scallops, twice-baked Dorset Blue Vinny cheese soufflé or the crab soup. Its two-course lunch is amazing value at £15.

Mallams (☎ 776757; www.mallamsrestaurant.co.uk; 5 Trinity Rd; 2/3 courses £23/29; ☑ dinner May-Sep, Mon-Sat Oct-Apr) A romantic harbourside eatery with subdued lighting and old stone. Ethically sourced fish features heavily – sustainable cod covered in a dill and parmesan crust and New Forest barramundi with Cajun spice. Top it off with a white and dark chocolate torte with raspberry sauce.

DORSET

DORSET

Getting There & Away

BOAT
Condor Ferries (☎ 0870 243 5140; www.condorferries .com) runs daily fast ferries between Weymouth and the Channel Islands (two to 2½ hours). Normal return fares start at £90 for a foot passenger, and £250 for a car and driver, but there are cheaper deals on day trips (adult/child return from £23/16).

BUS
There's one direct National Express coach to London (£25, 4¼ hours) a day.

Bus 10 runs to Dorchester (30 minutes, three per hour). Bus 31 stops in Dorchester en route to Lyme Regis (two hours, hourly) and Axminster. Bus X53 goes to Wareham (50 minutes, six daily, four on Sunday) and Bournemouth (£5.50, two hours), and to Abbotsbury (35 minutes), Lyme Regis (1½ hours) and Exeter (£5.50, three hours) in the opposite direction. Bus 1 travels regularly to Portland (30 minutes).

TRAIN
Trains run hourly to London (£41, three hours) via Dorchester South (11 minutes) and Bournemouth (£10.90, one hour), and every two hours to Dorchester West, Bath (£12.60, two hours) and Bristol (£14.60, 2¼ hours).

AROUND WEYMOUTH
Isle of Portland
01305 / pop 12,795
A hard, high comma of rock fused to Dorset by the ridge of Chesil Beach (opposite), in places Portland feels half finished. Its central plateau is pock-marked by the quarries used to extract its famous limestone and huge slabs of rock lie around. Here and there the crenellated minicastles of moneyed quarry owners suddenly pop up – not unlike surreal scenes from a David Lynch film. But the Isle is also strangely compelling. Proud, independent and decidedly different from the rest of Dorset, it's all the more intriguing because of it, and the stark beauty of its wind-whipped coasts, rich bird life and the activities on offer make it worthy of at least a day trip.

Portland is just over 4 miles long and 3 miles wide. The main settlement of Fortuneswell blurs into Castletown and Chiswell at the end of the road onto the Isle. The central plateau soars to 150m, taking in the village of Easton

in the middle. Portland Bill lies at the very southern tip, along with a summer-only **tourist office** (☎ 861233; Portland Bill; ☻ 11am-5pm Apr-Sep).

SIGHTS & ACTIVITIES
The red and white stripes of **Portland Bill Lighthouse** (☎ 820495; ☻ 11am-5pm Sun-Fri Apr-Sep) stick out above the remote headland. Climb to the top of its 13m tower and look down at the Race, a surging vortex of conflicting tides.

Portland Castle (EH; ☎ 820539; Castletown; adult/child £3.80/1.90; ☻ 10am-6pm Jul & Aug, till 5pm Apr-Jun & Sep, till 4pm Oct) looks surprisingly delicate but is one of the finest examples of the fortifications constructed during Henry VIII's castle-building spree. Inside you can try on period armour and enjoy great views over Portland Harbour.

From Mesolithic, through Roman and Tudor to the present day, Portland has a rich history. The Isle's **museum** (☎ 821804; 217 Wakeham St; adult/child £2.50/free; ☻ 10.30am-5pm Fri-Tue Easter-Oct) explores it with displays on fossils, shipwrecks and smuggling. Intriguingly, the first curator was Dr Marie Stopes, who went on to pioneer the birth-control pill.

Getting off Portland's sometimes bleak through-routes reveals a surprising side. Ancient terraces of fishermen's cottages wind down to the coast around **Chiswell**, while behind the museum a lane weaves past the ruins of the Norman **Rufus Castle** to good swimming at **Church Ope Cove** (via 150-odd steps). The exposed coast around Portland Bill has striking views and is particularly rich in **bird life** – in the spring expect flocks of migrants, in the summer look out for guillemots, kittiwakes and the odd puffin.

Portland offers extraordinary **rock climbing** on its precipitous cliffs. The usual safety and environmental rules apply – the tourist offices in Portland and Weymouth can advise. The waters round Portland offer a tempting range of **water sports**, from sailing and windsurfing to incredibly varied diving – see the boxed text, opposite.

SLEEPING & EATING
Portland YHA Hostel (☎ 0870 770 6000; www.yha.org.uk; Hardy House, Castle Rd; dm £19; **P**) Bright fabrics and pine jazz up this red-brick hostel of six-bed dorms on the fringes of Fortuneswell. You can't opt out of breakfast, which pushes the price up. Luckily it's good: Fairtrade *cafetière* (plunger) coffee, bacon, eggs and croissants.

WATER WONDERLAND

Stunning to look at, the seas around Weymouth and Portland are also a massive watery playground. So good, they're to host the sailing events for the 2012 Olympics. In part it's due to Portland Harbour – 890 hectares of sheltered water created by breakwaters begun by convict labour in the mid-1800s.

Weymouth Yacht Charters (☎ 01305-770283; www.weymouth-charters.co.uk; 11 Nothe Pde, Weymouth) offers yachting training for beginners (£200/365 for two/five days); bare-boat or skippered charters start from £350 for five days. **Weymouth and Portland National Sailing Academy** (☎ 0845 337 3214; www.wpnsa.org.uk; Portland Harbour) runs tuition for beginners (£155/295 for two/four days).

The Academy also holds windsurfing lessons (£90 per day) as does **Windtek** (☎ 01305-787900; www.windtek.co.uk; 109 Portland Rd, Wyke Regis; per 1/2 days £90/150) just after the bridge onto Portland. It also hires gear (£15 per hour) if you have a Royal Yachting Association card.

Underwater it's a diver's delight: there's a huge variety of depths, seascapes, and wrecks from paddle steamers and East Indiamen to WWII vessels. Rigid inflatable boats (RIBs) tend to run to shallower sites from Portland Harbour. The further, deeper dives accessible by hard boat, leave from Weymouth.

On Portland, **Underwater Explorers** (☎ 01305-824555; www.underwaterexplorers.co.uk; 15 Castletown, Portland) runs courses from a £85 a day to a four-day open-water qualification for £395. **Fathom & Blues** (☎ 01305-826789; www.fathomandblues.co.uk; Boscawen Centre, Castletown, Portland) offers a full range of PADI courses from a £95 taster day to an eight-day Divemaster (£550). It'll shuttle qualified divers to a site for between £16 and £34 and rent a range of equipment (from £50).

Scimitar Diving (☎ 07765 326728; www.scimitardiving.co.uk) excursions leave from Weymouth Harbour. Its hard boats shuttle to offshore dives for £40 per diver per day. It also rents a range of gear from £25.

Brackenbury House (☎ 826509; www.brackenbury house.co.uk; New Rd; s/d £26/52; P ⊠) A former manse, rich red carpets and dark woods fill this charming late-Victorian B&B. The bright rooms have cast-iron fireplaces and moulded flourishes on the ceilings. On the edge of Fortuneswell, on the road towards Easton.

Heights Hotel (☎ 821361; www.heightshotel.com; Portland; s/d/f £95/110/140; P ⊠ ▣) Plonked on top of Portland's central plateau, this firmly corporate, 65-room hotel has plush fabrics in the bedrooms and sparkly white bathrooms. There's a pool, sauna and steam room and expansive views towards Weymouth from its bistro-bar.

Cove House Inn (☎ 820895; Chiswell; mains £9; ☯ lunch & dinner) Right at the end of Chesil Beach, this fabulously friendly old fishermen's pub has oars, lead weights and black-and-white photos of shipwrecks hanging from its rough stone walls. The local fish is delicious – try its superfresh hand-dived scallops.

GETTING THERE & AWAY

Bus 1 runs from Weymouth to Fortuneswell in Portland every half-hour. Between June and September it goes on to Portland Bill. Between October and May bus 10 heads out to Portland Bill, but Monday to Friday only.

Chesil Beach
01305

One of the most breathtaking beaches in Britain, Chesil is a shade over 17 miles long, 15m high and moving inland at the rate of 5m a year. This mind-boggling, 100-million-tonne pebble ridge is the baby of the Jurassic Coast, a mere 6000 to 10,000 years old. It's thought the beach was formed when rising sea levels began depositing chert and flint on the much older bedrock, and its stones range from pea-sized in the west to hand-sized in the east. An energy-sapping hike up its shifting slopes takes you to dazzling views and the constant surge and rattle of sea on stones. Tucked behind is the Fleet, at 8 miles long, one of the most important lagoons in Europe.

Chesil Beach Centre (☎ 760579; Ferrybridge; admission free; ☯ 10am-5pm Apr-Sep, 11am-4pm Oct-Mar), just over the bridge to Portland, is a good place to get onto the ridge and find out about its origins and wildlife. At the west end of the beach, head for the (signed) car park just south of the Abbotsbury Sub Tropical Gardens. You can take one-hour **glass-bottomed**

DORSET

boat tours (☎ 759692; www.thefleetobserver.co.uk; Ferryman's Way, Wyke Regis; adult/child £6/4) of the lagoon that reveal murky waters and occasional sea squirts, anemones and wrasse. The tours run six to seven times daily from April up until October.

A visit to **Abbotsbury Swannery** (☎ 871858; New Barn Rd; adult/child £8/5; ☻ 10am-5pm or 6pm mid-Mar–Oct) puts you right in the middle of 600 nesting birds. Free flying, the swans are drawn by food and fresh water, and there's been a colony here for more than 600 years. You get to wander the network of trails snaking between waterways and see the extraordinary number of birds that nest beside and directly on the paths. It's an awe-inspiring experience – there are occasional territorial displays (think snuffling-cough and stand-up flapping) and even the liveliest children are stilled.

The village of Abbotsbury is an intensely thatched strip of honey-brown cottages, pubs and tearooms. A few miles west, the **Abbotsbury Sub Tropical Gardens** (☎ 871387; Bullers Way; adult/child £8/5; ☻ 10am-5pm or 6pm mid-Mar–Oct, 10am-4pm or dusk Nov–mid-Mar) are an 8-hectare indulgence – overflowing with the spikes and vivid petals of exotic plants from around the world.

There's camping at **East Fleet Farm** (☎ 785768; www.eastfleet.co.uk; Chickerell; tent sites £8-18; ☻ mid-Mar–Oct), a lagoonside, well-equipped site 2 miles from Portland. At the remote **West Fleet Holiday Farm** (☎ 782218; www.westfleetholidays.co.uk; Fleet; tent sites £10-17; ☻ Apr-Sep; ☻), 4 miles west, there's a pool, children's play area and bar in a cavernous barn.

LYME REGIS
☎ 01297 / pop 3504

Fantastically fossiliferous, Lyme Regis packs a heavyweight historical punch. Rock-hard relics of the past pop out at regular intervals from the surrounding cliffs – exposed by the landslides of a retreating coast. Now a pivot point of the World Heritage Site Jurassic Coast (p155), fossil fever is definitely in the air and everyone – from proper palaeontologists to those out for a bit of fun – can engage in a spot of coastal rummaging. Add sandy beaches and some delightful places to stay and eat, and you get a charming base for explorations.

The cultural credentials of Lyme (the Regis is dropped locally), are top notch. Jane Austen visited in 1804 and the town subsequently featured in *Persuasion*. Centuries later John Fowles was drawn here to write *The French Lieutenant's Woman*; the film version, starring Meryl Streep, later immortalised the iconic Cobb harbour defences in movie history. Way before that, Lyme got its royal charter from Edward I in 1284, was besieged by Royalists in 1644 and some 40 years later was the landing point for the Duke of Monmouth in his failed bid to seize the English throne.

A delightful, pastel-painted mishmash of architectural styles – thatches, terraces, gables and carved stone, Lyme fans out from two key roads, Broad St and Bridge St. Its **tourist office** (☎ 442138; www.westdorset.com; Church St; ☻ 10am-5pm Mon-Sat & 10am-4pm Sun Apr-Oct, 10am-3pm Mon-Sat Nov-Mar) is at the foot of town.

Sights & Activities

The **Cobb**, a curling harbour wall–cum–sea defence, was first built in the 13th century and it's hard to resist wandering its length for a wistful, sea-gazing Meryl moment at the tip. The Cobb's been strengthened over the centuries and doesn't present the elegant line it once did – Lyme's entire sea-defences saw extensive work in 2006 – extra shingle and Normandy sand were imported to bolster today's steeply shelving pebbles and gentle crescent of golden beach.

Fossil fever is catching – even for those with no previous palaeontologic tendencies. Regular **fossil walks** are run by Dinosaurland Fossil Museum and the Town Museum in the summer, or just pitch up for one led by **Dr Colin Dawes** (☎ 443758; adult/child £7/5, ☻ tours 1pm Sun year-round, plus Wed & Fri May-Sep); meet at the Old Forge Fossil Shop in Broad St. They last about 2½ hours.

Alternatively, search yourself: at low tide, head a mile east along the beach to **Black Ven**, a mudflow that brings fossil-filled deposits onto the shores. The sea washes away the silt exposing waves of prehistoric treasures. The site does come with safety warnings: it's only accessible within two hours of low tide (check at the tourist office for times) and it's easy to get cut off. Steer at least 20m clear of the highly unstable cliffs and be aware the rocks are very slippery. Responsible fossil collecting is positively encouraged – for more tips see the boxed text, p155. A mile along **Monmouth Beach** to the west, hunt out the extraordinary **ammonite pavement** – hundreds of fossilised, swirling sea creatures exposed in layers of rock. The beach is accessible at all stages of the tide, the best displays are around low water.

Mary Anning found the first full ichthyosaur skeleton near Lyme in 1814. The site of her former home is now the excellent **Lyme Regis Philpot Museum** (☎ 443370; www .lymeregismuseum.co.uk; Bridge St; adult/child £2.50/free; 🕙 10am-5pm Mon-Sat, 11am-5pm Sun Apr-Oct, Sat & Sun only Nov-Mar). An incredibly famous fossilist in her day, the bonneted Miss Anning did much to pioneer the science of modern-day palaeontology; the museum exhibits her story along with spectacular fossils and other prehistoric finds.

The **Dinosaurland Fossil Museum** (☎ 443541; www.dinosaurland.co.uk; Coombe St; adult/child £4/3; 🕙 10am-5pm mid-Feb–Nov) is a mini, indoor Jurassic Park – packed with the remains of belemnites, thrissops and the graceful plesiosaur. Its timeline emphasises what an insignificant blip humans are and the museum does a subtle, but good, education job. Lifelike dinosaur models will thrill youngsters – the fossilised tyrannosaurus eggs and 73kg dinosaur dung will have them in raptures.

A 2-mile hike west of Lyme along the coast path takes you into the lush rainforest-esque **Undercliff Nature Reserve**. It's a landscape of landslips – partly collapsed cliffs, exposed tree roots and tangles of brambles. Follow the signs from the Holmbush car park.

DORSET

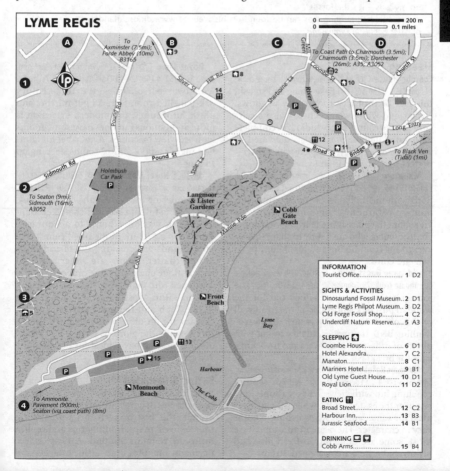

LYME REGIS

0 — 200 m
0 — 0.1 miles

DORSET

IN THE FOOTSTEPS OF FOSSILS

Steve Davies is a man with weathered legs and a gleam in his eye. And that gleam's never brighter than when, in his trademark shorts and trainers, he's heading off to the beach, leading a fossil hunting foray. Steve is the owner of the Dinosaurland Fossil Museum. So, what's the fascination?

'I love the hunting and gathering – the idea of collecting booty off the beach. I love just looking down and seeing something lying on the beach. It's just perfect – there it is a tiny little gold ammonite lying there waiting to be picked up – the sheer majesty of it all is mind-blowing.

'You never come close to seeing and understanding it all – there are always more to find and there's always more to learn. Then there's taking them back and spending hundreds of hours working on them, cleaning them for display.

'People's reactions are marvellous – you can see the ideas spark, and the thrill of the discovery. When children come in the museum it's 'wow!'. Then when we go out onto the beach and they find their own they are beside themselves with excitement.

'Before I came here, I used to work all over the world in the oil industry – but fossils have always been a passion and Lyme is so special – it's the history, traditions and the fossils still to be found. It kept me coming back and that's why I wanted to come to the area to live and bring up my kids – it's the fossils.'

Steve's fossil-hunting tips can be found on his website www.dinosaurland.co.uk, and in his booklet *Fossils In Lyme Regis*.

Sleeping

Coombe House (☎ 443849; www.coombe-house.co.uk; 41 Coombe St; d £50-56; P) Easy-going and stylish, this is a B&B of airy rooms, bay windows, wicker and white wood. There's also a self-contained, ground-floor studio flat, complete with minikitchen. Breakfast is delivered to your door on a trolley, complete with toaster – perfect for a lazy lie-in in Lyme.

Manaton (☎ 445138; www.manaton.net; Hill Rd; s £35, d £55-65; P ✗) A conventional but comfy B&B with magnolia décor, floral prints and modern bathrooms. Some rooms have sea views, but the place is made by the charming, chatty owners who are happy to share tips on everything from hiking and fossil hunting to fish and chips.

Old Lyme Guest House (☎ 442929; www.oldlyme guesthouse.co.uk; 29 Coombe St; s £34, d £70; P) The former town post office – look out for the wooden post box embedded in the front wall of this old stone house – is now an award-winning B&B. It provides ladylike rooms with plenty of frills, power showers and free-range eggs for breakfast.

Mariners Hotel (☎ 442753; www.hotellymeregis.co.uk; Silver St; s £40-47, d £80-94; P ✗) A 17th-century coaching inn with views; half the rooms look out over the eastern cliffs, while the garden is ideal for some languid sea-watching. Rooms vary in character. The beamed attic ones have most, some are done out in fresh lilac and yellow, but others are more pedestrian.

Royal Lion (☎ 445622; www.royallionhotel.com; Broad St; s £62, d £86-124, f £118-170; P ☒) A hotel with twin personalities: the 16th-century oak-panelled rooms are all gilt mirrors and plush furnishings; the modern extension is more anonymous but does have some rooms with sea-view balconies. A good bet for families, there's a pool and 12 rooms sleeping up to four.

our pick **Hotel Alexandra** (☎ 442010; www.hotel alexandra.co.uk; Pound St; s £60, d £100-150; P) Just like wandering into an Agatha Christie play, this hotel is full of class and character. Built in 1735, it was once home to a Countess. Today it's a picture of dignified calm – the only sounds are creaking floors and murmured chatter. Rooms are either scattered with antique chairs and fine drapes or gently revamped with marble bathrooms and bright, striped satin. Most have captivating views of the Cobb and the sea. Excellent, English classics are on offer in the galleried dining room, while the glorious terrace has a view of the sparkling bay – ideal for perusing the *Telegraph* in a panama hat.

Eating & Drinking

Jurassic Seafood (☎ 444345; 47 Silver St; mains £9-16; ☾ dinner) Bright and buzzy in blue and orange, this bistro revels in its prehistoric theme: fossil maps, hunting tips and replica dinosaur remains abound. A tasty, eclectic menu includes crab sushi, mussels and chips and local mackerel as well as salads and steaks.

ourpick **Broad Street** (☎ 445792; 57 Broad St; 3 courses £25; ☾ dinner Thu-Sat, plus Tue, Wed & Sun in high season) A refreshingly innovative restaurant. Décor is rough meets smooth: whitewashed walls and exposed stone; crisp white linen and beige Hessian. Seating is on old chapel chairs – complete with the slots for hymn sheets on the backs. The food also has flair; confit of duck, roast tomato and beetroot purée sits alongside pot-roast pollack with spinach and leeks. Impeccably sourced ingredients, their local credentials are outlined on the menu, include wild garlic gathered from the woods. Booking essential.

The trio of pubs clustered at the foot of the Cobb are great for harbourside bustle. The **Harbour Inn** (☎ 442299; Marine Pde; mains £5-10; ☾ lunch & dinner), with stone walls and wooden settles, pips the others for atmosphere and sheer range of pub grub. Alongside, the **Cobb Arms** (☎ 443242; Marine Pde) pulls a good pint.

Getting There & Away

Bus 31 runs to Dorchester (1¼ hours) and Weymouth (1¾ hours) hourly (every two hours on Sunday). Bus X53 goes west to Exeter (1¾ hours) and east to Weymouth (1½ hours, six daily, four on Sunday), but between April and October only.

AROUND LYME REGIS
Forde Abbey

A former Cistercian monastery, **Forde Abbey** (☎ 01460-221290; www.fordeabbey.co.uk; abbey adult/child £7.70/free, gardens £5.60/free; ☾ abbey noon-4pm Tue-Fri & Sun Apr-Oct, gardens 10am-4.30pm), was built in the 12th century, updated in the 17th and has been a private home since 1649. The building boasts magnificent plasterwork, ceilings and fine tapestries, but it's the outstanding gardens that are the main attraction: 12 hectares of lawns, ponds, shrubberies and flowerbeds with many rare and beautiful species. It's 10 miles north of Lyme Regis; public transport is a nonstarter.

DORSET

Devon

Devon is the kind of place you wish you'd grown up in and would want your children to. This gentle county is simple and sophisticated, quaint and ultra-cool, and fizzes with endless adventures. Elemental moors complement jagged cliffs; time-warp villages circle vibrant cityscapes. It's a place to recharge, regroup and reinvent – breathe deeply, become a beachcomber or gaze at glorious rural views. Hundreds of miles of coast tempt you into neoprene to be a surfer dude in the north or to swim, kayak and sail idyllic bays in the south. Take your pick of atmospheres: chic yachting havens, kiss-me-quick resorts or tranquil, ancient ports. You can eat lobster and crab fresh from the boats, at Michelin-starred restaurants or fishermen's stalls – the choice is yours.

Dartmoor, the biggest wilderness in southern England, offers exhilarating freedom; the chance to go wild-camping and see a stunning sky full of stars, then the next night lounge in luxury in a boutique hotel. Or discover a county laced with history: from stone circles, ruined castles and a classic cathedral, to stately homes, crime writers and Art Deco delights. The county revels in a strong ecovibe – relish those zero food-miles by tasting wine in the vineyard and veg plucked from the furrows in front of you. Devon is also where the cash-rich but time-poor from all over England come to down-size. Perhaps it should come with a warning: this county just might make you rethink your life.

HIGHLIGHTS

- Visit broodingly beautiful **Dartmoor** (p202), a get-away-from-it-all escape
- Surf a wave at **Croyde** (p213) and become an instant addict
- Crack the clues to Agatha Christie's secret **South Devon** (p181)
- Watch the boats bobbing at **Beer** (p174), a perfectly peaceful fishing village
- Enjoy the serenity at the gloriously Gothic **Exeter Cathedral** (p166)
- Sample Cabernet Sauvignon at **Sharpham Vineyard** (p184)
- Explore the maritime past and party present of **Plymouth** (p196)

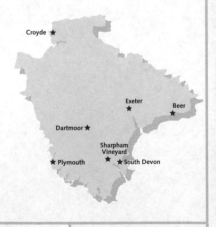

POPULATION: 1,074,919	AVE MAX SUMMER TEMP, TORQUAY: 20°C	NO OF THATCHED PROPERTIES IN DEVON: 4000

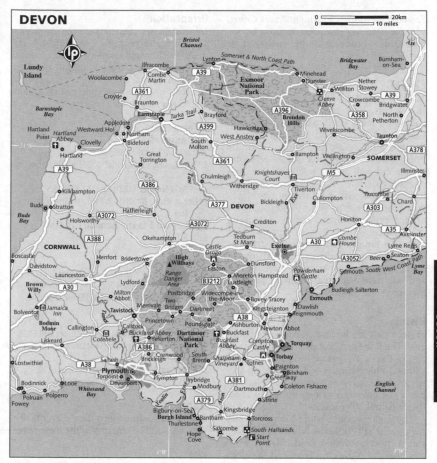

DEVON

DEVON

Orientation & Information

Somerset and Dorset frame Devon on the east, and the border flows south from Exmoor to Lyme Regis on the coast. One of Devon's two cities, Plymouth signals the western edge of the county, and the beginning of Cornwall. The city of Exeter lies 40 miles to the east. Dartmoor National Park occupies the centre of the county. A section of Exmoor National Park lies in Devon; however, most is in Somerset and we cover it in detail in that chapter (p113). Devon-wide transport is covered in the Transport chapter (p295).

Discover Devon (☎ 0870 6085531; www.discover devon.com) has plenty of useful information for planning your stay.

EXETER & AROUND

Well-heeled and comfortable, Exeter is steeped in evidence of its centuries-old role as the spiritual and administrative heart of Devon – relics include its exquisite, ancient cathedral and chunks of Roman wall. But the established co-exists with a buzzy youthful vibe – typified by a large student population and a burst of ultra-modern construction. The city is ringed by a hilly, pastoral landscape of deep green fields and flashes of vivid red soil, where thatched villages, such as Bickleigh, snuggle in valleys between working farms. Also within easy reach are the superb stately piles over at

Powderham Castle and Knightshayes Court, while at Tiverton you can hop on a horse-drawn canal boat and see the county at an even slower pace.

EXETER

☎ 01392 / pop 111,078

In pockets, Exeter has a collegiate feel: cobbled streets wind past medieval and Georgian buildings, all presided over by the graceful, reassuring presence of its fine cathedral. Fragments of the terracotta Roman city wall pop up to create lovely and unexpected views. But Exeter is far from locked in the past: a futuristic new shopping centre graces its skyline and thousands of university students ensure a kicking cultural scene. The city's vibrant quayside acts as a launch pad for cycling trips or kayaking down the River Exe – throw in some super-stylish places to stay and eat and you have a relaxed but lively base for further explorations.

History

Exeter's past can be read clearly in its buildings. The Romans marched in around AD 55 and put up a 17-hectare fortress, complete with a 2-mile defensive wall, crumbling sections of which remain. Saxon and Norman times saw growth: a castle went up in 1068, the cathedral 40 years later.

The Tudor woollen boom brought Exeter riches and half-timbered houses – all those sheep in surrounding fields meant wool was brought to the city, dyed, and the cloth exported via the quay to Europe.

By the late Georgian era, Exeter was a genteel urban centre, its merchants busy building elegant town houses, many of which now house hotels and B&Bs. The Blitz of WWII brought devastation. In just one night in 1942, 156 people died and over 12 hectares of the city were flattened – even the cathedral took a direct hit. The postwar years saw an ambitious rebuild in red brick and cream stone – look out for its clean lines above the high street shopfronts. Fast forward to 2007 and the attention-grabbing £220 million Princesshay shopping centre. Part blue cubes, part echoes of 1950s designs, its shimmering glass and steel pod now crouches in the centre, adding another architectural notch in the city's timeline.

Orientation

Central Exeter clusters between its elegant cathedral and peaceful Northernhay Gardens; the historic quayside is a 15-minute walk south. The city's bus station and Central train station are (appropriately) central; St David's, where most long distance trains arrive, is a mile to the northwest.

Information

BOOKSHOPS

Waterstone's (☎ 218392; 48-49 High St; ⏰ 9am-5.30pm Mon-Fri, 9am-6pm Sat, 10.30am-4.30pm Sun)

EMERGENCY & MEDICAL SERVICES

Police station (☎ 08452 777444; Heavitree Rd; ⏰ 24hr)
Royal Devon & Exeter Hospital (☎ 411611; Barrack Rd)

INTERNET ACCESS

Exeter Library (☎ 384200; Castle St; first 30min free, then per hr £3; ⏰ 9.30am-7pm Mon, Tue, Thu & Fri, 10am-5pm Wed, 9.30am-4pm Sat, 11am-2.30pm Sun)

LAUNDRY

St David's Laundrette (St David's Hill; per load £2.20; ⏰ 8am-9pm) On the junction of St David's Hill and Richmond Rd.
Soaps (☎ 491930; Isambard Pde; per load £1.70; ⏰ 8.15am-7.45pm Mon-Sat, 9.15am-5.45pm Sun)

MEDIA

The List magazine (50p) details events, listings, bars and restaurants in the Exeter area.

POST

Main branch (☎ 223344; Bedford St; ⏰ 9am-5.30pm Mon-Sat)

TOURIST INFORMATION

Quay House Interpretation & Visitor Centre (☎ 271611; The Quay; ⏰ 10am-5pm Easter-Oct, 11am-4pm Sat & Sun only Nov-Easter)
Tourist office (☎ 265700; www.exeter.gov.uk/visiting; Paris St; ⏰ 9am-5pm Mon-Sat, 10am-4pm Sun Jul & Aug)

Sights

EXETER CATHEDRAL

Magnificent in warm, honey-coloured stone, Exeter's **Cathedral Church of St Peter** (☎ 255573; www.exeter-cathedral.org.uk; The Close; suggested donation £3.50; ⏰ 9.30am-6.30pm Mon-Fri, 9am-5pm Sat, 7.30am-6.30pm Sun) is framed by lawns and wonky half-timbered buildings – a quintessentially

English scene often peopled by picnickers snacking to the sound of the bells.

The site's been a religious one since at least the 5th century but the Normans started the current building in 1114 and the towers of today's cathedral date from that period. In 1270 Bishop Bronescombe remodelled the whole building, a process that took 90 years, and introduced a mix of Early English and Decorated Gothic styles.

You enter via the gorgeous Great West Front. Above the door, scores of weather-worn figures line an image screen, which was originally brightly painted. Now it forms the largest collection of 14th-century sculpture in England. Inside, the ceiling is mesmerising – the longest unbroken Gothic vaulting in the world, it sweeps up to meet ornate ceiling bosses in gilt and vibrant colours. Look out for the 15th-century Exeter Clock, in the north transept. In keeping with medieval astronomy this shows the earth as a golden ball at the centre of the universe, with the sun, a fleur-de-lys, travelling round. Still ticking and whirring, it chimes on the hour. Further down, hunt out the tiny St James Chapel, built to replace the one destroyed in the Blitz in 1942. Note its unusual carvings: a cat, a mouse and, oddly, a rugby player.

In the **Refectory** (☎ 285988; ☯ 10am-4.45pm Mon-Sat) you can tuck into cakes, quiches and soups at trestle tables surrounded by vaulted ceilings, stained glass and busts of the great, the good and the dead.

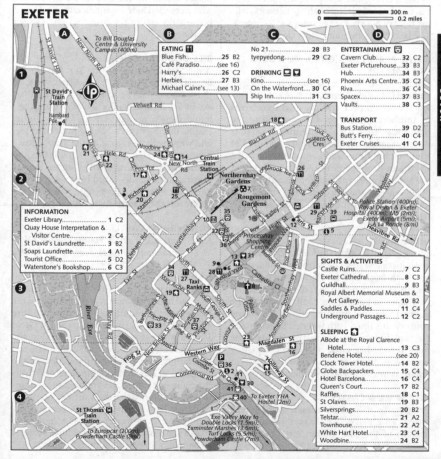

EXETER

0 — 300 m
0 — 0.2 miles

DEVON

To Bill Douglas Centre & University Campus (400m)
St David's Train Station
Isambard Pde
Velwell Rd
Howell Rd
Hele Rd
Woodbine Tce
New North Rd
Central Train Station
Blackall Rd
York Rd
Queens Cres
Northernhay Gardens
Rougemont Gardens
Richmond Rd
Station Yard
Queen St
Sidwell St
Cheeke St
To Police Station (400m);
Royal Devon & Exeter Hospital (400m); M5 (2mi);
Exeter Airport (5mi);
La Ronde (8mi)
Paris St
Heavitree Rd
Princesshay Shopping Centre
Post Office
High St
Cathedral Yard
Cathedral Cl
Palace Gate
Southernhay
Magdalen St
Holloway St
Western Way
The Quay
To Exeter YHA Hostel (2mi)
St Thomas Train Station
To Europcar (200m);
Powderham Castle (8mi)
Exe Valley Way to
Double Locks (1.5mi);
Exminster Marshes (3.5mi);
Turf Locks (5.5mi);
Powderham Castle (7mi)
River Exe
Bonhay Rd
Frog St
New Bridge St
Commercial Rd
Coombe St
Tower

Excellent 45-minute free guided tours run at 11am and 2.30pm Monday to Friday, 11am on Saturday and 4pm on Sunday, April to October. Evensong is at 5.30pm Monday to Friday and 3pm on Saturday and Sunday.

UNDERGROUND PASSAGES
Prepare to crouch down, don a hard hat and possibly get spooked in what is the only system of its kind open to the public in the country. These medieval, vaulted **passages** (☎ 665887; Paris St; adult/child £5/3.50; ☯ 9.30am-5.30pm Mon-Sat, 10.30am-4pm Sun Jun-Sep, 11.30am-5.30pm Tue-Fri, 9.30am-5.30pm Sat, 11.30am-4pm Sun May-Oct) were built to house pipes bringing fresh water to the city. Unlike modern utility companies, the authorities opted to have permanent access for repairs, rather than dig up the streets each time – genius. Guides lead you through the network, telling tales of ghosts, escape routes and cholera. The last tour is an hour before closing.

ROYAL ALBERT MEMORIAL MUSEUM & ART GALLERY
Roman Exeter features strongly in the city's **museum** (☎ 665858; Queen St; admission free; ☯ 10am-5pm Mon-Sat). Expect chunks of mosaic, bits of amphorae and a good re-creation of the bathhouse that used to lie under what is now Cathedral Green. There are also piles of south Devon flints, and a reconstruction of a Dartmoor Bronze Age roundhouse. Hunt out the tomb-like Egypt room, complete with a 3000-year-old mummy case and (mock-up) hieroglyphics on the walls. There are good, free quiz sheets for children.

GUILDHALL
The medieval **Guildhall** (☎ 665500; High St; admission free) is just a few steps away from the high street bustle, through an intricately carved oak door. A gloriously ornate barrel roof tops a structure that dates in parts from 1330, making it the oldest municipal building still in use in the country. It's lined with wooden benches and crests of dignitaries – the mayor still sits in the huge throne-like chair at the end. Opening hours depend on civic functions; drop in as you pass or call ahead for times.

CITY WALL & CASTLE
Fragments of Exeter's russet-red city wall weave an elusive, 2-mile trail around the fringes of the old Roman city. The most ancient bits are 2000 years old and with newer, particularly Civil War, defences built on top, it's perfect for playing a game of history detective – decoding the layers of the past. A surprising 70% is still standing and it springs up beside shops and car parks as well as parks, often accompanied by information panels.

Pick up a free City Wall Trail leaflet at the tourist office, the *Devon Archaeological Field Guide* number 12 from the Royal Albert Memorial Museum, or explore for yourself. The neighbouring Rougemont and Northernhay Gardens are particularly fertile hunting grounds. In the latter, at the end of Castle St, you can skirt the tree-fringed ruins of the city's 11th-century castle (but not go inside). The gatehouse is worth searching out – it has a plaque commemorating three Devon women who were tried here for witchcraft in 1685 and became the last in the country to be hanged for the crime.

BILL DOUGLAS CENTRE
A delightful homage to film and fun, the **Bill Douglas Centre** (☎ 264321; www.billdouglas.org; Old Library, Prince of Wales Rd; admission free; ☯ 10am-4pm Mon-Fri) is a compact collection of all things celluloid, from magic lanterns to Mickey Mouse. Inside, discover just what the butler did see, and why the flicks are called the flicks. Movie memorabilia reigns upstairs – Charlie Chaplin bottle stoppers mingle with Ginger Rogers playing cards, James Bond board games and *Star Wars* toys. It's a 15-minute walk from the centre, on the University of Exeter campus.

POWDERHAM CASTLE
Stately but still friendly **Powderham** (☎ 01626-890243; www.powderham.co.uk; adult/child £7.95/5.95; ☯ 10am-5.30pm Apr-Oct, closed Sat) is the historic home of the Earl of Devon. It was built in 1391, damaged in the Civil War and remodelled in the Victorian era, and has some of the best preserved Stuart and Regency furniture around. There's a fine wood-panelled Great Hall, a glimpse of life 'below stairs' in the kitchen, and parkland with 650 deer. The earl and family are still resident and, despite the grandeur of Powderham, for delightful fleeting moments it feels like you're actually wandering through someone's sitting room.

Powderham is on the River Exe near Kenton, 8 miles south of Exeter. Bus 85A runs from Exeter (20 minutes, every 15 minutes Monday to Saturday, every 30 minutes Sunday).

EXETER QUAY

The perfect place on a summer's day to forget you're in a city. The red stone warehouses that line the River Exe at **Exeter Quay** are home to antiques markets, pubs and restaurants, many with alfresco dining. There's been a quay on the site since Roman times, but by the 14th century the route to the sea had been cut off by an incredibly sharp piece of business practice. Those with vested interests in forcing trade to the port of Topsham to the south, built a weir across the river – severing the city's water link. Undeterred, John Trew built the first ship canal in Britain in 1563 to restore access to the sea.

The **Quay House Interpretation & Visitor Centre** (☎ 271611; The Quay; ⏲ 10am-5pm Easter-Oct, 11am-4pm Sat & Sun only Nov-Easter), with its small artefact and map collection, has more on the quay's past. There are more shops and cafés on the other side of the river. The bathtub-like **Butt's Ferry** (The Quay; adult/child 20/10p; ⏲ 11am-5pm Easter-Oct) is propelled across by a ferryman pulling on a wire – technically it's a floating bridge, one of only a handful in the country. The quay has open-air jazz on Sundays between June and September, and summertime **Slow Food Markets** (⏲ 10am-2pm Apr-Oct) on the third Saturday of the month. You can also hire bikes and kayaks (see below).

Activities

CYCLING, KAYAKING & WALKING

The foot and cycle paths along Exeter Quay join the Exe Valley Way and then head southeast to shadow both the canal and an ever-broadening estuary towards the sea. For the first 3 miles the route is a blend of heritage city, countryside and light industry. The excellent Double Locks pub (p171) is 1.5 miles down the cycle path from the quay; 2 miles further on is the start of the **Exminster Marshes nature reserve**, which is run by the Royal Society of the Protection of Birds (RSPB). One more great pub, the **Turf Locks Hotel** (☎ 833128), is another 2 miles inside the reserve. From there a rougher trail connects with a path to Powderham Castle (opposite). You can also navigate the 6-mile canal by kayak – an enjoyable, nontidal paddle past pubs.

Saddles & Paddles (☎ 424241; www.sadpad.com; 4 Kings Wharf, The Quay; ⏲ 9.30am-5.30pm), on Exeter quayside, rents out bikes (adult per hour/day £5/14, child per hour/day £4/10) and kayaks

and canoes (kayaks per hour/day £7/18, open canoe per hour/day £10/34).

The canal path picks up the end of the **Exe Valley Way**, a part-waymarked 57-mile hike north to the source of the river: Exe Head on Exmoor. Pick up a free leaflet at the tourist office, or contact **Discover Devon** (☎ 0870 608 5531; www.discoverdevon.com).

BOAT TRIPS

Exeter Cruises (☎ 07984-368442; adult/child £5/2.50) shuttle down the Exeter Ship Canal from Exeter Quay to the Double Locks pub. A connecting boat, the White Heather, then ferries passengers the extra 4 miles to the Turf Locks Hotel. The trip takes 45 minutes (five daily June to August, Saturday and Sunday only April, May and September).

Tours

Redcoat Guided Tours (☎ 265203; www.exeter.gov .uk/visiting; tours free) are hugely varied. Themes range from ghosts and murder to Romans and religion – there's even a torch-lit prowl through Exeter's Catacombs. Tours leave from Cathedral Yard or the quay. There are two to five daily from April to October, and two to three daily from November to March. Pick up a programme from the tourist office.

Festivals & Events

Exeter's big cultural party kicks off in mid-June for the two-week **Exeter Summer Festival** (☎ 265200; www.exeter.gov.uk/festival). A dozen venues stage a blend of serious classical music, contemporary folk, pulsating world rhythms, jazz, street theatre and comedy.

In February, **Animated Exeter** (☎ 265208; www .exeter.gov.uk/animatedexeter) is about much more than cartoons. Instead, it's a gloriously different filmic fortnight, which blends workshops, British classics, cuddly kids' films, 18 certificates (restricted to viewers who are 18 and over) and Japanese manga.

Sleeping

BUDGET

Globe Backpackers (☎ 215521; www.exeterbackpackers .co.uk; 71 Holloway St; dm £14, d £35; ✕ ▣ ▢) An excellent, clean and friendly hostel with high ceilings and woodland murals on the walls. There's a four-poster double room and dorms with six to 10 beds. You can even borrow plastic swords, Frisbees and water pistols from the games box.

DEVON

Exeter YHA Hostel (☎ 0870 770 5826; www.yha.org
.uk; 47 Countess Wear Rd; dm £15.50; **P** 🖳) This cream
17th-century building is tucked away in its
own peaceful grounds near the River Exe. The
2.5-mile trip into town can be a drag – catch
bus K or T from the high street, or 57 or 85
from the bus station to School Lane.

MIDRANGE

our pick **Raffles** (☎ 270200; www.raffles-exeter.co.uk;
11 Blackall Rd; s/d £38/66; **P**) Creaking with antiques and exuding atmosphere, this Victorian
B&B is a lovely blend of old woods and tasteful
modern fabrics. Plant stands and dado rails
add to the turn of the century feel and the late
19th-century prints include fetching adverts
for Pear's soap. Largely organic breakfasts,
a walled garden and much-coveted parking
make this a great value choice.

Woodbine (☎ 203302; www.woodbineguesthouse
.co.uk; 1 Woodbine Tce; s/d £39/66; ✖ 🖳) A bit of a
surprise sits behind this archetypal flower-
framed B&B façade: fresh, contemporary
rooms with low beds and flashes of burgundy.
There's even under-floor heating in the showers. Wonderfully tranquil, rooms at the back
overlook a square of green park.

Bendene Hotel (☎ 213526; www.bendene.co.uk; 15-16
Richmond Rd; s £27-50, d £45-80; **P** ✖ 🔊) Improbably, this compact Georgian terrace has its
own blue and cream outdoor swimming pool.
The floral and pine rooms come in a wide
variety of guises, from those with shared bathrooms to a four-poster option.

Townhouse (☎ 494994; www.townhouseexeter.co.uk;
54 St David's Hill; s/d £35/70; 🖳) Expect simple but
delightful rooms with stripped wooden floors
and clean, pared-down lines, spiced up by
dashes of intense colour. The Victorian exterior drips with ivy and all the rooms are
named after characters from books or plays.

White Hart Hotel (☎ 279897; www.roomattheinn
.info; 66 South St; s £60, d £70-75; **P** 🖳 🖳) One of
Exeter's oldest inns – they've been putting
people up here since the Plantagenets were on
the throne (1300s). The cobbled courtyard is
fringed by wisteria and the bar is book-lined
and beamed. Rooms are either traditional
(dark woods and rich drapes) or contemporary (laminate floors and light fabrics).

Silversprings (☎ 494040; www.silversprings.co.uk; 12
Richmond Rd; s £50, d £75-80, f 85-90, ste £100; **P** 🖳)
An oh-so-chichi Georgian townhouse that
will either leave you longing to recline and
varnish your nails, or slightly overwhelmed.

Rooms are all gilt mirrors, gold fabrics and
vibrant reds and greens. The best ones have
real coffee, a free half-bottle of wine and
fluffy bathrobes.

Queen's Court (☎ 272709; www.queenscourt-hotel
.co.uk; 6-8 Bystock Tce; s £85, d £93-109; 🖳) The owners of this early-Victorian townhouse have
clearly watched a few TV design shows:
it's packed with leather sofas, zebra prints,
bright satins, power showers and retro
Roberts radios. Refreshingly, prices fall at
the weekend.

Also recommended:

Telstar (☎ 272466; 75-77 St David's Hill; s £30-38,
d £55-68) A friendly, traditional B&B with plain rooms and
a tiny courtyard garden.

Clock Tower Hotel (☎ 424545; www.clocktowerhotel
.co.uk; 16 New North Rd; s £48, d £65-75, f £80-85;
P 🖳) Slightly anonymous décor but a good selection
of family rooms.

TOP END

St Olaves (☎ 217736; www.olaves.co.uk; Mary Arches St;
s £95, d £115-125, ste £155; **P**) This hotel's swirling spiral staircase is so gorgeous it's tempting to sleep beside it. But you better opt for
the bedrooms, which are Georgian with
contemporary twists, and feature rococo
furnishings, brass bedsteads and plush fabrics. The cheaper rooms can be a tad small.

our pick **Hotel Barcelona** (☎ 281000; www.alias
hotels.com; Magdalen St; room only rate: s £95, d £115-
135; **P** 🖳) A hotel conversion with more
wit than a festival full of comedians. The
fabulously clever revamp of this former eye
hospital has combined its medical past with
ultra arty twists. Plush deep-green carpets
cover the original hospital flooring; the hospital lift still ferries guests up and down. But
it's unlike any institution you've ever seen,
with rich woods, vivid furnishings, intricate
ironwork and deeply luxurious bathrooms.
There are also a few nods to the Beatles and
Antoni Gaudi. You can even sleep in the old
operating theatre (room 220) without a trolley bed (or a surgeon) in sight.

ABode at the Royal Clarence Hotel (☎ 319955;
www.abodehotels.co.uk/exeter; Cathedral Yard; r £125-
250) Georgian grandeur meets minimalist
chic. Curiously, wonky floors and stained
glass sit comfortably with recessed lighting,
pared-down furniture and neutral tones. The
rooms are classed as 'comfortable', 'enviable'
and 'fabulous'. The last is aptly named: bigger than most people's flats, it has slanted

ceilings and beams framing a grandstand view of the cathedral.

Eating

tyepyedong (☎ 251888; 175 Sidwell St; mains £6-8; ☺ lunch & dinner Mon-Sat) Tucked away in an unlikely terrace of modern shops, this fusion food and noodle bar has a pristine, modern feel. Eat great-value *udon* and *ramen* and sip your sake at long, gleaming bench tables. The lunchtime dish-and-a-drink deal costs £5.

Herbies (☎ 258473; 15 North St; mains £4-8; ☺ lunch Mon-Sat, dinner Tue-Sat) Cosy and gently groovy, Herbies has been cheerfully feeding Exeter's vegetarians for 20 years. Tuck into delicious butterbean and vegetable pie, Moroccan tagine or cashew nut loaf. It's strong on vegan dishes too.

Harry's (☎ 202234; 86 Longbrook St; mains £7-15; ☺ lunch & dinner) The kind of welcoming neighbourhood bistro you wish was on your own doorstep, but rarely is. The décor is wooden chairs, blackboards and gilt mirrors; the food includes goat's cheese and walnut burgers, char-grilled chicken and classic pizzas.

No 21 (☎ 210303; 21 Cathedral Yard; lunch mains £3-8, dinner mains £13-17; ☺ breakfast, lunch & dinner Tue-Sat, 9am-5pm Sun & Mon) A mellow eatery with subtle art on the walls and subtle lights on your food. There are imaginative fish, meat and veggie options – try the sea bass and chorizo or open mushroom ravioli.

Café Paradiso (☎ 281000; Magdalen St; lunch mains £4-8, dinner mains £11-20; ☺ lunch & dinner) Hotel Barcelona's funky restaurant is set in a futuristic glass-sided circus top, which is dotted with Rothko-esque artwork and (intriguingly) painted white bicycles. Lunch is chic, with dishes such as curried crayfish on granary baguettes. And there's stylish dining at night (dishes include wood-fired trout).

Blue Fish (☎ 493581; 44 Queen St; mains £10-24; ☺ lunch & dinner Mon-Sat) Crisp, clean design surrounds you as you tuck into fine foods, such as flambéed monkfish, pork stuffed with smoked cheese, or broccoli and blue cheese tagliatelle. There's a two-course lunch and early evening menu (before 7pm) for £10.

Michael Caine's (☎ 223638; Cathedral Yard; mains £21; ☺ breakfast, lunch & dinner) Housed in the Royal Clarence Hotel and run by a locally famous Michelin-starred chef, this restaurant offers a complex fusion of Westcountry ingredients and full-bodied French flavours. Try the monkfish with red wine butter and roasted

garlic or the Devon lamb with ratatouille. There's a bargain two-course lunch (£13) and a seven-course tasting menu (£58).

Drinking

Ship Inn (☎ 272040; Martin's Lane) Wood coats the ceiling, floors and even the walls at this citycentre, heavily beamed boozer. It claims to have been Sir Francis Drake's favourite pub – bet he wouldn't have recognised the tunes pulsing from the jukebox.

Kino (☎ 281000; Hotel Barcelona, Magdalen St) Full of movie-star glamour, Kino's centrepiece is a stunning 1930s-style bar. Original film posters line the walls and it's an irresistible place to sit, sip the seriously good cocktails and ponder your profile. It's open for members and guests only after 10pm.

On the Waterfront (☎ 210590; The Quay) In 1835 this was a warehouse; now its red-brick, barrel ceilings stretch back from a minimalist bar. There's typical pub-grub on offer for lunch and dinner (mains £7) and its tables stretch along the quayside – perfect for a riverside pint or a pizza.

Double Locks (☎ 256947; Canal Banks) A bit of a local legend, this atmospheric former lockhouse sits 2 miles south of the quay beside the Exeter Ship Canal. Scarred floorboards, creaking chairs, excellent ale and battered board games lend it a chilled vibe – helped by the real fires, waterside terrace and better than average bar food (available lunch and dinner, mains £7).

Entertainment

GALLERIES, THEATRES & CINEMAS

Phoenix Arts Centre (☎ 667080; www.exeterphoenix.org .uk; Gandy St) The city's art and soul, Phoenix is a vibrant hub of performance, music, dance, film, classes and workshops. There's a buzzing café bar too.

Exeter Picturehouse (☎ 435522; www.picturehouses .co.uk; 51 Bartholomew St West) This intimate independent cinema screens mainstream and art-house movies.

Spacex (☎ 431786; www.spacex.org.uk; 45 Preston St; admission free; ☺ 10am-5pm Tue-Sat) A consistently strong, contemporary art space, which stages regular free artists' talks.

Northcott Theatre (☎ 493493; www.northcott-thea tre.co.uk; Stocker Rd, University of Exeter Campus) Northcott stages a mix of home-grown and touring productions – look out for their open-air summer Shakespeare in Rougemont Gardens.

DEVON

NIGHTCLUBS

Hub (☎ 424628; 1 Mary Arches St) The Hub is a showcase for everything from thrash metal to alternative rock and DJs.

Cavern Club (☎ 495370; www.cavernclub.co.uk; 83-84 Queen St) A long-standing venue for big-name DJs and breaking acts from the indie scene.

Vaults (☎ 203939; 8 Gandy St) This arched red-brick basement bar is home to live DJs, party favourites, karaoke and cheese.

Riva (☎ 211347; www.rivaexeter.co.uk; The Quay) Enjoy R&B, hip hop and dancehall in the stone and brick cellar; disco and classic dance floor grooves are upstairs.

Getting There & Away

AIR

Regular services connect **Exeter International Airport** (☎ 367433; www.exeter-airport.co.uk) with cities such as Belfast, Leeds-Bradford, Glasgow, Manchester and Newcastle, and the Channel Islands and the Isles of Scilly. A key operator is **FlyBe** (☎ 0871 522 6100; www.fly be.com).

BUS

Bus X38 goes to Plymouth (£6, 1¼ hours, hourly). Bus X9 runs to Bude (£5.50, three hours, five Monday to Saturday, two on Sunday) via Okehampton. Bus X57 runs to Exmouth (25 minutes, every 20 minutes). Bus X52A runs to Sidmouth (45 minutes, hourly) and on to Seaton (one hour).

Bus X46 (hourly Monday to Saturday, three to eight Sunday) shuttles to Torquay (£6, one hour) and Paignton (£6, 1¼ hours); bus 85/85A (every 20 minutes Monday to Saturday, every 30 minutes Sunday) goes via Dawlish (one hour) to Teignmouth (£5, 1¼ hours).

Bus 82 (the Transmoor Link) heads across Dartmoor to Plymouth (£6, 2¼ hours), taking in Moretonhampstead (45 minutes) Postbridge (1¼ hours) and Princetown (one hour 20 minutes). Between July and September there are two buses a day Monday to Friday, and five on Saturday and Sunday. From October to June the service only runs on Saturday and Sunday (two buses each day).

TRAIN

Exeter St David's connects to London Paddington (£58, 2¾ hours, hourly), Bristol (from £19, 1¼ hours, every 30 minutes) and Penzance (from £14.90, three hours, hourly).

The picturesque Tarka Line connects Exeter Central with Barnstaple (from £6.90, 1¼ hours, every two hours Monday to Friday, four to six on Sunday).

Getting Around

TO/FROM THE AIRPORT

Buses 56 and 379 run from the bus station and Exeter St David's train station to Exeter Airport (20 to 30 minutes, hourly), 5 miles east of the city. The service stops at 6pm.

BUS

The one-day Explorer pass (adult/child £5/4) gives unlimited transport on Stagecoach's Exeter buses. Bus H links St David's and Central train stations and passes near the bus station.

CAR

The tourist office has a list of car-hire offices; try **Europcar** (☎ 275398; Water Lane; ⏰ 8.30am-5.30pm Mon-Fri, 8.30am-1pm Sat).

As well as there being city-centre car parks, park-and-ride buses run from Sowton (Bus PR4), Matford (Bus PR5) and Honiton Rd (PR2), every 10 minutes.

TAXI

Taxi ranks are at St David's train station and on the high street.

Capital Taxis (☎ 433433)
Club Cars (☎ 213030)
Gemini (☎ 666666)

AROUND EXETER

North of Exeter, the red hills roll away into Devon's rural heartland. It's one of the least touristy parts of the county – agriculture still holds sway here, towns are traditional and the pubs unreconstructed. As such, it provides a genuine insight into life in Devon's farming communities, while a horse-drawn canal trip and a stately home provide absorbing diversions on the journey north to Exmoor or the sea.

The biggest town is businesslike Tiverton. Its **tourist office** (☎ 255827; Phoenix Lane; ⏰ 9.15am-4.30pm Mon-Fri, 9.15am-3.30pm Sat) is a good source of area-wide information. The village of Bickleigh is on the A396 Exeter to Tiverton road.

Combe House

The sumptuous **Combe House** (☎ 01404-540400; www.thishotel.com; Gittisham; s £139-165, d £168-275, ste £370) is more like a National Trust property than a hotel. The great hall of this Elizabethan country manor has floor to ceiling wood panels, while ancient oak furniture and original Tudor paintings are everywhere. Indulge your taste for crisp cottons, monogrammed towels, rain showers and sumptuous throws. One room even has a vast copper washtub for a bath. It's set on a massive estate near Gittisham, 14 miles east of Exeter.

Bickleigh & Around
☎ 01884 / pop 239

For a dollop of picture-perfect thatched cottages, it's hard to top Bickleigh. The buildings cluster beside a 16th-century bridge over the rushing River Exe, with another clump just east of the main road. There's not much more to it really (apart from some good pubs), but it's an agreeable place to drink in the views.

The café-cum–craft centre at **Bickleigh Mill** (☎ 855419; www.bickleighmill.com; admission free; ⌚ 10am-5.30pm Mon-Wed & Sun, till 9.30pm Thu-Sat) houses a working 18th-century water wheel, while train buffs will enjoy chugging around the 2- and 7¼-gauge tracks of the **Devon Railway Centre** (☎ 855671; www.devonrailwaycentre.co.uk; adult/child £5.60/4.60; ⌚ 10.30am-5pm mid-Apr–mid-Sep).

SLEEPING & EATING
Willow Grove House (☎ 855263; mjhowes@bickleigh93.freeserve.co.uk; The Orchard; s/d £25/50) A modern B&B on the edge of Bickleigh, Willow Grove offers cheery, chintzy, tasselled rooms.

Fisherman's Cot (☎ 855237; fishermanscot@ep-ltd.com; s/d £70/80) An immense, thatched pub overlooking pretty Bickleigh bridge. Bedrooms can be a touch uniform; those over the pub are best, especially 10 and 11 with their beautiful beams and river views. The bar menu includes herb stuffed trout and Aberdeen Angus burgers (mains £12). Lunch and dinner are available, and meals are best enjoyed on the waterside terrace.

East Barton (☎ 855244; www.eastbarton.com; d £60-90) Plump for beams, four-poster beds and flowery furnishings at this 16th-century working farm beside the A396, slightly north of the village.

Beer Engine (☎ 01392-851282; Newton St Cyres; mains £9; ⌚ lunch & dinner) A dream for drinkers, the Beer Engine makes its own booze. This former railway hotel brews such cunningly named delights as Rail Ale, Piston Bitter and Sleeper Heavy. The grub slips down as smoothly as the beer; try the Devon bangers or 'ploughpersons' made with Quicke's

cheddar, produced just up the road. Newton St Cyres is 11 miles south of Bickleigh, and 5 miles north of Exeter.

GETTING THERE & AWAY
Buses 55 and 55A, B & C go from Exeter to Bickleigh (25 minutes, hourly Monday to Saturday, eight on Sundays) and on to Tiverton (12 minutes).

Bus 50 goes from Exeter to Newton St Cyres (10 minutes, every 30 minutes Monday to Saturday, hourly Sundays).

Tiverton Canal
High on a hill above town, the **Grand Western Canal Country Park** is an intriguing insight into life alongside one of these man-made, inland waterways. Built in 1814, it was originally intended to link up with a canal network stretching from Bristol to the English Channel. Reality fell short of that ambition, but tub boats carrying limestone from local quarries still worked this waterway for 130 years before the network declined, leaving only this 11-mile stretch. Canal-side displays chart its history. There's also a floating shop and café, and the chance to hire a row boat (per hour £4) or glide serenely along on a **horse drawn barge trip** (☎ 01884-253345; www.horseboat.co.uk; adult/child £8.20/5.70). There are normally one to two sailings daily between May and September; it's best to book.

Buses 55 and 55A, B & C link Tiverton with Exeter (45 minutes, hourly Monday to Saturday, eight on Sundays).

Knightshayes Court
This Victorian fantasy **manor house** (NT; ☎ 01884-254665; Bolham; adult/child £7.40/3.70; ⌚ 11am-5pm Sat-Thu late-Mar–Oct) was designed by the eccentric architect William Burges for the Tiverton MP John Heathcoat Mallory in 1869. Judging by the mix-and-match style of its construction, they never quite managed to agree on the eventual style of the house. Burges' obsession with the Middle Ages resulted in a plethora of stone curlicues, ornate mantles and carved figurines, but you'll also see lavish Victorian decoration, especially in the smoking and billiard rooms. The gardens are decidedly fancy too, featuring a waterlily pool and stately topiary.

Bus 398 runs from Tiverton to Bolham (10 minutes, six to eight daily Monday to Saturday), three-quarters of a mile away.

DEVON

SOUTH DEVON COAST

A coast of many characters, Devon's southern shore flows from Dorset to Cornwall and presents a dazzling display of seaside style en route. In the east, the beguiling fishing village of Beer leads onto the elegant Georgian terraces of Sidmouth, before Exmouth wades in with a wind- and kitesurfing burst of adrenaline. Exmouth also signals the beginning, or the end, of the Jurassic Coast (see the boxed text, p155). Next come kiss-me-quick Teignmouth and Torquay – the latter's excellent restaurants make it worth a detour for dinner. On to picture-postcard pretty Dartmouth, with more award-winning eateries, and captivating Salcombe, fringed by sandy coves and anchorage for a smart sailing set. Alongside, the rural South Hams offer simplicity, peace and space: undeveloped beaches, sparkling bays and inspiring cliffs. At the far west comes Plymouth, a city dripping with maritime history, overflowing with clubs and bars, and in the midst of a revitalising building boom.

THE EAST COAST
Beer
☎ 01297 / pop 1381

Somehow Beer manages to be thoroughly picturesque and a proper, working fishing village (not an imitation of one) at the same time. Multicoloured, snub-nosed boats line its steeply sloping beach, along with the winches and wires used to haul them ashore; deckchairs and crab pots lie scattered around. The village is set in a deep fissure in creamy-white cliffs and the main street is lined by waterfilled leats, and chalk and flint-faced houses, shops and pubs. With its unusual cave network and appealing places to stay and eat, the village is a charismatic base for exploring the east coast.

Although providing endless opportunities for jokes (sleeping in Beer, Beer garden and Beer Women's Institute), the village name actually comes from the old English for woodland (bere), because of the surrounding, densely forested slopes. The sea has always been a key source of income, but the catch hasn't always been scaly. In the 18th and 19th centuries, Beer was a smugglers' haven. The most celebrated excise-dodger was Jack Rattenbury, one of many to sneak barrels of French brandy ashore and secrete them in Beer Quarry Caves. Despite being arrested repeatedly and spending years in jail, Jack ensured local hero status by surviving to die in his bed at the age of 66.

Beer spills out from its central Fore St. It has no tourist office; the one in Sidmouth (see p176) can advise.

SIGHTS & ACTIVITIES

Beer stone is excellent masonry material and has been used in a wealth of buildings, including 24 cathedrals, the Tower of London and Windsor Castle. The Romans kick-started quarrying in the area and began the network of tunnels you can explore today at **Beer Quarry Caves** (☎ 680282; www.beerquarrycaves.fsnet.co.uk; adult/child £5.50/3.95; ◷ 10am-5pm Easter-Oct, 11am-4pm Oct). On the tour you see 2000-year-old tool marks on the walls, and a maze of arches and vaults dating from Saxon and Norman times to the early 20th century. You'll also hear tales of smugglers' hideaways and harsh conditions – the incessant ringing of hammer and chisel explains the origin of the phrase 'stone deaf'.

Check to see if the **Beer Heritage Centre** (admission free; ◷ hours vary) by the beach is open. It has tanks containing local sea life (starfish and sea anemones) and displays about fishing. It also explains how erosion has ensured the 130m high cliffs here are white, while 8 miles away at Sidmouth they're red. On the beach itself you can hire a beach hut (☎ 20756; per day £7), a deckchair (per half-day 60p) and, when the weather is good, a self-drive motor boat (☎ 07771 924857; per hour/half-/full day £10/50/80).

SLEEPING

our pick **Beer YHA Hostel** (☎ 0870 770 5690; www .yha.org.uk; Bovey Combe; dm £15; Ⓟ) Fancy a bunkbed bed with a view? In this hostel, dorms are decked out in pine and yellow, and some overlook the bay. Breakfasts are all-you-can-eat affairs of bacon, eggs and croissants. The suppertime pies are legendary (try the organic chicken). The local brew, Otter Ale, is among the tipples on sale in the bar.

Colebrooke House (☎ 20308; www.colebrookehouse .com; Fore St; s/d £35/58, f £78-84; Ⓟ ⊠) A family-friendly, late-Victorian terrace run by a former childminder – travel cots, high chairs and kid's cutlery are to hand. The breezy rooms are a palate of pastel shades and sleep two to five people. Wet walkers will find the drying room particularly welcome.

BOUNTY OR BOOTY?

On 20 January 2007, the coast around Beer was catapulted onto TV screens worldwide. Just 3 miles west, at the sleepy village of Branscombe, the 62,000-ton MSC *Napoli*, with 2318 containers onboard, had been beached. A dramatic enough sight, but what drew the cameras, and the crowds, was the contents of the 58 containers that found their way ashore. BMW motorbikes, wine bottles, and packets of shampoo and nappies littered the beach.

As the media coverage grew, the village was swamped by scavengers from across the country, carting goods up the steep streets in wheelbarrows. One woman, who was shipping her personal possessions from Sweden to South Africa, saw people rifling through them live on TV. Locals complained bitterly of mayhem and damage to their property before calm was restored. The morality and legality of the episode are still hotly debated. The UK's salvage laws meant that taking the goods wasn't illegal initially; not declaring them and using them was. Later the authorities evoked special powers, which prohibited taking goods.

Why had the *Napoli* been beached? She'd got into difficulties in French waters and was under tow to Portland when deepening gashes in her side prompted the call to run her aground off Branscombe. The move was severely criticised locally but justified by the authorities as the best way to limit fuel spillage – the local council is to hold a public inquiry. Pumping out her 3500 tonnes of oil took three weeks alone, removing her containers took four months and more than five months passed before her bow could be towed away. Resolving the rights and wrongs of it all could take years.

Durham House (☎ 20449; www.durhamhouse.org; Fore St; s/d £35/58, f £78-88; **P**) This laid-back, airy 1897 B&B is in the centre of the village. The rooms are a chilled combo of cream, light beams, wicker chairs and reclaimed pine. It's topped off with dashes of period charm: an arched doorway, bright tiles and stained glass.

Dolphin Hotel (☎ 20068; www.dolphinhotelbeer.co.uk; Fore St; s £32-36, d £64-72, f £96; **P**) Run by an affable, gently eccentric family, this 200-year-old hotel is full of laughter – helped by the giggle-inducing, distorting fairground mirrors beside the bar. Rooms are plainer and either feature high ceilings and solid wood furniture or the anonymous air of a modern extension.

EATING & DRINKING
Chappel & Son (snacks £3; ☼ 9am-5pm) One of two kiosks on the beach selling jacket potatoes and sarnies; try the delicious local crab ones. Or make your own with pre-cooked crab and lobster from the wet fish shop beside the causeway.

Anchor Inn (☎ 20386; Fore St; mains £7-12; ☼ lunch & dinner) A beer garden with a difference, this pub's terrace clings to the cliff. Inside, it's warm and welcoming, all worn wood and battered books. The restaurant whips up tasty medallions of pork, steaks and beer-battered cod 'n' chips.

Steamers (☎ 22922; New Cut; mains £14; ☼ lunch & dinner, closed Sun evening & Mon in winter) The place to go for a stylish supper – the décor here is exposed stone, purple velvet and arty chandeliers. Tuck into spicy sausage and king prawn pasta, tomato and sweet pepper tart and lots and lots of local fish. Just off the main street.

GETTING THERE & AWAY
Between April and October, bus X53 stops in Beer (two hourly, daily) en route between Exeter (one hour), Lyme Regis (1¼ hours) and Poole (£5.50, 3½ hours). Year-round from Monday to Saturday, bus 899 runs between Sidmouth and Seaton – some divert via Beer.

Sidmouth & Budleigh Salterton
☎ 01395 / pop 9955
Select Sidmouth, sedate Budleigh Salterton: the English seaside at its most stately, serene and salubrious. Here it's not so much kiss-me-quick as have a nap before a stroll. Sidmouth is the epitome of the Regency resort – hundreds of listed buildings line up elegantly behind its esplanade. In Budleigh Salterton a 3-mile level prom borders a pebbly beach flecked with fishing boats and backed by brightly painted huts. The resorts peep out from a shoreline of dramatic red, crumbling cliffs and in both you almost expect to see elderly ladies wearing white gloves, vicars in panama hats and Miss Marple dropping by for tea.

Each August Sidmouth is transformed by **Sidmouth Folk Week** (☎ 578627; www.sidmouth folkweek.co.uk), a vibrant festival of world and traditional music, which spills into scores of venues, as well as the streets. The **tourist office** (☎ 516441; www.visitsidmouth.co.uk; Ham Lane; ☻ 10am-4pm or 5pm Mon-Sat, 10am-1pm Sun Mar-Oct, 10am-1.30pm Mon-Sat Nov-Feb) stocks *Historic Sidmouth* (£2), which guides you around the town's blue plaques. Places worth hunting out are the 14th-century Old Ship pub in Old Fore St, and Fortfield Tce, which put up the Grand Duchess of Russia and her 100-strong retinue in 1831.

Budleigh Salterton is around 8 miles west; on its fringes is the village of East Budleigh, where Sir Walter Raleigh was born. The family pew, dated 1537, still sits in the village's All Saint's Church.

SLEEPING & EATING

Berwick House (☎ 513621; www.berwick-house.co.uk; Salcombe Rd, Sidmouth; s from £36, d £57-64; ⓟ ✗) This B&B's incredibly slanting attic room has the most character, and the least headspace. But it's the friendly owner who makes it stand out from the crowd, by making banana muffins and picking strawberries for breakfast.

Downderry House (☎ 442663; www.downderryhouse .co.uk; 10 Exmouth Rd, Budleigh Salterton; s £65-85, d £75-95; ⓟ) Set in sweeping lawns on the fringes of Budleigh Salterton, Downderry blends established elegance with boutique tweaks. It's brim-full of antique furniture and crisp cottons, and quality touches are everywhere: mini coffee machines in the rooms and little decanters of sherry.

our pick Salty Monk (☎ 513174; www.saltymonk .co.uk; Church St, Sidford; s £70, d £100-180; ⓟ 🖵) A place to indulge all the senses, this 16th-century restaurant-with-rooms panders to your comfort zone. Sink into an exquisite pared-down pod of a bath, then doze off in a chic low-level bed, or lounge under a peach canopy surrounded by beams and antiques. The food is deliciously imaginative: Devon sirloin with a baby pasty, and tomatoes topped with parmesan crisp and white truffle oil. Dinner is served nightly (two/three courses £30/33), but by reservation only. Lunch is Thursday to Saturday and it's best to book. It's 2 miles out of Sidmouth in Sidford, on the A3052.

Neil's Restaurant (☎ 519494; Radway Pl, Vicarage Rd, Sidmouth; mains £14; ☻ dinner Tue-Sat) Dishing up consistently the best fish in Sidmouth, Neil's delivers a smart, crisp dining experience. Try the tangy Beer crab with fresh mango or the grilled sea bass with roasted fennel.

GETTING THERE & AWAY

Bus 157 runs from Exmouth to Sidmouth (1¼ hours, hourly Monday to Saturday), via Budleigh Salterton (30 minutes). Bus 357 links Exmouth with Budleigh Salterton (30 minutes, hourly) on Sundays.

Bus 52 connects Sidmouth with Exeter (45 minutes, every 30 minutes daily).

Exmouth & Around

☎ 01395 / pop 35,430

Exmouth is a curious combination of well-worn Georgian resort and adrenaline frenzy. The town sits at the mouth of the River Exe and its exposed position draws fleets of wind- and kite-surfers who whip across the water on gusty days. The area also has good diving, a unique pint-sized National Trust property and is the beginning, or the end, of the Jurassic Coast (see the boxed text, p155).

The rusty red cliffs around Exmouth were formed in the desert conditions of the Triassic period 250 million years ago, making them among the oldest on the coast. In the 1800s the town was a fashionable, elegant watering hole with a whiff of scandal. Mary Ann Clarke, the Duke of York's mistress, lived here; in later life Lady Nelson resided here (after Horatio ran off with Lady Emma Hamilton); while Lady Byron (whose husband was quite the *Don Juan* himself) lived a few doors down.

Today, Exmouth is arranged behind its coarse sandy beach and promenade of refreshments, windbreaks and those odd, typically English constructions best described as bus-shelters-on-sea. The **tourist office** (☎ 222299; www.exmouthguide.co.uk; Alexandra Tce; ☻ 10am-5pm Mon-Sat, 10am-2pm Sun Apr-Sep) is in Manor Gardens. The bus and train stations are beside the estuary on the northwest edge of town.

SIGHTS & ACTIVITIES

À la Ronde (NT; ☎ 265514; Summer Lane, Exmouth; adult/child £5.20/2.60; ☻ 11am-5pm Sat-Wed late-Mar–Oct) is a DIY job with a difference. This delightfully quirky 16-sided cottage was built in 1796 for two spinster cousins to house a mass of curiosities acquired on a 10-year European grand tour. Its glass alcoves, low lintels and tiny doorways mean it's like clambering through a doll's house. Hunt out the cousins' own work: intricate paper cuts, a delicate feather frieze in the drawing room and the gallery plastered with a thousand sea-shells on the top floor (in a fabulous collision of old and new, this can only be seen via remote control CCTV from the butler's pantry). The house is 2 miles north of Exmouth on the A376; bus 57 (every 30 minutes) runs close by.

Edge (☎ 222551; www.edgewatersports.com; 3 Royal Ave; per half-day £60-75; ☼ 9.30am-5.30pm Mon-Sat, 10am-4pm Sun) runs kite- and windsurfing lessons from its base near the train station. **Jurassic Coast Diving** (☎ 268090; www.jcdiving.co.uk; Royal Ave; per day £75) organises a range of dives. The **Jurassic Coast cruises** (☎ 222144; www.stuartlinecruises .co.uk; adult/child 2-3hr cruise £7/5; ☼ Apr-Oct) leave from the marina; or hire your own **water taxi** (☎ 07970 918418; adult/child return £4/2; ☼ Apr-Oct) to take the 15-minute ride across the Exe to the wind-whipped, sandy wilderness that is Dawlish Warren Nature Reserve (right).

SLEEPING & EATING
New Moorings (☎ 223073; anneanddave@newmoorings .wanadoo.co.uk; 1 Morton Rd; s £27-40, d £54-64) The stone doorstop outside this red brick B&B says 'smile'; the owners are similarly warm and welcoming. The cream and brown rooms are simple and traditional; breakfasts include local, free-range eggs and organic sausages and bacon.

Dolphin Hotel (☎ 263832; www.dolphinhotelex mouth.co.uk; Morton Rd; s/d/f £38/74/144) Expect any colour but beige – bedrooms are alive with vivid yellows, rich reds and floating drapes, while the blue and red bathrooms swim with sea life themes. There's also a snazzy Moroccan bar, full of carved woods and immense leather sofas.

Royal Beacon Hotel (☎ 264886; www.royalbeacon hotel.co.uk; The Beacon; s £60-70, d £85-105, f £115) Established, personable and set in the same Regency terrace as Lady Nelson's old stomping ground. The best rooms have expansive sea views; all are comfy, and are decorated in dark woods, vanilla and candy stripes. Its Fennels Restaurant serves classic English dishes for lunch and dinner (mains £15) amid dark leather chairs and jazzy art, while there's a cosy Italian eatery called Donato's in the cellar (mains £9, open dinner Monday to Saturday).

GETTING THERE & AWAY
Trains shuttle to Exeter Central (25 minutes, every half hour Monday to Saturday, hourly

Sunday). Bus 57 goes to Exeter (25 minutes, every hald hour), while bus 157 runs to Budleigh Salterton (30 minutes, hourly Monday to Saturday) and then on to Sidmouth (1¼ hours).

TEIGNMOUTH & DAWLISH WARREN
☎ 01626 / pop 28,528
Hugging the shore where the River Teign meets the sea, Teignmouth is the picture of a faded resort: Georgian terraces back a seafront lined with rough, red-gold sand while a classic Victorian pier juts proudly out to sea. But Teignmouth is also home to a small port, which plies a coaster trade, and the tiny network of lanes nearby (with their salty pubs and ancient ferry slipway) lend the place a bustling, nautical air. A few miles to the north, the town of Dawlish is most notable for the nature reserve at nearby Dawlish Warren, a mass of wind-blasted dunes.

Teignmouth's **tourist office** (☎ 215666; www .southdevon.org.uk; The Den; ☼ 10am-5pm Mon-Sat Apr-Oct, plus 10am-4pm Sun Jul & Aug, 10am-4pm Mon-Sat Nov-Mar) is set just back from the pier at the grassy area called the Den. Teign St, with its collection of places to stay and eat, is towards the harbour, slightly upriver.

Sights & Activities
Teignmouth and Shaldon Museum (☎ 777041; 29 French St; adult/child £2/free; ☼ 10am-4.30pm Mon-Sat May–mid-Oct) displays an engaging potted history of local shipwrecks, treasure and Brunel's railway. It's due to close for a two-year revamp from autumn 2008.

It's thought the **Teign Ferry** (☎ 07880-713420; adult/child £1.30/70p; ☼ from 8am) service began life around the 10th century, while the distinctive black and white design of the current boat dates back to the time of Elizabeth I. This passenger service shuttles between Teignmouth and the tiny resort of Shaldon on the west bank of the river when required. Once over there, hunt out Ness Beach, accessed via a smuggler's tunnel hacked out of the rock. The ferry sails from Teignmouth's River Beach, just behind The Point (seafront) car park. The schedule varies; times are posted on boards on the beach.

Five miles north, the **Dawlish Warren Nature Reserve** clings to the coast at the mouth of the River Exe. This sand spit has a remarkable variety of habitats – from dunes and grasslands to salt marshes and mudflats – and is a key roost for wildfowl and wading birds. Arching out into the river, it's an exhilarating place, and the views across to Exmouth, up the Exe and out to sea, are superb. Bus 85/85A between Exeter and Torquay stops at Dawlish Warren, as do trains between Exeter (12 minutes, every one to two hours) and Torquay (30 minutes). Alternatively, enjoy a cracking water taxi journey from Exmouth (see p177) or hike the spray-spattered coastal path from Teignmouth (6 miles).

Sleeping

Britannia House (☎ 770051; www.britanniahouse.org; 26 Teign St; s/d £55/75) This 17th-century B&B in the heart of town packs a few surprises. Old cutlasses meet abstract art, and the gorgeous blood-red lounge is lined with exotic curios. The soothing bedrooms have comfy chairs and swish bathrooms, breakfast is a feast of local food while the walled garden is ideal for afternoon tea.

Thomas Luny House (☎ 772976; www.thomas-luny -house.co.uk; Teign St; s/d £65/92; Ⓟ ⊠) The essence of refined, restrained luxury, this 200-year-old town house oozes quality and is graced by heavy fabrics, antiques, wooden trunks and old sailing prints. The patio garden is an oasis of quiet calm.

Right on the seafront, the **Bay Hotel** (☎ 774123; www.bayhotelteignmouth.co.uk; 15 Powderham Tce; s/d £40/80; Ⓟ) has bright, fresh modern rooms, many with sea views.

Eating & Drinking

Teignmouth's eating scene is small but varied.

Zuko's (☎ 777181; 40 Northumberland Pl; mains £5; ☯ 10am-5pm Mon-Thu, 10am-10pm Fri & Sat, 10am-4pm Sun) This 1950s' diner is a riot of Americana, from the bits of convertible stuck on the wall to the juke-box cranking out rock 'n' roll. Unsurprisingly, they rustle up burgers, hotdogs and shakes, with some cocktails chucked in too.

Several pubs back onto River Beach, towards Teignmouth's port.

Ship (☎ 772674; 2 Queen St; mains £6.50; ☯ lunch & dinner, closed Tue & Sun evening) The Ship is a mellow, atmospheric old inn, all rustic tables, beams and wooden floors. Its waterside terrace is perfect for a pint and some good pub grub.

Owl and the Pussy Cat (☎ 775321; 3 Teign St; mains £10-16; ☯ lunch & dinner, closed Sun) A stylish, crisp restaurant that's brimming with Devon pro-

duce. Locally landed brill is teamed with buttered samphire, while Devon lamb and beef are combined with wild garlic. Enjoy it all in the leafy garden terrace.

Getting There & Away

Buses 85/85A go to Torquay (30 minutes, every 30 minutes) and Exeter (one hour, every 15 minutes). Trains runs to Exeter (30 minutes, every 30 minutes) and Torquay (20 minutes, every 30 minutes).

TORQUAY & PAIGNTON

☎ 01803 / pop 110,370

Bright and breezy Torquay is an archetypal Devon resort in a state of flux. For decades it's pitched itself as a slightly exotic 'English Riviera' – playing on a mild microclimate, palm trees, promenades and strings of twinkling fairy lights. Victorian villas and chintzy hotels stack up on its steep slopes like dominoes. But these days, Torquay is a bizarre blend of the boozed-up and the blue-rinsed – tourists are drawn by the resort's nightclubs and bars as well as its fudge shops and racks of slightly saucy postcards. Food aficionados are tempted by restaurants that rival those in the more obvious foodie hub of Dartmouth to the south. Throw in a batch of beaches, an azure circle of bay, an intriguing Agatha Christie connection and some great attractions (from zoos to caves), and it all makes for some grand days out beside the sea.

The Victorian Pier, beaches and arcades of Paignton, Torquay's smaller sister resort, lie a few miles south along the shores of Tor Bay. The joined-up version (Torbay) is applied to the area covering the two towns and the fishing port of Brixham.

History

Torquay's most famous residents are crime writer Agatha Christie and Basil Fawlty – the deranged hotelier memorably played by John Cleese in the classic British TV comedy *Fawlty Towers*. But Torquay was first inhabited by Neanderthals – literally. Evidence of Stone Age man has been found in the cave network of Kent's Cavern. The town itself was begun by a bunch of monks when an order of Premonstratensian canons founded a monastery in 1196 and built a quay on the shore near the settlement of Torre.

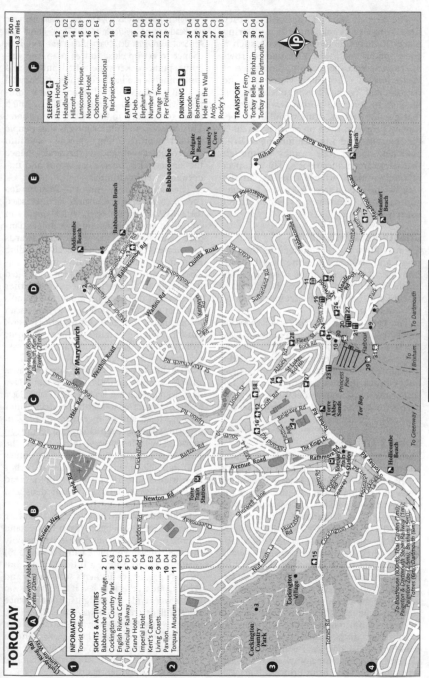

TORQUAY

INFORMATION	
Tourist Office....................	1 D4
SIGHTS & ACTIVITIES	
Babbacombe Model Village.	2 D1
Cockington Country Park....	3 A3
English Riviera Centre........	4 C3
Funicular Railway..............	5 D1
Grand Hotel......................	6 C4
Imperial Hotel...................	7 D4
Kent's Cavern....................	8 E3
Living Coasts...................	9 D4
Pavilion...........................	10 D4
Torquay Museum...............	11 D3

SLEEPING	
Haven Hotel......................	12 C3
Headland View..................	13 D2
Hillcroft...........................	14 C3
Lanscombe House..............	15 B3
Norwood Hotel..................	16 C3
Osborne............................	17 E4
Torquay International Backpackers...	18 C3

EATING	
Al-beb...............................	19 D3
Elephant...........................	20 D4
Number 7.........................	21 D4
Orange Tree......................	22 D4
Pier Point.........................	23 C4

DRINKING	
Barcode............................	24 D4
Bohemia...........................	25 D4
Hole in the Wall................	26 C3
Mojo................................	27 C4
Rocky's.............................	28 D3

TRANSPORT	
Greenway Ferry.................	29 C4
Torbay Belle to Brixham.....	30 D4
Torbay Belle to Dartmouth.	31 C4

DEVON

The French wars of the 18th century fired Torquay's development as a watering place (holidays in Europe weren't such a good option) and in the Victorian era rows of sea-view villas popped up, the Prince of Wales bagged a few sailing victories in the regattas, and Agatha Christie rollerskated on the pier. In the 1950s Torbay was such a hit that guesthouses sometimes couldn't cope, leaving people to sleep on beaches. In 2007 the resort secured a licence for one of Britain's new smaller-scale casinos – although that later came under review. The prospect of more roulette wheels spinning in the area has prompted fresh Monaco–Torquay comparisons. Comparisons which aren't entirely convincing.

Orientation & Information

Torquay flows into Paignton along the seafront, and stretches into the hills behind. The district of Babbacombe is on the cliffs northeast of central Torquay; the village of Cockington, set in a country park, sits to the southwest.

The **tourist office** (☎ 0870 707 0010; www.the englishriviera.co.uk; Vaughan Pde; ⊙ 9.30am-5.30pm Mon-Sat & 10am-4pm Sun May-Sep, 9.30am-5pm Mon-Sat Oct-Apr), beside Torquay Harbour, sells discounted tickets to local attractions, produces *Beach Bum* (a gay guide to the resort), and stocks leaflets detailing the great events run by the **Coast and Countryside Service** (www.countryside-trust.org.uk).

Sights & Activities

Torbay boasts no fewer than 20 beaches, and a surprising 22 miles of coast. Tourists flock to the central **Torre Abbey Sands** (covered by water at very high tides); the locals opt for the sand and shingle beaches below the 240ft red-clay cliffs at **Babbacombe**. These can be accessed by a glorious 1920s **funicular railway** (☎ 328750; adult/child return £1.60/1.15; ⊙ 9.30am-5.25pm). When the weather's foul, the wave machine and giant flumes of the pool at the **English Riviera Centre** (☎ 299992; Chestnut Ave; adult/child £3.60/2.85; ⊙ 9am-4pm, longer opening at peak times) draw the crowds.

Torbay Belle (☎ 528555) runs boat trips to Brixham (adult/child return £6/3) from North Quay in the Harbour, and to Dartmouth from Haldon Pier. The trips to Agatha Christie's garden at Greenway (see the boxed text, opposite) leave from Princess Pier.

Living Coasts (☎ 202470; www.livingcoasts.org .uk; Beacon Quay; adult/child £6.75/4.70; ⊙ 10am-6pm Apr-Sep, 10am-5pm Oct, 10am-4.30pm Nov-Mar) is a chance to get up close to free-roaming penguins, punk-rocker style tufted puffins and disarmingly cute bank cormorants. They all inhabit a massive netted-in enclosure, complete with mocked-up micro-habitats, which clings to the cliffs to the east of the harbour. This coastal zoo's philosophy is that people will act to protect things they've come into close contact with and understand – hence the keeper talks, open-plan layout and underwater viewing tunnels.

The same charity runs the **Paignton Zoo** (☎ 697500; www.paigntonzoo.org.uk; Totnes Rd; adult/child £11.35/7.60; ⊙ 10am-6pm), which majors in education and keeping and breeding endangered animals. It's amassed several awards for overseas conservation projects, breeding programmes and its innovative monkey enclosures – where animals are kept stimulated by having to forage for their food rather than have it delivered on a plate. The zoo's alphabet of animals ranges from American bison, tigers and tortoises to zebras. Look out for the free-swinging primates in lemur wood and the black rhinos, part of successful attempts at breeding.

At **Kent's Cavern** (☎ 215135; www.kents-cavern .co.uk; 89 Ilsham Rd; adult/child £7/5.50; ⊙ 10am-4.30pm Jul & Aug, 10am-4pm Mar-Jun & Sep-Oct, 11am-3.30pm Nov-Feb), expect a stalactite to drip water on your head and temperatures of 14°C in an atmospheric, prehistoric subterranean world. These caves were inhabited in the Stone Age, making them the oldest homes in Britain. The animals that roamed Torbay then were a mite different too – guides lead you past hyenas' lairs, cave bear dens and mammoth teeth.

Cockington Country Park is a 182-hectare patch of calm green space just a mile inland from Torbay's seafront bustle. Its heavily thatched village (complete with Lutyens pub) is pretty, if more than a little touristy, but the rose garden, craftsmen's workshops and cricket pitch (check to see if a match is on at the weekend) are delightful. **Babbacombe Model Village** (☎ 315315; www.model-village.co.uk; Hampton Ave; adult/child £8/5.50; ⊙ 10am to 11am-dusk) is a fabulously eccentric, 1.6-hectare world in miniature. Complete with a tiny Stonehenge, football stadium and beach, it's all inhabited by bizarre, Lilliputian people.

TORBAY'S CHRISTIE CONNECTION

Torquay is the birthplace of a one-woman publishing phenomenon: Dame Agatha Mary Clarissa Christie (1890–1976). In terms of book sales the detective writer is beaten only by the Bible and William Shakespeare, and her characters are world famous: Hercule Poirot, the moustachioed, immodest Belgian detective; and Miss Marple, the surprisingly perceptive busy-body spinster.

Born Agatha Miller in Torquay's Barton Rd, the young writer had already had her first piece published by the age of 11. By WWI she'd married Lt Archie Christie and was working as a nurse in the Red Cross Hospital in Torquay Town Hall – acquiring the knowledge of poisons that provided countless plotlines, including that of her first novel *The Mysterious Affair at Styles* (1920). Christie made her name with the cunning plot device she used in *The Murder of Roger Ackroyd* six years later. In the same year her mother died, Archie asked for a divorce and the writer mysteriously disappeared for 10 days – her abandoned car prompting a massive search. She was eventually discovered in a hotel in Harrogate, where she'd checked in under the name of the woman with whom her husband was having an affair. Christie always maintained she'd suffered amnesia – some critics saw it as a publicity stunt. Christie later married again, this time the archaeologist Sir Max Mallowan, and their trips to the Middle East provided masses of material for her work. By the time she died in 1976, Christie had written 75 novels and 33 plays.

Christie connections can be found at Torquay's **Beacon Cove**, where she had to be rescued from drowning; the **Pavilion**, where she met Archie; and the **Grand Hotel**, where she honeymooned. You can also detect Devon locations that appear in her books: in *Peril at End House* the Majestic Hotel is clearly Torquay's **Imperial**; her holiday home Greenway (p187) is Nasse House in *Dead Man's Folly*; Dartmouth's Royal Castle Hotel (p189) is the Royal George in *Ordeal by Innocence*; and Burgh Island Hotel (p195) features in fictional form in *And Then There Were None* and *Evil Under the Sun*.

Torquay's tourist office and website have an enjoyable *Agatha Christie Mile* leaflet (free) and also sells the excellent *Exploring Agatha Christie Country* (£4), by David Gerrard. **Torquay Museum** (☎ 293975; 529 Babbacombe Rd; adult/child £4/2.50; ⊙ 10am-5pm Mon-Sat & 1.30-5pm Sun Jul-Sep) displays an intriguing selection of Christie memorabilia, including family photos, handwritten notes and display cases devoted to her famous detectives. But the highlight is a visit to the lush gardens of Greenway, her home on the banks of the River Dart. The **Greenway Ferry** (☎ 844010) sails there either from Princess Pier in Torquay (adult/child return £16/9), or Dartmouth (adult/child £6/4). Boats sail only when the property is open (Wednesday to Saturday); times vary and it's best to book.

Sleeping

With eateries and sleeping options everywhere you turn, Torquay makes the best base out of the two resorts. There are particularly concentrated clusters of B&Bs around Avenue and Bridge Rds.

Torquay International Backpackers (☎ 299924; www.torquaybackpackers.co.uk; 119 Abbey Rd; dm/d £13/30) Relics of happy travels (world maps, board games and homemade wind chimes) are everywhere in this funky, friendly, laid-back hostel. Clean dorms sleep four to eight and feature bright colours and wooden bunks. The owner, Jane, hands out guitars and organises barbecues, beach trips and local pub tours.

Haven Hotel (☎ 293390; www.havenhotel.biz; 11 Scarborough Rd; s/d £35/60; P ⊠ 🖳) There's not a doily in sight at this cream, pristine B&B. Rooms are all clean modern lines with huge wood-framed mirrors and beige throws. The large, mounted soft-toy moose head above the front door (a nod to *Fawlty Towers*) adds a dash of comedy.

Norwood Hotel (☎ 294236; www.norwoodhotel torquay.co.uk; 60 Belgrave Rd; s/d/f £38/50/68; P) Expect four floors of lemon and gold, peach and satin in this friendly guesthouse. Sloping ceilings lend the top floor rooms a cosy feel. It's good for families, with four of the rooms sleeping three people, and the English Rivera Centre (with indoor pool) just 100m away.

Headland View (☎ 312612; www.headlandview.com; Babbacombe Downs; s/d £45/60; P) A B&B with a blast of the briny. Set high on the cliffs at Babbacombe, it's awash with nauticalia: from boat motifs on the curtains to 'welcome' life belts and salty sayings on the walls. Four rooms have tiny flower-filled balconies overlooking a cracking stretch of sea.

DEVON

DEVON

Lanscombe House (☎ 606938; www.lanscombe house.co.uk; Cockington Lane; s £50-60, d £75-110; P ⊠) Laura Ashley herself would love this design: a 19th-century house filled with lashings of tasteful fabrics, four poster beds, and freestanding slipper baths. Set on the edge of Cockington Village, it has a lovely English cottage garden where you can hear owls hoot at night.

Hillcroft (☎ 297247; www.thehillcroft.co.uk; 9 St Lukes Rd; d £75, ste £130-160; ⌨) This minihotel exudes boutique chic. Opt for French antiques and crisp lines or Asian-themed rooms with massive wooden furniture and exotic fabrics. Bathrooms range from the grotto-esque to the sleekly styled. The suite at the top is gorgeous and has broad views over the town.

Osborne (☎ 213311; www.osborne-torquay.co.uk; Hesketh Cres; d £130-205; P ⚲) The terrace of this grand hotel is more St Tropez than Torbay: think palm trees, white canvas parasols and utterly gorgeous sea views. Built in the style of a Georgian crescent, the Osborne has some rooms that are a touch bland but the ones overlooking the bay have period flourishes and binoculars to help you watch the boats go by.

Eating

Torbay sizzles with some seriously good restaurants, including one with a Michelin star, as well as the full complement of chippies.

Thai Garden (☎ 521540; 30 Palace Ave, Paignton; mains £7; ☾ lunch & dinner) Gloriously gilded Thai figurines and sparkly mirrors dot the interior, while fresh flavours fill a menu that includes extensive veggie options. Try the scallops with asparagus and spring onions.

Al-beb (☎ 211755; 64 Torwood St; meze £4, mains £9-13; ☾ dinner Tue-Sat) Take a virtual trip to north Africa courtesy of this brightly tiled Moroccan eatery crammed with woven fabrics and bright ceramics. It dishes up first-rate meze, tagine and couscous. Don't be surprised if a bit of belly dancing kicks-off too. If it's full, try the excellent Indian restaurant, Maha Bharat (☎ 215541) at No 52, which is also open for dinner (mains £7).

Boathouse (☎ 665066; Marine Dr; mains £6-12; ☾ lunch & dinner) Munch bistro standards (from steaks to spaghetti) and fresh fish at this breezy café on the seafront on the way to Paignton. You can hang out with a cappuccino on the sun-drenched terrace or sip a glass of white wine in chilled surrounds inside.

Pier Point (☎ 299935; Princess Pier; mains £5-20; ☾ lunch & dinner) You can eat right beside the water or in the cool, sleek dining room at this bistro-bar at the foot of the pier. Torbay mackerel with pesto, and local beef with creamed potatoes feature on the menu. There's also an extensive selection of wines, cocktails and cold beers.

Number 7 (☎ 295055; Beacon Tce; mains £15; ☾ lunch Wed-Sat, dinner daily) Fabulous smells fill the air at this buzzing harbourside fish bistro, and the menu is packed with super-fresh fruits of the sea. Number 7 specialises in local crab, lobster, skate and monkfish, often with an unexpected twist. Try the king scallops with vermouth or fish and prawn tempura.

Orange Tree (☎ 213936; 14 Park Hill Rd; mains £16, ☾ dinner) An award-winning brasserie, which blends continental flair and local fish, meat and game. Prepare to enjoy lemon sole with Armagnac and prawns, or Devon scrumpy pork (it's stuffed with apples), then loosen your belt for Vesuvius, a dark chocolate fondant cooked to order.

Elephant (☎ 200044; 3 Beacon Tce) One to remember, Torbay's Michelin-starred restaurant is full of imaginative flavour fusions: venison with vanilla and beetroot; sea bass with hog's pudding gnocchi. If that's a bit much, they'll do you a steak. There's fine dining in the Room (two/three courses £33/40; open dinner Tuesday to Saturday), or brasserie fare downstairs (mains £14; open lunch and dinner, closed Monday and Sunday evening).

Drinking & Entertainment

Torquay's bars splurge out from the harbour area; on Friday and Saturday nights it's swamped with the wide-eyed and legless.

Hole in the Wall (☎ 200755; 6 Park Lane) This heavily beamed, tardis-like boozer claims to be the oldest in Torquay – the part-cobbled floor is actually listed. At the front, there's a tiny alley-cum–beer terrace on which to enjoy an alfresco pint.

Barcode (☎ 200110; Palk St; ☾ to midnight, closed Mon & Tue evening) Quite simply the best bar in town, this is where Torbay's cool crowd hangs out. Raspberry red walls and twinkly lights surround huge, round cane chairs and a chimenea in the fireplace. The cocktails are works of art, and the snacks (£5) are tasty (try the homemade lamb and mint burgers).

Mojo (☎ 294882; Torbay Rd; ☾ nightly, to 1am Wed, Fri & Sat) This buzzing café-bar has a terrace overlooking Tor Bay. Inside it's all huge leather sofas and photos of jazz stars on the walls. Music is a mix of live bands, R&B and Latino with cheesy disco at the weekends.

The two-level **Bohemia** (☎ 292079; Torwood St; ☻ to 3am Fri, to 4am Sat) is the place for dance, house and R&B; while Torbay's gay venue, **Rocky's** (☎ 292279; Rock Rd; ☻ to 1am Mon-Thu, to 2am Fri & Sat), is a firm favourite with the fellas.

Getting There & Away

Bus 12 runs from Torquay to Paignton (20 minutes, every 10 minutes) and on to Brixham (40 minutes). Bus X80 goes to Totnes (one hour, every two hours) and on to Plymouth (1¾ hours). Bus 111 goes to Dartmouth (£5.20, 1¾ hours, hourly Monday to Saturday).

A branch train line runs from Exeter via Torquay (£6, 45 minutes, hourly) to Paignton (£6.30, 50 minutes). The **Paignton & Dartmouth Steam Railway** (☎ 555872; www.paignton-steamrailway .co.uk; adult/child return £7.40/5.10) offers a charming 7-mile trip (30 minutes) from Paignton to Kingswear on the River Dart, linked by ferry (six minutes) to Dartmouth. Generally four to nine trains run daily between April and October, with the exception of some Mondays, Wednesdays and Fridays in April, May and October (see the website for the full schedule).

BRIXHAM

☎ 01803 / pop 17,460

An appealing, pastel-painted row of fishermen's cottages leads down to Brixham's horseshoe harbour, signalling a very different place from the resort towns to the north. Here, gently tacky arcades co-exist with winding streets, brightly coloured boats and one of Britain's busiest working fishing ports. Although picturesque, Brixham is far from a neatly packaged resort, and its brand of gritty charm offers a more authentic glimpse of life along Devon's coast.

Information

The **tourist office** (☎ 0870 70 70 010; www.theeng lishriviera.co.uk; Old Market House, The Quay; ☻ 9.30am-5pm Mon-Sat, plus 10am-4pm Sun Apr-Oct) is right beside the harbour.

Sights & Activities

Among many things, Devon seafarer Sir Francis Drake (p196) carried out a treasure-seeking circumnavigation of the globe in the late 1500s. A full-sized replica of the vessel he travelled in, the **Golden Hind** (☎ 856223; adult/child £3/2; ☻ 10am-4pm Mar-Sep) is tied up in Brixham harbour. Though remarkably small, the original ship had a crew of 60. Today, you get to cross the ship's gangplank, peer inside the tiny captain's cabin, prowl around the poop deck and listen to tales of life in the officer's quarters delivered in suitably 'arrr, me-harteys' tones.

The displays at **Brixham Heritage Museum** (☎ 856267; www.brixhamheritage.org.uk; Bolton Cross; adult/child £2/1.5; ☻ 10am-5pm Mon-Fri, 10am-1pm Sat, closed Nov-Jan) explore the town's salty history, with exhibits on smuggling, the Brixham lifeboat and the unusual items dragged up by local trawlers.

It's worth hunting out the WWII defences of **Brixham Battery**. Its command posts, observation points, gun emplacements and searchlight positions are hidden away within the formal gardens at the end of North Furzeham Rd.

The unusual 1920s National Trust property of Coleton Fishacre (p187) lies 5 miles from Brixham, on the way to Dartmouth.

Sleeping

Sampford House (☎ 857761; www.sampfordhouse .com; 57 King St; s/d £35/60; P ✂) Judging by the roof height in this 18th-century fisherman's cottage, seafarers were much smaller 200 years ago – it has delightfully low ceilings and compact dimensions. The cream and peach bedrooms have little window seats and captivating views down onto the harbour.

Berry Head Hotel (☎ 853225; www.berryheadhotel .com; Berry Head Rd; s £91-107, d £108-164; P ✿) The Reverend Francis Lyte, who wrote *Abide With Me*, used to live here; now his abode is a top hotel with gorgeous vistas across Tor Bay. Built during the Napoleonic wars, it's a study of formal elegance, dotted with dark woods, floral fabrics and paintings of the Battle of Trafalgar.

Also recommended:

River Dart YHA Hostel (☎ 0870 770 5962; www.yha .org.uk; Galmpton; dm £14; P ☐ ☻) Four- to 12-bed dorms in a riverside Victorian mansion, 4 miles west of Brixham.

Quayside Hotel (☎ 855751; www.quaysidehotel .co.uk; King St; s £62, d £92-132; P) Harbour-view rooms are snazzy and warm-toned; inland ones are simpler and smaller.

Eating & Drinking

Chippies are sprinkled around the quay, but you can't beat a pot of prawns or fresh crab from one of the harbourside seafood booths: the best is **Browse Seafoods** (☎ 882484; ☮ Mon-Sat May-Sep, Tue-Sat Oct-Apr), next to the tourist office.

Maritime (☎ 853535; 79 King St) Quirky doesn't even begin to describe this dose of full-blooded British eccentricity. The inside of this pub is smothered in thousands of key rings, stone jugs and chamber pots, while Mr Tibbs, a parrot, wanders around the bar saying hello to customers (literally).

Poop Deck (☎ 858681; 14 The Quay; mains £8-17; ☮ dinner Tue-Sun, lunch Sat & Sun) A restaurant of riotous décor: pink walls, multicoloured tablecloths and hammocks slung from the ceiling. The equally eclectic menu includes king prawns in chilli and coriander, crab bisque and Greek salad, but the specialities are the delicious shellfish platters and Brixham fish, simply grilled.

Getting There & Away

Bus 12 runs to Paignton (20 minutes, every 10 minutes) and on to Torquay (40 minutes). Bus 22 goes to Kingswear (20 minutes, every 30 minutes Monday to Saturday, hourly Sunday), where you can catch the river ferry to Dartmouth.

The **Western Lady** (☎ 297292) runs ferries between Brixham and Torquay's Princess Pier (30 minutes, 10 daily May to October).

TOTNES & AROUND

☎ 01803 / pop 7443

After Torbay's kiss-me-quick delights, Totnes is decidedly different. It's got such a reputation for being alternative that locals wrote 'twinned with Narnia' under the town sign. This South Hams settlement has for decades been famous as a hippy haven – full of New Age shops and incense. The town still proudly flies the ecoflag, but the irony is that its brand of greener thinking is now being thought of as sensible, rather than laughable.

Totnes was founded in Saxon times, two key assets being its commanding position and access to the River Dart. In the 11th century the Normans stormed in and built the castle. Tudor times saw the town grow wealthy, especially from tin brought down from Dartmoor, and 60 fine merchants' houses still line the

central Fore St. Totnes' role as an alternative hub began in 1925 when Dorothy and Leonard Elmhurst bought the Dartington Estate, complete with its 14th-century hall, on the fringes of town. They set up an experiment in rural regeneration, established a progressive school and built some classic Modernist buildings, including High Cross House.

It led to the foundation of Dartington College of Arts in 1961, and for decades its trendy students have bolstered the town's ley lines and crystals image. But the immediate future is a little unclear – the whole school is due to merge with University College Falmouth by 2010 and decamp to Cornwall, a decision that prompted protests locally. But Totnes' alternative credentials remain: it's home to Riverford, one of the country's top organic food producers, as well as the pioneering Transition Town Totnes movement (see the boxed text, opposite).

Orientation & Information

Totnes radiates out from its Fore and High Sts, which wind up from the River Dart to the castle at the top. The **tourist office** (☎ 863168; www.totnesinformation.co.uk; Coronation Rd; ☮ 9.30am-5pm Mon-Sat) is towards the foot of town.

Sights & Activities

High Cross House (☎ 864114; Dartington Estate; adult/child £3.50/2.50; ☮ 10.30am-12.30pm & 2-4.30pm mid-Jul–Aug, 2-4.30pm Tue-Fri May–mid-Jul, Sep & Oct) is an exquisite example of a Modern Movement building, which teaches us that painting things in the garden bright colours isn't new. This white and vivid blue creation was constructed in 1932, making it one of the first examples of its kind in the country. A combination of rectilinear and curved lines, its starkly beautiful outline is deeply evocative of the period, as is the gorgeous interior – all pared-down shapes, smooth woods and understated elegance. High Cross sits alongside the main road inside the Dartington Hall Estate, which is 1.5 miles to the west of town. The **Ways With Words** (☎ 867373; www.wayswithwords.co.uk) literature festival draws key authors to Dartington in mid-July.

Sheltering in a tranquil riverside setting, **Sharpham Vineyard** (☎ 732203; www.sharpham.com; Ashprington; adult from £4; ☮ 10am-5pm Mon-Sat Mar-Dec, plus Sun Jun-Aug) evokes the hills of Chablis in the countryside of south Devon. Wander among the vines, learn about vinification

DEVON

CREATING AN ECOTOWN

In 2005 in Totnes, the seeds of an almighty ecoproject were sown. The first experiment of its kind in the UK, **Transition Town Totnes** (TTT; www.transitiontowns.org/totnes) began to look ahead to a world with less oil and work out its impact on every aspect of our lives: heating, car use, healthcare, schools, where and how we work, and the food, clothes and goods ferried into towns. A wealth of working groups has sprung up and hundreds of people are busy installing solar panels, planting food crops in public spaces and carrying out eco audits. They're even trialling the Totnes Pound, a parallel currency that aims to keep spending local. TTT's founder, Rob Hopkins, explains:

'It's about peak oil: the point after which the world begins to have less oil. When you consider that and climate change together, the challenges facing us are huge. Once we reach peak oil, there'll be restrictions on what can be imported, and towns will run into huge difficulties. The only way to prepare is to involve every section of the community and TTT acts as a catalyst to help people do that.

'Think of it as an iced cake. Totnes used to be self reliant. All the core elements (the cake) were produced locally; the luxuries (the icing) were imported, often by boat. Then the railways came and since then we've been importing the basics, the cake, from wherever we can get them cheapest and it's the locally produced items that are the extras. Since we began, at least 19 Transition Towns have sprung up across the UK. The move towards smaller, local economies is actually inevitable and any town that gets a head-start is ahead of the game.

'One way holidaymakers can really help is to spend money in truly local shops, cafés and restaurants – not the same old boring ones they have at home.'

---

techniques and indulge in tutored tastings. Handily, Sharpham also makes cheese on the estate, so you can nibble that while you sip too. The vineyard is 3 miles south of Totnes, signposted off the A381. Alternatively, walk from town along the Dart Valley Trail (ask at the tourist office for directions).

The Norman **Totnes Castle** (EH; ☎ 864406; adult/child £2.40/1.20; ☺ 10am-6pm Jul & Aug, 10am-5pm Apr-Jun & Sep, 10am-4pm Oct) is perfect for a bit of rampart clambering. The circular keep still clings to what is a massive man-made mound and there are buzzard's-eye views from the battlements over the town and surrounding fields. Kids in particular will love the tiny passageway leading to the latrine, little more than a hole in the wall.

Totnes Elizabethan Museum (☎ 863821; 70 Fore St; admission £1.50; ☺ 10.30am-5pm Mon-Fri Apr-Oct) is set in a house dating from 1575 and still retains many Tudor and Elizabethan features. Its displays explore the history of Totnes, and there's a room dedicated to the mathematician Charles Babbage, father of the modern computer.

The small but lovely **Devonshire Collection of Period Costume** (☎ 863168; High St; adult/child £2/80p; ☺ 11am-5pm Tue-Fri May-Sep) features beautifully displayed, annually changing selections from an extensive collection.

Canoe Adventures (☎ 865301; www.canoeadventures .co.uk; 5hr trips £17) organise trips on the Dart in 12-seater Canadian canoes. Staff often work in a campfire or a pub visit, and the monthly moonlit paddles are a treat.

Sleeping

Four Seasons (☎ 862146; www.fourseasonstotnes.co.uk; Bridgetown; s/d £40/60; P) Discover an inner penchant for flowery fabrics and pine at this traditional B&B on the outskirts of town. Expect patchwork quilts, lace and antiques. The slanted ceilings in the attic rooms make them the cosiest of the bunch.

Old Forge (☎ 862174; www.oldforgetotnes.com; Seymour Pl; s £52, d £62-82, f £107; P ⬜) This 600-year-old B&B used to be a smithy and the town jail. Thankfully, comfort has replaced incarceration: deep reds and sky blue furnishings cosy up to bright throws and spa baths. The delightful family room even has its own decked sun terrace. It's a 10-minute walk to town.

Steam Packet Inn (☎ 863880; www.steampacketinn .co.uk; St Peters Quay; d/f £80/110; P) Plucked from the pages of a design magazine, this wharfside warehouse's minimalist rooms are exquisite, with painted wood panels, willow arrangements and neutral tones. Ask for the river-view rooms, then sit back in style and watch the world float by. It's a five-minute amble downriver from Totnes.

our pick **Maltsters Arms** (☎ 732350; www.tuckenhay .com; d £85-95; Ⓟ) If you want something bland and conventional, don't stay here. The rooms in this old stone, creek-side pub ooze character; there's everything from silky and eastern to authentically nautical, with painted oil drums, real anchors and ship's rudders in one room. The three with gorgeous river views are easily the best; the inland Richmond room is much less fun. Avoid Saturday nights when you pay £15 to £25 extra. The pub dishes up tasty grub for lunch and dinner (mains £10 to £17). Try the roast guinea fowl or local oysters. It's in the hamlet of Tuckenhay, 4 miles south of Totnes.

Royal Seven Stars (☎ 862125; www.royalsevenstars .co.uk; The Plains; s £79, d £99-130, f £139; Ⓟ ⊠ ▣) They've been putting up travellers here since Charles II's day, and this grand old coaching-inn in the heart of Totnes is all 17th-century charm. Bay windows, bowed ceilings and slanting floors give it atmosphere, while rich throws, solid wood furniture and fancy bathrooms ensure modern comforts.

Eating & Drinking

Willow Vegetarian Restaurant (☎ 862605; 87 High St; mains £5; ☽ lunch Mon-Sat, dinner Wed, Fri & Sat) This rustic wholefood café sums up the spirit of New Age Totnes. Wobbly tables dot its bright dining room, and the menu is an array of couscous, quiches, hotpots, homemade cakes and Fairtrade drinks. It's strong on vegan dishes too.

Rumour (☎ 864682; 30 High St; mains £10.50-14; ☽ 10am-11pm Mon-Sat, 6-10.30pm Sun) A Totnes institution, this narrow, cosy pub-restaurant features low lighting, funky local art and free newspapers. Famous for its crispy pizzas (£5), it also rustles up dishes such as plaice with lemongrass and coconut rice, asparagus risotto and smoked chicken breast with ginger and chilli.

our pick **Riverford Field Kitchen** (☎ 762074; www .riverford.co.uk; Wash Barn, near Buckfastleigh; 2 courses adult/ child £14/7; ☽ lunch, booking required) An innovative bistro on a farm that aims for minimal food miles – the vegetables are picked to order from the fields in front of you, the meats are organic and locally sourced. Huge bench tables fill a futuristic, hangar-like canteen and chefs chop up artichokes and apples as you watch. Flavours and treatments are imaginative, from

the marinated grilled Moroccan lamb to the cumin and saffron with the veg. The ethos of picking only what's needed requires you to book; the planning laws demand you take either a guided or self-led tour of the fields. The farm is 3 miles west of Totnes. For excellent picnic supplies, look out for Riverford's organic food shop (closed Sunday) at the top of Totnes High St.

White Hart (☎ 847111; Dartington Estate; mains £9; ☽ lunch & dinner) This classy pub and restaurant is in the former kitchens of the beautiful 14th-century Dartington Hall. You enter via a soothing quadrangle of grass framed by ancient stone. The menu is strong on quality, with local meats, fish and veggie risottos spiced up with international flavours.

Entertainment

Dartington Hall & the Barn Theatre (☎ 847070; www .dartington.org/arts) The Great Hall and former barn on the Dartington Estate stage dance, drama and a wide range of arthouse flicks. Look out for the magical, open-air Shakespeare in the gardens in June. Ask someone to point you towards the Henry Moore sculpture in the grounds.

Getting There & Away

Bus X64 runs to Exeter (one hour, six daily Monday to Saturday, two Sunday). Bus X80 comes from Plymouth (1¼ hours, hourly), and on to Paignton (20 minutes) and Torquay (30 minutes).

Frequent trains go to Exeter (£8.80, 45 minutes) and Plymouth (£4.40, 30 minutes, hourly). The privately run **South Devon Railway** (☎ 0845 345 1420; www.southdevonrailway.org) is beside the main-line station. Trains chuff to Buckfastleigh (adult/child return £9/5.40, four or five daily Easter to October) on the edge of Dartmoor.

You can also cruise down the river to Dartmouth with River Link (p189).

DARTMOUTH

☎ 01803 / pop 5510

A bewitching blend of primary-coloured boats and delicately shaded houses, Dartmouth is hard to resist. Buildings cascade down steep, wooded slopes towards the River Dart, and 17th-century shops with splendidly carved and gilded fronts line narrow lanes. Its charms have drawn flotillas of yachts, and sometimes the trappings of a trendy sailing set risk imposing too many boutiques and up-market restaurants. But Dartmouth is also a busy port and a constantly shifting panorama of working vessels ensures an authentic tang of the sea. You don't have to have a yacht to enjoy this idyllic slice of the South Hams: fleets of ferries and hire boats mean everyone can get on the water. Enchanting and exhilarating hiking trails lead up the river or onto the cliffs, while Agatha Christie's summer home and a captivating Art Deco house wait in the wings.

History

Dartmouth's history is salty and compelling: ships headed off on the Crusades from here in the 12th century. The Pilgrim Fathers called in here en route from Southampton to America in 1620 – they only put in to Plymouth (to later depart from the much more famous Mayflower Steps, p198), because one of the boats sprang a leak. In WWII thousands of American servicemen set off from Dartmouth for the carnage of the Normandy landings. The hills above town are home to the Britannia Royal Naval College, the imposing 100-year-old mansion where the Royal Navy trains all its officers.

Information & Orientation

Dartmouth hugs the quay on the west side of Dart Estuary, its centre clustered around a tiny enclosed harbour known locally as 'the boat float'. The village of Kingswear on the Dart's east bank provides a key transport link to Torbay and is connected by an array of car and foot ferries. The Dart Valley Trail runs north up both sides of the river for 4 miles, then, on the west bank, continues for another 8 miles to Totnes.

The **tourist office** (☎ 834224; www.discoverdartmouth.com; Mayor's Ave; ☉ 10am-4pm Mon-Sat Feb & Mar, plus 10am-2pm Sun Apr-Oct) can advise on local walks.

Sights & Activities

Greenway (NT; ☎ 842382; Greenway Rd, Galmpton; adult/child £5.20/2.60; ☉ 10.30am-5pm Wed-Sat early-Mar–early-Oct), the utterly beguiling gardens of crime writer Agatha Christie (see the boxed text, p181), sit beside the River Dart near Dartmouth. Glorious woods hug the water. Speckled with splashes of magnolias, daffodils and hydrangeas, the planting creates intimate, secret spaces and the boathouse and

views over the river are enchanting. Although there's currently little evidence connecting the gardens to the crime writer, knowing she lived and wrote here creates a sense of intrigue. Christie was also inspired by the property – it doubles as Nasse House in *Dead Man's Folly*, with the boathouse making an appearance in a murder scene. Greenway is undergoing extensive renovation ahead of a planned opening in 2009 – you can sometimes watch the conservators working on the contents. The best way to arrive is on foot or by boat. Hike along the Dart Valley Trail from Kingswear (4 miles), or walk along the west bank from Dartmouth to the sleepy village of Dittisham (4 miles), then cross the river using the **Dartmouth–Dittisham Ferry** (☎ 844010; adult/child one way £4/3). It normally runs from 9am to 4.45pm, but if you're relying on it, call to check. Alternatively, sail upriver from Dartmouth on the **Greenway Ferry** (☎ 844010; adult/child £6/4). Boats run only when the property is open; times vary and it's best to book.

The Arts and Crafts style house of **Coleton Fishacre** (NT; ☎ 752466; Brownstone Rd, Kingswear; adult/child £6.40/3.20; ☉ garden 10.30am-5pm, house 11am-4.30pm Wed-Sun mid-Mar–Oct) sets the scene for a dollop of drama and long-lost glamour. It was built in 1926 for the D'Oyly Cartes, a family of theatre impresarios and owners of the Savoy Hotel and Claridge's. It's replete with gorgeous Art Deco embellishments: original Lalique tulip uplighters, comic bathroom tiles and a saloon that's reminiscent of a stage set – complete with tinkling piano. The grounds are like a three-act play, from the grassy terrace where croquet games were played to the scratch of a gramophone, to the deeply sloping subtropical gardens and the suddenly revealed vistas of the sea. You can hike to the property along a dramatic stretch of cliff path from Kingswear (4 miles) or drive. There's no public transport.

Guarding a promontory at the entrance to the Dart Estuary, **Dartmouth Castle** (EH; ☎ 833588; adult/child £3.90/2; ☉ 10am-6pm Jul & Aug, 10am-5pm Apr-Jun & Sep, 10am-4pm Oct, 10am-4pm Sat & Sun Nov-Mar) was built in the 14th century to protect the harbour from seaborne raids. These days it provides a fine panorama of houses tumbling down hillsides and the sea beyond – wandering around the battlements is fun too. It's connected by ferry (adult one way £1.20, every 15 minutes from 10am to 4.45pm) from South Embankment.

DEVON

DARTMOUTH

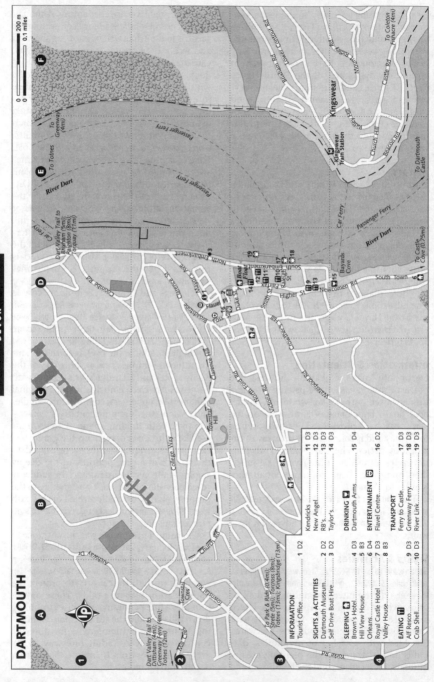

INFORMATION	
Tourist Office............................	1 D2

SIGHTS & ACTIVITIES	
Dartmouth Museum.....................	2 D2
Self Drive Boat Hire....................	3 D2

SLEEPING 🏠	
Brown's Hotel............................	4 D3
Hill View House.........................	5 B3
Orleans...................................	6 D4
Royal Castle Hotel......................	7 D3
Valley House.............................	8 B3

EATING 🍴	
Alf Resco.................................	9 D3
Crab Shell................................	10 D3
Kendricks................................	11 D3
New Angel................................	12 D3
RB's.......................................	13 D3
Taylor's...................................	14 D3

DRINKING 🍷	
Dartmouth Arms.........................	15 D4

ENTERTAINMENT 🎭	
Flavel Centre............................	16 D2

TRANSPORT	
Ferry to Castle...........................	17 D3
Greenway Ferry..........................	18 D3
River Link................................	19 D3

Kingswear

River Dart

The **Dartmouth Museum** (☎ 832923; Duke St; admission £1.50; ☺ 10am-4pm Mon-Sat Apr-Oct, 11am-3pm Mon-Sat Nov-Mar) displays a jumbled collection of costumes, swords, ships-in-bottles and vintage toys. The museum stands at the end of the **Butterwalk**, a row of wonky timber-framed houses that look as though they could collapse at any moment (although they have managed to remain standing since the late 17th century).

River Link (☎ 834488; www.riverlink.co.uk; adult/child return £9/6; ☺ Apr-Oct) runs cruises along the River Dart to Totnes (1¼ hours, two to four daily) from the pontoon at South Embankment.

You can chug about the Dart on a hired **motorboat** (☎ 834600; North Embankment; per 1 hr/day £25/100) or charter the **Enchantress** (☎ 07729-172977; per 2/4 people £150/300), a yacht complete with Richard the skipper. For a swim, clamber down the steps and join the locals at the tiny **Castle Cove** just round from the castle. It's also worth tracking down Dartmouth's quaintly cobbled **Bayard's Cove**, the quay from which the Pilgrim Fathers set sail, having put into Dartmouth for repairs.

Festivals & Events

Dartmouth International Music Festival (www .dartmouth-music-festival.org.uk) In mid-May this festival is a glorious melange of styles, from choirs and classical to country and western.

Royal Regatta (www.dartmouthregatta.co.uk) Dartmouth's big party is on the weekend of the last Friday in August with a carnival of water-related events that packs out the town.

Sleeping

Hill View House (☎ 839372; www.hillviewdartmouth .co.uk; 76 Victoria Rd; s £43-56, d £56-82; ☐) A B&B for the ecoconscious, here the emphasis is on environmentally friendly toiletries, natural cotton, long-life light bulbs and organic breakfasts. Some rooms are a touch small, but are tastefully decked out in cream and brown.

Valley House (☎ 834045; www.valleyhousedartmouth .com; 46 Victoria Rd; s £46-60, d £65; ℗) Set behind a flower-filled patio, this is a B&B with relatively plain rooms featuring white fitted wardrobes and silky fabrics ranging from light blue to gold. It's fairly central, the owners are very friendly and the price is good.

Brown's Hotel (☎ 832572; www.brownshoteldart mouth.co.uk; 29 Victoria Rd; s £65, d £85-170; ✂) How do you combine leather curtains, pheasant feather–covered lampshades, animal-print chairs and still make it look classy? Some-

how the owners of this smoothly sumptuous, imaginative hotel make it work. The smart breakfast room doubles as a tapas bar on Thursday, Friday and Saturday nights (tapas £4 to £9). Look out for their lobster and frites evenings.

Orleans (☎ 835450; www.orleans-guesthouse-dart mouth.co.uk; 24 South Town; d £85-95, ste £165; ℗) A guesthouse that combines utter opulence with cracking river views. Purple and gold fabrics team up with airy drapes, marble fireplaces and bare floorboards. You can sit in the bay window and enjoy a game of chess, if you can tear your eyes away from the boats on the water below.

our pick **Royal Castle Hotel** (☎ 833033; www.royal castle.co.uk; The Quay; s £95, d £155-199; ✂) Whisking you back to Tudor times, this exquisitely ancient hotel has stood plumb on Dartmouth's waterfront for 500 years. History seeps from the battered leather-bound books in the library and timbers from a Spanish man-o-war in the Galleon Bar, while antique chaise longues, massive carved chairs and velvet curtains deck the rooms. If you can, splash out on a river-facing room – the view onto the boat float and the quay is captivating. Pack a copy of Agatha Christie's *Ordeal by Innocence*; the crime writer used the hotel as inspiration for the Royal George in the novel.

Eating

With a celebrity chef dicing delicacies, Dartmouth has a reputation among gourmands. If you want a table in high summer, it's best to book.

our pick **Crab Shell** (☎ 839036; 1 Raleigh St; sandwiches £4; ☺ lunch, closed Jan-Mar) The shellfish in the sarnies made here has been landed on the quay a few steps away, and much of the fish has been smoked in Dartmouth. Opt to fill your bread with mackerel and horseradish mayo, kiln roast salmon with dill or classic, delicious crab. Excellent value.

Alf Resco (☎ 835880; Lower St; mains from £6; ☺ breakfast, lunch & dinner Wed-Sun) Tucked under a huge canvas awning, this cool café brings a dash of cosmopolitan charm to town. Rickety wooden chairs and old street signs are scattered around a front terrace, which makes a great place for a frothy latte or a ciabatta sandwich.

Kendricks (☎ 832328; 29 Fairfax Pl; mains £8-14; ☺ dinner) A cosy, reliable bistro, which blends local food and international flavours. There

DEVON

are crayfish tails and egg noodles, smoked salmon and blinis as well as monkfish, surf 'n' turf and homemade burgers too.

Taylor's (☎ 832748; 8 The Quay; mains £15, ❤ lunch Tue-Sat, dinner Fri & Sat, nightly Jul & Aug) You can watch the boats on the boat float from the huge bay windows here, while the menu takes care of your tastebuds. There's everything from grilled lobster and Dartmouth crab to Devon lamb or asparagus and goat's cheese tart.

RB's (☎ 832882; 33 Lower St; mains £12-18; ❤ dinner Wed-Mon) Sleek and very chic, RB's is all slim leather chairs, cream wood and brown napkins with sparkling silver rings. The food is pretty stylish too: local guinea fowl with bacon, pork wrapped in Parma ham, and vegetable and potato frittata. Save room for the treacle crumble tart with Devon clotted cream for pud.

New Angel (☎ 839425; 2 South Embankment; mains £18-23; ❤ breakfast, lunch & dinner, closed Mon & Sun evening) The fanciest, most famous joint in town. Awarded a Michelin star and run by celebrity TV chef John Burton Race (of *French Leave* fame), it serves up pheasant, Devon lamb and local fish with more than a dash of continental flair. There are also cookery courses (p53).

Drinking & Entertainment

Dartmouth Arms (☎ 832903; 26 Lower St; ❤ 11am-11pm) As an antidote to Dartmouth's sailing chic, join the locals for an unpretentious pint at the atmospheric Dartmouth Arms. There's polished wood everywhere, even on the ceilings, and navigational lights and cross-sections of ships dot the walls.

Flavel Centre (☎ 839530; www.theflavel.org.uk; Flavel Place) The Flavel Centre is the town's entertainment hub, hosting small-scale theatre and dance, as well as live music and films.

Getting There & Away

Bus 93 runs to Plymouth (£5.30, two hours, hourly Monday to Saturday, four on Sunday) via Kingsbridge (one hour). Bus 111 goes to Torquay (1¾ hours, hourly Monday to Saturday) via Totnes (30 minutes). Ferries shuttle across the river to Kingswear (car/pedestrian £3.30/1) every six minutes; they run from 6.30am to 10.45pm.

The charming Paignton & Dartmouth Steam Railway runs to Kingswear Station; for details, see p183.

THE SOUTH HAMS

South of Torbay, the Devon coast is transformed. Candy floss, promenades and arcades give way to the stylish sailing haven of Salcombe and an undeveloped shoreline studded with surfing beaches at Bantham and Bigbury-on-Sea. Inland lies a rolling, rural network of fields and woods draped with a string of mellow villages and market towns. It also holds a few surprises. At Start Bay you can sleep in a lighthouse and discover a ruined village. Or near Bigbury-on-Sea, drift off in Art Deco luxury and pop into a pub run by Marlene Dietrich's grandson.

The South Hams refers to a local council area, although the name 'ham' is said to come from the Saxon for 'sheltered place'. A good central source of information is www.somewhere-special.co.uk. The **South Devon AONB** (☎ 01803-861384) runs some inspiring outdoor activities; look out for their leaflets or visit www.southdevonaonb.org.uk.

Start Bay

A massive, elongated crescent, Start Bay is one of the most spectacular sections of coast in south Devon. The road south of Dartmouth climbs steeply via switchback gradients and hairpin bends, fields roll up to precipitous cliffs and villages cluster beside the sea. It's a landscape most people bypass, but it offers hidden gems: adventure sports, enchanting places to stay and unusual sights to explore, from a ruined village and a lighthouse to a massive freshwater lake.

Start Bay stretches from the village of Stoke Fleming, just south of Dartmouth, to Start Point, around 10 miles away. The A379 hugs the cliffs to pass through the village of Strete, the road then descends to Slapton Sands and the village of Torcross before veering off inland. At Torcross the coast path takes over, rising to pass the pint-sized fishing village of Beesands and the remains at South Hallsands before arriving at the lighthouse at Start Point. You can drive to the communities between Torcross and Start Point via a network of lanes, but hiking along the cliffs is a more atmospheric way to arrive. There is no tourist office in the bay; the one at Dartmouth can help.

SIGHTS & ACTIVITIES

The shells of the handful of houses that cling to the cliff at **South Hallsands** are all that remain of a thriving fishing village. In 1917 a severe storm literally washed this community out to sea. More than 20 cottages, a pub and a post office were lost overnight; remarkably, none of the 128 residents were killed. The disaster is blamed on the long-term dredging of Start Bay for building materials, which caused the village's protective strip of beach to disappear. You can't wander amid the ruins, but a viewing platform has displays that tell the story along with extraordinary sepia images of the village and its indomitable inhabitants. South Hallsands is 1 mile north of Start Point Lighthouse.

Start Point Lighthouse (☎ 01803-770606; www.trini tyhouse.co.uk; Start Point; adult/child £2.50/1.30; ☯ 11am-5pm Jul & Aug, noon-5pm Wed, Thu & Sun mid-Apr–Jun & Sep) is stuck right at the end of one of the most exposed peninsulas on the English coast; the land here juts almost a mile out to sea. Tours reveal just how remote life was for the lighthouse keepers before it was automated in 1993. You also get to climb the 28m tower for sweeping views of a boiling sea. No buses serve the lighthouse.

Slapton Sands (really a pebble beach) occupies a central, 3-mile stretch of Start Bay's shore, with **Slapton Ley National Nature Reserve** (www.slnnr.org.uk) tucked in behind. It contains the largest freshwater lake in the southwest and a series of trails, which wind past reedbeds, marshes and woods. At Torcross, look out for the **Sherman Tank Memorial**, which marks the deaths of more than 700American servicemen during WWII; they had been training here for D-Day when a German U-Boat torpedoed their landing craft.

SLEEPING

ourpick Seabreeze (☎ 01548-580697; www.seabreeze breaks.com; Torcross; s £48-88, d £60-110, f £70-120; **P** ✖) Fall asleep to a real-life soundtrack of the waves at this funky former fisherman's cottage. Just metres from the sea wall at Torcross, the stylish bedrooms all have slanting ceilings, whitewashed walls, artfully arranged pebbles and bits of weathered driftwood. The two seaview rooms have candy-striped window seats facing directly onto the bay. Choose to sip your breakfast cappuccino either ensconced in a cane chair on the terrace or tucked away in the totally chilled café.

Skerries (☎ 01803-770775; www.skerriesbandb.co.uk; Strete; s £47-50, d £75-80; **P**) Plump for one of two sea-view bedrooms at this superbly sited B&B

bordering the cliffs at Strete. The lighthouse room, with vistas from Start Point to the Dart Estuary, is best. The décor is aquamarine and cream, but with views like this you really don't notice the curtains.

Start Point Lighthouse (☎ 01386-701177; www .ruralretreats.co.uk; 2 nights from £491; **P**) Worth booking the babysitter for. Two cosy former lighthouse-keeper's cottages are full of old sea chests and comfy sofas, and one has a tiny seaview deck. Bring ear plugs (the signal sounds once a minute in fog) and hope for a clear night. The apartments sleep five to six people, and children under 11 are not permitted.

EATING

Britannia Shellfish (☎ 0845 0550711; Beesands; ☯ 10am-4.30pm) Directly opposite the fishing boats pulled up on the beach at Beesands, this tiny shop allows you to enjoy zero food miles. The pre-cooked crab and lobster and just-stopped-flapping bass, mackerel and skate are legendary. Look out for the new café too. The shop closes early and at weekends in winter; call to check.

Cricket Inn (☎ 01548-580215; Beesands; mains from £8; ☯ lunch & dinner) Fishermen have been served in this pub since 1867 and a few former seafarers still prop up the bar. Top-notch food includes steak and ale pie, and bangers and mash, but the pick is the locally landed crab or superb platters of fish 'n' chips.

Laughing Monk (☎ 01803-770639; Strete; mains £15; ☯ dinner Tue-Sat) This snug restaurant in Strete imaginatively fuses local and Mediterranean flavours. Try the French style fish soup, pine-nut crusted local lamb or Parma ham with celeriac – or there's always the crab and lobster landed at Beesands.

GETTING THERE & AWAY

Bus 93 runs from Dartmouth to Strete (20 minutes, hourly Monday to Saturday, four on Sunday) and on to Torcross (30 minutes) and Kingsbridge (one hour).

Kingsbridge & Around

☎ 01548 / pop 5845

Despite being on the same estuary as chi-chi Salcombe to the south, Kingsbridge has preserved the feel of a sleepy market town. At low tide the water drains out to leave mud flats, ensuring it's not so popular with yachting crews. So, instead this amiable community offers an authentic glimpse of rural Devon, and browsing its independent shops or lingering by its quay is a pleasant way to spend a few hours. Alternatively, tap into the adventure sports on offer in the area.

Kingsbridge's **tourist office** (☎ 853195; www .kingsbridgeinfo.co.uk; The Quay; 🕑 9am-5.30pm Mon-Sat May-Oct, 9am-5pm Nov-Apr, plus Sun 10am-4pm May-Sep) is by the quay. Fore St winds up to the **Cookworthy Museum of Rural Life** (☎ 853235; 108 Fore St; adult/child £2/1; 🕑 10.30am-5pm Mon-Sat Apr-Sep, to 4pm Oct), an engaging collection of school desks, cooking ranges, wagons and ploughs. **Mountain Water Experience** (☎ 550675; www.moun tainwaterexperience.co.uk; per half-/full day £20/55) offers a very different slice of Devon life: coasteering, caving, kayaking and bodyboarding are just some of the activities it runs in the surrounding area.

SLEEPING

Galleons Reach (☎ 853419; Embankment Rd; d £60; P) and **Haven Moorings** (☎ 852423, 07779-957910; 38 Embankment Rd; s/d £28/56; P) are two ordinary suburban houses with remarkable views. In both, furnishings are traditional and fairly plain, but the setting – low down beside the Kingsbridge estuary – is fabulous.

Hazelwood House (☎ 821232; www.hazelwoodhouse .com; Loddiswell; s £47, d £83-95; P) A calm Victorian country pile set deep in 27 hectares of breathtaking river valley. Polished floors and ancient furniture abound, meals are organic and there are occasional lectures and performances too. The decidedly New Age feel (the emphasis is on spirituality and healing) won't suit everyone. The house is 8 miles north of Kingsbridge.

EATING, DRINKING & ENTERTAINMENT

Mangetout (☎ 856620; 84 Fore St; 🕑 closed Sun) Tucked away at the top of town, this is a deli offering a smorgasbord of picnic goodies – from oozing soft local cheese to marinated olives and delicious breads.

Pig Finca (☎ 855777; The Quay; mains £10; 🕑 lunch & dinner Wed-Sat, lunch Tue) Act like a Sevillanos at this languidly cool bistro-bar, full of warm flavours and hot music. The interior is a riot of flowing fabric, iron tables and the odd pink plastic bust. Feast on serrano and chorizo or sip some manzanilla to tunes ranging from flamenco to Russian folk (sometimes it's live too).

The **Reel Cinema** (☎ 856636; www.thereelcinema .co.uk; Fore St) is Kingsbridge's own independent, family-run flicks.

GETTING THERE & AWAY

Bus 93 goes to Start Bay (20 minutes, every two hours Monday to Saturday, four on Sundays) and on to Dartmouth (one hour). The same service links Kingsbridge with Plymouth (one hour) in the west. Bus X64 goes to Salcombe (30 minutes, hourly Monday to Saturday, two on Sundays).

Salcombe

☎ 01548 / pop 1893

Oh-so-chic Salcombe sits charmingly at the mouth of the Kingsbridge Estuary, its network of ancient, winding streets bordered by sparkling waters and sandy coves. Its beauty has drawn waves of wealthy people and at times it's more South Kensington than south Devon. But despite the strings of shops selling sailing tops, delis and sleek restaurants, the port's undoubted appeal remains, and it offers tempting opportunities to catch a ferry to a beach, hike round a headland and soak up some nautical history.

HISTORY

Before it evolved into Chelsea-on-Sea, Salcombe was a salty seafaring port. In the 17th and 18th centuries its fishermen were working the Newfoundland Banks. By the 1800s scores of shipyards were turning out top-sail schooners, which sailed to the Azores to ferry fruit back to Britain. They sailed incredibly fast: a slow boat brought back only a rotting cargo. These days the numbers of fishermen and boat yards has dwindled dramatically, but the port has reinvented itself as a yachting haven. Enjoying a latte beside the lapping waters is undeniably lovely but the transformation has had a price – a massive 42% of properties here are second homes, many locals are firmly priced out of the market and in winter Salcombe resembles a ghost town.

ORIENTATION & INFORMATION

Salcombe centres round its harbour on the west bank of the Kingsbridge Estuary (technically a drowned valley, or ria, as no substantial river flows into it). Whitestrand Quay lies in the heart of town, Fore St runs south parallel to the water, becomes Cliff Rd, then leads to North and South Sands, 1.5 and 2 miles away. On the east side of the estuary, a string of sandy bays sit below the village of East Portlemouth. These coves and South Sands are linked to the centre of Salcombe by a fleet of ferries.

The **tourist office** (☎ 843927; www.salcombeinformation.co.uk; Market St; ☺ 9am-6pm Mon-Sat, 10am-6pm Sun Jul & Aug, 9am-5pm Apr-Jun & Sep-Oct, 10am-3pm Mon-Sat Nov-Mar), just back from Whitestrand Quay, can provide maps.

SIGHTS & ACTIVITIES
The **Maritime Museum** (Market St; admission £2.50; ☺ 10am-12.30pm & 2.30-4.30pm Apr-Oct), occupying just three rooms beside the tourist office, is an intriguing introduction to Salcombe's seafaring past. Bits of ship-building equipment and models of sleek schooners sit alongside treasure recovered from various local shipwrecks. Look out for the coin haul from the Salcombe Canon site: 500 gold Moroccan dinars dating from the 13th to the 17th centuries.

An Aladdin's cave of curios, **Overbeck's** (NT; ☎ 842893; Sharpitor; adult/child £5.80/2.90; ☺ 11am-5pm Sun-Fri mid-Mar–Sep, plus Sat late-Jul & Aug, 11am-4.30pm Sun-Thu Oct) is an Edwardian country house perched high on the cliffs at the mouth of the estuary in 3 hectares of lush, subtropical gardens. It's named after former owner Otto Overbeck, an inventor who pioneered a device called the Rejuvenator, which claimed to cure disease using electric currents – you can see one on display. Otto was also an inveterate collector and rooms are packed with a bizarre array of stuffed animals, snuff boxes and bits of nauticalia. There are also displays about the *Herzogin Cecilie*, a beautiful four-masted barque that came to grief off the south Devon coast in 1936 and sank in Starehole Bay around a mile south of the property. You can drive to Overbeck's or walk the steep 2¼ miles from Salcombe; just get to Cliff Rd and keep heading south until it's signposted.

It's hard to resist getting on the water in Salcombe. Rent a boat from **Whitestrand Boat Hire** (☎ 843818; Whitestrand Quay; per hr/half-day £20/50) or ride on the cheery **South Sands Ferry** (return adult/child £5.20/2.60; ☺ 9.45am-5.15pm Apr-Oct), where an ingenious motor-powered landing platform helps you ashore. The ferry runs every 30 minutes, and the trip takes 20 minutes. Alternatively, wander up Fore St to Ferry Steps for the five-minute putter across to the **beaches** below East Portlemouth (return adult/child

£2.40/1.40, every 30 minutes from 8am to 5.30pm, to 7pm August).

For an exhilarating and extraordinarily steep coastal **hike**, head south from South Sands along the cliff path towards Bolt Head (2 miles). A circular route leads back to town; pick up a map or ask the tourist office to advise.

SLEEPING
Higher Rew (☎ 842681; Malborough; www.higherrew.co.uk; sites £12; ☺ Apr-Oct) A fabulous, tranquil camp site (there's no pool) with good, clean facilities. Tucked away high in the fields around Salcombe, it's a mile's walk to South Sands.

Salcombe YHA Hostel (☎ 0870 770 6016; www.yha.org.uk; Sharpitor; dm £14; P) Actually set inside the National Trust property Overbeck's, this hostel offers a wide range of sleeping options, including a batch of family rooms and dorms that sleep six to eight. There's a licensed restaurant here and it runs sailing packages too.

Little Hill House (☎ 842530; little.hill@virgin.net; Little Hill; d £64-70) Tucked away at the top of town in a modern housing estate, this B&B displays a flair for design that lifts it above the crowd. Flourishes include solid dark woods, brown scatter cushions and Lloyd Loom furniture. Breakfast is a treat – everything except the baked beans is sourced from local farm shops.

our pick **Ria View** (☎ 842965; basweet@yahoo.co.uk; Devon Rd; d £68-78; P) The panorama on offer at this B&B is so scenic the rooms almost come as an extra. The décor is effortlessly stylish: cream and beige blends with peach and hints of dull gold, while the odd wicker sofa and leather headboard are scattered around. The views from the front rooms and the flower-filled deck are captivating – once you start watching the boats float past and the tide rise and fall, you might find it hard to tear yourself away. It's a few minutes' steep walk into town.

Tides Reach (☎ 843466; www.tidesreach.com; South Sands; d £214-274, f from £286; P ☻) The tide doesn't quite (reach), but South Sands does lie just across a lane. All rooms have sight of the sea, some have balconies, and the décor is pleasant and countrified rather than super-chic (think cosy fabric armchairs not sleek leather). Prices fall by up to £60 a room out of high season.

DEVON

EATING

For picnic supplies, **Salcombe Fishmongers** (☎ 844475; 11 Clifton Pl; ☒ 9am-5.30pm Mon-Sat), near the tourist office, sells everything from shellfish bisque and wet fish to gourmet crab sandwiches (with optional chilli sauce). Next door the Chelsea-style **Casse-Croute** (☎ 843003; 10 Clifton Pl; ☒ 8.30am-5.30pm, to 4.30pm winter, closed mid-Jan–mid-Feb) is a deli packed with charcuterie and organic artisanal breads.

Ferry Inn (☎ 844000; Fore St; ☒ lunch & dinner) This old pub's waterside terrace is right beside the ferry steps, ensuring briny views over to East Portlemouth. The atmosphere (busy and buzzing) is great – the bar food is good too.

Winking Prawn (☎ 842326; North Sands; mains £8-18; ☒ lunch & dinner Sat & Sun Oct-Mar) Overflowing with distressed driftwood-chic, this North Sands beach-side brasserie features huge rowing oars, red ensigns and a sea-view deck. It's a perfect spot to sample monkfish wrapped in bacon, black bream with mango and goat's cheese-themed veggie options. That or work through a pitcher of Pimm's.

Catch 55 (☎ 842646; 55 Fore St; mains £15; ☒ lunch Wed-Sun, dinner daily) Fish cooked every which way is the hallmark of this bustling bistro – mussels, local lobster and monkfish end up grilled, curried or covered in mornay sauce. Vegetarians and carnivores are catered for too.

GETTING THERE & AWAY

Bus X64 goes to Kingsbridge (30 minutes, hourly Monday to Saturday, two on Sundays). Bus 92 runs to Plymouth (three daily Monday to Saturday); on Sunday it becomes the 93 and involves a change onto the X64 at Kingsbridge.

Hope Cove to Burgh Island
☎ 01548

West of Salcombe the South Hams coast is a picture of unspoilt beauty, where exhilarating cliffs plunge down to reveal golden beaches and time-warp villages. It's a captivating stretch of shore, which manages to offer both simple pleasures and sophistication: the chance to catch crabs on harbour walls, learn to surf or stay in a sumptuous Art Deco Hotel.

There is no tourist office; those in Kingsbridge and Salcombe can help. The estuaries of the Rivers Avon and Erme cut deep into the landscape, edging the main A379 some 3 miles inland.

HOPE COVE

A couple of pint-sized sandy coves, a tiny harbour and a gathering of thatches – there's not much to Hope Cove, but what there is, is delightful. The village has a shop, a pub and a couple of places to stay and has managed to retain a sense of community, especially when compared with Salcombe to the east.

Hope is technically divided into the wonderfully named Inner and Outer Hope, although one leads to the other. The compact, curling harbour wall makes an ideal spot for a touch of **crabbing**. Alternatively, for some DIY archaeology, take the coast path a mile south to Bolt Tail and hunt out the 4.5m high grassy ramparts, which are the remains of an **Iron Age fort**.

Just up from the centre of the village, **Sand Pebbles** (☎ 561673; www.sandpebbles.co.uk; s £50, d £60-90; P) offers fairly traditional rooms, complete with candy-striped wallpaper and elegant chairs, as well as sea views from one room, sea glimpses from two others and a lovely sight of the bay from the terrace.

Set high on a hill, the **Cottage Hotel** (☎ 561555; www.hopecove.com; s £44, d £142-160; P) has a pleasantly old-fashioned feel, with family curios scattered around. The rear-facing bedrooms are very basic and share bathrooms – others are floral-themed and have wide sea views. The long, thin terrace is a perfect spot to combine wave-watching with afternoon tea. Prices include a five-course dinner.

The beer terrace of the **Hope and Anchor** (☎ 561294; mains from £6; ☒ lunch & dinner) pub is the place where everyone congregates for a pint – its bar menu features steaks and tasty soups.

Bus 162 runs to Kingsbridge (20 minutes, three daily Monday to Saturday).

THURLESTONE

A few miles west of Hope Cove, a compact rock arch sits in the middle of Thurlestone's sandy bay. A golf course lies between the beach and the sleepy village, which contains an atmospheric old pub and a swish modern hotel.

The **Village Inn** (☎ 563525; mains £9; ☒ lunch & dinner) is a snug study in stone and wood, with benches and settles inside, and picnic tables outside. The food is firmly local (the fish is brought in daily from Brixham); try the bream, River Exe mussels or char-grilled beefburger.

The **Thurlestone Hotel** (☎ 560382; www.thurle stone.co.uk; d £238-350, f from £264; P ✗ ⚊) serves up self-conscious glamour in the heart of rural south Devon. Smart blue parasols dot the grounds, glass screens shelter the almost-infinity pool and luxury reigns in the rooms, with super-fluffy bathrobes, crisp linens and balconies with sweeping sea views. Prices drop by as much as £80 a room in low season.

Bus 162 links Thurlestone to Kingsbridge (15 minutes, three daily Monday to Saturday) and Hope Cove (30 minutes).

BANTHAM

This pocket-sized village has the best surfing beach in south Devon – and hardly anything else. Its scattering of buildings, including a pub and a shop, stretches back from rolling dunes and (at low-tide) a magnificent expanse of sand.

Tucked at the east side of the mouth of the River Avon, Bantham's **beach** is refreshingly undeveloped – there's no kiosk and the toilet block is a five- to 10-minute walk from the sea. A cracking southwesterly swell draws waves of surfers here, stoked-up and itching to enjoy the most consistent break on the south coast. **Fir Tree Garage** (☎ 550063; ⏰ 9am-5pm Mon-Fri, 10am-4pm Sat & Sun), 5 miles northwest of the beach on the A379, rents out wetsuits (£7), bodyboards (£7) and longboards (£12.50); handily, hire is for 24 hours. For lessons, see Bigbury-on-Sea (right). Be aware: the currents at Bantham are potentially dangerous. Read the signs and follow the lifeguard's advice.

A sandy stroll from the beach, the 14th-century **Sloop Inn** (☎ 560489; www.sloopatbantham .co.uk; s/d/f £50/83/100; ⏰ lunch & dinner; P) makes a chilled-out base. The stylish rooms are decked out in neutral tones, suede headboards and floaty curtains. The bar has candles, an open fire and just the food (lunch and dinner) to fuel the next day's surfing. Try the tasty steaks, or whole sea bass (mains £12).

Buses don't run to Bantham. Drive, or hike along the cliff path from Thurlestone (2 miles). To get to Bigbury-on-Sea on the other side of the River Avon, either drive around the estuary via the village of Aveton Gifford (10 miles), or track down the very part-time **passenger ferry** (☎ 561196; ⏰ 10-11am & 3-4pm Mon-Sat Apr–mid-Sep).

BIGBURY-ON-SEA & BURGH ISLAND

From towering cliffs lined with impressive houses, Bigbury-on-Sea sweeps down suddenly to a sandy beach. The village is more developed than Bantham on the other side of the Avon Estuary but it has an ace in the pack: the intriguing Burgh Island, complete with Jazz Age hotel, which sits just offshore.

The temptation to try and ride the waves here is strong. **Discovery Surf School** (☎ 07813-639622; www.discoverysurf.com; 2hr lesson adult/child £30/25) runs classes, although locations change so booking is advised. For surfboard hire, see Bantham (left).

A slanting chunk of grass-topped rock, **Burgh Island** is connected to the mainland by an expanse of sand at low tide. At high tide the journey is made by a **sea-tractor**, an utterly eccentric device where the passenger platform is perched on stilts 6ft above the tractor's wheels and the waves. The 10.5-hectare island takes 20 minutes to walk around and it has its own pub, the 14th-century Pilchard Inn, an atmospheric spot for a pint on the terrace.

The **Henley Hotel** (☎ 810240; www.thehenleyhotel .co.uk; Folly Hill; s £60-70, d £100-120; P ✗) clings to the cliffs just inside the estuary, radiating a gentle elegance and charm. Lloyd Loom furniture, leafy houseplants and exotic rugs dot the interior, and the views down onto Bantham are extraordinary. Steps (150 of them) lead from the garden down the cliffs to the beach below.

our pick **Burgh Island Hotel** (☎ 810514; www .burghisland.com; s £230, d £320, ste £300-480; ✗) feels more like a film set than a place to sleep, with the huge, gleaming-white Art Deco building dominating the island. In its time, this grand hotel has put up Agatha Christie (who wrote *And Then There Were None* here) and Noel Coward as well as Prince Edward and Wallis Simpson. Thankfully it's kept much of its Jazz Age interior, and rooms merge flapper style with luxury modern flourishes: uplighters meet slipper baths, and rich woods meet retro radios. It's perfect for cocktails and croquet, and the views, as you'd expect, are superb.

The laid-back terrace of the **Oyster Shack** (☎ 810876; Milburn Orchard Farm, Stakes Hill; mains £14; ⏰ breakfast, lunch & dinner) is the place to indulge in local oysters, mussels, monkfish and crab; treatments range from grilled and traditional

DEVON

to spicy and Spanish. The shack lies just off the tidal road that hugs the estuary between Bigbury-on-Sea and Aveton Gifford to the northeast.

A few miles west, in the densely thatched village of Ringmore, the **Journey's End** (☎ 810205; mains £8; ☽ lunch & dinner, closed Mon) is a grand old pub run by the grandson of Marlene Dietrich. It's got great food, a friendly atmosphere and some superb movie-star stories.

Bigbury-on-Sea has one bus a week to Plymouth (1¼ hours), which also stops at Ringmore (20 minutes).

PLYMOUTH

☎ 01752 / pop 240,718

If parts of Devon are nature programmes or costume dramas, Plymouth is a healthy dose of reality TV. Gritty, and certainly not always pretty, its centre has been subjected to bursts of building even the architect's mother might question. But despite often being dismissed for its partying, poverty and urban problems, this is a city of huge spirit and great assets. It was bombed heavily in WWII but rose, literally, from the ashes. Its location, on the edge of a stunning natural harbour and just behind Dartmoor, brings endless possibilities for boat trips, sailing or hiking. The city's rich maritime history warrants exploration as does a waterfront Barbican area creaking with half-timbered houses and bobbing with boats. Add one of the country's best aquariums, a playful 1930s lido and a decid-edly lively nightlife, and you have a place to reconnect with the real before another foray into the delights of Devon's chocolate-box-pretty moors and shores.

History

Plymouth's history is dominated by the sea. The first recorded cargo left the city in 1211 and by the late 16th century it was the port of choice for explorers and adventurers. In just 12 years it said goodbye to Sir Francis Drake on his circumnavigation of the globe, Sir Walter Raleigh on his colony-building trip to Virginia, and the fleet that defeated the Spanish Armada. Plymouth also waved off the pilgrims who founded America, Charles Darwin, Captain Cook and count-less boats carrying emigrants to Australia and New Zealand. By the 1900s the Bar-bican area was packed with boats, and an incredibly vibrant community of fishermen, trawlers and herring packers.

During the 1940s Plymouth suffered hor-rendously at the hands of the Luftwaffe – a Royal Dockyard since 1690, it was now a key target. More than 1000 civilians died in the Blitz and the city centre was reduced to rubble – the ruins of a bombed-out church still stand at Charles Cross roundabout as a memorial. The post-war rebuild was dubbed Resurgam (I will rise again) and the crisp lines of these mid-20th-century buildings can be seen above the shopfronts lining the pedestrianised streets.

A DIFFERENT DRAKE

Sir Francis Drake (c 1540–96) was a man with a dashing image, which belies a different reality. To the English of the Tudor age he was a hero, an explorer and an adventurer. However, their Spanish counterparts dubbed him 'Drake – the master thief'. Drake was also involved, albeit briefly, in the slave trade. At 18, Drake enlisted on a boat owned by his relative John Hawkins. In 1562 Hawkins became the first English captain to ply the triangular slave trade when he kidnapped 400 Africans and sold them in the West Indies. Drake went on the last of Hawkins' three voyages, which enslaved a total of 1400 people.

In 1580 Drake sailed into Plymouth aboard the *Golden Hind*, having become the first man to circumnavigate the globe. His vessel was full of treasure looted from Spanish Colonies, securing the favour of Queen Elizabeth I and the money to buy Buckland Abbey (p206) on the outskirts of Plymouth. Eleven years later, Drake (legend has it) calmly insisted on finishing his game of bowls on Plymouth Hoe, despite hearing of the advance of the Spanish Armada. The first engagement happened just off Plymouth, the second at Portland Bill and eventually the Spanish fleet was chased to Calais and attacked with fire ships. Many escaped but were wrecked off the Scottish coast. Arguably Drake's past eventually caught up with him – in 1596 he died from fever while on a voyage against Spanish possessions in the West Indies and was buried at sea off modern Panama. His statue, looking more dignified than piratical, stands on Plymouth Hoe.

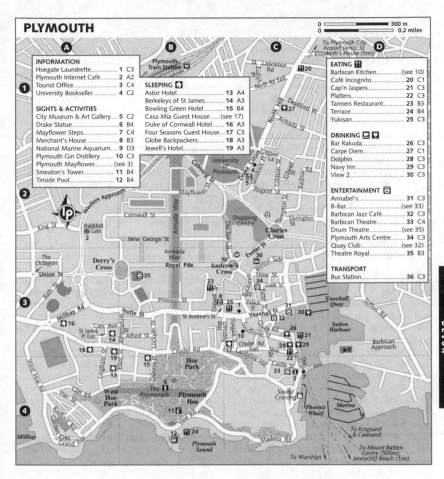

PLYMOUTH

INFORMATION	
Hoegate Laundrette...............	**1** C3
Plymouth Internet Café..........	**2** A2
Tourist Office........................	**3** C4
University Bookseller.............	**4** C2

SIGHTS & ACTIVITIES	
City Museum & Art Gallery....	**5** C2
Drake Statue........................	**6** B4
Mayflower Steps....................	**7** C4
Merchant's House.................	**8** B3
National Marine Aquarium.....	**9** D3
Plymouth Gin Distillery.........	**10** C3
Plymouth Mayflower...........	(see 3)
Smeaton's Tower..................	**11** B4
Tinside Pool........................	**12** B4

SLEEPING ⌂	
Astor Hotel..........................	**13** A4
Berkeleys of St James..........	**14** A3
Bowling Green Hotel.............	**15** B4
Casa Mia Guest House.........	(see 17)
Duke of Cornwall Hotel........	**16** A3
Four Seasons Guest House....	**17** A3
Globe Backpackers...............	**18** A3
Jewell's Hotel......................	**19** A3

EATING 🍴	
Barbican Kitchen..............	(see 10)
Café Incognito..................	**20** C1
Cap'n Jaspers...................	**21** C3
Platters...........................	**22** C3
Tanners Restaurant...........	**23** B3
Terrace............................	**24** B4
Yukisan...........................	**25** C3

DRINKING 🍷 🍸	
Bar Rakuda.......................	**26** C3
Carpe Diem......................	**27** C1
Dolphin...........................	**28** C3
Navy Inn..........................	**29** C3
View 2.............................	**30** C3

ENTERTAINMENT 🎭	
Annabel's.........................	**31** C3
B-Bar..............................	(see 33)
Barbican Jazz Café............	**32** C3
Barbican Theatre...............	**33** C4
Drum Theatre...................	(see 35)
Plymouth Arts Centre........	**34** C3
Quay Club.......................	(see 32)
Theatre Royal...................	**35** B3

TRANSPORT	
Bus Station......................	**36** C3

DEVON

The 21st century has seen large-scale re-development, including the £200 million, architectural mishmash of the Drake Circus shopping centre. The defence sector remains crucial to the city. Its Devonport Dockyard employs 2500 people, and scores of Royal Navy vessels and hundreds of troops are Plymouth-based – ensuring modern wars, from the Falklands to Afghanistan and the Gulf, have particular resonance.

Orientation

Plymouth's pedestrianised shopping centre is just south of the train station. Further south the Hoe, a grassy headland, over-looks the massive natural harbour that is Plymouth Sound; east of both lie the cob-bled streets of the Barbican, Plymouth's historic heartland.

Information

Hoegate Laundrette (☎ 223031; 55 Notte St; ◷ 8am-6pm Mon-Fri, 9am-1pm Sat)

Plymouth Internet Café (☎ 221777; 32 Frankfort Gate; per hr £4; ◷ 9am-5pm Mon-Sat, 10am-4pm Sun)

Police station (☎ 0845 2777444; Charles Cross; ◷ 24hr)

Post office (5 St Andrew's Cross; ◷ 9am-5.30pm Mon-Sat)

Tourist office (☎ 306330; www.visitplymouth.co.uk; 3-5 The Barbican; ◷ 9am-5pm Mon-Sat, 10am-4pm Sun Apr-Oct, 9am-5pm Mon-Fri, 10am-4pm Sat Nov-Mar) Housed inside the Plymouth Mayflower building.

ART ON THE BARBICAN

Seen by some as brilliant, by others as downright disturbing, the huge murals you'll see dotted about the Barbican are the work of the late, representational painter Robert Lenkiewicz (1941–2002; www.robertlenkiewicz.co.uk). The son of Jewish refugees from Germany and Poland, this brooding, eccentric philosopher was a fixture of the district for decades and has been described by some as a modern-day Rembrandt. Lenkiewicz developed a special bond with alcoholics, drug addicts and homeless people, often offering them a meal and a bed for the night. Exploring themes of death and obsession, he also achieved notoriety in the mid-1980s when he embalmed the body of a local tramp. Check out the biggest, and also the most peeling, of his works in the corner of the Parade, then track down the rest – one is in a café on Southside St.

In an utterly different artistic vein, the paintings of Plymouth-born Beryl Cook (1926–; www .berylcook.org) are renowned for their cheerful depictions of brash, large ladies sporting unfeasibly small clothes. Her exuberant, almost comic-book artwork features a dizzying variety of Barbican scenes, and one of the most popular local games is to try and spot (in the flesh) the type of characters that people her paintings. Look out for the gallery featuring her work in Southside St.

University Bookseller (☎ 660428; 42 Drake Circus; ⏱ 10am-4pm Mon-Sat)

Sights

BARBICAN

The Barbican is Plymouth's historic heart and soul. Its part-cobbled streets are lined with Tudor and Jacobean buildings, many of which are now galleries, craft shops restaurants and funky bars. The **Mayflower Steps** mark the final UK departure point of the Pilgrim Fathers – the band of settlers who founded New England's first permanent colony at Plymouth (Massachusetts) in 1620. Having left Southampton and been forced into Dartmouth because of an unseaworthy ship, they finally left Plymouth (England) on board the *Mayflower*. The rest, in this case the founding of America, is history. The steps themselves are small and although they look old, they aren't the original ones (you have to expect a bit of a rebuild over the last 400 years). The surrounding plaques help you navigate Plymouth's past – they mark the departure of the first emigrant ships to New Zealand, Captain Cook's voyages of discovery, the arrival of the first ever transatlantic flight in 1916 and, five decades later, the first solo circumnavigation of the globe by boat.

Plymouth Mayflower (3-5 The Barbican; admission £2; ⏱ 9am-5pm Mon-Sat, 10am-4pm Sun Apr-Oct, 9am-5pm Mon-Fri, 10am-4pm Sat Nov-Mar), directly behind, is an inventive, interactive series of exhibits that cracks through 10 centuries of history while giving enough detail for those who want to linger longer. It could make more of the impact on the world's indigenous populations of all this rampant British expansion, but it doesn't completely shy away from the now deeply offensive parts of the city's past – it identifies Plymouth captain, John Hawkins as the Englishman who established the blueprint for the triangular slave trade between England, Africa and the West Indies.

The futuristic glass lines of the **National Marine Aquarium** (☎ 220084; www.national-aquarium.co.uk; Rope Walk; adult/child £9.50/5.75; ⏱ 10am-6pm Apr-Oct, 10am-5pm Nov-Mar) are wittily sited next to the pungent Fish Market, providing an interesting dead-fish-live-fish juxtaposition. Here sharks swim in coral seas that teem with moray eels, turtles and vividly coloured fish. The Atlantic Reef tank is as big as a cinema screen and provides an insight into what's lurking just a few miles offshore on the Eddystone Reef. The aquarium focuses on conservation – look out for the tanks containing their breeding programmes of cardinal fish, corals and incredibly cute seahorses.

The **Plymouth Gin Distillery** (☎ 665292; www.ply mouthgin.com; 60 Southside St; tours £6; ⏱ 10.30am-4.30pm Mon-Sat, 11.30am-3.30pm Sun) offers a chance to tour the oldest producer of this kind of spirit in the world – they've been making gin in this heavily beamed building since 1793. The Royal Navy was responsible for taking it round the world in countless officer's messes and the brand was specified in the first recorded recipe for a dry martini in the 1930s, making it the spirit of choice for countless cocktails. You get to wander past the stills, sniff the sometimes surprising raw ingredients (called botanicals) and have a tutored tasting before indulging in a tipple in the restored medieval bar upstairs.

DEVON

PLYMOUTH HOE

The Hoe, a grassy headland 10 minutes' walk west of the Barbican, is where Sir Francis Drake supposedly insisted on finishing his game of bowls before setting off to defeat the advancing Spanish Armada. The fabled green on which he lingered was probably where his statue now stands.

Alongside, you can't miss the 70ft high, red and white candy-striped former lighthouse that is **Smeaton's Tower** (☎ 603300; The Hoe; admission £2.45; ⏰ 10am-4pm Apr-Oct, 10am-3pm Tue-Sat Nov-Mar). The whole structure used to stand on the Eddystone Reef 14 miles offshore before being moved here, brick by brick, in the 1880s. Now it provides an illuminating insight into the lives of past lighthouse keepers and (93 steps later) stunning views of the city, Dartmoor and the sea.

The Art Deco–style, open-air **Tinside Pool** (☎ 261915; Hoe Rd; adult/child £3.45/2/30; ⏰ noon-6pm Mon-Fri, 10am-6pm Sat & Sun late-May–early-Sep) curves out from the foot of the Hoe beside the sea. For decades this 1930s lido suffered from neglect, but now it's been delicately restored in cream and light and dark blue. Its unheated salt waters aren't quite as toe-curlingly cold as you might think and a dip here, within a pebble's throw of the expanse of Plymouth Sound, is a swim to remember.

MERCHANT'S HOUSE

The 17th-century **Merchant's House** (☎ 304774; 33 St Andrews St; adult/child £1.40/90p; ⏰ 10am-5pm Tue-Sat Apr-Sep) is packed with curiosities, from manacles, truncheons and a ducking stool to a replica 19th-century schoolroom and an entire Victorian chemist's shop where you get to try old-fashioned pill-rolling.

CITY MUSEUM & ART GALLERY

As well as a diverse programme of temporary exhibits, the **City Museum & Art Gallery** (☎ 304774; Drake Circus; admission free; ⏰ 10am-5.30pm Mon-Fri, 10am-5pm Sat) hosts collections of local history, porcelain and naval art. The Cottonian Collection includes some significant paintings, prints and etchings by artists including Plymouth-born Joshua Reynolds.

Activities

The **Kingsand and Cawsand ferry** (☎ 07833-936863; www.cawsandferry.com; adult/child return £7/5) is the pick of Plymouth's boat trips. Boats surge from the Mayflower Steps, across Plymouth

Sound to the old Cornish smuggling villages of Kingsand and Cawsand (30 minutes, four to five sailings daily mid-April to mid-September). There you can wander the narrow streets, soak up the atmosphere of some salty pubs and browse the handful of shops.

A little yellow ferry (one way £1.50, 10 minutes, every 30 minutes) shuttles from beside the Mayflower Steps across to the Mount Batten Peninsula. You can walk to rocky **Jennycliff beach** from there: get off the boat, walk west round the Napoleonic tower and stay on the coast path until the beach is signposted 15 minutes away on your right. At the **Mount Batten Centre** (☎ 404567; www .mount-batten-centre.com; 70 Lawrence Rd) you can learn to kayak (per two days £99) or sail (per two days £140).

Sound Cruising (☎ 671166; www.soundcruising .com; Phoenix Wharf; 1½hr trips £5) offers regular boat trips from Phoenix Wharf out to the warships at Plymouth's naval base. If you want to surf, the best beaches are Bigbury-on-Sea (p195) and Bantham (p195), 16 and 20 miles south respectively – you can hire equipment or take lessons.

Sleeping

BUDGET

Fertile B&B hunting grounds are just back from Hoe, especially around Citadel Rd.

Globe Backpackers (☎ 225158; www.exeterback packers.co.uk/plymouth; 172 Citadel Rd; dm/d £12/30) This traditional backpackers in an old five-floor terraced house is a bit worn but clean and friendly. The four- to eight-bed dorms have washbasins. There are free cooking oils, spices, tea and coffee in the kitchen, as well as a lounge, courtyard garden and hot baths for £1.50 a dip.

Jewell's Hotel (☎ 254760; 220 Citadel Rd; s £25, d £45-55, f £60-65) Traces of the 1800s linger in the high ceilings and ornate plasterwork of this fabulous value, friendly B&B in a lovely Victorian house. Rooms are bright and modern with lilac armchairs and filmy blue curtains, while top quality bathrooms add another layer of class.

Four Seasons Guest House (☎ 223591; www.foursea sonsguesthouse.co.uk; 207 Citadel Rd East; s £30-45, d £50-60, f £60; ✗) A place crammed full of little extras, from the big bowl of sweets by the door to the mounds of local produce for breakfast (try the Devon bacon and sausages). They've got the basics right too, with tastefully decorated rooms in calm gold and cream.

Casa Mia Guest House (☎ 265742; www.casa-mia -onthehoe.com; 201 Citadel Rd East; s/d/f £28/55/65; ☒) A riot of colourful flowers outside and a highly polished brass step hint at what to expect: a cheerful, traditional and spotlessly clean B&B. It's in a great location, tucked away from main roads and only a few minutes' walk to the Barbican and to town.

MIDRANGE & TOP END

Berkeleys of St James (☎ 221654; www.onthehoe.co.uk; 4 St James Pl East; s/d £40/60; Ⓟ) Superb breakfasts ensure this B&B stands out from the crowd. There's local hog's pudding, free range eggs from Cornwall, and bacon and sausages from the Devon organic producer Riverford. The cosy rooms are highly floral and it's all tucked away in a quiet square.

Bowling Green Hotel (☎ 209090; www.bowling greenhotel.co.uk; 10 Osborne Pl; s £46-56, d £66, f £76; Ⓟ) Some of the smart cream and white rooms in this family-run hotel look out onto the modern incarnation of Drake's famous bowling green. If you tire of watching people throw woods after jacks you can play chess in the conservatory.

Astor Hotel (☎ 225511; www.astorhotel.co.uk; 22 Elliot St; s £45-80, d £70-160, f £100-200, ste £124-400) This sumptuous Victorian-era hotel has a finish fit for film stars, with flouncy flourishes, four-poster beds and Jacuzzis in the suites. A place full of character, it's also run by one: Joseph, a charming, can-do guy who could write a handbook on customer service.

Duke of Cornwall Hotel (☎ 275850; www.thed ukeofcornwallhotel.com; Millbay Rd; s £94, d £87-160; Ⓟ ⓖ) This arresting, turret-topped pile is dotted with balconies and Gothic gables. The rooms here are massive, if just a touch old-fashioned. If you can afford it, the four-poster suite (with complementary champagne) is the one to choose. Prices fall by £30 a room at weekends.

St Elizabeth's House (☎ 344840; Longbrook St; r/ste £135/170; Ⓟ) A manor house in the 17th century and a convent until 2003, this minihotel now oozes boutique-chic. Free-standing slipper baths, oak furniture and Egyptian cotton grace the rooms; the suites feature palatial bathrooms and private terraces. It's set in the suburb-cum-village of Plympton St Maurice, 5 miles east of Plymouth.

Eating

CAFÉS

ourpick **Cap'n Jaspers** (☎ 262444; www.capn-jaspers .co.uk; Whitehouse Pier, Quay Rd; snacks £3-5; ☷ 7.45am-11.45pm) Unique, quirky and slightly insane, this Barbican institution has been delighting tourists and locals alike for decades. Motorised gadgets whirr around the counter and the tea spoons are attached by chains. The menu is of the burger and bacon butty school, and trying to eat their 'half a yard of hotdog' is a Plymouth rite of passage. Also on offer are fresh crab rolls – the filling could have been caught by the bloke sitting next to you, and his boat is probably tied up alongside.

Terrace (☎ 603533; Hoe Rd; lunches £3-6; ☷ breakfast & lunch) Tucked away beside the Tinside Lido, this bright and breezy café has one of the best locations in town, with panoramic views across Plymouth Sound and a selection of sandwiches, coffees and generous jacket potatoes.

Café Incognito (☎ 265999; 92 North Hill; lunches £3-6; ☷ 8am-8pm; ▣) An arty hangout between the university and the nightspots of Mutley Plain, this groovy café has free wi-fi and in term-time is packed with students writing essays. Robust bistro food includes chicken fajitas, memorable chilli and an utterly satisfying homemade sticky toffee pudding.

RESTAURANTS

ourpick **Barbican Kitchen** (☎ 604448; 60 Southside St; snacks £5, mains £11; ☷ lunch & dinner, closed Sun evening) The bistro-style baby sister of Tanners Restaurant (opposite) has a wood and stone interior with bursts of shocking pink and lime. The food is attention grabbing too – try the calves' livers with horseradish mash or maybe the honey, goat's cheese and apple crostini. The Devon beefburger, with a slab of stilton, is divine. It's all set in the atmospheric Plymouth Gin Distillery (p198).

Yukisan (☎ 250240; 51 Notte St; mains £14; ☷ lunch & dinner) Choose between a floor cushion or a chair in this stylish Japanese restaurant. There's wonderful sushi, light tempura, delicate monkfish with ginger and spring onions, and noodles worth mastering chopsticks for. Top-quality presentation and service too.

Platters (☎ 227262; 12 The Barbican; mains £16; ☷ lunch & dinner) The fish here is so fresh it's just stopped flapping – try the skate in but-

DEVON

ter or the locally caught sea bass. You could pay twice as much nearby and end up with something half as good. Gingham tablecloths complete the snug atmosphere.

Tanners Restaurant (☎ 252001; www.tannersrestaurant.com; Finewell St; 2-/3-course dinner £26/32; ☺ lunch & dinner Tue-Sat) Plymouth's top fine-dining restaurant is run by the (locally famous) Tanner brothers. Renowned for reinventing British and French classics, they dish up lamb with gnocchi, char-grilled asparagus with soft poached egg, and roasted quail with pancetta. Gourmands should try and book the five-course meal (£37).

Drinking

A proper Navy city, Plymouth has a more than lively nightlife. There are three main hubs: Union Street is clubland, Mutley Plain and North Hill have a slightly studenty vibe, while on the Barbican more restaurants lurk amid the bars. All three areas get rowdy, especially at weekends.

Bar Rakuda (☎ 221155; 11 Quay Rd) One of the best of a row of trendy quayside bars, Rakuda is ideal for a morning latté, a lunchtime mocha or a cocktail jug when the sun goes down.

Carpe Diem (☎ 252942; 50 North Hill; ☺ 11am-midnight) A beautifully lit, funky bar, done out in a kaleidoscope of colours. There's a heated, open air chill-out room and free wi-fi too.

View 2 (☎ 252564; Vauxhall Quay; ☺ to 2am, later at weekends) Tucked just round from the heart of the Barbican, this cool venue has its own waterside terrace, and is perfect for a lunchtime pizza or drink. In the evening, enjoy comedy, Latin and salsa, easy listening, soul, funk and R&B.

Dolphin (☎ 660876; 14 The Barbican) The Dolphin is an unreconstructed Barbican boozer, with scuffed tables, padded bench seats and an authentic, no-nonsense atmosphere. It's also painter Beryl Cook's local. The **Navy Inn** (☎ 301812), opposite, has impromptu Sunday lunchtime folk sessions.

Entertainment

NIGHTCLUBS

Barbican Jazz Café (☎ 672127; 11 The Parade; admission Fri & Sat £2; ☺ noon-2am Mon-Sat, noon-midnight Sun) Nightly jazz and guest DJs keep the crowd happy at this barrel-vaulted venue.

Quay Club (☎ 224144; 11 The Parade; ☺ 10am-2am, to 3am Fri, to 4am Sat) Next to the Jazz Café,

this cavernous club is a favourite with Plymouth's night owls, with rock and indie on Thursdays, funk, soul and Latin on Fridays, and chart and dance on Saturday.

Annabel's (☎ 260555; 88 Vauxhall St; ☺ to 2am Fri & Sat) This quirky cabaret-cum-dance venue has plush décor and intimate tables are lined up in front of a tiny stage, which is focus of an eclectic collection of acts. Upstairs the DJs fill the dance floor with crowd-pleasing tunes; downstairs you enter cocktail heaven.

THEATRES & CINEMAS

Theatre Royal (☎ 267222; www.theatreroyal.com; Royal Pde) Plymouth's main theatre stages large-scale touring and home-grown productions; its studio Drum Theatre is renowned for featuring new writing.

Barbican Theatre (☎ 267131; www.barbicantheatre.co.uk; Castle St) It's a tiny theatre with regular dance and drama, and a buzzing bar (the B-Bar).

Plymouth Arts Centre (☎ 206114; www.plymouthac.org.uk; 38 Looe St; ☺ 10am-8.30pm Mon-Sat, 5.30-8.30pm Sun) This place is a satisfying combination of exhibition space for innovative art, an independent cinema and a superb, licensed vegetarian café (open lunch Monday to Saturday, and dinner Tuesday to Saturday). It's a location to feed your body and your mind.

Getting There & Away

AIR

Plymouth City Airport (☎ 242620; www.plymouthairport.com; Derriford) is located 4 miles north of the centre. No buses run to the airport; instead, they stop at Derriford Roundabout, a 10-minute walk away. Regular buses to the roundabout, including bus 50 (30 minutes, every 15 to 30 minutes) leave from the city's Royal Pde.

BUS

National Express runs regular coach services to Birmingham (£42, 5½ hours, four daily), Bristol (£25, three hours, four daily), London (£28, five to six hours, eight daily) and also Penzance (£28, 3¼ hours, seven daily).

Bus X38 travels to Exeter (1¼ hours, hourly). The seasonal 'Transmoor Link' Bus 82 (five daily May to September, two on Saturday and Sunday only October to

April) goes across Dartmoor to Exeter via Princetown (45 minutes), Postbridge (one hour) and also Moretonhampstead (1¾ hours).

Bus X80 runs to Torquay (£5.20, 1¾ hours, every 30 minutes Monday to Saturday, two-hourly on Sunday) via Totnes (1¼ hours).

TRAIN

Services from Plymouth include those to London (£63, 3½ to four hours, every 30 minutes), Bristol (£40, two hours, two or three per hour), Exeter (£6.90, one hour, two or three per hour) and Penzance (£8.90, two hours, hourly).

DARTMOOR NATIONAL PARK

Steeped in history and shrouded in myth, Dartmoor is an ancient, compelling landscape. It's so different from the rest of Devon a visit can feel like falling into the third book of *The Lord of the Rings*. Exposed granite hills (tors) crest on the horizon, an array of crazy peaks linked by swathes of honey-tinged moors. On the fringes, streams tumble over moss-smothered boulders in woods of twisted trees. The centre is the higher moor, a vast, treeless-expanse. Moody and utterly empty

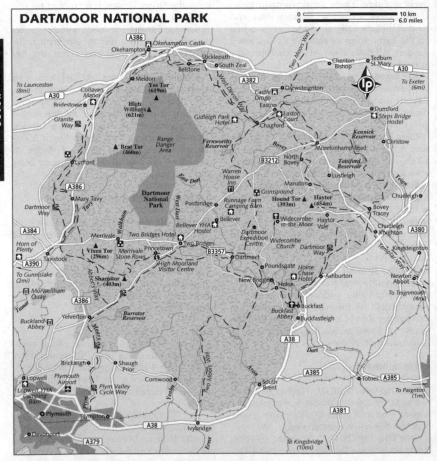

DARTMOOR NATIONAL PARK

DANGER

The military uses three different sections of the moor as training ranges, where live ammunition is used. The national park staff can explain their locations; they're also marked on Ordnance Survey maps. In general you're advised to check if the route you're planning falls within a range; if it does, find out if firing is taking place when you want to walk via the **Firing Information Service** (☎ 0800 458 4868; www.dartmoor-ranges.co.uk). In the day, red flags fly at the edges of the range if it's being used, and red flares burn at night. Even when there's no firing, beware of unidentified metal objects lying in the grass – don't touch anything you find, note its position and report it to the police or the **Commandant** (☎ 01837-650010).

---

you'll either find its desolate beauty exhilarating or chilling, or possibly a bit of both.

In many respects life on Dartmoor is the same as it's been for centuries, governed by the rhythms of season, weather and the livestock – the famous Dartmoor ponies are just some of the animals you'll see grazing. Peel back the picturesque and there's a core of hard reality – low stock prices mean that many farming this harsh environment struggle to make a profit. It's a mercurial place where the urban illusion of control over our surroundings is stripped away and the elements are in charge.

Dartmoor's stark, other-worldly nature inspired Sir Arthur Conan Doyle to write *The Hound of the Baskervilles* and in sleeting rain and swirling mists you suddenly see why; the moor becomes a bleak, wild place where tales of a phantom hound can seem very real indeed. Yet the same spot on a hot summer's day is idyllic, with swifts wheeling through an expanse of deep blue sky above sun-baked tors.

It makes Dartmoor a natural breakout zone with a checklist of charms: superb hiking, cycling, riding, climbing and white-water rafting; rustic pubs and fancy restaurants; wild-camping nooks and posh country-house hotels. The communities range from brooding Princetown and picturesque Widecombe-in-the-Moor to genteel Chagford, while everywhere lies evidence of 4000 years of human history: stone rows at Merrivale, Sir Francis Drake's former home and a copper mine near Tavistock, and at Chagford, the last castle to be built in England.

Orientation

Dartmoor occupies a massive 368 sq mile chunk of central Devon, its fringes only 7 miles from Plymouth and 6 miles from Exeter. The A38 dual carriageway borders its southeast edge, while the A30 skirts it to the north, heading from Exeter via Okehampton to Cornwall. The B3212 carves a path across the centre, linking Moretonhampstead, Postbridge and Princetown. From there the B3357 leads into Tavistock.

The northwest moor is the highest and most remote, peaking at 621m at High Willhays. The lower, southwest moor (400m to 500m) is particularly rich in prehistoric sites.

Information

The **Dartmoor National Park Authority** (DNPA; www.dartmoor-npa.gov.uk) runs the **High Moorland Visitors Centre** (☎ 01822-890414; ☼ 10am-5pm Apr-Oct, 10am-4pm Nov-Mar) in Princetown (p207) and smaller centres including ones at **Haytor** (☎ 01364-661520; ☼ 10am-5pm Easter-Oct, 10am-4pm Sat & Sun Nov & Dec) and **Postbridge** (☎ 01822-880272; ☼ 10am-5pm Easter-Oct, 10am-4pm Sat & Sun Nov & Dec).

A great source of information is the free, newspaper format *Dartmoor National Park Visitor Guide*, which details guided walks, events and transport. It's also full of good advice on how to take 'moor care' of this fragile environment. The DNPA website features the walks programme and downloads on everything from rock climbing to access for those with disabilities (see p290 for more information). DNPA centres can all advise on local walking and cycling routes while the bigger ones sell leaflets, books, Ordnance Survey (OS) maps, compasses, waterproofs and hiking socks. 'Ranger Ralph' activities are targeted towards children, while 'Letterboxing', a kind of massive navigational treasure hunt, is also likely to appeal. The **Dartmoor Tourist Association** (www.discoverdartmoor.co.uk) is another useful information source.

Be aware that feeding the endearing, semi-wild Dartmoor ponies isn't allowed. Vast tracts of the moor are unfenced grazing and you're very likely to round a bend and find cows, sheep or ponies in your path.

DEVON

COUNTLESS WAYS TO WANDER

When hiking this landscape, at times you'll stop and pinch yourself to see if it's real; the views from the tor tops are so spectacular. Half the entire moor (47,000 hectares) is open access and there are 450 miles of public rights of way to tread.

Hiking challenges include the 18-mile **Templar Way**, a two- to three-day walk that makes the mind-boggling transition from an isolated tor (Haytor) to the south Devon seaside town of Teignmouth, compete with amusements on the pier. A longer stretch is the stunning 117-mile (seven to eight day) **Two Moors Way**, a blockbuster traverse of the whole county from Lynmouth on Devon's north coast, across Exmoor, Dartmoor and countless fields to Wembury, just outside Plymouth in the south.

Jarrold's *Dartmoor, Short Walks* (£5.99) is a good introduction for family day strolls. The **DNPA** (www.dartmoor-npa.gov.uk) can advise on all types of self-guided trails and even has routes specifically designed to put children in charge. It also runs a range of guided walks. At £3 to £6 (free if you show your bus ticket), the walks feature themes such as Sherlock Holmes, myths, geology, industry and archaeology. Look out for their moonlit rambles amid stone rows.

The Ordnance Survey (OS) Outdoor Leisure 1:25,000 map No 28 *Dartmoor* covers the whole of the moor in good detail. You have a legal right to walk on footpaths, bridleways and byways. You can also walk on many other areas deemed to be open country. Be prepared for upland weather conditions: warm, waterproof clothing, water, hats and sunscreen are essential, as is a map and compass. The military uses some sections of moor for live firing (see p203).

Activities

Dartmoor is packed full of adventurous possibilities. There's more on sampling each of the following activities in the Outdoors chapter.

WHITE WATER RAFTING

The raging River Dart makes Dartmoor a top spot for thrillseekers. You can ride in a raft without any experience, but to shoot a rapid in a kayak you need more skill (BCU 2 star) and, if you're organising it yourself, a permit. Contact www.dartaccess.co.uk or the **British Canoe Union** (BCU; ☎ 0845 370 9500; www.bcu.org.uk). **CRS Adventures** (☎ 07891 635964; www.crsadventures.co.uk; Ashburton) runs a range of lessons and activities. Widecombe-in-the-Moor makes a good base. Environmental concerns mean rivers are only open in the winter.

CLIMBING

All those looming granite tors are irresistible to climbers. Experienced crags scramblers will have to book at some popular sites – the DNPA can provide a free leaflet and further advice. Or sign up for training locally – try the **Rock Centre** (☎ 01626-852717; www.rockcentre.co.uk; Rock House, Chudleigh; per half-/full day £15/25).

CYCLING

Tackle tough terrain or freewheel down a hill – on Dartmoor there are routes for everyone. The 11-mile **Granite Way** between Okehampton and Lydford traces the route of a former railway line and largely keeps away from roads. The traffic-free 7-mile **Plym Valley Cycle Way** leads from the moor to Plymouth, while the **Dartmoor Way** (www.dartmoorway.org.uk) is a 90-mile round-Dartmoor walking and cycling route with an option to detour across the middle of the moor.

Devon Cycle Hire (☎ 01837-861141; www.devoncyclehire.co.uk; Sourton Down, near Okehampton; adult/child per day £12/8; ☼ 9am-5pm Apr-Sep) rents out bikes at the start of the Granite Way. You can cycle on roads and public bridleways, but not on footpaths or across open countryside. The DNPA sells an off-road map and can advise about other routes.

PONY TREKKING & HORSE RIDING

There's a frontier feel to parts of the moor, which makes it perfect for saddling up and trotting out. A half-day horse ride costs around £30. Some of the stables:

Babeny Farm Riding Stables (☎ 01364-631296; Poundsgate)

Shilstone Rocks (☎ 01364-621281; Widecombe-in-the-Moor)

Skaigh Stables (☎ 01837-840917; www.skaighstables.co.uk; Belstone)

The *Dartmoor National Park Visitor Guide* has more options.

Sleeping & Eating

From spoil-yourself-silly luxury to snoozing under the stars, with some lovely thatched cottages in between, Dartmoor has the widest range of sleeping options around. Hiding amid the heather are some of the UK's most gorgeous country house hotels. We detail them in the later town sections – look out for the Horn of Plenty (p207) near Tavistock, Gidleigh Park (p210) near Chagford, and Holne Chase (p209) near Widecombe-in-the-Moor. Hardier options are the YHA hostels at Postbridge (p208) and Okehampton (p211), or the bare-bones camping barns at Lopwell (p206) near Tavistock, Postbridge (p208) and Widecombe-in-the-Moor (p209). Better still, go from one extreme to the other in successive nights and marvel at the difference.

Or kip under canvas. As well as a dozen or so formal sites on and around the moor, wild-camping is another option. Pitching a tent on some sections of the open moor is allowed, provided you stick to some simple but strict rules – pick up a free leaflet from DNPA, then pack your pack. And if you dream of nursing a pint in front of a blazing open fire in a cosy pub you're in luck; the moor is crackling with them

The **Dartmoor Tourist Association** (☎ 01822-890567; www.discoverdartmoor.com; High Moor Visitors Centre, Princetown) produces an annual *Dartmoor Guide* with full accommodation listings.

Getting There & Around

The DNPA advocates using public transport for environmental reasons and with a bit of planning using public transport is a real option. The *Discovery Guide to Dartmoor*, free from most Devon tourist offices and DNPA offices, details bus and train services in the park, as does **Traveline** (☎ 0871 200 22 33; www.travel inesw.com).

Buses travel to the park from various points including Totnes, Exeter, Plymouth and Okehampton. The Transmoor Link (bus 82, five daily May to September, two on Saturday and Sunday only October to April) runs between Exeter and Plymouth via Moretonhampstead, Warren House Inn, Postbridge, Princetown and Yelverton

The Dartmoor Sunday Rover ticket (adult/child £5/4, June to September) buys unlimited travel on most bus routes, and train travel on the scenic Tamar Valley line from Plymouth to Gunnislake. Buy tickets from bus drivers or at Plymouth train station.

DEVON

A MASS OF MONUMENTS

The sheer number and variety of prehistoric remains on Dartmoor means history's never been so much fun. With Stone Age burials and 19th-century tin workings, the moor is less a landscape and more a tangible timeline – in three dimensions.

Humans have lived on Dartmoor for around 10,000 years. Surprisingly it was originally covered in trees and the first clearings were made to help with hunting. Around 4000 BC the burials began; look out for cairns (rounded piles of stones) and cists (half buried stone boxes originally covered in granite slabs). The monuments started springing up in 2500 BC; you can see the stone circles and rows often with menhirs (standing stones) at the end. By the Bronze Age (around 1600 BC) the woods were being replaced by whole villages of dozens of roundhouses surrounded by sub-divided fields. Keep an eye out for these 'hut circles': clusters of low round walls, often enclosed by a sweeping stone barrier. A great one-stop shop to see all of these, from cairns and stone circles through to huts, is at the **Merrivale Stone Rows**, a five-minute walk south of the hamlet of Merrivale on the B3357 (Tavistock to Two Bridges road).

Eventually deforestation took its toll – by 1000 BC the soil became thin, the weather worsened and people moved away from the moor. But later sites also exist. Tin ore has been dug up from at least the 12th to the 19th centuries – search for 'tinners huts' on maps, and around gullies and ditches near streams. You'll also spot medieval crosses, crumbling farm buildings, granite quarries, abandoned stone tramways and the low walls of rabbit farms (called 'warrens') along with the rounded humps of the pillow mounds built for the rabbits to burrow into.

The DNPA (see p203) runs heritage-themed guided walks and shops and visitor centres stock countless leaflets and books. Or settle down, unfold the Ordnance Survey Outdoor Leisure *Dartmoor* map, pick a grid and see the past pop up all over the place.

The only main-line train station within easy reach of the park is Okehampton (p211).

TAVISTOCK & AROUND
☎ 01822 / pop 11,330

Peaceful and prosperous, Tavistock is graced by crenellated, turreted constructions built in the late 1800s out of warm, grey stone. But just 150 years ago this genteel market town was swept up in a copper mining boom, the population trebled and it rolled to a frontier feel: wild and rife with drunkenness and il-legitimacy. The copper market collapsed just decades later but this exotic past can be ex-plored at the mines at Morwellham Quay.

Tavistock sits on the western fringe of the moor. A cascading River Tavy flows through the town, which clusters around Bedford Sq, a parish church and an elegant town hall. The **tourist office** (☎ 612938; www.discoverdartmoor.com; Bedford Sq; ❍ 9.30am-5pm Mon-Sat Apr-Oct, 10am-4.30pm Mon, Tue, Fri & Sat Nov-Mar) is alongside the thriving pannier market (Tuesday to Saturday).

Sights
TAVISTOCK ABBEY & MUSEUM
A massive **abbey** used to occupy central Tavis-tock but was destroyed by a land-hungry Henry VIII in 1539. Fragments exist today; hunt out the chunk of cloisters near the parish church and the tower by the Tavy. The tourist office has town trail leaflets.

Abbey remnants sit in the traditional but excellent **museum** (☎ 612546; Bedford Sq; admission free; ❍ 11am-3pm Wed, Fri & Sat Apr-Oct) alongside artefacts of the copper heyday. Look out for clogs, shovels and photos revealing the harsh conditions masked by the mines' names: Vir-tuous Lady, Queen of the Tamar and Lady Bertha. You'll also see why there's a local place called Chipshop. A clue: it's nothing to do with fried fish.

MORWELLHAM QUAY
Morwellham Quay (☎ 832766; www.morwellham-quay .co.uk; adult/child £8.90/6; ❍ 10am-5.30pm Apr-Oct, 10am-4.30pm Nov-Mar) offers an intriguing insight into west Devon's copper boom as well as the chance to don some 19th-century clothes. In the 1860s this port beside the River Tamar was where tonnes of shimmering copper ore was loaded onto masted vessels. Mining went on here too and you get the chance to ex-plore the cottages, smithy and cooperage of this lost community as well as try on a bon-

net or waistcoat and promenade the streets. Costumed guides show you around but the highlight is the atmospheric trip into a cop-per mine on a little underground train. Part of the southwest's Mining World Heritage Site, Morwellham has secured £1.2 million for a new visitor centre. The last entry is two hours before closing. Morwellham Quay is 5 miles southwest of Tavistock.

BUCKLAND ABBEY
Built out of warm, honey-coloured stone, **Buckland Abbey** (NT; ☎ 853607; near Yelverton; adult/child £7.40/3.70; ❍ 10.30am-5.30pm Fri-Wed mid-Mar–Oct, 2-5pm Sat & Sun Nov–mid-Mar) dates back to the 14th century when it was a Cistercian monastery and an abbey church. It was turned into a family residence by Sir Richard Grenville before being bought by his cousin and nauti-cal rival Sir Francis Drake (p196) in 1581. A sumptuous interior includes Tudor plaster-work ceilings in the Great Hall and Drake's Chamber (where Drake's Drum is said to beat by itself when Britain is in danger of being invaded). There's also a monastic barn, a fine Elizabethan garden and a great programme of events – look out for the night-time moth hunts or the storytelling days.

Buckland Abbey is 7 miles south of Tavis-tock. From Plymouth take bus 83, 84 or 86 to Yelverton, then bus 55 (25 minutes, two hourly Monday to Saturday) to the village of Buckland Monachorum. It's then a sign-posted, mile walk.

Sleeping & Eating
Lopwell YHA Camping Barn (☎ 0870 770 8868; www .yha.org.uk; Lopwell; dm £6; ℗) Try and spot egrets, kingfishers and the splash of migrating salmon at this bolthole set in a densely wooded val-ley beside the River Tavy. Facilities include showers and a cooking area; the Plym Valley cycleway and great hikes are a few steps away. It's 8 miles from Tavistock.

April Cottage (☎ 613280; 12 Mount Tavy Rd; s/d £45/63; ℗) Enter this cosy B&B and enter a world in miniature. Every surface is cushioned, orna-mented and picture-framed. There's even a tiny conservatory and deck overlooking the rushing river. It's two minutes' walk from the centre of Tavistock.

Brown's Hotel (☎ 618686; www.brownsdevon.co.uk; 80 West St; s £80-90, d £120-210; ℗) A 17th-century coaching inn with bursts of boutique-chic: beams and exposed stone sit alongside stained glass and Egyptian flourishes. Sample a glass of water from its real Roman well as you tuck into tasty, stylish fare (try the sea bream with wild garlic) or tapas (£2 to £5). Lunch and dinner are available (two courses £18 to £32).

our pick Horn of Plenty (☎ 832528; www.thehornof plenty.co.uk; 2 course lunch/dinners £27/45; s £150-240, d £160-250; ☺ lunch & dinner; P) Effortlessly stylish and beautifully relaxed, this is a country house hotel chock-full of class. Swish rooms boast claw-foot baths and canopied beds; most have balconies or terraces. The classy, classic food includes Devon lamb with Madeira sauce or brill with sautéed squid and is best enjoyed on the vine-shaded terrace looking out over rolling Tamar Valley views. Take a tip from the locals and visit on a Monday, when dinner prices plunge to £28 for three courses. It's 3 miles from Tavistock.

The cheerful **Duke's Coffee House** (☎ 613718; 8-11 Pannier Market Arcade; ☺ 8.30am-5pm Mon-Sat) dishes up tasty café food amid market bustle.

Getting There & Away
Buses 83, 84 and 86 run from Plymouth (one hour, every 30 minutes Monday to Saturday, hourly Sunday). Bus 86 goes to Okehampton (45 minutes, hourly Monday to Saturday, two on Sunday), and bus 98 runs to Princetown (25 minutes, six daily Monday to Saturday).

LYDFORD
☎ 01822 / pop 2013
A winding string of ancient granite cottages, studded with two ruined castles and a gorgeous gorge, Lydford makes a perfectly peaceful night's stop. This tranquil backwater was once the administrative centre of the whole moor, and in the Saxon times of Aethelred II, royal coins were also minted here.

The 13th-century **castle** (admission free), now a compact, roofless cube, used to double as a jail and helped make 'Lydford Law' notorious as a 'hang 'em first, ask questions later' system. Half a mile southwest of the village, **Lydford Gorge** (NT; ☎ 820320; adult/child £5.20/2.60; ☺ 10am-4pm or 5pm late-Mar–Oct, 11am-3.30pm Sat & Sun Nov–late-Mar) is a rugged circuit of riverside walks topped by the spectacular White Lady waterfall and the bubbling water-rock combo of the Devil's Cauldron.

Sleeping & Eating
Lydford House (☎ 820347; www.lydfordhouse.com; Lydford; s/d £42/70; P ✗) Here, gently elegant,

tasteful rooms dotted with antiques look out over the tor tops. It's on the Granite Way cycle route to Okehampton and it offers bike hire (£10 per day); you can even stable your horse too. An Italian chef rustles up pasta, fish and steaks in the restaurant for dinner Wednesday to Monday (mains £8 to £15).

Castle Inn (☎ 820241; www.castleinnlydford.co.uk; s £55-60, d £65-80) The bar of this Elizabethan pub is the ultimate snug: lamp-light bathes bow ceilings and curving, high-backed benches. History oozes from the beams, flagstone floors and granite walls. Bedrooms range from charming and rustic to crisp and smart. Quality pub grub is available for lunch and dinner, and includes smoked trout with bubble and squeak (mains £6 to £10).

Getting There & Away
Bus 86 runs to Okehampton (15 minutes, eight daily Monday to Saturday, two on Sunday) and Tavistock (30 minutes, eight daily Monday to Saturday, two on Sunday).

PRINCETOWN
☎ 01822
Set in the heart of the remote, higher moor, Princetown is dominated by the grey, foreboding bulk of Dartmoor Prison. The gaol has dictated the town's fortunes for hundreds of years. When it stopped housing French and American prisoners of war in the early 1800s, Princetown fell into decline and parts of the town still have a bleak, neglected feel. But the settlement is also a useful insight into the hard realities of moorland life and makes an atmospheric base for some excellent walks.

The prison reopened as a convict jail in 1850 and just up from its looming gates the **Dartmoor Prison Heritage Centre** (☎ 892130; adult/child £2/1; ☺ 9.30am-12.30pm & 1.30-4.30pm, to 4pm Fri & Sun) provides a chilling insight into life inside – look out for the mock-up cell, straight jackets and manacles. Escapes feature too, including the tale of Frankie 'the mad axeman' Mitchell, who was supposedly sprung by the '60s gangster twins, the Krays. The centre also sells the bizarrely cheery garden ornaments made by the prisoners.

The **High Moorland Visitor Centre** (☎ 890414; www.dartmoor-npa.gov.uk; ☺ 10am-5pm Apr-Oct, 10am-4pm Nov-Mar) is a comprehensive information source, while its exhibition includes the evocative *Moor Memories* oral history archive. The centre used to be the Duchy Hotel, where Sir

Arthur Conan Doyle stayed while writing *The Hound of the Baskervilles* (superb reading on a foggy moorland night). Ask staff to point you towards Foxtor Mires (2 to 3 miles away), the inspiration for the book's Grimpen Mire; then detect the story's other locations.

All slate floors, beams and granite walls, the **Plume of Feathers** (☎ 890240; www.theplumeoffeathers .co.uk; Plymouth Hill; sites £13, dm/s/d £13/35/70; ☯ 11.30am-8.30pm; **P** ☯) in the heart of town serves up typical bar food. It also offers no-nonsense rooms with shared bathrooms, bunk-bed dorms and camping. The similar **Railway Inn** (☎ 890240; s/d £35/70; **P**) is next door.

Getting There & Away

Bus 82, the Transmoor Link, runs between Exeter (40 minutes, five daily May to September, two on Saturday and Sunday only October to April) and Plymouth (50 minutes) via Princetown, Postbridge (10 minutes) and Moretonhampstead (30 minutes).

Bus 98 runs to Tavistock (25 minutes, six daily Monday to Saturday).

POSTBRIDGE & AROUND
☎ 01822

Postbridge owes its popularity, and its name, to its ancient stone slab (or 'clapper') bridge, which is still remarkably sturdy despite being built in the 13th century. The village is just metres from the B3212 and although it's often busy with coach parties, it's still a delightful spot to dangle your feet in the icy East Dart river.

The village's time-warp shop does takeaway cream teas. The **DNPA centre** (☎ 880272; ☯ 10am-4pm Apr-Oct, plus some weekends Nov & Dec) in the car park sells a leaflet on local walks (£1.50). It's well worth it – just a few dozen metres away from the road the moor acquires a remote, mysterious edge.

Sleeping & Eating

Runnage Farm Camping Barn (☎ 0870 770 8868; www .yha.org.uk; dm £7; **P**) Bed down amid the bleating of sheep and lambs in this working farm's converted stables and hayloft. It's 1.5 miles from Postbridge; take the turning to the right off the Moretonhampstead road, signposted Widecombe.

Bellever YHA Hostel (☎ 0870 770 8868; www.yha .org.uk; Bellever; dm £14; **P**) This former farm on the edge of a conifer plantation amid swathes of open moor has bags of character: expect

a huge kitchen, lots of rustic stone walls, wooden stairs and cosy dorms. It's a mile south of the village.

Lydgate House Hotel (☎ 880209; www.lydgatehouse .co.uk; s £50-55, d £110-140; ☯ Mar-Oct; **P**) Oozing tranquillity, this beautifully furnished Victorian house is hidden away at the end of a moss-lined track. There are rich tapestries, linens and antique furniture inside, and birdsong and a rushing river outside. You can even feed the rescue sheep. It's a 10-minute walk from Postbridge.

our pick **Two Bridges** (☎ 890581; www.twobridges .co.uk; Two Bridges; s £90-115, d £130-180; **P**) Walking into this classic moorland hotel feels like slipping on a favourite pair of comfy but classy shoes – everything fits, perfectly. Lounge in the gently elegant rooms, with their huge inglenook fireplaces and squishy leather sofas. Former guests Wallace Simpson, Winston Churchill and Vivien Leigh probably liked it too. It's 3 miles south of Postbridge.

our pick **Warren House Inn** (☎ 880208; mains £4-9; ☯ food served noon-9pm Mon-Sat, noon-8.30pm Sun, to 4pm Mon & Tue Nov-Mar) Plonked amid miles of open moor, this former tin miner's haunt exudes the kind of hospitality you only get in a pub in the middle of nowhere. A Dartmoor legend, its stone floors, trestle tables and hearty food are given an extra glow by a fire that's reputedly been crackling since 1845. It's on the B3212, 2 miles north of Postbridge.

Getting There & Away

Bus 82, the Transmoor Link (five daily May to September, two on Saturday and Sunday only October to April), runs past Two Bridges, Postbridge and the Warren House Inn en route between Plymouth (approximately one hour) and Exeter (1½ hours).

WIDECOMBE-IN-THE-MOOR
☎ 01364 / pop 562

This is archetypal Dartmoor, down to the ponies grazing on the village green. Widecombe's honey-grey, 15th-century buildings circle a church whose 130ft tower has seen it dubbed the Cathedral of the Moor. Inside, search out the boards telling the fire-and-brimstone tale of the violent storm of 1638 – it knocked a pinnacle from the roof, killing several parishioners. As ever on Dartmoor the devil was blamed (said to be in search of souls).

The village is commemorated in the traditional English folksong of Widecombe Fair; the event of the same name takes place on the second Tuesday of September.

Sleeping & Eating

Dartmoor Expedition Centre (☎ 621249; www.dartmoorbase.co.uk; dm £10, loft room £12; P) A remote 300-year-old converted barn with dorm beds, real fires and hot showers. It's all best enjoyed after the climbing, orienteering, caving and hiking the centre organises. It's 2 miles west of Widecombe.

Higher Venton Farm (☎ 621235; www.ventonfarm .com; d £48/54; P) This 16th-century farmhouse could be used to define an architectural style: picture-postcard-thatch. With low lintels and winding stone stairs, there's not a straight line in the place. One room has a shared bathroom. It's a 15-minute walk to the village.

Holne Chase Hotel (☎ 631471; www.holne-chase .co.uk; Tavistock Rd; lunch mains £9, dinner 3 courses £35; s/d £120/160-180, ste £200; lunch & dinner, closed lunch Mon; P) Deeply luxurious but not too precious, this former hunting lodge has the delightfully lived in feel of a real country house. Most of the plush rooms have snug alcoves and views over the lushly wooded Dart Valley. The menu features locally smoked salmon and Dartmoor venison. It's open for lunch (mains £9) and dinner (three courses £35), but closed Monday lunch. It's 7 miles south of Widecombe.

Rugglestone Inn (☎ 621327; mains £4-9; lunch & dinner) This old pub is intimate and traditional, with a stone floor and low beams – plenty of locals can be found in front of its wood-burning stove. Tuck into handmade bangers and mash or fisherman's pie. It's a signposted, five-minute walk from the village.

Old Inn (☎ 621207; The Green; mains £9; lunch & dinner) This 14th-century hostelry right beside the village green has been carefully, if slightly incongruously, renovated in blond beams, light panelling and quirky quotes. It's somewhere to sip a cappuccino and dine on steak and ale pie or smoked fish crumble.

Getting There & Away

Bus 272 goes to Tavistock (1¼ hours, two daily late July to early September only) via Two Bridges (50 minutes) and Princetown (55 minutes).

Bus 274 runs to Okehampton (1¾ hours, three on summer Sundays only) via Moreton-hampstead. Several other buses stop at Widecombe on Sunday only as part of the Sunday Rover scheme; check with the DNPA.

MORETONHAMPSTEAD

☎ 01647 / pop 1721

Moretonhampstead has made a living from through-traffic for centuries and today a constant stream of cars and tractors still rumbles through its central square. Its roads are lined with a pleasant jumble of Georgian houses, shops, pubs and restaurants, and its bustle can be welcome after the remoteness of the higher moor.

The **tourist office** (☎ 400043; www.moretonhampstead.com; 11 The Square; 9.30am-5pm Apr-Oct, 10am-4pm Fri, Sat & Sun Nov-Mar) is in the centre.

Sleeping & Eating

Steps Bridge Hostel (☎ 252435; dm adult/child £8/11) Reminiscent of a Swiss chalet, this independent hostel is halfway up a steep wooded gorge – look out for heron and otters in the River Teign below. It's 4 miles east of town; bus 359 stops off en route to Exeter.

Sparrowhawk Backpackers (☎ 440318; www .sparrowhawkbackpackers.co.uk; 45 Ford St; dm/d £14/32) A pulse of vegetarian, ecofriendly funky-ness in the middle of town. The bright, light dorms are in a converted stable and there's a central courtyard, ringed by rickety outbuildings, in which to swap traveller's tales.

Cookshayes (☎ 440374; www.cookshayes.co.uk; 33 Court St; s/d £23/46; P) Ask for a room with a view of the fields edging the moor at this Victorian house. Rooms are fairly plain and traditional, except the four poster one which is a particularly vivid pink. It's a two-minute walk from town.

White Hart Hotel (☎ 441340; www.whitehartdart moor.co.uk; The Square; s £70-85, d £120-140; mains £14; lunch & dinner; P) The mail coaches used to change horses here in Georgian days; today it's a smoothly comfy hotel with tartan carpets, deep terracotta walls and CD players in the rooms. The food is tasty and substantial; try the steak with local blue cheese or sea bass with a pine-nut crust.

Getting There & Away

The Transmoor Link (bus 82) shuttles west to Princetown (40 minutes, five daily May to September, two on Saturday and Sunday only October to April) and Plymouth (1½ hours) or east to Exeter (45 minutes).

DEVON

Year-round, bus 359 goes to Exeter (15 minutes, seven daily Monday to Saturday).

CHAGFORD & AROUND
☎ 01647 / pop 1470

With its wonky thatches and cream and white fronted buildings, Chagford gathers around a busy square – at first glance it's every inch a timeless moorland town. But modern life peeps through: health food shops and contemporary pottery galleries now rub shoulders with purveyors of waxed-jackets and hip-flasks.

The nearest tourist office is in Moretonhampstead (p209). Chagford's biggest sight is the architectural curiosity that is **Castle Drogo** (NT; ☎ 433306; Drewsteignton; adult/child £7.40/3.70; 🕐 11am-5pm Wed-Mon late-Mar–Oct). This imposing grey edifice was the last castle to be built in England and was constructed between 1911 and 1931. It was designed by Sir Edwin Lutyens for self-made food-millionaire Julius Drewe. The brief was to combine the medieval grandeur of a castle and the comforts of a 20th-century country house. The result is a highly unusual property where crenellated battlements combine with comfortably carpeted interiors and (how practical) a good central heating system. The gardens are influenced by Gertrude Jekyll and the woods have spectacular views over Dartmoor and the Teign Gorge. Castle Drogo is 3 miles northeast of Chagford.

Sleeping & Eating

Easton Court (☎ 433469; www.easton.co.uk; Easton Cross; s £51-60, d £66-75; **P**) It's worth staying just for breakfast – choices include fresh fish or soufflé omelette. The rooms are lovely too, with their cast iron beds, soft sofas and view of wooded hills. It's 1.5 miles from Chagford.

Sandy Park (☎ 433267; www.sandyparkinn.co.uk; Sandy Park; s/d £50/80; **P**) Great pub, chic place to stay. Sip a pint of real ale in a bar with low ceilings and big fireplaces. Sample choice, locally sourced fish and meats in the restaurant (mains £6 to £12), then totter upstairs to sleep amid plump pillows and classic furnishings. The restaurant is open for lunch and dinner (except Sunday evening). It's a mile from Chagford.

Three Crowns Hotel (☎ 433444; www.chagford -accom.co.uk; High St; d £85) Seven centuries old and crowded with ghosts, this is an authentically atmospheric place for a drink and some solid

pub food (mains £8) – all overseen by the civil war style armour on the walls. The creaking bedrooms are full of dark woods.

Gidleigh Park (☎ 432367; www.gidleigh.com; s £340, d £440-1200; **P** 🖳) This prestigious oasis of ultimate luxury teams crests, crenellations and roaring fires with shimmering sanctuaries of blue marble, waterproof TVs and private saunas. That the restaurant has two Michelin stars says it all. Room rates include dinner; they fall to £290 for two B&B. The restaurant is open for lunch and dinner. Three courses cost £75, but crafty diners opt for the £27 two-course lunch between Monday and Thursday. It's 2 miles from Chagford.

Getting There & Away
Buses 178/179 run to Okehampton (one hour, two daily). Bus 173 travels to Moretonhampstead (15 minutes, twice a day Monday to Saturday) and Exeter (one hour).

OKEHAMPTON & AROUND
☎ 01837 / pop 6818

Okehampton huddles on the edge of the mind-expanding sweep of the higher moor. This breadth of bracken-covered slopes has no roads and no farms; just mile after mile of gorse and granite tors. Its proximity lends Okehampton a staging post feel and with its selection of traditional shops and pubs, it's a pleasant place to stock up before a foray into the wilderness.

The **tourist office** (☎ 53020; www.okehampton devon.co.uk; Museum Courtyard, 3 West St; 🕐 10am-5pm Mon-Sat Easter-Oct) can help with walking and cycling information.

Sights & Activities
There's a good network of **hiking trails** leading out of town, although parts fringe the military's live firing ranges (see the boxed text, p203).

The 11-mile **Granite Way** skirts the moor's western edge via an old dismantled railway to Lydford; **Devon Cycle Hire** (☎ 861141; www.devon cyclehire.co.uk; Sourton Down, near Okehampton; adult/ child per day £12/8; 🕐 9am-5pm Apr-Sep) is on the route itself.

For picturesque clambering it's hard to beat **Okehampton Castle** (EH; ☎ 52844; adult/child £3/1.50; 🕐 10am-5pm Apr-Jun & Sep, 10am-6pm Jul & Aug). A towering, crumbling ruin, it teeters on the top of a wooded spur just above the cascading River Okement. It's a Norman motte and bailey affair with the usual later extensions (in this case 14th-century), and you can wander amid its supposedly haunted walls.

From Okehampton a 5-mile hike through a boulder-strewn river-valley takes you to the village of Sticklepath and **Finch Foundry** (NT; ☎ 840046; adult/child £3.90/1.95; ☷ 11am-5pm Wed-Mon Mar-Oct). This tiny, water-powered forge dates from the 19th century but is still working and rings to the sound of metal being hammered.

Sleeping & Eating

Okehampton YHA Hostel (☎ 0870 770 5978; www .okehampton-yha.co.uk; Klondyke Rd; dm £13.95; ☐ ☷) This former railway shed, on the edge of Okehampton, has had a bright revamp and is now a hugely popular hostel. No doubt it's something to do with the sailing, rock-climbing and kayaking courses it runs.

Tors (☎ 840689; Belstone; s/d £30/60; ☐) Tucked away in the picturesque village of Belstone this welcoming country pub has views onto the moor. The rooms are simple and traditional, and the lunches and dinners are hearty (mains £8 to £15). It's 2 miles east of Okehampton.

Collaven Manor (☎ 861522; www.collavenmanor.co .uk; Sourton; s £63, d £104-142; ☐) It's a delightful, clematis-clad mini manorhouse with a wooden chandelier crowning a 16th-century hall. The restful rooms are lined with tapestries and window seats. If you're staying, venison stroganoff and guinea fowl in Madeira sauce feature on the menu (three courses £25.50); nonguests should phone to book. It's 5 miles west of Okehampton.

Getting There & Away

Bus X9 runs from Exeter (50 minutes, two hourly Monday to Saturday, two on Sunday) via Okehampton to Bude (one hour). Bus 179 heads to Chagford (30 minutes, two to three daily) and Moretonhampstead (50 minutes). Bus 86 goes to Barnstaple (1¾ hours, two-hourly Monday to Saturday, two on Sundays).

The **Dartmoor Railway** (☎ 55637; www.dartmoor railway.co.uk) runs diesel and steam services between Okehampton and Meldon (one way £3.50, 10 minutes, two to seven Tuesday, Saturday and Sunday April to October). There are six trains to Exeter on Sundays between June and mid-September.

NORTH DEVON COAST

Intensely rugged and in places utterly remote, this is a coast to inspire. It's crammed with drastically concertinaed cliffs, expansive sandy beaches and ancient fishing villages. But the shoreline is also dotted with classic, faded British seaside resorts, many of which are now trying to ride an incoming wave of surf culture. The result is a coast of twin personalities: coach parties and candyfloss meets partying beach bums and cutting-edge art. Occasionally uncomfortable, more often comic, these two cultures don't so much clash as sometimes bump – gently.

Away from the sea, a deeply rural hinterland has long had to battle hard times in the farming industry, but the shaded lanes that lead through tranquil villages reveal a place of almost forgotten charm, ripe with smells of the farm. The area offers a smorgasbord of delights: surfing lessons at cool Croyde, Damien Hirst's ultra-artistic restaurant in Ilfracombe, miles of sandy beaches near Braunton, the 30-mile Tarka Cycle Trail, impossibly pretty Clovelly, phenomenal rock formations at Hartland Point, and sitting on the horizon 10 miles out to sea the enigmatic chunk of granite that is Lundy Island.

The dramatic estuaries of the Rivers Taw and Torridge carve deep channels into the north Devon coast around the key towns of Barnstaple and Bideford. Though parts of Exmoor National Park fall within north Devon, we've covered the whole of Exmoor in our Somerset chapter (p113).

The **North Devon Marketing Bureau** (☎ 0845 241 2043; www.northdevon.com) is a good information source. Two good times to come is during the **North Devon Walking Festival** (www.walking northdevon.co.uk) in early May and the **North Devon Festival** (☎ 01271-324242; www.northdevonfes tival.org) in April, a gloriously vibrant mélange of classical music, fringe theatre, jazz, folk, art and literature staged in 80 venues across the area.

ILFRACOMBE & WOOLACOMBE
☎ 01271 / pop 10,842
Like a matinee idol past his prime, Ilfracombe has had a sagging, crumpled feel for years. Its heyday was as a Victorian watering hole and in places it still lives off faded grandeur – town houses with cast iron balconies edge its sloping

streets, while formal gardens, crazy golf and ropes of twinkling lights line the promenade. But digging a little deeper reveals the tweaks of a youthful face-lift in the form of some smart eateries and places to sleep. A Damien Hirst connection and the chance to go surfing or take a 'dip' in the past also make it worth a detour. The best local beach is 5 miles west at Woolacombe, a traditional family resort sitting at the head of 3 miles of sand.

Orientation & Information

Overlooked by a dinky 14th-century chapel, the cliffs crinkle in dramatic folds around Ilfracombe's tiny, sandy harbour. The shoreline then juts out in the 45° Capstone Hill before rejoining the Promenade and the twin, concrete domes of the **Landmark Theatre** (dubbed Madonna's Bra by locals). The **tourist office** (☎ 863001; www.visitilfracombe.co.uk; ☯ 10am-5pm Mon-Sat, plus Sun Apr-Oct) is inside.

Sights & Activities

If you're tempted by the waves, try the **Nick Thorn Hunter Surf Academy** (☎ 871337; www.nick thornhuntersurfacademy.com; wetsuit & board hire half-/full day £14/18; ☯ 9am-5pm Apr-Sep) on Woolacombe beach; lessons start from £30 for 2½ hours. For a leg-testing hike, head a few miles north up Woolacombe's coast path to the peaceful village of **Mortehoe**.

In Ilfracombe, **tunnelsbeaches** (☎ 879882; www .tunnelsbeaches.co.uk; Granville Rd; adult/child £1.95.1.50; ☯ 10am-5pm or 6pm Easter-Oct, plus 9am-7pm Jul & Aug) beautifully evokes the resort's glory days as a 19th-century bathing resort, and provides a spot for a swim at the same time. Walk through passageways hacked by hand out of solid rock to a pocket-sized beach and then enjoy a bracing dip in the tidal swimming pools. Displays convey an 1820s world of woollen bathing suits, segregated swimming and boating etiquette (gentlemen who cannot swim should never take ladies upon the water).

You can also catch the MS *Oldenburg* ferry to remote Lundy Island (see the box, p181) from Ilfracombe's harbour.

Sleeping & Eating

Ocean Backpackers (☎ 867835; www.oceanbackpackers .co.uk; 29 St James Pl; dm £10-13, d £34; P) Friendly and lively with compact, clean dorms, this hostel is in a great location near Ilfracombe's bus station and the harbour. There's a kitchen, pool table and a cave-like lounge too.

Norbury House Hotel (☎ 863888; www.norburyhouse .co.uk; Torrs Park; d £65-80, f & ste £80; ✖) Plush and stylish, this former gentleman's residence is dotted with contemporary artwork. Set on the hill overlooking Ilfracombe, there are impressive views from its terraced gardens.

Westwood (☎ 867443; www.west-wood.co.uk; Torrs Park Rd; d £80-95; P ☐) Modern, minimal and marvellous, this ultra-chic B&B is a study of neutral tones and dashes of vivid colour and is graced by pony-skin chaise longues and stand-alone baths. The rooms overlooking Ilfracombe have sea glimpses and there's an in-house spa treatment room.

Lundy House Hotel (☎ 870372; www.lundyhousehotel .co.uk; Chapel Hill; s £43-60, d £56-90; P ✖) Clinging to a cliff edge between Woolacombe and Mortehoe, this small hotel's stunning sea-view rooms float with airy drapes. The road-facing rooms are perfectly pleasant but not as captivating. There are panoramic views of Lundy Island from the terraced garden, which leads to the coast path and beaches below.

our pick **11, The Quay** (☎ 868090; www.11thequay .com; 11 The Quay, Ilfracombe; restaurant/bistro mains £20/10; ☯ restaurant lunch & dinner Wed-Sun, bistro lunch, dinner & snacks all day; ✖) Full of Chelsea chic and supremely distinctive, this eatery is owned by the controversial artist Damien Hirst – most famous for preserving dead cows and sharks. There's fine dining with superb views upstairs and a chichi bistro-café downstairs. Seared skate or Lundy lobster 'n' chips feature on the menu; Mr Hirst's artwork features on the walls, including chunks of his *Pharmacy* installation and, with delicious irony, fish in formaldehyde.

La Gendarmerie (☎ 865984; 63 Fore St; mains £13; ☯ dinner Wed-Sat, Sun bookings only) One of several smart restaurants winding up Ilfracombe's Fore St, this one is all wooden floors and exposed stone. Expect to eat local lobster, scallops and sea bass.

Getting There & Away

Buses 3 and 3A (40 minutes, every 30 minutes Monday to Saturday, hourly Sunday) run from Ilfracombe to Barnstaple. Bus 300 links Ilfracombe with Lynton (one hour) and Minehead (two hours) three times daily.

BARNSTAPLE & AROUND

☎ 01271 / pop 24,478

The commercial and administrative centre of north Devon, Barnstaple is also its transport hub and used to be notable as a major traffic bottleneck – all the area's main roads used to flow through its streets. But this businesslike town is now beginning to breathe again, thanks to a massive new bridge over the River Taw, designed to whisk 30,000 cars per day away from the centre.

The **tourist office** (☎ 375000; www.staynorthdevon .co.uk; The Square; ☼ 9.30am-5pm Mon-Sat) is inside the **museum** (☎ 346747; admission free; ☼ 9.30am-5pm Mon-Sat), a well-displayed cross-section of the area's history. Barnstaple is a handy jumping-off point for the Tarka Trail (below), while the **Queen's Theatre** (☎ 324242; www.northdevontheatres .org.uk; Boutport St) is a focal point of the area's theatrical and musical worlds. If your timing's right, drop by the vibrant **Pannier Market** (☎ 379084; High St; ☼ 9am-3.30pm or 4pm Tue, Wed, Fri & Sat) and the neighbouring **Butcher's Row** – fittingly some shops still sell meat, while others have super-fresh local fish. In the quiet streets nearby, search out the **parish church** with its crooked, lead spire.

Sleeping & Eating

Lower Yelland Farm (☎ 860101; www.loweryellandfarm .co.uk; Fremington; s £30-35, d £60; **P**) Breakfast on fresh eggs from rescue chickens and home-made jam at this charming 17th-century farmhouse. The cream rooms are light, calm and framed by flower boxes, while the Tarka Trail and a reserve teeming with birds are just 200m away. It's 3 miles west of Barnstaple off the B3233.

ourpick **Broomhill Art Hotel** (☎ 850262; www .broomhillart.co.uk; s/d £45/70; **P**) Funky, arty and very comfy, this innovative boutique hotel effortlessly blends contemporary design and antiques. Reached via a creaking, sweeping staircase, the bedrooms are packed with artwork and decked out with bursts of purple

velvet. The slow food mantra informs the cooking: meals are organic and local with a Mediterranean twist (three courses £13, tapas £9). Food is available for lunch Wednesday to Sunday, and dinner Friday and Saturday. The **sculpture garden** (adult/child £4.50/1.50; ☼ 11am-4pm daily Jul & Aug, Wed-Sun Sep-Jun, closed late-Dec–mid-Jan) sees slivers of polished steel and mystical figures hidden in the woods. Also look out for the huge red stiletto shoe. It's 2 miles north of Barnstaple on the B3230.

Getting There & Away

National Express services include those to London (£28), Bristol (£18.40) and Birmingham (£37). The Tarka railway line runs to Exeter (£6.90, one hour 15 minutes, hourly Monday to Saturday, six on Sunday).

Bus 315 shuttles to Exeter (2¼ hours, eight daily Monday to Saturday, two on Sunday) via Bideford (25 minutes). Bus 86 runs to Plymouth (3½ hours, eight daily Monday to Saturday, two on Sunday), also via Bideford.

CROYDE, BRAUNTON & AROUND
☎ 01271 / pop 8319

Croyde has the kind of cheerful, chilled vibe you'd expect from its role as north Devon's surf central. Here old world meets the new surfing wave washing these shores: thatched roofs peep out over racks of wetsuits, crowds of cool guys in board shorts sip beer outside 17th-century inns. Nearer the beach, green fields flow towards smooth dunes and the main draw is obvious: the line-up of powerful waves rolling in towards acres of sand.

This mini-Maui is reached through traffic-choked Braunton 2 miles inland, where butchers and bakers co-exist with a rising tide of neoprene and fibreglass. Braunton is also home to the **tourist office** (☎ 816400; www .brauntontic.co.uk; Bakehouse Centre; ☼ 10am-3.30pm or

---

A TRANQUIL CYCLING TRAIL

The 30-mile Tarka Trail gets its name from the Henry Williamson book *Tarka The Otter*, which was in turn inspired by the lush north Devon landscape. It starts at the coast and the initial 6-mile Braunton to Barnstaple stage makes for flat, family-friendly cycling alongside the banks of the River Taw (look out for wintering wildfowl such as curlew, red shank and even spoonbills). The final stretch, from Great Torrington to Meeth, winds through north Devon's lush, hilly farming heartland. The **North Devon Coast and Countryside Service** (☎ 01237-23655) and www .devon.gov.uk/tarkatrail has information about accommodation and bike hire. **Tarka Trail Cycle Hire** (☎ 01271-324202; half-/full day adult £7.50/10, child £5/7; ☼ 9.15am-5pm Apr-Oct) can be found at Barnstaple train station.

OUT OF THE WAY ADVENTURES

For a castaway, get-away-from-it-all bolthole, try Lundy Island. This slab of granite, 3 miles long by half a mile wide, is anchored on the horizon 10 miles off the north Devon coast. Though it looks elusive and mysterious from the mainland, it's actually only a two-hour ferry ride away. It's also a different world – in May and June, puffins nest on the 400ft cliffs, the only place in Devon where they do (fittingly Lundy means 'Puffin Island' in Norse). You'll see Lundy ponies, sika deer and Soay sheep, and basking sharks float by offshore. Pack a swimsuit – the wardens here lead snorkelling safaris. The island also has standing stones, a 13th-century castle and a couple of lighthouses to explore. Car-free, it's an extraordinarily peaceful place and, with rich star displays takes on a magical quality at night.

Lundy is run by the **Landmark Trust** (☎ 01628-825925; www.landmarktrust.org.uk). It has a shop and a welcoming pub, the **Marisco Tavern** (☎ 01237-431831; ☺ lunch & dinner).

Lundy's particular brand of remote charm doesn't appeal to everyone, but if bedding down on an offshore fragment of rock is your thing, camp near the Marisco Tavern (camp sites £14 to £20) or try one of the 20 holiday lets. These include cottages at the castle, apartments in a former lighthouse and the single-bed Radio Room – which used to house Lundy's wireless transmitter. Properties can be booked up months in advance, but it's worth checking nearer the time. In peak season, expect to pay £136 for two nights in a cottage that sleeps two, or £479 for the week. Bookings are made either through the Landmark Trust or the **Lundy Shore Office** (☎ 01271-863636; www.lundyisland.co.uk; ☺ 9am-5pm Mon-Fri, plus 9am-1pm Sat Apr-Oct), which doubles as the tourist office.

Between late March and October, the MS *Oldenburg* shuttles to the island from Ilfracombe or Bideford (day returns adult/child £29/14, two hours, three to four sailing per week). If you're staying overnight, the return fare rises to £49/25 for an adult/child. In winter there's a helicopter service (return adult/child £85/45) from Hartland Point – it only flies Mondays and Fridays between November and mid-March and can't be done as a day-trip. The Lundy Shore Office takes all transport bookings.

4pm Mon-Sat Easter-Oct, to 5pm plus Sun Jul & Aug, 10am-4pm Mon-Fri, 10am-3pm Sat Nov-Dec).

The water's hard to resist. **Le Sport** (☎ 890147; Hobbs Hill; ☺ 9am-5.30pm, 9am-9pm at peak times) is among those hiring wetsuits and boards (half-/full day £12/18). Surfing is harder than it looks, and beginners will definitely benefit from lessons; **Surf South West** (☎ 890400; www .surfsouthwest.com; Croyde Burrows Beach; per half-day £19; ☺ Mar-Nov) and **Surfing Croyde Bay** (☎ 891200; www.surfingcroydebay.co.uk; 8 Hobbs Hill, Croyde; 2½hr lesson adult/child £35/25) are both approved by the British Surfing Association. Just south of Croyde, Saunton Sands is a memorable 3-mile beach backed by the dunes and salt marshes of **Braunton Burrows**, an area awarded World Biosphere Reserve status by Unesco. It was also the main training ground for American troops before D Day and mock landing craft still sit poignantly in its tufted dunes near the southern tip – ask locally about how to hunt them out.

Sleeping & Eating

All that wonderful surf draws waves of crowds in the summer. Book ahead, even for camping,

which is on the pricey side; most sites ask for a minimum stay.

Bay View Farm (☎ 890501; www.bayviewfarm.co.uk; Croyde; sites from £20) An excellent, well equipped and very organised camp site on the way into the village from Braunton.

Mitchum's Campsites (☎ 890233; www.croydebay .co.uk; Croyde) Mitchums has two locations: one in Croyde village and one by the beach. They're only open on certain weekends in summer and rates vary widely – expect to pay up to £24 to £30 per night.

Chapel Farm (☎ 890429; www.chapelfarmcroyde.co.uk; Hobbs Hill, Croyde; s £25-30 d £56-68; **P**) Walls and ceilings shoot off at atmospherically random angles in this thatched cob farmhouse, formerly a home to monks. Some of the light, pretty rooms are share bathrooms. Self catering is available too.

Thatch (☎ 890349; 14 Hobbs Hill, Croyde; d £50-70, f £50-120; **P**) A cavernous, cob pub where surfers gather to swap tales of beach breaks, walls and barrels. The beamed rooms have smart, modern twists (delicate creams, browns and subtle checks) and some share bathrooms.

A touch noisy, but then most people staying are in the bar, which serves hearty, nacho-and-burger style food (breakfast, lunch and dinner are available).

Saunton Sands Hotel (☎ 890212; www.brend-hotels .co.uk; Saunton Sands; d £184-228, B&B £194-240; **P** **R**) Dominating the cliff, this is a delightful Art Deco, wedding-cake white creation, all clean lines and curves. The 1930s style doesn't extend to the bedrooms, which can feel a little uniform, but the pool and the mind-expanding beach views are superb.

Corner Bistro (☎ 813897; 8 The Square, Braunton; mains £6-12; ☺ 9am-2pm Mon & Wed-Sat, plus 7-9pm Fri & Sat, 9am-noon Sun) If you're passing through Braunton, check out this bright, terracotta eatery done out in crisp linens and driftwood. Try their Devon crab salad or fishcakes with buttered spinach.

Getting There & Away

Bus 308 bus runs from Barnstaple to Braunton (20 minutes), then on to Saunton Sands (25 minutes) and Croyde (30 minutes) hourly Monday to Saturday only.

BIDEFORD & APPLEDORE

☎ 01237 / pop 26,042

The graceful expanse of the Taw-Torridge estuary has shaped the communities along its banks for centuries, and still does. Bideford stretches along a river quay, with shops, pubs and houses climbing the hills behind. Fewer boats are now tied up alongside, although the MS *Oldenburg* still makes regular crossings to Lundy Island (opposite). Bideford's **tourist office** (☎ 477676; www.torridge.gov.uk/tourism; Victoria Park; ☺ 10am-5pm Mon-Sat, 10am-1pm Sun) is at the northern end of the quay.

Three miles downriver, Appledore provides expansive views over miles of wide water towards distant clusters of white houses and shifting sand dunes. Lined with flowerboxes and pastel-pretty terraces, some of its streets are too narrow for cars – making for unusually tranquil wanderings. Track down sepia images of Appledore's shipbuilding glory days alongside the disused **dry dock** at the end of the quay.

A 7-mile drive south from Bideford, the market town of **Great Torrington** has a brace of quality sights. **Rosemoor** (☎ 01805-624067; www.rhs .org.uk; adult/child £6/2; ☺ 10am-6pm Apr-Sep, 10am-5pm Oct-Mar), one of only four Royal Horticultural Society gardens in England, is a vivid, fragrant

delight, full of colour, serenity and arboreal inspiration. It's signposted off the A3124.

Torrington 1646 (☎ 01805-626146; www.torrington -1646.co.uk; South St, Great Torrington; adult/child £6.95/4.75; ☺ 10.30am-5pm Mon-Sat Mar-Sep, 11am-4pm Mon-Fri Oct-Feb) is an irrepressible re-creation of the town's role in a key English Civil War battle. Cheeky costumed guides regale you with tales of leech-breeders, urine-takers and Puritans – laughter and learning at the same time. The last entrance is 3pm.

Sleeping & Eating

Raleigh House (☎ 459202; www.appledorebandb.co.uk; 9 Myrtle St, Appledore; ste £70) A superb value, mini-suite in an 18th-century terrace is a minute's walk from Appledore's quay. The private lounge and bedroom luxuriate in restful, neutral tones, and the bright bathroom features blues and white woods.

Bensons (☎ 424093; 20 The Quay; mains from £11) Gently sophisticated and hugely popular, this relaxed Appledore restaurant serves up simple, quality food. Try the local lemon sole with buttered spinach or the sea bass and shallots. It's open for dinner Tuesday to Thursday only if you've pre-booked; reservations are also recommended for Friday and Saturday nights.

The rooms at the **Seagate Hotel** (☎ 472589; www.seagatehotel.co.uk; The Quay; s/d £46/75; **P**), right on Appledore's riverfront, are comfortable if a little bland. The **Champion of Wales** (☎ 425993; Meeting St) or the **Coach and Horses** (☎ 474470; Market St) are the places to head for an atmospheric pint.

Getting There & Away

Bus 2 (10 daily) links Appledore with Bideford (20 minutes) and Barnstaple (one hour).

WESTWARD HO!

☎ 01237 / pop 1933

Westward Ho! is the only place name in England with an exclamation mark, which seems a bit of a waste really. This unremarkable resort has a suburbs-meets-seaside feel and owes its existence to the best-selling 1855 novel *Westward Ho!* by Charles Kingsley, which featured this stretch of coast. Developers targeted the spot, built a resort here and gave it the same name to cash in on the book's popularity.

The town's beach is more deserving of exclamatory punctuation – a vast 2-mile expanse of sand backed by a natural pebble ridge. Very high tides push this defensive barrier inland.

The stones used to be thrown back in gloriously eccentric English style by Potwallopers (only those locals who had two fires and a pot) at a wild, annual village bun-fight. These days the pebble management is done more prosaically by bulldozers but the Potwallopers Festival, with its music and marquees, still happens on the Spring Bank Holiday.

The nearest tourist office is in Bideford (p215). **Surfers** (☎ 474534; Golf Links Rd; per half/full day surfboards £10/20, wetsuits £5/10, bodyboards £5/10; ☺ 10am-5pm or 8pm) rents out equipment. For tuition, try **North Devon Surf School** (☎ 01598-710818; www.northdevonsurfschool.co.uk; per half-/full day £25/45) at the northern end of the beach – booking is essential.

Sleeping & Eating

Waterfront Inn (☎ 474737; Golf Links Rd; s/d/f £40/65/80; ℗) A minute from the beach, this aquamarine, modern building has dark-pine rooms with a motel feel. But they're bright, a fair size and have sparkling bathrooms. From noon to 9pm, the pub serves the usual grub, from bar snacks to steaks (mains £5 to £11).

Culloden House (☎ 479421; www.culloden-house .co.uk; Foseth Hill; s £30-45, d £60-70, f £100; ℗ ☒) All moulded cornices and stained glass, this lovely 1865 gentleman's residence is built, apparently, in domestic Gothic style. It's halfway up a hill and the best bedrooms have expansive sea views – choose from brisk blues and white or refined greens and creams.

Getting There & Away

Bus 1 runs to Bideford (15 minutes, every 30 minutes Monday to Saturday) and Barnstaple (one hour).

CLOVELLY

☎ 01237 / pop 1616

Clovelly is almost impossibly beautiful. Its white cottages cascade down cliffs to meet a curving crab claw of a harbour, which is lined with lobster pots and set against a deep blue. If quaint is defined by cobbled streets, then Clovelly wins any quaint contest hands down. These 'cobbles' are actually large pebbles and have been used to build walls in the village as well as to surface its incredibly steep, winding lanes. The stones can also be found scattered on the tiny beach far below. It gives the place an integrated, organic feel – as if it's flowing down the hills to the sea. The village is privately owned (you have to pay to get in)

and inevitably, it's heavily tourist targeted, but even the sometimes stage-set feel can't detract from its underlying appeal, best appreciated in the calm of a summer's evening when the coach parties have gone.

The uneven, energy-sapping streets are so steep cars can't negotiate them so supplies are brought in by sledge – look out for them, often big breadbaskets on runners, leaning outside people's homes. They're a reminder that this picture-postcard village is home to hundreds of tenants and some of their rents are fixed as low as an enviable £400 a year. Although Clovelly is often branded artificial, around 98% of the houses are lived in (in some Westcountry villages almost half the properties are second homes).

Sights

Clovelly is entered through an overwhelming **visitor's centre** (☎ 431781; www.clovelly.co.uk; adult/child £4.95/3.25; ☺ 8.45am-6.30pm Jun-Sep, 9am-5pm Apr & May, 10am-4pm Nov-Apr). Technically you have to cross private land to enter the village, but if you're walking the South West Coast Path they may let you in for free. Between Easter and October, there's a regular Land Rover shuttle (£2, 10am to 5.45pm) from the visitor centre to the foot of the severe slope.

Charles Kingsley, author of *The Water Babies*, lived in Clovelly as a child and it's claimed it inspired him to write the classic children's story. Once inside the village you can visit his former house, the **Kingsley Museum** (admission free; ☺ 8.45am-6.30pm Jun-Sep, 9am-5pm Apr & May, 10am-4pm Nov-Apr), as well as an old fisherman's cottage and two chapels.

Sleeping & Eating

Steart Farm (☎ 431836; steart@tiscali.co.uk; Buck's Cross; sites £10.10) Three hillside terraces for tents give this camp site a secluded feel. There are splendid views over the bay and the owners even turn on underfloor heating in the showers when it's cold. There is distant noise from the A39, and the camp site is 3 miles from Clovelly.

Donkey Shoe Cottage (☎ 431601; www.donkeysh oecottage.co.uk; 21 High St; s/d £24/48; ☒) In a superb spot in the heart of Clovelly, this ancient terraced house has surprisingly snazzy touches, with bedrooms in raspberry or green. You can see the sea from all rooms, but the view is best from number 3, under the eaves. Rooms have shared bathroom.

Round House (☎ 451687; www.the-round-house
.co.uk; Horns Cross; s/d £40/65; P ✗) A character-
full converted barn and mill – ask for the
unusual round bedroom, which sits above
the similarly circular guest lounge. There's a
free cream tea on arrival and their own fresh
eggs for breakfast. It's 4 miles from Clovelly
beside the A39.

ourpick **Red Lion Hotel** (☎ 431237; www.clovelly
.co.uk; s £58-94, d £127-157) Right on Clovelly quay,
these are not so much rooms with a view, as
views with a room. The hardest decision is
whether to look out over the sea or the harbour – both are captivating. Rooms are fresh
and dotted with Lloyd Loom style furniture.
Tuck into sea bass and local beef in the restaurant (mains £15 to £20, open for dinner). Or
try handmade fish cakes and pub grub in the
bar (mains £5 to £10, open lunch and dinner),
overlooked by a locally caught, stuffed shark's
head on the wall.

Getting There & Away
Bus 319 goes to Clovelly from Bideford (30
minutes, four to six Monday to Saturday, two
on Sunday between May and September only)
and on to Hartland (20 minutes).

HARTLAND PENINSULA
☎ 01237 / pop 1873
A rugged, right-angle of land, the Hartland
Peninsula has the kind of coast that makes you
gasp. It feels like the edge of Devon, and it is –
the county goes no further west from here
and only a few miles south before the cliffs
surge off into Cornwall. Tucked away from
traffic through-routes, its unspoilt coastline
produces gorgeous sunsets, and its remoteness
ensures stunning star displays at night.

There is no tourist office on the Hartland
Peninsula; contact the one in Bideford (p215).
The village of Hartland, a couple of miles inland from Hartland Point, has a number of
shops and pubs.

Hartland Point & Quay
The cliffs at **Hartland Quay** are among the most
spectacular in the region. Strata of russet rock
have been scrunched vertical by incredible
natural force to stick out at crazy angles – not
unlike a giant, deeply folded lasagne. The quay
has an atmospheric, rocky beach and a com-
pact **Shipwreck Museum** (☎ 441218; adult/child £1/50p;
☿ 11am-5pm Easter-Oct), which uses artefacts and
powerful photographs to evoke some of the

hundreds of vessels that have foundered on
the jagged shore. There's also a welcoming
pub (below).

At the tip of this peninsula, the coast
around **Hartland Point** offers superb hiking.
Tucked just under the point is the short white
column of a lighthouse built in 1874. You
can't go in but there's a viewing platform just
to the west, where you can also see the rusting
hull fragments of the coaster *Johanna*. She
came to grief on New Year's Eve in 1982 (the
crew were rescued by the Clovelly lifeboat);
the ship's bell now sits in the Shipwreck Museum at Hartland Quay. There's a kiosk and
a car park (£1.30) at the point, but it's not
served by bus.

The 12th-century **Hartland Abbey** (☎ 441264;
www.hartlandabbey.com; adult/child £8/2.50; ☿ gardens
12.30-5pm, house 2-5pm Wed, Thu & Sun Apr & May, Sun-
Thu Jun-Sep) is a warm grey, sumptuous, stately
home, rich in history and plush furnishings.
It was a monastery until Henry VIII grabbed
it in the Dissolution; he then gave it to the
sergeant of his wine cellar in 1539. It boasts
fine murals, ancient documents, paintings by
English masters and Victorian photos. The
intimate paths in the lush gardens were created by Gertrude Jekyll, a frequent guest. The
abbey is midway between Hartland village and
Hartland Quay.

SLEEPING & EATING
West Titchbury Farm (☎ 441287; Hartland Point; s/d/f
£24/45/50; P) Space and silence surround this
beamed 17th-century working farm half a
mile from the coast path at Hartland Point.
Two of the simple, traditional rooms share a
bathroom, while one has its own. There's a
grassed, walled garden at the front from which
to enjoy unspoilt rural views.

Hartland Quay Hotel (☎ 441218; www.hartland
quayhotel.com; s/d £35/70; P ✗) This cosy, established hotel is in a grandstand location
just above the quay. The bedrooms are fairly
plain, but who cares – you're here for the
view, and most look out onto a swirling sea.
Locals pack the lively, friendly bar, which
serves up hearty pub grub (mains £6 to £9)
for lunch and dinner.

GETTING THERE & AWAY
Bus 319 goes to Hartland village from Bide-
ford (40 minutes) via Clovelly (four to six
Monday to Saturday year-round, two on
Sunday between May and September only).

Cornwall

> And gorse turns tawny orange, seen beside
> Pale drifts of primroses cascading wide
> To where the slate falls sheer into the tide.
>
> *Sir John Betjeman, Cornish Cliffs*

Jutting out into the churning sea and cut off from south Devon by the broad River Tamar, Cornwall (or Kernow, as its usually known around these shores) has always seen itself as a nation apart from the rest of England – another country, not just another English county.

This slender sliver of land was one of the last great bastions of Celtic culture, and there's no doubt that there's something different in the air this far west. It's a place that mixes artistic inspiration and natural majesty in equal measures: heather, gorse and wildflowers blanket the craggy headlands; tiny fishing villages huddle in the lee of granite bluffs; cackling gulls and kittiwakes cut ribbons across an open sky. Far from being a cultural boondocks, Cornwall has recently garnered a reputation as one of Britain's most creative corners, a place where you can feed your brain, your appetite and your soul all at once: world-class museums and groundbreaking greenhouses sit side-by-side with designer restaurants, hugger-mugger pubs and surfers' bars, and every twist and turn in the coast offers a fresh panorama of postcard views.

With so much scenic splendour, it's hardly surprising that Cornwall is also one of the nation's favourite getaways, and on sunny summer days it can seem like half of Britain is jostling for that last patch of unclaimed sand. Better to visit during the quieter shoulder months, or most atmospheric of all, during the roaring surf and bitter winds of Cornwall's feral winter.

CORNWALL

HIGHLIGHTS

- Watch a gig race or stroll the Abbey Gardens on the **Isles of Scilly** (p253)
- Marvel at the architectural audacity of the **Eden Project** (p268)
- Explore the spooky monuments and standing stones of **West Penwith** (p241)
- Play lord of the manor around the great estates of **Lanhydrock** (p275) and **Cotehele** (p277)
- Top the summit of **Brown Willy** (p275), Cornwall's highest point
- Savour a pint at a creekside pub on the **River Helford** (p252)

Brown Willy ★
Cotehele ★
Lanhydrock ★
Eden Project ★★
West Penwith ★
Isles of Scilly ★
★ Helford

| POPULATION: 501,267 | ANNUAL HOURS OF SUNSHINE ISLES OF SCILLY: 1500 | PASTIES PRODUCED PER WEEK: 3 million |

Orientation & Information

Cornwall stretches from the River Tamar and the granite hump of Dartmoor in the east all the way to mainland England's most westerly point at Land's End. The principal administrative town, Truro, sits bang in the middle of the county; to the north are the lofty cliffs and surfing beaches of the north coast, while the south coast is a gentler landscape of fields, river estuaries and quiet beaches. The main A30 road cuts through the middle of the county, running roughly parallel with the main-line railway between London Paddington and Penzance; a second major road (the A38) runs east from Plymouth across the Tamar Bridge and along Cornwall's southern edge. See p291 for more detail on ways to get to and from the county and p295 for countywide travel.

Cornwall 24 (www.cornwall24.co.uk) Lively (and usually heated) Cornwall discussion forum.

Cornwall Beach Guide (www.cornwallbeachguide .co.uk) Online guide to the county's finest sand.

Cornwall Online (www.cornwall-online.co.uk) A community-based site with guides to accommodation, walks, attractions, villages and activities.

THE NORTH COAST

If it's the classic Cornish combination of lofty cliffs, sweeping bays and white-horse surf you're after, then make a beeline for the north Cornwall coast. Battered by Atlantic

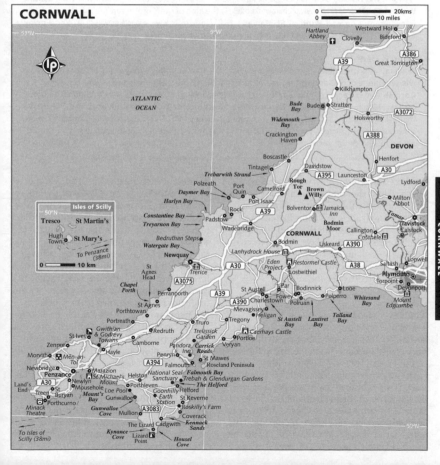

CULINARY KERNOW

Cornwall's cuisine has undergone a renaissance in recent years, with celebrity chefs setting up everywhere you look and gourmet shops springing up across the county. But while Jamie Oliver, Rick Stein and chums take all the plaudits, Cornwall's real stars are its small local producers. Here's a list of our favourite places; for more suggestions check out www.foodfromcornwall .co.uk and www.foodtrails.co.uk, or swing by the annual **Cornwall Food and Drink Festival** (www .cornwallfoodanddrinkfestival.co.uk) held every November in Truro.

The Cornish Classic

The best countywide suppliers of traditionally made pasties are **Rowe the Bakers** (www.wcrowe .com) and **Pengenna Pasties** (www.pengennapasties.co.uk), while Ann Muller's **Lizard Pasty Shop** (p251) on the Lizard and **Chough Bakery** (☎ 01841-533361; www.thechoughbakery.co.uk) in Padstow have both received the seal of approval from Mr Stein.

Seafood

If it's seafood that floats your boat, the best place for fresh fish is straight from the docks. In Newlyn, **WH Harvey & Sons** (☎ 01736-362983) specialises in crab and lobster, while the **Pilchard Works** (☎ 01736-332112; www.pilchardworks.co.uk) is the king of the 'Cornish sardine', aka the pilchard. Elsewhere in Cornwall **Wing of St Mawes** (☎ 01726-861666; www.wingofstmawes.co.uk) and **Fowey Fish** (☎ 01726-832422; www.foweyfish.com) are well-known local fishmongers.

Wine & Beer

Cornwall also specialises in its own local brews. The **Camel Valley Vineyard** (p275) has an award-winning range of reds and whites, as well as a sparkling wine that's champagne in all but name. The **Cornish Cyder Farm** (☎ 01872-573356; info@thecornishcyderfarm.co.uk) produces traditional scrumpy on a working farm in Penhallow. Cornish ale-brewers include **Skinner's Brewery** (☎ 01872-245689; www.skinnersbrewery.com; Truro) and the **St Austell Brewery** (☎ 01726-66022; www.staustellbrewery.co.uk); both supply pubs across the county. Downing a pint of Storm or Tribute is an essential Cornish experience and not to be missed.

breakers and whipped by year-round winds, the stretch of shoreline between Bude and St Ives is arguably the county's most dramatic. Unsurprisingly, this was John Betjeman's favourite corner of Cornwall, but it's far from a well-kept secret these days; the north coast has become a magnet for everyone from beach babes and wannabe surfers to gourmet chefs and celebrity second-homers.

BUDE

☎ 01288 / pop 9242

Travelling west along the grandiosely titled Atlantic Hwy (aka the A39), the first town across the Cornish border is Bude. Nestled at the end of the River Neet and a 19th-century canal (currently undergoing a £3.8 million face-lift), Bude has established itself as a popular family getaway and surfing hangout thanks to its fantastic nearby beaches. Closest to town is **Summerleaze**, a classic bucket-and-spade affair with bags of space at low tide, and just to the north is **Crooklets**, a stretch of sand that often

has decent surf, but gets crowded. For quieter waves try the little cove at **Duckpool**, a couple of miles north. Three miles south of town, **Widemouth Bay** (pronounced widmouth) is another family favourite that's usually jam-packed when the weather's fine, while 5 miles beyond the cliff-backed beach of **Crackington Haven** is Bude's most eye-catching stretch of sand. A little further south is **The Strangles**, where you'll need to break out your birthday suit – it's one of Cornwall's best-known naturist beaches.

There's not that much to Bude itself, other than a smattering of surf stores, cafés and pasty shops, but it's worth strolling down to the town **museum** (☎ 353576; adult/child £1/free; ☀ noon-5pm Mon-Sat Apr-Oct), by the old sea lock, to see its exhibits on Bude's industrial and seafaring heritage.

The **Bude visitor centre** (☎ 354240; www.visitbude .info; The Crescent; ☀ 10am-5pm Mon-Sat, plus 10am-4pm Sun in summer) is in a car park at the end of town, near the rather extravagantly named **Bude Castle**. This small faux-fortress was built in 1830 by the

Cheese

Cornwall's most famous cheese is yarg, a strong, semihard cheese, traditionally wrapped in nettles to develop its distinctive greeny rind. Other local cheeses include Cornish Blue, Cornish Brie and several delicious goat's cheeses; contact **Lynher Dairies** (☎ 01872-870789; www.lynherdairies.co.uk; near Truro), the **Cornish Cheese Co** (☎ 01579-363660; www.cornishcheese.co.uk; Liskeard) or the **Cheese Shop** (☎ 01872-270742; 29 Ferris Town, Truro).

Farm shops

Not just for veg but also organic and traditionally reared meat and eggs, organic cheeses, fruit from private orchards, homemade jams and cakes. Among the best:

Trevelyan Farm (☎ 01736-710410; Perranuthnoe; ☷ 8am-6pm Mon-Sat, 9-5pm Sun) It's located near Penzance.

Gear Farm (☎ 01326-221977; www.lizardleaves.com; St Martin, near Helston)

Cornish Organics (☎ 01209-202579; Four Lanes, near Redruth)

Trevathan Farm (☎ 01208-880164; www.trevathanfarm.com; St Endellion, near Port Isaac; ☷ 9.30am-5.30pm summer)

Lobbs (☎ 01726-844411; www.lobbsfarmshop.com; St Ewe, near Heligan Gardens; ☷ 9.30am-5pm Mon-Sat, 10.30am-4.30pm Sun)

Indulgences

On the gourmet side, **Trenance Chocolate** (p251) in Mullion produces delightful handmade chocolates, while **Roskilly's Farm** (p251) in St Keverne makes award-winning ice creams, yogurts and sorbet. The **Halzephron Herb Farm** (☎ 01326-240652; Gunwalloe) specialises in herbs, marinades and sauces, while the **Buttermilk Shop** (☎ 0845 644 4251; www.buttermilkfudge.co.uk; St Eval), near Wadebridge, still uses traditional copper pans to make its Cornish fudge.

There is a tea plantation in the region – **Tregothnan Estate** (☎ 01872-520000; www.tregothnan. co.uk) near Truro, which sells four brands including afternoon, green and Earl Grey – as well as a coffee producer, **Origin Coffee** (☎ 01326-340320).

crackpot Cornish inventor Sir Goldsworthy Gurney, whose contraptions included a steam-powered carriage, an oxy-hydrogen blowtorch, a musical glass piano and the pioneering 'Bude Light', a super-bright oil-lamp, which later found fame illuminating the House of Commons and Trafalgar Square in London.

Sleeping & Eating

Dylan's Guesthouse (☎ 354705; www.dylansguest houseinbude.co.uk; Downs View; s/d £40/60) Our favourite Bude B&B, with nine fresh, uncluttered rooms decked out in white linen, chocolate throws and pleasant pine, plus Freeview TV, sea prints and groovy chrome-tinged bathroom fixtures. Cheap, sweet and contemporary.

Falcon Hotel (☎ 352005; www.falconhotel.com; d £60; P) This white turret-topped hotel opposite Bude Canal began life as an 18th-century lodging house, but depressingly few traces of its Georgian heritage remain. The plain, peach and pistachio flavoured

rooms are comfy enough, with the odd frill and four-poster, and some have views over the canal.

Camelot Hotel (☎ 0800-7812536; www.camelot -hotel.co.uk; Downs View; s/d £49/98; P ☐) A more traditional option with cheery rooms snuggling behind a whitewashed, garden-wrapped façade. Few surprises, but the simple spic-and-span rooms won't break the bank and the brekkie is stuffed with local produce.

Life's a Beach (☎ 355222; Summerleaze Beach; lunch £4-6, dinner mains £15-17; ☷ Mon-Sat) By day a chaotic California-style beach café churning out ciabattas, coffees and ice creams for the Summerleaze crowd; by night something altogether slinkier – a snazzy bistro serving whole bream, wok-fried tiger prawns and slow-cooked lamb.

Getting There & Away

Bus 595 (three hours, six daily Monday to Saturday, four on Sunday) travels from Bude along the coast via Widemouth, Crackington

CORNWALL

ORGANIC FANTASTIC

our pick **Bangors Organic** (☎ 01288-361297; www.bangorsorganic.co.uk; Poundstock, Bude; r £84-105, ste £97-120; **P**) You can forget about food miles at this fantastic all-organic B&B. The owners grow much of their own produce, from eggs and onions to chickens and courgettes, and everything else is sourced from nearby farms. The stunning rooms are spread over several lodges; the Lundy and Menhir Rooms in the main house are lovely, but for real luxury ask for the split-level Stables Suite, with its stripped-wood floor, freestanding bath and loft-style TV lounge. For breakfast tuck into home-baked focaccia, malthouse loaves, smoked kippers and dry-cured bacon. Why can't all B&Bs be this good?

Haven and Boscastle. From Boscastle the 594 (11 daily Monday to Saturday, four on Sunday) continues to Tintagel and Camelford.

BOSCASTLE
☎ 01840

You couldn't ask for a more picturesque setting for the ancient harbour of Boscastle, burrowed at the base of a steep coombe along Cornwall's wild north shore. But Boscastle's chocolate-box setting backfired in dramatic fashion in August 2004, when the village was devastated by the worst flash floods to hit Britain in more than 50 years. A month's rainfall fell in just a few short hours, sending a tidal wave of 440 million gallons of water tearing through the village, carrying trees, cars and buildings in its wake, and forcing the emergency evacuation of the village by naval helicopter.

The episode was startlingly reminiscent of the flood that levelled the Exmoor village of Lynton (p120) in 1952, killing more than 50 people. Miraculously no one died in the Boscastle flood. Though many of the damaged buildings have been restored or rebuilt, Boscastle's still not quite back to its former self; huge flood-prevention schemes have been installed upriver to prevent future flooding, but no one's sure whether the floods were simply a freak event or a sign of things to come in a world of global warming.

The **visitor centre** (☎ 250010; boscastlevc@btconnect .com; ✆ 10am-5pm Mar-Oct) has been moved from its old home in the main visitor car park to a new location beside the harbour.

Nearby is the quirky **Museum of Witchcraft** (☎ 250111; The Harbour; admission £2.50; ✆ 10.30am-6pm Mon-Sat, 11.30am-6pm Sun) and its eclectic collection of witch-related memorabilia (the world's largest, apparently). Among its artefacts are spooky poppets (a kind of voodoo doll), wooden witch mirrors, enchanted skulls, and a hideous cast-iron 'witch's bridle' designed to extract confessions from suspected hags. Not for the faint-hearted (or the pointy-hatted).

A 3-mile wooded walk leads inland along the River Valency to the **Church of St Juliot**, which the young architect Thomas Hardy was contracted to restore in 1870; he ended up marrying the rector's sister-in-law, Emma Lavinia Gifford, and you can now stay at their former love nest (see below). Several other walking trails snake around the Boscastle scenery – ask at the tourist office for maps and guides.

Sleeping & Eating

Old Rectory (☎ 250225; www.stjuliot.com; St Juliot; d £76-84; ✆ Mar-Nov; **P**) Flowering shrubs and overhanging trees line the drive of this sumptuous double-gabled house, formerly the home of St Juliot's parson, and the place where Thomas Hardy wooed his wife-to-be. Heavy furniture, patterned drapes and eclectic bits of Victoriana pepper the three Hardy-themed rooms, or you could plump for a wood-burner stable with private entrance.

Wellington Hotel (☎ 250202; www.boscastle-wellington.com; The Harbour; d £76-140; **P**) Closer to a fortified castle than a coaching inn, the grand old Welly has welcomed weary travellers for more than 500 years (previous guests include Edward VII, Thomas Hardy and Guy Gibson of *Dambusters* fame). Post-flood, it's back in business as the top traditional hotel in town – bag a turret room for an antique atmosphere, chunky rugs, gentlemen's armchairs and unbeatable views.

Bottreaux Hotel (☎ 250231; www.boscastlecornwall .co.uk; d £80-95; **P**) This elegant little guesthouse makes an ideal Boscastle bolthole, away from the tourist fizz of the main drag but still near the sights. All the rooms are Boscastle-themed, and the best have huge king-size beds, seagrass floors and ghosted-glass sinks.

Other options:

Riverside Hotel (☎ 250216; www.hotelriverside.co.uk; s/d £35/65) Old building meets fresh, modern rooms at this reliable B&B in the heart of the village.

St Christopher's (☎ 250412; www.st-christophers -boscastle.co.uk; High St; d £56-70) Flouncy rooms in tints of lemon and rose inside a former merchant's house; the owners will pack you lunch if you ask sweetly.

Getting There & Away

Buses run between Bude and Boscastle; see p221 for details.

TINTAGEL

☎ 01840 / pop 1822

The spectre of King Arthur looms over the village of Tintagel and its spectacular clifftop **castle** (EH; ☎ 770328; adult/child £4.50/2.30; ⊙ 10am-6pm Apr-Sep, 10am-5pm Oct, 10am-4pm Nov-Mar). Though the present-day ruins mostly date from the 13th century, archaeological digs have revealed the foundations of a much earlier fortress, fuelling speculation that the legendary king may have been born at the castle as local legend claims. Part of the crumbling stronghold stands on a rock tower cut off from the mainland, accessed via a bridge and steep steps (vertigo sufferers beware) and it's still possible to make out several sturdy walls and the castle's interior layout.

Below the castle is a natural **sea cave** rumoured (inevitably) to have been Merlin's hide-out, while a short walk inland is the tiny Norman **Church of St Materiana**, in a fabulous wind-blown spot above Glebe Cliff.

After the natural splendour of the Tintagel headland, the village itself is pretty disappointing, with a motley collection of tearooms, tacky souvenir shops and crystal sellers strung out on the main street. The rickety **Old Post Office** (NT; ☎ 770024; Fore St; adult/child £2.70/1.35; ⊙ 11am-5.30pm daily Jul & Aug, 11am-5.30pm Sun-Fri Mar-Jun & Sep, 11am-4pm Sun-Fri Oct) is worth a look. A beautiful example of a traditional 16th-century Cornish longhouse, it was used as a post office during the 19th century. Rather less authentic are **King Arthur's Great Halls** (☎ 770526; adult/child £3/2; ⊙ 10am-5pm), a weird Arthurian homage built by the retired millionaire Frederick Glasscock

---

THE ONCE AND FUTURE KING

For many people the southwest is inextricably bound up with the legend of **King Arthur**, the mythic warrior-king, heroic knight and fabled protector of the British Isles. The fantastic tale of Merlin, Guinevere, Lancelot and Arthur and his Knights of the Round Table has inspired everything from epic narrative poems to a Disney cartoon, but despite endless hours of research, countless archaeological digs and hundreds of dubious movies, it's still a matter of complete conjecture if Arthur even really existed.

So here are the facts. There was a soldier by the name of Arthur or Arthurus who led a fierce counter-attack against invading Celts sometime in the 6th century; a Welsh monk called Nennius is the first to mention Arthur by name in his *Historia Brittonum*, a historical text written around 800, although Arthur is noticeably absent in the works of other chroniclers of the period such as Bede and Gildas.

The 12th-century historian Geoffrey of Monmouth – a notoriously unreliable scholar – was the first to lay down the basics of Arthur's biography, including his birth and death (c AD 500–42), as well as his genealogy, childhood and ascension to the throne. But Geoffrey almost certainly used a large dollop of Celtic myth to embellish his historical facts, and it's possible he just made much of it up for the sake of a good yarn (naughty chap). However the seed of Arthur's legend had been sewn; later writers including Chrétien de Troyes and Thomas Mallory substantially embellished the story, and Mallory's epic poem *Le Morte d'Arthur*, published in the late 15th century, inspired later retellings including Tennyson's *Idylls of the King* and TH White's *The Once & Future King*.

Many areas in the southwest have staked their claim on an Arthurian connection. Glastonbury Abbey (p107) is the supposed burial place of Arthur and Queen Guinevere, while Glastonbury Tor (p106) is rumoured to be the legendary Isle of Avalon, where Arthur was carried after being mortally wounded by his illegitimate son/nephew, Mordred. But Cornwall has by far the most King Arthur connections, including Tintagel (above), supposedly the site of Arthur's stronghold and Merlin's Cave. To the north is Slaughterbridge (p275), near Camelford, asserted to be the site of Arthur's last battle at Camlann, while Dozmary Pool (p276) and Loe Pool (p249) both claim to be the mystical home of the Lady of the Lake.

in the 1930s. Fake stone thrones, round tables and 72 stained-glass windows gamely attempt to bring Arthur's tale to life, but it just goes to prove the old adage that money definitely can't buy you taste.

The well-stocked **tourist office** (☎ 779084; tintagelvc@btconnect.com; Bossiney Rd; ☙ 10am-5pm Mar-Oct, 10.30am-4pm Nov-Feb) has plenty of background on the Arthur story, as well as good walking guides to the area.

Sleeping & Eating

Headland Caravan & Camping (☎ 770239; headland .caravan@btconnect.com; Atlantic Rd; sites £15-17) Spacious camp site on the opposite headland to the castle, with a laundry, small shop and Atlantic views.

Bosayne Guest House (☎ 770514; www.bosayne .co.uk; Atlantic Rd; d £50-60) This Victorian town house is your best bet in Tintagel village. The décor is bright and cheery, livened up by cast-iron beds and mini-fridges, although the attic rooms feel a bit boxy.

Camelot Castle Hotel (☎ 770202; www.camelotcastle .com; Atlantic Rd; r £78-200; **P**) This comically kitsch hotel stands in a glorious location opposite the castle, and was built in 1899 for Victorian tourists by the Cornish architect Sylvanus Trevail. The décor has hardly changed since – ancient carpets, battered TVs and 70s furniture colonise the antediluvian rooms, but the sea views are striking, and there's even a grand Arthurian lounge complete with round table. Daft, dated fun.

Mill House (☎ 770200; themillhouseinn.co.uk; Trebarwith; d £90-110; ▣) In a peaceful valley halfway between Tintagel and Port Isaac, this converted mill is crammed with Cornish character: an atmospheric bar-restaurant boasting heavy wooden beams, solid Delabole slate and high-grade food (mains £13.95 to £16.25), plus nine elegant rooms finished in calming creams, crisp linen and dark wood.

Lewis's Tea Rooms (☎ 770427; Bossiney Rd; lunches £4.75-6.25) This ivy-covered house serves up Tintagel's top cream teas, either in the sunny front garden or the suitably frilly salon inside.

Getting There & Away

For buses to and from Tintagel, see p221.

PORT ISAAC

☎ 01208

With its heavy-duty harbour and atmospheric alleyways, cottages and slender *opes* (lanes),

Port Isaac is one of north Cornwall's most attractive ports. Its aesthetic appeal certainly isn't lost on second-homers and film directors – umpteen celebs have their holiday homes in Port Isaac, and the British film *Saving Grace* and the TV series of *Doc Martin* both used the village as a ready-made backdrop. It's a lovely base for exploring Cornwall's northwest corner; there's a clutch of top-notch pubs and restaurants, as well as a tangle of atmospheric backstreets (look out for Squeezy Belly Alley), plus the neighbouring harbour of **Port Gaverne**. Just south of Port Isaac is the rocky cove of **Port Quin**, an old fishing cove now owned by the National Trust, and a great spot for digging in the rock pools to see what the tide's brought in.

Sleeping & Eating

Anchorage (☎ 880629; www.anchorageportisaac.co.uk; d from £56) Soothing views, simple rooms and a warm and welcoming owner make this uphill B&B worth considering if you're on a budget.

ourpick Old School Hotel (☎ 880721; www.the oldschoolhotel.co.uk; Fore St; d from £60; **P**) Laurence Llewellyn-Bowen (who owns a house in Port Isaac) helped out with the redesign of this quirky, utterly delightful small hotel, originally Port Isaac's schoolhouse. The 14 rooms are named after school subjects and are eccentrically furnished in mix-and-match style. Some are festooned with scatter cushions, pin stripes, and bold primary colours, others boast exposed stone walls, curved-oak trusses, higgledy-piggledy layouts and arched windows overlooking the harbour. One to savour. Meals are available (mains from £14).

Port Gaverne Inn (☎ 880244; Port Gaverne; d £60; **P**) A classic, old coastal inn with all the shipshape trappings (log fires, low-beamed bar, slate flagstones) and an ever-faithful local crowd, plus cholesterol-packed pub staples and cosy old-school rooms.

Bay Hotel (☎ 880380; jacki.burns@talk21.com; The Terrace; d £75-99; **P**) An upmarket B&B with smartly furnished rooms and a vaguely Victorian air; gourmet teas and a well-stocked honesty bar keep it a cut above its competitors.

Long Cross Hotel (☎ 880243; www.longcrosshotel .co.uk; Trelights; d £100-150; **P** ▣) Gorgeous digs with a gentlemanly feel in this Trelights town house; chilled-colour throws, black-leather armchairs and lustrous wood furniture in the rooms, some with views, some not.

Honeymooners should book the garden at the bottom-of-the-garden 'Love Shack', with its open-plan sitting room and free-standing shower, while families can plump for a stonking great converted stable.

Golden Lion (☎ 880386; Fore St) Another salty old boozer just a stone's throw from the slipway, with seaside tables and St Austell ales on tap.

Getting There & Away

The 584 bus (hourly Monday to Saturday) scuttles between Wadebridge and Camelford, stopping at Port Quin, Port Isaac and Port Gaverne.

Space is tight for cars in Port Isaac, so your best bet is to park in the main car park at the top of the village and take a stroll down the hill.

PADSTOW & AROUND

☎ 01841 / pop 3162

The epicentre of Cornwall's culinary scene is Padstow, a workaday fishing harbour turned gastronomic giant thanks to celebrity chef, TV star and local food champion Rick Stein. Before Stein pitched up in Padstow the town was principally a centre for the north-coast fishing industry, but over the last decade the place has been reinvented as a kind of pocket-sized Knightsbridge-by-the-sea, with a profusion of posh boutiques and upmarket eateries sitting side-by-side with the huddle of homely pubs, pasty shops and cafés around the old harbour. It's a curious mix, but despite its chichi surface, it's hard not to be charmed by Padstow's seaside setting, and if you're looking for a taste of contemporary Cornish cuisine then this is definitely the place.

The **tourist office** (☎ 533449; padstowtic@btconnect .com; North Quay; ☼ 10am-5pm Mon-Sat) offers the usual selection of leaflets, maps and walking trails, as well as tickets for boat trips and the Eden Project.

Sights & Activities

PRIDEAUX PLACE

Much favoured by directors of costume dramas, the stately manor house of **Prideaux Place** (☎ 532 411; www.prideauxplace.co.uk; admission £7, grounds only £2; ☼ 12.30-5pm Sun-Thu Easter Sun–mid-Apr & mid-May–Oct) was built by the Prideaux-Brune family, purportedly descendants of William the Conqueror. Fans of English architecture will be in seventh heaven, with a feast of state rooms, grand staircases and ornately carved ceilings. Youngsters will be less thrilled, but can always keep an eye out for one of the ghosts said to stalk the house's creaky corridors.

ST ENODOC CHURCH

Across the estuary from Padstow is the ultraexclusive enclave of **Rock**, for long the second-home venue of choice for well-heeled celebrities and rich retirees. Before the moneybags rolled in, the area's claim to fame was poet John Betjeman; he spent many summer holidays in the area, both as nipper and grown-up, and recalled this stretch of coastline in many of his poems – notably in *Trebetherick*, with its classic (and much-quoted) lines:

Sand in the sandwiches, wasps in the tea,
Sun on our bathing dresses heavy with the wet,
Squelch of the bladder-wrack waiting for the sea.

After his death in 1984, Betjeman was buried in the tranquil hilltop chapel of St Enodoc, just north of Rock. The walk up to the church is worth the effort, with sweeping views across the Camel Estuary and Daymer Bay, and you can still visit the old boy's grave, unmissable thanks to its florid slate headstone.

CORNWALL

GOING NATIVE

Tired of boring old B&Bs and sardine-can camp sites? Then we've got just the answer. **Cornish Tipi Holidays** (☎ 01208 880781; www.cornish-tipi-holidays.co.uk; Pendoggett, St Kew; per week £495-555) offers traditionally made tepees in an idyllic quarry filled with foxgloves and birdsong, 10 minutes' drive from Port Isaac. **Yurtworks** (☎ 850670; www.yurtworks.co.uk; St Breward; per week £275-345), offers ash-framed Mongolian yurts filled with posh rugs, puffy cushions and wood-burning stoves in a woodland spot on Bodmin Moor; it's all fittingly ecofriendly (composting toilet, charcoal, hen-laid eggs) and offers courses in bushcraft skills including longbow making and yurt making. Ray Mears would be proud.

'OSS ANTICS

Padstow is famous for its chaotic **'Obby 'Oss ceremony**, an annual May Day festival (or 2 May if it falls on a Sunday), believed to derive from an ancient pagan fertility rite. The ritual begins just before midnight on 30 April, when revellers announce to the innkeeper at the Golden Lion that summer is 'a-come'. At 10am the next morning the Blue Ribbon (or Peace) Oss – a man garbed in a huge hooped sailcloth dress and snapping horse headdress – dances around the town, accompanied by a baton-wielding 'teazer' and a retinue of flower-covered musicians, dancers, singers and drummers, all singing the traditional May Song. An hour later he's followed by the Old (or Red) Oss with his own team of musicians and dancers, then by a day of revelling, sing-ing, carousing and general high jinks, before the 'osses are both 'stabled' for another year. It's all eerily reminiscent of the classic British horror flick *The Wicker Man*, but unlike Edward Woodward's unfortunate Sgt Howie you'll need to book ahead if you're planning on staying in town.

CAMEL TRAIL

In his autobiography *Summoned By Bells* Betjeman fondly remembered the train ride to Cornwall from Waterloo, especially the coastal stretch between Bodmin and Padstow. Although the railway line closed in the late 1960s, it's been redeveloped as the Camel Trail, one of Cornwall's most popular cycling tracks. The trail starts in Padstow and runs east through Wadebridge (5.8 miles), Bodmin (11 miles) to Poley's Bridge (17 miles) on Bodmin Moor (see p273). The Padstow–Wadebridge section makes a lovely half-day excursion from Pad-stow, either on foot or two wheels, but it gets crowded in summer; the Wadebridge–Bodmin section is much quieter and just as scenic.

Bikes can be hired from both ends; in Padstow, **Padstow Cycle Hire** (☎ 533533; www .padstowcyclehire.com; South Quay; ⊙ 9am-5pm) and **Brinhams** (☎ 532594; South Quay; ⊙ 9am-5pm) hire bikes for around £10 to £15 per day.

BOAT TRIPS

Several boat trips chug out into the Camel Estuary. One, the **Jubilee Queen** (☎ 521093) offers trips (adult £6) around the bay and offshore islands, with a chance of spotting sea birds, seals and even a basking shark in summer. For a more exciting pace there are 15-minute **speedboat trips** (☎ 07811 113380; ⊙ Easter-Oct) past the treacherous sandbank of Doom Bar and the beaches of Daymer Bay, Polzeath, Hawkers Cove and Tregirls. The **Boy Darren** (☎ 07800 553329) runs daily mackerel and wreck fishing trips.

The *Black Tor* ferry crosses the estuary (£2 return) to Rock between 8am and 7.50pm in summer and to 4.30pm in winter, supple-mented by a nightly **water taxi** (☎ 862815; adult/child return £5/3) from 7pm to midnight April to mid-July, September and October; 7.30pm to midnight mid-July and August – handy if you've had a night out in Polzeath.

BEACHES

Padstow is ringed by stunning beaches. A few miles west around Trevose Head are the surfing beaches of **Constantine** and **Harlyn Bays**, both with crystal-clear water and great swimming; the attractive coves of **Mother Ivey's Bay** and **Treyarnon** are often chock-a-block with people from the nearby caravan parks. Further along the coast is **Porthcothan**, framed by steep cliffs and usually less tour-isty than its neighbours.

On the opposite side of the estuary from Padstow is **Polzeath**, which usually plays second fiddle to Newquay in the surf-ing stakes, but is actually a more pleas-ant place to learn to ride the waves. **Surf's Up Surf School** (☎ 862003; www.surfsupsurfschool .com) and **Animal Surf Academy** (☎ 0870 242 2856; asa@wavehunters.co.uk) have outlets on the beach, and **Ann's Cottage** (☎ 869924; www.annscottagesurf .co.uk) rents boards, wetsuits and fins (check its website for surfing tips and beach web-cams). Polzeath is a popular hangout for the north coast's beach crowd, with plenty of surfers' bars and ramshackle pubs to keep you entertained.

Sleeping

If the prices in Padstow are too rich for your pocket, you'll find cheaper sleeps along the estuary in Wadebridge. The surrounding countryside is packed with camp sites; we've suggested a couple, but the tourist office has full details.

HOSTELS & CAMPSITES

Dennis Cove (☎ 532349; www.denniscove.co.uk; camp sites £10-15; ☺ Easter-Oct) Popular family campground 10 minutes' walk from Padstow beside the Camel Trail. There's room for campers and caravans, plus a shiny shower block and laundry area – and the seaside is just steps away.

Padstow Touring Park (☎ 532061; www.padstowtour ingpark.co.uk; Trerethern; camp sites £14.50-25.50; ☺ Easter-Oct) Another well-run field camp site, signposted a mile from Padstow. Choose a standard site or upgrade to superior (with electricity hook-up) or Kernow (with private bathroom and water tap).

Treyarnon Bay YHA Hostel (☎ 0870 770 6076; Tregonnan; dm £15.50; ☐P☐X☐☐) This 1930s beach house has been rejigged into arguably Cornwall's best hostel, in an unbeatable spot above Treyarnon Bay, topped off by a café with home-cooking, designer lounge and comfy dorms with top-drawer sea views. Summer BBQs, surf packages, beach games and tent space are available, too.

HOTELS & B&BS

Molesworth Manor (☎ 540292; www.molesworthmanor .co.uk; Little Petherick; d £56-104; ☐P☐) Live (or at least sleep) like the lord of the manor at this eye-shreddingly grand mansion in Little Petherick, with a plethora of (slightly shabby) heritage-style rooms stuffed with rocking horses, mahogany wardrobes and vintage rugs, and a converted cottage in the manor grounds.

Ballaminers House (☎ 540933; www.ballamin ershouse.co.uk; Little Petherick; tw/d £60/80; ☐P☐) Once owned by the Prideaux clan, this smart stone farmhouse outside Padstow represents a happy marriage between old-world atmosphere and modern elegance. Expect calming and uncluttered rooms, dotted with Balinese furniture, antique chests and glossy magazines, plus sweeping views of fields and farmland from every window.

Althea Library (☎ 532717; www.althealibrary.co.uk; 27 High St; d £74-116; ☐P☐X☐) As cosy as they come, this homely guesthouse has three rooms squashed in under the roof beams of a listed cottage, plus a roomier 'nook suite' annexe. Guests can use a little A-frame lounge, complete with CD player and board games for those inevitable rainy days.

Treverbyn House (☎ 532855; www.treverbynhouse .com; Station Rd; d from £75) Harry Potter would feel at home at this imposing villa, complete with five colour-coded rooms (eg lilac, pink, green)

plus an extra-romantic turret hideaway. Pine beds, pocket-sprung mattresses, roll-top baths and a choice of three breakfasts make this a top Padstow choice.

St Ervan Manor (☎ 01841 540255; info@stervanmanor .co.uk; St Ervan; r £140-160; ☐P☐X☐) Having bagged several national awards, this palatial B&B is rightly one of Padstow's most prestigious places to stay. It's pricey, but worth every penny, with lavish bedrooms, a regal lounge, private garden as well as a Michelin-starred restaurant.

Eating

London Inn (☎ 532444; Lanadwell St) One of a brace of fishermen's boozers on Lanadwell St, fronted by flower baskets and stocked with crab sarnies, local music and St Austell ales.

Rojano's (☎ 532796; 9 Mill Sq; pizzas £4-8, pasta £6-10; ☺ lunch & dinner Tue-Sun) Despite all the fine dining on offer in town, sometimes nothing more than a plain old bowl of pasta will do. Thankfully this laid-back restaurant can cater for your cravings, with all the Italian standards from authentic bolognese to pizzas spun on the premises.

Rick Stein's Café (☎ 532700; Middle St; mains £8.50-15; ☺ closed Sun) Stripped-down versions of Stein's Seafood Restaurant fare are on offer at this continental backstreet café-bistro. It's buzzy and busy, with a faint seaside feel; everything from homemade carrot cake to grilled mackerel fillets colonise the specials blackboard.

Margot's Bistro (☎ 533441; 11 Duke St; mains £11.50-14.95; ☺ lunch & dinner Tue-Sat) Just nine tables at this dinky little bistro, so you'll need to book, but for those in the know this is one of Padstow's gems, with a fresh British menu taking in baked cod, guinea fowl and sticky toffee pudding.

Pescadou (☎ 532359; South Quay; mains £14-18; ☺ lunch & dinner) Fish, fish and more fish distinguishes this brightly-toned brasserie in the town's old excise house, but if you're tired of turbot you could always plump for rumpsteak or corn-fed chicken washed down by Duchy Bitter at the Old Custom House next door.

No 6 (☎ 532093; 6 Middle St; mains from around £15; ☺ dinner Wed-Sun) Another first-rate place to add to Padstow's packed address book, with a Mediterranean-inspired menu, a commitment to local produce, and a choice of quiet courtyard or intimate white-walled dining room.

THE STEIN EFFECT

Building on the success of the original Seafood Restaurant, Stein's property portfolio has swelled to encompass half of Padstow. If you can't bag a table at the Seafood or the spin-off café, you could munch on a muffin from the **Stein Patisserie** (Lanadwell St; 9am-7pm Mon-Sat, 10am-5pm Sun), dine in style at **St Petroc's Bistro** (New St; lunch & dinner), or tuck into boutique battered cod from **Stein's Fish & Chips** (South Quay; noon-2.30pm & 5-9pm, takeaway noon-9pm). Still not sick of Stein? Swing by the **Stein Deli** (South Quay; 9am-7pm Mon-Sat, 10am-5pm Sun) next door for chutneys and cheeses, pick up his cookbooks at the **Stein Gift Shop** (Middle St; 9am-7pm Mon-Sat, 10am-5pm Sun), follow a cookery course at the Seafood School, or kip at **St Edmunds House** (St Edmunds La; r £260) or **St Petroc's Hotel** (New St; d £125-195). Stein gets notoriously tetchy at the merest mention of Pad-stein – but really, Rick, it's hardly surprising, is it?

Contact the **Stein central switchboard** (532700; www.rickstein.com) for all enquiries.

Most of the chefs are ex–Gordon Ramsay, so odds are this place'll have the Michelin seal before the year is out.

Seafood Restaurant (532700; www.rickstein.com; Riverside; mains £17.50-45; lunch & dinner) The brick that built the Stein empire, and still the best of the bunch. It's less starchy than you might think, with a conservatory for predinner tipples, a bubbly dining room draped with potted plants and local art, and a chaotic kitchen glimpsed through swing doors. Unsurprisingly, superb seafood is the menu's cornerstone, and pretty much all the produce is certified Cornish. You'll need friends in high places to get a table, but this is one place that lives up to the hype.

Getting There & Away

Bus 555 goes to Bodmin Parkway (50 minutes, at least hourly Monday to Saturday) via Little Petherick, St Issey and Wadebridge. The 556 (hourly Monday to Saturday, six on Sunday) travels down the coast via several beaches including Trevone, Harlyn and Porthcothan, veering inland to Newquay airport (50 minutes) and Newquay (one hour 20 minutes).

NEWQUAY

01637 / pop 19,423
Hawaii smacks headlong into Ibiza on the streets of Newquay, the capital of British surfing and Cornwall's busiest and brashest tourist town. Strung out along the cliffs above a cluster of white-sand beaches, it's a weird mix of family resort, theme park and full-on party town, where sun-bleached surfers jostle for space with boozed-up clubbers, high-heeled hen parties and white-shirted footie fans. Love it or loathe it, there's no escaping the fact that Newquay sits slap bang in the centre of one of

Cornwall's best bits of coastline, but in summer it can be pretty hard to see beyond the chiming amusement arcades, greasy spoons and chucked-away chip wrappers. If you're looking to appreciate the area's more natural charms, it's probably best to give summer a miss and come back when the beer boys have hightailed it for home.

Information

Laundrette (875901; 1 Beach Pde, Beach Rd)
Laundrette (876558; Manor Rd)
Post office (08457 223344; East St)
Quintdown (875242; 11 Trevena Tce; per min 5p; 10am-5.30pm Mon-Sat) Internet access.
Tad & Nick's Talk'n'Surf (874868; 72 Fore St; per min/hr 5p/£3; 10am-6pm) Internet access.
Tourist office (854020; www.newquay.co.uk; Marcus Hill; 9.30am-5.30pm Mon-Sat, 9.30am-12.30pm Sun)
www.newquaynet.com Useful local listings site, with an events calendar and club guide.

Sights & Activities
BEACHES

The town beaches of **Great Western**, **Tolcarne** and **Towan** are nearly always crammed to capacity with windbreaks and beach tents thanks to their proximity to town. Things are usually quieter along the coastline at **Lusty Glaze** and **Porth**, while surfers haunt the ever-reliable waves of **Fistral**, England's most famous surfing beach, and the location for the annual Rip Curl Boardmasters surfing festival. Despite the summer crowds, all the town beaches offer decent facilities and great swimming, plus beach lifeguards throughout the season.

If the town beaches are too hectic, you'll find more elbow-room further afield. Some 3 miles southwest is **Crantock**, sandwiched between the twin headlands of East and West Pentire, and backed by grassy dunes and the fast-flowing River Gannel. Further west is the family favourite of **Holywell Bay**, with powder-soft sand and rockpools and caves to explore at low tide.

East of Newquay is the broad, flat beach of **Watergate Bay**, home to the latest branch of Jamie Oliver's Fifteen restaurant and a fast-growing centre for adventure sports. A few miles further east are the stately rock towers of **Bedruthan Steps** (sometimes called Carnewas), a haven for sea birds and an irresistible challenge for the county's rock climbers. Though the beach practically disappears at high tide, Bedruthan is always a spectacular spot for a clifftop stroll, and there's a small National Trust café where you can seek shelter when the Atlantic wind gets up.

OTHER SIGHTS

On the headland between Towan and Fistral stands the 14th-century **Huer's House**, a lookout once used for spotting approaching pilchard shoals. Until they were fished out in the 20th century, these shoals were enormous: one catch of 1868 netted a record 16.5 million fish.

Back towards town, the **Blue Reef Aquarium** (☎ 878134; www.bluereefaquarium.co.uk; Towan Promenade; adult/child/family £7.95/5.50/22; ⏰ 10am-5pm) on Towan Beach is home to some weird and wonderful underwater characters, including jellyfish, seahorses, octopi and rays. Several

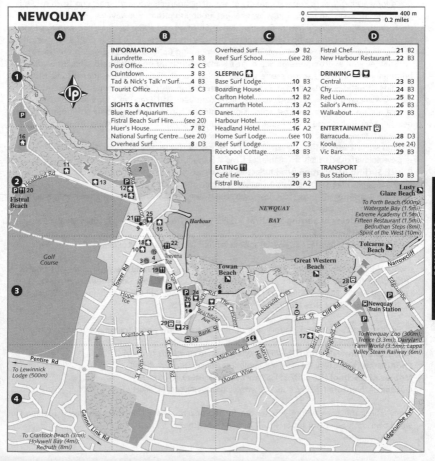

NEWQUAY

0 ────── 400 m
0 ────── 0.2 miles

INFORMATION		
Laundrette	1	B3
Post Office	2	C3
Quintdown	3	B3
Tad & Nick's Talk'n'Surf	4	B3
Tourist Office	5	C3

SIGHTS & ACTIVITIES		
Blue Reef Aquarium	6	C3
Fistral Beach Surf Hire	(see 20)	
Huer's House	7	B2
National Surfing Centre	(see 20)	
Overhead Surf	8	D3

Overhead Surf	9	B2
Reef Surf School	(see 28)	

SLEEPING		
Base Surf Lodge	10	B3
Boarding House	11	A2
Carlton Hotel	12	B2
Carnmarth Hotel	13	A2
Danes	14	B2
Harbour Hotel	15	B2
Headland Hotel	16	A2
Home Surf Lodge	(see 10)	
Reef Surf Lodge	17	C3
Rockpool Cottage	18	B3

EATING		
Café Irie	19	B3
Fistral Blu	20	A2

Fistral Chef	21	B2
New Harbour Restaurant	22	B3

DRINKING		
Central	23	B3
Chy	24	B3
Red Lion	25	B2
Sailor's Arms	26	B3
Walkabout	27	B3

ENTERTAINMENT		
Barracuda	28	D3
Koola	(see 24)	
Vic Bars	29	B3

TRANSPORT		
Bus Station	30	B3

CORNWALL

tanks are open-topped so you can touch the fish.

More wild beasties reside at **Newquay Zoo** (☎ 873342; www.newquayzoo.co.uk; Trenance Gardens; adult/child/family £8.95/6/25; ☯ 9:30am-6pm Apr-Sep, 10am-5pm Oct-Mar), 10 minutes' walk along Edgcumbe Ave, or a quick (and mortifying) trip aboard the tourist choo-choo. The zoo's resident population ranges from red pandas, sloths and penguins to great-horned owls and an African lion called Connie; latest arrivals include red-fronted macaws, two ruffed lemurs and a litter of impossibly cute baby marmosets. Budding David Bellamys can play keeper for a day for £85.

Newquay is surrounded by several other family-friendly attractions that'll entertain the kids and have the parents reaching for the hipflask. Pony rides, billy goats and cow milking are on offer at **Dairyland Farm World** (☎ 510246; www.dairylandfarmworld.com; adult/child/family £7.95/6.95/28; ☯ 10am-5pm late Mar-Oct). Alternatively, you could see the world (in plastic Brobdingnagian form) at the **World in Miniature** (☎ 01872-572828; Halt Rd, Goonhavern) or ride the rails aboard Ronnie Corbett–sized

---

SURF'S UP, DUDE

With a bevy of world-class beaches and Britain's most reliable swells, Newquay is the UK's premier place for learning to surf. You'll see plenty of wannabe boarders wandering around town decked out in the latest kit, but surprisingly few ever get around to hitting the waves – and for those who do, it can be a notoriously frustrating experience. Surfing has a steep learning curve, but as long as you're not expecting to be Laird Hamilton in a day, most people find that after a few lessons they've mastered the basics of catching a wave, 'popping-up' and standing up on the board.

Whether you're a complete novice or just want to brush up on your board skills, Newquay is brimming over with surf schools, offering everything from half-day taster lessons (£25 to £30) to full-blown multiday 'surfaris' (from £135). Make sure you go with a BSA-accredited operator (British Surfing Association; www.britsurf.co.uk), which guarantees you'll receive a high level of coaching from a qualified teacher. The best schools offer minibus trips to some of Cornwall's other surfing beaches (not just Fistral) and of high-quality equipment; don't be shy to shop around.

Reputable operators:

Animal Surf Academy (Polzeath; ☎ 0870 242 2856; asa@wavehunters.co.uk; Tolcarne; ☎ 01637-858808; asa@overheadsurf.co.uk) Outlets on Tolcarne Beach and at Polzeath, near Padstow.

British Surfing Association (www.nationalsurfingcentre.com; Fistral; ☎ 01637-850737; Lusty Glaze; ☎ 01637-851487) The BSA has its National Surfing Centre on Fistral Beach.

Extreme Academy (☎ 01637-860840; www.extremeacademy.co.uk; Watergate Bay) Also offers lessons in kitebuggying, mountainboarding and waveskiing.

Gwithian Academy of Surfing (☎ 01736-755493; www.surfacademy.co.uk) Another excellent operator based at Gwithian Beach (p239).

Reef Surf School (☎ 01637-879059; Great Western Beach; www.reefsurfschool.com)

If you're just looking to hire equipment, lots of surf shops around Newquay hire out boards (£10/25/45 for one/three/seven days) and wetsuits (£5/12/25 for one/three/seven days). Try **Overhead Surf** (☎ 01637-850808; ☯ 9am-6pm; Great Western Beach 19 Cliff Rd; Harbour Beach 1 Beacon Rd) or **Fistral Beach Surf Hire** (☎ 01637-850584; Fistral Beach).

For seasoned surfers looking for more thrills and spills, how about trying kitesurfing, coasteering or sea kayaking?

Adventure Cornwall (☎ 01726-870844; www.adventurecornwall.co.uk; Fowey)

EboAdventure (☎ 0800 781 6861; www.penhaleadventure.com; Holywell Bay)

Mobius Kite School (☎ 01637-831383; www.mobiusonline.co.uk; Cubert)

Outdoor Adventure (☎ 01288 362900; www.outdooradventure.co.uk; Bude)

Lastly, check the swell before you set out for the beach – www.a1surf.com and www.magicseaweed.com both have surf reports for Cornwall's beaches.

steam trains at **Lappa Valla Steam Railway** (☎ 01872-510317; www.lappavalley.co.uk; St Newlyn East; adult/child/family £9.20/7.50/29; ☼ 10.30am-5pm Apr-Sep, 10.30am-4pm Tue-Thu & Sun Oct & Nov). Weirdest of all, at **Spirit of the West** (☎ 881160; www .wildwestthemepark.co.uk; adult/child/family £7/5/22; ☼ 10.30am-5pm Sun-Thu May-Sep) near St Columb, dodgily dressed Cornish gunslingers shoot it out around a *gin-u-wine* Wild West theme park, stables, saloon and all. Yee-ha, pardner. Weird.

Sleeping

BUDGET

Newquay is stuffed with hostels and surf lodges catering for the influx of surfers and stag-dos, but look before you book – some are in dire need of some TLC (or demolition, depending on your point of view).

Base Surf Lodge (☎ 874852; www.basesurflodge .com; 20 Tower Rd; dm £15-20) A superior surf lodge; slatted blinds, tiled floors and big sunset murals brighten up the lounge-bar, while pine bunk beds and off-white walls characterise the upstairs dorms.

Reef Surf Lodge (☎ 879058; www.reefsurflodge .info; 10-12 Berry Rd; dm £15-29.50; ☐) Don't be fooled by the flashy website – underneath the glitzy trappings of plasma-screen TVs and retro furniture, this is still your bog-standard surf lodge. It's cleaner, smarter and more efficient than many others round town, but the beds are saggy and it gets chronically overbooked.

Home Surf Lodge (☎ 873387; 18 Tower Rd; dm £16-20; ☐) Next door to Base, this is a more basic affair, with the usual boarding-school dorm rooms, plus free net access and a DVD lounge and licensed bar.

Boarding House (☎ 873258; www.theboardinghouse .co.uk; 32 Headland Rd; dm £20-25; ☐) The pick of Newquay's surf lodges sits on Towan Headland, with a lively-café-bar peppered with yucca plants and Indonesian furniture. There's a great sundeck overlooking the golf course but, as usual, the dorm beds are crammed in tighter than a tin of pilchards.

Camping

Porth Beach (☎ 876531; www.porthbeach.co.uk; sites £14-27) Popular tourist park just off Porth, with packed-in sites, hook-ups for power and satellite TV, and an award-winning loo block.

MIDRANGE & TOP-END

Danes (☎ 878130; www.thedanes.co.uk; 4 Dane Rd; d £50-60) Decent if dull rooms in a slightly school-marmish guesthouse on Dane Rd, redeemed by its weekly rates.

Rockpool Cottage (☎ 870848; www.rockpoolcottage .co.uk; 92 Fore St; d from £60) Laminate floors, white walls, pine furniture and an excellent brekkie in bed make this a top choice; plus it's run by an ex-surfing champion, so surfing tips come gratis.

Carlton Hotel (☎ 872658; www.carltonhotelnewquay .co.uk; 6 Dane Rd; d £60-70; ⓟ ☒) Swanky rooms, frilly edged beds, DVD players and country-cream furnishings run throughout this upmarket (and slightly snooty) B&B, on a quiet terrace just off Headland Rd.

Carnmarth Hotel (☎ 872519; www.carnmarth .com; Headland Rd; d depending on season £65-100; ⓟ ▯) Newquay's package-holiday image might be about to change thanks to the Carnmarth, which is slowly swapping its out-of-date trappings for a pared-back, minimal aesthetic. Rooms are erratic, but most boast calm neutral tones and unfussy furniture. The funky decked C-Bar is a highlight, too.

Headland Hotel (☎ 872211; www.headlandhotel .co.uk; Fistral Beach; d £80-302; ⓟ ▯ ▣) Memorably featured in the film of Roald Dahl's *The Witches*, this red-brick pile stands aloof on the Fistral Headland. It's all about old-style pampering – the ritzy rooms range from budget singles to ornate sea-view suites, and the facilities include heated swimming pools, tennis courts and a nine-hole golf course.

Harbour Hotel (☎ 873040; www.harbourhotel.co.uk; North Quay Hill; s/d £90/140; ▯) This intimate hotel is a real find, with a fantastic harbour aspect and beach-view balconies that feel far removed from the summertime throng. Bedrooms are classic in feel, with wrought-iron bedsteads, pleated cotton sheets and polished furniture, backed up by a conservatory and swish bar downstairs.

Eating

Café Irie (☎ 859200; Fore St; lunch £3-6) Run by surfers for surfers, this technicolour twin-floored café is famous for its hot chocolate – just the ticket after a cold morning in the ocean swell – plus veggie wraps, piping-hot jacket potatoes and gooey cakes.

CORNWALL

Fistral Chef (☎ 850718; 2 Beacon Rd; breakfasts £2-6, mains £6-10; ✆ breakfast & lunch) Fantastic fry-ups and chunky sandwiches are the mainstays of this popular all-day café, which champions its all-day breakfast as the best in town and opens for Thai meals several nights a week.

Fistral Blu (☎ 879444; Fistral Beach; mains £7-19; ✆ lunch & dinner) Right on Fistral Beach, this modern glass-fronted eatery experiments with Thai and Mediterranean flavours, as well as Cornish standards such as fish pie and local scallops. Less formal fare is available at the downstairs café.

Lewinnick Lodge (☎ 878117; Pentire Headland; mains £9-12.25) Nestled on Pentire Head, this lively gastropub wins the sea-view prize hands down, with a grassy terrace and gloss-wood dining room offering panoramic Atlantic vistas. The food's not bad, either, with mains including rump steak, chargrilled chicken and confit of duck.

New Harbour Restaurant (☎ 874062; South Quay Hill; mains £10-15; ✆ lunch & dinner) Refined dining by the harbourside, with fishy treats from roast cod, crab claws and monkfish medallions to a king-sized *fruits de mers*. Food is cooked in the outside grill-shack while you sip cold Chablis with a view of bobbing fishing boats. Divine.

Chy (☎ 873415; www.the-chy.co.uk; 12 Beach Rd; mains £11-18) Chrome, wood and leather dominate this stylish café-bar with a patio above Towan Beach. Perfect for a gourmet breakfast or lunchtime salad, or pitch up late when the DJs take to the decks, the beers flow and the beautiful people arrive en masse.

Drinking & Entertainment

Newquay is Cornwall's party central, but come prepared for alco-pops and cheesy choons rather than anything classy. Most have a weekend cover-charge and stay open till 2am or 3am.

Koola (☎ 873415; www.thekoola.com; 12 Beach Rd) Underneath Chy, Koola is the choice for connoisseur clubbers, with regular house, Latin and drum and bass nights, and a regular slot for local boys Jelly Jazz.

Walkabout (☎ 853000; The Crescent; ✆ noon-11pm Mon, Wed & Sun, noon-2am Tue, noon-midnight Thu & Fri, noon-1am Sat) This cavernous Aussie-styled bar is popular for big-screen sports and cocktail nights, plus party, pop and house DJs on weekends.

Central (☎ 878310; 11 Central Sq) Bang in the centre of town, the rowdy Central is a Newquay institution for a pre-club warm-up, and the spacious front terrace is always overflowing when the weather's warm.

Red Lion (☎ 871195; North Quay Hill) Old surfer's pub with regular live music and plenty of ales on tap.

Vic Bars (☎ 872671; King St) Grungy venue that's good for local bands on Friday and Saturday night.

Barracuda (☎ 875800; www.barracudanewquay.com; 27-29 Cliff Rd; ✆ 9pm-3am) One of Newquay's biggest nightclubs, hosting everything from karaoke to hen parties and big-name house DJs.

Sailor's Arms (☎ 872838; Fore St) Notoriously low-rent pub-club where the main emphasis is on rock-bottom booze. Shy and retiring types should steer clear.

Getting There & Away

Newquay Airport (☎ 860600; www.newquaycornwall airport.com) has regular flights to various UK cities. Ryanair has at least one daily flight to London Stansted, while Air Southwest has up to four daily flights to London Gatwick via Plymouth. Other UK airports served include Cardiff, Dublin, Belfast, Edinburgh and the Isles of Scilly. Bus 556 travels hourly to the airport from Newquay from 9am to 6pm, with a few buses in the evening; if you need to catch an earlier flight, you can book a minibus transfer with **Summercourt Travel** (☎ 01726-861108). The fare to the airport is a flat £10, or £5 per person for two people. Short- and long-term parking is also available at the airport.

The 585/586 bus is the most frequent to Truro (50 minutes, twice-hourly Monday to Saturday), while the hourly 587 follows a slower route to Truro along the coast via Crantock (15 minutes), Holywell Bay (20 minutes) and Perranporth (50 minutes).

There are trains every couple of hours between Newquay and Par (£5.20 one way, 45 minutes), on the main London–Penzance line.

TRERICE

Built in 1751, the charming Elizabethan manor of **Trerice** (NT; ☎ 01637-875404; admission £6; 🕑 11am-5pm Sun-Fri Mar-Oct, gardens from 10.30am) is famous for the elaborate barrel-roofed ceiling of the Great Chamber, but has plenty of other intriguing features, including ornate fireplaces, original plasterwork and a fine collection of period furniture. There's also an odd lawnmower museum in the barn, with more than 100 grass-cutters going back over a century.

Trerice is about 3 miles southeast of Newquay. Bus 526 runs from Newquay to Kestle Mill, about a mile from the manor house.

PERRANPORTH

☎ 01872 / pop 4003

With 3 miles of sand and excellent surf, Perranporth is one of the most popular beach towns on the north coast, and it's nearly always jam-packed with day-trippers and coach tours throughout the peak months. Off-season the town is practically deserted, so you'll have plenty of space to stroll the sands or try your hand at some kitesurfing or bodyboarding.

On the southern side of the beach a cliff staircase winds up to a giant **sundial**, built to commemorate the millennium and show Cornish time (rather than Greenwich Mean Time). Nearby **Penhale Sands** is also occasionally frequented by naturists, much to the chagrin of the MOD, who own a training camp nearby – after all, who knows what the sight of some wobbling flesh might do to those unsuspecting young recruits?

The **tourist office** (☎ 573368; www.perraninfo.co.uk) is on Cliff Rd.

Sleeping & Eating

Perran's hotels and B&Bs are pretty uninspiring, although there are some lovely coastal camp sites nearby.

Perranporth Camping and Touring Park (☎ 572174; Budnick; sites £8-18; 🕑 Easter-Oct) A five-minute walk from the Penhale dunes, this busy camp site offers plenty of space for tents and caravans, although the facilities are fairly basic.

Tollgate Farm Touring Park (☎ 572130; Budnick Hill; sites from £11; 🕑 Easter-Oct) This farm-based campground a mile from town offers sites spread over four areas, with a small children's play area, sparkling shower block and coastal views.

Seiner's Arms (☎ 573118; Beach Rd; d from £60) This old pub-hotel isn't too attractive, but it's handy for the beach. The rooms could do with a 21st-century spruce-up (net curtains and carpets in the bathrooms, anyone?); ask for one of the upstairs rooms for unbeatable sea views.

St Georges Country Hotel (☎ 572184; www.stgeorgescountryhouse.co.uk; St George's Hill; s £45, d £80-90, f £90-100; 🅿 🖳) This former mine-captain's house is the best place in Perran. It is homely and welcoming, with eight well-kept rooms including a four-poster suite, countryside views and a stonking home-cooked breakfast (including eggs sourced from the owner's chickens).

Watering Hole (☎ 572888; Perranporth Beach; mains £3-8) Sunk into the sands, this breezy beach bar makes a fine place for a cold beer as the sun goes down. Surfer dudes and beach chicks rub shoulders with day-tripping families on the outside wooden deck; look out for bands on weekends and beach barbies on summer evenings.

Getting There & Away

Bus T1 travels to Truro (50 minutes, four to six daily Monday to Saturday) via St Agnes, while Bus 501 travels along the coast between Newquay (20 minutes, three daily except on Saturday) and St Ives (1½ hours, four daily except on Saturday). The more regular bus 587 stops off in Perran at least once every hour en route from Newquay to Truro.

ST AGNES & PORTHTOWAN

☎ 01872 / pop 7257

Abandoned engine houses and ghostly chimney stacks litter the hilltops around St Agnes, which once resounded to the thump and clang of mine pumps and steam engines, and now echoes with the strains of crashing surf and calling gulls. Miners' cottages and stone-fronted houses hint at the town's former

CORNWALL

CORNWALL'S BEST BEACHES

- **For families:** Holywell Bay (p229), Perranporth (p233), Kennack Sands (p250), Summerleaze (p220)

- **For surfers:** Fistral (p228), Gwithian (p239), Crooklets (p220), Polzeath (p226)

- **For hikers:** Porthgwarra (p243), Lantic Bay (p270)

- **For views:** Bedruthan Steps (p229), Chapel Porth (below), Kynance Cove (p250)

- **For solitude:** Housel Bay (p250), Porth Chapel (p243)

- **For starkers sunbathers:** The Strangles (p220)

- **For outdoor sports:** Watergate Bay (p229), Widemouth Bay (p220)

prosperity as one of the centres for Cornish tin-mining. A century or two ago there were several mines working the area's rich mineral lodes, including **Wheal Coates**, which hugs the cliffside above the lovely cove of **Chapel Porth** a mile or so from St Agnes. From here a dizzying cliff path goes along the clifftops via awesome views of **St Agnes Head**, before tumbling down to the sandy beach at **Trevaunance Cove**.

A couple of miles west from St Agnes is the small coastal town of Porthtowan, with a wide sandy beach with that's always popular with surfers and bodyboarders, and a brilliant beach bar.

Sleeping & Eating

Presingoll Farm (☎ 552333; Penwinnick Rd; camp site for 2 adults £11; **P** **&**) The handiest camp site is near the Presingoll Barns pottery shop, spread over 1.5 hectares with a small shop, laundry and guest freezers.

Penkerris (☎ 552262; www.penkerris.co.uk; Penwinnick Rd; s £34.50-49.50, d £49-59; **P**) On the edge of Aggie, this is a British B&B of the old school, so fans of floral furnishings and pastel colour schemes will feel right at home. The rooms are small, chintzy and simple, and only three have bathrooms. Downstairs there's a log-fire lounge and a pleasant garden with views of the creeper-covered house.

Driftwood Spars (☎ 01872-552428; www.driftwood spars.com; d from £98; **P**) This laid-back beach-front pub at Trevaunance Cove has long been the haunt of choice for Aggie's surfers, bohos and ale-drinkers, with bars swimming in maritime paraphernalia, and a bright and breezy seafood restaurant (mains £11.95 to £16.95).

Rose-in-Vale Hotel (☎ 552202; www.rose-in-vale -hotel.co.uk; Mithian; d from £130; **P** **🛏**) This former mine-captain's manor house has been transformed into a country getaway par excellence. Surrounded by lawns and flower-filled grounds, the hotel offers effortlessly elegant rooms, decorated in country fashion; the pick is the Rose Suite, with a grand bathroom and luxurious sitting area.

Blue Bar (☎ 01209-890329; www.blue-bar.co.uk; Porthtowan; mains £6-13; 🕑 lunch & dinner Thu-Sun) Over at Porthtowan, this thriving beach hangout brings some Bondi flair to Cornwall's social scene. It's all suitably surfy inside, with bold primary colours and an open-plan interior, plus tables overlooking the beach tailor-made for sinking a cold one at sundown.

Tap House (☎ 553095; 1 Peterville) A lively pub at the bottom of St Agnes where you can sup some local ale and rub shoulders with Aggie's younger set.

Getting There & Away

Bus T1 travels from St Agnes to Perranporth (15 minutes, every two hours), and in the opposite direction to Truro (30 minutes, at least hourly) from Monday to Saturday. The 501 (four daily Sunday to Friday) meanders along the north coast between St Ives and Newquay, stopping at most places en route, including St Agnes.

WEST CORNWALL

While most visitors head for the tourist honey traps of the north coast, the wild west of Cornwall receives relatively few visitors outside St Ives and Land's End. And that's a real shame, as it's one of Cornwall's most starkly beautiful areas; stone monuments rise up from the hilltops, ancient moorland buts up against gorse-topped cliffs, and forgotten mine stacks stand in sharp relief against the skyline. Take some time and you'll discover some amazing coves along the snaking coastal path, as well as a clifftop theatre, a restored tin mine and the most atmospheric ancient sites this side of Stonehenge.

ST IVES

☎ 01736 / pop 9870

While Padstow grabs the gourmets and Newquay nabs the nightlife, St Ives is the humming heart of the Cornish art scene. Nestled beside a shimmering curve of sea near the holiday hot spot of Carbis Bay, St Ives was historically one of Cornwall's most important pilchard harbours, but reinvented itself as a haven for the arts after a stream of influential painters and sculptors set up their studios along the town's cobbled streets during the 1920s and '30s. Art galleries aplenty still line St Ives' meandering alleyways, but in recent years they've been joined by a hotchpotch of bars, bistros, surf shops and seafood cafés, especially around the horseshoe harbourside. The only drawback is the inevitable tourist traffic, but despite its popularity St Ives remains one of Cornwall's most eclectic and intriguing seaside escapes.

Information

Library (☎ 795377; 1 Gabriel St; Net access per hr £3)
Post office (☎ 795004; 11 Tregenna Hill; ☉ 9am-5.30pm Mon-Fri, 9am-12.30pm Sat)
Tourist office (☎ 796297; ivtic@penwith.gov.uk; Street-an-Pol; ☉ 9am-5.30pm Mon-Fri, 9am-5pm Sat, 10am-4pm Sun) Inside the Guildhall.

www.stives-cornwall.co.uk Official town website with accommodation and activity guides.

Sights & Activities
GALLERIES

There's no shortage of art galleries to nose around in St Ives, but the stunning **Tate St Ives** (☎ 796226; www.tate.org.uk/stives; Porthmeor Beach; adult/child £5.75/3.25, joint ticket with Barbara Hepworth museum £8.75/4.50; ☉ 10am-5pm Mar-Oct, 10am-4pm Tue-Sun Nov-Feb) is the centrepiece. Hovering like a white concrete curl above Porthmeor Beach, the gallery is every bit as impressive as its sister institutions in London and Liverpool. With its curving galleries, plate-glass windows and glittering white walls, the gallery's design evokes its natural seaside surroundings; its fantastic collection of modern art is especially rich in works by artists connected with the St Ives School. Terry Frost, Naum Gabo, Patrick Heron, Ben Nicholson, the potter Bernard Leach and the naïve Cornish painter Alfred Wallis are all represented, alongside several striking sculptures by Dame Barbara Hepworth. On the top floor is a stylish café-bar with a fantastic patio overlooking Porthmeor Beach.

Elsewhere around St Ives, the **Sloop Craft Centre** is a treasure trove of tiny artists' studios

---

SHINING A LIGHT ON CORNWALL

It's got spectacular natural scenery, a thriving culinary landscape, world-class gardens and a rich artistic heritage, not to mention groundbreaking ventures such as the Eden Project and the Combined Universities of Cornwall, so it's hardly surprising that Cornwall has established a reputation as one of the country's most creative counties. According to Helen Gilchrist, editor of *Stranger Magazine* (www.stranger-mag.com), Kernow (Cornwall) is definitely where it's at.

'Cornwall is a unique place, not just because of the natural landscape, but because of the people and our unique culture and heritage. I grew up here but, like many young people, moved away to study at university. I then spent several years working as a freelance writer in London, but I always wanted to move home. Cornwall gets in your blood – there's something about it that draws you back. So after years of umming and ahhing, I finally decided to just get on with it, move home and set up the magazine.'

Since its launch in 2005, *Stranger* has proved a huge hit with local audiences thanks to its buzzy mix of local coverage combined with lifestyle, music, cultural and environmental features. But it's not just a local thing – the magazine has a rapidly growing readership upcountry, with subscribers as far afield as London, Bristol and Birmingham.

'People are genuinely interested in what's going on down here. Since we started, I've noticed huge changes in Cornwall and the way it's perceived by the rest of Britain. Of course we've got great surfing and beautiful coastline, but we've also got an amazing cultural scene, with all sorts of art, music and outdoor theatre going on, and there are exciting bars, galleries and restaurants springing up every day. The aim of the magazine was to shine a light on some of these things and show what an exciting place Cornwall is. We're incredibly lucky to live down here. I can't think of anywhere else I'd rather be.'

CORNWALL

selling everything from handmade jewellery to driftwood furniture. The **St Ives Society of Artists** (☎ 795582; www.stivessocietyofartists.com) – one of Cornwall's oldest and most influential artists' collectives, founded in 1929 – still has its gallery in a converted church on Norway Sq, with a separate 'Mariners Gallery' in the former crypt.

BARBARA HEPWORTH MUSEUM & SCULPTURE GARDEN

Barbara Hepworth was one of the leading abstract sculptors of the 20th century, and a key figure in the St Ives art scene, so it seems fitting that her former studio has been transformed into a moving **museum** (☎ 796226; www.tate.org.uk/stives; Barnoon Hill; adult/child £4.75/2.75, joint ticket with Tate St Ives £8.75/4.50; ☻ 10am-5.30pm Mar-Oct, 10am-4.30pm Tue-Sun Nov-Feb). The studio has remained practically untouched since her death in a fire in 1975, and the adjoining garden contains some of her most famous sculptures. Hepworth was known for her use of geometric shapes and striking mix of natural materials and sculpted metal; many of her pieces show a fascination with pagan or primitive motifs, inspired by her fascination with Cornwall's prehistoric monuments. Works to look out for amongst the shrubs include the harplike *Garden Sculpture (Model for Meridian)* and the huge *Four Square*, the largest work Hepworth ever created. Her art is also dotted around the rest of town; there's a Hepworth sculpture outside the Guildhall,

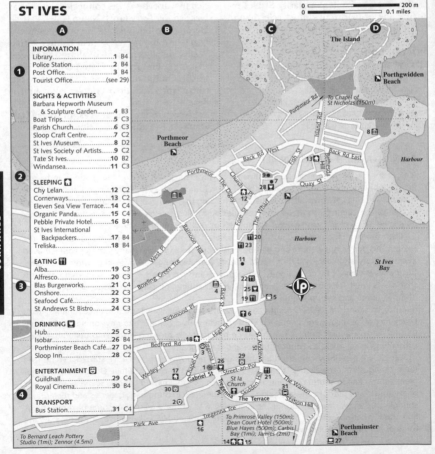

ST IVES

INFORMATION	
Library...................................1	B4
Police Station.......................2	B4
Post Office............................3	B4
Tourist Office...............(see 29)	

SIGHTS & ACTIVITIES	
Barbara Hepworth Museum	
& Sculpture Garden..........4	B3
Boat Trips..............................5	C3
Parish Church........................6	C3
Sloop Craft Centre................7	C2
St Ives Museum.....................8	D2
St Ives Society of Artists......9	C2
Tate St Ives........................10	B2
Windansea..........................11	C3

SLEEPING 🏠	
Chy Lelan...........................12	C2
Cornerways.........................13	C2
Eleven Sea View Terrace.....14	C4
Organic Panda....................15	C4
Pebble Private Hotel...........16	B4
St Ives International	
Backpackers....................17	B4
Treliska...............................18	B4

EATING 🍴	
Alba...................................19	C3
Alfresco..............................20	C3
Blas Burgerworks................21	C4
Onshore.............................22	C3
Seafood Café......................23	C3
St Andrews St Bistro...........24	C3

DRINKING 🍷	
Hub....................................25	C3
Isobar................................26	B4
Porthminster Beach Café.....27	D4
Sloop Inn............................28	C2

ENTERTAINMENT 🎭	
Guildhall.............................29	C4
Royal Cinema......................30	B4

TRANSPORT	
Bus Station.........................31	C4

200 m
0.1 miles

The Island

Porthgwidden Beach

Porthmeor Beach

To Chapel of St Nicholas (150m)

Harbour

St Ives Bay

Porthminster Beach

To Bernard Leach Pottery Studio (1mi); Zennor (4.5mi)

To Primrose Valley (150m); Dean Court Hotel (500m); Blue Hayes (500m); Carbis Bay (1mi); James (2mi)

and her moving *Madonna And Child* inside St Ia Church commemorates her son Paul Skeaping, who was killed in an air crash in 1953.

BERNARD LEACH POTTERY

While Hepworth was breaking new sculptural ground, the gifted potter Bernard Leach was hard at work reinventing British ceramics in his studio in Higher Stennack. Drawing inspiration from Japanese and Oriental sculpture, and using a hand-constructed kiln based on ones he had seen in Japan, Leach's pottery created a unique fusion of Western and Eastern ideas with a strong emphasis on function rather than form. His former **studio** (☎ 796398; www.leachpottery.com; adult/child £2.50/1.50; ☙ 10am-5pm Mon-Sat) displays many examples of his work, supplemented by a showroom selling work by eight modern potters.

ST IVES MUSEUM

Housed in a pierside building variously used as a pilchard-packing factory, laundry, cinema, sailors' mission and copper mine, the **St Ives Museum** (☎ 796005; admission £1.50; ☙ 10am-5pm Mon-Fri, 10am-4pm Sat Mar-Oct) is a typically haphazard local-history museum, with artefacts ranging from shipwreck salvage to photos of famous St Ives artists and a replica of a Cornish kitchen.

BEACHES

Near the museum, tucked under the grassy headland known under The Island, is the little cove of **Porthgwidden**, a pleasant picnic spot and a handy paddling spot for the little 'uns. On the promontory is the pre-14th-century **Chapel of St Nicholas**, patron saint of children and sailors, and the oldest (and certainly smallest) church in St Ives.

On the other side of town is **Porthminster**, with an attractive arc of soft golden sand that's usually sheltered from the wind by the cliffs, but inevitably gets busy on warm days. Below the Tate is **Porthmeor**, top choice for swimmers and novice surfers thanks to its gentle swells, and with a handy beach café just below the Tate. Along the coast is the touristy beach of **Carbis Bay**.

Several places around Porthmeor Beach and Fore St rent wetsuits and surfboards; try **Windansea** (☎ 794830; 25 Fore St) or the BSA-approved **St Ives Surf School** (☎ 0966 498021; Porthmeor Beach).

BOAT TRIPS

Sea-fishing trips and coastal cruises to the grey-seal colony on Seal Island (£8) are run by the **St Ives Pleasure Boat Association** (☎ 796080/07712 386162) and lots of other operators on the harbour.

Sleeping

Guesthouses are 10-a-penny in St Ives, but prices (and space) are at a premium in the high season, so you might find better value in Carbis Bay.

Pebble Private Hotel (☎ 794168; www.pebble-hotel .co.uk; 4 Park Ave; s £30-42, d £60-88; ☒) Groovy B&B where the emphasis is firmly on fun furniture and memorable design. Technicolour shades, fluffy cushions, flock curtains and glinting sinks make this a favourite sleep for hip young things, but families will feel hemmed in.

Treliska (☎ 797678; www.treliska.com; 3 Bedford Rd; s/d £45/64; ☒) Another glitzy guesthouse that's a world away from chintzy curtains and flock wallpaper. Here it's all clean lines, chrome bath taps and pine furniture – and it's bang in the heart of town.

Dean Court Hotel (☎ 796023; www.deancourthotel .com; Trelyon Ave; d £80-104; ℗) Upmarket 12-room hotel in a double-fronted Victorian town house, with panoramic views across the bay, clifftop gardens and spacious heritage-style rooms (six of which have sea views).

Organic Panda (☎ 793890; www.organicpanda.co.uk; 1 Pednolver Tce; d £90-100; ℗) Sleep with a clear conscience at this B&B in Carbis Bay, run by artistic owners along all-organic lines. The rooms are simple without being bland – spotty cushions, technicolour artwork and timber-salvage beds keep the funk factor high, while digiboxes and wi-fi will please the techno-savvy.

Jamies (☎ 794718; Wheal Whidden, Carbis Bay; s/d £80/100; ℗) This detached 1920s sea-view villa attracts a more genteel crowd thanks to its cream-and-check rooms and starchy service. If scented soap, fluffy bathrobes and Egyptian cotton sheets are a selling point, you'll be dead happy.

Eleven Sea View Terrace (☎ 798440; www.11stives .co.uk; 11 Sea View Tce; d £100-110; ℗) Creams, checks and cappuccino carpets distinguish this chic B&B above town, where local art lines the corridors and even the hand-creams are artisan-made. The two front rooms have town views, while the rear one overlooks a garden patio;

CORNWALL

for more space ask for the newly converted holiday flat (£500 to £800 per week).

Blue Hayes (☎ 797129; www.bluehayes.co.uk; Trelyon Ave; r £140-170; **P**) A favourite of the Sunday supplements, this luxurious hotel has a flavour of the Côte d'Azur, thanks to its manicured grounds, balustraded breakfast terrace and five pampertastic rooms (all designated as suites). Molton Brown bathstuffs, body-jet showers, tasteful lamps and lounge chairs help conjure the luxury air.

our pick **Primrose Valley** (☎ 794939; www.primrose online.co.uk; Porthminster Beach; d £105-145, ste £160-225; **P**) This fantastic hideaway is one of St Ives' secret gems; a swish guesthouse-cum-boutique hotel with 10 individual rooms, eco-friendly credentials and an eye for interior design to rival most metropolitan hotels. All the rooms have characteristic quirks – some boast blonde wood, leather armchairs and exposed brick, while others flourish with sea blues and pastel purples, offset by Philippe Starck lights and mosaic-lined bathrooms. Throw in a locally sourced breakfast, Manhattan-style lounge-bar and fab location near Porthminster Beach, and you have one of the best little boltholes in Cornwall.

St Ives International Backpackers (☎ 799444; www.backpackers.co.uk/st-ives; The Stennack; dm £10.95-16.95; 🖳) Housed in a Wesleyan Chapel, this shabby backpackers is pretty grungy, with cramped dorms, battered beds and threadbare carpets, but it's handy for town.

Cornerways (☎ 796706; www.cornerwaysstives.com; 1 Bethesda Pl; d £50-80) Tiny little flower-covered cottage on a backstreet in Downalong, where the central location compensates for the incey-wincey rooms.

Chy Lelan (☎ 797560; www.chylelan.co.uk; Bunkers Hill; d £50-60; ✖) 17th-century guesthouse with fresh, light rooms bang in the middle of town.

Eating

Most of the action is located around the harbourside, but there are some treats along the town's back-lanes too.

Blas Burgerworks (☎ 797272; The Warren; burgers £4-8; 🕑 lunch) The humble burger becomes a work of art at this designer burger joint, where the gourmet creations range from beetburgers in sunflower baps to black bean chilli burgers. The recycled boxes and napkins are a nice touch, too.

Seafood Café (☎ 794004; 45 Fore St; lunch £3.95-7.95, dinner £10.95-16.95) Fish of every description comes straight off the day boats into the kitchen of this café, from weaver and turbot to

sea bream and shark steaks. The ciabattas, club sandwiches and cakes are also really good.

Onshore (☎ 796000; The Wharf; pizzas £7-16; 🕑 lunch & dinner) A roaring wood-fired oven and handmade pizza bases keep the punters happy at this glass-fronted pizzeria near the old lifeboat station.

Porthminster Beach Café (☎ 795352; Porthminster Beach; lunch £7.95-11.95, dinner £16.90-18.90) There's a buzzy Riviera vibe around this beachside café with a breezy patio deck just off Porthminster's sands. Despite the moniker, it's more bistro than beach café – pitch up for Lavazza coffee and breakfast patisseries or a steaming lunch bowl of garlic mussels or Cornish scallops.

our pick **St Andrews St Bistro** (☎ 797074; 16 Andrews St; mains £9-16; 🕑 lunch Sun, dinner Wed-Sun) A hectic heap of North African rugs, *objets d'art* and oddball furniture covers this fantastic bistro, where the modern British menu is jazzed up by traces of African and Middle Eastern cuisine. Artisan bread, lentil curries, grilled fish and spicy casseroles all feature, and you'll be as chuffed with your choice whether you're a veggie or a carnivore.

Alfresco (☎ 793737; The Wharf; mains £10-18; 🕑 lunch & dinner) Watch the world spin by at this wharfside bistro, with just a few tiny wood tables and sliding doors opening onto the harbour. It's especially strong on seafood, with a sideline in Italian-influenced salads and risottos.

Alba (☎ 797222; Old Lifeboat House; mains £14-18; 🕑 lunch & dinner) Long a watchword for sophisticated seafood, the Alba continues to turn out amazing food in a contemporary split-level space where you can watch the chefs at work. Line-caught fish, skate tempura and pan-fried squid are some of the exotic treats in store.

Drinking

Hub (☎ 799099; The Wharf; 🕑 10am-late) After-dark action is thin on the ground in St Ives; thankfully this funky open-plan café-bar fills the void, with DJs and live music by night, and lattes and hot chocolate by day.

Isobar (☎ 796042; www.theisobar.co.uk; Tregenna Pl; 🕑 to 2am) St Ives's sole club, split into two levels; chrome-edge chill-out bar on the ground floor, hot-and-heavy dance floor upstairs. Funk, house, techno and cheesy disco played throughout the week.

Sloop Inn (☎ 796584; The Wharf) Old Speckled Hen, Doom Bar and Bass ales make this beam-ceilinged boozer a favourite with St Ives' old boys. Settle into a booth seat for the night, or bag a spot on one of the wharfside tables.

Entertainment

Royal Cinema (☎ 796843; www.merlincinemas.co.uk; The Stennack) Shows new films and often has cheap matinees.

Guildhall (☎ 796888; 1 Street-an-Pol) Regular programmes of music and theatre, especially during the St Ives September Festival.

Getting There & Away

Buses 17/17A/17B (twice hourly Monday to Saturday, hourly on Sunday) regularly link St Ives to Penzance; the 343 bus (five daily Monday to Saturday) trundles around the coast to Penzance via Zennor and Land's End.

The pretty coastal railway from St Erth (£2.50, 20 minutes, hourly) links up with the main London–Penzance line.

GWITHIAN & GODREVY TOWANS

Cornwall has its fair share of glorious bays, but the beaches at Gwithian and Godrevy Towans are tough to top. Backed by grassy headlands and windblown *towans* (Cornish for sand dunes), at low tide the beaches combine to form Hayle's '3 miles of golden sand'. It's a favourite spot for locals, surfers and summer visitors, but there's usually ample room for everyone (though not always in the beach car parks). At the southwestern end is the Hayle Estuary and the old Hayle harbour, once one of the county's busiest

THE MERMAID OF ZENNOR

Zennor's most famous legend tells the story of local lad Matthew Trewhella, famous for his fine singing voice and dashing good looks. Every night Matthew would sing the closing hymn in the Church of St Senara, and his singing was said to have attracted the attentions of a mermaid living in nearby Pendour Cove. Disguising herself with a long dress, and being careful to conceal her long tail, the mermaid came ashore one Sunday to find the source of this magnificent voice, and as soon as Matthew and the mermaid laid eyes on one another they fell madly in love. After the service Matthew followed this beautiful stranger out towards the clifftops, and neither he nor the mermaid were ever seen again. It's said that if you sit on the cliffs at twilight you might still hear the faint strains of Matthew and his beloved mermaid singing somewhere in the waves beyond Pendour Cove.

industrial ports, but disused since the mid-20th century; at the other end of the *towans* is Godrevy Lighthouse, inspiration for Virginia Woolf's stream-of-consciousness classic *To The Lighthouse*.

There are a couple of beach cafés behind the dunes, including the **Sunset Surf Café** (☎ 01736-752575; 10 Gwithian Towans; 🕑 10am-5pm in season) and the **Godrevy Café** (☎ 01736-757999; sandwiches & light meals £3-8; 🕑 10am-5pm daily, plus 6-11pm Thu-Sat), which does sandwiches, risottos, veggie wraps and crumbly cakes, as well as late-night meals from Thursday to Saturday.

ZENNOR & PENDEEN
☎ 01736

The wild B3306 coast road between St Ives and St Just is one of Cornwall's most scenic, winding through an eye-popping panorama of chequerboard fields and granite-strewn moorland. Five miles west from St Ives is Zennor, a cluster of houses and a village pub set around the granite **Church of St Senara**. DH Lawrence famously sojourned here between 1915 and 1917, a period which spawned *Women in Love* and was recounted in his autobiographical novel *Kangaroo;* but the village is also famous for its mythological associations with the Mermaid of Zennor (see the boxed text, above). Two carved bench ends commemorate the legend with intricate designs of a mermaid holding a mirror and comb; the mermaid's favourite haunt of **Pendour Cove** is along the cliff path.

Downhill from the church, the **Wayside Folk Museum** (☎ 796945; admission £3; 🕑 10.30am-5pm Sun-Fri May-Sep, 11am-5pm Sun-Fri Apr & Oct) houses a treasure trove of artefacts gathered by the magpie-minded collector Colonel 'Freddie' Hirst in the 1930s, from blacksmiths' hammers and cobblers' tools to an 18th-century kitchen and two reclaimed watermills.

Tin mining was once the staple industry in this wild corner of Cornwall, and engine houses still punctuate the crag-backed coastline. The last to close was **Geevor Tin Mine** (☎ 788662; www.geevor.com; adult/child £7.50/4.50; 🕑 hourly tours 10am-4pm Easter-October), just south of Pendeen, which now provides a fascinating insight into the harsh working conditions of a Cornish tinner. Above ground you can wander around the old mining machinery where the tin ore was extracted, while below ground you can venture into the old mine itself – a claustrophobic maze of echoing shafts and dank tunnels where miners worked by tallow candles, enduring ever-present dangers of rockfalls, air pollution and underground explosions.

More of Cornwall's mining heritage comes to life at the **Levant Engine House** (☎ 786156; levant@nationaltrust.org.uk; adult £5; 🕑 11am-5pm Sun & Wed-Fri Jul-Sep, plus Tue Jun, Wed & Fri Apr, May & Oct, 11am-4pm or Fri Nov-Mar), one of Cornwall's oldest beam engines, where you can see the original pump-shafts in action. Clinging to the cliffs nearby is **Botallack Mine**, one of Cornwall's most dramatic engine houses, which has abandoned mine shafts extending right out beneath the raging Atlantic waves.

Sleeping & Eating
Old Chapel Backpackers Hostel (☎ 798307; www .backpackers.co.uk/zennor; dm/f £12/50; P) Zennor's old Wesleyan chapel is now an excellent independent hostel, with smart, well-kept dorms, some the perfect size for a family stay. The huge downstairs café is a popular stop-off for coastal hikers who flock here for the homemade cakes and doorstep sandwiches.

Tregeraint House (☎ 797061; sueewilson@yahoo .co.uk; s/d £35/60) This Cornish cottage, just west of Zennor village, makes a fabulous place to escape the outside world. Run by local potter Sue Wilson, the house offers just a couple of Alice-sized rooms, complete with rustic furniture and granite-slab fireplaces, and nothing but coast and moorland for miles around.

Tinner's Arms (☎ 792697; lunches from £7-10) DH Lawrence's favourite drinking den is a fine example of an old Cornish inn, with the requisite slate roof, roaring fireplaces and a refreshing lack of commercial clutter. Next door the 'White House' has been spotlessly converted to provide, fresh, modern rooms (singles/doubles £40/70).

Getting There & Away

Bus 343 (five daily Monday to Saturday) crosses the moorland between Penzance and St Ives via Zennor, while the 344A travels along the coast from St Ives to Zennor and St Just once per day Monday to Friday and twice daily on Saturday.

PENWITH'S ANCIENT SITES

West Penwith is astonishingly rich with **prehistoric monuments**. The area's granite hilltops are littered with quoits, tombs and ancient settlements left behind by Cornwall's earliest settlers, many predating the first phases of construction at Stonehenge and Avebury. Little is known about the lives of these Neolithic builders, or what they were trying to achieve with their upstanding brand of architecture, but one thing's for certain – they certainly knew an eye-catching location when they saw one.

Quoits & Standing Stones

Most of the Penwith monuments mark the location of ancient burial sites. The most dramatic are the quoits, three or more upright stones topped by a capstone, built on top of a chamber tomb. Most quoits were probably once covered by a barrow of earth or stones, but over the centuries these have often been worn away to reveal the supporting structure. The most impressive is **Lanyon Quoit**, between Madron and Morvah, a classically shaped quoit topped by a huge 13.5-tonne capstone. In the 18th century, the monument was tall enough to accommodate a man on horseback, but a storm in 1815 blew the quoit down and broke one of the four uprights; it was

re-erected nine years later. There are several other quoits in the area, including **Zennor Quoit** and nearby **Sperris Quoit**, as well as the partially collapsed **Mulfra Quoit** (off the road between Treen and New Mill) and **Chûn Quoit** (near the Chûn Castle hillfort; below).

Five miles southeast from Morvah is the curiously curvy **Mên-an-tol** (from the Cornish for stone-of-the-hole), a weird formation consisting of two upright menhirs flanking a hollow stone. Local legend states that squeezing through the stone will either get you pregnant or cure you of rickets, but the truth is no-one has the foggiest what this strange stone signifies. The Mên-an-tol is a 15-minute walk from a back road between Madron and the coastal B3306, but there are no signs marking the start of the track, so you might need an OS map to find it.

Hillforts & Settlements

The area is also dotted with the remains of ancient hillforts. **Chûn Castle** is signposted from the road past Mên-an-tol, and lies about a mile east of Chûn Quoit. A pile of rubble and two upright stones marking the old gateway are all that remains of this once-mighty fortress, but archaeologists have found all kinds of prehistoric relics including weapons, pottery and evidence of tin smelting. In the 18th century the walls stood 4.5m high, but much of the stone was plundered for construction projects, including the building of Penzance's north pier.

Perhaps the most atmospheric ruins of all are at the Iron Age village of **Chysauster** (☎ 07831 757934; adult/child £2.40/1.20; ☻ 10am-6pm Jul & Aug, 10am-5pm Apr-Jun & Sep, 10am-4pm Oct), one of the best-preserved ancient settlements in Britain. Consisting of eight stone-walled houses, each with its own central courtyard, it's a remarkably domestic place that gives you a real sense of Iron Age daily life – you can still see the stone hearths and platforms used to grind corn, and you wander around the small gardens where the residents kept livestock and grew arable crops. Not quite two-up, two-down, perhaps, but still eerily familiar all the same.

Stone Circles

Cornwall's stone circles aren't quite on the same scale as Stonehenge and Avebury, but they're still hugely atmospheric. The **Merry Maidens**, a ring of 19 stones near Lamorna, are

CORNWALL

supposedly the petrified remains of a group of local ladies turned to stone for dancing on a Sunday. Nearby are the twin **Pipers**, who earned the same fate for daring to tootle a tune on a Sunday. There's a similar circle east of the Mên-an-Tol, the **Nine Maidens**; the name derives from the Cornish word *maedn* (later *mên*) meaning stone.

ST JUST
☎ 01736 / pop 4690

The stern granite settlement of St Just might not be quite the hive of activity it was during the heyday of Cornish tin-mining, but it's still a lively hub for Penwith's artistic community. All roads lead to the central Market Sq, ringed by grey granite buildings, the small parish church and the **Plen-an-gwary**, an open-air auditorium once used to stage outdoor theatre, mystery plays, Methodist sermons and Cornish wrestling. These days it's more popular for lunchtime picnics, although plays and outdoor concerts are still sometimes performed there.

Jutting out from the cliffs a couple of miles from St Just is **Cape Cornwall**, a rocky curve of headland topped by an abandoned chimney stack (the last remains of the Cape Cornwall Mine, which closed in 1875). Below the cape is the rocky beach of **Priest's Cove**, while nearby are the ruins of **St Helen's Oratory**, supposedly one of the first Christian chapels built in West Cornwall.

Sleeping & Eating

Kelynack Caravan & Camping Park (☎ 787633; francis&wendykelynackholidays.co.uk; sites from £10) This sheltered campground offers sites for tents and caravans, plus a bunk barn and chalets. Facilities include a laundry, shop, table tennis and a resident donkey and Shetland pony to entertain the kids.

Land's End YHA (☎ 0870 770 5906; landsend@yha .org.uk; dm £18; P) Despite its name, this small hostel is closer to St Just than Land's End, but makes a good base for backpackers and hikers on the coast path. The smallish three- or four-bed rooms are good value for families, and there's camping and cycle storage outside. The hostel is a mile south of St Just in the Cot Valley.

Bosavern House (☎ 788301; www.bosavern.com; d £54-60; P) Things are not so refined at this flock-heavy B&B, a mile south of St Just, but the coast-view rooms are still reasonably

priced and the owners are very friendly. Other plus points include the local-produce brekkie and afternoon cream teas, but the rooms could do with a contemporary revamp.

Boscean Country Hotel (☎ 788748; www.boscean countryhotel.co.uk; d from £70; P) A former gentleman's residence turned modest hotel, in a smart whitewashed house surrounded by secluded countryside. Original features (oak staircase, tiled fireplaces, wood panelling) are mirrored by brass bedsteads and classic English décor.

Cookbook (☎ 787266; 4 Cape Cornwall St; lunch £4-8, dinner from £8; 10am-5pm, plus from 7pm Sat) Another bohemian hangout, where wonderful home-cooked food rubs shoulders with a huge range of secondhand books. The soups, cakes and sarnies are super, and the coffee's served in mugs made by a local potter.

Kegen Teg (☎ 788562; 12 Market Sq; mains £6-10; 9am-4.30pm Mon-Sat) St Just's artsy types flock to this wholefood café for its handmade smoothies, Fairtrade coffee and sticky cakes. There's always a daily-changing soup on the menu, and the sandwiches, chillis, curries and stews are all prepared with loving care.

Getting There & Away

Buses 17 and 17A travel between St Just, Penzance (40 minutes) and St Ives (1½ hours, once or twice hourly Monday to Saturday); there's also an hourly 17B bus on Sundays. Less useful is the 344A bus, which stops in St Just once or twice daily Monday to Friday en route along the coast from St Ives.

SENNEN
☎ 01736 / pop 829

Nestled on the edge of the huge arc of Whitesand Bay, Sennen Cove boasts the largest stretch of golden sand in West Penwith, popular with swimmers, surfers and sun-worshippers, and also a good starting point for the coastal hike to Land's End. If you want to find out what the weather (or the surf) is up to down at the cove, there are three handy webcams at www.sennen -cove.com.

The **Round House & Capstan Gallery** (☎ 871859; www.round-house.co.uk; 10am-5pm) is located in a circular building that once housed the massive capstan used to haul fishing boats from the water. It now sells work by local artists, including handmade jewellery and driftwood furniture. Nearby are a couple of small shops and cafés where you can stock up on beach supplies and ice creams.

Sleeping options in Sennen itself are limited; the cosiest B&B is rose-pink **Myrtle Cottage** (☎ 871698; s/d from £20/40), with three basic rooms and a popular cream-tea café below. Campers are spoilt for choice: try **Trevedra Farm** (☎ 871835; sites £13-15; ☼ Easter-Oct), off the A30, or **Sennen Cove** (☎ 871588; ☼ Easter-Oct). Both sites are very popular, and tend to get overcrowded in summer. Light sleepers beware.

The 17th-century **Old Success Inn** (☎ 871232; s £31, d £88-96) is the best place to grab something more substantial than a sandwich, and it's also the main drinking den for locals and Sennen's lifeboat crew. Rooms are available.

Inland from the cove, the **Whitesands Seafood and Grill** (☎ 871776; www.whitesandshotel.co.uk; r £75-110; **P**) has five fun rooms all themed after a different capital city – choose from stripped-back Washington, minimalist London or rustic Nairobi. For budget travellers there's an 18-bed surf lodge and a couple of tepees for that Cherokee-meets-Cornish camping experience. Meals are available (mains £10.95 to £16.95).

LAND'S END

A mile from Whitesand Bay, the Penwith Peninsula comes to a screeching stop at Land's End, the most westerly point on the British mainland and the last port of call for countless charity walkers on the 874-mile slog from John O' Groats. The scenery doesn't get much more dramatic – black granite cliffs and heather-covered headland teeter above the booming Atlantic surf, and on a clear day you can glimpse the Isles of Scilly, 28 miles out to sea. Why someone felt the experience would be enhanced by building a tawdry theme park is anyone's guess, but nevertheless the **Legendary Land's Experience** (☎ 0870 458 0099; www .landsend-landmark.co.uk; adult/child/family £9.95/5.95/21.95; ☼ 10am-5pm summer, till 3pm winter) continues to lure in the summertime crowds. Connoisseurs of kitsch might enjoy the five exhibits – in an ironic sort of way – which include an Air Sea Rescue show, a small animal farm, a cringeworthy semihistorical *son et lumière* show called *The Last Labyrinth*, and an exhibition on *Doctor Who*. Wiser heads will just pay for the car park (£3) and head off in search of their own scenic thrills and spills.

Various trails wind their way around the Land's End headland and its roll call of rocks,

including **Dr Syntax's Head**, **Dr Johnson's Head** and the **Armed Knight**. It's a great place for a bit of wildlife-spotting, with plenty of sea-bird colonies nearby and the occasional glimpse of dolphins or seals offshore; bring binoculars in case.

Getting There & Away

Buses 1/1A/101 travel the route from Penzance to Land's End (one hour, eight to 12 Monday to Saturday, five on Sunday). The 345 (two daily Monday to Friday, one on Saturday) takes slightly longer and travels via Newlyn, Mousehole and the Minack. Bus 201 travels from St Ives to Land's End (one hour 20 minutes, three daily May to October).

PORTHCURNO
☎ 01736

From the rugged promontory of Land's End, the coastline sweeps in a jagged curve towards the pretty coves of **Porthgwarra** and **Porth Chapel**, both accessible from the coast path. Further east is the sheltered wedge of sand of **Porthcurno** and the gravity-defying **Minack Theatre** (☎ 810181; www.minack.com; tickets from £8.50), which is carved into the cliffs above the beach and exists thanks to one indomitable English eccentric, Rowena Cade.

Originally from Derbyshire, Cade bought the headland for £100 in the 1920s and, inspired by classical auditoria and a burning passion for Shakespeare, she spent the next 30 years developing the theatre by hand, carting much of the wood, sand and stone up from the beach in a battered wheelbarrow. The first production of *The Tempest* was performed in 1932 on a rickety stage lit by batteries and car headlights; 70 years later the Minack is a full-blown theatrical venue with a season running from mid-May to mid-September. With its vertigo-inducing seating and circular amphitheatre thrusting out over the Atlantic, it's an unforgettable place to watch a play – although aficionados bring umbrellas and blankets in case the British weather decides to take centre stage.

Above the theatre there's a café and **visitor centre** (adult/child under 12yr £3.50/free; ☼ 9.30am-5.30pm daily Apr–mid-Sep, except Wed & Fri afternoons May–mid-Sep, 10am-5pm late Sep & Oct, 10am-4pm Nov-Mar) that explores the Rowena Cade story; you can wander around the auditorium unless there's a matinee.

CORNWALL

Behind the beach, the **Porthcurno Telegraph Museum** (☎ 810966; www.porthcurno.org.uk; adult/child £4.50/2.50; ☺ 10am-5pm Thu-Tue, 10am-7.30pm Wed May-Sep, 10am-5pm Sun & Mon Nov-Mar) is located in the underground tunnels of the old Porthcurno telegraph station, once the hub for a network of subterranean telegraph cables stretching halfway around the globe. These days the museum houses some intriguing exhibits exploring the history of telecommunications, including mahogany telephones and cutting-edge speaking tubes.

Eating

Porthcurno Beach Café (☎ 810834; ☺ 9am-5.30pm Easter-Oct) This pleasant little café sells Cornish fudge, biscuits and beach fare, as well as Lavazza coffee and a wicked range of home-made cakes (including apricot flapjacks and an irresistible lemon drizzle cake).

Logan Rock Inn (☎ 810495) A gorgeous little kiddleywink, with all the ingredients for a classic Cornish snug – head-scraping ceilings, wooden seats, a crackling coal fire, brassy trinkets and warm beer on tap. Look out for a copy of the original bill presented to young Lieutenant Goldsmith on one of the walls.

Getting There & Away

Porthcurno is 3 miles from Land's End and 9 miles from Penzance; follow the brown signposts from the main road for the Minack Theatre. Buses 1/1A/101 stop at Porthcurno (12 to 14 Monday to Saturday, four on Sunday May to October), or you could catch the 345 bus (two daily Monday to Friday, one on Saturday) from Penzance or St Just.

MOUSEHOLE & NEWLYN

☎ 01736 / pop 4075

With its quiet cliffs and hidden coves, the remote coastline between Treen and Mousehole feels rooted in another century. A hundred years ago this was one of Britain's richest fishing grounds, and most of the small inlets were home to communities of mackerel and pilchard fishermen, especially around **Penberth**, **Lamorna** and the old fishing harbour of Mousehole (pronounced *mowzel*). These days the fishing trade has moved east to Newlyn, and Mousehole has reinvented itself as a seaside getaway and a notorious hot spot for second-home ownership (it's thought that over half of Mousehole's houses are now used as holiday lets or second homes). Despite its problems

Mousehole remains one of Cornwall's prettiest villages, with a tight-packed knot of slate-roofed cottages and cob buildings gathered around the harbour, best seen in December when the village streets are illuminated by an extravagant set of **Christmas Lights**. Mousehole is also the setting for a much-loved children's fable, *The Mousehole Cat*, as well as the best place to indulge in a portion of Stargazy Pie (see the boxed text, p48).

The nearby harbour of **Newlyn**, 3 miles down the Penzance road, has somehow weathered the ongoing storms within the Cornish fishing industry and remains one of the southwest's busiest working ports. Every August the town celebrates its piscatorial prowess at the annual **Newlyn Fish Festival** (www.newlynfishfestival.org.uk), and it's still the best place in Cornwall to pick up a fresh mackerel fillet or a lobster straight from the pot.

During the 19th century Newlyn became famous for its colony of artists, spearheaded by the Irish-born Stanhope Forbes, who aimed to capture the hardy spirit and rustic customs of Cornwall's fishermen in his canvases. Most of his work is now owned by national museums and private collectors, although the Penlee Gallery (p246) has a few of his minor paintings alongside work by other artists of the Newlyn School.

Newlyn's artistic associations live on at the cutting-edge **Newlyn Art Gallery** (☎ 363715; www.newlynartgallery.co.uk; New Rd), recently reopened after a £4 million face-lift, along with a new outpost in the former telephone exchange opposite the Acorn Arts Centre. The art here is definitely of a contemporary slant; for more traditional work there are more small galleries sprinkled along Newlyn's main street.

Sleeping & Eating

Kerris Farm (☎ 731309; www.kerrisfarm.co.uk; d with/without bathroom £60/52; ☺ Feb-Nov; **P**) Offers clean and cosy rooms in a working family

---

TOP FIVE CORNISH KIDDLEYWINKS

- Pandora Inn (p263)
- Ferryboat Inn (p252)
- Halzephron Inn (p249)
- Turk's Head (p258)
- Logan Rock Inn (left)

farmhouse in the village of Paul, just uphill from Mousehole.

Old Flowershed (☎ 731239; vanillavilla1@btinternet .com; Love La; d with 2-night minimum £55) Tired of tea trays and '70s bathroom suites? Then try this unusual B&B, in a single-room timber cabin at the bottom of an old flower farm. Luxury it ain't, but it's packed with charm plus a little wooden verandah for a twilight tipple. Breakfast arrives every morning in a hamper, so brekkie in bed is *de rigueur*.

Old Coastguard Hotel (☎ 731720; www.oldcoast guardhotel.co.uk; s £60, d £110-170; (P)) Mediterranean chic hits Mousehole at this swish hotel, with posh, pretty rooms divided between the main house and a separate lodge down by the water. Gingham checks and soothing sea colours characterise the bedrooms, while the restaurant (three-course menu £39) is all stripped-back simplicity – blinding white tablecloths, gleaming floors and windows over the sea.

Cornish Range Restaurant with Rooms (☎ 731488; www.cornishrange.com; d £100) This tiny place is a well-kept seafood secret, housed in a tiny converted pilchard-processing factory. The food (mains £12.50 to £18.95) is fresh, local and fantastic, but the pocket-sized dining room is often crammed so reservations are essential. Upstairs the three rooms chuck out the chintz in favour of muted colours and wicker motifs. Classy.

Ship Inn (☎ 731234; South Cliff; s/d £40/65) The pubs around Newlyn are on the rowdy side, so your best bet for a pint and a pie (mains £6 to £10) is this venerable inn in the heart of Mousehole. It's especially popular in December, when the Ship's the traditional place to tuck into some stargazy pie (see the boxed text, p48).

Getting There & Away

If you're driving to Mousehole, it's best to park outside the village, as driving through the narrow streets in high summer can be a real headache.

The quickest bus to Mousehole is the 6/6A from Penzance (20 minutes, half-hourly Monday to Saturday, every hour on Sunday).

PENZANCE

☎ 01736 / pop 21,168

Gulls wheel overhead, fishing trawlers ply the waterways and there's a scent of brine on the breeze around the elegant old harbour town of Penzance. Stretching along the western edge of Mount's Bay, Penzance has marked the end of the line for the Great Western Railway since the 1860s, and the town still feels one step removed from the rest of Cornwall. There's an air of faded grandeur around Penzance's streets, though these days the town's fine architecture is offset by the usual smattering of high-street chains and corporate shopfronts; but unlike many of its sister towns up the coast, Penzance seems to have resisted the urge for over-gentrification and still boasts the kind of rough-edged authenticity many of Cornwall's daintier towns lost long ago. It's also an ideal launch pad for exploring Land's End and the Penwith Peninsula.

Information

Library (☎ 363954; Morrab Rd; per hr £3) Internet access.

Polyclean Laundrette (☎ 364815; 4 East Tce; ⊗ 7.30am-7.30pm)

Post office (☎ 362464; 113 Market Jew St; ⊗ 9.30am-5.30pm Mon-Fri, 9.30am-12.30pm Sat)

Tourist office (☎ 362207; pztic@penwith.gov.uk; Station Approach; ⊗ 9am-5pm Mon-Sat, 10am-1pm Sun) Next to the bus station.

www.penzance.co.uk Useful local guide to Penzance and the surrounding area.

Sights

As with Truro and Falmouth further east, Penzance's wealth was founded largely on the import-export trade, and most of the town's Georgian and Regency town houses were built for the merchants and sea captains who once plied their trade out of the harbour. The best examples can be seen along Chapel St and Queen St; look out for the extraordinary **Egyptian House**, which looks like a bizarre cross between a Georgian town house and an Egyptian sarcophagus and was originally built for a wealthy mineralogist, John Lavin, as a geological museum.

At the top of Market Jew St is a statue to Penzance's most famous son, **Humphry Davy** (1778–1829), the pioneering 'chemical philosopher', amateur poet and fanatical trout fisherman. Davy was responsible for an astonishing number of scientific advances: the discovery of six new elements (including potassium, sodium and strontium), the invention of the miner's safety lamp and the use of nitrous oxide (or laughing gas) as a medical anaesthetic. He also penned reams of

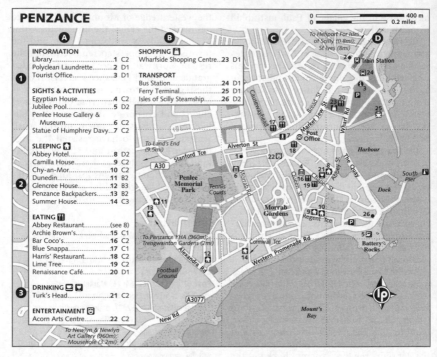

PENZANCE

0 — 400 m
0 — 0.2 miles

INFORMATION
Library..............................1 C2
Polyclean Laundrette.........2 D1
Tourist Office....................3 D1

SIGHTS & ACTIVITIES
Egyptian House...................4 C2
Jubilee Pool........................5 D2
Penlee House Gallery &
Museum...........................6 C2
Statue of Humphrey Davy...7 C2

SLEEPING
Abbey Hotel.......................8 D2
Camilla House.....................9 C2
Chy-an-Mor.......................10 C2
Dunedin............................11 B2
Glencree House..................12 B3
Penzance Backpackers........13 B2
Summer House....................14 C3

EATING
Abbey Restaurant.............(see 8)
Archie Brown's...................15 C1
Bar Coco's........................16 C1
Blue Snappa......................17 C1
Harris' Restaurant..............18 C2
Lime Tree.........................19 C2
Renaissance Café..............20 D1

DRINKING
Turk's Head.......................21 C2

ENTERTAINMENT
Acorn Arts Centre..............22 C2

SHOPPING
Wharfside Shopping Centre...23 D1

TRANSPORT
Bus Station......................24 D1
Ferry Terminal...................25 D1
Isles of Scilly Steamship.......26 D2

Map labels: To Heliport For Isles of Scilly (0.8mi); St Ives (8mi); Train Station; Causewayhead; Broad St; Market Jew St; Post Office; To Land's End (9.5mi); Alverton St; Stanford Tce; A30; Penlee Memorial Park; Tennis Courts; Morrab Rd; Harbour; The Quay; South Pier; Dock; Queen St; Abbey St; Chapel St; Morrab Gardens; Regent Tce; To Penzance YHA (960m); Trengwainton Gardens (2mi); Cornwall Tce; Western Promenade Rd; Alexandra Rd; Football Ground; Battery Rocks; A3077; New Rd; Mount's Bay; To Newlyn & Newlyn Art Gallery (960m); Mousehole (3.2mi)

---

amateur poetry and befriended some of the 19th century's best-known Romantic writers, including Samuel Taylor Coleridge, although whether it was Davy's amateur verse or his ready supply of chemical narcotics that most interested Coleridge is a moot point.

Penlee House Gallery & Museum (☎ 363625; www.penleehouse.org.uk; Morrab Rd; adult/child £3/free, free Sat; ☺ 10am-5pm Mon-Sat May-Sep, 10.30am-4.30pm Mon-Sat Oct-Apr) has a fine collection of paintings by artists of the Newlyn and Lamorna Schools (including Stanhope Forbes, whose 1922 work *On Paul Hill* was purchased by the museum in 2006), alongside more contemporary work. The lovely landscaped gardens are also worth a stroll.

Penzance's 19th-century **promenade** stretches along the sea wall between the South Pier and New Rd. At the eastern end is the **Jubilee Pool** (www.jubileepool.co.uk; adult/child/family £3.85/2.75/12.20; ☺ 11am-7pm May-Sep), a classic 1930s Art Deco lido. Since falling into disrepair in the 1980s, it's been thoroughly spruced-up and is now open to alfresco bathers throughout the summer – just don't expect the water to be warm.

Sleeping

B&Bs are 10-a-penny along Alexandra and Morrab Rds, so you shouldn't have too much trouble finding somewhere to stay.

BUDGET

Penzance Backpackers (☎ 363836; www.pzbackpack .com; Alexandra Rd; dm/d per person £14/15; ☺) This indie hostel isn't as well-equipped as its YHA compatriot, but it's more laid-back. Squeezed into a converted house on Alexandra Rd, the rooms and kitchen are small and a touch tatty, but it's clean, fun and friendly, so globe-trotting backpackers will feel right at home here.

Penzance YHA Hostel (☎ 0870 770 5992; penzance @yha.org.uk; Castle Horneck, Alverton; dm £15.50; ℗ ☺) This excellent YHA hostel is on the Penzance outskirts, housed inside a Georgian mansion with its own gardens and woodland. Most of the rooms are in austere four- to eight-bed dorms, but the onsite facilities are fantastic, with a café, games room, TV lounge and cycle store, plus space for campers. Buses 5 and 6 run to Alverton; jump off at the Pirate Inn and walk the 500m to the hostel.

CORNWALL

Glencree House (☎ 362026; www.glencreehouse
.co.uk; 2 Mennaye Rd; r £40-50 depending on season) This is
a great budget B&B, offering eight slightly old-
fashioned rooms, most with bathroom, including a couple with a modest sea view. Despite
the uninspiring interior, it's worth a look for
the wallet-friendly price tag and the slap-up
breakfast, which includes smoked kippers,
fruit teas, cafetière coffee and veggie options.

MIDRANGE & TOP END
Dunedin (☎ 362652; Alexandra Rd; s £35, d £55-65; 🖳)
Comfy, simply furnished rooms on the B&B
ghetto of Alexandra Rd, with the added bonus
of free wi-fi.

Chy-an-Mor (☎ 363441; Regent Tce; s £35, d £64-80;
🅿) Second billing on Regent Tce behind
Camilla House goes to this reliable guesthouse, decked out in standard-issue shades
and off-the-shelf furnishings, but worth considering for the seafront location.

Camilla House (☎ 363771; www.camillahouse.
co.uk; 12 Regent Tce; d £70-75; 🅿 🖳) In a terrace of
better-than-average B&Bs, Camilla House
stands out for its classy rooms, period features
and environmentally conscious stance. Rooms
are 'Classic' or 'Standard', but most people
will plump for one with a view over the prom.
Fluffy bathrobes, pillow treats and supremely
helpful owners seal the deal.

Summer House (☎ 363744; www.summerhouse-corn
wall.com; Cornwall Tce; s £85, d £95-120; 🕑 closed Nov-Mar;
🅿 ❌) This elegant Penzance town house
near the promenade was an artist's hideaway,
but it's been lovingly converted into a stylish
hotel mixing Knightsbridge chic with hints
of the seaside. Checks, pinstripes and cheery
colours characterise the five bedrooms, and
downstairs there's a Mediterranean restaurant
with alfresco terrace.

our pick **Abbey Hotel** (☎ 366906; www.theabbeyon
line.co.uk; Abbey St; d £130-180) This 17th-century
sea-captain's house turned heritage hotel is
a stunner, shunning modish minimalism in
favour of burnished antiques, vintage rugs
and a warren of wood-floored corridors. All
the rooms have their own offbeat style and
higgledy-piggledy layout – our favourites are
Room 4, with its cupboard-cum-bathroom,
and the spacious suite complete with its own
booklined lounge.

Eating
Archie Brown's (☎ 362828; Bread St; mains £3-6;
🕑 9.30am-5pm Mon-Sat) Sticky cakes, wedge sar-

nies and hearty soups take top billing at this
longstanding wholefood café, with cheap,
filling eats in the sunny 1st-floor café, plus a
vegetarian smorgasbord of lentils, pulses and
wholegrains in the ground-floor shop.

Renaissance Café (☎ 366277; 6 Wharfside Shopping
Centre; mains £5-12; 🕑 lunch & dinner) Light streams in
through floor-to-ceiling windows at this contemporary café, hidden away in the Wharfside
Shopping Centre overlooking Mount's Bay.
Club sandwiches, ciabattas and salads feature,
with more-substantial mains by night and
late-night music at weekends.

Blue Snappa (☎ 333352; 35 Market Pl; mains £5.95-
11.50; 🕑 9.30am-11pm Mon-Thu, 9.30am-1am Fri & Sat,
10.30am-5pm Sun) Expect fusion food and a lively,
buzzy atmosphere at this surfy bar-brasserie
where you can tuck into a gourmet burger or
Thai stir-fry or just sink a few cold brews.

Bar Coco's (☎ 350222; 13 Chapel St; tapas £2-6, mains
from £8; 🕑 closed Sun) Bringing a little piece of
southern Spain to Chapel St, this popular
tapas bar is as good for a morning latte as for
a late-night *cerveza*, and is usually crammed
with paid-up members of Penzance's arty
crowd.

Lime Tree (☎ 332555; 16 Chapel St; mains £16-20;
🕑 lunch & dinner Tue-Sat) With a relaxed townhouse setting and cosy front-room atmosphere, dining at the Lime Tree feels like
having supper at a friend's house – assuming
your friend is a gourmet chef with a passion
for global cuisine. Cornish duck breast, sea
bass and John Dory fillet for mains, chased
down by homemade bread and vanilla *crème
brûlée*.

Harris' Restaurant (☎ 364408; 46 New St; mains
£16-20; lunch Mon, lunch & dinner Tue-Sat) Penzance's
original fine-dining restaurant is still going
strong after 30-odd years. Times have moved
on but the menu at Harris' is still mostly classic French, serving up local game and fish
dishes in the scarlet-tinted, napkin-laced dining room.

Abbey Restaurant (☎ 330680; mains £16.25-19.50,
2/3 course menu £19/23; 🕑 dinner daily, plus lunch Fri & Sat
Apr-Aug, dinner Wed-Sun plus lunch Fri & Sat Oct-Mar) This
cutting-edge British bistro has been garnering
serious praise, not least from the boffins at
the AA and Michelin guides. Underpinned
by top-quality produce, the Abbey turns out
consistently fabulous food in the light-filled
dining room, and nibbles, cocktails and aper-
itifs in the crimson-walled bar downstairs.
It's not cheap, but tucking into your roast

CORNWALL

monkfish or hot chocolate soufflé, you'll feel it's money well spent.

Drinking & Entertainment

Turk's Head (☎ 363093; Chapel St) Penzance isn't short of a boozer or two, but the old Turk's Head – purportedly the town's oldest pub – is a personal favourite. Tobacco-stained walls, patchy carpets and a battered bar just add to the atmosphere of a well-used (and much-loved) watering hole.

Acorn Arts Centre (☎ 363545; www.acorn-theatre.co.uk; Parade St) This venerable arts centre hosts a varied programme of film, theatre, comedy and live bands in its unusual twin-tiered auditorium.

Getting There & Away

Penzance is well-served by local buses: the 301 to St Ives (one hour 10 minutes, at least hourly) via Marazion and Hayle, and the No 1/1A to Land's End (one hour, eight to twelve Monday to Saturday, five on Sunday) via Newlyn, Porthcurno, Sennen and Treen. The 18/X18 is the quickest service to Truro (hourly Monday to Saturday), or you could catch a National Express coach.

Penzance is the last stop on the main train line from London Paddington (£117, six hours, eight to 10 daily) via Truro. There are frequent trains on the lovely coast-hugging line from Penzance to St Ives (£4.80, 20 minutes, hourly) via St Erth.

ST MICHAEL'S MOUNT

Looming up from the waters of Mount's Bay, the craggy-cliffed island abbey of **St Michael's Mount** (NT; ☎ 710507; www.stmichaelsmount.co.uk; adult/child £6.40/3.20; ☺ house 10.30am-5.30pm Sun-Fri May-Sep, 10.30am-5pm Apr, Oct & Nov, gardens 10.30am-5.30pm Mon-Fri May & Jun, 10.30am-5.30pm Thu & Fri Jul-Nov) is one of Cornwall's iconic landmarks. Connected to the mainland by a cobbled causeway that's submerged by the rising tide, there's been a monastery here since at least the 5th century, but the mount was being used long before as a trading port for tin and copper, and it's almost certainly the isle of Icstis referenced by classical authors. After the Norman conquest, the island was given to the Benedictine monks of Mont St Michel in Normandy, who raised a new chapel on the site in 1135. The mount later served as a fortified stronghold and is now the family home of the St Aubyns, although since 1954

the island has been under the stewardship of the National Trust.

The best way to reach the castle is at low tide via the stone-topped causeway, although you can hop aboard a ferry (£1) from Marazion at other times. From the island's stone harbour, it's a lung-busting climb up to the castle itself, which spans the spectrum of architectural styles from the late Middle Ages to the Georgian era. The tiny island chapel with its wonderful rose window and 15th-century alabaster panels is a highlight; there's also the rococo Blue Drawing Room, the ornate library, the island garrison and the hunting friezes and ornate plasterwork of the Chevy Chase Room (named after a medieval hunting ditty, not the *National Lampoon* star). Around the island's edge, sub-tropical gardens hover precariously above the cliffs.

THE LIZARD

Cornwall's southern coastline takes a sudden wild turn around the Lizard Peninsula, where open fields and flat heaths plunge into a melee of ink-black cliffs, churning surf and saw-tooth rocks. Cut off from the rest of Cornwall by the River Helford and ringed by treacherous seas, the Lizard was once the heartland of Cornwall's smuggling community and an ill-famed graveyard for ships, and the peninsula still has a wild, untamed edge. The Lizard has long been Cornwall's secret corner, and if you're looking for somewhere to stalk the cliffs, drink in the views or escape the rat race, this is definitely the place.

Get the regional low-down on Cornwall's wildest corner at www.theliz ard.co.uk.

Helston & Around

☎ 01326 / pop 9780

The only town on the Lizard is Helston, once a bustling river port and Stannary town, and now the peninsula's main place to stock up on supplies. The eccentric **Folk Museum**, housed in the town's former butter market, has background on the furry dance (see the boxed text, p250), as well as a 5-tonne cider press dating from the 18th-century, some bizarre Victorian fire-fighting contraptions and a display on local hero Bob Fitzsimmons, the first man to simultaneously hold the world titles for middleweight, light heavyweight and heavyweight boxing.

Three miles southwest of Helston is the port of **Porthleven**, where the stout double-walled harbour is crowned by a brace of cannons recovered from the wreck of the HMS *Anson,* which foundered on Loe Bar in 1807. This traumatic event inspired the local cabinet-maker Henry Trengrouse to devote his life to inventing more effective life-saving tools; among his fine inventions were the winch-powered 'Bosun's Chair' and also a pioneering rocket-propelled rescue line. Porthleven is also renowned among British surfers for its right-hand reef break. Colloquially known as 'The Beauty and the Beast', it's definitely for hard-core boarders only – you'll probably end up getting acquainted with the harbour wall if you don't know what you're doing.

A mile south is the shingly bank of Loe Bar and the saltwater lake of **Loe Pool**, where King Arthur's magic blade Excalibur was rumoured to have been returned to the water (a claim hotly contested by Dozmary Pool; p276). Several woodland walks wind their way around the lake banks, but the swimming off Loe Bar is dangerous due to the strong tides, so if you fancy a dip you're better off heading south to **Halzephron Cove** and **Gunwalloe Cove**, where you'll also find the titchy 15th-century Church of St Winwaloe half-buried in the sand. There are several legends of buried treasure at Gunwalloe – the swashbuckling pirate John Avery, alias Long Ben, supposedly buried a fabulous gold hoard in the Gunwalloe dunes, so you might want to bring that old metal detector along just in case.

SLEEPING

Greystones (☎ 565583; mawbb@tiscali.co.uk; 40 West End, Porthleven; s/d £25/50) Solid, pastel bedrooms in a pleasant end-of-terrace house in Porthleven; pick of the bunch is the attic room complete with skylight and essential sea scenes.

An Mordros Hotel (☎ 562236; www.anmordroshotel .com; Peverall Tce, Porthleven; r from £50) An Mordros means 'sound of the sea' in Cornish, and it's aptly named; this simple hotel is a short walk from Porthleven Harbour and its bevy of restaurants and pubs. Bag one of the front rooms if you can for the harbour outlook.

Tregathenan House (☎ 569840; www.tregathenan .co.uk; Sithney, Helston; s/d £35/60; P) A more traditional guesthouse in a squat, 17th-century country manor just outside Helston. The farmhouse-style furniture and simple furnishings characterise the three guest rooms, all named after local beaches, but the main attraction here is the ridiculously tranquil country setting.

Beacon Crag (☎ 573690; www.beaconcrag.com; Beacon Crag, Porthleven; d £75-95; P 🖳) A bewitching B&B in 2 hectares of private clifftop grounds above Porthleven. Built for a local artist, the Victorian villa has been renovated with flat-screen TVs and tasteful tones of chocolate, slate and cream, and most rooms have bay windows with the kind of coastal view you'd normally pay through the nose for.

EATING & DRINKING

Blue Anchor (☎ 562821; 50 Coinagehall St, Helston; mains from £8) Six centuries of beer-brewing later and this wonderful old inn is still packing in the punters, mainly thanks to its home-brewed Spingo ale (ask at the bar to see the vats). Flagstone floors, wooden beams, roaring hearths and a traditional skittle alley add up to one of Cornwall's finest drinking dens.

Halzephron Inn (☎ 240406; Gunwalloe; mains £10.95-15.10; P) Nooks and crannies abound at this whitewashed alehouse above Gunwalloe Cove. It is known for its superior food, rich smuggling history and opera-singer owner; these days it's a perfect bolthole after a day spent exploring the nearby coast path.

our pick Kota (☎ 562407; Harbour Head, Porthleven; mains £10.95-21; ☽ lunch & dinner in summer, lunch Thu-Sat & dinner Tue-Sat in winter) Malaysian meets Maori at this rustic-chic converted mill, where the food blends Pacific Rim flavours with Cornish ingredients – Falmouth bay scallops with a soy-coriander dressing, Thai-spiced crab bisque or sweet potato and smoked chilli soup. Pitch up between 6pm and 7pm for the cut-price two-course menu (£12). Rooms are available for £60 to £80 a double.

GETTING THERE & AWAY

The Lizard's transportation hub is Helston, served by **Truronian** (☎ 01872-273453; www.truro nian.co.uk). Bus T1 runs from Truro to Helston (50 minutes, at least hourly Monday to Saturday, five on Sunday); for onward connections to the Lizard village, catch bus T34 from the Tesco car park in Helston.

For getting around the Lizard, the most useful bus is the T2, which runs from Helston to Goonhilly (20 minutes), Coverack (25 minutes) and St Keverne (40 minutes, 15 daily Monday to Saturday), stopping at Gweek twice daily.

CORNWALL

CORNWALL'S FURRY FLING

Helston is famous for its annual **Flora Day**, held every year on 8 May. Believed to be the last remnant of a pagan celebration marking the coming of spring, this ancient festival is a peculiar mixture of street dance, musical parade and floral pageant. Local residents dress up in traditional finery and the town is covered in blossoms collected from the surrounding countryside. The day itself is marked by several stately dances; the first is at 7am, followed by the lively Hal-An-Tow pageant and a children's dance. The main highlight of the day is the formal Furry Dance, which kicks off at noon and proceeds around the town's streets; participants take part by invitation only, and the dance is always led by a local couple. The final dance of the day is at 5pm, before the entire town descends on the local pubs for a hard-earned pint or six. Unsurprisingly, the Victorians took a dim view of the proceedings, and the festival was banned in the 19th century for promoting 'drunken revelry'.

The T3 Lizard Rambler (two daily Monday to Saturday) travels from Helston around the coast via Mawgan (20 minutes), Helford (35 minutes), Manaccan (40 minutes), Porthallow (50 minutes), St Keverne and Roskilly's Farm (one hour) and Coverack (one hour 10 minutes).

A Day Rover ticket valid on all Truronian buses costs £16/6/4 for a family/adult/child.

Lizard Point & Around

☎ 01326

Tucked away on the Lizard's west side is the village of **Mullion**, handily plonked near three of the peninsula's prettiest coves. A mile south is **Mullion Cove**, home to a cluster of fishing boats and a granite-walled harbour, but discerning beach lovers will head for the softer sand and swimmable surf at **Polurrian** or **Poldhu Cove** a mile to the north.

Five miles south from Mullion, Britain reaches its southernmost fringe around the sea-pummelled cliffs of Lizard Point, notorious as one of the most deadly coastal areas in Britain. Hundreds of vessels have come to grief on the peninsula's rocky shores, from Spanish treasure galleons and transport tankers to tiny Cornish fishing smacks; with all those wrecks it's a mecca for treasure hunters and scuba divers, as well as coastal walkers who flock to the clifftops to bask in the scenery.

With its conglomeration of fudge sellers and *pisky* (pixie) stores, Lizard village itself makes a pretty disappointing gateway, so most people park in the village and make the mile-long walk to Lizard Point and the 18th-century **Lizard Lighthouse**. Like nearly all Cornwall's lighthouses, the Lizard was automated in the '90s, and is now controlled by the flick of a switch 400 miles away in Essex.

Below the lighthouse, a rough track leads down to the disused lifeboat station and a shingly cove, pounded by endless white surf rolling in from the Atlantic, and sometimes visited by the odd inquisitive seal, dolphin or Cornish chough. Energetic types can explore coastal trails to the secluded beaches of **Housel Bay** and **Church Cove**, or venture north to **Cadgwith**, where a chocolate-box collection of thatched houses and fishermen's cottages huddle at the foot of a lung-straining hill. You might even catch sight of a gig boat or two plying the waters on a warm summer day.

The most popular beach near Lizard Point is **Kennack Sands**, a good family paddling spot with good sand, seaweed-stocked rockpools and a brace of beach shops. Across the peninsula is the National Trust beach of **Kynance Cove** (NT; ☎ 561407; lizard@nationaltrust.org.uk) tucked under towering cliffs and flower-covered headland, and once an important source of the red-green serpentine rock favoured by Victorian knick-knack makers. A steep trail leads down from the car park to the cove and its ecofriendly **tearoom**, ideal for cakes, sandwiches and cream teas.

SLEEPING

Lizard YHA Hostel (☎ 0870 770 6120; lizard@yha.org.uk; dm £15.50; ☼ Apr-Oct) Few top-end hotels can boast the kind of spectacular sea view enjoyed by this gloriously situated hostel, in a renovated Victorian hotel right below the lighthouse on Lizard Point.

Old Vicarage (☎ 240898; bandbmullion@hotmail.com; Mullion; s/d £41.50/73) Top-notch rooms in a historic Mullion vicarage, once frequented by Arthur Conan Doyle and converted with grace and style. Garden views and the country location are the selling points, while families will appreciate the good-sized rooms and spacious bathrooms.

Housel Bay Hotel (☎ 01326 290417; www.houselbay .com; The Lizard; d £64-136; **P**) This grand gabled manor was constructed by a group of Victorian entrepreneurs to offer its discerning guests the sort of stirring views and luxurious rooms they'd expect from a Cornish country house. A century later it's still a gorgeous place to stay, with plenty of period pieces and a charming old-world atmosphere.

Mullion Cove Hotel (☎ 240328; www.mullioncove .com; Mullion Cove; r £79-120; **P** 🐕) This old Victorian mansion is hardly cutting-edge, but if it's cliff views and comfy rooms you want then it could be just the ticket. Hovering over Mullion Cove, the hotel has choices from 'garden suites' to 'superior plus' sea-view rooms; the décor's flouncy and faded, but you couldn't ask for a better seafront location.

Lanwednack House (☎ 290877; www.landewednack .uniquehomestays.com; Church Cove; d £100-150; 🐕 **P**) A slice of real Lizard luxury, this restored rectory sits in 0.8 hectares of grounds and mixes country chic with metropolitan-style; kick back in the heated pool, lounge in the antique-stuffed drawing room, or order a four-course meal from your own private chef. Wow.

Polurrian Hotel (☎ 240083; www.polurrianhotel.com; Mullion; r £160-206; 🐕 **P**) Things are upmarket at this Edwardian pile perched above Polurrian Cove, offering 39 poshly furnished bedrooms, self-catering suites and kid-friendly facilities (including tennis, table football, Playstations and a toddlers' playroom). It's undeniably smart, but might be too precious for some.

EATING

Trenance Chocolate (☎ 241499; www.trenancechoco late.co.uk; Mullion) Cornwall's best-known chocmaker is opposite the turn-off to Mullion village. Boxes of choccies and truffles are available plus fudge and shortbread laced with Rodda's Cornish Clotted Cream.

Colroger Creamery (☎ 241007; Lender Lane, Mullion) This miniature deli is chock-full of Cornish delicacies (chutneys, jams, bickies). It also runs a dinky next-door bistro (three-course menu £22.50), open for dinner Tuesday, Thursday and Friday and lunch on Sunday.

Lizard Pasty Shop (☎ 290889; The Lizard; pasties £2-4; ☯ Tue-Sat) Renowned as Rick Stein's favourite pasty-maker, this traditional bakery, run by local lady Ann Muller, churns out handmade pasties using only traditional ingredients.

Thanks to Mr Stein you'll need to get there early to be sure of bagging one.

Old Inn (☎ 240240; Mullion; mains £6-12) Sporting prints and nautical trinkets adorn the walls of this thatched 16th-century pub in Mullion, blessed with a surfeit of Cornish ales, a fine front patio and superior pub food (crab salads, club sandwiches, battered cod). Double rooms start at £60.

GETTING THERE & AWAY

For bus transport to Lizard, see the Helston section (p249).

St Keverne & Around

☎ 01326 / pop 2107

Centred around a sleepy market square ringed by stone cottages and a brace of smuggler's pubs, St Keverne is one of the Lizard's oldest market towns. The spire of the parish church has been a vital day-mark for sailors and fishermen for more than five centuries, and the nearby coastline is dotted with typically Cornish fishing ports, including **Porthoustock**, **Porthallow** (locally pronounced *pralla*) and the arc-shaped harbour of **Coverack**, once an infamous haunt for smuggled contraband, now a haven for the Lizard's artistic community.

Just outside St Keverne is **Roskilly's Farm** (☎ 280479; www.roskillys.co.uk; ☯ 10am-6pm), an ice-cream maker and organic farm, which has scooped several awards for its lip-smacking organic ice creams, yogurts, fudges, sorbets and fruit jams. There's an onsite shop and tearoom (see p252), and you can watch the cows being milked every day from 4.30pm to 5.30pm.

Spread over the barren Goonhilly Downs five miles west of St Keverne are the vast satellite dishes of **Goonhilly Earth Station** (☎ 0800 679593; www.goonhilly.bt.com; adult/child £6.75/4.75; ☯ 10am-6pm late May-Sep, 10am-5pm Apr-late May, Sep & Oct, 10am-4pm Tue-Sun Feb & Mar), one of the world's first satellite stations, and still the UK's main hub for international telecommunications. The multimedia visitor centre has interactive exhibits and offers guided tours of the site, including the chance to climb up 'Arthur', one of the site's largest satellite dishes (for some reason the Goonhilly dishes are all named after Arthurian characters).

SLEEPING

Coverack YHA Hostel (☎ 0870 770 5780; coverack@yha .org.uk; Coverack; dm £14; ☯ Mar-Oct) Great hostel

CORNWALL

inside a converted gentleman's residence on the hillside above Coverack. The rooms are light and bright, split over a couple of floors and arranged in three-, four- and eight-bed dorms. It feels cramped when it's full, but there's space outside for camping and BBQs, and you bed down in one of the hostel's tepees like a bona-fide Blackfoot.

EATING
Croust House (☎ 280479; www.roskillys.co.uk; ☷ 10am-6pm) The farm restaurant-tearooms at Roskilly's is a truly local operation – practically everything on the table has been sourced straight from the farm, from the ham in your sandwich to the milk in your tea. Homemade pasties, pies, soups, casseroles and pizzas are all on offer, plus a selection of over 50 ice creams, including hokey-pokey crunch and orange and mascarpone.

Old Lifeboat House (☎ 280899; Coverack; mains from £8; ☷ dinner) A lovely little seafood diner serving up classic fish dishes in a cramped and endearingly chaotic setting above Coverack harbour.

The Helford
☎ 01326
Flowing along the northern edge of the Lizard along a tranquil estuary lined with overhanging oaks and hidden creeks, the River Helford feels far removed from the rest of the Lizard Peninsula. It's famous for its historical links with Cornwall's smuggling fraternity, largely thanks to the literary invention of Daphne du Maurier, who named her classic novel *Frenchman's Creek* after one of the many inlets that pock the river's shingle-strewn banks. These days the Helford is one of Cornwall's most exclusive postcodes, with rock-star mansions and palatial country getaways sprinkled along the riverbanks, especially around **Helford village**. There are lots of little coves to explore on both banks of the river, as well as a traditional oyster fishery at Porth Navas and a couple of fantastic riverside pubs.

Helford River Boats (☎ 250770; www.helford-river-boats.co.uk) run passenger ferries (10am to 6pm April to October) that cross the river between Helford Passage and Helford village, and a Garden Ferry (10.30am to 4.30pm Tuesday to Sunday) that runs from Helford village to Trebah, Glendurgan and the Budock Vean Hotel (p261) on request. You can also hire motorboats (£50/80/100 per two hours/four

hours/day), rowboats (£30/50/70), and kayaks (£20/30/50).

TREBAH & GLENDURGAN GARDENS
Across the water from Trelowarren are the neighbouring estates of Trebah and Glendurgan, both founded by members of the Fox family, who made their fortune importing exotic plants from the New World. **Glendurgan** (NT; ☎ 250906; glendurgan@nationaltrust.org.uk; admission £5; ☷ 10.30am-5.30pm Tue-Sat Feb-Oct) was one of the first great Cornish pleasure gardens, established by Alfred Fox in the 1820s It was specifically designed to show off the weird and wonderful plants being brought back from the far corners of the empire, from rhododendrons, magnolias and camellias from Nepal and India right through Canadian maples, New Zealand tree ferns and Chilean monkey puzzle trees. Tumbling down a stunning subtropical valley, the garden offers breathtaking views of the River Helford, as well as an ornamental maze and a secluded beach near **Durgan** village.

Just west is **Trebah** (☎ 250448; www.trebahgarden.co.uk; admission £6.50 Mar-Oct, £3 Nov-Feb; ☷ 10.30am-6.30pm, last entry 5pm), planted in 1840 by Charles Fox, Alfred's younger brother. It's less formal and a touch wilder than Glendurgan, with giant rhododendrons, massive gunnera and jungle ferns lining the sides of a steep ravine leading down to a shingle beach. Charles Fox was a celebrated polymath and a notorious stickler for detail; according to the story, he made his head gardener construct a scaffold to indicate the height of each individual tree, barking out his orders from an attic window via a megaphone and telescope. Certainly makes Alan Titchmarsh look tame.

NATIONAL SEAL SANCTUARY
Further west along the river near Gweek, the 'ahh' factor goes into overdrive at the **National Seal Sanctuary** (☎ 221361; www.sealsanctuary.co.uk; adult/child £10.95/6.95; ☷ 10am-5pm May-Sep, 9am-4pm Oct-Apr), which cares for sick and orphaned seals washed up along the Cornish coastline before returning them to the wild.

PUBS
Ferryboat Inn (☎ 01326-250625; Helford Passage; mains £5-15) This riverfront pub is an old fave with locals and visiting yachties. On summer nights the creekside patio is packed with a lively crowd tucking into beer-battered fish or

triple-decker club sandwiches. In winter it's the quintessential smuggler's pub, perfect for Sunday lunch in front of a roaring log fire.

Shipwright's Arms (☎ 231235; Helford village; mains from £8) Just across the water, this heart-meltingly pretty thatched pub in Helford village is another classic place to dine by the waterside. There are real ales on tap, crab and lobster salads on the blackboard and rickety tables where you can dine out on the view.

GETTING THERE & AWAY
For buses to the Helford see Helston (p249).

ISLES OF SCILLY

☎ 01720

Sprinkled across the Atlantic Ocean 28 miles southwest of Land's End, the Isles of Scilly offer a taste of what life must have been like in England a century ago. Rush-hour traffic, trilling telephones and summertime roadworks seem like a distant memory as soon as you set foot on this miniature archipelago of 140 tiny islands, only five of which are inhabited. On Scilly the nearest thing to noise pollution is the screech of seagulls and the crash of waves breaking on the shore; it's a place where the accumulated hum of the outside world is left behind and life is dictated by the whims of the weather and the tide. Even the main island of St Mary's, which welcomes the vast majority of the islands' visitors, is hardly a bustling metropolis, while the smaller islands of Tresco, Bryher, St Martin's and St Agnes are home to just a few hardy castaways. Whether it's solitary walks, empty beaches or clear, cool water you're looking for, Scilly certainly won't disappoint – just don't expect to get back on that chopper any time soon.

Orientation & Information
Peak season on Scilly is from May to September, when you'll find most of the B&Bs and hotels are fully booked weeks ahead, while many businesses simply shut down in winter, which can make visiting out of season tricky. All the islands, except Tresco, have a basic camping area, but even these are often booked up during the busiest months.

There are loads of self-catering cottages available – contact the tourist office for full listings, or call **Island Properties** (☎ 422082; St Mary's) or **Sibley's Island Homes** (☎ 422431; sibleys@scilly.fsnet.co.uk).

The island's main website is at www.simplyscilly.co.uk, while the locally run website www.scillyonline.co.uk has plenty of other useful info.

Hospital (☎ 422392; ⊗ 24hr)
Isles of Scilly Tourist Board (☎ 422536; tic@scilly .gov.uk; Hugh Town, St Mary's; ⊗ 8.30am-6pm Mon-Fri, 9am-5pm Sat, 9am-2pm Sun summer, shorter hours winter) The islands' only tourist office.
Police station (Garrison Lane, Hugh Town, St Mary's; ⊗ 9am-10pm) Staffed by a trio of part-time bobbies.

Getting There & Away
There's no transport to or from the islands on a Sunday. Look out for special Saver and Daytrip fares, as well as discount coupons in the local papers.

AIR
The **Isles of Scilly Skybus** (☎ 0845 710 5555; www .ios-travel.co.uk) flies between St Mary's and Land's End (adult/child return £125/76.50, 15 minutes) and Newquay (£145/88, 30 minutes) several times daily year-round (except Sunday). Cheaper Saver fares are available for flights leaving Land's End after 2pm, or leaving St Mary's before noon. There's also at least one daily flight to Exeter (£232/138, 50 minutes), Bristol (£278/162, one hour 10 minutes) and Southampton (£298/170, 1½ hours) in summer.

British International (☎ 01736-363871; www.isle sofscillyhelicopter.com) helicopters fly to St Mary's (20 minutes, 11 daily Monday to Friday, 17 on Saturday late June to late September; seven to 10 daily late September to late March) and Tresco (20 minutes, four to six daily Monday to Saturday April to October, four daily November to March) from Penzance heliport.

Standard return fares are £152/90 for an adult/child; cheap day returns (£102/65) and reduced fares for midweek travel or last-minute bookings are also sometimes available. Parking at the heliport costs £6 per day.

BOAT
The *Scillonian* ferry (☎ 0845 710 5555; www.ios -travel.co.uk) sails between Penzance and St Mary's (adult/child return £92/46, two hours 40 minutes, once per day Monday to Saturday). The crossing can be notoriously rough – landlubbers might be better off taking the chopper.

CORNWALL

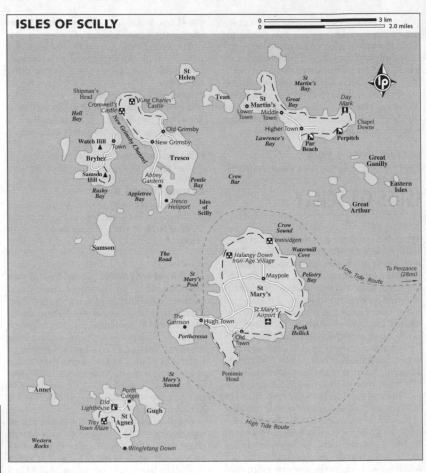

ISLES OF SCILLY

Getting Around

Regular interisland launches sail from St Mary's harbour daily in summer to the other main islands. The boats usually leave in the early morning and return in late afternoon. A return trip to most offshore islands costs £6.80; make sure you label your luggage clearly so it can be deposited at the right harbour. The official boats are operated by the St Mary's Boatmen's Association, but there are several other operators – check the boards on Hugh St and the Old Quay.

The airport bus service (£3) departs from The Strand in Hugh Town 40 minutes before each flight. A bus service runs around St Mary's several times daily in summer (£1 to all destinations).

There are a couple of bus tours of St Mary's; contact **Heritage Tours** (☎ 422387) or the **Island Rover** (☎ 422131; www.islandrover.co.uk), which offers a twice-daily trip (£6) around St Mary's in a vintage open-topped bus. Ferry passengers can buy tickets on board the boat.

Bikes are available from **Buccaboo Hire** (☎ 422289; Porthcressa, Hugh Town) and **St Mary's Bike Hire** (☎ 422289; The Strand, High Town) for around £8 per day.

For taxis, try **Island Taxis** (☎ 422126), **Scilly Cabs** (☎ 422901) or **St Mary's Taxis** (☎ 422555).

ST MARY'S

First stop for most visitors (unless you happen to be arriving by private yacht) is St Mary's, the largest and busiest of the islands, and also where you'll find the vast majority of hotels, shops, restaurants and B&Bs. Just over 3 miles at its widest point, St Mary's is shaped like a crooked circle, with a claw-shaped peninsula at its southwestern edge – home to the island's capital, Hugh Town, and the docking point for the *Scillonian* ferry. The main airport is a mile east at Old Town, while most of the best beaches and sights are tucked along the coastline to the northeast.

Sights & Activities

Most of the action on St Mary's centres on Hugh Town, which sits on a low-lying sliver of land between the main island and the old Garrison, and often finds itself swamped by Atlantic swells during the winter months. By Scilly standards, it can feel pretty hectic in summer; ice cream–toting trippers mill around the many souvenir shops and cafés along the main thoroughfares of The Strand and Hugh St, or dip their toes in the waters off Town Beach and Porthcressa Beach.

The **Isles of Scilly Museum** (☎ 422337; Church St; adult/child £2/50p; ⏲ 10am-4.30pm summer, 10am-noon Mon-Sat winter, or by arrangement) has some fantastically atmospheric exhibits, including lots of archive photos of the islands, various artefacts recovered from shipwrecks (including muskets, a cannon and a ship's bell) and a fully rigged pilot gig dating from 1877.

A mile east of Hugh Town, reached via a pleasant coast path around Peninnis Head, is the island's former harbour at **Old Town**, home to a few small cafés, a village pub, a working pottery and a pleasant beach. The graveyard of the tiny Old Town Church contains a memorial to Augustus Smith, founder of the Abbey Garden, as well as the grave of former prime minister Harold Wilson, who often holidayed on the Scillys.

There are lots of small inlets scattered around the island's coastline, best reached on foot or by bike: Porth Hellick, Watermill Cove and the relatively remote Pelistry Bay are worth seeking out. St Mary's also has some unique ancient sites, notably the Iron Age village at Halangy Down, a mile north of Hugh Town, and the Neolithic barrows at Bant's Carn and Porth Hellick.

DIVING & BOAT TRIPS

For diving on St Mary's, contact **Island Sea Safaris** (☎ 422732), who also offers white-knuckle speedboat rides (£18 to £25) around the islands and snorkelling trips to the local seal colonies (£36).

The traditional sport of **gig racing** is still popular on Scilly. These six-oared wooden boats were originally used to race out to rescue foundering ships, but these days gig racing is a highly competitive sport. Races are held most weekends, and every April or May St Mary's hosts the **World Pilot Gig Championships**, which attracts teams from as far away as Holland and the USA.

Tours

Scilly Walks (☎ 423326; www.scillywalks.co.uk) leads three-hour archaeological and historical tours, costing £5/2.50 per adult/child, as well as visits to other offshore islands. Twitchers should get in touch with **Will Wagstaff** (☎ 422212), who runs bird-watching tours.

Sleeping

Blue Carn Cottage (☎ 422214; Old Town; d £62-68) Removed from the relative bustle of Hugh Town, this whitewashed B&B near Old Town is a truly welcoming affair, run by a family of Scilly flower farmers. DVD players and cosy surroundings distinguish the rooms, while there's a game-stocked guest lounge and huge breakfasts with Fairtrade ingredients.

Pelistry Cottage (☎ 422506; www.scillyholidays .com; The Parade; d £73) A clean and simple guesthouse in the heart of Hugh Town. The rooms are hardly cutting edge – floral bedspreads, shipshape prints and fibreboard furniture are about as exciting as things get – but the Aga (type of cooking range) breakfast makes up for the underwhelming rooms.

Amaryllis (☎ 423387; earlsamaryllis@aol.com; d £90) Perched on Buzza Hill with views of Porthcressa and St Agnes, this fine guesthouse is the one for people looking for a hilltop hideaway; kids aren't allowed here. The spacious lounge, tended gardens and good evening food are a bonus, too.

Star Castle Hotel (☎ 422317; www.star-castle.co.uk; The Garrison; standard rooms £188-268, ste £282-310, incl dinner; ⊠ 🍷) Shaped like an eight-pointed star, this former fort on Garrison Point is one of the fanciest places to stay on Scilly, with higgledy-piggledy, heritage-themed rooms filled with plush sofas and vast beds, and a couple of top-class restaurants serving a bevy of fishy treats.

St Mary's Hall Hotel (☎ 422316; www.stmaryshallho tel.co.uk; r £210-280; ⊠) Another indulgent hotel

CORNWALL

dashed with Italianate luxury, in a renovated mansion originally built for a holidaying nobleman. Grand wooden staircases, *objets d'art* and panelled walls cover the public rooms, while you can plump for a choice of 'Godolphin' or Count Leon rooms, or super-plush designer suites with LCD TVs and a galley kitchen. Posh, but well overpriced.

Campsite (☎ 422670; tedmoulson@cs.com; Tower Cottage, Garrison Farm; tent sites £4.50-8) Field space and basic washing facilities are about all you'll find at St Mary's campground.

Evergreen Cottage (☎ 422711; www.evergreencot tageguesthouse.co.uk; The Parade; d £58-69) White cob cottage opposite The Park, with plenty of low-ceilinged atmosphere and a garden patio out front.

Crebinick Guest House (☎ 422968; www.crebinick .co.uk; Church St; d £66-80; ☒) Homely rooms in a stout 18th-century house, in Hugh Town, with helpful tips on hand from its Scilly owners.

TRESCO

A short boat hop across the channel from St Mary's brings you to Tresco, the second-largest island, once owned by the monks of Tavistock Abbey. The main attraction is the **Abbey Garden** (☎ 424105; www.tresco.co.uk/stay/abbey -garden; admission £9; ☟ 9.30am-4pm), first laid out in 1834 on the site of a 10th-century Benedictine abbey. The terraced gardens feature more than 5000 subtropical plants, including species from Brazil, New Zealand and South Africa. The admission price includes entry to the Valhalla collection, made up of figureheads and nameplates salvaged from the many ships which have foundered off Tresco's shores.

Around the edge of the island are several well-hidden beaches, including the sand and shell beach of **Appletree Bay**, and the more grandiose curve of sand at **Pentle Bay**, both near the Abbey Garden. On the northwest side of the island are the ruins of two naval forts – **King Charles' Castle** was the first to be built in the 1550s, but was later superseded by the cannon tower of **Cromwell's Castle** nearby.

There are only two places to stay on the island, apart from self-catering cottages. The **New Inn** (☎ 422844; newinn@tresco.co.uk; d £180-210; ☒) has been whetting Scillonian whistles for several centuries, and is still the hub of island life. The upstairs rooms are smartly finished with subtle colours and all mod-cons, and a few boast views over the channel to Bryher. The dining here (mains £5 to £18) has made Michelin's *Eating Out in Pubs*.

This eye-poppingly expensive **Island Hotel** (☎ 422883; islandhotel@tresco.co.uk; r £150-440; ☒ ☒) has bedrooms spread across several wings, with a choice of either private garden patios or glorious sea-view balconies. The décor throughout is elegance personified, ranging from gingham-checked bedrooms to luxurious suites decked out in gold and navy blue, but at these prices it's hardly surprising most people head back to St Mary's after a day's sightseeing.

BRYHER & SAMSON

Just over 70 people scrape along on the re-mote island of Bryher, the Scilly's smallest and wildest inhabited island. Blanketed with heather and bracken, and topped by a range of miniature hills, it's a tough place to try and eke out an existence: fishing and flower-growing are just about the island's only industries, and even those are showing signs of decline. Most of the houses are near the harbour in **Bryher Town**, which sits on the shoreline near the deep anchorage of **New Grimsby Channel**, a favourite stop for visiting yachts. Just to the north of the shops is the modest summit of **Watch Hill**, from where you can drink in one of the finest views in all of Scilly, with a fantastic panorama taking in most of the island chain.

Bryher's eastern side is exposed to the full force of the Atlantic weather, and the appro-priately named **Hell Bay** makes a powerful sight during a winter gale. Things are usually much more tranquil to the south at **Rushy Bay**, a se-cluded cove that's often all but deserted. From the quay, occasional boats visit local seal and bird colonies and deserted **Samson Island**, where the ruined cottages are all that's left of the last island settlers who moved out in 1855.

Bryher's accommodation is pretty limited, and most places are usually fully booked weeks ahead. There are a couple of B&Bs, including **Soleil d'Or** (☎ 422003; June@scillybug .freeserve.co.uk), a modern three bedroom bun-galow on the east side of the island, and **Bank Cottage** (☎ 422612; mac.mace@homecall.co.uk), a more old-fashioned Scillonian cottage with flow-ery rooms, a self-catering kitchen and a cute barbecue patio.

If you're feeling flush, by far the best place to stay on the island – and arguably in all of Scilly – is the superexclusive **Hell Bay Hotel** (☎ 422947; hellbay@aol.com; d incl dinner £420-550; ☒), a lavish island getaway with a selection of suites mixing light New England–style furnishings with sunny golds, sea blues and pale-wood beams. Most have their own sitting rooms, private balconies, and gorgeous bathrooms, but at this price you'd expect nothing less than perfection.

The **campsite** (☎ 422886; www.bryhercampsite .co.uk; sites £7.50) is essentially a field with some outdoor sinks and an old shower block – definitely one for hardy campers. Bikes (£8), canoes (£15) and windsurfers (£15) are available for hire.

There are a couple of places to eat on Bryher, including sandwiches and cakes at the **Vine Café** (☎ 423168) and more filling mains at **Fraggle Rock** (☎ 422222), near the post office. For self-catering supplies, the island's post office sells fruit, veg, bread and tinned goods.

ST MARTIN'S

The third-largest and furthest north of the islands, St Martin's is one of the main centres for Scilly's flower-growing industry. The main settlement is Higher Town, where you'll find a small village shop and **Scilly Diving** (☎ 422848; www.scillydiving.com), which offers dive trips (from £36) in the fantastically clear waters around St Martin's. A short way to the west are the tightly huddled cottages of **Middle Town**, and a little further on is the cluster of houses around **Lower Town**, where you'll also find the island pub and a small jetty.

One of the largest beaches on the island is **Par Beach**, right next to the main quay, while on the island's southern shore is **Lawrence's Bay**, which reveals a broad sweep of sandy

flats at low tide. Along the northern side is **Great Bay**, arguably the finest beach in the Scillys; from the western end, you can cross to White Island at low tide. If you walk east along the windswept northern cliffs you'll find the Day Mark, a red-and-white candy-striped landmark built in 1683, and the secluded cove of **Perpitch**.

Seven miles offshore is the Seven Stones reef, notorious for the 1967 shipwreck of the tanker *Torrey Canyon*, which resulted in one of Britain's most disastrous oil spills. The vessel was bombed by the RAF several times in an attempt to sink the ship and burn off the spill; eventually it broke up after several days, but still polluted more than 120 miles of coastline around Cornwall and northern France.

Also worth a visit is **St Martin's Vineyard** (☎ 423418), the most southwesterly (and certainly the smallest) winery in Britain. Tours of the vineyard with owners Val and Graham Thomas are offered from 11am to 4pm on weekdays throughout the summer.

Sleeping & Eating

Campsite (☎ 422888; www.stmartinscampsite.co.uk; Middle Town; camp site £6.50-8.50) The island's 50-place campground is near Lawrence's Bay at the western end of the island; the facilities (as ever on Scilly) are rudimentary, with water standpipes and coin-op showers, but you couldn't ask for a more beautiful location.

Polreath (☎ 422046; Higher Town; d £80-100, weekly stays only in summer; ✕) This is a robust granite

---

THE LOST LANDS OF LYONESSE

One of Cornwall's oldest legends relates to the fabled kingdom of Lyonesse, which stretched from the land of Belerion (present-day Cornwall) to the Isles of Scilly. According to the story, at some point not too long ago this beautiful land was suddenly engulfed by the sea; the sole survivor was a man named Trevilian, who outrode the advancing waves on a swift white horse, taking refuge in a cave near Marazion. His descendants, the aristocratic Trevelyan family, still bear a white horse rising from the waves on their family crest.

Despite the fanciful story, this legend just might be rooted in fact. As late as the 4th century Roman historians were still referring to the Isles of Scilly as one large island, and there are various points around the islands' coastline where Bronze Age fields have been drowned by the rising tide. There are also submerged woods around the Cornish coast, including one in Mount's Bay, where ancient tree stumps are sometimes exposed at exceptionally low tides, and it's known that the end of the last Ice Age brought about a major sea-level rise around much of the British Isles. Whether Lyonesse ever existed still remains something of a mystery, but local fishermen swear that submerged buildings can sometimes be seen around the Seven Stones Lighthouse of Mount's Bay, and it's said that from Land's End you can still sometimes hear the tolling of Lyonesse's church bells on the evening breeze.

cottage – one of the few B&Bs on the island. Squeeze yourself into one of the titchy, traditional rooms or sip a cool lemonade in the sunny conservatory; cream teas, baguettes and light bites are also on offer six days per week and sometimes you'll even get a hot evening meal too.

St Martin's on the Isle (☎ 422090; www.stmartinshotel.co.uk; d £290-460; ✕ ⊠) Scilly certainly has its share of pamper-palace hotels, and St Martin's is no exception. Sparkling rooms, a lavish pool, manicured grounds and a private jetty make this one of the top-rated hotels in the islands, but you'll need to raid the piggy bank if you want to secure a sea view. The contemporary Tean Restaurant (three-course menu £42.50) is a gourmet treat too – venison, foie gras and squab pigeon all find their way onto the upmarket *carte*.

ST AGNES

Even by Scilly standards, the rocky island of St Agnes is quiet; when the last day boats have departed for St Mary's, the island is practically deserted, so aspiring Robinson Crusoes will feel right at home. The most southerly of the Scilly Isles, St Agnes is studded with peaceful coves, rugged reefs and a scattering of prehistoric sites, and it's a place many visitors never quite manage to reach.

The main quay is at **Porth Conger**, near the decommissioned **Old Lighthouse**, from where the road leads to two lovely inlets at Periglis Cove and St Warna's Cove, named after the patron saint of shipwrecks. The coast path between the coves passes the tiny **Troy Town Maze**, a concentric maze of stones that's thought to be around two centuries old, but might be based on a prehistoric original. The southern side of the island is mostly taken up by the bracken-strewn sweep of **Wingletang Down**, while on the east side the little beach of **Covean** is a handsome place to settle down for an afternoon sunbathe. At low tide a sand bar connects St Martin's with the small island of Gugh, famous for its Bronze Age remains and the slanting menhir known as the **Old Man of Gugh**. Take care not to be cut off by the rising tide, which comes in fast and is too strong for swimming.

Offshore boat trips are operated by **St Agnes Boating** (☎ 422704; www.st-agnes-boating.co.uk) to St Mary's (£6.60), the offshore islands (£7) and longer trips to the Western Rocks (£122) and the Bishops Rock Lighthouse (£14).

Sleeping & Eating

The **campsite** (☎ 422360; www.troytownscilly.co.uk; Troy Town Farm; tent sites £7.50) is at Troy Town Farm in the southwestern corner of the island. Flush loos, hot and cold water basins and token-operated showers are all available, but the site is quite exposed to the Atlantic wind, though the views are out of this world.

The island's nicest B&B is **Covean Cottage** (☎ 422620; s £20-24, d £58-70), a small granite house near Covean Beach with four frilly rooms and a friendly owner who'll happily pack you a picnic lunch if you ask, complete with scones and other sticky treats.

Alternatively try **Coastguards** (☎ 422373; d from £60), an atmospheric B&B in a row of fishermen's cottages not far from the post office.

our pick **Turk's Head** (☎ 422434; mains £6.50-10.95) Quite possibly our favourite pub in the entire country, Britain's most southerly alehouse is a real beauty. Model ships and seafaring photos line the walls, great pub food (swordfish, crab-cakes, veggie chillis) is served up in the wood-panelled bar, and you can carry your pint down to the slipway as the sun goes down. You might even be treated to a sea shanty if the local lads are in the mood. Wonderful in every way. Rooms are also available (doubles £64 to £70).

THE SOUTH COAST

In contrast to the plunging crags and surfable swells of the North Coast, Cornwall's southern shore presents a much more tranquil side to the county, with a patchwork landscape of flowery hedgerows, tree-lined lanes and broad green fields rolling gently down to the water's edge. Sheltered from the brunt of the biting Atlantic winds, it's also where you'll find many of Cornwall's fine gardens, including Trelissick, Caerhays Castle and the Lost Gardens of Heligan.

FALMOUTH

☎ 01326 / pop 20,775
Strategically situated at the end of the Fal Estuary, overlooking the entrance to the Carrick Roads, the port of Falmouth has been a maritime hub for more than 500 years. Boasting the world's third-deepest natural harbour, Falmouth flourished as a trading port and naval harbour after the

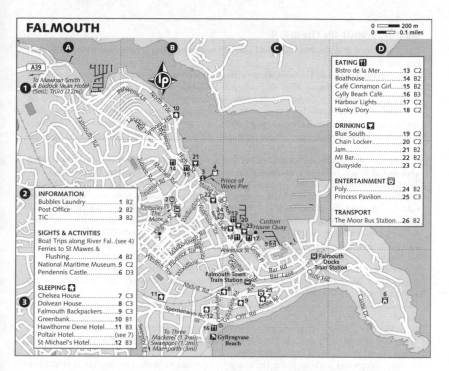

FALMOUTH

0 —— 200 m
0 —— 0.1 miles

EATING 🍴
Bistro de la Mer............13 C2
Boathouse......................14 B2
Café Cinnamon Girl........15 B2
Gylly Beach Café............16 B3
Harbour Lights...............17 C2
Hunky Dory....................18 C2

DRINKING 🍸
Blue South.....................19 C2
Chain Locker..................20 C2
Jam...............................21 B2
MI Bar...........................22 B2
Quayside.......................23 C2

ENTERTAINMENT 🎭
Poly...............................24 B2
Princess Pavilion............25 C3

TRANSPORT
The Moor Bus Station....26 B2

② **INFORMATION**
Bubbles Laundry.............1 B2
Post Office......................2 B2
TIC.................................3 B2

SIGHTS & ACTIVITIES
Boat Trips along River Fal..(see 4)
Ferries to St Mawes &
Flushing.........................4 B2
National Maritime Museum.5 C2
Pendennis Castle.............6 D3

③ **SLEEPING** 🛏
Chelsea House.................7 C3
Dolvean House................8 C3
Falmouth Backpackers.....9 C3
Greenbank....................10 B1
Hawthorne Dene Hotel....11 B3
Poltair Hotel...............(see 7)
St Michael's Hotel..........12 B3

---

river at Truro silted up. The town reached its heyday during the era of the Falmouth Packet Service, which carried mail, bullion and supplies between Britain and its overseas colonies between 1689 and 1850. The days of the tall ships, tea clippers and naval galleons may be long gone, but the town remains an important centre for shipping and repairs, and since 2003 it's also been home to the southwestern outpost of the National Maritime Museum. More recently, especially since the spanking new campus of the CUC (Combined Universities of Cornwall) opened up the road in Penryn, it's also gained a buzzy after-dark scene, with a medley of bars and brasseries dotted along its central street.

Information

Bubbles Laundry (☎ 311291; 99 Killigrew St; ⏰ 8am-7pm Mon-Fri, 9am-7pm Sat, 10am-3pm Sun)
Post office (☎ 318916; The Moor; ⏰ 9am-5.30pm Mon-Sat)
Tourist office (☎ 312300; falmouthtic@yahoo.co.uk; 11 Market Strand, Prince of Wales Pier; ⏰ 9.30am-5.15pm Mon-Fri, 9.45am-5.15pm Sat)

Sights & Activities

NATIONAL MARITIME MUSEUM

Falmouth's illustrious seafaring takes centre stage at the **National Maritime Museum Cornwall** (☎ 313388; www.nmmc.co.uk; Discovery Quay; adult/child £7.50/5; ⏰ 10am-5pm; ♿), situated on the town's heavily redeveloped dockside. The museum houses one of the largest maritime collections in the UK, second only to its sister museum in Greenwich in London. At the heart of the complex is the huge Flotilla Gallery, where boats dangle from the ceiling by slender steel wires, while suspended walkways wind their way around the collection of yachts, schooners, punts and canoes. Other highlights include the Set Sail exhibit, which tells the story of nine groundbreaking boats, and the Lookout, with a 360-degree panorama of Falmouth Bay. The museum even has its own harbourfront pontoon.

PENDENNIS CASTLE

Perched on the promontory of Pendennis Point, **Pendennis Castle** (EH; ☎ 316594; adult/child £5.40/2.70; ⏰ 10am-6pm Jul & Aug, 10am-5pm Apr-Jun & Sep, 10am-4pm Oct-Mar) was constructed from

CORNWALL

MESSING ABOUT ON THE RIVER

Down on Prince of Wales Pier you'll find several companies offering boat trips around Falmouth Bay and the Fal Estuary.

Enterprise Boats (☎ 01326-374241; www.enterprise-boats.co.uk) operates three wooden-hulled boats along the picturesque River Fal, calling at **Trelissick Gardens** (p262; adult/child one way £4.50/3) and Smuggler's Cottage at **Tolverne** en route to **Truro** (return £10/5). Depending on the tides, the boats sometimes stop at Malpas, 3 miles downriver from Truro; free double-deckers connect with the harbourmaster's office near the city centre. There are also trips from Truro to **St Mawes** (return £10/5). Boat trips run every two hours or so in both directions depending on the time of year.

Other companies offer similar routes but only travel as far as Trelissick and Tolverne; try **K&S Cruises** (☎ 01326-211056) and **Newman's Cruises** (☎ 01872-580309). **Twinstar Cruises** (☎ 01326-211446) is the only company with its own catamaran, and also offers cruises along the River Helford and Frenchman's Creek. Most of the companies offer an onboard commentary detailing local wildlife and points of interest such as Pill Creek (setting of the film *Treasure Island*), Tregothnan (the Seat of Lord Falmouth and the site of Cornwall's only tea plantation), and embarkation points for US troops during the D-Day invasions. The website at **Fal River Links** (☎ 01872-861914; www .falriverlinks.co.uk) has contact details and timetables for all the companies, plus suggestions for local walks including the Oyster Way, a 3-hour ramble from Tolverne to St Mawes.

Passenger ferries (☎ 01872-861910; www.kingharryscornwall.co.uk/ferries) cross to St Mawes (return £7/4.50) and the small yachting village of **Flushing** from the pier every hour in summer, and a few times daily in winter except Sunday.

1540 to 1545 by Henry VIII as one of a chain of fortresses designed to defend the British mainland from Spanish and French invasion. Falmouth's deepwater harbour made the town a key strategic asset, and Pendennis was built, along with its sister fortress of St Mawes (p266), to defend the harbour and the entrance to the Carrick Roads. During the Civil War, the castle was engaged in a five-month siege under the command of Captain John Arundell of Trerice (p233), and later became a defensive gun battery during WWII.

These days the guns have fallen silent, but you can still experience a taste of Tudor warfare on the castle's reconstructed gun-deck with its impressive collection of vintage cannons. The history of the fortress is explored inside the old artillery barracks, and outside you can visit the old underground magazine, Guardhouse and Observation Post. Regular outdoor concerts are held in the castle grounds during summer; rather less tuneful is the deafening retort of the Noonday Gun, which rings out everyday at noon sharp.

BEACHES

Falmouth is blessed with a trio of town beaches. Most popular is **Gyllyngvase**, a flat sandy beach backed by a funky café. A pleasant half-hour stroll along the headland is

Swanpool, backed by a small inland lagoon and nature reserve, populated by grebes, coots, kingfishers and mute swans. A couple of miles further along the coast is **Maenporth**, trammelled by cliffs and a fine spot for some sheltered swimming. There's also a small beach café (open 9am to 6pm in season) selling drinks, snacks and ice creams. All three beaches are accessible from the coast path, or you can catch the X89 bus from town. There are car parks at Swanpool and Maenporth, but they fill up quickly in summer.

Sleeping

Falmouth Backpackers (☎ 319996; www.falmouth backpackers.co.uk; 9 Gyllyngvase Tce; dm £16-17, s/d from £20/36) Plonked on a back street near Princess Pavilion, this indie hostel is handy for Gyllyngvase and the town centre. Dorm rooms are plain and patchy, arranged in three- to six-bed configurations, and include a basic brekkie of tea and toast. Summer barbies are often provided by the genial owners.

Chelsea House (☎ 212230; www.chelseahousehotel .com; 2 Emslie Rd; s £35-40, d £55-76; ✗) Shh, keep it a secret – three of Falmouth's best-value B&Bs are tucked away on this quiet terrace behind the Promenade. This is the pick, with a 'Ships and Castle' family room, a four-poster 'Pendennis' suite and a miniscule 'Captain's

Cabin' in the attic. Homemade marmalade and three types of Danish pastry grace the breakfast table.

Hawthorne Dene Hotel (☎ 311427; www.haw thornedenehotel.co.uk; 12 Pennance Rd; s £40, d from £75; **P**) Edwardian elegance rules the roost at this family-run hotel, from the old photos adorning the walls to the antique dining room and booklined gentleman's lounge (complete with log fire). The rooms are antiquated, but most have sea views, springy beds and the odd period curio.

Dolvean House (☎ 313658; www.dolvean.co.uk; 50 Melvill Rd; s £40, d £80-90; **⌨**) Falmouth's only five-star B&B is a cut above the norm, but won't be to everyone's taste. The 10 rooms are flouncy and feminine – expect lashings of lace, tasteful tones, brass bedheads and frilly trimmings – but they're all plush and posh, with treats including DVD players and wi-fi. Shame about the busy road.

Greenbank (☎ 312440; www.greenbank-hotel.co.uk; Harbourside; standard d £120-150, executive £150-215, ste £260; **P**) Ships in bottles and model boats cruise around Falmouth's original upmarket hotel, plonked on the edge of town with a top-drawer harbour view. Rooms are 'Standard' (classic colours, pine furniture, quilted bedspreads) or 'Executive' (deluge showers, king-size beds, and the odd zebra stripe or Dalmatian print); the Sheldrake Suite even has its own brass-mounted telescope.

Budock Vean Hotel (☎ 250288; www.budock.co.uk; Mawnan Smith; d £214-240; **P ⌨ ☏**) Another stalwart on Cornwall's luxury-hotel scene, this riverside beauty sits on the Helford's north bank, with huge rooms (some with private sitting rooms), four lounges, a health spa, tennis courts, 13 hectares of parkland and even a private jetty. It's more country-chic than boutique, but a wonderful place to wallow.

Poltair Hotel (☎ 313158; www.poltair.co.uk; Emslie Rd; s £24-30, d £48-60) Great value double-fronted guest-house, with eleven spic-and-span rooms and a luxurious top-floor 'Beachcomber' suite.

St Michael's Hotel (☎ 312707; www.stmichaelshotel .co.uk; Gyllyngvase Beach, d £136-178) By far the best of the Gyllyngvase Beach hotels, St Michael's offers luxurious sea-themed rooms and all the top-end trimmings (spa, swimming pool, sauna).

Eating

Harbour Lights (☎ 316934; Arwenack St; fish & chips £3-4; ❤ lunch & dinner) Sometimes you can't do better than a good old-fashioned fish supper, and this place does the best cod 'n' chips in town (sustainably sourced, of course). There's even a nice little dining room overlooking the quay.

Café Cinnamon Girl (☎ 211457; 4-6 Old Brewery Yard; lunch & sandwiches from £5.50; ❤ 9.30am-5pm Mon-Sat; ⌨) Look no further for lunch than this cute little organic café, locally famous for its bumper-sized sandwiches, homemade soups and trademark roasted veg. The free wi-fi's a bonus.

Gylly Beach Café (☎ 312884; Gyllyngvase Beach; mains £5.50-8.95; ❤ 9.30am-11pm summer, 10.30am-5pm winter) A popular den for Falmouth's beach-going crowd, this environmentally friendly, fair-trade hangout offers tempting café food right on the sands of Gyllyngvase. There are DJs and drinks promos several nights a week, and the weekend breakfasts are recommended (check out the Canadian pancakes).

Three Mackerel (☎ 311886; Swanpool Beach; mains £12-20; ❤ lunch & dinner) Not exactly handy for town, but a fine choice for beachside dining if you're down Swanpool way. Sophisticated Med-style dishes and barbecue-grilled tapas are served on the beach-view sundeck in summer, or in the sparkly dining room on inclement days.

Bistro de la Mer (☎ 316509; 28 Arwenack St; mains £14.95-19.95; ❤ lunch & dinner) An old favourite with Falmouth foodies, this snug little bistro brings a soupçon of Gallic flair to Arwenack St. The tables here are packed in tight and you'll be elbow-to-elbow with your neighbours, but the menu's authentically French and makes great use of fresh Cornish fish and seafood.

Boathouse (☎ 315425; Trevethan Hill; ❤ noon-3pm & 6-11pm Fri & Sat, noon-12.30am Mon-Thu, noon-midnight Sun) The gastropub label is bandied about all too easily, but this is the real deal – an excellent pub-cum-bistro with an imaginative menu of burgers, ciabattas and heartier mains, along with a tempting selection of local brews.

Hunky Dory (☎ 212997; 46 Arwenack St; mains £15.95-18.50; ❤ dinner) Local seafood takes top billing at this laid-back restaurant, split over two floors of a listed building near the old Customs House. The menu is bang up-to-date, blending European and Asian flavours with top-notch Cornish produce, and the setting is nicely minimal, mixing Mediterranean tones with pale wood and rough whitewashed walls.

CORNWALL

MARVELLOUS MOLLUSCS

The River Helford is home to one of the last traditional **oyster fisheries** in the UK. Oysters have been farmed in this corner of Cornwall for at least 500 years. The earliest known reference to Cornish oyster fishing comes from a document dating from 1506 belonging to the Manor of Earthen (once part of the Trelowarren Estate), which stakes a claim for the best fish and shellfish from the Helford for the lord of the manor. By the mid-19th century oyster fisheries in the Helford and Fal Estuaries were supplying large fish markets as far away as Plymouth and London, a trade which was to flourish for the next hundred years. The industry suffered a catastrophic decline in the late 1980s after the introduction of a parasite from the USA devastated stocks of native British oysters. Thankfully oyster production is up and running again on the Helford, and every October Falmouth hosts an annual **Oyster Festival** (www.falmouthoysterfestival.co.uk) in celebration of this blooming bivalve, with a programme of live music, cookery demonstrations and food markets, not to mention oodles of oyster guzzling.

Drinking

Chain Locker (☎ 311685, Quay St) Shiver-me-timbers – a classic old sea-dog of a pub, with the all-important low ceilings, heart-stopping ales and hugger-mugger atmosphere.

Quayside (☎ 312113; Arwenack St) Just along the quay from the Chain Locker, this busy boozer is the place for a sunset pint, with picnic tables beside the harbour and a twin-floored pub selling German lager and local beers.

MI Bar (☎ 316909; Church St; ☼ 7pm-midnight Mon-Wed, 7pm-2am Thu & Fri, noon-2am Sat, noon-midnight Sun) For something slicker, try this stripped-back bar with pool tables, live bands, big-screen sports and casino nights.

Blue South (☎ 212122; 35-37 Arwenack St; ☼ 11am-11pm) Sister venue to the Blue Bar on Porthtowan, this beachy bar offers a similarly chilled vibe, with deep sofas, draft beers and a menu of munchie mains.

Jam (☎ 219123; 32 High St) Impossibly funky music emporium-cum-cappuccino bar, with a just-so selection of vinyl and CDs, great coffee and leather sofas to lounge around on. *Nice…*

Entertainment

Poly (☎ 314566; www.thepoly.org; Church St) The old Falmouth Arts Centre has had a recent revamp as an arthouse cinema, and shows all the brilliant European films and low-budget Brit flicks you never get to see down the Odeon.

Princess Pavilion (☎ 211222; princesspavilion@carric kleisure.org.uk; 41 Melvill Rd) The town's main venue for live events, with gigs, theatre and tribute bands aplenty, and the annual **Cornwall Film Festival** (☎ 01209-204655; www.cornwallfilmfestival.com) every November.

Getting There & Away

The quickest bus from Falmouth to Truro is the 89 (30 minutes, hourly Mondays to Saturdays), which continues to Newquay as the 90. Bus 88 (50 minutes, half-hourly Monday to Saturday) via Penryn takes longer but is more frequent. For all the town beaches, catch the 400 (hourly Monday to Saturday, five on Sunday).

Ponsharden Park & Float Service (☎ 319417; www .ponsharden.co.uk; ☼ 10am-6pm Mon-Fri May-Sep) runs three hourly ferries from Ponsharden car park to Customs House Quay. On Sunday, the ferry doesn't run and there is only a bus into Falmouth. The Falmouth Float Pass includes all-day car parking and costs £10 per car for up to two people, or £14 per car for up to seven people; the St Mawes Explorer costs £15.50 per car for two people, or £22.50 per car for up to seven people. You'll also qualify for discounted entry to the National Maritime Museum.

Falmouth is at the end of the branch line from Truro (£2.90 one way, 20 minutes, hourly Monday to Saturday), stopping at Penryn, Falmouth Town and Falmouth Docks.

TRELISSICK GARDENS

Rolling fields and world-class rhododendrons sum up **Trelissick Gardens** (NT; ☎ 01872-862090; trelissick@nationaltrust.org.uk; adult/child £5.80/2.90; ☼ 10.30am-5.30pm Feb-Oct, 11am-4pm Nov-Feb), another of Cornwall's glorious country estates. Stretching for 200 hectares above the Carrick Roads, the heart of the estate is the 19th-century neo-Gothic mansion built for Thomas Daniell in 1825, which stands in a fabulous position overlooking lushly wooded fields to the River Fal. Although the house is closed to the public, you can see the refurbished Georgian stable block and stroll through the ornamental gardens, renowned for their rhododendrons, camellias and hydrangeas. There's also a garden shop, gallery and top-notch teashop. Aspiring aristocrats can stay in the 19th-century water tower – contact **National Trust Holiday Cottages** (☎ 0870 458 4422; cottages@nationaltrust.org.uk) for details.

If you need to burn off those teatime scones, you can follow one of several lovely walks and riverside trails around the estate. Look out for the deep-sea tankers that moor up along the riverbank – 50 years ago many American destroyers destined for the D Day beaches were hidden along the quiet creeks nearby.

TRURO

☎ 01872 / pop 17,431

Cobbled streets and high-street chainstores meet in the cathedral city of Truro, the county's capital and its main administrative and commercial centre. Nestled at the bottom of a bowl-shaped valley fed by the Rivers Allen, Kenwyn and Truro, the city has a long history as a stannary town and industrial hub, although it's now principally of interest to shoppers, office workers and weekend drinkers. Traces of its rich heritage remain in the Georgian town houses and Victorian villas dotted around the city. It's also where you'll find the main county museum and a lively choice of bars and bistros.

Information

Library (☎ 279205; Union Place; per hr £3; ☯ 9am-6pm Mon-Fri, 9am-4pm Sat) Internet access.

Post office (High Cross; ☯ 9am-5.30pm Mon-Sat)

Royal Cornwall Hospital (☎ 250000; Treliske) 24hr accident and emergency.

Police station (Tregolls Rd; ☯ 8am-6pm)

Tourist office (☎ 274555; tic@truro.gov.uk; Boscawen St; ☯ 9am-5.30pm Mon-Fri, 9am-5pm Sat)

Truro Launderette (☎ 272005; Chapel Hill)

Waterstone's (☎ 225765; 11 Boscawen St; ☯ 9am-5.30pm Mon-Sat, 10am-4pm Sun) Large chain bookshop selling travel guides, fiction and general-interest titles.

Sights

OLD CITY

Truro grew up around a hilltop castle on the site of the present-day Crown Court, but the town's history really began in the 14th century when it became one of the county's four stannary towns (where tin was assayed, stamped and taxed). Until the 18th century it was also a busy port, but suffered a serious setback when the river became clogged with silt. These days Truro's old quays exist only in name, including **Lemon Quay** and **Back Quay**, both near the Hall for Cornwall.

While the lucrative shipping trade moved to Falmouth, Truro turned its attentions to mining and manufacturing, and the town enjoyed a huge financial boom after the arrival of the railway in 1859. Fine Georgian mansions and grand town houses sprang up to accommodate Truro's industrial magnates; the finest examples can be seen along **Falmouth Rd**, **Strangways Tce**, **Walsingham Pl** and **Lemon St**.

TRURO CATHEDRAL

Plonked like a neo-Gothic supertanker in the heart of town, the three-spired **Truro Cathedral** (☎ 276782; www.trurocathedral.org.uk; High Cross; suggested donation £4) dominates the city skyline from every angle. Built on the site of the 16th-century parish church of St Mary's (part of which now forms the cathedral's South

---

THE SMUGGLERS' SNUG

our pick **Pandora Inn** (☎ 01326-372678; Restronguet Creek; mains £4-12) Prepare to fall in love with the Pandora, one of Cornwall's oldest and best-loved waterside pubs, ensconced in a heart-melting spot by Restronguet Creek. Foot-thick walls, scuffed-wood tables, ship's lanterns and a huge abandoned anchor outside conjure up the smugglers'-den vibe, and you can sink your drinks on the pontoon to the sound of clanking yacht masts. Hardy souls can even sample some of the Pandora's fabled smuggler's rum: at 80% proof, though, you might need to arrange for a taxi home. Or an ambulance.

The Pandora sits on the edge of Restronguet Creek, about 0.7 miles northeast of the village of Mylor Bridge. Heading south on the main A39 road from Truro to Falmouth, take the right-hand turn to Flushing and Mylor Bridge; follow signs for Mylor Bridge and look out for the left turn onto the brake-squeakingly Restronguet Hill. The pub's right at the bottom by the dock.

Aisle), the new cathedral was a massive technical and financial undertaking for its architect John Loughborough Pearson. Although the foundation stones were laid in 1880, the building wasn't completed until 1910 – the first new cathedral to be built in Britain since St Paul's. The cathedral's famous features include its collection of Victorian stained-glass windows (including ones dedicated to Cornish mining and the Methodist preacher John Wesley), an ornate memorial to the Robartes family (owners of Lanhydrock House) and the huge Father Willis Organ, built in 1887, and almost identical to one produced by its maker Henry Willis for Coventry Cathedral in 1886.

ROYAL CORNWALL MUSEUM

The **Royal Cornwall Museum** (☎ 272205; www.royal cornwallmuseum.org.uk; River St; admission free; ☺ 10am-5pm Mon-Sat) on River St is Cornwall's oldest and largest museum, and houses most of the main collection relating to the county's archaeological and historical past.

SHOPS & GALLERIES

All the main high street chains are dotted along Boscawen St and Pydar St, but more intriguing shops and craft sellers are found around **Lemon St Market**. Across the street, the **Lemon St Gallery** (☎ 275757; 13 Lemon St; ☺ 10.30am-5.30pm Mon-Sat) often hosts high-profile exhibitions by local artists.

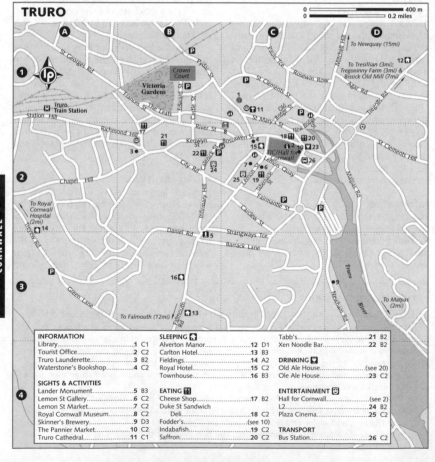

Sleeping

Tregoninny Farm (☎ 520145; www.tregoninny.com; Tresillian; d from £50, cottages £400-700 per wk; P) This delightful B&B is arranged around a central courtyard in Tresillian, 3 miles from Truro, and offers a selection of light, airy rooms and self-catering cottages across several converted farm buildings.

Carlton Hotel (☎ 223938; www.carltonhotel.co.uk; 49 Falmouth Rd; s £42.50-50, d £60-70; P ✖) The furnishings are bog-standard B&B (pastel colours, easy-clean carpets, ancient kettles), but extras such as Sky TV and a guest sauna and Jacuzzi sweeten the deal at this old package-tour favourite.

Bissick Old Mill (☎ 01726-882557; www.bissickoldmill.co.uk; Ladock; d £75, ste £95; P ▢) You'll need wheels to reach this beautiful converted mill in Ladock, about 7 miles northeast of town. It's got all the boutique credentials; Egyptian cotton sheets, handmade soap, fresh fruit and in-room fridges, plus self-contained cottages for longer stays.

Royal Hotel (☎ 270345; www.royalhotelcornwall.co.uk; Lemon St; s £75, d £95-120; P ▢) This hotel with a Georgian front looks old-world, but don't be fooled by the vintage exterior. Inside the 34 rooms are zingy and modern, distinguished by citrus tints and stripped-back furniture. Behind the main hotel are nine corporate-style 'aparthotels' complete with workspaces, dishwashers and designer striplights.

Alverton Manor (☎ 276633; reception@alvertonmanor.co.uk; Tregolls Rd; s £90, d £95-200, ste £225; P) This converted convent is Truro's top hotel, but the style is definitely more country than contemporary. Antique wardrobes, burnished sleigh beds and flowery drapes in the generously proportioned bedrooms; the best have views over the hotel's manicured grounds.

Fieldings (☎ 262783; www.fieldingsintruro.com; 35 Treyew Rd; s/d £22/44) Homely guesthouse run by a local husband-and-wife team.

Townhouse (☎ 277374; 20 Falmouth Rd; s £45, d £65-75; P ✖) A practical if wholly unremarkable B&B just uphill from the town centre.

Eating

Duke St Sandwich Deli (☎ 320025; 10 Duke St; sandwiches £2.50-5; ☽ 9am-5.30pm Mon-Sat) Gourmet sandwiches and handmade ciabattas form the cornerstone of this great sandwich shop, which also sells a selection of Cornish jams, chutneys and cheeses.

Fodder's (☎ 271384; Pannier Market, Lemon Quay; mains £6-9; ☽ 9am-5.30pm Mon-Sat) Hidden away above the old Truro Pannier Market, this chaotic wholefood café's been around for donkey's years but is still churning out its chunky butties, thick bean soups and carrot cakes.

Xen Noodle Bar (☎ 222998; 47-49 Calenick St; mains £6-9; ☽ lunch & dinner) Ditch the Chinese dragons and paper lanterns – this resolutely modern noodle bar brings the Oriental experience bang up-to-date, with a menu of Szechuan, Hong Kong and Canton flavours as well as Chinese classics.

Saffron (☎ 263771; 5 Quay St; mains £9-16; ☽ dinner Tue-Sat) This tiny bistro has been a well-kept secret for years, but it's now tough to bag a table without booking. Hardly surprising, as the inventive menu is arguably the best in town, with daily changing mains veering from spider crab chowder to pan-fried monkfish.

Tabb's (☎ 262110; 85 Kenwyn St; mains £12.50-21.50; ☽ lunch Tue-Fri, dinner Tue-Sat) Lilac walls, leather chairs and slate floors create a slightly stuffy atmosphere, but there's no arguing with the food – Cornish meats, hand-baked bread and local seafood all feature, and the owner's renowned for his petits fours.

Indabafish (☎ 274700; Tabernacle St; mains £14-18; ☽ dinner) Plate-glass windows, chrome fixtures and overhead pipes make this swish fish emporium feel metropolitan-modern, but the menu's all about classic, straight-forward seafood, from Falmouth oysters to Newlyn lobster.

Drinking

Kasbah (☎ 272276; 3 Quay St) Shades of Morocco hang heavy over this perennially popular wine bar, which is always stuffed with 30-something boozers and runs a late-licence on weekends.

Old Ale House (☎ 271122; Quay St) The pick of Truro's pubs, and a welcome change if you're getting sick of minimalist décor and designer cocktails. Here it's all burnished wood and beer mats; a selection of daily ales are chalked up behind the bar, and there's often a jazz troupe at weekends.

Heron (☎ 272773; Malpas; ☽ 11am-3pm & 6-11pm Mon-Sat, 7-10.30pm Sun) Two miles from the city along the river estuary, this creekside pub serves good beer and excellent grub, with outside benches where you sup your pint.

CORNWALL

Entertainment

Hall for Cornwall (☎ 262466; www.hallforcornwall .co.uk; Lemon Quay) The county's main venue for touring theatre and music, housed in Truro's former town hall on Lemon Quay.

Plaza Cinema (☎ 272894; www.wtwcinemas .co.uk; Lemon St) A four-screen cinema showing mainstream releases.

L2 (☎ 222023; Calenick St; cover charge £3-5; ⌚ 9pm-1.30am Mon, 9.30pm-1am Wed-Thu, 9.30pm-2.30am Fri & Sat) Truro's biggest nightclub, with five themed nights including the popular Tranz@ction club night on Friday. Things get notoriously rowdy at kicking-out time.

Getting There & Away

There are regular buses from Truro to most of the rest of Cornwall; useful lines include the 88 to Falmouth (30 minutes, at least hourly Monday to Saturday, hourly on Sunday), 14 to St Ives (1½ hours, hourly Monday to Saturday), X18 to Penzance (1½ hours, hourly Monday to Saturday) and the T50 to St Mawes (one hour, every two hours Monday to Saturday).

Truro is halfway along the main line through Cornwall, with onward connections to Penzance, Plymouth and London Paddington, and a branch line to Falmouth

THE ROSELAND

South of Truro, the mudflats and tidal estuaries of the River Fal seep into the deep water of the Carrick Roads, which divides the quiet parishes of Mylor and Feock from the Roseland Peninsula. The name derives from the Cornish word *ros*, meaning promontory, and it's still a tough place to reach unless you've got your own boat; the only route across is via the old King Harry Ferry (opposite), which links Trelissick on the west bank with Philleigh on the east; if you miss the last boat it's a 30-mile round trip by road. The Roseland is a lovely, quiet corner of Cornwall, filled with crop fields, grazing cattle and meandering backlanes, along with little-visited inlets studded along the southern coastline.

St Mawes & Around
☎ 01326

Across the waterway from Falmouth is the chichi harbour of St Mawes, best known for its unusual clover-shaped **castle** (EH; ☎ 01326-270526; adult/child £3.90/2; ⌚ 10am-6pm Jul & Aug, 10am-5pm Apr-Jun & Sep, 10am-4pm Oct, 10am-4pm Fri-Mon Nov-Mar). Designed to work in tandem with its sister

fortress of Pendennis (p259), St Mawes is one of the best preserved of Henry's chain of coastal fortresses; the last time it saw action was during the Civil War, when it surrendered without a fight to the Parliamentarian General Fairfax in 1646. The preserved stonework is particularly impressive, and the views from the central keep are superb; look out for the murky *oubliettes*, narrow shafts that once housed unfortunate inmates.

The countryside around St Mawes is well worth delving into. Across the River Percuil from St Mawes is the promontory of St Anthony's Head, where you'll find a candy-striped lighthouse and the old St Anthony gun battery, as well as the charming 12th-century church of **St-Anthony-in-Roseland**. Further east you'll stumble across the steep streets of **Portscatho** and the beaches of **Carne** and **Pendower**, which join at low tide to form one of the best expanses of sand on Cornwall's south coast. North from St Mawes is the beautiful churchyard of **St-Just-in-Roseland**, a jumble of wildflowers and overhanging yews tumbling down to a boat-filled creek.

East towards the sweep of Veryan Bay is the harbour of **Portloe**, an old wreckers' hangout on the South West Coast Path, while the village of **Veryan** sits a little way inland around a central green and duck pond; it's famous for the twin roundhouses at the top of the village (the lack of corners apparently made them devil-proof).

SLEEPING

Braganza (☎ 270281; braganzak@googlemail.com; Grove Hill; s/d £35/70) An imposing Regency house on the hillside with cluttered, comfy rooms loaded with knackered trinkets and shabby-chic furniture; bag a front room for the stunning harbour overlook.

St Mawes Hotel (☎ 270266; www.stmaweshotel.co.uk; d £90-120) Can't stretch to the Tresanton? Fear not – this mustard-coloured 'bar-with-beds' has five jazzily finished rooms, including three with a sea view to match the Tresanton's priciest suites. Noise from the ground-floor café is the only drawback.

Driftwood Hotel (☎ 580644; www.driftwoodhotel .co.uk; near Portscatho; r £190-220; P) It's another wallet-buster, but the Driftwood is a seaside escape *par excellence*. New England colours and a mix of wicker, scrubbed wood, chocolate checks and sea-stripe blues conjure up the feeling of a beach house by the sea, and there are shells and pebble-filled jars all over the place just to reinforce the vibe.

Hotel Tresanton (☎ 270055; www.tresanton.com; d £230-295, ste £315) Celebrities and sojourning film stars have graced the Riviera-style terraces of this fantastic hotel, run by renowned hotelier Olga Polizzi. Chilled checks, sea stripes and deluxe fabrics in the bedrooms, natural woods and nautical shades in the bathrooms, and luxuries including a private cinema, motor launch and award-winning bistro. One for the album.

EATING
Rising Sun (☎ 270233; St Mawes Harbour; mains £5-10) A popular pub near the water's edge, with a lovely enclosed patio out front that makes a fine place for a gammon steak or a bowl of scampi and chips.

Victory Inn (☎ 270324; Victory Steps; mains £6-12) This flower-covered pub combines traditional trappings (slate roof, warm beers, outside tables) with an up-to date restaurant (all wicker chairs and twisted willow), with swordfish, bass fillets and skate on the menu.

GETTING THERE & AWAY
The T50 runs to Truro (one hour, every two hours Monday to Saturday).

The **King Harry Ferry** (☎ 01872-862312; www .kingharry-info.co.uk; cars one way/return £4.50/6.50, pedestrians/bikes one way 20p/50p) is one of the world's last chain-operated ferries, and makes the crossing over the River Fal every 20 minutes. The last ferry from the Truro side is 9.30pm, from Roseland side 9.20pm; one hour earlier on Sunday.

For ferries to Falmouth, see p260.

MEVAGISSEY & AROUND
☎ 01726 / pop 3785

Flower-fronted cottages, salty old pubs and a small fishing fleet shelter behind a double granite breakwater in Mevagissey, another of Cornwall's quintessentially pretty fishing ports. It won't take you long to explore the town's meandering open spaces, but there are several intriguing sights within easy reach, including the large sandy beach at **Pentewan**, popular with holidaymakers from the nearby chalet park, and the pocket-sized harbour of **Gorran Haven**. In summer, ferries run from Mevagissey Harbour along the coast to Fowey (adult/child return £10/5, four to six daily May to September).

Sights
LOST GARDENS OF HELIGAN
Before he embarked on his Eden adventure, Tim Smit's pet project was the **Lost Gardens of Heligan** (☎ 845100; www.heligan.com; Pentewan; adult/child £8.50/5; ☺ 10am-6pm Mar-Oct, 10am-5pm Nov-Feb). During the 19th century, Heligan was the family seat of the Tremayne family and one of Cornwall's great country gardens, but following the outbreak of WWI (where most of its staff were killed), the garden and the house slid into disrepair. For the next five decades Heligan languished, overgrown and forgotten, until the early 1990s when Smit and his team of volunteers began the arduous task of restoring the garden to its former splendour. Over the last decade the garden has yielded up its secrets: tropical greenhouses, a Victorian kitchen garden, a fairy grotto and a spectacular 'Lost Valley' filled with palms and exotic blooms. It's also home to the world's largest rhododendron, which measures a majestic 25m from root to tip and can be seen in all its glory on Flora's Green, right in the middle of the gardens.

Heligan is 1.5 miles from Mevagissey and 7 miles from St Austell. Bus 25 leaves from St Austell station (30 minutes, nine daily), or you can catch Bus 526 (six daily, two on Sunday), which travels from Newquay via St Austell station.

CAERHAYS CASTLE
West of Mevagissey, past gorse-topped headland around Dodman Point, is the graceful curve of **Porthluney Cove**, a sheltered beach backed by woods, pastureland and a WWII pillbox. Behind the beach is **Caerhays Castle**, (☎ 501310; www.caerhays.co.uk; combined ticket to house & garden adult/child £9.50/3.50, house or grounds only £5.50/2.50; ☺ house tours hourly noon-3pm Mon-Fri Mar-May, gardens 10am-5pm mid-Feb–May), a crenellated country mansion originally built for the Trevanions and later remodelled under the guidance of John Nash (who designed Buckingham Palace and Brighton Pavilion). The house is a classic chunk of Victorian extravagance, with a centrepiece staircase, book-lined library and chandelier-strewn rooms; outside are stately grounds covered in camellias, towering rhododendrons and the National Magnolia Collection. The house and gardens are only open in spring; if you want to visit the house, you'll have to book ahead for one of the hourly guided tours.

CORNWALL

Sleeping & Eating

Honeycombe House (☎ 843750; www.honeycombehouse
.co.uk; d £60-68; **P**) It's a stiff walk uphill to this
sweet B&B, but the super outlook is worth the
effort. Creamy walls and light pine define the
rooms; if you're a view-junky make sure you
ask for Victoria or Albert, which both have
great balconies overlooking the harbour and
Mevagissey Bay.

Tremarne Hotel (☎ 842213; www.tremarne-hotel
.co.uk; Polkirt; d £74-116; **P** **⌨**) It's more a smart
B&B than a hotel, but lovely all the same;
dinky rooms in pale palettes, all with pocket-
sprung beds and field or sea views; add
twisty-columned four-posters and baby-soft
cotton sheets as you move up the price scale.
The house is nearer Portmellon than Mevagissey, but that just means you're closer to
the beach.

Trevalsa Court (☎ 842468; www.trevalsa-hotel
.co.uk; School Hill, Mevagissey; s £79, d £128-196; **P** **▯**)
Twelve eclectic rooms in a stately Edward-
ian pile above Mevagissey, mixing restoration
with retro; some have settees, abstract prints
and sleigh beds, others stylish bedlamps and
mullioned windows over the bay. Elsewhere
there's a wood-clad lounge scattered with
deep sofas and cushioned window seats and
a sunwashed terrace on the hillside.

Fountain Inn (☎ 842320; St George's Sq; pub meals
£5-8) Mevagissey doesn't seem to have caught
Cornwall's culinary wave just yet, but who
cares when you've got a pub this good? The
oldest (and saltiest) pub in town has two bars
in original oak and slate, plus a smugglers'

tunnel to the harbour, Camra-approved
(Campaign for Real Ale) St Austell ales, and
a menu of beer-battered cod and Malaysian
curries.

Getting There & Away

The hourly bus 26B wanders inland to St
Austell (20 minutes) before cutting back to
Fowey (50 minutes), while the twice-daily
526 goes to Heligan (10 minutes) and Gorran
Haven (20 minutes).

EDEN PROJECT

Looming up from the bottom of an abandoned clay pit near St Austell like a lunar-
landing station, the giant biomes of the **Eden
Project** (☎ 01726-811911; www.edenproject.com; Bodelva;
adult/child/family £14/5/35; ◷ 10am-6pm Apr-Oct, 10am-
4.30pm Nov-Mar) have established themselves
as Cornwall's best-known (and best-loved)
landmark since opening their futuristic doors
in early 2001. The three giant greenhouses –
the largest on earth – were dreamt up by ex-
record producer Tim Smit (also the brains behind the Lost Gardens of Heligan; see p267),
and re-create natural habitats from across the
world, from the steaming rainforests of South
America to the dry deserts of Mexico and the
open savannahs of the South African veld.

From the main visitor centre, a winding
pathway leads down into the landscaped pit
and the three biomes. The **Humid Tropics Biome** –
the world's biggest, a staggering 240m high –
houses orchids, ferns, climbing plants and
tropical trees; there's even a manmade waterfall, a miniature banana plantation and a resident population of butterflies. Things are less
steamy in the **Warm Temperate Biome**, which
mirrors the arid regions of the Mediterranean,
California and South Africa, while the **Outside
Biome** takes in practically everywhere from
Cornish farmland to the American Prairie.
Beside the biomes is an education centre (constructed according to the Fibonacci sequence,
one of nature's most fundamental building
blocks), and the surrounding grounds are livened up by all kinds of exotic plants and bits
of outlandish artwork. It's an amazing and
hugely ambitious project, and also a model
of environmental sustainability – packaging
is reused or recycled, power comes from sustainable sources or microgenerators, and even
the rainwater is recycled to flush the loos.

In summer, the biomes form the backdrop
for the **Eden Sessions**, a series of gigs held in a

SEASIDE SWANK

Lugger Hotel (☎ 01872 501322; www.lugger
hotel.co.uk; Portloe; r depending on season £160-
280) Teetering over the harbour's edge in
the beautiful old fishing town of Portloe,
this supremely indulgent boutique hotel
makes the consummate romantic getaway.
Higgledy-piggledy rooms dot the old smugglers' inn and adjoining fishermen's cottages, making for some imaginative layouts;
expect rough oak beams, clean, contemporary furnishings and huge, decadent beds.
Downstairs the elegant restaurant serves
fishy treats straight off the boats, and the
panoramic portside terrace makes the ideal
place for watching the sun go down. When
did the British seaside get this sexy?

purpose-built arena (previous artists include Amy Winehouse, José Gonzalez, Goldfrapp and The Magic Numbers), while in winter, a full-size covered ice-rink springs up for the winter-themed **Time of Gifts** festival. Planned projects include the Edge, an ambitious new building designed to explore global challenges such as climate change, environmental disaster and overpopulation.

As you might expect, Eden is hugely popular and can get very crowded in summer. Thankfully there are lots of ways to beat the queues; you can buy your tickets in advance from tourist offices, or book via the website, and if you're visiting regularly you can buy an annual pass for no extra charge.

The Eden Project is 3 miles northeast of St Austell. **Truronian** (☎ 01872-273453) runs buses from St Austell, Newquay, Helston, Falmouth and Truro; combined bus and admission tickets are available onboard. If you arrive by car you'll have to park in one of the onsite car parks and catch a shuttle bus down to the biomes. Alternatively, if you arrive by bike, you'll get £3 off the admission price.

FOWEY
☎ 01726 / pop 2273

A jumble of pastel-coloured houses and tiered terraces teetering on a wooded hillside above the River Fowey, the historic maritime port of Fowey (pronounced foy) has long been one of the southwest's most important ports. Sea captains, free traders and scurrilous pirates have all called the town home, and during the Middle Ages it was a crucial port for warships and galleons charged with protecting

the British mainland against Catholic invasion. Fowey later became a key harbour for exporting Cornish china clay, mined at the pits around nearby St Austell, but over recent years the tugboats and freighters have mostly been replaced by swanky yachts and sailboats. In many ways Fowey feels rather like Padstow's south coast sister; a workaday port turned well-heeled holiday town, with a gaggle of portside pubs, posh hotels and bistros overlooking the pretty waterfront.

Sights & Activities

The **tourist office** (☎ 833616; www.fowey.co.uk; 5 South St; ☑ 9am-5.30pm Mon-Sat, 10am-5pm Sun) houses a literary centre devoted to Fowey's most famous resident, the British thriller writer **Daphne du Maurier** (1907–89), who lived most of her life in a house at nearby Polridmouth Cove. Every May, Fowey hosts the **Daphne du Maurier Literary Festival** (www.dumaurier.org) in her honour, with book readings, gigs and live events.

Right in the centre of town is the 15th-century **Church of St Finbarrus**, which marks the southern end of the **Saints' Way**, a 26-mile waymarked trail running to Padstow on the northern coast. East of the church, the smart terrace of The Esplanade leads down to the small beach of **Readymoney Cove**. Henry VIII constructed the small fort of **St Catherine's Castle** (EH; admission free) above the beach to protect the town against Spanish raids; though it's mostly ruined you can still stroll around the cannon emplacements and a section of the old battlements.

In the opposite direction, Fore St leads down to the harbour, where various scenic boat trips trundle out onto the river and a every 15 minutes a **passenger ferry** (foot passengers and bikes only; £1) travels across to the harbour of **Polruan**, over the river from Fowey. Depending on the season, the ferry leaves either from Town Quay or Whitehouse Slip – check the boards for the next sailing. It operates daily from about 7.15am to 11pm in summer and until 7pm in winter; Sunday start is 10am.

Further out of town, the **Bodinnick Ferry** (car/pedestrian £2.20/1; ☑ last ferry 8.45pm Apr-Oct, 7pm Nov-Mar) carries cars, bikes and foot passengers to Bodinnick. If you're on foot, the scenic 4-mile Hall Walk leads from Bodinnick along the river to Polruan, from where you can catch the passenger ferry back to Fowey.

Along the coast towards Looe there are several excellent beaches, but you'll have to

CORNWALL

strap on the walking shoes and dig out the OS map. **Lansallos** is a small sand and shingle beach reached by a half-mile trail from Lansallos village, while **Lantic Bay** is a lovely soft-sand cove reached via a steep cliff-path, although rip-tides make the swimming here a little dicey.

The local legend of *Tristan and Iseult*, (retold by everyone from Béroul and Shakespeare to Wagner and Kneehigh Theatre), supposedly has its roots in Fowey. According to the story, the Cornish King Mark was betrothed to the beautiful maiden Iseult, but she fell in love with King Mark's nephew Tristan after drinking a love potion by mistake (with predictably tragic results). Just outside the town is the Iron Age hillfort of **Castle Dore**, supposedly King Mark's fortress, although little remains save for a few scattered stones and raised banks. The **Tristan Stone** is another local curiosity; standing by the main Fowey road, this granite block is inscribed in Latin with the legend *Drustanus Hic Iacit/Filius Cunomorus* (here lies Drustanus, son of Cunomorus). Fanciful types have taken this to refer to the legendary Tristan and King Mark.

Sleeping

Golant YHA Hostel (☎ 0870 770 5832; golant@yha.org.uk; Penquite House; dm £15.50; 🖳) Set in 1.2 private hectares, this wonderful old Georgian manor house has spacious dorms, estuary views and organised trips including Bodmin Moor hikes and night-time badger watching. There's even a rentable tepee for aspiring Apaches.

Globe Posting House Hotel (☎ 833322; 19 Fore St; s £22.50, d £45-55; 🗶) A tiny cob-walled cottage in the middle of Fore St, with a clutch of snug, low-ceilinged rooms arranged around its rabbit-warren corridors.

Fowey Marine Guest House (☎ 833920; www.fowey marine.com; 21-27 Station Rd; s/d £45/65) Bright, newly refurbished rooms with an East Coast feel at this harbour guesthouse, run by a friendly husband-and-wife team; it's right opposite the harbour car park, so it's handy for those with wheels.

Tredudwell Manor (☎ 870226; www.tredudwell manor.co.uk; Lanteglos-by-Fowey; r £74-94; 🅿) Deep in the countryside across the River Fowey, this stunning Queen Anne manorhouse is one of those places where you have to pinch yourself to make sure it's not make-believe; a huge country mansion bedecked in oil portraits,

spiral staircases and surrounded by hectares of private grounds.

Marina Hotel (☎ 833315; www.themarinahotel.co.uk; The Esplanade; d £108-152) Accolades aplenty mean this chic town-house hotel stays fully booked most of the year; spread over three buildings, the quietly elegant rooms mix nautical style with luxurious bath goodies, deluge showers and the odd sleigh bed. The pricier rooms boast private balconies over the river.

Old Quay House (☎ 833302; 28 Fore St; www.the oldquayhouse.com; d £160-210) This is another boutique beauty that provides further evidence of Fowey's exclusive edge. Natural fabrics, rattan chairs and achingly tasteful tones are dotted around the architect-designed interior, offset by reminders of the building's seafaring past; seven rooms have estuary-view balconies.

Eating

King of Prussia (☎ 627208; www.kingofprussiafowey.com; Town Quay) The king of Fowey's many pubs takes its name from the local 'free trader' John Carter, and makes a lovely spot for a quayside pint or a quick lunchtime sandwich.

Sam's (☎ 832273; 20 Fore St; mains £4-10) Forget razor-sharp napkins and snooty service – this great little local's favourite is like a cross between *Cheers* and a backstreet French bistro. Squeeze into one of the booths, sink a beer and tuck into mussels, calamari rings or stacked-up Samburgers. If it's full, try Sam's Other Place (☎ 833636) at 41 Fore St. No bookings or credit cards.

Food For Thought (☎ 832221; 4 Town Quay; menu £19.95; 🕑 lunch & dinner) There's a French Riviera feel around this smart restaurant on Town Quay, with an excellent fixed-price menu filled with fishy treats and an outside terrace shaded by navy-blue awnings.

Getting There & Away

Bus 25 from St Austell (55 minutes, half-hourly) runs to Fowey via Par, the closest train station.

RESTORMEL CASTLE

High on a hilltop above Lostwithiel, the ruined castle at **Restormel** (☎ 01208-872687; adult/child £2.40/1.20; 🕑 10am-6pm Jul & Aug, 10am-5pm Apr-Jun & Sep, 10am-4pm Oct) was originally built by Edward the Black Prince (the first Duke of Cornwall), although he only stayed there twice during his entire reign. It's one of the best-preserved circular keeps in the country, and affords brilliant views across the river and fields from its crenellated battlements.

POLPERRO

☎ 01503 / pop 1584

Nestled at the bottom of a steep valley bounded by wooded cliffs, the little port of Polperro is the picture of a Cornish fishing village. With its tightly packed warren of fishermen's bothies, cob cottages and squeeze-guts alleyways, the village was once a key pilchard port and a notorious smugglers' haven. Though you'll still glimpse the occasional fishing smack and rowing boat bobbing beside the granite quay, these days Polperro is geared towards the holiday trade and, despite the tourist clutter, it's still a bewitching place.

The main car park is 750m outside the village, from where it's a 15-minute stroll down to the old quayside, ringed by slate-topped houses and fishermen's stores. Alternatively, lazy souls can jump aboard one of the dinky trams (one way/return 75p/£1.30) and horse-drawn carts (return £1.50 including a free ice cream).

The **Polperro Heritage Museum** (☎ 272423; adult/child £1.75/50p; ⏱ 11am-5pm Easter-Oct) occupies an old pilchard-processing factory overlooking the harbour. The ramshackle building houses fishing memorabilia, model boats, Victorian paintings and vintage pilchard barrels, as well as plenty of period photos of Polperro in its heyday. There's also a small display relating to one of the town's most notorious smuggling episodes, when the crew of the local boat *Lottery* were involved in the murder of a Customs Officer; one of the crew, Tom Potter, was subsequently hanged for the crime. A cutlass belonging to one of his cohorts, Robert Mark, is also on display.

Regular boat trips from Polperro Harbour travel along the coast to Polruan and Fowey (adult one way/return £9/14, child £6/10), and there are some fine coastal walks along the clifftops to nearby **Talland Bay**.

Sleeping

Watchers (☎ 272296; The Warren; d from £50) This little bolthole above the harbour boasts one of Polperro's finest views, best appreciated from the lovely glass-fronted conservatory-cum-dining room. The rooms are traditional and very cosy, with lots of old knick-knacks and vintage wood.

Cottles (☎ 272578; Longcoombe Lane; s £45, d £60-65; Ⓟ) On the hillside above the main car park, this slate-roofed cottage is distinguished by its hideaway rooms and a lovely suntrap conservatory, plus Reiki sessions and Indian head massages from the ever-so-slightly New Age owners.

Penryn House (☎ 272157; d £70-80; Ⓟ) Set back from the village's main street, this is a pleasant, uncomplicated B&B, with smallish bathrooms characterised by stalwart shades of cream and magnolia, pretty seaside prints and simple pine furniture.

Eating & Drinking

Three Pilchards (☎ 272233; The Quay; mains £6-10) For more homely fare, head for this whitewashed Polperro kiddleywink near the quay; just the spot for a fresh crab sandwich washed down with an ale or three.

our pick **Couch's Great House Restaurant** (☎ 272554; Saxon Bridge; 3-/4-course menu £23/27; ⏱ from 4.30pm Sun, from 6.15pm Mon, Tue & Thu-Sat) A real heavy-hitter, run by a former pupil of Gordon Ramsay, Raymond Blanc and Marco-Pierre White. Wooden beams, reclaimed stoves and Art Nouveau furniture meet a menu tripping from pan-roasted sea bass to hand-reared beef and Cornish cheeses. For true gut-busters, there's a seven-course gourmet tasting menu (£30) from Sunday to Thursday, with dishes prepared after consultation with the head chef.

Getting There & Away

Buses 572 and 573 make the trip over to West and East Looe (30 minutes) every hour Monday to Saturday. The 573 also travels on to the train station at Liskeard (one hour).

LOOE

☎ 01503 / pop 5280

Squaring up across the River Looe spanned by a seven-arched Victorian bridge, the fortunes of East and West Looe have been inextricably bound up with the sea for the last eight centuries. In contrast to Fowey, its long-standing rival along the coast, Cornwall's cultural renaissance hasn't yet reached as far east as Looe. Chip shops and chintzy B&Bs still reign supreme here, especially in East Looe, although things are more upmarket across the river on Hannafore Point.

The heart of the action is concentrated on East Looe, where you'll find the majority of

CORNWALL

the town's shops, pubs and restaurants, as well as the **tourist office** (☎ 262072; looetic@btconnect .com; The Guildhall; ☻ 10am-2pm). By the early 19th century Looe had already established itself as a thriving holiday spot, and one of the county's first bathing machines was installed around 1800 at the sandy beach beside **Banjo Pier** (named for its circular shape rather than any George Formby connections). For more seclusion, head east for the expanse of sand at **Second Beach**, or make the trip across the river to **Hannafore Beach**, with grassy banks for picnics, and rock pools to delve in at low tide.

The town's **museum** (adult/child £1.50/50p; ☻ 11.30am-4.30pm Sun-Fri), in the centre of East Looe, is worth a look for local history exhibits, as well as a chance to peek inside the 15th-century guildhall. Outside the museum is the half-tonne Finbacker cannon, dredged up from the quay and thought to belong to a Swedish warship.

Boat trips set out from **Buller Quay** for destinations up and down the coastline. One of the most atmospheric is an old **RNLI Lifeboat** (☎ 263110), which makes trips over to St George's Island (adult/child £5/3), as well as trips to Polperro and Fowey (£19/12). There are plenty of other operators – check the signs on the quay for the next sailings and leave your name in one of the books once you've made your choice. Glass bottom boats also venture into the bay in search of local marine life (£10/7).

Looe is also famous for its **sea-fishing** – the national headquarters for the **Shark Anglers' Club** (☎ 262642) is just behind Buller's Quay. Expect to pay around £20/£30 for a half/full day of shark or reef angling, or £10 for a couple of hours' mackerel fishing.

Hidden away on the hilltop above East Looe, the **Monkey Sanctuary** (☎ 262532; www.mon keysanctuary.org; St Martins; adult/child £6/3.50; ☻ 11am-4.30pm Sun-Thu Easter-Sep) is home to a colony of ridiculously cute woolly monkeys, who spend most of their days larking about in the treetops of their wooded enclosure. Altogether now – *I want to be like you-oo-oo....*

If the little ones have still got the wildlife bug, **Porfell Animal Land** (☎ 220211; www.porfell animalland.co.uk; Trecangate; adult/child £6/5; ☻ 10am-6pm Feb & Apr-Nov, Sat & Sun only Mar), just off the B3359 from Looe, is another excellent wildlife centre with a menagerie of meerkats, lemurs and marmosets, as well as a capybara called Bert.

Sleeping

Beach House (☎ 262598; www.thebeachhouselooe.com; Hannafore Point; d £80-110; P) The guesthouse goes grandiose at this double-gabled house overlooking Hannafore Point. All the rooms are named after Cornish beaches, and while none are massive, the balconies, puffy beds and breakfast pancakes make for a luxurious night's stay.

Trehaven Manor (☎ 262028; www.trehavenhotel .co.uk; Station Rd; d £82-120; P) Things are more old-world at this converted manorhouse above East Looe. Antique wardrobes, original fireplaces and deep armchairs create a tangible whiff of yesteryear – the superior rooms have maximum space and river views (rooms 6 and 8 are the best).

Barclay House (☎ 262929; www.barclayhouse.co.uk; St Martins Rd, East Looe; d from £110; P ▢ ▨) Some of Looe's B&Bs would make Basil Fawlty blush with embarrassment, but this swish hotel in East Looe offers an altogether more cultured experience. Classy modern fixtures and bold colourways of aquamarine, gold and pistachio distinguish the rooms, and several offer views across river and countryside.

Schooner Point (☎ 262670; www.schoonerpoint .co.uk; 1 Trelawney Tce; d £50-55; P) Pastel-shaded but chintz-free B&B with great veggie breakfasts and a handy location for town.

Polraen (☎ 263956; www.polraen.co.uk; Sandplace; d £75-85; P) Traditionally themed B&B in an 18th-century house five minutes from Looe, with an award-winning landlady.

Eating

Treleavens (☎ 220969; Fore St; ice creams £1.50-2.00) This award-winning ice-cream firm is an irresistible treat; traditionalists can go for vanilla and chocolate, while adventurous souls plump for blackcurrants and cream or apple-and-blackberry crumble.

Mawgan's (☎ 265331; Higher Market St; mains £14-18; ☻ dinner Thu-Tue) Slow Food takes centre stage at this faintly fussy restaurant in East Looe. Cornish produce and organic ingredients are used wherever possible, and the rustic dining makes a pleasant place to while away the evening; the Cornish cheeseboard is particularly worth investigating. No children under 15.

Old Sail Loft (☎ 262131; The Quay; mains £15.95-29.95, 3-course menu £22.50; ☻ lunch Thu-Mon, dinner Wed-Mon) Inside an old fishermen's store, this excellent seafood restaurant combines maritime character with continental flair –

think stripy canvas chairs crossed with rough wooden tables and hefty beams, and a menu wriggling with lobster, sea bass and local fish.

Getting There & Away

Bus 572 travels to Plymouth (one hour 10 minutes, hourly Monday to Saturday) while Bus 573 goes to Liskeard (30 minutes, hourly Monday to Saturday, five on Sunday). Both buses travel over to Polperro (thirty minutes) in the opposite direction.

Trains travel the scenic Looe Valley Line from Liskeard (£2.50, 30 minutes, 11 daily Monday to Saturday, eight on Sunday), on the London–Penzance line.

BODMIN MOOR

Hugging the edge of the Devon border, the stark, barren expanse of Bodmin Moor is one of the county's wildest, weirdest landscapes. Pockmarked by bogs and treeless heaths, Cornwall's 'roof' is often overlooked by visitors, but it's well worth taking the time to ex-plore; lofty peaks loom on the horizon, stone circles and eerie monuments are scattered across the hills, and ancient churches nestle at the foot of granite tors. It's also home to the peaks of Rough Tor (pronounced row-tor; 400m) and Brown Willy (419m), and a fabled menagerie of fairies, buccas, sprites and giants, as well as the infamous Beast of Bodmin Moor – a large black catlike creature that's been seen for many years but still has the scientific boffins baffled.

BODMIN & AROUND

☎ 01208 / pop 12,778

On the western side of the moor is the stout market town of Bodmin, which grew up around a large 7th-century monastery founded by St Petroc, and later became one of the county's main stannary towns. Although much of Bodmin's bureaucratic power moved over to Truro in the late 19th century, Bodmin remained the seat for the county court until the mid 1990s. You can now visit the old courtroom inside the town hall, as well as the ruins of Bodmin Jail, Cornwall's infamous lock-up, where unfortunate law-breakers were

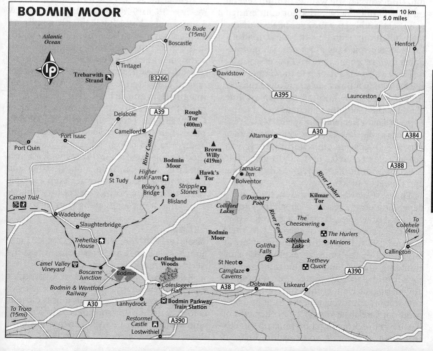

either banged up or, in more serious cases, introduced to the hangman's noose.

Bodmin tourist office (☎ 76616; bodmintic@visit .org.uk; Mount Folly; ☺ 10am-5pm Mon-Sat) is housed inside the Shire Hall, where you'll also find the **Charlotte Dymond Courtroom Experience** (adult/child £3.75/2.25; ☺ 11am-4pm Mon-Sat Easter-Oct, 11am-4pm Mon-Fri Nov-Easter), in which one of Cornwall's most infamous court cases is re-created in the old county courtroom. Using film, audio and several dodgy fibreglass dummies, the exhibit relives the events of the 1884 trial, during which the young farmhand Matthew Weeks was condemned for the murder of local woman Charlotte Dymond, despite dubious evidence and widespread scepticism at the time. At the end you can cast your own verdict and take a peek into the old holding cells below the court.

A crowd of 20,000 people turned up (many aboard special trains laid on for the occasion) to gawk at Weeks' execution at **Bodmin Jail** (☎ 76292; www.bodminjail.org; adult/child £5/3; ☺ 10am-dusk), once the county's main prison and now a popular hangout for local spook-hunters. Though much of the original jail has fallen into ruin, you can still wander around several cells, including the one used for condemned prisoners, and keep your eyes peeled for the many phantoms who stalk the jail's corridors. Chances are you'll see more rubbish mannequins than revenants, but you never know.

The jail also sits adjacent to the Camel Trail (p226), which follows the abandoned railway route to Padstow. Though this classic line closed in the 1960s, the venerable steam trains of the **Bodmin & Wenford Railway** (☎ 0845 125-9678; www.bodminandwenfordrailway.co.uk; adult return depending on route £7.50-10.00) are still chuffing their way between along a stretch of standard-gauge line between Bodmin Parkway, Bodmin General and Boscarne Junction.

There are between four and six trains daily depending on the season – check the site for fares and timetables. It makes a great day trip, and the trains are still decked out in their original 1950s livery. You can jump off at either end of the route to explore the surrounding area. Along the Bodmin General to Bodmin Parkway route, the train stops at Colesslogget Halt, from where a half-mile path leads to the lovely walking trails and bike routes of **Cardinham Woods**. The other end of the line at Boscarne Junction joins up directly with the Camel Trail; you can hire bikes at

Bodmin General station from **Bodmin Cycle Hire** (☎ 73555).

Sleeping

Castle Canyke Farmhouse (☎ 79109; www.castlecanyke .co.uk; Prior's Barn Rd; d £60-70; P) Rough stone walls meet designer prints and tailor's dummies at this impeccably designed B&B on the edge of Bodmin, with three fancy rooms kitted out with DVD players and power showers.

Bedknobs (☎ 77553; www.bedknobs.co.uk; Castle St; s £50-65, d £65-85; P ⌨) Green issues come to the fore at this ecosavvy guesthouse, one of only two Cornish B&Bs to sweep the Green Tourism Gold Award. Three refined rooms, all named after trees, have minifridges, 21-inch TVs and wi-fi connection, while locally sourced sausages, eggs and bacon grace the breakfast table.

Higher Lank Farm (☎ 850716; www.higherlankfarm .co.uk; St Breward; r from £85) A working farm that's tailor-made for kids – in fact, you'll have to have a toddler under five to stay here. Little 'uns can help feed the pigs, groom the ponies and gather the eggs, while grown-ups kick back for a slap-up, farm-fresh feed.

Trehellas House (☎ 73336; www.trehellashouse.co.uk; Washaway; s £60, d £90-120; P ⌨) Once an inn, now a grand manorhouse hotel, this place pulls out all the stops; countrified rooms in two buildings, a great restaurant and a picturesque rural setting hemmed in by woods and fields.

South Tregleath Farm (☎ 01208-72692; www.south -tregleath.co.uk; d from £70; P ⌨ ⌨) Architectural imagination and artistic flair combine to make this one of the nicest farmstays in all of Cornwall. Forget cob walls and inglenook fireplaces: here it's all silky wood, bamboo screens and restrained colour schemes. Despite the modern interiors, it's still very much a working farm. Kids can help milk the cows and collect the eggs, and there are even a couple of rent-a-dogs to borrow for country walkies if you haven't brought along your own.

Eating

Maple Leaf (☎ 72206; 14 Honey St; ☺ Mon-Sat) Light lunches, lasagnes and fresh cream teas are served in this down-home café.

Hole in The Wall (☎ 72397; Crockwell St; mains around £8) Good restaurants are hard to come by in Bodmin, so your best bet is this murky old pub, a former debtor's prison covered in old rifles and vintage swords, with a menu of Sharps beers and freshly-cooked pub rations.

CORNWALL

BOTTOMS UP!

Two miles west of Bodmin, the **Camel Valley Vineyard** (www.camelvalley.com) has been producing award-winning Cornish wines in a secluded valley vineyard for more than 15 years, from world-class whites to a sparkling champagne that manages to give the authentic French variety a real run for its money. There are three tours available, including a basic trip around the vineyard (£4.50; at 2.30pm Monday to Friday April to September), a grand tour and tasting session (£6.50; 5pm Wednesday April to September), and a full-blown day tour (£33; at 10.30am, enquire for dates) including a buffet lunch and a personal tour conducted by the vineyard manager. Naturally there's plenty of opportunity to taste the various vintages, and a well-stocked shop if you fancy taking a few cases home. *Santé!*

Getting There & Away

Bus 529 travels to St Austell (one hour, hourly Monday to Saturday), while the 555 goes from outside the Shire Hall to Bodmin Parkway (15 minutes, hourly Monday to Saturday), on the London to Penzance train line, and in the opposite direction to Padstow and Wadebridge. The Bodmin & Wenford Railway (see p274) links Bodmin Parkway with Bodmin and the Camel Trail.

LANHYDROCK

Set in 365 hectares of sweeping grounds above the River Fowey, the 16th-century manor house of **Lanhydrock** (NT; ☎ 01208-73320; house & gardens adult/child £9.40/4.70, gardens only £5.30/2.65; ☾ house 11am-5.30pm Tue-Sun Mar-Sep, 11am-5pm Tue-Sun Oct, gardens 10am-6pm year-round) was devastated by fire in 1881, but was later rebuilt in lavish style. Formerly owned by the high-faluting Robartes family, the house offers a fascinating insight into *Upstairs Downstairs* life in Victorian England. Highlights include the gentlemen's smoking room (complete with old Etonian photos, moose heads and tiger-skin rugs), the children's toy-strewn nursery and the huge original kitchens with their gargantuan ovens and pioneering water-cooled coldstore. There's also a fabulous plaster ceiling in the Long Gallery, which somehow managed to escape the fire, and a small museum exploring the house's long history.

Lanhydrock is 2.5 miles southeast of Bodmin. Bus 554 runs from Bodmin Parkway train station three times daily.

CAMELFORD & THE NORTHERN MOOR

The northern stretch of the moor is dominated by the twin peaks of Brown Willy and Rough Tor, which rise from flat heathland 4 miles southeast from the little town of Camelford. Thanks to its vaguely similar name, Camel-ford has been linked with both Camelot (King Arthur's mythic castle) and Camlann (the site of his last battle), but the name probably derives from the Cornish *cam-hayle*, meaning curving river. The Arthur connections were given further credence by the discovery of an inscribed stone in nearby **Slaughterbridge**, supposedly marking the location of Arthur's last battle, although the stone more probably marks the site of a decisive battle between the Saxon king Egbert and the Celts in the late 9th century. The **Arthurian Centre** (☎ 01840-213947; adult/child £3/2; 10am-5pm Easter-Oct) in Slaughterbridge explores the various legends, and marks the start of a short woodland trail where you can check out the stone itself.

Camelford is also – bizarrely – home to the **British Cycling Museum** (☎ 212811; Old Station; adult/child £2.50/1.50; ☾ 10am-5pm Sun-Thu), which houses more than 400 weird and wonderful velocipedes, from a classic penny-farthing to Chris Boardman's Olympic medal-winning bike frame. The museum is a mile north of town on the B3266 to Boscastle.

If you're steadier on two legs than on two wheels, Camelford makes a good launching pad for the trek to **Rough Tor** and **Brown Willy**, Cornwall's highest hump. Despite its saucy name – a perennial source of entertainment for local schoolkids – Brown Willy is actually a corruption of *brone whella*, Cornish for 'high hill'. The best route heads from the car park at Rough Tor Ford, 3 miles south of Camelford, along a well-marked trail; it's generally easy-going, although the last section to the summit is rocky and quite steep. From the summit of Rough Tor it's another 1.5 miles southeast to the top of Brown Willy; both peaks can be tackled in two or three hours, though as always you'll need decent boots, hiking gear and a well-packed lunch. If the weather's foggy or soggy you might be better

CORNWALL

off waiting for another day. Walking routes and OS maps are sold at the Bodmin and Camelford tourist offices.

Sleeping & Eating

Penlea House (☎ 212194; jandrews04@supanet.com; Station Rd; s/d £20/40; (P)) A small B&B in the traditional British style (ancient kettles, dated bathroom suites, faded wallpaper), but handy for town and dead cheap.

Countryman Hotel (☎ 212250; countrymanhotel@bt openworld.com; Victoria Rd; s/d £40/60; (P)) A pleasant hotel on Camelford's outskirts that's a favourite for hikers and bikers, as it sits just off Rte 3 on the National Cycle Network. The rooms are hardly spectacular but have all the mod-cons, and guided walks can be arranged by the owners.

Mason's Arms (☎ 213309; Market Pl; mains £5-9) This is a cream-coloured 18th-century pub that serves good grub and the usual selection of local beers, with a garden backing onto the River Camel.

Getting There & Away

Bus 594 (which goes hourly Monday to Saturday) travels along the coast from Camelford to Tintagel (15 minutes) and on to Boscastle (20 minutes).

JAMAICA INN & THE CENTRAL MOOR

Standing in a desolate spot in the middle of the moor, beside the old coaching road through Bolventor, the **Jamaica Inn** (☎ 01566-86250; www .jamaicainn.co.uk; s £65, d £70-100; (P)) became Britain's most infamous pub practically overnight thanks to Daphne du Maurier's classic adventure story, published in 1936. The book was apparently conceived when she became lost on the moor during an impromptu riding trip and sought shelter in the inn, where she was entertained with spooky tales and smuggling yarns by the local parson from Altarnun Church.

These days the inn has been joined by a **Museum of Smuggling**, with a section devoted to du Maurier, housing her original writing desk and a pack of her favourite ciggies (du Maurier brand, of course, named after her actor father Gerald). Though the rooms have been ruthlessly modernised since du Maurier's day, a few still have four-poster beds and moor views, but you might find yourself stuck in the concrete annexe rather than in the inn itself during busy periods.

About a mile south from the inn is **Dozmary Pool**, said to have been where Arthur's sword, Excalibur, was thrown by Sir Bedivere after Arthur's death. To the west, near the hummock of Hawk's Tor, are the **Stripple Stones**, a circular alignment that once enclosed 28 stones, although only four remain standing. Jamaica Inn also makes a useful base for the 4-mile walk north to Brown Willy.

On the eastern edge of the moor along the main A30 road is **Launceston**, mainly worth visiting for its ruined 11th-century **castle** (EH; ☎ 01566-772365; admission £2; ⏰ 10am-6pm Jul & Aug, 10am-5pm Apr-Jun & Sep, 10am-4pm Oct).

Sleeping

Other than Jamaica Inn itself, the nearby villages of Altarnun, St Tudy and Blisland make good overnight stops.

Cabilla Manor (☎ 821224; www.cabilla.co.uk; Mount; d from £60; (P)) Hidden away at the end of a private track, this working farmhouse is owned by the British explorer Robin-Hanbury Tenison, and offers several smartly designed rooms packed with vintage carpets, booklined shelves and curios from across the globe.

Lavethan (☎ 851387; near Blisland; s £40-50, d £70-80; (P) (☰)) This Grade II–listed house has been around since the Domesday Book, and makes a supremely peaceful getaway. The rambling farmhouse sits in a quiet valley surrounded by sheep-filled fields, and the rooms mix heritage wallpaper with deep fireplaces, stone lintels and corniced ceilings.

Polrode Mill Cottage (☎ 850203; www.polrodemill cottage.co.uk; St Tudy; r £70-90; (P)) Brass beds, beams and roll-top baths make this sweet cottage B&B one of our favourite Bodmin Moor bases, with a valley setting and a super home-grown breakfast using garden-grown veggies and home-laid eggs.

Eating

Rising Sun (☎ 01566-86636; Altarnun; mains £6-8) Another friendly beerhouse, with lots of hand-pump ales, slate flagstones and crannied corners, plus chicken and chips and chillis on the blackboard.

Blisland Inn (☎ 01208-850739; Blisland; mains £6.95-10.95) Popular with Camel Trail bikers and Camra-enthusiasts, this cheery local inn is covered inside with beer badges and wood beams; the menu features hearty fare including steak pie and moussaka, and there's a family room with dominoes, pool and table skittles.

Getting There & Away

Buses are almost nonexistent in this section of the moor, so you'll need your own wheels, although the 225 (three daily Monday to Friday) runs between Altarnun and Launceston.

LISKEARD & THE SOUTHERN MOOR

East of Jamaica Inn and Dozmary Pool, the moor sweeps across an autumn-coloured landscape of rocks and grassland towards Twelve Men's Moor and the high point of Kilmar Tor (396m). Three miles east of Siblyback Lake, the small village of **Minions** stands near the moor's most interesting prehistoric monuments. The **Hurlers**, two stone rings said to be the remains of men turned to stone for playing the Cornish sport of hurling on a Sunday, while nearby is the **Cheesewring**, a strange pillar of piled-up stones said to be the work of local giants, but actually a result of natural erosion. Three miles south, near Darite, is **Trethevy Quoit** – sometimes known as King Arthur's Quoit or the Giant's House – another example of Cornwall's distinctive Neolithic burial chambers, standing almost 15ft high.

Moor and heath give way to woods and river valleys along the moor's southern edge. The serene little village of **St Neot**, lined with slate-topped cottages and overhanging trees, is home to a gorgeous 15th-century **parish church**, blessed with spectacular medieval stained glass and one of John Betjeman's favourite Cornish churches. A couple of miles east of St Neot are the rushing waters of **Golitha Falls**, a celebrated beauty spot and nature reserve surrounded by the last remains of the vast oak woodland which once covered much of the moor.

Just to the south are the slate caves of **Carnglaze Caverns** (☎ 01579-320251; www.carnglaze .com; adult/child £6/4; ☼ 10am-5pm), with a series of cathedral-like caverns and an eerie subterranean lake. Concerts and live shows are often held in the caverns – check the website for a full events calendar.

The area's main town is **Liskeard**, useful for supplies or as a gateway to the moor for train travellers on the London–Penzance line. If you're really stuck for things to do, there's always **Magnificent Music Machines** (☎ 01579-343108; admission £5; ☼ Easter-Oct), in St Keyne, where the attractions include self-playing pianos, a Berlin street organ and a Wurlitzer that once graced Brighton's Regent Cinema.

Sleeping & Eating

Lampen Farm (☎ 01579-320284; www.lampenfarm.fsnet .co.uk; St Neot; d £54-56; Ⓟ) A peaceful farmstay just steps from St Neot, offering cosy, flock-flavoured accommodation in a 16th-century farmhouse.

Treverbyn Manor (☎ 01579-326105; www.treverbyn vean.co.uk; Twowatersfoot, near Liskeard; s £60, d £90-100; Ⓟ) Standing in glorious grounds above the Glynn Valley, this fabulous Hogwartsesque manorhouse is an aristocratic treat. The rooms are reached via a winding staircase, and feature bay windows, enamel baths and original Victorian fittings, while cream teas are served in the Great Hall with its Minstrel's Gallery and mullion windows.

London Inn (☎ 320263; mains from £8) Packed with Cornish character, this old coaching inn in the shadow of St Neot church combines slate fireplaces and wood-timbered walls with a great bar menu; live music often livens up the bar at weekends.

Getting There & Away

The 274 (four services daily Monday to Friday) from Liskeard to St Neot is just about the only bus in the southern moor.

COTEHELE

Dating from Tudor times, the manor house at **Cotehele** (NT; ☎ 01579-351346; St Dominick; adult/child £8.40/4.20, garden & mill only £5/2.50; ☼ 11am-4.30pm Sat-Thu Apr-Oct) served as the family seat of the aristocratic Edgcumbe dynasty for over 400 years. It's stocked with some of Britain's finest Tudor interiors, best seen in the great hall, and dotted throughout with impressive tapestries, furniture and suits of armour. It's also notoriously haunted – several ghostly figures are said to wander through the house, accompanied by music and a peculiar herbal smell.

Outside, the lovely terraced gardens include both a Victorian summerhouse and a medieval dovecote. **Cotehele Quay** is part of the National Maritime Museum and has displays on local boat-building and river trade, while the restored **Cotehele Mill** is a 15-minute walk away.

Cotehele is 7 miles southwest of Tavistock. Bus 190 travels to Cotehele from Gunnislake station via Callington (40 minutes) four times daily on Sunday.

CORNWALL

Directory

CONTENTS

This chapter gives practical information for the region. For details on specific parts of the southwest, turn to the relevant county chapter.

ACCOMMODATION

As varied as the weather in an English summer, there's somewhere to sleep to suit all tastes in the southwest. From lighthouses to luxury estates, from chintzy B&Bs to camping barns, from boutique hotels to bijou cottages. Pampered or primitive, it's all here; the best is detailed throughout this book.

We often split sleeping sections into three price bands: budget (under £60), midrange (£60 to £130) and top end (more than £130). These rates are the full price during high season for a double room. In general you get what you pay for: some of the budget options are very basic, while you'll be cosseted and coddled at the luxury end. Overall standards are good. In many places prices and demand rise in the main tourist season, broadly Easter to October, with a peak during the school holidays of July and August. Irritatingly in some cities, Bath for example, you often have to pay more at weekends throughout the year. Some sleeping options are only open in the holiday season – we've noted it where this is the case.

Accommodation in the UK is graded by stars (five being superplush). In general it's a reasonable gauge to what's on offer, but it can't be a guarantee of good service. Equally, as hotels and guesthouse have to pay to be classified some excellent but small gems don't bother. The **regional tourist board** (☎ 0870 442 0880; www.visitsouthwest.co.uk) is a good central resource; it also lists ecofriendly places to stay and those accessible to people with disabilities.

B&Bs & Guesthouses

More personal than a hotel but more comfy than camping – that's the great British B&B (bed and breakfast), and it's alive and well across the Westcountry. B&Bs range from larger, professional affairs to eccentric enclaves where your presence appears to come as a surprise to the proprietor. Styles vary from crisp white linen in smart city streets through to rustic rooms in remote villages and clashing carpets in kiss-me-quick resorts. Some still have shared bathrooms but the surge towards the en suite can mean everything's been crammed into an unfeasibly small space, providing great comic potential; you may have a toilet – but is that the only place to sit? Most B&Bs serve the kind of belt-busting breakfast that means you don't have to eat till the evening.

BOOK ACCOMMODATION ONLINE

For more accommodation reviews and recommendations by Lonely Planet authors, check out the online booking service at www.lonelyplanet.com. You'll find the true, insider lowdown on the best places to stay. Reviews are thorough and independent. Best of all, you can book online.

Prices vary wildly. Expect to pay anything from £40 for a double with shared bathroom, to £60 for a double room with a private bathroom. Rates can go beyond £95. Single travellers normally face a premium paying up to 75% of the double rate.

Here are some more B&B tips:

■ Some don't take credit or debit cards and instead require cash or cheque.

■ Advance bookings are a good idea and are essential in busy places during peak periods.

■ In most towns there's an area where B&Bs cluster – search it out then play spot the 'Vacancy' sign.

■ In cities, some are for long-term residents or those on welfare only.

■ Rates may rise at busy times, but some places cut prices for longer stays.

■ When booking, check where the B&B is actually located. In country areas, postal addresses often include the nearest town, which may be up to 20 miles away.

Bunkhouses & Camping Barns

Basic, budget places to bed down for the night, bunkhouses and camping barns are aimed primarily at hikers and cyclists and are normally in gorgeously rural locations.

Facilities vary but bunkhouses tend to have more to them; expect dorm-style accommodation as well as bathroom and cooking facilities, but you'll still need to bring a sleeping bag. Camping barns are more primitive, often just a sleeping platform with cold running water and a flush toilet. So bring all your camping kit except the tent.

Rates for both categories are normally around £6 to £15. Some are run by the Youth Hostels Association, some are independent – we give details in the county chapters. They are concentrated in Dartmoor (p205) and Ex-

moor (p116); contact the **Dartmoor National Park Authority** (DNPA; ☎ 01822-890414; www.dartmoor-npa .gov.uk) and the **Exmoor National Park Authority** (ENPA; ☎ 01398-323841; www.exmoor-nationalpark.gov .uk). The **YHA** (☎ 0870 770 8868; www.yha.org.uk) also has information.

Camping

There's nothing quite like waking up at 4am with your face squashed up against a flysheet and your feet in the open air; camping either appeals or it doesn't. If it does the southwest has some stunning sites – from farmers' fields equipped with a toilet, a tap, views of the sea and nothing else to facility-laden sites (think bouncy castles and pools) within striking distance of resorts. In this book we quote prices per camp site for two people – regionwide costs range from £5 to £20.

On Dartmoor you can experience wild-camping at its best. Pitching a tent on certain parts of the open moor is allowed, provided some simple rules are followed. These are largely to do with choosing a sensible place to camp, avoiding damage and dealing with waste; the DNPA produces a free leaflet. If you'll be fiddling with flysheets a lot, consider joining the **Camping and Caravanning Club** (☎ 0845 130 7632; www.campingandcaravanningclub.co.uk). Membership is £33 a year and you get the guide *Your Big Sites Book* free.

Hostels

Be they official or unofficial, the southwest is peppered with hostels offering a cheap 'n' cheerful sleeping experience. They range from funky backpackers in city centres, through to surfers' crash pads in Cornwall and dignified old houses in rural Dorset. In the summer they're popular places so book ahead, conversely some close in the winter so check before turning up.

YHA HOSTELS

There are around 30 **Youth Hostels Association** (YHA; ☎ 0870 770 8868; www.yha.org.uk) hostels scattered around the southwest, making it perfectly possible to tour the region using them as bases. YHA hostels have a more establishment feel than independent ones and are sometimes roamed by excitable school groups – although the 'youth' in the title is a misnomer; you can join however old you are. Facilities are modern and many have double and family rooms with bathrooms, as well as dormitories. Some specialise in activities and many are in old buildings full of character in rural or clifftop locations, although they feature in or near cities such as Exeter (p170), Bath (p96) and Bristol (p83). There are even two in Cornwall where you can sleep in a tepee – Golant (p270) and Coverack (p251). Dorm beds are normally £12 to £15 per night for adults (although some charge £20) and £9 to £10 for under 18s. YHA membership is £16 for over 25s, £10 if you're aged 16 to 25.

INDEPENDENT HOSTELS

With a distinctly backpacker vibe, the southwest's independent hostels are the place to revel in the region's chilled-out atmosphere. Expect to come across cool city-centre pads, decks with beach views and no-one bothering about sandy feet. Again, having a regionwide network means you can tour staying exclusively in them. Among the ones we feature are those in Bath (p96), Bristol (p83), Bournemouth (p127), Exeter (p169), Ilfracombe (p212), Newquay (p231), Torquay (p181) and Plymouth (p199), and at Moretonhampstead (p209) on Dartmoor. Predictably quality varies; unsavoury ones exist among the many friendly, funky and clean options.

It's not unusual for dorms to be mixed-sex, prices average around £13 for a bed, but some peak at £20 in high season. Many have double rooms, which cost around £30. Some, but not all, have internet and laundry facilities. The *Independent Hostels Guide* (www.independenthostelguide.co.uk) is a useful resource.

Hotels

What separates hotels from B&Bs is uniformity; both of our expectations and the facilities they provide. While guesthouses can be gloriously idiosyncratic, at hotels things are often posher, bigger and more consistent. Some are undoubtedly bland, but others are supremely relaxing places to stay.

The Westcountry has a scattering of boutique hotels and beats other regions on the kind of luxurious coastal and country-house options that are travel experiences in themselves.

Hotel rates vary from £50/70 for singles/doubles to £100/130 and way beyond. Rooms normally have private facilities. There's sometimes a cheeky 'sea-view supplement'; anything from £5 extra a night for a glimpse of glittering water.

If atmosphere isn't a priority, chain hotels can be ideal: consistent, cheap and conveniently sited along main roads or in city centres. Double rooms with **Travelodge** (☎ 0870 085 0950; www.travelodge.co.uk) vary from £15 to £46.

Pubs & Inns

What could be more civilised than having a fabulous meal in a convivial country inn, sampling some real ale, then heading upstairs to sleep? The local pub is also at the heart of community life; join in with the conversation and you really feel part of things. Accommodation can be stylish or seedy; sometimes rooms are a little too reminiscent of the atmosphere downstairs in the bar.

Prices too vary considerably, from £30/40 for a single/double to £60/70 and beyond. For more on pubs, see p51.

BOUTIQUE BEAUTIES

Some of our top recommendations for sleeping in style in the southwest:

- Combe House (p172), near Exeter
- Hotel Barcelona (p170), Exeter
- Burgh Island Hotel (p195), south Devon
- Horn of Plenty (p207), Tavistock
- Gidleigh Park (p210), Dartmoor
- Holne Chase Hotel (p209), near Widecombe-in-the-Moor on Dartmoor
- Hotel Tresanton (p267), St Mawes
- Primrose Valley (p238), St Ives
- Lugger Hotel (p268), Portloe
- Marina Hotel (p270), Fowey

LIGHT SLEEPER

Fancy solitude, cliffs and cracking views? Then bed down for the night at a working lighthouse. Trinity House, which looks after navigation aids, has turned some of its former lighthouse-keepers' cottages into bijou holiday lets. Snugly sleeping between two and six people, the network of 16 in the southwest stretches from Woolacombe in north Devon, around the tip of Cornwall, via one at Start Point (p191) in south Devon to Swanage in Dorset.

The lighthouses can be booked through **Rural Retreats** (☎ 01386-701177; www.ruralretreats.co.uk); prices range from £460 for two people in March to around £1000 for five in July. For safety reasons some don't take children; others stress strict supervision is required. A final thought: as well as nodding off to the rhythmic crash of the surf and the cry of the gulls, you could also jolt awake to the blast of a fog horn – many recommend you bring ear plugs just in case it's more than a little misty.

Rental Accommodation

Renting a fully equipped cottage or apartment gives you the freedom of lazy lie-ins, eating in and having somewhere to shelter if it rains (perish the thought). Across the southwest there are snazzy flats, fishermen's cottages and idyllic country retreats waiting to be booked. Lets often sleep four to six people, although some sleep two and others up to 10.

Sometimes reality bites; that 'quaint' rural cottage is actually cold, damp and cut off in the middle of a desolate moor – ask a few questions before you make your booking. Knowing the wider context is also handy here. Inflated house prices are a huge problem in the southwest and the buying of second homes and holiday lets are seen by many as being partly to blame. Often locals can't afford to buy a house in the place where they grew up, yet some properties stand empty most of the year. In some communities almost 50% of the houses are second homes. Once it has become a holiday home, rentals can help bring money into the region but it's worth being aware of the situation and opting to channel your cash into truly local shops, services and produce.

The tourist board has a number of properties on its books; specialist firms also exist. **Stilwell's** (☎ 0870 197 6964; www.stilwell.co.uk) has a good range. Other, local, firms include **West Country Cottages** (☎ 01803-814000; www.westcountrycottages.co.uk) and **Classic Cottages** (☎ 01326-555555; www.classic.co.uk). Or sleep cheek by jowl with history, and support a heritage charity; try the **National Trust** (NT; ☎ 0870 4584422; www.nationaltrustcottages.co.uk) for scores of atmospheric places to lay your head in the region.

Many properties are rented by the week and prices vary hugely according to size, location and the season. During off peak expect to pay around £200 a week for a cottage for two; this can rise to £500 between July and September. A four-person cottage can cost £300 to £500 in peak season, while a waterfront cottage sleeping eight, in a tourist hot spot, can be £1500 a week in the height of summer. Kitchen equipment is normally included, along with bed linen and towels. Book ahead, as the popular ones get snapped up early.

University Accommodation

While the region's students are frantically earning money in the holidays, university accommodation can provide cheap, handy places to stay – sometimes in city-centre locations, sometimes on leafy campuses. Normally available during July and August, prices range between £12 to £36 per person per night, often in single rooms with bathrooms. Some places to try:

Bournemouth University (01202-595385; www.bournemouth.ac.uk/accommodation)
University of Bath (01225-386622; www.bath.ac.uk/hospitality/salesandevents)
University of Bristol (0117-954 5740; www.bristol.ac.uk/accom)
University of Exeter (01392-262524; www.ex.ac.uk/accommodation)
University of Plymouth (01752-232061; www.plymouth.ac.uk)

ACTIVITIES

Breathe deeply, race about, go wandering or simply chill-out – the southwest region is brimming with adventurous pursuits or opportunities to get away from the rat race. See the Southwest Outdoors chapter (p61) for some ideas.

BUSINESS HOURS

Banks, Shops & Offices

Despite the occasional 'back in 10 minutes' that stretches to an hour, most shops in the southwest have fairly regular hours: Monday to Saturday 9am to 5.30pm, with many in urban areas also open 10am to 4pm on Sundays. Throughout this book those are the hours we've used as a standard; we won't specify unless they differ. As elsewhere, convenience stores are more 'convenient' and stay open into the evening; in many of the bigger towns and cities some are 24 hours. But in rural areas stores can shut at lunchtime and on Sunday, while sometimes whole streets full of shops close on Wednesday or Saturday afternoon. Many banks and businesses operate Monday to Friday 9am to 5pm, while post offices are unpredictable; in big cities expect normal shop hours, in some rural areas consult the seaweed and guess – it's much more sporadic.

Museums & Sights

For the region's attractions the maxim is bigger equals open more often – blockbuster sights have longer hours and fewer days when they're closed completely, the rest tend to target tourist peaks. More sights are open more often between Easter (March/April) and October, and they often have longer hours in July and August. Some cut hours drastically or close completely in the winter. We list opening times for sights and activities.

Pubs, Bars & Clubs

Despite a much heralded change in the law to allow longer opening hours, many pubs have stuck to the same time groove: 11am to 11pm, sometimes later at weekends. Again we won't specify unless it's different. In general, drinking dens in larger towns and cities are more likely to be pulling pints later, while some rural pubs close for the afternoon. Visitors to the UK will notice people order drinks at the bar.

In clubs you can cut your best moves until 1am, 2am, or later – as it varies we'll specify when they'll turf you out on your musical ear.

Restaurants & Cafés

When will eateries be open? How long is a piece of spaghetti? Places may be either open for lunch or dinner, or both, while some serve breakfast too. We indicate which it is alongside each entry – taking standard hours to be noon to 2pm for lunch, and 6pm to 10pm for dinner. Where it's different, we'll say. Overall the usual big-city rules apply: you're more likely to scoop a mocha or land some sushi at 11pm in Bristol than in sleepy Budleigh Salterton.

CHILDREN

It's reassuring to know in our digital, virtual world that irrigating a sand castle with an incoming tide still appeals. Packed with beaches, moors and bucket loads of attractions, the southwest is a delight for kids – and adults who've lost touch with childlike joys.

The **regional tourist board** (☎ 0870 442 0880) has two specific websites aimed at children and parents: www.easypreschoolsouthwest .co.uk and www.familyholidaysouthwest .co.uk, which detail locations such as beaches that have lifeguards and toilets, as well as family-friendly attractions. Across the southwest tourist offices are rich sources of more localised leaflets and advice. Look out too for events aimed at children organised by National Park Authorities (NPAs), local authorities, museums and heritage organisations; these are often great fun, educational and cheap, too – see the boxed text, p72.

You'll experience many of the same kinds of issues travelling with youngsters in the southwest as the rest of England. Some hotels, restaurants, pubs and attractions are equipped for and welcome children – others clearly aren't and don't. As elsewhere some people will frown on breast feeding, while others will barely notice.

While many of the key tourist beaches have lifeguards, by no means all do and where it does exist cover is seasonal (often Easter to September) and tends to finish at 6pm. The **RNLI** (☎ 0845 122 6999; www.rnli.org.uk) lists where and when it provides lifeguards. For other advice, ranging from holiday checklists to avoiding car-journey rows, see www.babygoes2 .com (which also has a miniguide to Cornwall). For Plymouth, www.parents-guide-to -plymouth.co.uk is a useful resource.

CLIMATE CHARTS

The southwest is one of the warmest regions in the country and has the highest sea temperatures in the UK (remember that as you shiver). It's also the wettest – which they don't mention in the tourist brochures. The Westcountry's gloriously unpredictable weather is outlined on p17. Here are the stats:

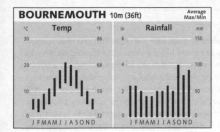

BOURNEMOUTH 10m (36ft) — Average Max/Min

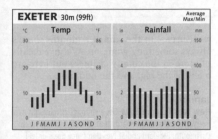

EXETER 30m (99ft) — Average Max/Min

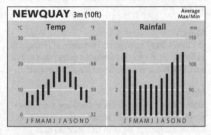

NEWQUAY 3m (10ft) — Average Max/Min

CUSTOMS

What you can bring into the UK depends on where you set out from; a key distinction is normally whether it's inside or outside the EU.

Duty Free

If you bring duty-free goods from outside the EU, the limits include 200 cigarettes, 2L of still wine, plus 1L of spirits or 2L of fortified wine (such as port or sherry), 60cc of perfume, and other duty-free goods (including beer) to the value of £145.

Tax & Duty Paid

In many cases there's no limit to the amount or value of goods you can bring from within the EU (if taxes have been paid), provided it's for your own use. Customs officials use guidelines to distinguish between what's personal and what's commercial, allowing you to bring in 3200 cigarettes, 200 cigars, 10L of spirits, 20L of fortified wine, 90L of wine and 110L of beer.

Be aware if travelling from some newer EU member countries (including Bulgaria, the Czech Republic, Poland and Romania); at the time of writing some limits do apply. Generally it's a 200-cigarette maximum. For more details see www.hmce.gov.uk or search for 'customs allowances' at www .visitbritain.com.

DANGERS & ANNOYANCES

Compared with the world's trouble spots England is a safe place and the southwest corner of it particularly so; it has the joint-lowest crime figures in the country. Of course, crime can happen anywhere and in the big cities you still need to be careful, especially at night. In some places, particularly where there are concentrations of bars and clubs, women should think twice before walking alone at night, and men in particular should beware of becoming embroiled in a fight. Stash luggage and valuables out of sight in cars, even at remote moorland and seaside beauty spots, which are sometimes targeted by thieves.

On the main city streets muggers, bag-snatchers and pickpockets are relatively rare, but money and important documents are best kept out of sight and reach, rather than in hand or shoulder bags. If you're staying in hostels take a padlock for the lockers and keep stuff packed away.

Other dangers come in the form of the great outdoors. The lifesaving charity, the RNLI has to rescue hundreds of people each year in the southwest – see its sea-safety advice, p69. The region has some of the biggest tidal ranges in the world, and the clear, sandy route out of that secluded cove can soon disappear under feet of water. Less dramatically, kit left on the sand when you went in the surf could be a soggy, scattered mess when you get back. Times of high and low tide are often outlined at popular beaches, as well as on local BBC TV and radio, and in newspapers. Small yellow booklets of tide times are available from newsagents and local shops (£1.20).

While stunning to hike, the region's beautiful cliffs, hills and moors are also often remote so prepare for upland weather conditions – see p64 for safety advice. For details on how to avoid and treat hypothermia see p300.

> **GULL CULL?**
>
> Nothing evokes a sense of the seaside past or present quite like the wheeling cry of a seagull. Unfortunately in the southwest these days, gulls are more likely to prompt celluloid flashbacks of *The Birds*. Their demands to be fed have become so insistent many locals see them as a pest – they're blamed for digging things out of bins, tearing open rubbish bags, intimidating picnickers and sometimes even plucking food right out of your hand. Things have reached such a pitch that there are periodic calls for gull culls. The birds' defenders counter by blaming people for feeding them and argue intensive fishing by humans forces the birds inland. Either way, those who do chuck a gull a chip become the focus of a Hitchcockean swarm of flapping, screeching birds and some very dirty looks from the locals.

DISCOUNT CARDS

We outline regional railcards in our Transport chapter (p298), as well as national train (p294) and bus passes (p293). Otherwise there are no specific discount cards available for visitors to the southwest.

At a national level, having membership of the YHA (p280) secures discounts at some music, book and outdoor shops. The Westcountry has a superb sprinkling of historic buildings and membership of a heritage organisation can prove a great deal. You can join the **National Trust** (NT; ☎ 0870 458 4000; www.nationaltrust.org.uk) at one of its many southwest properties. Individual admissions average £6 for adults and £4 for children, while annual adult membership is £43.50; families pay £29 to £77.50 and five- to 25-year-olds £19.50. Overseas visitors can buy seven- or 14-day passes at £18 or £23 per person, with cheaper rates for couples and families. They have to be bought outside the UK; you can do so online.

English Heritage (EH; ☎ 0870 333 1181; www.english-heritage.org.uk) also has a good selection of properties regionwide, prices average £3 to £4 for adults and £2 for children. You can join at some properties: annual adult membership is £40 (over 60s £28), for couples it's £69 (senior couples £45), while students and those under 19 pay £25. Again overseas visitors can get into most sites with a special pass – an adult seven-/14-day one costs £19/23, equivalent passes for two adults are £36/43; family passes are £40/48.

FESTIVALS & EVENTS

Its status as a holiday destination, and a growing reputation as a laid-back, chilled-out corner of England, ensures the southwest is home to countless festivals. From folk to oysters, the quirky and traditional to the hip and surfy – in the summer months there's always something going on. We give details of more in the county chapters but here are a few of the big, and the odd, ones.

January
New Year Celebrations Kiss a stranger at midnight as everyone works hard towards that collective hangover. In Dartmouth, Bideford and St Ives don fancy dress or feel left out.

March
St Piran's Day Process across sand dunes of Perranporth on 5th March, in honour of Cornwall's patron saint or look out for his flag: a white cross on a black background.

May
'Obby 'Oss All singing, drums and whirling dance, this ancient fertility rite parades around Cornwall's Padstow harbour and through the town on 1 May; see p226.
Flora Day A traditional celebration of spring's arrival in early May. The Floral, or Furry Dance, leads elegantly through the streets of Helston, Cornwall; see p250.
Bath International Music Festival (www.bathmusicfest.org.uk) A world-class celebration of classical and opera plus jazz and world music, taking place late May to early June. Some of it is outdoors and free; see p96.
Bath Fringe Festival (www.bathfringe.co.uk) Also late May to early June, comedy, drama and music collide for the oldest bash of its type in the country; see p96.

June
Glastonbury Festival (www.glastonburyfestivals.co.uk) The mother of all music festivals takes place in late June near the village of Pilton, Somerset. Rich in hippy history, these days it's a mad, mud-soaked or heat-baked rite of passage for Brits; see p109.

July
Ways With Words (www.wayswithwords.co.uk) Seriously good literature festival in early July amid the idyllic medieval surrounding of Dartington Hall, Devon; see p184.

Eden Sessions (www.edenproject.com) July/August sees big names from the world of rock and pop draw a cool crowd to the warm biomes of the Eden Project in Cornwall; see p268.

August

Rip Curl Boardmasters (www.ripcurlboardmasters .com) Hard-core cool and frenetic – the biggest surf, skate and music festival in Europe is held in early August in Newquay, Cornwall (let's hope the sea's not a flat calm); see p228.

Sidmouth Folk Week (www.sidmouthfolkweek.co.uk) Open up your musical mind as British folk and world artists perform at gigs all round this Devon resort in early August; see p176.

British Fireworks Championships (www.british fireworks.co.uk) A two-night contest of sky-filling colour bursts over Plymouth, Devon, in mid-August. Fantastic, fun and free.

Port Eliot Lit Fest (www.porteliotlitfest.com) Dubbed 'Glastonbury for books': magical, gentle and quirky you get to camp beside a Cornish country house too. Held at St Germans, Cornwall, in mid-August.

October

Falmouth Oyster Festival (www.falmouthoysterfes tival.co.uk) Cookery demos, boat races and music – there's also a chance to slurp, gulp or chew at this celebration of Cornish seafood, held late October.

November

Guy Fawkes Day Melt a marshmallow and chorus collective 'oohs' and 'aahs' at bonfires and firework displays around the region on 5 November. Join the big, free display at Plymouth Hoe.

Blazing Tar Barrels Watch, and watch out, as people carry flaming barrels soaked in tar through crowded streets of Ottery St Mary, Devon on 5 November. There's even a children's event – bless 'em.

December

Christmas Lights Garlands of glowing bulbs deck cottages, buildings and boats mid-December to early January as the tiny Cornish fishing village of Mousehole lights up the festive season in stunning style; see p244.

New Year's Eve Celebrations Party hats at the ready, here we go again – see January, p284.

FOOD

With tasty cheese, deeply flavoursome organic meats, fresh fish, and some top alcoholic brews around – you'll leave the southwest with a happy (if larger) stomach. See our Food & Drink chapter (p47) for

what to expect, then sample the delights in this guide – we list prices per main dish.

GAY & LESBIAN TRAVELLERS

England is relatively tolerant towards lesbians and gay men and the southwest generally follows that trend. Bristol has a fairly vibrant gay scene (see p88), Bournemouth (see p128) has a cluster of venues and Torquay produces *Beach Bum* – a gay guide to the resort. Gay clubs and bars can also be found in other major cities, although there's often not a huge range and in some places gay venues don't exist at all. Everywhere the usual instincts about how open you want to be about your sexuality are the best guide; you can be the victim of homophobia, or not, in the most surprising places.

Even in the deepest rural areas individual gay businesses, be they lesbian-owned B&Bs or exclusively gay hotels are thriving – see the wittily titled www.queery.org.uk, which has a good searchable database, and www.ukgay guides.co.uk, with links to several southwest websites. The **Intercom Trust** (☎ 0845 602 0818; www.intercomtrust.org.uk) runs a lesbian and gay switchboard for Devon, Cornwall, Dorset and Somerset. For other info, listings and contacts see monthly national magazines *Gay Times* (www.gaytimes.co.uk) and *Diva* (www.divam ag.co.uk).

HOLIDAYS

In England, most businesses and banks close on official public or 'bank' holidays:
New Year's Day 1 January
Easter (Good Friday to Easter Monday inclusive) March/April
May Day first Monday in May
Spring Bank Holiday last Monday in May
Summer Bank Holiday last Monday in August
Christmas Day 25 December
Boxing Day 26 December

If a public holiday falls on a weekend, the nearest Monday is usually taken as a holiday instead.

Some small museums and places of interest close on bank holidays, but larger attractions specifically gear up for their busiest times. Nearly everything closes on Christmas Day. A useful guide is if a place closes on Sunday, it'll probably be shut on bank holidays as well.

The main school holidays:
Easter Holiday Week before and week after Easter.

Summer Holiday Third week of July to first week of September.
Christmas Holiday Mid-December to first week of January.

There are also three week-long 'half-term' school holidays – usually late February (or early March), late May and late October. The southwest is one of the UK's busiest vacation destinations; at holiday times, especially the summer ones, roads can get clogged, resorts become booked out and prices go up.

INSURANCE

Things can go wrong anywhere and if you're an overseas visitor, travel insurance is highly recommended; see p299 for more on health insurance. Worldwide travel insurance is available at www.lonelyplanet.com/travel_services. You can buy, extend and claim online anytime – even if you're already on the road.

INTERNET ACCESS

While not as packed with wi-fi zones as some parts of the UK, the southwest has plugged into the information superhighway – it's a great leveller for a region that's otherwise out on a limb. You'll be able to log on at internet cafés, hotels and hostels in the region's cities and towns. Prices vary, but are around £1 to £2 per hour. Public libraries often have free access but sometimes run booking systems and limit sessions to half an hour. There are more wi-fi venues in bigger cities – charges range from nothing to £5 per hour.

In some remoter parts there won't be internet access at all, but just where you think there's no chance of checking your emails, up pops a wireless-enabled coffee shop in a sleepy market town. In this book we use an internet icon (🖥) if a place has PCs for public use. Overseas visitors who want to connect using a laptop and cable may find it doesn't fit in English sockets; adaptors are easy to buy at electrical stores.

LEGAL MATTERS
Driving Crimes & Transport Fines

Drink driving is a serious offence and can result in imprisonment. For more information, and details about speed limits and parking rules, see p297.

On buses and trains, people without a valid ticket for their journey may be fined on the spot, usually around £20, and/or required to pay the full fare.

Drugs

In the southwest, as elsewhere in England, illegal drugs are fairly widely available, especially in clubs. All the usual dangers apply and there have been much-publicised deaths associated with ecstasy. The government reclassified cannabis in 2002: possession remains a criminal offence, but the punishment for carrying a small amount is usually a warning. Dealers face far stiffer penalties, as do people caught with any other 'recreational' drugs.

MAPS

If you're driving around the Westcountry a regional road atlas will save frustration, 'interesting' diversions and circling leafy lanes – several times; aim for a scale of about 1:200,000 (3 miles to 1 inch). Cities have their own A–Zs, look out too for county-specific map books that feature a number of key towns and cities. Most road atlases cost around £7 to £10.

Ordnance Survey (OS; www.ordnancesurvey.co.uk) is a UK mapping institution and its products are available in bookshops and local stores across the region. If you're walking or cycling its *Landranger* (1:50,000) series (£7) can be ideal, although many prefer the greater detail of the OS *Explorer* (1:25,000) range (£8).

LEGAL AGE

England has a curious relationship with its sons and daughters – despite (or perhaps because of) the fact that everyone has actually been a young person, there's a pervasive distrust of their actions and judgements. The result is a very blurred line marking when a child becomes an adult. For matters sexual the age of consent in England is 16 (gay and straight). You're also judged to be responsible enough to marry at 16 (with permission from parents), but not to buy alcohol – that has to wait till you're 18. Bizarrely you can buy cigarettes at 16.

You usually have to be 18 to enter a pub or bar, although the rules are different if you have a meal. Some bars and clubs are over-21 only – in theory.

MONEY

Paper versions of the dear old pound sterling come in £5, £10, £20, £50 and higher denominations. Avoid £50 notes – many shops won't accept them and most people have never seen one. Other currencies aren't accepted. A guide to exchange rates is given on the inside front cover of this book and for likely costs, see p17.

ATMs

ATMs (normally called 'cash machines') wait to replenish pockets all over the region's cities and towns – but some smaller communities don't have banks with hole-in-the-wall cash machines, so a cheque book or small emergency cash stash is a good idea. Alternatives can be the stand-alone cash machines in convenience stores (charges may apply) or 'cash back' – see the following section.

Debit & Credit Cards

Visa, MasterCard and AmEx credit cards, and debit cards such as Switch and Maestro are widely accepted, but some of the region's smaller businesses, such as pubs or B&Bs, only take cash or cheque.

Nearly all credit and debit cards now use the 'chip & pin' system; instead of signing, you enter a PIN (personal identification number). If you're from overseas, and your card isn't 'chip & pin' enabled, you can sign in the usual way.

Most supermarkets and often convenience stores have a 'cash back' system: you spend more than £5, and you can withdraw a relatively small amount of cash and (sadly) add it to your bill, which you pay using your debit card.

It's a real pain if your only card gets lost – take a back-up.

Moneychangers

You can change money, or convert travellers cheques to cash, at many banks in the Westcountry, and also at some post offices, where rates are particularly fair.

Tipping & Bargaining

The best tip here is: leave one if the service or food was good – you're not obliged to if it wasn't. The usual amount is around 10%, both in restaurants and cafés, 15% if you're feeling particularly appreciative. Some restaurants include a service charge in the bill so check to avoid tipping twice without knowing. If you particularly want to reward the waiting or cooking staff and are paying by card ask if they actually receive the bonus – sometimes it goes to the establishment, in that case leave cash.

Taxi drivers tend to be tipped 10%, although if they've added 50p to your fare for 'luggage' and then left you to wrestle with it, you might not feel inclined to add the extra.

The British don't tend to bargain, although it can happen at markets and antiques shops. Do ask if there are student or senior discounts for attractions, theatre tickets and transport fares; there normally are.

Travellers Cheques

Travellers cheques (TCs) offer protection from theft and so are safer than wads of cash, but are rarely used in England – credit/debit cards and ATMs have become the norm. If you do prefer TCs, note that they are rarely accepted for purchases (except at large hotels), so for cash you'll still need to go to a bank.

POST

Post boxes are an easily identifiable cherry-red and the service delivered by the Royal Mail is equally reassuring: a 1st-class letter (34p) posted within the UK often arrives the next day, 2nd class costs 24p and takes up to three working days. A letter to an EU country costs from 48p; the wider world can be reached from 54p; postcards overseas are 54p. Prices tend to rise every few years, see www.royalmail.com for the latest.

SOLO TRAVELLERS

If you're travelling alone you're likely to be disadvantaged financially – simply because of accommodation costs. On average, the cost of a single room in hotels and B&Bs is up to 75% of the double rate. Sometimes in peak season it's the full room rate. Of course, this doesn't apply to hostel dorm beds, which may or may not be a consolation.

Day to day, safety won't be a main concern, but women in particular should carefully consider their routes if walking at night in some parts of the main cities, especially deserted areas or those around clusters of bars and clubs. Because of general safety concerns some organisations recommend people don't walk alone on cliffs and moors and advise informing someone of your route. Similarly lifesaving groups advise against doing some water sports on your own.

Although it's not that common, a woman won't cause a stir by dining alone (as ever, a book comes in very handy) or settling down with a paper in a country pub. If you head alone into a city club or bar it'll probably be assumed, accurately or not, you're there with one purpose in mind.

TELEPHONE

In its classic red phone boxes England used to have a design icon – now it has transparent cubicles, with a large open panel at the bottom. While the loss of most cosy red cubby-holes is often bemoaned, in reality they were fuggy, unsavoury places; stinking of stale cigarette smoke and worse. Boxes accept coins (a 40p minimum for local and national numbers) and usually credit/debit cards. In some phone boxes you can also send text messages at 10p each, and use the internet at £1 for the first 15 minutes then 10p per 90 seconds after that.

As well as the usual area codes (☎ 020 for London, ☎ 01752 for Plymouth etc, separated from the individual number by a hyphen in this book), other codes and charges from a British Telecom (BT) line include: ☎ 080 free; ☎ 084 local-call rate; ☎ 087 national-call rate and ☎ 09 a premium rate – which should be specified alongside, so you know the cost before you call. Calling a mobile phone is more expensive than dialling a landline; codes usually start with ☎ 07.

International Calls

To call somewhere outside the UK dial ☎ 00, then the country code (☎ 1 for USA, ☎ 61 for Australia etc), the area code (you usually drop the initial zero) and the subscriber number.

Direct-dialled calls to most overseas countries can be made from most public telephones, and it's usually cheaper between 8pm and 8am Monday to Friday and at weekends. You can often save money by buying a phonecard (denominated £5, £10 or £20) with a PIN that you use from any phone by dialling an access number (you don't insert it into the machine). There are dozens of cards, usually available from city newsagents, with rates of the various companies often vividly displayed.

To make a reverse-charge (collect) call, dial ☎ 155 for the international operator.

It's an expensive option, but then you won't be paying.

To call England from abroad, dial your country's international access code, then ☎ 44 (the UK's country code), then the area code (dropping the first 0) and then the phone number.

Local & National calls

Local calls (within 35 miles) are cheaper than national calls, and are often cheaper again from 6pm to 8am Monday to Friday, and from midnight Friday to midnight Sunday. From private phones, rates vary between telecom providers. From BT public phones local and national calls are charged at 40p for the first 20 minutes, then 10p for each following 10 minutes.

For the operator, call ☎ 100. For directory inquiries, a host of agencies compete for your business and charge from 10p to 40p; numbers include ☎ 118192, ☎ 118118, ☎ 118500 and ☎ 118811.

Mobile Phones

Remote cliff paths, beaches, moors and city streets – you'll find people nattering on mobile phones pretty much everywhere in the southwest. But because of the geography different networks have different areas where there's poor or no reception – it's a bit pot luck but you can often get a signal a few miles away.

Phones in the UK use GSM 900/1800, which is compatible with Europe and Australia but not with North America or Japan (although phones that work globally are increasingly common).

Beware if your phone is registered overseas, calling someone just up the road will be routed internationally and charged accordingly. An option is to buy a local SIM card (around £30), which includes a UK number, and use that in your own handset (as long as your phone isn't locked by your home network).

A second option is to buy a pay-as-you-go phone (from around £30); to stay in credit, you buy 'top-up' cards at newsagents.

TIME

Whichever time zone you're in it's measured relative to GMT or Greenwich Mean Time (also known as Universal Time Coordinated – UTC). So if it is noon in London, it is 4am on the same day in San Francisco, 7am in New York and 10pm in Sydney.

British Summer Time (BST) is one hour ahead of GMT from late March to late October.

TOURIST INFORMATION

If travelling from abroad, **VisitBritain** (www.visit britain.com) and **enjoyEngland** (www.visitengland.com), are both good sources of national information, while the **regional tourist board** (☎ 0870 442 0880; www.visitsouthwest.co.uk) is an introduction to the southwest. This book lists city, county and district organisations throughout.

Local Tourist Offices

Universally helpful, consistently cheerful and brimming with local knowledge, staff at tourist offices are an invaluable holiday resource. You'll find offices throughout the southwest – predictably ones in the bigger cities are busier, larger and open for longer hours. Some tourist offices are run by national parks. Many hand out free town maps, are crammed with leaflets and sell a good selection of walking maps and local books. Staff can also often help with booking accommodation. Many offices keep regular business hours although in quiet areas they can close from October to March.

You'll also come across some Tourist Information Points, these range from a collection of leaflets in a local post office to a big, plastic-covered map in a lay-by.

Tourist Offices Abroad

Some VisitBritain's offices overseas are listed below. Otherwise, check locations under www.visitbritain.com and click 'change language' to your own to bring up the relevant details. Offices where we note an address can deal with walk-in visitors; for the others it's phone or email only.

Australia (☎ 02-9021 4400; www.visitbritain.com.au; Level 2, 15 Blue St, North Sydney, NSW 2060)
Canada (☎ 1 888 847 4885; www.visitbritain.ca)
New Zealand (☎ 0800 700741; www.visitbritain.co.nz)
USA (☎ 1 800 462 2748; www.visitbritain.us; 7th fl, 551 Fifth Ave, New York, NY 10176)

TOURS

If you want to kick back and let someone else guide you through the Westcountry, you're in luck – there's range of options:
Devon in a Day (☎ 01404-813706; www.devon-in -a-day.co.uk) A range of guided minibus day trips to the county's best bits. It's £300 for six passengers.

Footscape (☎ 01300-341792; www.footscape.co.uk) This three-night journey through the heart of Thomas Hardy's Dorset can be done as a self-guided walk or accompanied tour. From £225 per person including B&B accommodation.
Livingstone Colbourne (☎ 01409-221939; www .livingstonecolbourne.co.uk) Luxury, bespoke tours of Devon and Cornwall, specialising in antiques, history and local produce. From £350 per person, per day – including hotel rooms, all meals and admission charges.
Railtours Southwest (☎ 01752-562009; www .railtours-southwest.co.uk) Guided day tours, part train, part coach, focusing on Devon and east Cornwall's scenic railway lines. From £18 per person.
Road Trip (☎ 0845 200 6791; www.roadtrip.co.uk) Backpacker central – leaving from London routes include weekend trips to Bath and Stonehenge and a five-day regionwide haul. From around £100, including a dorm bed.
Treading Softly (☎ 07780-984609; www.treading softly.co.uk) Guided walking tours of Dartmoor, strong on archaeology and local culture. A five-night trip costs from £800 per person, including hotel accommodation.
Wessex Heritage Tours (☎ 01935-862394; www .wessexheritage.com) Includes guided trips to Bath, Stonehenge and the Jurassic Coast from £345 for three days, including entrance fees but not accommodation.

The regional tourist board has a list of other tour firms, some trips only run in the summer months.

Alternatively, go and hand pick a guide who specialises in your particular passion. The national **Institute of Tourist Guiding** (☎ 020-7953 1257; www.itg.org.uk) and its local branch, the **Association of West Country Tourist Guides** (www .swtourguides.co.uk) have members whose interests are as diverse as Daphne du Maurier, military history and the southwest's links with America. These 'Blue Badge Guides' have to undergo training and assessment before they're registered.

Or grab this guidebook, hop on a bus or a train and delight in your own explorations, some gorgeous railway lines are highlighted in the boxed text, p298.

TRAVELLERS WITH DISABILITIES

It'll come as no surprise to people with disabilities that conditions in the southwest, like elsewhere throughout the country, are patchy. In places, genuine and successful efforts have been made to make things accessible, in others they haven't and the situation is woeful. Sometimes the best of

DIRECTORY

intentions are defeated by heritage and geography, in others quite simply more needs to be done.

Modern developments are required to have wheelchair access and in some places ramps, lifts and other facilities have been put into existing properties, but again it's by no means universal. You might also find it's inconsistent within a building: a posh restaurant with ramps and excellent wheelchair-access loos, but tables 10 inches apart.

For long-distance travel, coaches can present problems but staff will help whenever possible (see the 'Why chose us?' section of www.nationalexpress.com). On trains, there's often more room and better facilities; in some modern carriages all the signs are repeated in Braille. If getting on the train proves difficult there's normally a telephone and a sign detailing how to request help. In cities and towns in the southwest you may find buses with lower floors, but it's unlikely in rural areas. Some firms have taxis that take wheelchairs.

Exploring the region's wilder spaces can present obvious challenges, but real efforts have been made. These include on the **South West Coast Path** (☎ 01392-383560; www.southwest coastpath.com), where some of the more remote parts (as well as resort sections) have been made more accessible. You can search for easier-access options on its website; for more on the trail itself see p63. The **DNPA** (DNPA; ☎ 01822-890414; www.dartmoor-npa.gov.uk) produces the *Easy Going Dartmoor* booklet for less-mobile visitors –this outlines facilities and has a good range of accessible routes to explore. The DNPA also has a regular minibus tour for those with disabilities.

The regional tourist board runs www.acces siblesouthwest.co.uk, a searchable directory which includes accommodation, attractions, beaches and toilets. It's a little thin in places but the accessibility checks are detailed and it makes a good starting point.

National sources of information:

All Go Here (www.allgohere.com) Comprehensive details on hotels and travel.

Disability UK (www.disabilityuk.com) Huge information resource, including shop-mobility schemes.

Good Access Guide (www.goodaccessguide.co.uk) The name says it all.

Holiday Care Service (☎ 0845 124 9971; www .holidaycare.org.uk) Publisher of numerous booklets on UK travel.

Royal Association for Disability & Rehabilitation (Radar; ☎ 020-7250 3222; www.radar.org.uk) Published titles include *Holidays in Britain & Ireland*.

WORK

Many EU citizens looking to fund their trip by earning some cash are in luck – they often don't need a permit to work in England. After recent expansions of the EU, people from some new member states have been required to register, while those from other states have been required to apply for a permit. For the latest, check www.working intheuk.gov.uk, the official government site. Nationals from countries in the European Economic Area (EEA), including Iceland, Liechtenstein, Norway and Switzerland, do not need a work permit.

Those from outside the EU normally do need a permit and if this is the main purpose of your visit, you must be sponsored by an English company. Exceptions include Commonwealth citizens with a UK-born parent; a Certificate of Entitlement to the Right of Abode allows you to live and work in England free of immigration control. If one of your grandparents was born in the UK you may be eligible for an Ancestry Employment Certificate allowing full-time work for up to four years. Commonwealth citizens under 31 without UK ancestry are allowed to take temporary work during their holiday, but need a Working Holiday Entry Certificate – which must be obtained in advance and is valid for four years. You're not allowed to engage in business, pursue a career or work as a professional athlete or entertainer, but au pair placements are generally permitted. The situation can change, so double-checking at www.workingintheuk .gov.uk is advised.

Other useful websites include www.bunac .org (advice on six-month work permits for students from the USA) and www.working holidayguru.com (aimed mainly at Australians coming to Europe).

Transport

CONTENTS

GETTING THERE & AWAY

Without denying its undoubted delights, the southwest is at the end of England and sometimes getting there feels like it: it's quicker to take a train from London to Paris than it is to Plymouth. At its worst it can involve seven-hour coach trips, sluggish rail journeys and roads clogged with bank-holiday traffic. At its best, the Westcountry's charms are less than a few hours away. Besides, one of the reasons people are drawn to the far west is that it's different – if it was more accessible it would also be more the same.

Traveline (☎ 0871 200 2233; www.traveline.org .uk; calls per min 10p) details UK-wide train and coach timetables and journey durations. Remember flights, tours and rail tickets can be booked online at www.lonelyplanet .com/travel_services.

AIR

A sign of the budget-flight times is the sheer number of regional airports across what is actually a very small country. The southwest has its share with many services flying daily. Costs vary insanely and depend on when you book and when you want to fly – once tax has been added, expect to pay around £35 to £100 for return flights to the region from within the British Isles. Those coming from

---

CLIMATE CHANGE & TRAVEL

Climate change is a serious threat to the ecosystems that humans rely upon, and air travel is the fastest-growing contributor to the problem. Lonely Planet regards travel, overall, as a global benefit, but believes we all have a responsibility to limit our personal impact on global warming.

Flying & Climate Change

Pretty much every form of motorised travel generates CO_2 (the main cause of human-induced climate change) but planes are far and away the worst offenders, not just because of the sheer distances they allow us to travel, but because they release greenhouse gases high into the atmosphere. The statistics are frightening: two people taking a return flight between Europe and the USA will contribute as much to climate change as an average household's gas and electricity consumption over a whole year.

Carbon-Offset Schemes

Climatecare.org and other websites use 'carbon calculators' that allow travellers to offset the level of greenhouse gases they are responsible for with financial contributions to sustainable travel schemes that reduce global warming – including projects in India, Honduras, Kazakhstan and Uganda.

Lonely Planet, together with Rough Guides and other concerned partners in the travel industry, support the carbon-offset scheme run by climatecare.org. Lonely Planet offsets all of its staff and author travel.

For more information check out our website: www.lonelyplanet.com.

outside the country will often need to land at one of Britain's main international airports, then travel on to the southwest.

Airlines

Air Southwest (☎ 0870 241 8202; www.airsouthwest .com) Flies from Bristol to Leeds-Bradford and Manchester. Also connects Newquay with Cardiff, Cork, Dublin, Leeds-Bradford, London (Gatwick) and Manchester. Links Plymouth with Leeds-Bradford, Jersey, London (Gatwick) and Manchester.

Aurigny (☎ 0871 871 0717; www.aurigny.com) Flies between Bristol and Guernsey.

Blue Islands (☎ 08456 20 21 22; www.blueislands .com) Links Bournemouth with the Channel Islands.

bmibaby (☎ 0871 224 0 224; www.bmibaby.com) Shuttles between Newquay and Manchester.

British Airways (☎ 0870 850 9850; www.britishair ways.com) Daily flights between Newquay and London (Gatwick).

British International (☎ 01736-363871; www .islesofscillyhelicopter.com) Operates helicopter flights between Penzance and St Mary's and Tresco on the Isles of Scilly – flights run Monday to Saturday throughout the year (adult £120 to £152, child £75 to £90). Day trips cost £100 for adults; £65 for children.

easyJet (☎ 0871 244 2366; www.easyjet.com) Flies between Bristol and Belfast, Glasgow, Edinburgh, Inverness, Newcastle and a range of European destinations.

Flybe (☎ 0871 522 6100; www.flybe.com) Links Exeter with Aberdeen, Belfast, the Channel Islands, Dublin, Edinburgh, Glasgow, Leeds-Bradford, Manchester, Newcastle, Norwich and a scattering of cities across Europe. It also flies between Bristol and Jersey and connects Newquay with Belfast and Edinburgh.

Ryanair (☎ 0871 246 0000; www.ryanair.com) Connects Bournemouth and Dublin; Bristol with Glasgow and Dublin; and Newquay with London (Stansted).

Skybus (☎ 0845 710 5555; www.islesofscilly-travel .co.uk) Run by the Isles of Scilly Steamship Company and operates fixed-wing flights linking St Mary's Airport on the islands with Bristol (adult/child return £280/165), Exeter (adult £190 to £232, child £115 to £140), Land's End (adult return £100 to £125, child £65 to £80), Newquay (adult return £120 to £145, child £75 to £90) and Southampton (adult/child return £300/170). In the summer there are several flights a day between Monday and Saturday, although this can reduce to a weekly flight from just Land's End and Newquay in the depths of winter. Cheaper day trips also run in the summer from Land's End and Newquay. For more details on getting to the Isles of Scilly, see p253.

Airports

Bristol is the biggest regional airport, with some transatlantic as well as European flights, Exeter and to a lesser extent Bournemouth link with a sprinkling of destinations on the Continent.

Bournemouth Airport (BOH; ☎ 0120-236 4000; www.bournemouthairport.com)

Bristol International Airport (BRS; ☎ 0870 121 2747; www.bristolairport.co.uk) See p88.

Exeter International Airport (EXT; ☎ 01392-367 433; www.exeter-airport.co.uk) See p172.

Land's End Airport (LEQ; ☎ 01736-788771; www .islesofscilly-travel.co.uk/leq) See p253.

Newquay Cornwall Airport (NQY; ☎ 01637-860600; www.newquay-airport.co.uk)

Plymouth City Airport (PLH; ☎ 01752-242620; www .plymouthairport.com) See p201.

St Mary's Airport (ISC; ☎ 01720-423104; www.scilly .gov.uk; Isles of Scilly) See p253.

LAND
Bus

Hopping on a bus is a cheap and reliable way to get to the region, although journey times are normally longer than the train. **National Express** (☎ 08705 80 80 80; www.nation alexpress.com) has a good network of routes. Services from London Victoria coach station include between four and 15 direct departures daily to: Bath (adult return £24, 3½ hours); Bournemouth (£25, two to three hours); Bristol (£24, 2½ hours); Exeter (£38, 4½ hours); Penzance (£45, 8½ to 11 hours); Plymouth (£40, six hours); Torquay (£40, five to eight hours) and Truro (£50, seven to 10 hours). There is also one direct service a day from the capital to Newquay (£50, seven hours). Other key routes are from the midlands and the north. Between one and eight direct services leave Birmingham daily for

---

THINGS CHANGE

The information in this chapter is particularly vulnerable to change: fares are volatile, schedules alter, rules are amended and special deals come and go. You should get opinions, quotes and advice from as many airlines and travel agencies as possible, and be 100% clear on each ticket's restrictions before parting with your hard-earned cash. You should also be fully aware of visa regulations and security requirements for international travel. The details given in this chapter are pointers and are no substitute for your own up-to-date research.

Bournemouth (adult return £45, six hours); Bristol (£25, two hours); Exeter (£40, 4½ hours); Newquay (£60, seven hours); Penzance (£60, nine hours); Plymouth (£50, five to six hours) and Torquay (£45, six hours). Numerous other journeys are possible with changes. Special deals (or 'fun fares') can be a real bargain.

BUS PASSES & DISCOUNTS

A Young Person's Coach Card costs £10 and secures up to 30% off National Express fares for students and those under 26. People over 60 can travel half-price in many instances (without signing up for a discount card); family cards, at £8 and £16, mean one or two children respectively can travel free.

For those visiting the UK a National Express Xplorer passes allows unlimited travel for seven days (£79), 14 days (£139) and 28 days (£219). You don't need to book journeys in advance; if the coach has a spare seat you can take it. This deal is only available to non-Brits and has to be bought either abroad or at specific centres, none of which are in the southwest.

Car & Motorcycle

The overwhelming majority of visitors to the southwest come by car and sometimes they overwhelm the road network – considering other options could lead to a more relaxing stay. London's circular M25 leads onto the M4, which links into the M5 around Bristol. The M5 winds south to Exeter – making for good jumping-off points for Bath, Somerset and Exmoor on the way. From the midlands and the north, the M6 links up with the M5 at Birmingham.

Beyond Exeter two dual carriageways lead further west; the A30 snakes north around Dartmoor and into Cornwall, the A38 heads south via Plymouth and beyond. Dorset is reached via the M3 which ends at Southampton – an alternative route west is to take the A303 from the M3 which heads towards Somerset via Stonehenge.

The region's main dual-carriageway roads are generally good and have plenty of petrol and service stations. Off season they can be a delight to drive, but in the height of summer where two lanes contract into one, serious snarls can occur. Overheated cars and agitated people are not uncommon – check your engine coolant and pack your patience along with your swimsuit.

London to Exeter is about 170 miles and should take around 3½ to four hours. You can drive the 240 miles between Birmingham and Newquay in around five hours; Leeds to Bath is about 220 miles with a journey time of approximately four hours. The epic Glasgow to Torquay road trip is around 450 miles – an eight-hour haul. For all times, expect to add anything from half an hour to two hours (and more) for summer delays. For more on driving within the region see p296.

Train

Despite being as susceptible as the rest of the country to cancelled trains and bizarrely timed engineering works, in general rail links to the southwest are good. Services between the major cities tend to run at least hourly.

National Rail Enquiries (☎ 08457 484950; www.nationalrail.co.uk) is the best starting point for times and fares, it can also direct you to the individual train firms to buy the ticket. Services run by **First Great Western** (☎ 08457 000125; www.firstgreatwestern.co.uk) include those leaving London Paddington for Bath, Bristol, Exeter, Penzance, Plymouth and Taunton and Truro. It also operates to Gatwick Airport and runs branch lines to Dorchester, Exmouth, Falmouth, Newquay, St Ives, Torquay and Weymouth.

CrossCountry (www.crosscountrytrains.co.uk), part of Arriva, has wrested one of the regional rail franchises from Virgin and will now link the southwest with the midlands, Scotland and the north. Stations served include Aberdeen, Birmingham, Edinburgh, Glasgow, Leeds, Newcastle, Cardiff and the main southwest stations between Bristol and Penzance, as well as the Reading–Bournemouth link. At time of writing CrossCountry hadn't an established phone number – check the firm's website or call National Rail Enquiries.

South West Trains (☎ 0845 600 0650; www.southwesttrains.co.uk) runs services between London Waterloo and Axminster, Exeter, Salisbury and Yeovil. It also links Waterloo with Bournemouth, Christchurch, Dorchester, Poole and Weymouth.

Travel times and costs vary; the latter wildly, depending on how far in advance

TRANSPORT

TRANSPORT

you book and when you want to travel. Off peak days and hours are best. Some sample journey durations and fares: an off-peak adult return between London and Bath (1½ hours each way) can cost under £20; from Glasgow to Penzance (10 hours) it's around £100; or between Birmingham and Plymouth (3½ hours) about £80.

TICKETS

You can buy train tickets on the spot, which is fine for short journeys, but the extra you tend to pay can mount up over long distances. Some top tips for making savings:

- Buy as far in advance as you can (up to 12 weeks); the earlier you book, the cheaper it gets.
- Avoid peak commuter and holiday times; this can save hundreds of pounds.
- Buying two one-way tickets can be cheaper than a return, sometimes dramatically so.
- Check if splitting tickets (eg London–Bristol, Bristol–Plymouth) will save money; ridiculously it often does.
- Visit www.thetrainline.com for up-to-date deals and more hints.

Children under five travel free on trains; those aged between five and 15 pay half-price, except on tickets already heavily discounted. Seniors also get discounts, but again not on already heavily discounted fares.

TRAIN PASSES

Major train stations sell railcards, which cost around £20, are valid for one year and secure a third off most train fares; on Family and Network cards, children get a 60% discount. You might need proof of age and a passport photo. For full details see www.railcard.co.uk, or ask at a train station.

Family Railcard Covers up to four adults and four children travelling together.

Senior Railcard For anyone over 60.

Young Person's Railcard You must be 16 to 25, or a full-time UK student.

An All Line Rover Card (adults £375/565 for seven/14 days, child £245/375 for seven/14 days) gives unlimited travel on the rail network and can be purchased by anyone. A Disabled Person's Railcard costs £18 and secures a third off most standard fares for the holder and an accompanying adult.

BICYCLES ON TRAINS

Bikes can be taken on the majority of long-distance train journeys for £1 to £3, but space limitations and sometimes complicated advance-booking regulations can make it difficult. For more info contact **National Rail Enquiries** (☎ 08457 484950; www .nationalrail.co.uk).

On local trains and shorter trips in rural areas there's generally much less trouble; bikes can be taken free of charge on a first-come-first-served basis. Even so, there may be space limits.

For overseas visitors **BritRail Passes** (www.brit rail.com) are a good option, but must be bought before arriving in the UK from a specialist travel agency. There are many kinds, two key types are listed below. We've quoted adult prices – children's passes are usually half-price (or free with some adult passes) and seniors get discounts too.

BritRail England Consecutive Unlimited travel on all trains in England for four, eight, 15 or 30 days costs US$185/265/399/599.

BritRail England Flexipass Options for a set number of unlimited days' travel within a 60-day period. Four days costs US$235, eight days US$340 and 15 days US$515.

Of the other international passes, Eurail cards are not accepted in England, and InterRail cards are only valid if bought in another mainland European country.

SEA

The southwest is a region of seafarers, so chugging in on a ferry is a fitting way to arrive; you also get to see some superb scenery. **Brittany Ferries** (☎ 0870 366 5333; www.brittany-ferries.com) sails between Plymouth and Roscoff in France (six to eight hours, one to three daily) and Santander in northern Spain (20 hours, two per week). It also shuttles between Poole and Cherbourg in France (2¼ to 6½ hours, one to three daily). Prices vary dramatically: in general its cheaper to take a nonpeak, midweek, day crossing and return within five days – prices rise for 10-day trips, and again for more than 10. Opting for a cabin also pushes the price up. Some sample fares: a 10-day Roscoff to Plymouth return, midweek in August costs around £115 for an adult foot passenger, £425 for two people and a car. The bill for travelling in the same period between Santander and Plymouth is £150 return per foot passenger (£230 for a cabin) and £720 (£870 with a cabin) for two people and a car. A comparable Poole-to-Cherbourg return costs around £86 per foot passenger, £330 for a car and two passengers.

Condor Ferries (☎ 0870 243 5140; www.condorferries .com) runs daily fast ferries between Poole and Weymouth and the Channel Islands (two to 2½ hours). Return fares start at £90 for a foot passenger, £250 for a car and driver – it's also possible to carry the connection on to St Malo.

GETTING AROUND

The southwest is a relatively compact destination with good concentrations of attractions and environments to explore. The vast majority of people drive (then complain about the traffic) and in some cases that will prove the most practical way to get around. In other places the public-transport system could meet all your needs, making many of the options following worth investigating. Or try people power – with ribbons of coast path, vast tracts of moors and miles of gentle cycle tracks you can cast timetables aside and let your legs do the work. See p65 for some impetus and inspiration.

For bus, train or coach travel the regional **Traveline** (☎ 0871 200 2233; www.travelinesw.com) service is an excellent online planning tool and a good single source of information once on the road. Calls from a landline cost 10p per minute.

AIR

With only 200 road miles separating Bristol from the end of Cornwall, you're unlikely to want to fly within the region, especially once you factor in costs and the environmental impact. Air Southwest runs services between Bristol and Newquay (£27, 45 minutes, one or two daily except Saturday) and between Bristol and Plymouth (£27, 35 minutes, one or two daily).

Skybus and British International operate plane and helicopter hops to the Isles of Scilly, while between early November and mid-March you can also take a helicopter flight to Lundy Island (p214; adult/child return £85/45), a tiny chunk of granite 10

miles off the coast of north Devon. Flights run only on Monday and Friday and there's just one flight a day, so it can't be done as a day trip. For more information and bookings contact **Lundy Shore Office** (☎ 01271 863636; www .lundyisland.co.uk).

BICYCLE

Whether superfit and looking for an epic trip, or after a few gentle meanders, cycling is a feasible way to explore the region. Some excellent, largely traffic-free cycle routes make it even more attractive. See p65 for more.

BOAT

The Isles of Scilly and Lundy aside, you don't have to get on a boat to get around the southwest, but it can be fun if you do. The deep rivers and wide estuaries that cut into the landscape sometimes make ferries the fastest, most scenic, route from A to B. At other times peak-period traffic queues make you wonder if that 20-mile road detour wasn't a better idea after all.

Some ferries take cars, people and bikes, but some only carry foot passengers. The key car-ferry routes run all year while some of the other routes are seasonal. In all cases the boat isn't the only way to reach a destination; you can go by road (or sometimes path), although it will mean a detour that can be significant, especially if you're relying on leg power.

Some, unfailingly picturesque, routes:

Bodinnick–Fowey An atmospheric crossing to a pretty port; see p269.

Dartmouth–Kingswear Boat pushed, this chugs across a stunning estuary; see p190.

Falmouth–St Mawes An exhilarating trip across the fringes of the sea; see p260.

King Harry A 32-car shuttle to Cornwall's Roseland Peninsula; see p267.

Mudeford Ferry A potter to a strip of sand between Christchurch and the sea; see p133.

Salcombe–East Portlemouth A dash from yachting haven to golden sands; see p193.

There are also scores of other little ferries dotted around the southwest. Offering countless mini-adventures, they open up coast and coves and are a timeless way to make a journey; breathing spaces to connect with the past and the place. As a general rule, if you see one you fancy – hop on it, then explore.

Isles of Scilly Travel (☎ 0845 710 5555; www.isle sofscilly-travel.co.uk) operates the archipelago's emblematic ferry the *Scillonian* between Penzance and St Mary's (adult return £70 to £92, child £35 to £46; two hours 40 minutes). It's for foot passengers only with one (sometimes two) sailings Monday to Saturday, between Easter and early November. There are also Sunday sailings in August.

BUS & COACH
Bus Passes
The First Bus & Rail Card (one/seven days £11/44) allows unlimited travel on First Great Western trains and most First buses in Cornwall and Devon. The pass can be bought from bus drivers and main train stations. The Firstday Southwest (adult £7) is valid on First buses not only in Devon and Cornwall, but also in Bristol, Somerset, Gloucestershire and Dorset.

The PlusBus scheme allows you to add on bus travel around many main towns (including Plymouth, Exeter, Truro, Falmouth, Penzance and Bodmin) to your train ticket from around £2 per day – ask at any train station or consult www.plusbus.info.

Stagecoach Devon's Day Explorer (adult £5) allows one day's travel on its Devon buses, while the Goldrider pass (£18) is valid for a week.

Regional Travel
Getting around the southwest by coach can be a good option – if you do get stuck in traffic at least you're not the one fuming at the wheel. Journey durations can be similar to the train, but overall the bus tends to take longer, although it can be cheaper.

National Express (see p292) runs frequent services between the cities, towns and resorts in the region. Return fares for some sample adult, direct, journeys are: from Bristol to: Exeter (£16, two hours, four daily), Newquay (£36, five hours, one per day), Plymouth (£30, 2½ to three hours, four daily), St Ives (£45, six hours, two daily), Torquay (£21, three hours, three daily) and Weymouth (£20, 2¾ hours). The firm also serves a range of other places including Barnstaple, Bath, Penzance, Poole, Falmouth, Glastonbury and Taunton. See above for tips on bus passes.

For shorter trips within the region bus services may well meet your needs – especially in urban areas and those places popular with holidaymakers. However, keep in mind that connections to some rural areas can be as

infrequent as one a day, or even one or two a week.

The regional **Traveline** (☎ 0871 200 2233; www .travelinesw.com; calls per min 10p) has a comprehensive and easy-to-search database of times and destinations, and can connect you to the individual bus operators. You can pick up timetables for district-wide routes from tourist offices.

One of the region's main operators is **First** (☎ 0845 600 1420; www.firstgroup.com), which is the key operator in: Cornwall; north, south, east Devon and Dartmoor; west Dorset; and Somerset. First also provides key services around Bristol and Bath.

In Cornwall **Truronian** (☎ 01872-273453; www .truronian.com) serves the south – Truro, Falmouth, St Austell, the Lizard, Camborne and Redruth, while **Western Greyhound** (☎ 01637-871871; www .westerngreyhound.com) operates in north and west Cornwall, Bodmin Moor and St Austell.

Stagecoach Devon (☎ 01392-427711; www.stage coachbus.com) runs mostly local services and buses from Plymouth to Exeter or Totnes, and **Wilts & Dorset** (☎ 01202-673555; www.wdbus.co.uk; Poole) has services in east and central Dorset.

Within Cities
The region's cities have good bus services, although some wind down at about 11pm. If you're going to be taking a few local bus rides consider taking a day pass (with names such as Day Rover, Wayfarer or Explorer); single fares vary but expect prices in the £1.20 to £1.50 range (for short trips, we have not included fares). Three-day passes can be a great bargain – often they can be bought on your first bus, and may include local rail services.

We mention passes in specific chapters, but it's always worth asking ticket clerks, bus drivers and at tourist offices for the latest deals.

CAR & MOTORCYCLE
There's no doubt having your own car frees you from timetables, luggage and imposed destinations. In the southwest it will also let you in for parking hassle, nasty petrol bills and traffic jams; be aware: in the summer even on a clear road when the sign before a bend says 'traffic queuing ahead' – it's probably going to be true.

Petrol and diesel cost around 95p per litre at the time of writing, although fuel prices rise

Road Distances (miles)

	Barnstable	Bath	Bournemouth	Bristol	Exeter	Lyme Regis	Newquay	Penzance	Plymouth	Salcombe	Truro	Yeovil
Barnstable	---											
Bath	120	---										
Bournemouth	123	67	---									
Bristol	93	12	80	---								
Exeter	43	100	84	75	---							
Lyme Regis	65	66	56	67	33	---						
Newquay	78	180	170	167	84	117	---					
Penzance	110	215	196	193	110	145	32	---				
Plymouth	67	140	128	118	43	75	50	79	---			
Salcombe	90	145	130	120	48	78	77	104	25	---		
Truro	85	190	175	170	87	122	16	29	57	80	---	
Yeovil	75	42	50	42	50	33	135	160	90	94	134	---

as you get away from cities and large towns. If you are heading off the main routes it's worth filling up, sometimes petrol stations are few and far between and may not be open late or on Sunday.

Satellite navigation causes a few glitches for the unwary; prompting a wealth of local folklore about caravans stuck down unfeasibly small Dorset lanes, and holidaymakers arriving at the banks of a Cornish river expecting a route across that simply isn't there.

Hire

Hiring a car in England isn't cheap; you should expect to pay around £250 per week for a small car (unlimited mileage) although rates rise at busy times. Rental offices are at cities and bigger towns across the southwest. Some key firms:

Avis (☎ 0844 581 0147; www.avis.co.uk)
Europcar (☎ 0845 758 5375; www.europcar.co.uk)
Hertz (☎ 0870 850 2677; www.hertz.co.uk)
National (☎ 800 227 7368; www.nationalcar.com)
UK Car Hire (www.uk-car hire.net) Online rental broker website.

Parking

Every few years the regional press features stories of a parking space at a key Westcountry resort selling for tens of thousands of pounds. This tells us several things – first, that the world is indeed a crazy place; second, that finding somewhere legal to leave your car can be a big challenge. Charges vary but range from 60p for 30 minutes, through £1.20 for an hour to £5 for the day. Many places have 'Park and Ride' (often £2.50) which allow you to deposit the car at the edge of town then ride to the centre on regular buses provided.

Visitors will need to know yellow lines (single or double) along the edge of the road indicate restrictions. Find the nearby sign that spells out when you can and can't park – parking fines are around £30.

Road Rules

A foreign driving licence is valid in England for up to 12 months. If you plan to bring a car from Europe, it's illegal to drive without (at least) third-party insurance. Some other important rules:

■ drive on the left

TRANSPORT

- wear fitted seat belts in cars
- wear crash helmets on motorcycles
- give way to your right at junctions and roundabouts
- always use the left-hand lane on motorways and dual carriageways, unless overtaking
- don't use a mobile phone while driving unless it's fully hands-free

Speed limits are 30mph (48km/h) in built-up areas, 60mph (96km/h) on main roads, and 70mph (112km/h) on motorways and dual carriageways. Drinking and driving is taken very seriously; you're allowed a blood-alcohol level of 80mg per 100mL – campaigners want it reduced to 50mg per 100mL.

All drivers should read the *Highway Code*. It's often stocked by tourist offices and is available online at www.highwaycode.gov.uk.

HITCHING

Hitching is not as common as it used to be in England, possibly because few drivers give lifts any more. It is possible if you don't mind long waits, although travellers should understand that they're taking a small but potentially serious risk, and we don't recommend it. If you decide to go by thumb, note that it's illegal to hitch on motorways; you must use approach roads or service stations.

LOCAL TRANSPORT
Bus

See p296 for city-bus transport information.

Taxi

There are two main sorts of taxi in England. The famous metered black cabs (although they can be different colours) can be hailed in the street; minicabs can only be called by phone. In the cities taxis cost £2 to £3 per mile, and in rural areas, it can be about half this. If you call **National Cabline** (☎ 0800 123444) from a landline phone, the service will pinpoint your location and transfer you to an approved local company.

TOURS

Whether you want someone else to do the work or to tap into local knowledge, a tour can bring a whole new emphasis to your trip.

Crime writers, history, hiking, cycling – there are tours focusing on a huge range of interests and ways of travelling the region. For details of some available possibilities see p289.

TRAIN

Even if it's not your main means of transport, taking a trip on a local train can be a scenic, ecofriendly break from driving and parking-related stress. Within the southwest services between cities are good, while a network of branch lines connects the peripheries. Key routes are Castle Cary to Weymouth, Exeter to Barnstaple, Exeter to Exmouth, Liskeard to Looe, Newton Abbot to Paignton, Par to Newquay, Plymouth to Gunnislake, St Erth to St Ives and Truro to Falmouth. There is also a good rail connection between Bristol and Bath.

The website of **Great Scenic Railways of Devon & Cornwall** (www.carfreedaysout.com) has a wealth of information on picturesque railways and details integrated walk options. There are cracking views between Plymouth and Gunnislake; Exeter and Newton Abbot; and Plymouth and Liskeard. Steam trains also chuff their way attractively along some sections of track. They're run as private businesses – look out for the ones linking Paignton with Kingswear (p183) and Buckfastleigh with Totnes (p186) in south Devon; the West Somerset Railway (p109); and the Swanage Steam Railway (p136) in south Dorset.

Rail Passes

Regional passes include the Freedom of the SouthWest Rover, which covers an area west of (and including) Salisbury, Bath, Bristol and Weymouth. It allows an adult eight days' unlimited, off-peak travel in a 15-day period for £95, or three days' travel in a week for £70.

The Devon and Cornwall Rover ticket allows unlimited, off-peak travel across Devon's and Cornwall's train network; eight days' travel in 15 costs an adult £60, three days' travel in one week is £40. The passes are accepted by all the national train companies and can be bought either from them or at many train stations.

For details of the First Bus & Rail Card, see p296.

Health

CONTENTS

Despite critical, page-high newspaper headlines, in relative terms England's National Health Service (NHS) is one of the best, free health-care systems in the world. The kind of treatment you'll receive in the southwest is broadly similar to the rest of the country, although some areas are relatively remote and have less extensive health-care systems. On the other hand, some of the region's hospitals are less crowded than their big-city counterparts in the rest of the country. The region is by and large a healthy place to travel and hygiene standards are generally high.

BEFORE YOU GO

No immunisations are mandatory for visiting England. If you're an EU citizen, a European Health Insurance Card (EHIC) covers you for most medical care, but not nonemergencies or emergency repatriation. You have to apply for a card in your own country before travelling. Non-EU citizens should find out

---

TRAVEL HEALTH WEBSITES

If visiting England from overseas it's usually a good idea to consult your government's travel-health website before departure.

- Australia (www.smartraveller.gov.au)
- Canada (www.hc-sc.gc.ca/english /index_e.html)
- USA (www.cdc.gov/travel)

---

if there is a reciprocal arrangement for free medical care between their country and the UK, and if so, the precise terms of the arrangement; search for the 'overseas visitors' section of the Department of Health website: www.dh.gov.uk.

Everyone, regardless of nationality, is entitled to free treatment at NHS Accident and Emergency (A&E) departments but, crucially, charges may apply once that care transfers to another department. Travel insurance is advisable. Consider a policy that covers you for the worst possible scenario, such as that emergency flight home.

INTERNET RESOURCES

The WHO's website (www.who.int/ith) is the definitive resource. Other useful sites include www.mdtravelhealth.com (world wide travel-health recommendations, updated daily), www.ageconcern.org.uk (advice on travel for the elderly) and www.mariestopes .org.uk (information on women's health and contraception).

IN TRANSIT

DEEP VEIN THROMBOSIS (DVT)

Blood clots may form in the legs during plane flights, chiefly because of prolonged immobility. The longer the flight, the greater the risk. The chief symptom of DVT is swelling or pain of the foot, ankle or calf, usually but not always on just one side. If a blood clot travels to the lungs, it may cause chest pain and breathing difficulties. Travellers with any of these symptoms should seek medical attention immediately.

To prevent the development of DVT on long flights walk about the cabin, contract the leg muscles while sitting, drink plenty of fluids and avoid alcohol and tobacco.

JET LAG & MOTION SICKNESS

To avoid jet lag (common when crossing more than five time zones) try drinking plenty of nonalchoholic fluids and eating light meals. On arrival, get exposure to natural sunlight and readjust your schedule (for meals, sleep and so on) as soon as possible.

Antihistamines such as dimenhydrinate (Dramamine) and meclizine (Antivert, Bonine) are usually the first choice for treating motion sickness. A herbal alternative is ginger.

IN SOUTHWEST ENGLAND

As you'd expect, good health care is readily available across the region and there's the usual range of services, from doctors' surgeries in villages to major city hospitals. If you have a medical emergency dial ☎ 999 and ask for an ambulance. For everything else contact the 24-hour helpline NHS Direct (☎ 0845 4647; www.nhsdirect.nhs.uk); it can provide a range of health-care advice, including the location and hours of the nearest doctor's surgery, A&E departments, local chemists, opticians and dentists. For minor illnesses high-street pharmacists can give valuable advice and sell over-the-counter medication. The standard of dental care is good, but it's always sensible to have a dental check-up before a long trip.

ENVIRONMENTAL HAZARDS
Bites & Stings
Adders, Britain's only venomous snakes and a protected species, are not uncommon in the region's hills, moors and coast paths. They will only attack if harassed or threatened. Although an adder's venom poses little danger to a healthy adult human, the bite is very painful and does require medical attention. If you are bitten don't panic. Immobilise the limb with a splint (eg a stick) and apply a bandage over the site firmly, similar to a bandage over a sprain. Do not apply a tourniquet, or cut or suck the bite. Get the victim to medical help as soon as possible.

Ticks are increasingly common in the countryside, some carry Lymes Disease – a relatively uncommon but potentially serious illness. To prevent bites use insect repellent and wear long trousers tucked into socks and long-sleeved shirts. At the end of the day check you're tick-free; if you are bitten, remove the tick as soon as possible by grasping it close to the skin with tweezers and twisting anti-clockwise. Lymes Disease may appear as an expanding, reddish round rash in the area of

the bite, for as long as 30 days later. Symptoms include influenza, mild headaches and aching muscles and joints. The condition is treatable with antibiotics but early diagnosis is best.

Bees and wasps cause real problems only to those with a severe allergy (anaphylaxis). If you have a severe allergy to bee or wasp stings carry an 'epipen' or similar adrenaline injection.

Hypothermia
The southwest isn't mountainous but it's still possible to get caught out on the remoter hills and moors or when coming into contact with water. On high ground prepare for upland, rapidly changing weather conditions – carry waterproofs and warm layers, inform others of your route and check the weather before you go. Hypothermia starts with shivering, loss of judgement and clumsiness. Unless rewarming occurs, the sufferer deteriorates into apathy, confusion and coma. Prevent further heat loss by seeking shelter, warm dry clothing, hot sweet drinks and shared bodily warmth.

Sunburn
Some of the highest malignant skin cancer rates in England and Wales occur in the southwest – the coastline and outdoor lifestyle are often blamed. Experts remind UK nationals they still need sunscreen even at home. Stay out of the sun between 11am and 3pm, cover up, use factor 15+ sunscreen and UV sunglasses and take extra care of children.

Water
Tap-water quality in Britain is generally very high and you should have no problem drinking it. Common sense still applies – look out for signs, on trains for example, warning it's not safe to drink. Don't drink from streams in the countryside – you can't be sure what's in the water, or what it's flowed through.

WOMEN'S HEALTH
Emotional stress, exhaustion and travelling through different time zones can all contribute to an upset in the menstrual pattern. If using oral contraceptives, remember some antibiotics, diarrhoea and vomiting can stop them from working. Travelling during pregnancy is usually possible but you should always consult your doctor. The most risky times for travel are during the first 12 weeks of pregnancy and after 30 weeks.

Glossary

aga – a large, heat-retaining cooking range, commonly used in farmhouse kitchens
AONB – Area of Outstanding Natural Beauty

beach break – a wave that breaks on a beach (rather than a reef)
Brizzle – Bristol
BSA – British Surfing Association
bucca – a type of spirit or sprite, usually living in mines

cairn – rounded pile of stones
Camra – Campaign for Real Ale
chine – a narrow river valley in Dorset
cists – half buried stone boxes originally covered in granite slabs
coombe – a narrow river valley in Cornwall
crib – Cornish word for lunch

DNPA – Dartmoor National Park Authority
day-mark – an onshore landmark used as a navigational aid by fishermen and sailors

EH – English Heritage
emmet – Cornish word for tourist
ENPA – Exmoor National Park Authority

firkin – type of barrel traditionally used to carry beer or cider
flicks – the movies
flip-flop – a casual beach sandal (called *thongs* in Australasia)
Freeview – digital TV accessed via a set-top box

gert lush – Bristolian for very nice
grockle – common word for tourist in Devon, Dorset and Somerset
grommet – a young surfer

hunkypunk – type of gargoyle used in Somerset churches that serves no purpose

Kernow – traditional name for Cornwall in the Cornish language
kiddleywink – old smugglers' term for a pub or inn

longboard – surfboard over 2.5m (8ft) in length
lychgate – church gateway with a covered roof

menhirs – standing stones
minster – cathedral or large church; originally connected to a monastery

NPA – National Park Authority
NT – National Trust

offshore – when the wind is blowing out to sea (opposite to onshore)
onshore – when the wind is blowing towards the land (opposite to offshore)
ope – narrow alleyway in Cornwall and Devon

pilchard – an immature sardine
pisky – pixie

Quidditch – a fictional sport developed by JK Rowling, found in the internationally bestselling Harry Potter novels and films
quoit – a circle of stone pillars topped by a flat capstone, thought to mark an ancient burial site

ramble – short, easy walk
rip – a powerful undercurrent near the shore
RNLI – Royal National Lifeboat Institution, a charity that saves lives at sea

sarnies – slang for sandwiches
scrumpy – traditional term for cider made from 'scrumped' (stolen) apples
SSSI – Site of Special Scientific Interest
swede – dialect word for turnip

tor – hill or pillar made of rock or granite
towan – Cornish word for sand dune

wheal – Cornish word for tin or copper mine
withy – dialect word for willow

yarg – type of Cornish cheese, traditionally wrapped in nettles

The Authors

OLIVER BERRY
Coordinating Author; History; The Culture; Environment; Bristol, Bath & Somerset; Cornwall

Oliver graduated from University College London with a degree in English and now works as a freelance writer and photographer. He's been proud to call the land of Kernow home for most of the last 28 years, and is always looking for excuses to wander the county's beaches and clifftops; writing a guidebook is the best one yet. For this book he braved the bone-chilling waters of Cornwall's north coast, swapped dowsing tips with druids in Glastonbury, took a crash course in Kernewek and got thoroughly lost in the Isles of Scilly. He'd do it all again tomorrow given half a chance. Oliver has received several awards for his writing including the *Guardian's* Young Travel Writer of the Year.

BELINDA DIXON
The Culture; Food & Drink; Southwest Outdoors; Dorset, Devon, Directory, Transport

Belinda was drawn to the southwest in 1993 to do a post-grad course (having been impressed by the palm trees on the campus) and, like the best West Country limpets, has proved hard to shift since. She spends as much time as possible in the sea, but can also be seen and heard writing and broadcasting in the region. Her personal highlights from this latest Lonely Planet adventure are finding her very own ammonite in Lyme Regis, catching the waves in north Devon and rigorously testing the ever-tasty food and drink of the South Hams.

LONELY PLANET AUTHORS

Why is our travel information the best in the world? It's simple: our authors are independent, dedicated travellers. They don't research using just the internet or phone, and they don't take freebies in exchange for positive coverage. They travel widely, to all the popular spots and off the beaten track. They personally visit thousands of hotels, restaurants, cafés, bars, galleries, palaces, museums and more – and they take pride in getting all the details right, and telling it how it is. Think you can do it? Find out how at lonelyplanet.com.

Behind the Scenes

THIS BOOK

This is the exciting 1st edition of *Devon, Cornwall & Southwest England*. It was commissioned in Lonely Planet's London office, and produced by the following:

Commissioning Editor Clifton Wilkinson
Coordinating Editors Yvonne Byron, Evan Jones
Coordinating Cartographer Jolyon Philcox
Coordinating Layout Designer Paul Iacono
Managing Editors Bruce Evans, Geoff Howard
Managing Cartographer Mark Griffiths
Managing Layout Designers Adam McCrow
Assisting Editors Susie Ashworth, Katie Evans, Margedd Heliosz
Assisting Cartographers Barbara Benson, Anna Clarkson, Damien Demaj, Julie Dodkins, Valentina Kremenchutskaya, Sophie Richards, Andrew Smith, Simon Tillema, Anita Banh, Csanad Csutoros, Herman So, Corey Hutchinson
Assisting Layout Designers Wibowo Rusli
Cover Designer Marika Mercer
Project Manager Fabrice Rocher

Thanks to Eoin Dunleavy, Dr Caroline Evans, Laura Jane, David Burnett, Sin Choo, Mark Germanchis, Sasha Baskett, Trent Paton, James Hardy, Wayne Murphy, Emma McNicol, Lyahna Spencer, Celia Wood

THANKS
OLIVER BERRY

There are way too many people as always to fit into a short paragraph of thanks, but here goes: Mark Jenkin on the good ship *Ark,* Helen Gilchrist, Clare

---

LONELY PLANET: TRAVEL WIDELY, TREAD LIGHTLY, GIVE SUSTAINABLY

The Lonely Planet Story

The story begins with a classic travel adventure: Tony and Maureen Wheeler's 1972 journey across Europe and Asia to Australia. There was no useful information about the overland trail then, so Tony and Maureen published the first Lonely Planet guidebook to meet a growing need.

From a kitchen table, Lonely Planet has grown to become the largest independent travel publisher in the world, with offices in Melbourne (Australia), Oakland (USA) and London (UK). Today Lonely Planet guidebooks cover the globe. There is an ever-growing list of books and information in a variety of media. Some things haven't changed. The main aim is still to make it possible for adventurous individuals to get out there – to explore and better understand the world.

The Lonely Planet Foundation

The Lonely Planet Foundation proudly supports nimble nonprofit institutions working for change in the world. Each year the foundation donates 5% of Lonely Planet company profits to projects selected by staff and authors. Our partners range from Kabissa, which provides small nonprofits across Africa with access to technology, to the Foundation for Developing Cambodian Orphans, which supports girls at risk of falling victim to sex traffickers.

Our nonprofit partners are linked by a grass-roots approach to the areas of health, education or sustainable tourism. Many projects we support – such as one with BaAka (Pygmy) children in the forested areas of Central African Republic – choose to focus on women and children as one of the most effective ways to support the whole community.

Sometimes foundation assistance is as simple as helping to preserve a local ruin like the Minaret of Jam in Afghanistan; this incredible monument now draws intrepid tourists to the area and its restoration has greatly improved options for local people.

Just as travel is often about learning to see with new eyes, so many of the groups we work with aim to change the way people see themselves and the future for their children and communities.

Howdle and all the *Stranger* team, all the boys over at o-region, Jock McClaverty, the Hobo (my ever-present companion), Adam Laity and Bec Gee for the idea of watching Hitchcock films in scout huts, TSP and of course Susie Berry, who underpinned the whole affair. At the Planet, special thanks to Cliff Wilkinson for doing a sterling job on keeping us sane and on the straight and narrow; to the map team in Melbourne, especially Jolyon Philcox for making sense of the scrawl; to Yvonne Byron for her eagle eye for detail; and to Belinda Dixon for all the feedback and supportive words throughout those long, long nights of write-up.

BELINDA DIXON

Thanks to LP's editors and cartos, Cliff for the gig and curing me (ish) of potentially fatal dangling participles. Coordinating author Oliver (Tom) Berry deserves thoroughly nice things for years to come for tact, support and gentle advice: OTB, I thank you! Thanks also to: tourist information staff across Devon and Dorset; ferrymen, publicans and B&B and restaurant owners regionwide; Taste of the West for pasty stats; the rangers of Dartmoor and Exmoor National Parks; and the RNLI for keeping a weather eye. Also the Exeter Llewellyn-Hills for wise words and a place to stay, and J for editing extraordinaire.

ACKNOWLEDGMENTS

Many thanks to the following for the use of their content:

Globe on title page ©Mountain High Maps 1993 Digital Wisdom, Inc.

Internal photographs p6 (#2), Nigel Hicks/Alamy; p6 (#1), Jeff Morgan built environment/Alamy; p6 (#4), Paul Glendell/Alamy; p8 (#5), p10 (#1), Tim Cuff/Alamy; p8 (#4), Guy Edwardes Photography/Alamy; p9 (# 2), Buzz Pictures/Alamy; p9 (#1), Penny Tweedie/Alamy; p10 (#5), Barry Lewis/Alamy; p11 (#4), John Martin/Alamy; p11 (#2), Paul White/Alamy; p12 (#1), David Cantrille/Alamy; p12 (#2), Robert Harding Picture Library Ltd/Alamy; p142 (#1), Kevin Britland/Alamy; p142 (#4), Vaughan Brean/Alamy; p143 (#2), Thomas Dobner/Alamy; p143 (#3), Mike Greenslade/Alamy; p144 (#1), Banana Pancake/Alamy; p145 (#2), FoodPix/Alamy, p145 (#3), Adrian Sherratt/Alamy; p145 (#4), p147 (#3), Marc Hill/Alamy; p146 (#1), Nick Gregory/Alamy; p147 (#2), Matt Cardy/Thermae Bath Spa. All other photographs by Lonely Planet Images, and by Chris Mellor p5; Jon Davison p7 (#3); Glenn Beanland p141; Barbara Van Zanten p148.

All images are the copyright of the photographers unless otherwise indicated. Many of the images in this guide are available for licensing from Lonely Planet Images: www.lonelyplanet images.com.

Index

000 Map pages
000 Photograph pages

GreenDex

Everyone's 'going green' these days and the southwest of England is leading the way in many areas, from organic farming to renewable energy. But how do you know which businesses are actually eco-friendly and which are simply jumping on the eco/sustainable bandwagon?

The following sights, activities, and eating and accommodation choices have all been selected by our authors because they meet our criteria for sustainable tourism; for more background on issues affecting the region see the Environment chapter.

If you think we've missed anywhere out, or if you disagree with our choices, email us at talk2us@lonelyplanet.com.au and set us straight for next time.

ABBREVIATIONS

Ba	Bath
Br	Bristol
C	Cornwall
De	Devon
Do	Dorset
S	Somerset

ACCOMMODATION

Bedknobs, Bodmin (C) 274
Berkeleys of St James, Plymouth (De) 200
Broomhill Art Hotel, Barnstaple (De) 213
Cornish Tipi Holidays, St Kew (C) 225
Hazelwood House, Loddiswell (De) 192
Headland View, Torquay (De) 181
Hill View House, Dartmouth (De) 189
Little Hill House, Salcombe (De) 193
Organic Panda, St Ives (C) 237
Primrose Valley, St Ives (C) 238
Royal Castle Hotel, Dartmouth (De) 189
Skerries, Start Bay (De) 191
Sparrowhawk Backpackers, Widecombe (De) 209
Yurthworks, St Breward (C) 225

EATING

Bell Street Café, Shaftesbury (Do) 153
Blue Fig, Wimborne (Do) 134
Bordeaux Quay (Br) 86
Britannia Shellfish, Start Bay (De) 191
Broad Street, Weymouth (Do) 163
Café Kino (Br) 85
Croust House, St Keverne (C) 252
Green, The, Sherborne (Do) 152
Gylly Beach Café, Falmouth (C) 261
Mallams, Weymouth (Do) 157
Riverford Field Kitchen, Totnes (De) 186
Roskilly's Farm, St Keverne (C) 251
Willow Vegetarian Restaurant, Totnes (De) 186

SIGHTS & ACTIVITIES

Blackdown Hills Hedge Association, Taunton (S) 109
Eden Project (C) 268, 11, 146
Great Scenic Railways of Devon & Cornwall 298
It's Not Easy Being Green courses, Tywardreath (C) 269
Roskilly's Farm, St Keverne (C) 251
Somerset willow 112
Sustrans 65
Transition Town Totnes (De) 185

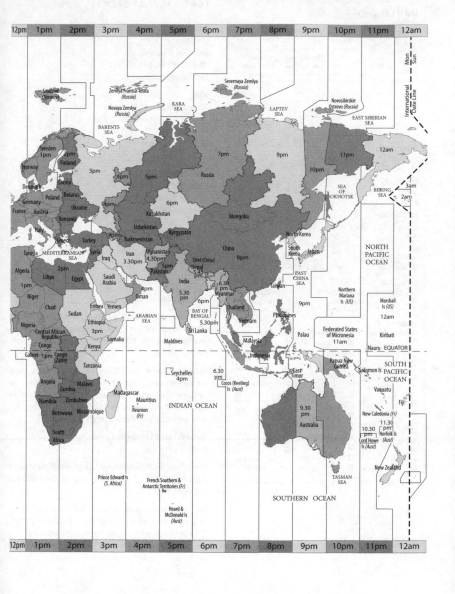

316

MAP LEGEND

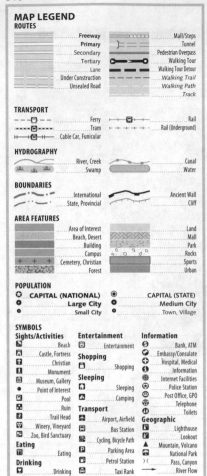

LONELY PLANET OFFICES

Australia
Head Office
Locked Bag 1, Footscray, Victoria 3011
☎ 03 8379 8000, fax 03 8379 8111
talk2us@lonelyplanet.com.au

USA
150 Linden St, Oakland, CA 94607
☎ 510 893 8555, toll free 800 275 8555
fax 510 893 8572
info@lonelyplanet.com

UK
2nd Floor 186 City Rd,
London EC1V 2NT UK
☎ 020 7106 2100, fax 020 7106 2101
go@lonelyplanet.co.uk

Published by Lonely Planet Publications Pty Ltd
ABN 36 005 607 983

© Lonely Planet Publications Pty Ltd 2008

© photographers as indicated 2008

Cover photograph: Surfboards at Polzeath Beach, Cornwall, England UK, Nick Hanna/Photolibrary. Many of the images in this guide are available for licensing from Lonely Planet Images: www.lonely planetimages.com.

All rights reserved. No part of this publication may be copied, stored in a retrieval system, or transmitted in any form by any means, electronic, mechanical, recording or otherwise, except brief extracts for the purpose of review, and no part of this publication may be sold or hired, without the written permission of the publisher.

Printed by Hang Tai Printing Company.
Printed in China.

Lonely Planet and the Lonely Planet logo are trademarks of Lonely Planet and are registered in the US Patent and Trademark Office and in other countries.

Lonely Planet does not allow its name or logo to be appropriated by commercial establishments, such as retailers, restaurants or hotels. Please let us know of any misuses: www.lonelyplanet.com/ip.

Although the authors and Lonely Planet have taken all reasonable care in preparing this book, we make no warranty about the accuracy or completeness of its content and, to the maximum extent permitted, disclaim all liability arising from its use.